# SOCIETY'S PROBLEMS

# SOCIETY'S PROBLEMS

## Sources and Consequences

**D. Stanley Eitzen**
Colorado State University

**Allyn and Bacon**
Boston London Sydney Toronto

A Division of Simon & Schuster
160 Gould Street
Needham Heights, MA 02194



Series Editor: Karen Hanson
Cover Administrator: Linda K. Dickinson
Manufacturing Buyer: Tamara McCracken
Editorial Production Service: Kathy Smith

**Library of Congress Cataloging-in-Publication Data**

Eitzen, D. Stanley.
Society's problems.

1. United States—Social conditions.
2. Social problems. 3. Social institutions
—United States. I. Title.
HN59.2.E33 1989 306′.0973 88-33291
ISBN 0-205-11979-4

Printed in the United States of America

10 9 8 7 6 5 4 3 2 1 93 92 91 90 89

# Contents

# Preface

The organization of this book and the selection of the articles are based on the fundamental assumption that the sources of social problems are found in the structure of society. Social problems are *not,* as is commonly believed, rooted in original sin, the genes, aberrant personalities, or flawed culture. They result from the organization of society itself. This emphasis on social structure is at the core of sociology. The sociological perspective requires a critical stance toward all social forms. Sociologists ask: How does the social system really work? Who really has the power? Who benefits under the existing social arrangements and who does not? The articles in this book ask and answer such questions. They examine critically both parts of and the totality of society. Thus, they will sensitize the reader to the inconsistencies present in society. But, more important, they will show how society actually perpetuates social problems. In the process, by addressing society as it is, they will expose existing myths, stereotypes, and official dogma.

As editor of this volume, my choices of articles were not based on the fiction of my value neutrality. They were based on my understanding of the structural sources and consequences of social problems and on my values. As I said in the preface to the fourth edition of *Social Problems:*

> I oppose social arrangements that prevent people from developing their full potential. This means that I reject political and social repression, educational elitism, institutional barriers to racial and sexual equality, economic exploitation, and official indifference to human suffering. Stating my feelings positively, I favor equality of opportunity, the right to dissent, justice, an economic system that minimizes inequality, and a political system that maximizes citizen input in decisions and provides for an adequate health care system and acceptable living conditions for all persons.[1]

While my values guided the selection of articles to be included, the writings herein are not biased—that is, they are not distorted and scientifically invalid. The study of social problems cannot be value-free for the problems examined and the strategies employed to solve them tend either to support or to undermine existing social arrangements. While both types are surely political, there is a strong tendency to label

[1]D. Stanley Eitzen, *Social Problems,* 4th ed. (Boston: Allyn and Bacon, 1989), p. x.

as political only the research that challenges the system. And, given the topic of this book, we shall examine in detail the latter type of research. To reiterate, although the analyses in this book are, by definition, political and value-laden, they are important to our understanding of the structural sources of social problems.

The book is divided into three major parts. The first part examines the key institutions of society—the economy and the polity—and how they work to perpetuate social problems. The second part focuses on inequality based on the exigencies of class, race, and gender. The topics covered include the new poverty, homelessness, hunger, the intractability of urban racial inequality, women's poverty, and pay equity. The final part focuses on specialized problems of certain institutions, for example, the family and child care, and the seeming epidemic of black teenage pregnancy; the workplace and inequality, worker exploitation, and the consequences of the changing economy for cities and populations; health care delivery to the poor, the problem with privatizing health care, the politics of tobacco, and the AIDS crisis; the concentration of power in the media and the effects of media violence on consumers, especially children; the criminal justice system, which defines and punishes criminals; and finally, issues involving the ultimate problems of national security (war, defense, priorities, and waste).

The articles have been selected to describe, explore, and analyze various social problems. They represent a sample of the thinking on these complex subjects, and should not be considered to be exhaustive or to present the only interpretations or answers. They have been selected for several reasons—they may provide rich details about a particular problem, they may explore and interpret a problem in an interesting and provocative way, or they may provide a potential solution to a problem. In every instance their inclusion is intended to provide the reader with insight and interpretation that might kindle interest and understanding into society's crucial problems.

# SOCIETY'S PROBLEMS

# The Sociology of Society's Problems

*D. Stanley Eitzen*

Social problems are *social* in origin and effect. The source of social problems is the organization of society, the normal ways that the social institutions of society function to distribute goods and services, to allocate jobs, to make societal decisions, to provide for defense, to educate youth, to disseminate information, to deliver health care, and to set laws and sanction the violators of those laws. Whenever these structural arrangements endanger human life—through the indiscriminate use of natural resources, the pollution of air, water, and land, or through war—there is a social problem. Whenever these structural arrangements are unfair to certain populations because of class (the poor), race (blacks, Hispanics, or Native Americans), or gender (women), there is a social problem. The focus, then, is on how the society operates and who benefits and who does not under the existing social patterns. In other words, we ask: Is the system biased? Are the societal rewards skewed? Do some categories of persons suffer or profit because of the way juries are selected, or because of the seniority system in the workplace, or by the way health care is provided?

To ask these kinds of questions diverts attention away from "problem" people and toward society's institutions as the generators and perpetrators of social problems. These kinds of questions are contrary to the strong tendency of most persons to perceive social problems and prescribe remedies from a psychological perspective. Typically, most persons blame the poor for their plight without seeing the maldistribution of wealth or the racism and sexism that limit education and job advancement, and thwart self-esteem. They blame poor black women for high illegitimacy rates and welfare dependency without reference to urban blight, extremely high unemployment rates for black males, and the cost of child care coupled with a very low minimum wage. They blame the homeless without understanding the sudden downward mobility of newly divorced women with children, the gentrification of inner cities, and the deinstitutionalization policies of state mental hospitals. They blame black and Hispanic males for high crime rates and have no appreciation for the structural limits placed on their upward social mobility, the government data that exaggerates the crimes of the poor and hides white-collar and corporate crimes, and the unjust system of justice. They tend to blame the recently unemployed without understanding the fundamental transformation of the economy from one based on manufacturing to one based on services and which is now global in scope rather than local or regional. The point of these examples is that most of us tend to find the basis for social problems within "problem" persons, those flawed by personal defect, rather than in the organization of society. We blame these "problem" individuals because their behaviors deviate from the standards of society. Because people do not ordinarily examine critically the normal way that things are done in society, they tend to question the exceptions. The system is not only taken for granted, but it also has an aura of sacredness about it. Consider, for example, the acceptance of capitalism in American society. Capitalism is not only accepted; it is revered. Capitalism is promoted and rarely, if ever, criticized by government, the schools, and by the churches. Yet capitalism promotes massive inequities and private gain without consideration for humane or societal consequences. This incongruence of our economic system with human needs is somehow obscured from our vision and understanding. This book directs our attention to such inconsistencies.

The critical examination of society is the heart of good sociology. The subject matter of sociology is social structure—the patterned social arrangements that emanate from social interaction. These arrangements are created by people and, therefore, are neither sacred nor perfect. The sociological perspective demands the critical assessment of these arrangements. The organization of this book and the essays selected are based on that premise.

Before you embark on this sociological journey, you should be aware of two dangers in the system-blame approach to social problems. Taken to an extreme, this orientation presents a rigidly deterministic explanation of social problems by viewing individuals as robots controlled totally by their social environment. Such a view, of course, goes too far. Individuals make choices between alternative courses of action. Oppressed people can join together to change oppressive social structures, as history demonstrates. A balanced view, then, acknowledges that individuals are not puppets controlled completely by the strings of society. Yet it must be recognized that society exerts powerful forces on individuals from the outside (laws, customs, sanctions) and from within (what we have been taught).

The second danger of the system-blame approach is that if it is accepted as dogma, then individuals are absolved from the responsibility of their actions. To take such a stance argues that society should never restrict problem people. That view invites anarchy and further complications from some individuals who are dangerous and who clearly require society's control. A realistic approach to social problems recognizes this.

While there are dangers to the system-blame approach, this clearly is the way to explain and understand social problems. Social problems, to reiterate, are social in origin and consequence. The key to understanding social problems is social structure and that theme dominates the selections in this book. The important implication of this is that the solutions to social problems require not changing "problem" people, but changing the structure of society.

# Part 1
# WEALTH AND POWER: THE BIAS OF THE SYSTEM

This section addresses the two "master" institutions of society—the economy and the polity. Institutions are social arrangements that channel behavior in prescribed ways in the important areas of social life. They are interrelated sets of normative elements—norms, values, and role expectations—that the people making up the society have devised and passed on to succeeding generations in order to provide solutions to society's perpetually unfinished business. The way that society is organized to produce and distribute goods and services (the economy) and the way it is organized to wield power (the polity) are the crucial determinants in the way the other institutions are organized. In other words, the economy and the polity shape the family, education, and religion—not the other way around.

The institutions of the economy and the polity are inexorably intertwined. The state is *not* a neutral agent of the people, but is biased in favor of those with wealth—the rich and the largest corporations. Contrary to popular belief, the United States is neither a society of equal opportunity nor a model of justice. Rather, in many fundamental ways, American Society is an "upside down" society, with the few benefiting at the expense of the many.

This section is divided into two chapters. Chapter 1 focuses on the economy. Joe Feagin's essay shows how private enterprise *causes* social problems. The following three articles by Morton Mintz, Mark Dowie, and Ronald Brownstein provide clear and representative examples of how corporate decisions are based on profit rather than humane considerations, with disastrous consequences for the victims and society. The final selection by the National Conference of Catholic Bishops examines capitalism critically and proposes structural solutions.

Chapter 2 begins with Michael Patrick Allen's essay on the relationship between money and political power in the United States. The remaining three articles examine specific problems generated by the polity. James H. Jones chronicles the amazing story of a government-sponsored medical experiment that used humans as unknowing guinea pigs. Samuel Epstein's article shows how the government has allowed political considerations to outweigh medical ones to the detriment of cancer research. The final selection, by D. Stanley Eitzen and Maxine Baca Zinn, considers how the policies of the Reagan Administration have resulted in greater inequality and hardships for particular segments of society.

# Chapter 1
# THE ECONOMY

## The Social Costs of Private Enterprise

*Joe R. Feagin*

### Introduction

Many social problems are the direct result of private enterprise. The emergence and expansion of capitalistic production has created numerous societal problems which are conventionally viewed as inevitable, isolated, or temporary, but which are actually the recurring social costs of the U.S. political–economic system. Periodically citizens' groups have targeted these costs for remedial action, making clear their discontent. Social costs include air and water pollution, toxic waste, the destruction of wildlife, soils, and forest resources, unemployment, and poverty. Those who control the private production of goods and services often give little attention to the dangerous byproducts and negative side effects of their routine activities. Pollution grows until the Love Canal area is unsafe to live in. Basic resources are consumed so fast that they disappear, ozone layers which protect humans from too much sunlight are destroyed by deodorant sprays, and forests are stripped until oxygen levels decline. These losses do not enter into the traditional cost accounting of private corporations (see Kapp, 1950).

Environmental costs are not the only losses from private enterprise. There are the direct human costs of private production—losses which can be seen in injuries and deaths from workplace accidents and occupational diseases as well as in unemployment and its related poverty. Much human wreckage seen in these problems is the direct result of the unbridled private operation of capitalistic enterprise. There are yet other costs. There is the psychopathological impact of privately controlled production, the mental and other stress burdens imposed, ranging from a hyper-consumerist ethic, to neurocirculatory diseases from workplace stress and violent personal crime resulting from chronic unemployment. Many such problems are conventionally seen as noneconomic, as somehow unrelated to basic political–economic institutions. On the contrary, these problems are intimately related to the everyday operation of market capitalism.

---

Joe R. Feagin, "The Social Costs of Private Enterprise," *Research in Social Problems and Public Policy* 3 (1984), pp. 115–116; 122–133. 

---

See Statistical Appendix Tables A–1, A–15, and A–17.

It is the purpose of this essay to argue for a reinvigorated theory of social problems which views such problems as grounded in or shaped by the fundamental political-economic conditions of this society: the structure and process of modern capitalism.

## What Are Social Costs?

Exactly what are social costs? They are the negative consequences of private for-profit production; they are the costs which are not paid for by the individual firm; they are costs which are shifted onto other people, onto third parties including individuals and whole communities. In capitalistic societies, generally speaking, investment and production decisions are made without a satisfactory prior accounting of societal consequences (Kapp, 1950:xv, 13–25). Costs are calculated at the micro-economic level of the individual company in terms of its profits, its future net revenues, its share of the market. Decision-making by this criterion will seek to reduce internal costs and to ignore many social costs which can be displaced onto third persons. Many social problems are created because decision-making affecting whole communities is made at the level of the individual firm, where decision makers use a narrow accounting method that aims at achievement of in-house cost savings and profits. A company's accounts generally do not figure the larger social costs into their internal budget sheets: "These costs don't show up on any firm's ledger; no accountant writes them down. They're not charged against the income the firm makes from selling its products and services" (Smith, 1979:3).

But the social costs do not occur accidentally or because companies cannot plan adequately for the future. Indeed, very large corporations are "the most ardent and successful planners in the United States" (Carnoy and Shearer, 1980:233). Corporate capitalists and top managers, for many decades, have planned what products to make, the product cycle, the level of profit considered acceptable, product design, mass market advertising, overseas market expansion, and congressional lobbying. Modern capitalism is not a planless array of small companies competing in a free market system. Capitalism is dominated by large corporations with large planning staffs who may try to coordinate their activities, often successfully, with a few other companies. They plan for higher profits and expanded markets, but seldom plan to *reduce* social costs.

Why are firms able to create social problems by shifting their social costs off onto other people? Because they have greater economic and political power. In a society with a vast inequality in income and in the ability to make decisions about jobs and resources, the production and distribution decisions of companies, particularly large firms, are hard for ordinary citizens to resist or change. And challenging the great power and resource inequality is made difficult by the fact that many social costs (e.g., cancer from extensive workplace pollution) may take a long time to show up in individuals or in a community.

"Free enterprise" markets are sacred in U.S. society. Conservatives and liberals alike accept decisions aimed at the market as the primary adjudicator of what is or is not produced, with governmental production and intervention seen as secondary. Indeed, this society is frequently portrayed as one big market where virtually everything is for sale. But market prices do not necessarily reflect the larger social costs. An individual firm's market-oriented decision to produce a given product for sale can look positive if seen solely in terms of that firm's internal cost accounting. But when numerous companies make decisions in this fashion which create, for example, high unemployment from corporate relocation or cancer-causing pollution, it becomes clear that the market process can be very negative for the larger social or community context.

## A Closer Look at Profits

Corporate profit seeking is at the heart of social costs. Profit decisions are in private hands. The business creed's emphasis on profits is still widely accepted. For four decades Warner and Swasey corporate ads, for example, have aggressively argued that attacks on profits "show their foreign accent" and are made by "furtive people" (Sutton, Harris, Kaysen, and Tobin, 1956:70). Billboards across the nation proclaim that "profits mean jobs." The idea that profit seeking can be antisocial is explicitly rejected. President C. E. Wilson of General Electric once emphasized this view. "Certainly there is nothing antisocial in profit. I think the truth of the matter is that—given access to all as buyers and sellers—the profit earned by the wise businessman is a measure of the service he has rendered to his market, in terms of a value placed on those services by the buyers, individually and collectively" (Sutton, Harris, Kaysen, and Tobin, 1956:72). The need for societal growth, according to a recent Boston Federal Reserve Bank booklet (1974:27), is a common justification for profit seeking: "In a private enterprise system the hope for profits encourages new production, investment and economic growth." There is often a "consumer-is-king" theory which goes along with this view. Corporate executives argue that they *only* make what consumers demand, neglecting the role advertising and marketing play in creating demand. Competition, it was further argued by G. E.'s Wilson, "will assure that the profits which are earned are not excessive" (Sutton, Harris, Kaysen, and Tobin, 1956:73). Ultimately capitalists and top corporate executives make the broad investment decisions, within which latitude lower-level managers and ordinary workers can act.

Business schools have taught that short-run, maximized profitability is the central goal of business. Thus a recent review of the business school literature found that managers are taught to make decisions based on such factors as short-run profitability, market share, and annual sales growth. Luria and Russell (1981:30:34) found a graph used in the teaching curriculum of Harvard Business School. The graph instructs young managers how to invest. It indicates that a "dog" company (or subsidiary) is one with sales growth under 8 percent a year and with a market share less than that of its nearest competitor. A "star" company (or subsidiary) has a market share substantially greater than that of its nearest competitor and a sales growth of at least 8–10 percent per year. A cash "cow" is a company with a large market share but sales growth rates under 8–10 percent per year. Fledgling managers learn that they should disinvest in "dogs" and "cows" and invest in more profitable "stars" or near-stars.

But this type of investment decision-making ignores, among other things, the many social costs of investment or disinvestment. For example, job-creating investments with modest profitability (a "dog"?) can have an impact beyond an individual company. Such modest-profit investments can generate small businesses in an area, thus indirectly creating greater employment. And by creating jobs, other gains come such as less government expenditure for unemployment insurance, welfare, and policing. Typically such factors are not included in the firm-level decision making process about capital investments.

Even the corporate managers of big corporations are taught that their powerful firms should be run as investment portfolios, with their various subsidiaries seen as profit centers competing with one another for the highest levels of net revenue. Short-term profitability is emphasized here as elsewhere; if one business subsidiary declines a bit, it should be abandoned and the money invested elsewhere. Companies are thus managed like investment portfolios; resources are quickly shifted to keep the portfolio viable. Some operations are to be "milked" for cash, and thus killed off, for investments elsewhere. The operations of a subsidiary company or subdivision which do well become places for expanded investment.

Recently, even two business school professors, Robert H. Hayes and William J. Abernathy, have argued that this extreme short-vision philosophy may be responsible for the difficulties faced by American corporations, such as their frequent losing out in competing with Japanese firms (Wayne, 1983:F1). The real cause of these difficulties does not lie in lower Japanese labor costs or even in subsidies to firms from the Japanese government, but rather in the philosophy which emphasizes rate of return in the short run as the measure of corporate success. As Leslie Wayne (1983:F1) wrote in the *New York Times* recently, this U.S. corporate approach "piles its rewards on executives who force through impressive short-term performance, at indeterminate cost to long-term health. Fearing any dip in today's profits, American companies keep research and technology on short rations, skimping the investment critically needed to insure competitiveness tomorrow."

Hayes and Abernathy have argued that this serious neglect of long-term technological investments for short-term profits and fancy financial techniques is responsible for the relative decline of U.S. business; Japan is doing better because corporations there give much greater emphasis to quality control, to preventive maintenance of machinery, and to good worker-manager relations.[1] They further argue that American executives' concern for short-term profits has led to cost-cutting approaches which make manufacturing more standardized at the expense of innovation in technology. The short-term profitability corporate orientation has resulted not only in serious social costs for the larger society but also in problems in long-run health and profitability for corporations themselves (Wayne, 1982:F21).

Many corporate executives are aware of citizen criticism of their profit seeking and seek to develop a better public image of their companies. Some try to mix into their public image a publicized concern for community service. The chairperson of the board of Aetna Life and Casualty recently expressed this idea:"Experience has taught us that in addition to helping others the pursuit of social goals can significantly strengthen a corporation's capacity to achieve its primary corporate purpose of being profitable" (Research and Policy Committee, CED, 1982:82). The social goals he mentions here would likely include such things as charitable contributions, but he notes the primary goal of profits. As a top executive quoted in a recent report on urban problems by the Committee for Economic Development (CED)[2] explains, corporate philanthropy and community involvement are aimed at enhancing the images of corporations and at enhancing profit and production: "the principal function of the business corporation is to produce goods and services in a manner that will provide for an expanding base of production" (Research Policy Committee, CED, 1982:82).

In its 1981 *Annual Report* Eaton, a $3.2 billion conglomerate making electronic and automotive products, notes that its "first and most important contribution to society" is "to provide jobs, produce goods and earn profits" (Eaton Corporation, 1982:18). But it also adds that it contributes $2.8 million a year to civic, health, and cultural organizations as well as to colleges "of importance to the company." The signed statement by the two top executives at the beginning of this *Annual Report* accents the point that public policy in the next decade will emphasize the "clear need of the productive sector of the economy for nourishment" and a "de-emphasis on social programs." These executives look favorably on the new emphasis on wealth: "In short, we expect there to be an emphasis in the '80s on the creation of wealth, rather than its redistribution" (Eaton Corporation, 1982:5). The tension between basic corporation goals and societal needs seems clear in these views of profitability.

## Traditional Answers to the Dilemma of Social Costs

For the most part, business executives, traditional economists and other social scientists have accepted official measures of this society's health and development such as national income, corporate profits, and Gross National Profit (GNP). But these widely accepted statistics are, at least in part, misleading because they do not give an accurate picture of total societal health. The negative social costs are omitted. Measuring the growth and progress of a society in terms of GNP or profits can be misleading, for when unemployment-related crime goes up and people buy more burglar alarms, GNP and the profits of certain businesses increase, but the society has not "progressed." When Americans are less healthy and spend more on medical care the GNP increases, but the American people as a whole have not necessarily become more healthy or prosperous. When more is spent on a variety of harmful items and sales and profits go up, so does the GNP, which many assume to be a good sign. Yet that is often not the case. From the perspective of a society's total economic health, GNP-type statistics are not adequate because they mix together measures of societal illness as well as health.

Uncounted social costs have traditionally been ignored or viewed in traditional economic theory as "market defects," "externalities," or "transaction costs." One systematic study of the dominant business creed has noted that certain problems of capitalism such as systematic unemployment "have received little attention in the business creed, except indirect and polemical treatment in the form of attacks on the welfare state or on the dangers of workers' demands for security" (Sutton, Harris, Kaysen, and Tobin, 1956:51). A variety of traditional theories has been presented to try to account for a few selected social costs. Some analysts speak of a "market breakdown." Others emphasize that some social costs are just an inevitable part of industrialization or technological change. Population growth is the major villain for yet other analysts. Some observers blame consumers themselves for their wasteful desires, seeing corporations as responding to consumer wants. While all these explanations are relevant to social problems, they do not seem to be as central to many problems as the character of the process of capitalistic production and distribution itself (Kapp, 1950:xiv).

## The Many Faces of Capitalism: Specific Social Costs

We can now turn to the concrete ways in which modern capitalism persists in generating and shaping the problems faced by citizens of this society. We have only the space here to trace out a few major examples.[3]

### Air, Water, and Land Pollution

Enterprises oriented to short-term profitability tend to ignore environmental costs, which are as a result paid for by third parties, such as people affected by industrial smog in cities like Los Angeles and Houston or by radioactive airborne and groundborne waste from nuclear power plants. Air pollution can cause major losses to property, such as the deterioration of paint on houses, and it causes losses to human beings in the form of cancer and other debilitating diseases. Polluted urban air has been linked to an increased probability of respiratory diseases and asthma. Today much unnecessary air pollution is generated by manufacturing and other industrial concerns, either by their day-to-day operations or by the products they produce. Oil, utility, steel, chemical, metals, and auto companies create much U.S. air pollution. For example, in the 1970s for several summers steel mills in Alabama, a state with weakly enforced pollution standards, polluted the air so heavily that a very severe health hazard was created, not only for the people there but for people in nearby states as well.

Another societal cost from private enterprise production can be seen in the chemical waste pollution generated by thousands of chemical and other manufacturing plants. A recent report of the U.S. Surgeon General predicted that in the 1980s people in many communities will face environmental emergencies created by toxic chemical wastes which have not been properly disposed of. The Environmental Protection Agency (EPA) has estimated that U.S. chemical companies and other economic organizations account for 77 billion pounds of dangerous chemical waste annually. Included are such chemicals a biphenyl (PCB), trichloroethylene, benzene, nitroglycerine, mercury, arsenic, and biological agents (No author, ''The Poisoning of America,'' 1980:58–63).

Frequently toxic wastes are stored in metal drums and other containers, and are improperly and unsafely distributed above ground or underground, in back lots, on farmland, or in lakes and rivers. Some waste has been disposed of openly; in other cases companies have paid truckers to haul it off and dump it at night in rural areas. No one knows where all the major dump sites are or how much waste has actually been deposited. The federal EPA has estimated that there are at least 2,000 disposal sites with potential for creating serious health hazards. A number of observers have called the thousands of dump sites ticking ''time bombs.'' Some of these bombs have already gone off. There were three major explosions and fires in the New York area in the middle of 1979. One explosion, in a dump with tens of thousands of barrels of chemicals, rocked parts of northern New Jersey and Manhattan. Chemical wastes were responsible for major fires and toxic fumes in Carlstadt and Perth Amboy, New Jersey, where people were evacuated from nearby residential areas. Moreover, underground water pools have recently been found to be seriously contaminated with chemical wastes in New Jersey townships, twenty-two towns in Massachusetts, and several areas in the Midwest (No author, ''The Poisoning of America,'' (1980:59–63).

Large-scale programs to eliminate these types of life-threatening pollution typically require *considerable* monetary expenditures. As a general rule, profit-oriented corporations will not voluntarily take the large-scale action necessary to pay for such social costs. In most cases these firms fight pollution controls as government interference, because they know that in the short run *their profits* will fall as they spend more money for pollution control equipment. Influential capitalists such as David Rockefeller, one-time head of Chase Manhattan Bank, have said that ''unrealistic pollution abatement costs on industry'' will make companies uncompetitive in the world market. Moreover, one recent survey of executives in multinational corporations discovered many who felt that expenditures for pollution controls would make their firms less profitable (Barnet and Muller, 1974:343–344).

Citizen protests against chemical pollution such as that at Love Canal in New York have heavily pressured local and federal governments to pass laws and set up regulations partially limiting the extent of pollution. Ironically, some polluting corporations are now in the position of making profits from cleaning up the pollution caused by their own industry. Most chemical companies now have pollution abatement divisions responsible for cleanup procedures, processes, and devices. The cleanup costs are often subsidized by governments. Martin Gellen has pointed out that the chemical industry is ''in the enviable position of reaping sizable profits by attempting to clean up rivers and lakes (at public expense) which they have profitably polluted in the first place'' (Hunt and Sherman, 1981:198).

## The Throwaway Economy

A major series of crises facing U.S. society has to do with mineral, oil, and gas resources. Cheap oil–gas energy will be very expensive for American society in the long run, since cheap energy has made possible such enterprises as the large-automobile industry, the synthetic packaging industry, and the aluminum industry. Had cheap energy not been available, those industries might well have never developed as they did.

The packaging industry has moved substantially in the direction of throwaway containers. Yet production of throwaway bottles takes four times as much energy and throwaway cans three times as much energy as returnable bottles. Shifting the beer and soft drink industries back to returnable containers would sharply reduce energy demand. A small increase in convenience to corporations and their consumers brings societal problems in the form of higher consumer prices for products and energy, and manufacturers of throwaway containers meanwhile reap substantial profits from ecologically unsound packaging technologies. Throwaway products can often be profitable from a corporate point of view, since there is always additional demand. They also create a marketing flexibility preferred by corporations. Long-term reusable products, whether pop bottles or cars, can be a profit-oriented executive's nightmare. Built-in obsolescence seems to be a central feature of production (Hannon, 1975:115–117). Whether this wasteful packaging can continue, given the ever rising cost of raw materials, remains to be seen.

## Hyper-Consumerism and Its Waste

The wasteful consumption of resources by industries is tied to the creation of *hyper-consumerism* among rank-and-file citizens. Hunt and Sherman (1981:196) have dramatized the point that modern capitalistic advertising, marketing, and other socialization processes "make consumption-hungry, irrational, compulsive buying machines of us all." While this exaggerates the point, nonetheless multi-billion-dollar advertising and public relations work are critical to creating environmental and energy problems, since the primary goal of their activities is to generate hyper-consumerism, to convince consumers to buy products (in large quantities) they do not need or products that are of questionable ecological value. Coupled with advertising is industrial designing, where many people work hard to design such unnecessary commodity features as chrome fins for automobiles, electric hairbrushes, and "sexy" packages for many products. Many marketing people then devise ways of selling such products to consumers. Hundreds of thousands of Americans work daily to design and package products that no one really needs. Billions of dollars are spent annually to entice consumers to buy attractively packaged and advertised goods. Products need to be packaged, but far more effort goes into packaging than is necessary to hold products (Papenek, 1971:xxi, 171–190).

Some advertising may be necessary for information purposes; but billions are spent in persuading consumers to buy the products made. Corporate apologists assert that the consumer is "king" or "queen" of the market and that consumers demand the products they make. But do consumers really demand deodorant sprays that destroy the earth's ozone layer, twenty kinds of toothpaste, and poorly designed, or gas guzzling automobiles with built-in obsolescence? Another problem with the conventional argument is that many consumers "demand" products that industry may not want to supply, such as high-speed mass transit and long lasting, energy-efficient autos.

Much waste is created by the commitment of corporate officials to product differentiation. Every year or so automobiles are changed in terms of exterior design, then are presented to consumers as something "new" they cannot do without. Over the last decade Americans increased their consumption of synthetic food additives—coloring, artificial flavors, texturizers, preservatives—by nearly 100 percent, from 5 pounds per person per year to nearly 10 pounds per person per year. An estimated 4 million pounds of color dyes are eaten by consumers each year (Schell, 1979:37–38). Today food technology has become a massive operation attempting to make vegetables, fruits, meats, milk products, and processed foods look better than they are in reality and to create "new" artificial products. Each new chemical additive can potentially bring great new profits to the company developing it. And additives help food corporations disguise lesser quality products from consumers.

Under capitalism almost everything, numerous observers have noted, can become a commodity for sale. The market orientation is pervasive. In a series of books Erich Fromm has emphasized how a commodity-oriented market society regularly alienates its members from themselves: "Man," he notes,

> experiences himself as a thing to be employed successfully on the market. He does not experience himself as an active agent, as the bearer of human powers. His aim is to sell himself successfully on the market. His sense of self does not stem from his activity as a loving and thinking individual, but from his socio-economic role. . . . If you ask a man, "Who are you?" he answers, "I am a manufacturer," "I am a clerk,". . . . This is the way he experiences himself, not as a man, with love, fear, convictions, doubts, but as that abstraction, alienated from his real nature, which fulfills a certain function in the social system. (Fromm, 1965:129–130)

In a commodity-oriented market society the evaluation of human beings, their friendliness, "personality," and ability in dollars-and-cents terms is commonplace. An alienated sense of self is yet another social cost of capitalism.

## Social Costs at the Workplace

Much of the price for a business system centered on short-term profits and annual cost-benefit accounting is paid by workers in the form of accidents and diseases, including delayed-effect diseases such as cancers. Workplace safety can cut into profits. Ralph Nader has commented that "as a form of violence, job casualties are statistically at least three times more serious than street crime, and with each new discovery or documentation of a hitherto neglected exposure to gases, chemicals, particulates, radiation, or noise, the epidemic looms larger and more pervasive"

(Nader, 1973:xiii). Recent surveys by federal health agencies have found a third of all workers in factories are working in situations where they are exposed to serious health hazards. Yet the majority are not aware of the unsafe conditions; capitalistic employers often by intention keep workers uninformed of the workplace hazards because greater worker awareness and democratic participation in workplace decisions would corrode private control of workplaces by employers.

An estimated 6,000 workers are killed and 2.7 million are seriously injured on the job annually. These are corporate figures, so they are doubtless lower than the real figures. Indeed, some observers argue that 10,000 workers are killed on the job annually, with serious injuries totalling 8 to 10 million. In the six decades after 1900 accident rates in manufacturing declined, but from the mid-1960s to the late 1970s the accident rate climbed. Corporate fines for fatal accidents usually run $10,000 or less, so that large corporations need not fear regulatory agencies. When profits are in the hundreds of millions, a few fines might well be regarded as a ''cost'' of doing business (Reutter, 1980:58–68).

However, workplace accidents have been sharply reduced in European countries where pure capitalistic operations have been replaced by nationalized enterprises with more worker or public input. For example, in Britain the nationalized coal industry has a fatal injury rate less than 20 percent of the death rate in the U.S. coal industry. In Britain, unions have joint consultation with management on safety issues. In addition, millions of U.S. workers are regularly exposed to high levels of cancer-causing materials. Longterm exposure to dangerous dust, radiation, and chemicals kills, according to the National Institute for Occupational Safety and Health, at least 100,000 Americans each year, and perhaps several times that figure (Epstein, 1978:80–81).[4]

## Social Costs of Light Water Nuclear Reactors

A common defense of nuclear power plants is that they provide not only major sources of energy for electricity but also thousands of jobs, directly in the plants themselves and indirectly in the businesses using nuclear-generated electricity. Nuclear industry executives frequently tell consumers that they will have to face brownouts and blackouts without nuclear power; that consumers' standard of living is linked to building dozens of power plants. Yet in a recent book on nuclear power David E. Lilienthal (1979), the first chairman of the Atomic Energy Commission (AEC), has sharply criticized the decisions of private industry and even the AEC to develop the now widely used ''light water'' nuclear reactors to generate electricity. In his book Lilienthal attacks this existing nuclear technology as ''immature'' and ''too complex'' and as having too many places ''at which something can go wrong.'' Remarkably candid, Lilienthal (1979) emphatically criticizes the choice of light water reactor technology as ''chosen too hastily'' and ''for short-run commercial gain.''

One environmental problem of power reactors is the disposal of the toxic radioactive waste regularly generated by power plants. The waste includes radioactive waste regularly generated by power plants. The waste includes radioactive isotopes of cesium and iodine, as well as plutonium. Plutonium is a very dangerous element and is lethal in amounts too small to see. It remains dangerously radioactive for many generations. As yet, we have no permanent disposal sites for waste plutonium and similar materials. Radioactive wastes stored in the state of Washington have already seeped out of storage tanks and into the underground water system.

Most serious of all are major nuclear power plant accidents. There have already been a number of serious accidents and near disasters. In the early 1960s three workers in an Idaho reactor testing station were killed when a radioactive core in a reactor went out of control and exploded. In the mid-1960s the Fermi experimental nuclear reactor near Detroit was closed down because of a failure of coolant systems. The core melted but was finally brought under control. A major catastrophe was narrowly missed, and a few years later the plant was permanently closed down. In the mid-1970s there was a near disaster at Browns Ferry nuclear power plant in Alabama.

The accident at Three Mile Island in Pennsylvania made clear the social costs of capitalism. As elsewhere, the rush to construct light water reactors in central Pennsylvania has been justified by its cheaper costs compared with alternatives. Yet nowhere in the rush to develop this nuclear technology was there a careful projection of the long-term social costs, including routine and emergency cleanup costs. The Three Mile Island accident shows what these social and human costs are. The accident created such fear in nearby areas that the miscarriage rate for women increased; unborn infants died. Half a billion dollars had been spent on the cleanup by mid-1982; informal estimates suggest that another $2 billion will be required to decontaminate completely the Three Mile Island power plant facility. Who is paying and who will pay these costs? Electric consumers covered by the utility there have already paid for part of it in higher electric rates. The federal taxpayer will probably pay, in one way or another, for much of the cleanup cost. Such longterm costs as these have not been figured into the costs of building and operating nuclear power plants, at least in public announcements by the nuclear industry.

And the Three Mile Island accident was minor compared to what could conceivably happen. A Brookhaven National Laboratory report estimated what the casualties would be from a large nuclear reactor disaster (a complete meltdown) a few miles from a major city; an accident might kill 45,000 people, injure 100,000, and make an area the size of the state of Pennsylvania unusable for a long period of time. The 1965 report was not released by the government until 1973, out of fear that the public response might have stopped nuclear reactor construction (Olson, 1976:22–28). Nuclear industry advocates admit that there is a 50–50 chance of such a major core meltdown accident happening once during the total operating lifetimes of all existing and planned power plants, but from their point of view this is an "acceptable risk."

## Unemployment and Underemployment

Late in 1982 eleven million Americans were officially unemployed, just 10.4 percent of the labor force, the highest percentage since the Depression. These Americans were only the tip of the iceberg. Many more millions were out of work: some were discouraged workers who had been out of work so long they had given up looking, some were working part-time but wanted full-time work, some such as unemployed illegal aliens just did not get into the official statistics. And tens of millions more Americans were sub-employed, that is, their wages were too low to support a family at a minimally decent standard of living. Yet other millions of workers were working at jobs which did not make use of their skills or education.

The U.S. political-economic system regularly generates large numbers of unemployed workers; periodically depression-level (20–30 percent unemployed) percentages of unemployed workers are created in many parts of the country. Judging from its daily realities, modern capitalism does seem to require *high* levels of unemployment. The human costs associated with unemployment are substantial. Workers who are unemployed for very long use up their savings, so houses and cars are repossessed by banks. Illnesses, physical and psychological, may increase; family tensions may increase. Workers who have built up communities—churches, schools, streets, water systems—may be forced to move elsewhere, leaving behind towns and cities in decay for lack of workers to pay local taxes. A common occurrence in the last decade has been the closing down of a plant in a community, often in the northern states, and the investment of the capital saved in corporate operations elsewhere, in the Sunbelt or in the Third World. Thousands of plants and other corporate facilities have been closed because the level of profits was not up to the corporate standard. Even profit-making plants are closed if the profit level is not high enough, no matter what the social costs for workers and surrounding communities may be (Bluestone, Harrison, and Baker, 1981:12–13).

Other social problems are linked to unemployment and subemployment, which sharply reduce the income resources of large groups in the U.S. population. Much property crime, for example, is committed by young people (especially nonwhites) who have little hope for decent-paying jobs, whose family backgrounds are replete with unemployment or poverty, or who have gone into a life of drugs to block the unpleasant realities of life around them (Quinney, 1979:166–167, 221–225). Physical and mental illnesses are endemic in high unemployment areas. This society pays a high price in human losses for persisting unemployment and subemployment. Historically, as poorer ethnic groups (e.g., the Irish, the Italians) have moved up into stable, decent-paying employment property thefts and other crimes have declined among them. . . .

## Notes

1. Even in Japan, however, the criterion of profitability leads to a neglect of human factors, and thus to societal problems. The point here is that some, though by no means all, societal problems are *lessened* when capitalists modify their actions to include long-term and human relations issues.
2. The CED is one of the most important corporate policy making organizations at the national level. Its research staff reports to a board of directors which is made up of top (presidents, board chairs) corporate executives. Its policy reports have shaped federal and state government policy.

3. An earlier discussion of some examples cited in this section appeared in Feagin (1982:314-319, 343-345, 361-365).
4. Even the threat of lawsuits need not be a serious deterrent, since for every company which is successfully sued, hundreds if not thousands more laugh "all the way to the bank." Moreover, a company facing lawsuits can dodge them, even though still profitable, by filing for limited bankruptcy under friendly laws.

## References


Alcaly, Roger E. and Helen Bodain
1977 "New York's fiscal crisis and the economy." Pp. 30-58 in Roger E. Alcaly and David Mermelstein (eds.), The Fiscal Crisis of American Cities. New York: Random House Vintage Books.

Albert, Michael and Robin Hahnel
1981 Socialism Today and Tomorrow. Boston. South End Press.

Auletta, Ken
1980 The Streets Were Paved With Gold. New York: Random House Vintage Books.

Barnet, Richard J. and Ronald E. Muller
1974 Global Reach. New York: Simon and Schuster

Bassis, Michael S., Gelles, Richard J. and Ann Levine
1982 Social Problems. New York: Harcourt Brace Jovanovich Inc.

Bayles, Fred
1981 "Hizzoner the socialist." The Boston Phoenix, May 26, 1981, pp. 2, 8.

Bluestone, Barry, Harrison, Bennett, and Lawrence Baker
1981 Corporate Flight. Washington, D.C.: Progressive Alliance.

Braverman, Harry
1974 Labor and Monopoly Control. New York: Monthly Review Press.

Boston Federal Reserve Bank
1974 Introducing Economics. Boston: Boston Federal Reserve Bank.

Boyte, Harry C.
1980 The Backyard Revolution. Philadelphia: Temple University Press.

Carnoy, Martin and Derek Shearer
1980 Economic Democracy. Armonk, N. Y.: M. E. Sharpe.

Classen, Alfred
1980 "The policy perspective: social problems as investment opportunities." Social Problems 27: 526-539.

Drier, Peter
1984 "The tenants movement." In L. Sawers and W. Tabb (eds.), Marxism and the Metropolis, Second Edition. New York: Oxford Press.

Eaton Corporation
1982 1981 Annual Report.

Epstein, Samuel S.
1978 The Politics of Cancer. San Francisco: Sierra Club Books.

Etzioni, Amitai
1976 Social Problems. Englewood Cliffs, N.J.: Prentice-Hall, Inc.

Feagin, Joe R.
1982 Social Problems: A Critical Power-Conflict Perspective. Englewood Cliffs, N.J.: Prentice-Hall, Inc.

Fromm, Erich
1965 The Sane Society. New York: Fawcett World Library, Premier Books.

Hannon, Bruce
1975 "Bottles, cans, and energy use." Pp. 114-121 in B. Commoner, H. Boksenbaum, and M. Corr (eds.), Human Welfare: The End Use for Power. New York: Macmillan.

Horton, Paul B. and Gerald Leslie
1981 The Sociology of Social Problems. Englewood Cliffs, N. J.: Prentice-Hall, Inc.

Hunt, E. K. and Howard Sherman
1981 Economics. Fourth edition. New York: Harper and Row.

Kapp, Karl W.
1950 The Social Costs of Private Enterprise. New York: Schocken Books.

Lauer, Robert H.
1982 Social Problems and the Quality of Life.

Second edition. Dubuque, Iowa: William C. Brown.

Leibig, Michael
1980 Social Investments and the Law: The Case for Alternative Investments, Washington, D.C.: Conference on Alternative State and Local Policies.

Lilienthal, David E.
1979 Atomic Energy. New York: Harper and Row.

Lindblom, Charles E. and David K. Cohen
1979 Usable Knowledge. New Haven: Yale University Press.

Lindorff, Dave
1981 "About-face in Santa Monica." The Village Voice, December 2-8, 1981, p. 20.

Lindsey, Robert
1982 "Jane Fonda's exercise salons aiding her husband's candidacy." New York Times, May 2, 1982, p. Y-11.

Luria, Dan and Jack Russell
1981 Rational Reindustrialization: An Economic Development Agenda for Detroit. Detroit: Widgetripper Press.

Merton, Robert K.
1971 "Social problems and sociological theory." Pp. 793-845 in Robert K. Merton and Robert Nisbet (eds.), Contemporary Social Problems. New York: Harcourt Brace Jovanovich Inc.

Mills, C. Wright
1963 "The professional ideology of social pathologists." Pp. 526-532 in I. L. Horowitz (ed.), Power, Politics, and People. New York: Ballantine Books.

Moynihan, Daniel P.
1969 Maximum Feasible Misunderstanding. New York: Free Press.

Nader, Ralph
1973 "Preface." Pp. xiii-xiv in Joseph A. Page and Mary-Win O'Brien, Bitter Wages. New York: Grossman.

Nickerson, Colin
1981 "Red mayor in the green mountains." Rolling Stone, May 28, 1981, pp. 13-14.

Nisbet, Robert
1971 "The study of social problems." Pp. 1-28, in Robert K. Merton and Robert Nisbet (eds.), Contemporary Social Problems. New York: Harcourt Brace Jovanovich Inc.

No Author
1980 "The Poisoning of America." Time, September 22, 1980, pp. 58-63.

No Author
1981 "Capital moves: who's left behind." Dollars and Sense, April, 1981, pp. 7-9.

Olson, Mckinley C.
1976 Unacceptable Risk. New York: Bantam Books.

Papanek, Victor
1971 Design for the Real World. New York: Random House.

Perlman, Janice
1979 "Grassroots empowerment and government response." Social Policy. 10:16-19.

Perrow, Charles
1982 "Not risk but power." Contemporary Sociology 11:298-300.

Quinney, Richard
1979 Criminology. Second edition. Boston: Little Brown.

Research Policy Committee, Committee for Economic Development (CED)
1982 Public-Private Partnership: An Opportunity for Urban Communities. New York: Committee for Economic Development.

Reutter, Mark
1980 "The invisible risk." Mother Jones 5:48-58.

Sagan, Leonard
1981 "Have the nuclear power risk assessors failed?" Pp. 321-344 in George G. Berg and H. David Maillie (eds.), Measurement of Risks. New York: Plenum Press.

Schell, Orville
1979 "What this country needs is a stronger white rat." Mother Jones 4:37-41.

Schwing, Richard C. and Walter A. Albers (eds.)
1980 Societal Risk Assessment: How Safe is Safe Enough? New York: Plenum Press.

Smigel, Edwin O.
1971 "The sociology of a social problems handbook." Pp. ix-xiv in Edwin O. Smigel (ed.), Handbook on the Study of Social Problems. Chicago: Rand McNally.

Smith, David
1979 The Public Balance Sheet. Washington, D. C.: Conference on Alternative State and Local Policies.

Sutton, Francis X., Harris, Seymour E., Kayser, Karl, and James Tobin
1956 The American Business Creed. Cambridge: Harvard University Press.

Wayne, Leslie
1982 "Management gospel gone wrong." New York Times, May 30, 1982, p. F1, 21.

Webb, Lee and William Schwecke
1979 Public Employee Pension Funds: New Strategies for Investment. Washington, D. C.: Conference on Alternative State and Local Policies.

# A Crime Against Women: A.H. Robins and the Dalkon Shield

*Morton Mintz*

In January 1971, the A.H. Robins Company began to sell the Dalkon Shield, promoting it as the "modern, superior," "second generation" and—most importantly—"safe" intrauterine device for birth control. Robins, a major pharmaceutical manufacturer in Richmond, Virginia, distributed 4.5 million of the IUDs in eighty countries before halting sales in the mid-1970s. There followed a catastrophe without precedent in the annals of medicine and law.

The seriously injured victims number in the tens of thousands. Nearly all suffered life-threatening forms of the infections known as pelvic inflammatory disease (PID). In the United States alone, PID killed at least eighteen women who had been wearing Shields. Most of the infections impaired or destroyed the women's ability to bear children.

Not only was the Shield unsafe, it was surprisingly ineffective. The number of wearers who became pregnant with the devices in place was on the order of 110,000, or 5 percent—a rate nearly five times the one falsely claimed in advertising and promotion to physicians and women, and a rate sharply higher than that for many other IUDs. More than ordinary commercial puffery, the exaggerated and bogus claims led women to reject more effective birth control in favor of the Shield; and this led directly to consequences far worse than unwanted pregnancies. Statistically, half of all women who become pregnant with an IUD miscarry. But in fact, of the estimated 110,000 women who conceived while wearing the Dalkon Shield, 66,000—or 60 percent—miscarried. Most suffered the previously rare miscarriages called spontaneous abortions in either the first or second trimester. Others, in the fourth to sixth months of pregnancy, experienced the still rarer infected miscarriages, or septic spontaneous abortions. By the count of the Food and Drug Administration (FDA), 248 women in this country alone endured this dangerous, Shield-related complication; for 15 of them, these septic abortions were fatal.

Moreover, hundreds of women throughout the world who conceived while wearing the Shield gave birth prematurely, in the final trimester, to children with grave congenital defects including blindness, cerebral palsy, and mental retardation, or that were stillborn. No one can pinpoint the exact number of such women, partly

---

Morton Mintz, "A Crime Against Women: A.H. Robins and the Dalkon Shield." This article is reprinted from the *Multinational Monitor 7* (January 15, 1986), pp. 1–7. *Multinational Monitor* is a monthly news magazine published by Essential Information, Inc., P.O. Box 19405, Washington, D.C. 20036. $22 individual.

because no one knows how many times women or their doctors failed to make a proper connection between the Shield and the premature birth of a defective baby.

Robins distributed about 2.86 million Shields in the United States, and doctors implanted them, by the company's estimate, in 2.2 million women. Abroad, Robins distributed about 1.71 million Shields, and in June 1974 it estimated that 800,000 to one million were implanted. The Agency for International Development (AID) bought more than 697,000 Shields for use in the Third World. Whatever the precise numbers of Shield insertions in African, Asian, Middle Eastern, Caribbean, Latin American, and South American countries, poor medical conditions made lethal complications more likely. If a Shield wearer became infected, "where there are no doctors, no antibiotics, she's going to die," said Dr. Richard P. Dickey, a former member of the FDA's obstetrical and gynecological devices advisory panel.

The A.H. Robins Company twice explored the possibility of buying the rights to an intrauterine device. The first time was in 1965, when Dr. Jack Freund, the vice-president who headed the medical department, became interested in the Lippes Loop. The second time was in 1970, when the Dalkon Shield became available. The Loop episode was a dry run, in a sense; it offers a glimpse of the considerations that influenced the Robins executives.

Dr. Freund asked Dr. Frederick Clark, the medical director, for what Clark called "preliminary comment on the IUCD [intrauterine contraceptive device], with specific attention to the Lippes Loop."

On July 12, 1965 Clark wrote a memo listing the pros and cons. One favorable entry was, "Trend is up and likely to continue. Old fears on use receding." A second "pro" was that a new-drug application (NDA) would not have to be filed with the

Countries Where A.H. Robins Sold the Dalkon Shield

| | | | |
|---|---|---|---|
| Arab Republic of Egypt | France | Laos | Saudi Arabia |
| Argentina | Ghana | Lebanon | Singapore |
| Australia | Great Britain | Lesotho | Somalia |
| Austria | Greece | Liberia | South Africa |
| Bangladesh | Guatemala | Libya | Spain |
| Belgium | Haiti | Luxembourg | Sri Lanka |
| Brazil | Honduras | Malaysia | Sudan |
| Canada | Hong Kong | Mexico | Suriname |
| Chile | Iceland | Netherlands | Swaziland |
| Colombia | India | Nicaragua | Sweden |
| Costa Rica | Indonesia | Nigeria | Switzerland |
| Cyprus | Iran | Norway | Syria |
| Denmark | Iraq | Pakistan | Taiwan |
| Dominican Republic | Israel | Panama | Tanzania |
| Ecuador | Italy | Paraguay | Thailand |
| El Salvador | Jamaica | Peru | Tunisia |
| Ethiopia | Japan | Philippines | Uganda |
| Federal Republic | Jordan | Portugal | Venezuela |
| of Germany | Kenya | Puerto Rico | Virgin Islands |
| Finland | Kuwait | Samoa | Zambia |

FDA. The absence of an NDA requirement arose from an absurdity in the Food, Drug, and Cosmetic Act that would play a crucial role in the Dalkon Shield disaster.

The 1938 law as amended in 1962 requires a manufacturer to submit to the FDA an expanded NDA showing "substantial evidence"—derived from adequate and well-controlled clinical investigations—of effectiveness in the uses for which the company was recommending the product, including reliable and sufficient animal and clinical testing for safety.

But the law had a ridiculous loophole: with no premarket clearance, a manufacturer could put on sale an untested, hazardous device. Only after it had caused injury or death could the FDA—if it was prepared to carry the legal burden—go to court for an injunction to halt interstate sales.

Like so much legislation that would benefit the public rather than special interests that finance political campaigns, a device bill had always lacked an active constituency. This made it easy for Congress to turn its back on the fundamental contradiction; if it required the FDA to regulate a drug taken into the body for a specific purpose, such as birth control, how could it not compel the agency to regulate a device inserted into the body for an identical purpose?

The indications are overwhelming—from the history of the Robins company, from the words of both the elder and the younger Robins, and from innumerable documents—that had a device law been on the books, the company would never have seriously considered the Dalkon Shield. Without regulation, the company could be in the birth-control market in matter of months. With regulation it would have to monitor 1,500 to 2,000 users for no less than two years and then submit the results to the FDA. Without regulation, it could put the Shield on sale without prior testing for safety in either animals or humans.

In the end, in the case of the Lippes Loop, the highest levels of the Robins Company decided not to acquire the device. In 1970, Robins, which had specialized in bowel and cold medications through most of its first century, got a second crack at the IUD market. Less than a month after they had been approached about buying the Dalkon Shield, Robins officials signed the papers buying the patent rights to the Shield for $750,000 from the Dalkon Corporation.

By late 1970, the A.H. Robins Company had trained an aggressive force of several hundred salesmen—who had never sold a gynecological product and who seldom if ever called on obstetrician-gynecologists—to sell Dalkon Shields. Robins estimated the production cost of a Shield, to be priced at $4.35, would be only twenty-five cents. Although it carefully examined marketing and manufacturing, A.H. Robins, like the Dalkon Corporation before it, had not undertaken to test the Shield for safety in either animals or women. The only study of efficacy—done by Hugh Davis—had been questioned by Robins's own senior physicians.

Not only did Robins fail to initiate its own testing; it actively turned down a series of proposals from outside the company for studies that had the potential to provide an early warning of the pelvic infections that would turn up in actual use.

In January 1971, Robins began to sell Dalkon Shields in the United States and ultimately in seventy-nine other countries. The marketing campaign was a dazzling success. Over the next twelve months, according to company estimates made for internal purposes, 56 of each 100 IUDs inserted in American women were Shields; in 1972, 59 of each 100.

On June 23, 1972, almost two years after Robins purchased the Shield, a Midwestern physician sent an alarming letter to A.H. Robins. Six women in whom he had implanted the Dalkon Shield had become pregnant while it was in place, and five of them had gone on to suffer life-threatening spontaneous infected abortions. His report was not the first to link the Shield to infected pregnancies. Rather it was the sheer number in a single physician's experience that made the report ominous. Yet another aspect made the warning unique, and that was its source: Thad Earl—an Ohio general practitioner who was one of the very first physicians to insert the Shield and who, even then, as a $30,000-a-year consultant to Robins, was busily promoting it. Earl's warning had the potential, in the judgment of Bradley Post, a leading plaintiffs' attorney, to save "most of the women who have been killed and maimed by this device."

In late May 1974, almost two years after Thad Earl's warning and amid increasing problems associated with the Dalkon Shield, FDA officials asked the company to halt distribution until the bureau's OB-GYN advisory committee could take up the matter at a two-day meeting in early June. The company declined. Its reasons are illuminated by a May 24 memo, brought to light by later litigation: ". . . if this product is taken off the market it will be a 'confession of liability' and Robins would lose many of the pending lawsuits."

On May 30, the Center for Disease Control told the FDA of the results of the questionnaire it had mailed in 1973 to 35,544 medical and osteopathic physicians. The survey yielded reports on 3,502 women who were hospitalized with IUD-related disease and injury in the first six months of 1973. The key findings, not made public for several weeks, were dismaying for Shield wearers.

The ratio of "complicated pregnancies to other diagnoses is twice as high for Dalkon Shield wearers as it is for all other (including unknown) types of IUDs," the survey found. Moreover, among the hospitalized women who have never borne a child and were fitted with small-size IUDs, more than 73 percent had worn Shields. The incidence of pregnancy with complications was 61.6 percent among Shield wearers, compared with 29.6 percent for the Lippes Loop and 6.9 percent for the Saf-T-Coil. For pelvic infection: Shield, 49.8 percent; Loops 32.6 percent; Saf-T-Coil, 7.7 percent. For "other infection": Shield, 50.8 percent; Loop, 30.2 percent; Saf-T-Coil, 9.5 percent.

At the June meeting, the FDA's device advisers concluded that in preventing pregnancy, the small-size Shield "is less effective than other IUDs," while the standard-size Shield "is no more effective and possibly less effective." They also concluded, 5 to 0, with two abstentions, "that the risk of septic abortion and septicemia is greater than with other IUDs." Furthermore, they judged, 4 to 2, that the Shield carries a comparatively greater risk of death. Finally, by a vote of 4 to 3 they recommended withdrawal of the Shield from the market "for a lack of demonstrated safety." As of that time, according to Robins's testimony, the company knew of six fatal and seventy nonfatal spontaneous septic abortions in American Shield users.

On June 24, officials with the FDA's device bureau urged FDA Commissioner Alexander Schmidt to take a forceful action: ask Robins to cease distribution of Shields and "recall all stocks of the device which have not been implanted." If Robins refused, Dr. Schmidt would designate the Shield a "health hazard" and order a "Class 1 Recall." This would enable the agency to get a court injunction.

The drug committee then met and evaluated the same body of information. Without spelling out its reasons, it voted, 4 to 2, simply to recommend withdrawal of the Shield from the market.

FDA officials, however, rejected the recall and withdrawal concluding that "the inability of the advisory committees to come out with something more forceful" left the agency unable "to support the charge that the device was a hazard to health."

Meanwhile, Robins, accepting the inevitability of some kind of agency move, sought the weakest possible regulatory action, a legally voluntary suspension of sales, because it would inflict the least damage on the company's defense against Shield lawsuits and on its reputation. Moreover, the company would be free to resume sales of the Shield if it would develop a safer model.

On June 26—after the reported toll of fatal spontaneous abortions had risen to 7 and of nonfatal to 103—Commissioner Schmidt accepted Robins's proposal to suspend sales, pending a hearing by the two FDA advisory bodies. The FDA and Robins announced the action two days later.

Inside the company, Claiborne Robins, A.H. Robins chief executive officer, was jubilant. He had once again managed to dodge regulation and get the FDA to do precisely what he wished. He sent an exultant memo that hinted at how a regulatory staff trying to protect the public can be blindsided by corporate legions with access to agency bosses. Stated the memo: "I would like to congratulate you . . . for the outstanding job you all have done . . . We had all felt that the decision would be political, and to have Dr. Schmidt announce his action—taken against the vote of the panels—was indicative of the input of our teams which had been working constantly with the FDA during the period leading up to the announcement."

Although Robins had agreed to suspend sales in the United States in 1974, the company continued to distribute Shields abroad for as long as nine months—"at the request of . . . specific governments," Robins swore at a deposition in January 1984. Asked who had told him that, he replied, "I don't know that. It seems to me I saw a memo somewhere, but I don't remember when or where."

In El Salvador in 1975—a year after the suspension of Shield sales here the only IUD some clinic's doctors were inserting was the Shield. Some clinics in El Salvador continued to implant Shields until 1980.

By 1983, however, the manufacturer of the Dalkon Shield had seen grim omens appear in three cities. In St. Paul, federal juries made two awards of punitive damages to Shield victims, one for $1,750,000 and another for $50,500. These dealt a heavy blow to the A.H. Robins Company, partly because it had no insurance coverage for exemplary damages, and partly because the awards would inevitably encourage other victims to seek to punish the manufacturer.

In Philadelphia, a federal jury, barred from awarding punitive damages to a Shield user who had suffered a pelvic infection and loss of her ability to bear children, set a record for compensatory damages: $5.15 million. This was bad news for Robins, but perhaps worse for Aetna Casualty & Surety Company which, in its 1977 agreement with Robins, had undertaken to pay the bills for *all* awards of compensatory damages—even those arising from "the supplying of false and misleading information."

From the vantage point of Robins and Aetna, however, a development in Minneapolis on December 9 was the most ominous of all: the six federal judges of the District of Minnesota assigned twenty-one Shield cases to Miles W. Lord, the activist, blunt-spoken Chief Judge. Over the next three months, Lord would be intensely and personally involved in trying to expedite Shield litigation, which was clogging the federal and state courts of Minnesota. (See *Lord's Justice.*)

For Robins, the growing number of awards of punitive damages had become a plague. In the February 29, 1984 package settlement, Robins had to pay $2,050,000 to dispose of two jury awards of punitive damages. On June 4, the Colorado Supreme Court upheld the record $6.2 million award of punitive damages. Strikingly, Robins paid the award rather than appeal. On June 6, a jury made a $1.4 million exemplary award to Melissa Mample, a cerebral-palsied child in Boise, Idaho, whose mother had given birth with a Shield in place. By June 30, juries had awarded punitive damages in eight cases, totaling $17.2 million. Shield victims who specified only the exemplary awards had filed suits in excess of $12 billion more.

For relief, Robins turned to the United States Senate, where the Commerce Committee had before it a bill to establish national uniform standards for the liability of manufacturers whose products are alleged to have caused avoidable disease and injury to consumers and workers. In addition to President Reagan, two large coalitions of about three hundred businesses and trade associations supported the bill, whose principal sponsor was Senator Robert W. Kasten, Jr. (R-Wis.). Over a period of four years starting on January 1, 1979, their political action committees gave $626,918 to members of the Commerce Committee. A new committee member, Paul S. Trible, Jr.—a Republican from Robins's home state of Virginia—received $117,593, the largest single share.

In early 1984, it was Paul Trible who introduced an amendment under which a manufacturer of any kind would have to pay punitive damages only once—to the first litigant to persuade a jury that the company had been grossly negligent or had recklessly disregarded safety.

A few days later, a Trible spokesman told me that the senator had introduced the amendment—which critics called "the Robins bail-out"—after being contacted by Robins.

Trible's amendment aroused the anger of women's groups, trial lawyers, consumer advocates, unions and newspapers. Sensing the threat to his political future, Trible first said he would weaken his amendment and then dropped it altogether.

Although Robins was increasingly embattled, its status as a large, international conglomerate with diverse lines of business and some thirty foreign subsidiaries protected it financially. This was reflected in the company's report for the three months ending June 30, 1984. Because of a 430 percent increase in Shield litigation expenses, the company said, net earnings fell 70 percent, to $4,069,000. But sales rose 11 percent to $151,992,000—the best second quarter in Robins's history.

Still, the Shield took its toll. On April 2, Robins held a press conference in Richmond to announce the creation of a $615 million reserve fund for paying Shield claims until the year 2002. The payment through December 31, 1984, having been $314.6 million, the total now would approach the $1 billion level. G.E.R. Stiles, senior vice-president and financial officer, revealed that a study by an outside consultant indicated that the Shield may have injured roughly 87,000 or 88,000 of the 2.2 million American women who wore it, that the ultimate total of those who would sue or file claims would be approximately 20,000, and that the $615 million would suffice for compensatory damages for all existing and expected claims. But Stiles left considerable doubt that the $615 million would be adequate, mainly because it allowed neither for punitive damages—although billions of dollars in such damages were being sought—nor for lawsuits by foreign Shield users, who by 1985 had begun to sue Robins in American courts.

Even without such future woes, the $615 million fund caused Robins to report a 1984 net loss of $416 million, a sum larger than the company's net worth, and large enough to wipe out all shareholder dividends through the end of 1986.

The setbacks for Robins continued into 1985. On January 21, the Eleventh United States Circuit Court of Appeals in Miami ruled that Dr. Louis Keith, the long-time Robins consultant and Northwestern University professor of OB-GYN, might have committed perjury, and the FBI began an investigation.

On February 21, special masters Peter Thompson and Thomas Bartsh, who had been sent to Richmond a year earlier to seek compliance with Judge Lord's document-production order, filed a report. Their summary began:

> We conclude that Plaintiffs have established a strong *prima facie* case that A.H. Robins Co., Inc., has, with the knowledge and participation of in-house counsel, engaged in an ongoing fraud by knowingly misrepresenting the nature, quality, safety, and efficacy of the Dalkon Shield. The ongoing fraud has also involved the destruction or withholding of relevant evidence.

They said of the four studies cited in the eight-page "Progress Report" advertisement that Robins published in the final four months of 1972: "Robins officials knew that the results of the studies were inaccurate and misleading."

On May 3, 1985, in Wichita, a Sedgwick County jury awarded punitive damages of $7.5 million—a new record in Shield litigation—and $1.1 million in compensatory damages to Loretta Tetuan, thirty-three, who lost her uterus and ovaries after wearing a Shield for nine years.

On August 21, a startling development occurred in Judge Merhige's court in

Richmond, one that caused the price of a share of Robins's stock to fall to $8 from a 1985 high of over $24, and one that made most every front page in the country. The company asked to be allowed to reorganize under Chapter 11 of the Bankruptcy Code, so that it could be protected from lawsuits by creditors—Shield victims, above all—while it devised a plan to pay its debts. Robins did not claim to be financially shaky. Rather, it invoked "the continuing burden of litigation," much as the financially healthy Manville Corporation had done in 1982, when it pioneered using Chapter 11 as a refuge from lawsuits, brought in its case by victims of asbestos-related diseases.

The next day, Merhige suspended proceedings in thousands of Shield lawsuits, saying that "everything is stayed in every court." Many plaintiffs' lawyers denounced Robins for a "sham" and "unjustified" action that would let it pay everyone to whom it owes money except Shield victims.

On August 23, a motion to dismiss Robins's petition was filed by the National Women's Health Network, which twice had sought worldwide Shield recalls—in a 1981 court action and in a 1983 FDA petition.

Today, more than a decade after Shield sales officially ended, its legacies of death, disease, injury, and pain persist. Even women who have had the Shield removed are not out of danger. Because PID is not an affliction that is simply treated and is then over and done with, large numbers of former Dalkon Shield wearers suffer chronic pain and illness, sometimes requiring repeated hospitalization and surgery; many have waged desperate battles to bear children despite severe damage to their reproductive systems. Not even women who currently wear the Shield with no apparent problem are safe: they run the risk of suddenly being striken by PID. In the words of Judge Lord, they are wearing "a deadly depth charge in their wombs, ready to explode at any time."

The exact number of women still wearing the Shield is unknown. By early 1983, some Food and Drug Administration officials and OB-GYNs were confident that few American women, probably only hundreds, still used it. Other qualified observers, however, were estimating the figure to be much higher, anywhere from 80,000 to more than half a million. Certainly the response to Robins's own call-back campaign of October 1984 suggests that the higher figures are closer to the mark. By February 1, 1985, a $4-million advertising drive, which urged women still wearing the Shields to have them removed at Robins's expense, had drawn more than 16,000 phone calls on toll-free hotlines; by the end of March, 4,437 women had filed claims for Shield removals. The claims were flowing in at the dramatic rate of more than one hundred a week.

And what of women in the seventy-nine other countries where the Shield was distributed? The company told the FDA that it had notified first the countries' ambassadors in Washington and then their senior health officials at home of its Shield-removal campaign in the United States, and had "sought direction on whether a similar program would be appropriate in those countries." By early April 1985, Australia, Canada, and the United Kingdom had requested, and the company had put into effect, one or another kind of removal program. New Zealand, too, was considering a program. Sixteen other countries had simply acknowledged receipt of Robins's letter. Eight others—Denmark, Mexico, Norway, Pakistan, the Philippines, South Africa, Tanzania, and Zambia—had declined any removal program. From the rest of the countries, of which there were fifty-one, Robins had received no response almost a half-year after inviting one. If this record suggests indifference to the health and safety to women, at least partial explanation may be found in the company's adamant refusal to admit to the special dangers inherent in its device. "Robins believes that serious scientific questions exist about whether the Dalkon Shield poses a significantly different risk of infection than other IUDs," it said in an interim report to the FDA.

Another measure of the extent of the damage is provided by the lawsuits and unlitigated claims filed by Shield wearers in the United States. Nearly all of these women had suffered PID followed by damage to or loss of their ability to bear children. Through June 30, 1985, by the company's own count, the total number of cases was 14,330 and new ones were being filed at a rate of fifteen a day. Through June 30, 1985, Robins and its former Shield insurer Aetna Life & Casualty Company, had paid out $378.3 million to dispose of cases, plus $107.3 million in legal expenses. Juries have awarded $24.8 million in punitive or exemplary damages, which are intended to punish wanton or reckless behavior and to deter its repetition or emulation.

Still, no summary of suits and claims can come close to accounting for the total number of Shield injuries. By Robins's own conservative estimate in April 1985, 4 percent of the wearers were injured—that is, nearly 90,000 women in the United States alone. It was 10 years after Robins was forced to discontinue sales that the company began a recall. Surely it is reasonable to suggest that many Shield victims might not have died, and that thousands of other women would not have suffered pain and agony, if Robins had acted earlier. But Robins consistently claimed—and continues to claim—that the Dalkon Shield was safe and effective when "properly used." Robins executives insist that they did not know of any special hazard. But they did know, and they chose to do nothing—until it was too late.

## Addendum: Lord's Justice

*Miles W. Lord, Chief U.S. District Judge for Minnesota, was assigned 21 Shield cases on December 9, 1983. When the victims and Robins agreed to settle out of court some months later, Lord read the following statement to three officers of the A.H. Robins Company who under the settlement had been required to appear before him. The three officers were E. Claiborne Robins, Jr., president and chief executive officer; Carl D. Lunsford, senior vice-president for research and development; and William A. Forrest, Jr., vice-president and general counsel.*

"I did not know." "It was not me," "Look elsewhere." Time and time again, each of you has used this kind of argument in refusing to acknowledge your responsibility and in pretending to the world that the chief officers and the directors of your gigantic multinational corporation have no responsibility for the company's acts and omissions.

In a speech I gave several years ago . . . I suggested to the hundreds of ministers of the gospel who constitute the Minnesota Council of Churches that the accumulation of corporate wrongs is, in my mind, a manifestation of individual sin.

You, Mr. Robins, have been heard to boast many times that the growth and prosperity of this company is a direct result of its having been in the Robins family for three generations. The stamp of the Robins family is upon it. The corporation is built in the image of the Robins mentality.

You, Dr. Lunsford, as director of the company's most sensitive and important subdivision, have violated every ethical precept to which every doctor under your supervision must pledge as he gives the oath of Hippocrates and assumes the mantle of one who would help and cure and nurture unto the physical needs of the populace.

You, Mr. Forrest, are a lawyer—one who, upon finding his client in trouble, should counsel and guide him along a course which will comport with the legal, moral, and ethical principles which must bind us all. You have not brought honor to your profession, Mr. Forrest.

Gentlemen, the results of these activities and attitudes on your part have been catastrophic. Today as you sit here attempting once more to extricate yourselves from the legal consequences of your acts, none of you has faced up to the fact that more than nine thousand women have made claims that they gave up part of their womanhood so that your company might prosper. It is alleged that others gave their lives so you might so prosper. And there stand behind them legions more who have been injured but who have not sought relief in the courts of this land.

If one poor young man were, by some act of his—without authority or consent—to inflict such damage upon one woman, he would be jailed for a good portion of the rest of his life. And yet your company without warning to women invaded their bodies by the millions and caused them injuries by the thousands. And when the time came for these women to make their claims against your company, you attacked their characters. You inquired into their sexual practices and into the identity of their sex partners. You . . . ruined families and reputations and careers—in order to intimidate those who would raise their voices against you. You introduced issues that had no relationship whatsoever to the fact that you planted in the bodies of these women instruments of death, of mutilation, of disease.

Mr. Forrest, you have told me that you are working with members of the Congress of the United States to ask them to find a way of forgiving you from punitive damages which might otherwise be imposed. Yet the profits of your company continue to mount. Your last financial report boasts of new records for sales and earnings, with a profit of more than $58 million in 1983. And all the while, insofar as this court is able to determine you three men and your company still engage in the selfsame course of wrongdoing in which you originally commenced. Until such time as your company indicates that it is willing to cease and desist this deception and seek out and advise victims, your remonstrances to Congress and to the courts of this country are indeed hollow and cynical. The company has not suffered, nor have you men personally. You are collectively being enriched by millions of dollars each year.

Mr. Robins, Mr. Forrest, Dr. Lunsford: You have not been rehabilitated. Under your direction, your company has in fact continued to allow women, tens of thousands of women, to wear this device—a deadly depth charge in their wombs, ready to explode at any time . . . The only conceivable reasons you have not recalled this product are that it would hurt your balance sheet and alert women who already have been harmed that you may be liable for their injuries. You have taken the bottom line as your guiding beacon, and the low road as your route. This is corporate irresponsibility at its meanest.

. . . The policy of delay and obfuscation practiced by your lawyers in courts throughout this country has made it possible for you and your insurance company, Aetna Casualty and Surety Company, to delay the payment of these claims for such a long period that the interest you earn in the interim covers the cost of these cases. You, in essence, pay nothing out of your pocket to settle these cases . . .

Your company seeks to segment and fragment the litigation of these cases nationwide. The courts of this country are now burdened with more than three thousand Dalkon Shield cases. The sheer number of claims and the dilatory tactics used by your company's attorneys clog court calendars and consume vast amounts of judicial and jury time . . .

Another of your callous legal tactics is to force women of little means to withstand the onslaught of your well-financed, nationwide team of attorneys, and to default if they cannot keep pace. You target your worst tactics for the meek and the poor.

. . . If this were a case in equity, I would order that your company make an effort to locate each and every woman who still wears this device and recall your product. But this court does not have the power to do so. I must therefore resort to moral persuasion and a personal appeal to each of you. Mr. Robins, Mr. Forrest, and Dr. Lunsford: You are the people with the power to recall. You are the corporate conscience.

Please in the name of humanity, lift your eyes above the bottom line. You, the men in charge, must surely have hearts and souls and consciences . . .

Please, gentlemen, give consideration to tracking down the victims and sparing them the agony that will surely be theirs.

# The Dumping of Hazardous Products on Foreign Markets

*Mark Dowie*

Tom Mboya was the hope of the western world. Bright, energetic, popular and inclined to be democratic—he was a born leader who, Washington hoped, would rise to power in Kenya and help keep Africa safe for United States commerce. In 1969 he was shot down in the streets of Nairobi. An emergency rescue squad was by his side in minutes. They plugged him into the latest gadget in resuscitative technology—a brand new U.S. export called the Res-Q-Aire. What the rescue team didn't know as they watched Tom Mboya's life slip away was that this marvelous device had been recalled from the American market by the U.S. government because it was found to be totally ineffective. The patient died.

Losing Mboya to the Res-Q-Aire was perhaps a subtle retribution for the U.S., for to this day we allow our business leaders to sell, mostly to Third World nations, shiploads of defective medical devices, lethal drugs, known carcinogens, toxic pesticides, contaminated foods and other products found unfit for American consumption.

Ten years after Mboya's assassination, in fact, Kenya itself remains a major market for unsafe, ineffective and contaminated American products. At the 1977 meeting of the United Nations Environmental Program, Kenyan Minister of Water Development Dr. D. J. Kiano warned that developing nations would no longer tolerate being used as "dumping grounds for products that have not been adequately tested" and that their people should not be used as "guinea pigs" for chemicals.

The prevailing sentiment in Washington contrasts considerably with Dr. Kiano's. Say the word "dumping" in federal government circles and the predominant response will be "Oh, yes, 'dumping.' Really must be stopped. It's outrageous, not in our economic interests at all . . . unscrupulous bastards. . . . "

Sounds as if we've solved the problem, doesn't it, except what our bureaucrats are talking about, one discovers, is foreign corporations "dumping," low-priced goods on the American market—Japanese cars, Taiwanese televisions, Hong Kong stereos, Australian beef, etc. The export of banned and hazardous products, which *Mother Jones* calls "dumping," is considered business as usual.

As the following articles make painfully clear, dumping is, in fact, *big* business as usual. It involves not only manufacturers and retailers, a vast array of export brokers, tramp steamers, black marketeers and go-betweens who traffic an esti-

---

Mark Dowie, "The Dumping of Hazardous Products on Foreign Markets," *Mother Jones 4* (November 1979), pp. 23–25, 37–38, 44. 

mated $1.2 billion worth of unsafe goods overseas every year, but also the United States Export-Import Bank, which finances large dumps; the Commerce, State and Treasury Departments, which have the statutory authority to stop or control dumping, but won't; and a President who, in his quiet way, subverts the efforts of the few progressive members of Congress who seek to pass uniform anti-dumping legislation.

Hard evidence of dumping and its tragic consequences has repeatedly been brought to the attention of federal agencies, the Congress and the White House. Here are some examples:

- 400 Iraqis died in 1972 and 5,000 were hospitalized after consuming the by-products of 8,000 tons of wheat and barley coated with an organic mercury fungicide, whose use had been banned in the U.S.
- An undisclosed number of farmers and over 1,000 water buffalos died suddenly in Egypt after being exposed to leptophos, a chemical pesticide which was never registered for domestic use by the Environmental Protection Agency (EPA) but was exported to at least 30 countries.
- After the Dalkon Shield intrauterine device killed at least 17 women in the United States, the manufacturer withdrew it from the domestic market. It was sold overseas after the American recall and is still in common use in some countries.
- No one knows how many children may develop cancer since several million children's garments treated with a carcinogenic fire retardant called Tris were shipped overseas after being forced off the domestic market by the Consumer Product Safety Commission (CPSC).
- Lomotil, an effective anti-diarrhea medicine sold only by prescription in the U.S. because it is fatal in amounts just slightly over the recommended doses, was sold over the counter in Sudan, in packages proclaiming it was "used by astronauts during Gemini and Apollo space flights" and recommended for use by children as young as 12 months.
- Winstrol, a synthetic male hormone, which was found to stunt the growth of American children, is freely available in Brazil, where it is recommended as an appetite stimulant for children.
- Depo-Provera, an injectable contraceptive banned for such use in the United States because it caused malignant tumors in beagles and monkeys, is sold by the Upjohn Co. in 70 other countries, where it is widely used in U.S.-sponsored population control programs.
- 450,000 baby pacifiers of the type that has caused choking deaths have been exported by at least five manufacturers since a ban was proposed by the CPSC. 120,000 teething rings that did not meet recently established CPSC standards were cleared for export and are on sale right now in Australia.

Occasionally, a particularly scandalous dump like one of these will come to the attention of conscientious Americans. Most dumps, however, are performed quietly, the product moving unnoticed in the fast flow of normal trade between nations.

And dumping is not limited to chemicals and consumer products. When a firm's production facilities and industrial equipment are condemned by the Occupational Safety and Health Administration, the manufacturer often simply closes up shop and moves the factory to Mexico or Jamaica, where occupational health standards are virtually nonexistent. Even entire technologies are dumped. Nuclear power, which seems certain to receive a ''hazardous'' classification before long in the U.S., is today being dumped on energy-starved nations like the Philippines and India.

We are only beginning to discover how toxic and carcinogenic are some of the chemicals we use, chemicals with the potential to affect the entire global environment and human gene pool. Moreover, the number of other consumer products that maim or kill shows no sign of diminishing. The list of banned and hazardous products is, thus, bound to grow, which *should* make dumping a major international issue for the 1980s.

Early in our investigation, however, we discovered that exposing dumpers was more challenging than we thought it would be. ''They're really smugglers,'' said one of our team in a story meeting. ''The only difference between drug smugglers and dumpers is that the products are usually moving in opposite directions.''

There is another difference: the government protects dumpers. We talked to countless officials in countless agencies and departments of the government while researching this story—a few of them outspoken opponents of dumping. They would tell us about contaminated foods, baby pacifiers, pesticides and drugs that were being dumped overseas. They often knew how many of each item were shipped to specific countries, but they would never tell us the brand names, the manufacturers or the names of the export brokers. The answer was always the same. ''I'm sorry, that's proprietary information . . . trade secret . . . confidential corporate information.'' And as we shall see, government protection afforded to dumpers goes way beyond this kind of cover.

Although the bottom line motive is always profit, hazardous products are dumped to solve different problems. For nonmanufacturers—wholesalers, retailers, brokers, importers and exporters—the problem is generally just a matter of inventory. Salvation often comes in the form of a broker, offering to buy the banned goods at a ''close-out'' price for resale in an unnamed (read, Third World) market.

It's not that simple, however, for manufacturers who have invested capital in tools, dies, assembly plants, personnel, machines and land. When a company like A. H. Robins foresees the withdrawal of a product like the Dalkon Shield intrauterine device, it dumps a million units on foreign countries, voluntarily withdraws the product and closes up shop. The company takes a small loss buying back recalled inventory (which it writes off), and its capital investment is amortized.

## Carter Dumps Dumping

It was Tris that brought dumping into the political arena. And the political arena for dumping is Washington. Tris (2,3-dibromopropyl) phosphate is a fire-retardant chemical used to treat synthetic flammable fabrics. In June of 1977, after Tris was found to cause cancer in animals, millions of pairs of infant pajamas and tons of children's sleepwear were suddenly withdrawn from the U.S. market by the CPSC. When some of the manufacturers, stuck with huge repurchased inventories of these carcinogenic garments, threatened to dump them on the overseas markets, the CPSC claimed at first that it had no statutory authority to stop them from doing so. In fact, although the CPSC, the EPA and the FDA together have removed over 500 pesticides, drugs and consumer products from the American market for health, safety or environmental reasons, the patchwork of regulations obfuscates what limited power these agencies have to prohibit the export of dangerous products.

When President Carter, who *does* have the authority to stop dumping with a simple Executive Order, learned of the Tris situation, he authorized the formation of an Interagency Working Group to develop a uniform national policy on dumping. Although such task forces can provide a valuable forum for intra-government communication and often make important policy recommendations, the Interagency Working Group on Hazardous Substances Export Policy (HSEP)—chaired by Carter's Special Assistant for Consumer Affairs, Esther Peterson—is, in fact, being used to table the issue until our balance of trade improves. Dumping, you see, is exporting; and although banned and hazardous products represent only about one percent of our total trade, every percent seems to count when we are consistently running a trade deficit of over $25 billion a year.

To determine why the task force report is still nonexistent, we took our investigation to Washington. In a long series of interviews with task force members and White House staff the reason for the delay became clear. The President, intimidated by Congress, is unwilling to take the issue to the Hill, in the face of growing "export fever" and antiregulatory sentiment.

Edward Cohen, staff counsel to both the HSEP task force and the White House Office of Consumer Affairs, asked us to turn off our tape recorder as he explained the dilemma. He also told us he was "one of the good guys in the story." We can't quote what he told us when the recorder was off, but since we don't believe him, it really doesn't matter. Cohen refused to tell us the names of any agency representatives on the task force and throughout our investigation went to elaborate lengths to stop any flow of information to our researchers. When we asked him for innocuous background material on the task force, Cohen exercised "executive privilege" and gave us nothing, forcing us to file Freedom of Information requests with the 16 agencies and departments in the task force. Despite White House efforts to discourage compliance with our requests, we obtained the material from friendly sources in the agencies. More on the contents later.

During the interview, Cohen struggled to remember the correct name of the task force. The records, files and minutes from past meetings were stuffed in a cardboard box under a radiator in his otherwise tidy office. It was clear that dumping and HSEP had slipped a notch or two on the White House agenda. Cohen admitted eventually that it was barely on his own agenda. He persisted, however, in his "good guy" stance.

When we persisted with our investigation, Cohen realized he had a public relations problem on his hands. In fact, when we called the White House to interview Esther Peterson recently, Cohen turned up unexpectedly on the line to tell us he was working on a fourth policy draft for task force review. But when we talked to representatives from all but three of the agencies involved, most barely remembered the task force and felt that the issue was dead. And Cohen recently told Ralph Nader's office that if the fourth draft is not approved, the entire matter will be dropped.

The President can place any product he wants on the Commodity Control List, which makes exportation of the product absolutely illegal. There are three statutory justifications for placing a commodity on this list: scarcity, national security and foreign relations.

When Tris-treated clothing was found to be a cancer threat to infants and it became clear that President Carter wasn't going to do anything to stop its export, an alarmed S. John Byington, chairman of the CPSC, wrote in June 1977 to Secretary of Commerce Juanita Kreps, whose department administers the Commodity Control List. Byington asked her to place the garments on the list, pointing out to her that their export would have "serious implications for foreign policy."

On October 7, nearly four months and, as it turns out, many pajama dumps later, Kreps answered Byington. She had taken the time to consult the State Department, which "has advised me that the controls on Tris and Tris-treated garments are not, in the language of the statute, 'necessary to further significantly the foreign policy of the U.S. to fulfill its international responsibilities.'"

Frustrated by months of bureaucratic waffling, the CPSC finally reversed its position on June 14, 1978 by prohibiting the export of Tris-treated sleepwear.

This delay, obfuscation and inactivity are all too typical. Records of Interagency Working Group meetings, which we were able to obtain despite White House efforts to stonewall us, show that Commerce and State Department representatives are doing everything in their power to prevent the adoption of a uniform policy on dumping.

Although President Carter has mumbled a word or two about the ethics of exporting, he clearly does not consider the use of safe products a human right for non-Americans. In fact, his actions on this matter have pleased the most conservative pro-dumping forces.

On September 26, 1978, the day before the HSEP task force was due for release, Carter issued a public statement on exports. The wording of the statement so clearly subverted the intent of any reforms the task force might have conceivably proposed that it's little wonder not a word has been heard from the group since.

## Notification Before the Dump

The liberal compromise on the dumping issue is notification. Invoking the principles of national sovereignty, self-determination and free trade, government officials and legislators have devised a system whereby foreign governments are notified whenever a product is banned, deregulated, suspended or cancelled by an American regulatory agency. The notification system is handled by the State Department, whose policy statement on the subject reads, in part, "No country should establish itself as the arbiter of others' health and safety standards. Individual governments are generally in the best position to establish standards of public health and safety."

Based on this judgment, an unwieldy and ineffective notification procedure allegedly places announcements in the hands of the proper foreign government officials, telling them a certain drug has been found to be toxic or that babies have strangled in particular brands of cribs.

The main problem with notification is the logic behind it. Other governments are generally *not* in a position to establish safety standards, let alone control imports into their countries. In fact, the countries where most of our banned and hazardous products are dumped lack regulatory agencies, testing laboratories or well-staffed customs departments. In 1978, Nigeria's Environmental Protection Ministry was one person. He recently told the U.S. EPA that it didn't matter whether or not he was notified when a pesticide was suspended; there was nothing he could do to stop its importation.

When our EPA, FDA or CPSC finds a product to be hazardous, they notify our State Department as required or as a matter of protocol. State, which we have found to be no opponent of dumping, is then supposed to send a communiqué to each American embassy overseas. Each embassy is, in turn, supposed to notify the appropriate foreign officials. However, the Commerce, Consumer and Monetary Affairs Subcommittee of the House Committee on Government Operations discovered in hearings held in July of 1978 that the agencies frequently neglected to inform the State Department when they banned a product. For example, the EPA failed to notify State after suspending such notorious pesticides as kepone, chlordane and heptachlor. The Government Accounting Office (GAO) also discovered and testified to the same subcommittee that even when the agencies did notify State, the communiqués rarely went further than the U.S. embassies overseas—they almost never reached the foreign officials who might have been able to warn foreign buyers or intercept shipments. One embassy official even admitted to the GAO that he "did not routinely forward notification of chemicals not registered in the host country because it may adversely affect U.S. exporting." The GAO would not tell us the name or location of the official they quoted, but said the sentiment was not unusual.

Some of the foreign officials who have been notified have complained that the communiqués are vague and ambiguous, or else so highly technical that they are incomprehensible.

Of course, even if clear notification about a product were to reach officials in an importing nation, there is nothing to stop the exporters from changing a product's brand name before they ship.

## It's All Coming Back

Perhaps the only aspect of the whole dumping travesty that has kept the issue alive in Washington is reimportation. Congressmembers and bureaucrats who would otherwise ignore or even encourage dumping become irate upon learning that a hazardous product is being reimported (smuggled) into the U.S. for sale, or that an imported fruit or vegetable contains residue of a pesticide long-since suspended for American use. Even Esther Peterson, in a memo to the President, expressed concern about reimportation.

Remember, it is perfectly legal to dump hazardous products abroad. There are, however, strict measures to prevent reimportation. The FDA allows manufacturers to export banned drugs, stale-dated drugs and even unapproved new drugs if they are shipped under "an investigational protocol" (for experimentation on other people). But one of the stipulations for the export of drugs removed from the American marketplace is that they never be offered for domestic sale again.

The CPSC, however, can prohibit the export of goods forced off the American market. It can also stop exports that present "an unreasonable risk to persons in the U.S." (through their reimportation, for example), but the CPSC admits that proving unreasonable risk is "very difficult."

## How to Stop It

The White House Office of Consumer Affairs remains confident that a uniform policy on the export of banned and hazardous products will protect foreign consumers. Our investigations, however, indicate that the corporate dumping urge is rooted in a criminal mentality and that dumpers will, as they already have, find new ways to circumvent whatever legal and regulatory barriers stand between their warehouses and profitable markets for their deadly goods.

Global corporations, with their worldwide network of subsidiaries, high technology and marketing systems, far outstrip the puny regulatory efforts of a government that considers corporate crime a minor nuisance at worst. Nothing short of a complete moral transformation of the corporate ethos will stop dumping. Until that unlikely transformation takes place, we recommend the following:

- Dumping must be clearly defined by statute, and one term, such as "illegal for export," should be applied to American products found to be too dangerous for use here and, hence, anywhere. We should recognize that there are a few—a very few—products that are unsafe for use in the U.S. for which the benefits far outweigh the risks in other countries—for example, certain drugs used to treat tropical diseases or pesticides used to kill the malaria-carrying mosquito. In such cases, when the foreign government is apprised of the risk, the products should be cleared for export to that country only.
- Dumping should be made a criminal offense.
- The government, which already controls exports through the Commodity Control List and the Bureau of Census (where all exports of over $250 are registered), must accept the responsibility of monitoring the outflow of banned and hazardous products. This responsibility should be taken from the Department of Commerce, where it represents an untenable conflict of interest.
- Notification of product bans, suspensions, cancellations and withdrawals

from registration should be made *directly* by the U.S. regulatory agencies to appropriate foreign officials, in language that can be understood.

- The State Department should be relieved af any anti-dumping responsibility, since it has so deliberately failed to coordinate an effective notification program.

Until all of the above are accomplished, the President should use his powers to stop dumping immediately.

## What Dumping Really Is

Executives in major exporting corporations, with the strong support of Commerce Secretary Juanita Kreps, argue that if the export of banned and hazardous products is prohibited by statute or Executive Order, foreign buyers will merely turn to European or other suppliers, as they have in the past for weapons and ammunition. Other developed nations do dump; Germany dumps at least as many toxic pesticides as the U.S., and no nation on earth can match Switzerland for dumping baby formula. However, the assumption that foreign buyers will import known toxins and recognized lethal products from one country when they can't get them from another is patently ridiculous.

American business leaders, who tout themselves as the most ethical businesspeople in the world, should lead the way in ending dumping worldwide. It's in their best interest to do so, for by dumping toxins on the Third World they are actually poisoning the very markets they seek to develop. Perhaps one day they will even see dumping for what it really is—a subtle genocide.

## Addendum: A Dumper's Guide to Tricks of the Trade

Dumpers have proven themselves to be a highly imaginative lot. Here are a few of the tricks they have devised to circumvent regulatory agencies at home and suspicious importers abroad.

*The Name Change:* When a product is withdrawn from the American market, receiving a lot of bad publicity in the process; the astute dumper simply changes its name.

*The Last Minute Pullout:* When it looks as if a chemical being tested by the Environmental Protection Agency won't pass, the manufacturer will withdraw the application for registration and then label the chemical "for export only." That way, the manufacturer doesn't have to notify the importing country that the chemical is banned in the U.S.

*Dump the Whole Factory:* Many companies, particularly pesticide manufacturers, will simply close down their American plants and begin manufacturing a hazardous product in a country close to a good market.

*The Formula Change:* A favorite with drug and pesticide companies. Changing a formula slightly by adding or subtracting an inert ingredient prevents detection by spectrometers and other scanning devices keyed to certain molecular structures.

*The Skip:* Brazil—a prime drug market with its large population and virulent tropical diseases—has a law that says no one may import a drug that is not approved for use in the country of origin. A real challenge for the wily dumper. How does he do it?

Guatemala has no such law; in fact, Guatemala spends very little each year regulating drugs. So, the drug is first shipped to Guatemala, which becomes the export nation.

*The Ingredient Dump:* Your product winds up being banned. Don't dump it. Some wise-ass reporter from *Mother Jones* will find a bill of lading and expose you. Export the ingredients separately—perhaps via different routes—to a small recombining facility or assembly plant you have set up where you're dumping it, or in a country along the way. Reassemble them and dump the product.

# The Corporate Roots of Environmental Pollution

*Ronald Brownstein*

When officials at, say, the Dow Chemical Company proceed with the production and sale of a product such as 2,4,5-T despite the serious questions raised about its safety, the company traditionally has been removed from the consequences of its officials' decisions in several ways. The officials themselves are unlikely ever to actually manufacture or be sprayed with the substance. (Some overzealous public-relations personnel have been known to eat a small sample of 2,4,5-T now and then at public debates over its safety. No one appears to be doing that anymore.) And when the product damages property or people, society and not the company bears the cost. These "external" costs figure neither in the prices of the product nor the ledger sheets of the corporation. But, for society, the costs can be immense: the degradation of the environment and the loss of its use; the expense of treating illness and compensating for disability; the shortened lives and diminished opportunities.

That these costs are real is beyond dispute. But in the calculations of the balance sheet—barring successful law suits, which are infrequent—they are nonexistent. This shifting onto the general public costs in the billions of dollars annually stands in stark contrast to the strident demands of business to keep industry free from outside control. "A business enterprise that pollutes the environment is . . . being subsidized by society," writes environmentalist Barry Commoner. "To this extent, the enterprise, though free, is not wholly private."[1]

With society bearing the costs of industry's byproducts, corporations have had little economic incentive to reduce the harmful effects of their activities. George Kush, director of chemical waste management of the National Solid Wastes Management Association, put the matter bluntly: "Without federal regulations to enforce the safe management of all hazardous wastes . . . *there has not been any real incentive, given the highly competitive nature of the business community,* for companies to adopt adequate disposal procedures at the risk of losing their competitive edge through increased costs. . . ."[2] (Emphasis added.)

It is tempting to point to the poisoned children of Love Canal as an "incentive . . . for companies to adopt adequate disposal procedures." But the chemical industry, in particular, has lately asserted that these dangers are the responsibility of all segments of society, since all society uses chemical products. Commenting on the Superfund proposal—signed into law by former president Jimmy Carter in Decem-

---

Ronald Brownstein, "The Corporate Roots of Environmental Pollution. From *Who's Poisoning America?* by Ralph Nader, Ronald Brownstein, and John Richard.  (pp. 32–41)

ber 1980 to pay for the cleanup of hazardous dumpsites with money provided by the chemical and related industries—Jackson B. Browning, the director of health, safety and environmental affairs at Union Carbide, capsulized this attitude: "[Hazardous wastes] are an integral by-product of our industrial society, and represent by-products of the daily life of every citizen. The problems associated with abandoned hazardous waste disposal sites reflect more than 100 years of industrial development in the Nation. . . . The problem is societal in scope and the mechanisms for coping with it should reflect its societal nature, just as the benefits of resolving the problems will extend to all elements of the country."[3]

Even Browning is unlikely, however, to convincingly argue that society as a whole benefits from chemicals as much as Union Carbide, whose chemical sales in 1979 stood at a robust $5.3 billion.[4] Nor has society had the benefit of full—or, often, any—information about the hazards associated with production or disposal of the products people use in great volume. In a more fundamental sense, in fact, the prices of products that don't reflect the "external" factors of production mislead consumers about the true costs. In sum, the costs are socialized. But the profits are kept private.

Environmental regulation, observed the CEQ, "was based on the clear recognition that existing market prices were giving incorrect signals to consumers by understating what society was giving up to have goods whose production resulted in pollution."[5] The exclusion of these costs from price has upheld the demand for products whose costs were rippling beyond the marketplace, through all segments of society: in the air we breathe, in the water we drink, in the food we eat.

Opposition to environmental regulation usually is couched in concerns about decreasing corporate productivity and competitiveness in world markets. A federal consultant, however, has projected the annual productivity decline between 1970 and 1986 owing to environmental regulations at only .1 percent annually.[6] Scholarly researchers have found evidence that regulation actually can increase overall productivity by spurring technological change. A March 1980 report commissioned by the Senate Committee on Governmental Affairs observed, "Research and development aimed at compliance with health or safety regulations can increase overall productivity because the production system becomes more tightly enclosed, reducing emissions, or because the instruments used to control it are improved."[7] Recycling resources can save voluminous amounts of energy, cutting costs as well as reducing the need for waste disposal.

A company's political effectiveness hardly would be served by acknowledging its resistance to pay for proper management of the wastes produced by new technologies. Political effectiveness is an issue quite apart from truth, however. The historic resistance is best exemplified by the dumping of hazardous wastes. Hooker Chemical could have paid $4 million, in 1979 dollars, to properly dispose of its wastes at Love Canal.[8] Hooker chose instead to dump the wastes indiscriminately—sometimes simply pouring the wastes directly into the disposal site—and to cover them so inadequately that barrels repeatedly surfaced after heavy rain or snowfall. Hooker knew as early as 1958—20 years before 240 families were forced from their homes—that wastes were surfacing from the dump and children were being injured by the substances.[9]

Another reflection of the natural propensity of businesses to minimize expenditures is a figure they regularly trot out to demonstrate how heavily harassed they are by government: the cost of compliance with federal environmental laws. From the evidence already presented it should be apparent that federal laws have entirely stanched neither the flow of toxics into the environment nor the increase of environmental disease. But the laws have provided steady, and in some cases significant, improvements in the problems they were enacted to affect. Of the $55.9 billion estimated to have been spent by industry (and municipalities) on pollution control in 1979, $36.9 billion, or 66 percent, was spent in direct response to federal directives.[10] These increased expenditures contributed only .3 percentage points to the annual rise of the consumer price index and, by stimulating the pollution-control industry, actually increased employment.[11] This money represents incremental improvements in environmental quality that by definition would not have been undertaken by industry on its own. It also represents the vast gulf in the level of environmental contamination that many corporate managers—as opposed to the general society—are willing to accept.

The inexorable drive to expand production and to find new markets for products also is a significant factor in the environmental equation, particularly as it applies to the chemical industry. Traditionally, Dow Chemical or Monsanto have not asked whether society needs a new pesticide. They have asked only whether they can develop a market for it. And since the petrochemical industry is so capital-intensive, so dependent on elaborate, expensive equipment, the economies of scale are considerable. These economic factors are further stimuli to expand production and create new markets.

Even before the current offensive against regulation, the business community had vigorously resisted attempts to make it incorporate the societal costs of its activities. To keep these costs from becoming apparent, corporations have not been averse to covering up, downplaying or outright lying. Dr. Wilhelm C. Hueper, a prominent environmental physician, recognized this almost 40 years ago:

> Industrial concerns are in general not particularly anxious to have the occurrence of occupational cancer among their employees or of environmental cancer among the consumers of their products made a matter of public records. Such publicity might reflect unfavorably on their business activities and oblige them to undertake extensive and expensive technical and sanitary changes. . . . It is therefore not an uncommon practice by the parties financially interested in such matters to keep information on the occurrence of industrial cancer well under cover.[12]

Cover-ups or misrepresentations of impending dangers were key factors in each of the environmental disasters considered in this book. Because they were concealed, the dangers spread far beyond their original boundaries.

—Hooker Chemical knew in 1958 that wastes were surfacing at the Love Canal, but did not warn local residents of the danger.
—The Allied Chemical Corporation determined in animal tests as early as 1949 that Kepone attacks the nervous system, causing the tremors that were the trademark of the disaster made public in the mid-1970s.
—General Electric admitted at hearings on its discharge of PCBs into the Hudson River that the substance was involved in the illnesses of at least 65 of its workers over a 15-year period.
—The Nuclear Fuel Services Corporation, which operated the West Valley nuclear reprocessing plant now the responsibility of the state and federal governments, frequently hired temporary workers. These workers were given little or no instruction and no information about the potential hazards of radiation, yet were used to clean highly contaminated areas until the employees reached their annual dose limit of radiation—sometimes in only two or three days.
—Velsicol Chemical Company officials were indicted for falsely telling FDA investigators that PBB was not stored near feed additives. (The charge was dropped in October 1980 after Velsicol pleaded no contest to misdemeanor charges on the same incident.) The officials' statements were made shortly after the contamination of Michigan cattle feed with the toxic chemical PBB was discovered. In fact, employees have revealed, feed additives not only were stored near PBB, but were manufactured and processed on machinery that often contained PBB residues, spreading the contamination.
—The Reserve Mining Company, testifying at 1947 hearings on its application to dump tailings into Lake Superior, failed to reveal the results of a report it had commissioned that showed the dumping would seriously disrupt the food balance for fish near the plant. The report presaged the environmental disruption that followed. Twenty-five years later, during a trial that considered ending its lake discharges, Reserve claimed that land disposal was unfeasible and withheld a report it had commissioned on how to move the tailings onto land.
—The Dow Chemical Company knew in 1964 that 2,4,5-T was contaminated with dioxin, a highly toxic, carcinogenic and mutagenic chemical. That was six years before any action was taken on the chemical.[13]

No matter how prodigious the concealment efforts, they cannot keep all dangers out of the public eye. But the intricate regulatory system for weeding out unsafe chemicals and pesticides has ground to a virtual halt under an administrative siege from the affected industries. Only a handful of pesticides—DDT, aldrin and dieldrin and a few others—have been removed from use, and those only after the bureaucratic equivalent of war. Each ban has followed the compilation of voluminous records, the filing of countless motions by highly paid Washington law firms, and repeated trips to courthouse after courthouse for what must seem to government lawyers like Sisyphean rounds of appeal.

While these painstaking efforts drag on, the pesticides under dispute continue to be used. Of course, they are joined in the market place by new products every year.

And, while the EPA has been prodded to each of its bans by environmental groups, the overall impetus is not in the direction of more spirited action. Two EPA lawyers who resigned from the agency in 1976 complained that the EPA has failed "to take effective action under existing authority [because of] . . . industry pressure brought to bear through Congressional committees."[14] That pressure still is a deterrent to action, especially now that some representatives are pushing to end EPA regulation of pesticides altogether.

Occupational health regulation similarly has been stymied by intractable resistance. Since being formed 10 years ago, the Occupational Safety and Health Administration (OSHA) has been able to promulgate exposure standards for only 22 substances. In 1979, as the political climate further cooled and congressional rhetoric about over-regulation heated up, no standards were promulgated. And those standards that have been issued have typically had to withstand suits brought by trade associations in order to become law.

Pressure against taking aggressive action on environmental problems comes not only from industry, and from Congress, but additionally from White House officials—such as officials on the Council on Wage and Price Stability—concerned about the short-run inflationary impact of new regulation. This concern also keeps down the budgets of regulatory agencies, often leaving them with inadequate resources. Consequently, statutes that look fine in the law books—and were passed only after monumental legislative struggles—are only spottily enforced.

Consider the monitoring of the nation's food supply, a massive and complex but undeniably essential task. The program to oversee the safety of food has two components: setting standards for the maximum amount of contaminants permitted and monitoring to ensure compliance with the standards. On both ends, the government's program falls short.

Setting standards for pesticide residues begins with an evaluation of a pesticide's effects on health, usually gauged through animal studies. A General Accounting Office review of EPA files on 36 chemicals from which tolerances—maximum permissable levels of residues—had been set found that 7 lacked cancer and reproductive-effect studies, 14 lacked birth-defect studies, and 23 lacked mutation studies.[15] This random sample reflects an overall trend. "EPA files are replete with safety test data gaps," determined the Oversight Subcommittee of the House Commerce Committee in its 1978 report on carcinogens in food.[16] Moreover, that the chemical companies themselves supply the health-effects information casts doubts on the entire process. The oversight subcommittee concluded: "There is no federal compliance testing program to evaluate these data. As a result, EPA is forced to set many tolerances on unverified test data which may not fully assess the potential dangers of the pesticide in question."[17]

Compounding the problem of faulty data is the methodology used to derive a tolerance. Before a tolerance can be set, a "food factor" is determined that indicates how much of any single product—and its accompanying pesticide residue—an average person will eat during a year. Because averaging lumps together consumers and nonconsumers, the food factor is a consumption figure that understates the amounts that those who eat the product actually consume. "You need only to eat 7.5 ounces of avocado [per year] for instance—about the amount of avocado that is contained in a single avocado—before you begin to exceed the level that EPA assumes as the usage level [for the entire year] in setting up tolerances," said Lowell Dodge, then-counsel to the Oversight Subcommittee.[18]

The program for monitoring compliance with these standards also has been inadequate. The Food and Drug Administration (FDA) and the Department of Agriculture tests do not cover all the pesticides and animal drugs for which tolerances have been set; thus for all intents and purposes even some compounds for which tolerances have been set are unregulated.

Residue monitoring is also inadequate because, as Assistant Agriculture Secretary Carol Tucker Foreman testified in 1979, it is "not a preventative program."[19] It does not keep contaminated animals off the market. By the time the test results for a sample animal are available, even the meat in violation of the standards has been wrapped, bought and cooked. The Oversight Subcommittee estimated from the test results the FDA eventually received that 1.9 million tons of beef and 1.1 million tons of swine with illegal residues were sold to the public in 1976.[20]

The vast amounts of meat sold are another factor multiplying the inherent weaknesses in the program. According to Foreman, the cost of testing all beef and poultry marketed, with conventional technology, would be "about $100 billion" annually.[21] And, after the current testing procedure, little meat or poultry would remain to be eaten. Obviously, then, even if the EPA and FDA programs were drastically improved, no regulation could clean up the national food system after the fact—especially since many scientists believe no safe level of exposure to a carcinogen can be set. The only way to effectively eliminate the contamination is to cut it off at its source. But for all the testimonials given to selective pesticide use, pesticide sales continue to increase by leaps and bounds. This increased use confounds any efforts to reduce the level of food contamination. And the failure to prevent at the first steps in the food chain the increased pesticide use—use that is carefully nurtured by chemical and some farm groups and is protected, as the EPA has learned, by their supporters in Congress—is the crucial breakdown in the entire regulatory chain.

Shortfalls like these, failures of even the modest steps taken toward solving the vast environmental problem, illustrate the need to strenghten the oversight system. But the system is not being strengthened. Even as new environmental hazards are being identified, and the agony of their human victims understood, the regulatory system revealing them is under assault. Business lobbyists, with their mushrooming political action committees, have gone on the offensive and no longer are merely resisting regulation and tying up the process, but are taking their case to Congress and attacking the health-regulation enforcement system itself.

"The days when business people can sit back in the bushes and not participate in the public decision-making process," Dow Chemical President Paul Oreffice declared in 1978, "are over."[22] Oreffice may have understated the activity of business interests in the American political process for the past 200 years. But his assessment of the current mood was on target: If ever there were any businesses out there in the bushes, they are not there any longer.

One after another in the past two years, industries of all kinds have come to Washington, fighting what they have termed "regulatory overkill" and "excessive regulation."[23]

In advertisement after advertisement, trade associations and individual corporations have hammered home the claim that regulation is strangling business in red tape, wasting taxpayer money and aiming to create an unreachable, "zero-risk" society. "Pollution takes many forms," Mobil recently opined on the op-ed page of the *New York Times;* "In the American experience, by far the most damaging form has been stagnation. Economic stagnation."[24] And from the National Cotton Council: "OVER-REGULATION COULD COST YOU THE SHIRT OFF YOUR BACK. You might never get to wear cotton again. Not if the government has its way. . . ."[25] Accompanying this message, prominently placed in major magazines, is a picture of several muscular young businessmen with ties and vests but no shirts, presumably because government regulation has made cotton a thing of the past.

Nowhere in this picture are any of the 30,000 considerably less affluent, less vigorous men and women who have contracted byssinosis from breathing cotton dust on the job. But the omission may be fitting. The entire debate over regulation—with the demands for cost-benefit analysis of laws designed to save lives—has had a certain air of unreality to it, as though the suffering of workers in the plants or the families exposed to pesticide drift could be filed away as statistics under the category of business costs, and thereafter forgotten. The debate over regulation has subjected the lives of workers and the violent pollution of the air, water and land, perhaps more blatantly than ever before, to the calculus of short-range profit and myopic management.

## Notes

1. Barry Commoner, *The Closing Circle* (Bantam Books, 1972), p. 267.
2. Kush made the remark at the American Chemical Society Annual Meeting in Washington, D. C., September 10, 1979; it was quoted in the *Journal of Commerce,* September 11, 1979.
3. Jackson B. Browning, "Hazardous Wastes: Action On a National Problem," *Environmental Forum,* vol. I, no. I, October 1979.
4. "Rising Prices Spur Sales of Leading Chemical Producers," *Chemical & Engineering News,* May 5, 1980, p. 40.
5. *Environmental Quality: The Tenth Annual Report of the Council on Environmental Quality,* p. 643 (hereafter, *Tenth Annual Report,* CEQ).
6. Mark Green and Norman Waitzman, *Business War on the Law* (Corporate Accountability Research Group, 1979), p. 52.
7. Center for Policy Alternatives at the Massachusetts Institute of Technology, *Benefits of Environmental, Health, and Safety Regulation,* prepared for the Senate Committee on Governmental Affairs, March 25, 1980, p. 14.
8. *Hazardous Waste Disposal,* Hearings before the Subcommittee on Oversight and Investigations, House Interstate and Foreign Commerce Committee, p. 23.

9. Ibid., p. 665.
10. *Eleventh Annual Report,* CEQ, pp. 393–396.
11. Ibid., pp. 657–659.
12. Quoted in a statement by Representative George Miller (D-California), *Congressional Record,* July 27, 1979, pp. E 3922–3923.
13. For more discussion of each of these issues, see "House Hearing is Told Dow Knew in 1964 That Defoliant was Toxic," *New York Times,* July 23, 1980.
14. "Effort to Assess Pesticide Safety is Bogged Down," *New York Times,* December 12, 1977.
15. *Cancer-Causing Chemicals in Food,* report of the Subcommittee on Oversight and Investigations, House Interstate and Foreign Commerce Committee, December 1978, p. 25.
16. Ibid., p. 18.
17. Ibid., p. 19.
18. Ibid., p. 12.
19. Testimony of Carol Tucker Foreman, assistant secretary for food and consumer services, USDA, before the Oversight and Investigations Subcommittee of the House Interstate and Foreign Commerce Committee, September 28, 1979, p. 4.
20. *Cancer-Causing Chemicals in Food,* p. 26.
21. Foreman testimony, p. 4.
22. "No Time To Sit Back," *Chemical Week,* June 28, 1978.
23. Testimony of Richard L. Lesher, president of the U.S. Chamber of Commerce, before the Senate Labor and Human Resources Committee, April 1, 1980, p. 9.
24. Mobil's ad first appeared on May 4, 1972. See the *New York Times,* March 20, 1980, for a reprint.
25. The Cotton Council, the cotton industry trade association, took out this ad in several publications in spring 1980.

# The Church and the Future of the U.S. Economy

*National Conference of Catholic Bishops*

1. Every perspective on economic life that is human, moral, and Christian must be shaped by three questions: What does the economy do *for* people? What does it do *to* people? And how do people *participate* in it? The economy is a human reality: men and women working together to develop and care for the whole of God's creation. All this work must serve the material and spiritual well-being of people. It influences what people hope for themselves and their loved ones. It affects the way they act together in society. It influences their very faith in God.[1]

2. The Second Vatican Council declared that "the joys and hopes, the griefs and anxieties of the people of this age, especially those who are poor or in any way afflicted, these too are the joys and hopes, the griefs and anxieties of the followers of Christ."[2] There are many signs of hope in U.S. economic life today:

- Many fathers and mothers skillfully balance the arduous responsibilities of work and family life. There are parents who pursue a purposeful and modest way of life and by their example encourage their children to follow a similar path. A large number of women and men, drawing on their religious tradition, recognize the challenging vocation of family life and child rearing in a culture that emphasizes material display and self-gratification.
- Conscientious business people seek new and more equitable ways to organize resources and the workplace. They face hard choices over expanding or retrenching, shifting investments, hiring or firing.

---



---

*See Statistical Appendix Tables A–1, A–6, A–8, A–9, A–10, A–11, A–12, A–13, A–14, A–15, A–16, A–17, A–18, and A–20.

[1]Vatican Council II, *The Pastoral Constitution on the Church in the Modern World,* 33 [Note: This pastoral letter frequently refers to documents of the Second Vatican Council, papal encyclicals, and other official teachings of the Roman Catholic Church. Most of these texts have been published by the United States Catholic Conference Office of Publishing and Promotion Services; many are available in collections, though no single collection is comprehensive.]

[2]*Pastoral Constitution,* 1.

- Young people choosing their life's work ask whether success and security are compatible with service to others.
- Workers whose labor may be toilsome or repetitive try daily to ennoble their work with a spirit of solidarity and friendship.
- New immigrants brave dislocations while hoping for the opportunities realized by the millions who came before them.

3. These signs of hope are not the whole story. There have been failures—some of them massive and ugly:

- Poor and homeless people sleep in community shelters and in our church basements; the hungry line up in soup lines.
- Unemployment gnaws at the self-respect of both middle-aged persons who have lost jobs and the young who cannot find them.
- Hardworking men and women wonder if the system of enterprise that helped them yesterday might destroy their jobs and their communities tomorrow.
- Families confront major new challenges: dwindling social supports for family stability; economic pressures that force both parents of young children to work outside the home; a driven pace of life among the successful that can sap love and commitment; lack of hope among those who have less or nothing at all. Very different kinds of families bear different burdens of our economic system.
- Farmers face the loss of their land and way of life; young people find it difficult to choose farming as a vocation; farming communities are threatened; migrant farmworkers break their backs in serf-like conditions for disgracefully low wages.

4. *And beyond our own shores, the reality of 800 million people living in absolute poverty and 450 million malnourished or facing starvation casts an ominous shadow over all these hopes and problems at home.*

5. Anyone who sees all this will understand our concern as pastors and bishops. People shape the economy and in turn are shaped by it. Economic arrangements can be sources of fulfillment, of hope, of community—or of frustration, isolation, and even despair. They teach virtues—or vices—and day by day help mold our characters. They affect the quality of people's lives; at the extreme even determining whether people live or die. Serious economic choices go beyond purely technical issues to fundamental questions of value and human purpose.[3] We believe that in facing these questions the Christian religious and moral tradition can make an important contribution.

---

[3]See ibid., 10, 42, 43; Congregation for the Doctrine of the Faith, *Instruction on Christian Freedom and Liberation,* (Washington, D.C.: USCC Office of Publishing and Promotion Services, 1986), 34–36.

## A. The U.S. Economy Today: Memory and Hope

6. The United States is among the most economically powerful nations on earth. In its short history the U.S. economy has grown to provide an unprecedented standard of living for most of its people. The nation has created productive work for millions of immigrants and enabled them to broaden their freedoms, improve their families' quality of life, and contribute to the building of a great nation. Those who came to this country from other lands often understood their new lives in the light of biblical faith. They thought of themselves as entering a promised land of political freedom and economic opportunity. The United States *is* a land of vast natural resources and fertile soil. It *has* encouraged citizens to undertake bold ventures. Through hard work, self-sacrifice, and cooperation, families have flourished; towns, cities, and a powerful nation have been created.

7. But we should recall this history with sober humility. The American experiment in social, political, and economic life has involved serious conflict and suffering. Our nation was born in the face of injustice to native Americans, and its independence was paid for with the blood of revolution. Slavery stained the commercial life of the land through its first two hundred and fifty years and was ended only by a violent civil war. The establishment of women's suffrage, the protection of industrial workers, the elimination of child labor, the response to the Great Depression of the 1930s, and the civil rights movement of the 1960s all involved a sustained struggle to transform the political and economic institutions of the nation.

8. The U.S. value system emphasizes economic freedom. It also recognizes that the market is limited by fundamental human rights. Some things are never to be bought or sold.[4] This conviction has prompted positive steps to modify the operation of the market when it harms vulnerable members of society. Labor unions help workers resist exploitation. Through their government, the people of the United States have provided support for education, access to food, unemployment compensation, security in old age, and protection of the environment. The market system contributes to the success of the U.S. economy, but so do many efforts to forge economic institutions and public policies that enable *all* to share in the riches of the nation. The country's economy has been built through a creative struggle; entrepreneurs, business people, workers, unions, consumers, and government have all played essential roles.

9. The task of the United States today is as demanding as that faced by our forebears. Abraham Lincoln's words at Gettysburg are a reminder that complacency today would be a betrayal of our nation's history: "It is for us, the living, rather

---

[4]See Pope John Paul II, *On Human Work* (1981), 14; and Pope Paul VI, *Octogesima Adveniens* (1971), 35. See also Arthur Okun, *Equality and Efficiency: The Big Tradeoff* (Washington, D.C.: The Brookings Institution, 1975), ch. 1; Michael Walzer, *Spheres of Justice: A Defense of Pluralism and Equality* (New York: Basic Books, 1983), ch. 4; Jon P. Gunnemann, "Capitalism and Commutative Justice," paper presented at the 1985 meeting of the Society of Christian Ethics.

to be dedicated here to the unfinished work . . . they have thus far nobly advanced."[5] There is unfinished business in the American experiment in freedom and justice for all.

## B. Urgent Problems of Today

10. The preeminent role of the United States in an increasingly interdependent global economy is a central sign of our times.[6] The United States is still the world's economic giant. Decisions made here have immediate effects in other countries; decisions made abroad have immediate consequences for steelworkers in Pittsburgh, oil company employees in Houston, and farmers in Iowa. U.S. economic growth is vitally dependent on resources from other countries and on their purchases of our goods and services. Many jobs in U.S. industry and agriculture depend on our ability to export manufactured goods and food.

11. In some industries the mobility of capital and technology makes wages the main variable in the cost of production. Overseas competitors with the same technology but with wage rates as low as one-tenth of ours put enormous pressure on U.S. firms to cut wages, relocate abroad, or close. U.S. workers and their communities should not be expected to bear these burdens alone.

12. All people on this globe share a common ecological environment that is under increasing pressure. Depletion of soil, water, and other natural resources endangers the future. Pollution of air and water threatens the delicate balance of the biosphere on which future generations will depend.[7] The resources of the earth have been created by God for the benefit of all, and we who are alive today hold them in trust. This is a challenge to develop a new ecological ethic that will help shape a future that is both just and sustainable.

13. In short, nations separated by geography, culture, and ideology are linked in a complex commercial, financial, technological, and environmental network. These links have two direct consequences. First, they create hope for a new form of community among all peoples, one built on dignity, solidarity, and justice. Second, this rising global awareness calls for greater attention to the stark inequities across countries in the standards of living and control of resources. We must not look at the welfare of U.S. citizens as the only good to be sought. Nor may we overlook the disparities of power in the relationships between this nation and the developing countries. The United States is the major supplier of food to other countries, a major source of arms sales to developing nations, and a powerful influence in multilateral institutions such as the International Monetary Fund, the World Bank, and

---

[5]Abraham Lincoln, Address at Dedication of National Cemetery at Gettysburg, November 19, 1863.

[6]Pope John XXIII, *Peace on Earth* (1963), 130–131.

[7]Synod of Bishops, *Justice in the World* (1971), 8; Pope John Paul II, *Redeemer of Man* (1979), 15.

the United Nations. What Americans see as a growing interdependence is regarded by many in the less developed countries as a pattern of domination and dependence.

14. Within this larger international setting, there are also a number of challenges to the domestic economy that call for creativity and courage. The promise of the "American dream"—freedom for all persons to develop their God-given talents to the full—remains unfulfilled for millions in the United States today.

15. Several areas of U.S. economic life demand special attention. Unemployment is the most basic. Despite the large number of new jobs the U.S. economy has generated in the past decade, approximately 8 million people seeking work in this country are unable to find it, and many more are so discouraged they have stopped looking.[8] Over the past two decades the nation has come to tolerate an increasing level of unemployment. The 6 to 7 percent rate deemed acceptable today would have been intolerable twenty years ago. Among the unemployed are a disproportionate number of blacks, Hispanics, young people, or women who are the sole support of their families.[9] Some cities and states have many more unemployed persons than others as a result of economic forces that have little to do with people's desire to work. Unemployment is a tragedy no matter whom it strikes, but the tragedy is compounded by the unequal and unfair way it is distributed in our society.

16. Harsh poverty plagues our country despite its great wealth. More than 33 million Americans are poor; by any reasonable standard another 20 to 30 million are needy. Poverty is increasing in the United States, not decreasing.[10] For a people who believe in "progress," this should be cause for alarm. These burdens fall most heavily on blacks, Hispanics, and Native Americans. Even more disturbing is the large increase in the number of women and children living in poverty. Today children are the largest single group among the poor. This tragic fact seriously threatens the nation's future. That so many people are poor in a nation as rich as ours is a social and moral scandal that we cannot ignore.

17. Many working people and middle-class Americans live dangerously close to poverty. A rising number of families must rely on the wages of two or even three members just to get by. From 1968 to 1978 nearly a quarter of the U.S. population was in poverty part of the time and received welfare benefits in at least one year.[11] The loss of a job, illness, or the breakup of a marriage may be all it takes to push people into poverty.

18. The lack of a mutually supportive relation between family life and economic

---

[8]U.S. Department of Labor, Bureau of Labor Statistics, *The Employment Situation: August 1985* (September 1985), Table A–1.

[9]Ibid.

[10]U.S. Bureau of the Census, Current Population Reports, Series P–60, 145, *Money Income and Poverty Status of Families and Persons in the United States: 1983* (Washington, D.C.: U.S. Government Printing Office, 1984), 20.

[11]Greg H. Duncan, *Years of Poverty, Years of Plenty: The Changing Economic Fortunes of American Workers and Their Families* (Ann Arbor, Mich.: Institute for Social Research, University of Michigan, 1984).

life is one of the most serious problems facing the United States today.[12] The economic and cultural strength of the nation is directly linked to the stability and health of its families.[13] When families thrive, spouses contribute to the common good through their work at home, in the community, and in their jobs; and children develop a sense of their own worth and of their responsibility to serve others. When families are weak or break down entirely, the dignity of parents and children is threatened. High cultural and economic costs are inflicted on society at large.

19. The precarious economic situation of so many people and so many families calls for examination of U.S. economic arrangements. Christian conviction and the American promise of liberty and justice for all give the poor and the vulnerable a special claim on the nation's concern. They also challenge all members of the Church to help build a more just society.

20. The investment of human creativity and material resources in the production of the weapons of war makes these economic problems even more difficult to solve. Defense Department expenditures in the United States are almost $300 billion per year. The rivalry and mutual fear between superpowers divert into projects that threaten death, minds, and money that could better human life. Developing countries engage in arms races they can ill afford, often with the encouragement of the superpowers. Some of the poorest countries of the world use scarce resources to buy planes, guns, and other weapons when they lack the food, education, and health care their people need. Defense policies must be evaluated and assessed in light of their real contribution to freedom, justice, and peace for the citizens of our own and other nations. We have developed a perspective on these multiple moral concerns in our 1983 pastoral letter, *The Challenge of Peace: God's Promise and Our Response*.[14] When weapons or strategies make questionable contributions to security, peace, and justice and will also be very expensive, spending priorities should be redirected to more pressing social needs.[15]

21. Many other social and economic challenges require careful analysis: the movement of many industries from the Snowbelt to the Sunbelt, the federal deficit and interest rates, corporate mergers and takeovers, the effects of new technologies such as robotics and information systems in U.S. industry, immigration policy, growing international traffic in drugs, and the trade imbalance. All of these issues do not provide a complete portrait of the economy. Rather they are symptoms of more fundamental currents shaping U.S. economic life today: the struggle to find meaning and value in human work, efforts to support individual freedom in the context of renewed social cooperation, the urgent need to create equitable forms of

---

[12]See Pope John Paul II, *Familiaris Consortio* (1981), 46.

[13]*Pastoral Constitution,* 47.

[14]National Conference of Catholic Bishops, *The Challenge of Peace: God's Promise and Our Response* (Washington, D.C.: USCC Office of Publishing and Promotion Services, 1983).

[15]Cardinal Joseph L. Bernardin and Cardinal John J. O'Connor, Testimony before the House Foreign Relations Committee, June 26, 1984, *Origins* 14:10 (August 10, 1984): 157.

global interdependence in a world now marked by extreme inequality. These deeper currents are cultural and moral in content. They show that the long-range challenges facing the nation call for sustained reflection on the values that guide economic choices and are embodied in economic institutions. Such explicit reflection on the ethical content of economic choices and policies must become an integral part of the way Christians relate religious belief to the realities of everyday life. In this way, the "split between the faith which many profess and their daily lives,"[16] which Vatican II counted among the more serious errors of the modern age, will begin to be bridged.

## C. The Need for Moral Vision

22. Sustaining a common culture and a common commitment to moral values is not easy in our world. Modern economic life is based on a division of labor into specialized jobs and professions. Since the industrial revolution, people have had to define themselves and their work ever more narrowly to find a niche in the economy. The benefits of this are evident in the satisfaction many people derive from contributing their specialized skills to society. But the costs are social fragmentation, a decline in seeing how one's work serves the whole community, and an increased emphasis on personal goals and private interests.[17] This is vividly clear in discussions of economic justice. Here it is often difficult to find a common ground among people with different backgrounds and concerns. One of our chief hopes in writing this letter is to encourage and contribute to the development of this common ground.[18]

23. Strengthening common moral vision is essential if the economy is to serve all people more fairly. Many middle-class Americans feel themselves in the grip of economic demands and cultural pressures that go far beyond the individual family's capacity to cope. Without constructive guidance in making decisions with serious moral implications, men and women who hold positions of responsibility in corporations or government find their duties exacting a heavy price. We want these reflections to help them contribute to a more just economy.

24. The quality of the national discussion about our economic future will affect the poor most of all, in this country and throughout the world. The life and dignity of millions of men, women, and children hang in the balance. Decisions must be judged in light of what they do *for* the poor, what they do *to* the poor, and what they enable the poor to do *for themselves*. The fundamental moral criterion for all

---

[16] *Pastoral Constitution,* 43.

[17] See, for example, Peter Berger, Brigitte Berger, and Hansfried Kellner, *The Homeless Mind: Modernization and Consciousness* (New York: Vintage, 1974).

[18] For a recent study of the importance and difficulty of achieving such a common language and vision see Robert N. Bellah, Richard Madsen, William M. Sullivan, Ann Swidler, and Stephen M. Tipton, *Habits of the Heart: Individualism and Commitment in American Life* (Berkeley, Calif.: University of California Press, 1985). See also Martin E. Marty, *The Public Church* (New York: Crossroads, 1981).

economic decisions, policies, and institutions is this: They must be at the service of *all people, especially the poor.*

25. This letter is based on a long tradition of Catholic social thought, rooted in the Bible and developed over the past century by the popes and the Second Vatican Council in response to modern economic conditions. This tradition insists that human dignity, realized in community with others and with the whole of God's creation, is the norm against which every social institution must be measured.[19]

26. This teaching has a rich history. It is also dynamic and growing.[20] Pope Paul VI insisted that all Christian communities have the responsibility "to analyze with objectivity the situation which is proper to their own country, to shed on it the light of the Gospel's unalterable words and to draw principles of reflection, norms of judgment, and directives for action from the social teaching of the Church."[21] Therefore, we build on the past work of our own bishops' conference, including the 1919 Program of Social Reconstruction and other pastoral letters.[22] In addition many people from the Catholic, Protestant, and Jewish communities, in academic, business or political life, and from many different economic backgrounds have also provided guidance. We want to make the legacy of Christian social thought a living, growing resource that can inspire hope and help shape the future.

27. We write, then, first of all to provide guidance for members of our own Church as they seek to form their consciences about economic matters. No one may claim the name Christian and be comfortable in the face of the hunger, homelessness, insecurity, and injustice found in this country and the world. At the same time, we want to add our voice to the public debate about the directions in which the U.S. economy should be moving. We seek the cooperation and support of those who do not share our faith or tradition. The common bond of humanity that links all persons is the source of our belief that the country can attain a renewed public moral vision. The questions are basic and the answers are often elusive; they challenge us to serious and sustained attention to economic justice.

---

[19]Pope John XXIII, *Mater et magistra* (1961), 219; *Pastoral Constitution,* 40.

[20]Congregation for the Doctrine of the Faith, *Instruction on Certain Aspects of the Theology of Liberation* (Washington, D.C.: USCC Office of Publishing and Promotion Services, 1984); Pope Paul VI, *Octogesima Adveniens* (1971), 42.

[21]*Octogesima Adveniens,* 4.

[22]Administrative Committee of the National Catholic War Council, *Program of Social Reconstruction,* February 12, 1919. Other notable statements on the economy by our predecessors are *The Present Crisis,* April 25, 1933; *Statement on Church and Social Order,* February 4, 1940; *The Economy: Human Dimensions,* November 20, 1975. These and numerous other statements of the U.S. Catholic episcopate can be found in Hugh J. Nolan, ed., *Pastoral Letters of the United States Catholic Bishops,* 4 vols. (Washington, D.C.: USCC Office of Publishing and Promotion Services, 1984).

# Chapter 2
# THE POLITY

## Wealth and Power

*Michael Patrick Allen*

It is usually assumed that the wealthy are also powerful. To begin with, it is not unusual for the members of corporate rich families to exercise some degree of control over those corporations in which they are major stockholders. Indeed, family members often serve as officers and directors of those corporations. As a result, they exercise considerable economic power. However, economic power is not the same as political power. Despite a few notable exceptions, only a few scions of corporate rich families have ever been elected or appointed to political office. Nevertheless, economic power can be translated into certain forms of political power. For example, the members of wealthy capitalist families are typically among the major contributors to political campaigns. Of course, campaign contributions, even substantial ones, do not permit contributors to dictate the actions of elected officials. After all, most candidates for political office receive contributions, both large and small, from many individuals and organizations. As a general rule, however, elected officials who plan to seek reelection at some point generally try to avoid antagonizing those who have contributed or might someday contribute generously to their campaigns. In fact, candidates who seek large campaign contributions from the members of corporate rich families must typically demonstrate that their political goals and beliefs are consistent with the economic interests of those families and their corporations. In this way, the members of these families are able to influence the selection of candidates for political office.

The corporate rich are powerful, but they are not omnipotent. There are definite limits to their power. After all, there are many examples of government actions that have not been entirely consistent with the economic interests of wealthy capitalist families and their corporations. The existence of formally progressive transfer taxes, for example, confirms that the corporate rich have been unable to prevent the passage of

---



---

See Statistical Appendix Tables A-1, A-3, and A-6.

legislation that is clearly inimical to their interests. In this particular case, widespread popular sentiment in favor of the redistribution of wealth through the imposition of progressive taxes has simply overwhelmed the ability of the corporate rich to influence legislation. Although they have been unable to prevent the passage of progressive transfer taxes, the corporate rich have been able to introduce changes into these tax laws that have mitigated the effects of these taxes. Wealthy entrepreneurs and their descendants derive much of their political power from their campaign contributions, but they are able to influence the formation of public opinion and public policy in other ways as well. In fact, the corporate rich derive much of their political power from their control over major corporations and foundations. The ability of corporate rich families to control the major media corporations in America enables them to wield a subtle but pervasive influence on public opinion. Similarly, the ability of corporate rich families to control major foundations that, in turn, provide grants to policy-research institutions enables them to influence the formulation of public policy.

## Deep Pockets

The relationship between wealth and power is especially apparent in the case of political campaign contributions. Corporate rich families are able to exert considerable political influence by virtue of the fact that they are usually among the largest contributors to political campaigns. Although a large contribution does not guarantee that a politician will invariably serve the interests of a particular contributor, such a contribution usually does ensure a contributor immediate access to that politician. For example, W. Clement Stone, the founder of Combined American Insurance Company and a major contributor to the Republican party in both 1968 and 1972, once claimed that he talked with President Nixon over the telephone about once a month. In a few cases, major contributors have actually sought specific forms of administrative or legislative relief in return for their contributions. In any event, campaign contributions are an important part of the candidate-selection process because candidates are not likely to win their elections unless they can raise sufficient campaign contributions. As a rule, individuals contribute money only to those candidates who share their political views. The members of corporate rich families typically contribute to candidates who share their opposition to government regulations that benefit either workers or consumers at the expense of corporate profits. Moreover, they are especially supportive of candidates who promise to reduce those taxes levied on wealthy capitalist families and their corporations. As one observer puts it, "a candidate is an extension of the political views of those from whom he receives money."

The dependence of politicians on the members of corporate rich families for campaign contributions has a long and somewhat ignoble history in American politics. One of the first researchers to examine the relationship between wealthy contributors and elected officials was Ferdinand Lundberg. In his classic study *America's Sixty Families,* Lundberg concluded unequivocally that "it is an established fact that vast sums about which the general public seldom hears are used to prostitute virtually all elections." One of the first public investigations of political campaign contributions was conducted in 1912 by the Senate Privileges and Elections Committee. This investigation revealed that both political parties relied heavily on large contributions from major corporations and members of their founding families. In 1904, for example, the Republican National Committee received large contributions from such wealthy individuals as Edward H. Harriman, Mark A. Hanna, Henry C. Frick, T. Coleman du Pont, and Charles W. Post. The presidential nominee of the Republican party that year was Theodore Roosevelt. Although he publicly denounced the immorality of great wealth and the power of big business, President Roosevelt failed to mount any serious challenges to the privileges of the corporate rich or the power of the large corporations. Indeed, the actions that he initiated against a few corporations often served to obviate more radical challenges to the economic interests of the majority of corporate rich families and their corporations.

In recent years, the enactment and enforcement of more stringent federal campaign disclosure laws have revealed the full extent of contributions by members of corporate rich families to both presidential and congressional campaigns. Using information from a variety of sources, Herbert Alexander, a noted political scientist, has identified the major contributors to every presidential election since 1960. In each of these elections, a significant proportion of all the money raised for political campaigns at the national level was contributed by a few hundred wealthy contributors. In 1960, for example, there were 95 individuals who contributed $10,000 or more to the major political parties and their candidates. These contributions accounted for just over 16 percent of the $9.5 million raised from all individuals by these parties and their candidates. By 1968, there were 424 individuals who contributed $10,000 or more to the major political parties and their candidates. In that year, contributions from these 424 contributors accounted for over 40 percent of the $29 million raised from all individuals by the major political parties and their candidates. In each of these elections, most of the large contributors were members of corporate rich families. Between 1960 and 1968, for example, 75 individuals who were members of either the Rockefeller, du Pont, or Mellon family contributed a total of $2.7 million to political campaigns at the national level. However, this total includes at least $1.5 million contributed to the unsuccessful presidential campaigns of Nelson Rockefeller by other members of the Rockefeller family between 1960 and 1968.

The campaign contributions of the corporate rich to presidential campaigns have followed a consistent pattern over the past several decades. By and large, the members of wealthy capitalist families have directed the bulk of their contributions to the Republican party and its candidates. As a result of this largesse, Republican candidates have been better financed than their Democratic opponents. Although the corporate rich have contributed the vast bulk of their campaign funds to the Republican party in most presidential elections, they have not neglected the Democratic party entirely. As a rule, many of the wealthy contributors to the Democratic party over the years have been either Jews, Catholics, or Southerners. Of course, members of these groups have traditionally been Democrats. Moreover, even wealthy Jews, Catholics, and Southerners have often been excluded from elite positions by Protestant Northerners from established upper-class families. Moreover, incumbent presidents, even those who are Democrats, often receive generous campaign contributions from members of the corporate rich. For example, when President Roosevelt ran for reelection for the first time in 1936, he received large contributions from such scions of corporate rich families as Doris Duke Cromwell, Marjorie Post Davies, Joseph Medill Patterson, W. Averell Harriman, and Augustus A. Busch, Jr. Of course, his Republican opponent received substantially larger campaign contributions from several members of the Rockefeller, du Pont, Mellon, and Pew families. In many cases, those wealthy individuals who contributed to the Democratic party and its candidates were considered mavericks even by members of their own family.

The ability of corporate rich families to influence political campaigns by means of their contributions to particular candidates and parties may have reached its peak in the presidential election of 1972. The presidential campaign that year, between Richard M. Nixon and George F. McGovern, was very expensive, and the corporate rich responded to the challenge with their customary largesse. In all, the 1,254 largest contributors that year gave $51.3 million to the major presidential candidates and their parties. Moreover, 284 individuals lent a total of $11.8 million to these campaigns. The Republican party and its candidate, who was also the incumbent president, collected far more from wealthy entrepreneurs and their families than the Democratic party and its candidate, who proposed more progressive gift and estate taxes. For example, the top 20 contributors to the Nixon campaign gave a total of just over $8 million. Much of this money went directly to the Committee to Re-Elect the President. Conversely, the top 20 contributors to the McGovern campaign gave a total of less than $3 million. Almost all of the largest contributors to the Nixon campaign, as well as many of the largest contributors to the McGovern campaign, were members of corporate rich families. Major contributors to the Nixon campaign included such wealthy entrepreneurs as W. Clement Stone, Daniel Terra, and Ray Kroc, as well as such scions of corporate rich families as Richard M. Scaife, Arthur K. Watson, and Walter Annenberg. Among the major contributors to the McGovern campaign were several liberal members of the corporate rich, including Stewart R. Mott, Max Palevsky, and Anne Labouisse Peretz.

Many of the activities associated with the Watergate scandal, which eventually led to the resignation of President Nixon, were financed with illegal or misappropriated campaign contributions. In 1974, as a result of the disclosure of these financial abuses, Congress passed several amendments to the Federal Election Campaign Act. These and subsequent amendments established limits on the amount of money that individuals could contribute to any candidate for federal office. Specifically, these reforms prohibited individuals from contributing more than $1,000 to a candidate for each primary, runoff, or general election. Moreover, individuals were prohibited from contributing more than $5,000 to any political action committee or more than $20,000 to the national committee of any political party. In general, these reforms set an annual limit of $25,000 on individual contributions to candidates for federal office. However, because these limits apply to individuals, it is possible for a married couple to double these amounts. The Federal Election Campaign Act also limits the campaign expenditures of the candidates for federal office, including congressional candidates, and provides for some public financing of federal elections. These campaign-financing reforms have served to reduce the importance of large contributors to presidential and congressional campaigns. Nevertheless, wealthy contributors are still important, particularly in primary elections. For example, presidential candidates cannot continue to receive public funds unless they receive a sufficient proportion of the votes cast in the state primaries.

Even the Federal Election Campaign Act has failed to sever the tie between wealth and power entirely. For example, as the result of recent court decisions, individuals are free to pay for advertisements on behalf of a candidate. The Supreme Court concluded that any limitations on individual expenditures advocating the election of a candidate represent an infringement of the constitutional right of free speech. Consequently, an individual is free to make independent expenditures on advertisements on behalf of a candidate as long as those expenditures are not coordinated with the candidate or any of his or her committees. One of the first major campaign contributors to exploit this ruling was Stewart R. Mott. One of the children of Charles S. Mott, a principal stockholder in General Motors, Stewart Mott has contributed generously to a number of moderate or liberal presidential candidates in recent years. Faced with the limitations on campaign contributions imposed by the Federal Election Campaign Act, Mott decided to use independent expenditures to influence the 1980 election. To begin with, he spent $90,000 on advertisements advocating the nomination of John Anderson, a moderate, as the presidential candidate of the Republican party. Later, he established his own direct-mail company, Mott Enterprises, which extended John Anderson, by then an independent presidential candidate, a $500,000 line of credit for direct-mail solicitations. As Mott later boasted, "I've figured out how to be a fat cat again." Another gap in the Federal Election Campaign Act involves political campaigns by the members of wealthy families. Under the present law, there is no limit to the amount individuals can spend on their own political campaigns.

No family in American history has spent as much on politics as the Rockefeller family. The first member of the family to run for elected office was Nelson A. Rockefeller. In 1958, he defeated the incumbent governor of New York, W. Averell Harriman, who was also a scion of a corporate rich family. They both spent so much money on the campaign that newspapers referred to it as "the millionaires' sweepstakes." In all, he was elected governor of New York for four successive terms, longer than any other governor. He never hesitated to use his own money or money from other family members to finance his campaigns. Between 1958 and 1972, Nelson Rockefeller spent a total of $3 million of his own money on his four gubernatorial and three presidential campaigns. His family contributed another $14 million during that same period. It is not known how much his brother, Winthrop Rockefeller, spent on his four gubernatorial campaigns in the state of Arkansas. It may have been as much as $10 million. The biggest spender of them all, however, is undoubtedly John D. Rockefeller IV, the nephew of Nelson and Winthrop Rockefeller. After serving four years in the West Virginia state legislature, Jay Rockefeller decided to run for governor in 1970. He lost the election, but four years later he ran again. This time he spent over $11 million of his own money on the campaign and won. No one had ever spent so much money on a gubernatorial campaign in a state the size of West Virginia. In 1984, Jay Rockefeller decided to run for the Senate. He spent $12 million of his own money on the campaign and won. In all, Jay Rockefeller has spent well over $25 million of his own money on his political campaigns.

In the past, only a few scions of corporate rich families have sought political office. There is the example of James M. Cox, the newspaper publisher and founder of Cox Enterprises, who served as governor of Ohio before he became the presidential candidate of the Democratic party in 1920. However, as political campaigns have become increasingly expensive, candidates who are wealthy enough to finance their own primary campaigns have enjoyed a distinct advantage over their opponents. Scions of wealthy families have generally sought the prestige and security of the Senate. For example, H. John Heinz III, whose great-grandfather founded the H.J. Heinz Company, was elected to the Senate from Pennsylvania in 1976. In all, he spent $2.6 million of his own money during the campaign. That same year, John C. Danforth, whose grandfather founded Ralston Purina, was elected to the Senate from Missouri. Although wealth typically provides a candidate with a distinct advantage, it is not always a decisive advantage. In 1982, Mark Dayton, a great-grandson of the founder of the Dayton Hudson Company, spent $6.7 million of his own money on his unsuccessful campaign for the Senate from Minnesota. During the campaign, Dayton referred to his wealth as his "original sin." However, eight other members of the Dayton family, who were apparently unrepentant about their wealth, contributed to his opponent. Other members of corporate rich families have pursued governorships. Pierre S. du Pont IV, whose family still controls E.I. du Pont de Nemours and Company, served as governor of Delaware for eight years. More recently, Lewis E. Lehrman, whose father founded Rite-Aid Corporation, spent $6 million of his own money on an unsuccessful campaign for governor of New York.

The corporate rich are not reluctant to exercise their political power to their own advantage. For example, members of corporate rich families have occasionally lobbied the Congress and the president to enact special legislation for their benefit. A case in point involves the du Pont family. In 1949, the Justice Department filed an antitrust suit against the members of the du Pont family and their various holding companies on the grounds that their control of both E.I. du Pont de Nemours and Company and General Motors violated the Clayton Antitrust Act. At that point, Pierre S. du Pont, his siblings, and their descendants owned, directly and indirectly, over 26 percent of the stock in Du Pont. In turn, Du Pont owned almost 23 percent of the stock in General Motors. Members of the du Pont family also served as directors of both Du Pont and General Motors. Five years later, the presiding judge dismissed the antitrust complaint. However, the Justice Department appealed the decision to the Supreme Court, which overruled the District Court decision in 1957. After five more years of legal skirmishes, the presiding judge finally entered a final judgment that required Du Pont to divest itself of its General Motors stock by 1965. According to the terms of this decree, Du Pont was required to distribute its General Motors stock to its own stockholders in three installments. Similarly, Christiana Securities, the main holding company of the du Pont family, was required to sell some of this General Motors stock and distribute the rest to its stockholders. The judgment also required several members of the du Pont family, particularly those who were large stockholders in Christiana Securities, to sell a portion of this General Motors stock.

The divestiture order raised serious tax problems for the members of the du Pont family. Du Pont was required to distribute General Motors stock then worth approximately $3 billion to its stockholders. Because the members of the du Pont family owned, either directly or indirectly, at least 26 percent of the stock in Du Pont, they were due to receive about $790 million in General Motors stock. Even though this stock was due to be received in three separate installments over a period of four years, this stock distribution would create enormous tax liabilities because the tax laws treated such distributions as income. Specifically, the du Ponts were faced with the prospect of paying as much as $550 million in income taxes on this General Motors stock. Even before the final divestiture order was issued, special bills were introduced in both the House and the Senate to provide Du Pont stockholders, including the du Ponts, with tax relief. In general, these bills required Du Pont stockholders to pay relatively low capital-gains taxes on only a portion of the value of the General Motors stock they received as a result of these distributions. President Kennedy signed the special Du Pont tax-relief bill in 1962. By 1964, however, the du Ponts were seeking additional tax relief. Because General Motors stock had doubled in value since 1962, the tax liabilities of the du Ponts on the last distribution of General Motors stock were also about to double. Yielding to a concerted lobbying effort, the Treasury Department ruled that the final distribution of General Motors stock was a tax-free distribution. In all, the du Ponts probably saved at least $350 million in income taxes as a result of these government actions.

On occasion, individual members of the corporate rich have lobbied Congress to pass special legislation for their benefit alone. One of the most blatant political maneuvers of this sort involved H. Ross Perot, the founder of Electronic Data Systems. In 1975, as the House Ways and Means Committee was about to finish its work on a major tax-reform bill, one of its members introduced a very unusual amendment. This amendment would permit any taxpayers who had capital losses of more than $30,000 in one year to receive a corresponding refund of any taxes they paid on capital gains during the previous three years. A few weeks earlier, the Senate Finance Committee had included a similar amendment in its version of the tax bill. The main beneficiary of this amendment was H. Ross Perot. In fact, the proposed amendment had been prepared by his lawyer, who was also a former commissioner of the Internal Revenue Service. It seems that Perot had paid roughly $18 million in capital-gains taxes on the sale of $57 million worth of Electronic Data

Systems stock in 1971. Three years later, he lost approximately $15 million when a brokerage house that he had financed became bankrupt. This amendment would have entitled him to a tax refund of about $15 million in 1974. H. Ross Perot had some reason to believe that his amendment might pass. Earlier in 1974, he had contributed $90,000 to various congressional candidates, more than any other individual. Moreover, $55,000 of this went to members of the House Ways and Means Committee and the Senate Finance Committee. This amendment was eliminated only after the details of the Perot amendment and his campaign contributions were published in several major newspapers.

A more recent and more successful attempt by the members of a corporate rich family to amend the tax laws for their own benefit involves the Gallo family. Ernest and Julio Gallo and their four children are the owners of a large wine company worth roughly $600 million. When the House Ways and Means Committee began considering a tax-reform package in 1985, one of the proposed changes in gift and estate taxes was the imposition of a new "generation-skipping tax." The existing law contained a provision for taxing distributions from generation-skipping trusts, but the proposed law would tax direct gifts and bequests from grandparents to grandchildren as well. However, the proposed law included a $1 million exclusion for each grandparent. Under this law, for example, the Gallo brothers and their wives would have been able to transfer a total of $4 million in company stock to their grandchildren before they had to pay generation-skipping taxes. Ernest and Julio Gallo, who planned to distribute some of their stock in the family company to their twenty grandchildren, wanted a more generous exclusion. An amendment to the proposed generation-skipping tax that would grant an additional $2 million exclusion to each grandparent for each grandchild was introduced. Indeed, a temporary version of the "Gallo Amendment," as it came to be known, was included in the final tax law. The passage of this amendment may have been aided by the fact that Ernest and Julio Gallo and their wives had contributed over $276,000 to various federal campaigns since 1977. In any event, the Gallos now have until 1990 to transfer a total of $84 million worth of stock in the family corporation to their twenty grandchildren without paying any generation-skipping taxes.

Sometimes, special legislation is introduced in order to enable the descendants of a wealthy entrepreneur to maintain control of their family corporation. For example, the Pew family sought to change the tax laws in 1971 so they could retain their control over Sun Company. The Tax Reform Act of 1969 was the first attempt by the federal government to regulate the activities of tax-exempt private foundations. One of the key provisions of this legislation was a minimum payout rate that required private foundations to disburse 6 percent of the market value of their assets each year. One of the foundations threatened by this provision was the Pew Memorial Trust, which was endowed and controlled by members of the Pew family. Indeed, the descendants of Joseph N. Pew have been able to retain almost absolute control over Sun Company through their control of the Pew Memorial Trust, which, in turn, owns about 22 percent of Sun Company stock. The problem facing the Pews was the fact that Sun Company stock paid very small dividends. In 1971, a member of the House of Representatives from Pennsylvania, the home of Sun Company, the Pew Memorial Trust, and the Pew family, introduced a bill that would have greatly reduced the minimum payout requirement as it applied to the Pew Memorial Trust. The Treasury Department later recommended passage of a bill that reduced the minimum payout provision from 6 percent to 5 percent of foundation assets and extended the deadline for full compliance from 1975 to 1978. Although both bills eventually failed to gain passage, the Pews did receive some assistance from the Republican administration. It was the least they could expect, because they had contributed over $142,000 to national Republican organizations in 1968.

The members of corporate rich families are sometimes able to amend the laws of particular states to suit their own purposes. For example, the Getty family had the laws governing estates and trusts in the state of California changed in order to resolve a lingering family feud. By 1984, the three surviving sons and fifteen grandchildren of J. Paul Getty were the beneficiaries of a trust worth roughly $3 billion. One of the sons, Gordon P. Getty, was the sole trustee of this trust. However, many of the beneficiaries, including his brothers and several of his nieces and nephews, did not approve of his management of the trust. To begin with, many of them felt that he had exposed the trust to unnecessary capital-gains taxes when he agreed to the acquisition of Getty Oil Company by Texaco in 1984. Although the trust received just over $4 billion in cash for its Getty Oil stock, it also incurred state and federal tax liabilities of nearly $1 billion as a result of this sale. During this period, several family members brought suit to have Gordon Getty removed as the trustee of the family trust. After months of litigation, the various descendants of J. Paul Getty finally agreed to split the trust into several smaller trusts, one for each branch of the family. This arrangement would enable the members of each branch of the family to choose the trustees for their trusts. There was one problem with this solution. The laws of the state of California did not contain any explicit provision for dividing a trust into a series of separate trusts. Within a matter of weeks, a bill that allowed the Gettys to resolve their family feud by dividing their trust into separate trusts was passed by the state legislature and signed by the governor.

Even though they are major contributors to many political campaigns, it is not easy for the corporate rich to obtain the passage of preferential legislation. Legislative relief in the form of a change in the law requires the cooperation of the members of various congressional committees and the assent of a majority of the members of both the Senate and the House of Representatives. It is difficult to convince a majority of the members of both houses of Congress to vote for a law that benefits only the members of a few wealthy families. They are much more likely to vote for a law that purports to benefit a large segment of the population, even if the bulk of the benefits accrue to the members of corporate rich families. In 1981, for example, President Reagan advocated several changes in both the income tax and the transfer tax that were very beneficial to the corporate rich. In particular, his tax-reform package contained a provision that would eventually reduce the federal transfer tax on gifts and estates from a maximum rate of 70 percent to a maximum rate of 50 percent. In order to gain legislative support for this provision, the proponents of the Economic Recovery Tax Act argued that the small family farm in America was being destroyed because farm families could not afford to pay the transfer taxes incurred whenever a farm passed from one generation of family members to the next. Because the maximum transfer tax rate applied only to gifts and estates in excess of $5 million, however, the family farms that stood to benefit the most from this change in the law were hardly small. Indeed, the main beneficiaries of this reduction in the maximum transfer tax rate were the corporate rich.

## The Privileged Class

The members of corporate rich families are clearly more powerful and influential than the members of most other families. First and foremost, they are principal stockholders in large corporations. In many cases, family members also serve as officers and directors of these corporations. To the extent that they control major corporations, the members of wealthy capitalist families are able to exercise tremendous economic power. For example, corporations have the power to build new plants and close old ones. In this way, they affect the welfare and even the survival of entire communities. Consequently, government officials, at both the state and local levels, are generally very solicitous of these corporations and the families that control them. At the national level, corporations are sometimes able to influence government policy by lobbying members of Congress for or against particular pieces of legislation. The members of corporate rich families also exercise considerable social power by virtue of the fact that they often control large philanthropic foundations. Almost all of the large foundations in America were endowed by members of wealthy capitalist families. Moreover, many of these foundations are still controlled by these donors or their descendants. As a result, corporate rich families often determine which organizations and causes receive grants from these foundations. The control that these families exert over these foundations enables them to influence civic and cultural affairs at the local, regional, and national levels.

Economic power is not always translated directly into political power. Indeed, the political power exercised by the corporate rich is subtle yet pervasive. For example, only a few scions of wealthy capitalist families are actively involved in politics. Those descendants of wealthy entrepreneurs who have entered electoral politics have usually done so as a means of personal fulfillment. In fact, many of the most important decisions are made by elites who occupy formal positions of authority in major institutions and organizations. These elites are usually affluent, but they rarely possess great wealth. Consequently, the corporate rich must exercise their political power primarily by influencing these elites. In the case of elected officials, the members of wealthy capitalist families are able to influence the selection of candidates by their campaign contributions. Large campaign contributions from the members of wealthy capitalist families provide a distinct financial advantage to those candidates who are willing to defer to the economic interests of these families and their corporations. Similarly, the members of corporate rich families sometimes use their foundations to fund conservative policy-research institutions that, in turn, issue reports and studies advocating policies that are consistent with their economic interests.

In terms of political power, it is important to distinguish between the power of the corporate rich as individuals or families and the power of the corporate rich as a class. Although the boundaries between different social classes in America are vague and indeterminate, the corporate rich belong to a distinct and coherent social class. Specifically, corporate rich families form the core of the capitalist class in America. The members of these families constitute an identifiable social class for several reasons. First and foremost, they represent a social class inasmuch as the members of different families share certain economic interests. These shared economic interests stem from the fact that wealthy entrepreneurs and their descendants are typically principal stockholders in large corporations. As a result, they share a common interest in corporate profitability. The members of these families also constitute a distinct social class because their economic interests are often opposed to the economic interests of other large segments of the population. For example, the corporate rich are generally opposed to many of the government regulations enacted on the behalf of workers and consumers, at least to the extent that they impinge upon the profits of their corporations. In this regard, the corporate rich have important allies among the legions of small-business proprietors across the nation. Although they do not possess great wealth, the proprietors of small businesses have many of the same economic interests and political objectives as the members of wealthy capitalist families.

The corporate rich have also forged alliances with other powerful groups in American society. In particular, the members of established corporate rich families have derived certain political advantages from their acceptance into the national upper class. Although the capitalist class and the upper class overlap to a significant extent, they are not identical. On the one hand, the capitalist class is defined in terms of economic interest and comprises primarily the officers, directors, and principal stockholders of corporations. The upper class, on the other hand, is defined in terms of social status and comprises the members of families that have been socially prominent for several generations. The fortunes of many upper-class families have become depleted over the years, and the members of these families are often unable to subsist comfortably on the incomes provided by their investments. Consequently, many of the scions of these established families have been compelled to take positions in business and government. Of course, they usually obtain positions that are commensurate with their social status. For example, scions of upper-class families often become partners in large investment banks, lawyers in prestigious law firms, professors at elite colleges and universities, or senior government officials. Some of these individuals from upper-class families eventually occupy positions of authority in the major institutions and organizations. In short, there is a great deal of overlap between the upper class and the power elite. The integration of corporate rich families into the upper class serves, therefore, to augment their power and influence at the national level.

The essential question is not whether or not the members of corporate rich families exercise an inordinate amount of political power. It is abundantly clear that they are one of the most powerful groups in American society. Rather, it is whether or not these wealthy capitalist families as a class represent a dominant or ruling class. The corporate rich are obviously powerful, but they are far from omnipotent. Indeed, the very existence of progressive income and transfer taxes, for example, demonstrates that the members of wealthy capitalist families have not been able to prevent the passage of legislation inimical to their economic interests. By and large, the corporate rich favor substantial reductions in the level of government expenditures accompanied by corresponding reductions in taxes. At the same time, most of them accept, albeit reluctantly, the necessity for some minimal level of taxation. They understand that government, at the local, state, and national levels, performs many important functions that contribute to the profitability of their corporations. Corporations are dependent upon government at one level or another for the provision of important facilities and services, such as highway construction, police and fire protection, and education. Moreover, state and local governments, with the assistance of the federal government, are responsible for providing social welfare services to ameliorate the effects of unemployment. Last but not least, these corporations also rely on the fiscal and monetary policies of the federal government to maintain stable rates of economic growth.

The members of corporate rich families may be resigned to the necessity of taxes, even to the inevitability of progressive taxes, but they are not about to relinquish their fortunes without a struggle. After all, wealth is the foundation of the corporate rich family and the source of all its privileges. Consequently, the members of these families take every opportunity to preserve their fortunes. As Karl Marx once proclaimed, "tax struggle is the oldest form of class struggle." The corporate rich have conducted their struggle against taxes on two levels. As individuals and families, they have employed elaborate strategies to avoid or reduce the taxes on their gifts and estates. On occasion, they have even sought special legislation or Internal Revenue Service rulings to relieve particular tax problems. Moreover, as a class, the members of corporate rich families have sometimes induced members of Congress, as well as presidents, to endorse tax reforms that have included reductions in the taxes on intergenerational transfers of wealth. Over the years, these efforts have produced a tax system that is formally progressive but still permits wealthy capitalist families to transfer the bulk of their wealth intact from one generation to the next. In the final analysis, the issue is not whether the corporate rich in America have lost any important political battles, but whether they have lost the war. For the members of these families, the most important war is the war for wealth. Although the corporate rich have lost some significant political battles, such as the imposition of progressive transfer taxes, they have certainly not lost the war for wealth.

# Bad Blood: The Tuskegee Syphilis Experiment

*James H. Jones*

In late July of 1972, Jean Heller of the Associated Press broke the story: for forty years the United States Public Health Service (PHS) had been conducting a study of the effects of untreated syphilis on black men in Macon County, Alabama, in and around the county seat of Tuskegee. The Tuskegee Study, as the experiment had come to be called, involved a substantial number of men: 399 who had syphilis and an additional 201 who were free of the disease chosen to serve as controls. All of the syphilitic men were in the late stage of the disease when the study began.[1]

Under examination by the press the PHS was not able to locate a formal protocol for the experiment. Later it was learned that one never existed; procedures, it seemed, had simply evolved. A variety of tests and medical examinations were performed on the men during scores of visits by PHS physicians over the years, but the basic procedures called for periodic blood testing and routine autopsies to supplement the information that was obtained through clinical examinations. The fact that only men who had late, so-called tertiary, syphilis were selected for the study indicated that the investigators were eager to learn more about the serious complications that result during the final phase of the disease.

The PHS officers were not disappointed. Published reports on the experiment consistently showed higher rates of mortality and morbidity among the syphilitics than the controls. In fact, the press reported that as of 1969 at least 28 and perhaps as many as 100 men had died as a direct result of complications caused by syphilis. Others had developed serious syphilis-related heart conditions that may have contributed to their deaths.[2]

The Tuskegee Study had nothing to do with treatment. No new drugs were tested; neither was any effort made to establish the efficacy of old forms of treatment. It was a nontherapeutic experiment, aimed at compiling data on the effects of the spontaneous evolution of syphilis on black males. The magnitude of the risks taken with the lives of the subjects becomes clearer once a few basic facts about the disease are known.

Syphilis is a highly contagious disease caused by the *Treponema pallidum,* a delicate organism that is microscopic in size and resembles a corkscrew in shape. The disease may be acquired or congenital. In acquired syphilis, the spirochete (as the *Treponema pallidum* is also called) enters the body through the skin or mucous

---

membrane, usually during sexual intercourse, though infection may also occur from other forms of bodily contact such as kissing. Congenital syphilis is transmitted to the fetus in the infected mother when the spirochete penetrates the placental barrier.

From the onset of infection syphilis is a generalized disease involving tissues throughout the entire body. Once they wiggle their way through the skin or mucous membrane, the spirochetes begin to multiply at a frightening rate. First they enter the lymph capillaries where they are hurried along to the nearest lymph gland. There they multiply and work their way into the bloodstream. Within days the spirochetes invade every part of the body.

Three stages mark the development of the disease: primary, secondary, and tertiary. The primary stage lasts from ten to sixty days starting from the time of infection. During this "first incubation period," the primary lesion of syphilis, the chancre, appears at the point of contact, usually on the genitals. The chancre, typically a slightly elevated, round ulcer, rarely causes personal discomfort and may be so small as to go unnoticed. If it does not become secondarily infected, the chancre will heal without treatment within a month or two, leaving a scar that persists for several months.[3]

While the chancre is healing, the second stage begins. Within six weeks to six months, a rash appears signaling the development of secondary syphilis. The rash may resemble measles, chicken pox, or any number of skin eruptions, though occasionally it is so mild as to go unnoticed. Bones and joints often become painful, and circulatory disturbances such as cardiac palpitations may develop. Fever, indigestion, headaches, or other nonspecific symptoms may accompany the rash. In some cases skin lesions develop into moist ulcers teeming with spirochetes, a condition that is especially severe when the rash appears in the mouth and causes open sores that are viciously infectious. Scalp hair may drop out in patches, creating a "moth-eaten" appearance. The greatest proliferation and most widespread distribution of spirochetes throughout the body occurs in secondary syphilis.[4]

Secondary syphilis gives way in most cases, even without treatment, to a period of latency that may last from a few weeks to thirty years. As if by magic, all symptoms of the disease seem to disappear, and the syphilitic patient does not associate with the disease's earlier symptoms the occasional skin infections, periodic chest pains, eye disorders, and vague discomforts that may follow. But the spirochetes do not vanish once the disease becomes latent. They bore into the bone marrow, lymph glands, vital organs, and central nervous systems of their victims. In some cases the disease seems to follow a policy of peaceful coexistence, and its hosts are able to enjoy full and long lives. Even so, autopsies in such cases often reveal syphilitic lesions in vital organs as contributing causes of death. For many syphilitic patients, however, the disease remains latent only two or three years. Then the delusion of a truce is shattered by the appearance of signs and symptoms that denote the tertiary stage.

It is during late syphilis, as the tertiary stage is also called, that the disease inflicts the greatest damage. Gummy or rubbery tumors (so-called gummas), the characteristic lesions of late syphilis, appear, resulting from the concentration of spirochetes in the body's tissues with destruction of vital structures. These tumors often coalesce on the skin forming large ulcers covered with a crust consisting of several layers of dried exuded matter. Their assaults on bone structure produce deterioration that resembles osteomyelitis or bone tuberculosis. The small tumors may be absorbed, leaving slight scarred depressions, or they may cause wholesale destruction of the bone, such as the horrible mutilation that occurs when nasal and palate bones are eaten away. The liver may also be attacked; here the result is scarring and deformity of the organ that impede circulation from the intestines.

The cardiovascular and central nervous sytems are frequent and often fatal targets of late syphilis. The tumors may attack the walls of the heart or the blood vessels. When the aorta is involved, the walls become weakened, scar tissue forms over the lesion, the artery dilates, and the valves of the heart no longer open and close properly and begin to leak. The stretching of the vessel walls may produce an aneurysm, a balloonlike bulge in the aorta. If the bulge bursts, and sooner or later most do, the result is sudden death.

The results of neurosyphilis are equally devastating. Syphilis is spread to the brain through the blood vessels, and while the disease can take several forms, the best known is paresis, a general softening of the brain that produces progressive paralysis and insanity. Tabes dorsalis, another form of neurosyphilis, produces a stumbling, foot-slapping gait in its victims due to the destruction of nerve cells in the spinal cord. Syphilis can also attack the optic nerve, causing blindness, or the eighth cranial nerve, inflicting deafness. Since nerve cells lack regenerative power, all such damage is permanent.

The germ that causes syphilis, the stages of the disease's development, and the complications that can result from untreated syphilis were all known to medical science in 1932—the year the Tuskegee Study began.

Since the effects of the disease are so serious, reporters in 1972 wondered why the men agreed to cooperate. The press quickly established that the subjects were mostly poor and illiterate, and that the PHS had offered them incentives to participate. The men received free physical examinations, free rides to and from the clinics, hot meals on examination days, free treatment for minor ailments, and a guarantee that burial stipends would be paid to their survivors. Though the latter sum was very modest (fifty dollars in 1932 with periodic increases to allow for inflation), it represented the only form of burial insurance that many of the men had.

What the health officials had told the men in 1932 was far more difficult to determine. An officer of the venereal disease branch of the Center for Disease Control in Atlanta, the agency that was in charge of the Tuskegee Study in 1972, assured reporters that the participants were told at the beginning that they had syphilis and were told what the disease could do to them, and that they were given the opportunity to withdraw from the program any time and receive treatment. But a physician with firsthand knowledge of the experiment's early years directly contradicted this statement. Dr. J. W. Williams, who was serving his internship at Andrews Hospital at the Tuskegee Institute in 1932 and assisted in the experiment's clinical work, stated that neither the interns nor the subjects knew what the study involved. "The people who came in were not told what was being done," Dr. Williams said. "We told them we wanted to test them. They were not told, so far as I know, what they were being treated for or what they were not being treated for." As far as he could tell, the subjects "thought they were being treated for rheumatism or bad stomachs." He did recall administering to the men what he thought were drugs to combat syphilis, and yet as he thought back on the matter, Dr. Williams conjectured that "some may have been a placebo." He was absolutely certain of one point: "We didn't tell them we were looking for syphilis. I don't think they would have known what that was."[5]

A subject in the experiment said much the same thing. Charles Pollard recalled clearly the day in 1932 when some men came by and told him that he would receive a free physical examination if he appeared the next day at a nearby one-room school. "So I went on over and they told me I had bad blood," Pollard recalled. "And that's what they've been telling me ever since. They come around from time to time and check me over and they say, 'Charlie, you've got bad blood.'"[6]

An official of the Center for Disease Control (CDC) stated that he understood the term "bad blood" was a synonym for syphilis in the black community. Pollard replied, "That could be true. But I never heard no such thing. All I knew was that they just kept saying I had the bad blood—they never mentioned syphilis to me, not even once." Moreover, he thought that he had been receiving treatment for "bad blood" from the first meeting on, for Pollard added: "They been doctoring me off and on ever since then, and they gave me a blood tonic."[7]

The PHS's version of the Tuskegee Study came under attack from yet another quarter when Dr. Reginald G. James told his story to reporters. Between 1939 and 1941 he had been involved with public health work in Macon County—specifically the diagnosis and treatment of syphilis. Assigned to work with him was Eunice Rivers, a black nurse employed by the Public Health Service to keep track of the participants in the Tuskegee Study. "When we found one of the men from the Tuskegee Study," Dr. James recalled, "she would say, 'He's under study and not to be treated.'" These encounters left him, by his own description, "distraught and disturbed," but whenever he insisted on treating such a patient, the man never returned. "They were being advised they shouldn't take treatments or they would be dropped from the study," Dr. James stated. The penalty for being dropped, he explained, was the loss of the benefits that they had been promised for participating.[8]

Once her identity became known, Nurse Rivers excited considerable interest, but she steadfastly refused to talk with reporters. Details of her role in the experiment came to light when newsmen discovered an article about the Tuskegee Study that appeared in *Public Health Reports* in 1953. Involved with the study from its beginning, Nurse Rivers served as the liaison between the researchers and the subjects. She lived in Tuskegee and provided the continuity in personnel that was vital. For while the names and faces of the "government doctors" changed many times over the years, Nurse Rivers remained a constant. She served as a facilitator, bridging the many barriers that stemmed from the educational and cultural gap between the physicians and the subjects. Most important, the men trusted her.[9]

As the years passed the men came to understand that they were members of a social club and burial society called "Miss Rivers' Lodge." She kept track of them and made certain that they showed up to be examined whenever the "government doctors" came to town. She often called for them at their homes in a shiny station wagon with the government emblem on the front door and chauffeured them to and from the place of examination. According to the *Public Health Reports* article, these rides became "a mark of distinction for many of the men who enjoyed waving to their neighbors as they drove by." There was nothing to indicate that the members of "Miss Rivers' Lodge" knew they were participating in a deadly serious experiment.[10]

Spokesmen for the Public Health Service were quick to point out that the experiment was never kept secret, as many newspapers had incorrectly reported when the story first broke. Far from being clandestine, the Tuskegee Study had been the subject of numerous reports in medical journals and had been openly discussed in conferences at professional meetings. An official told reporters that more than a dozen articles had appeared in some of the nation's best medical journals, describing the basic procedures of the study to a combined readership of well over a hundred thousand physicians. He denied that the Public Health Service had acted alone in the experiment, calling it a cooperative project that involved the Alabama State Department of Health, the Tuskegee Institute, the Tuskegee Medical Society, and the Macon County Health Department.[11]

Apologists for the Tuskegee Study contended that it was at best problematic whether the syphilitic subjects could have been helped by the treatment that was available when the study began. In the early 1930s treatment consisted of mercury and two arsenic compounds called arsphenamine and neoarsphenamine, known also by their generic name, salvarsan. The drugs were highly toxic and often produced serious and occasionally fatal reactions in patients. The treatment was painful and usually required more than a year to complete. As one CDC officer put it, the drugs offered "more potential harm for the patient than potential benefit."[12]

PHS officials argued that these facts suggested that the experiment had not been conceived in a moral vacuum. For if the state of the medical art in the early 1930s had nothing better than dangerous and less than totally effective treatment to offer, then it followed that, in the balance, little harm was done by leaving the men untreated.[13]

Discrediting the efficacy of mercury and salvarsan helped blunt the issue of withholding treatment during the early years, but public health officials had a great deal more difficulty explaining why penicillin was denied in the 1940s. One PHS spokesman ventured that it probably was not "a one-man decision" and added philosophically, "These things seldom are." He called the denial of penicillin treatment in the 1940s "the most critical moral issue about this experiment" and admitted that from the present perspective "one cannot see any reason that they could not have been treated at that time.'' Another spokesman declared: ''I don't know why the decision was made in 1946 not to stop the program.''[14]

The thrust of these comments was to shift the responsibility for the Tuskegee Study to the physician who directed the experiment during the 1940s. Without naming anyone, an official told reporters: ''Whoever was director of the VD section at that time, in 1946 or 1947, would be the most logical candidate if you had to pin it down.'' That statement pointed an accusing finger at Dr. John R. Heller, a retired PHS officer who had served as the director of the division of venereal disease between 1943 and 1948. When asked to comment, Dr. Heller declined to accept responsibility for the study and shocked reporters by declaring: ''There was nothing in the experiment that was unethical or unscientific.''[15]

The current local health officer of Macon County shared this view, telling reporters that he probably would not have given the men penicillin in the 1940s either. He explained this curious devotion to what nineteenth-century physicians would have called ''therapeutic nihilism'' by emphasizing that penicillin was a new and largely untested drug in the 1940s. Thus, in his opinion, the denial of penicillin was a defensible medical decision.[16]

A CDC spokesman said it was ''very dubious'' that the participants in the Tuskegee Study would have benefited from penicillin after 1955. In fact, treatment might have done more harm than good. The introduction of vigorous therapy after so many years might lead to allergic drug reactions, he warned. Without debating the ethics of the Tuskegee Study, the CDC spokesman pointed to a generation gap as a reason to refrain from criticizing it. ''We are trying to apply 1972 medical treatment standards to those of 1932,'' cautioned one official. Another officer reminded the public that the study began when attitudes toward treatment and experimentation were much different. ''At this point in time,'' the officer stated, ''with our current knowledge of treatment and the disease and the revolutionary change in approach to human experimentation, I don't believe the program would be undertaken.''[17]

Journalists tended to accept the argument that the denial of penicillin during the 1940s was the crucial ethical issue. Most did not question the decision to withhold earlier forms of treatment because they apparently accepted the judgment that the cure was as bad as the disease. But a few journalists and editors argued that the Tuskegee Study presented a moral problem long before the men were denied treatment with penicillin. ''To say, as did an official of the Center for Disease Control, that the experiment posed 'a serious moral problem' after penicillin became available is only to address part of the situation,'' declared the *St. Louis Post-Dispatch.* ''The fact is that in an effort to determine from autopsies what effects syphilis has on the body, the government from the moment the experiment began withheld the best available treatment for a particularly cruel disease. The immorality of the experiment was inherent in its premise.''[18]

Viewed in this light, it was predictable that penicillin would not be given to the men. *Time* magazine might decry the failure to administer the drug as ''almost beyond belief or human compassion,'' but along with many other publications it failed to recognize a crucial point. Having made the decision to withhold treatment at the outset, investigators were not likely to experience a moral crisis when a new and improved form of treatment was developed. Their failure to administer penicillin resulted from the initial decision to withhold all treatment. The only valid distinction that can be made between the two acts is that the denial of penicillin held more dire consequences for the men in the study. The *Chicago Sun Times* placed these separate actions in the proper perspective: ''Whoever made the decision to withhold penicillin compounded the original immorality of the project.''[19]

In their public comments, the CDC spokesmen tried to present the Tuskegee Study as a medical matter involving clinical decisions that may or may not have been valid. The antiseptic quality of their statements left journalists cold, prompting an exasperated North Carolina editor to declare: ''Perhaps there are responsible people with heavy consciences about their own or their organizations' roles in this study, but thus far there is an appalling amount of 'So what?' in the comments about it.'' ABC's Harry Reasoner agreed. On national television, he expressed bewilderment that the PHS could be ''only mildly uncomfortable'' with an experiment that ''used human beings as laboratory animals in a long and inefficient study of how long it takes syphilis to kill someone.''[20]

The human dimension dominated the public discussions of the Tuskegee Study. The scientific merits of the experiment, real or imagined, were passed over almost without comment. Not being scientists, the journalists, public officials, and concerned citizens who protested the study did not really care how long it takes syphilis to kill people or what percentages of syphilis victims are fortunate enough to live to ripe old age with the disease. From their perspective the PHS was guilty of playing fast and loose with the lives of these men to indulge scientific curiosity.[21]

Many physicians had a different view. Their letters defending the study appeared in editorial pages across the country, but their most heated counterattacks were delivered in professional journals. The most spirited example was an editorial in the *Southern Medical Journal* by Dr. R. H. Kampmeir of Vanderbilt University's School of Medicine. No admirer of the press, he blasted reporters for their ''complete disregard for their abysmal ignorance,'' and accused them of banging out ''anything on their typewriters which will make headlines.'' As one of the few remaining physicians with experience treating syphilis in the 1930s, Dr. Kampmeir promised to ''put this 'tempest in a teapot' into proper historical perspective.''[22]

Dr. Kampmeir correctly pointed out that there had been only one experiment dealing with the effects of untreated syphilis prior to the Tuskegee Study. A Norwegian investigator had reviewed the medical records of nearly two thousand untreated syphilitic patients who had been examined at an Oslo clinic between 1891 and 1910. A follow-up had been published in 1929, and that was the state of published medical experimentation on the subject before the Tuskegee Study began. Dr. Kampmeir did not explain why the Oslo Study needed to be repeated.

The Vanderbilt physician repeated the argument that penicillin would not have benefited the men, but he broke new ground by asserting that the men themselves were responsible for the illnesses and deaths they sustained from syphilis. The PHS was not to blame, Dr. Kampmeir explained, because "in our free society, antisyphilis treatment had never been forced." He further reported that many of the men in the study had received some treatment for syphilis down through the years and insisted that others could have secured treatment had they so desired. He admitted that the untreated syphilitics suffered a higher mortality rate than the controls, observing coolly: "This is not surprising. No one has ever implied that syphilis is a benign infection." His failure to discuss the social mandate of physicians to prevent harm and to heal the sick whenever possible seemed to reduce the Hippocratic oath to a solemn obligation not to deny treatment upon demand.[23]

Journalists looked at the Tuskegee Study and reached different conclusions, raising a host of ethical issues. Not since the Nuremberg trials of Nazi scientists had the American people been confronted with a medical *cause célèbre* that captured so many headlines and sparked so much discussion. For many it was a shocking revelation of the potential for scientific abuse in their own country. "That it has happened in this country in our time makes the tragedy more poignant," wrote the editor of the *Philadelphia Inquirer.* Others thought the experiment totally "un-American" and agreed with Senator John Sparkman of Alabama, who denounced it as "absolutely appalling" and "a disgrace to the American concept of justice and humanity." Some despaired of ever again being able to hold their heads high. A resident of the nation's capital asked: "If this is true, how in the name of God can we look others in the eye and say: 'This is a decent country.'"[24]

Perhaps self-doubts such as these would have been less intense if a federal agency had not been responsible for the experiment. No one doubted that private citizens abused one another and had to be restrained from doing so. But the revelation that the Public Health Service had conducted the study was especially distressing. The editor of the *Providence Sunday Journal* admitted that he was shocked by "the flagrant immorality of what occurred under the auspices of the United States Government." A curious reversal of roles seemed to have taken place in Alabama: Instead of protecting its citizens against such experiments, the government was conducting them.[25]

Memories of Nazi Germany haunted some people as the broader implications of the PHS's role in the experiment became apparent. A man in Tennessee reminded health officials in Atlanta that "Adolf Hitler allowed similar degradation of human dignity in inhumane medical experiments on humans living under the Third Reich," and confessed that he was "much distressed at the comparison." A New York editor had difficulty believing that "such stomach-turning callousness could happen outside the wretched quackeries spawned by Nazi Germany."[26]

The specter of Nazi Germany prompted some Americans to equate the Tuskegee Study with genocide. A civil rights leader in Atlanta, Georgia, charged that the study amounted to "nothing less than an official, premeditated policy of genocide." A student at the Tuskegee Institute agreed. To him, the experiment was "but another act of genocide by whites," an act that "again exposed the nature of whitey: a savage barbarian and a devil."[27]

Most editors stopped short of calling the Tuskegee Study genocide or charging that PHS officials were little better than Nazis. But they were certain that racism played a part in what happened in Alabama. "How condescending and void of credibility are the claims that racial considerations had nothing to do with the fact that 600 [all] of the subjects were black," declared the *Afro-American* of Baltimore, Maryland. That PHS officials had kept straight faces while denying any racial overtones to the experiment prompted the editors of this influential black paper to charge "that there are still federal officials who feel they can do anything where black people are concerned."[28]

The *Los Angeles Times* echoed this view. In deftly chosen words, the editors qualified their accusation that PHS officials had persuaded hundreds of black men to become "human guinea pigs" by adding: "Well, perhaps not quite that [human guinea pigs] because the doctors obviously did not regard their subjects as completely human." A Pennsylvania editor stated that such an experiment "could only happen to blacks." To support this view, the *New Courier* of Pittsburgh implied that American society was so racist that scientists could abuse blacks with impunity.[29]

Other observers thought that social class was the real issue, that poor people, regardless of their race, were the ones in danger. Somehow people from the lower class always seemed to supply a disproportionate share of subjects for scientific research. Their plight, in the words of a North Carolina editor, offered "a reminder that the basic rights of Americans, particularly the poor, the illiterate and the friendless, are still subject to violation in the name of scientific research." To a journalist in Colorado, the Tuskegee Study demonstrated that "the Public Health Service sees the poor, the black, the illiterate and the defenseless in American society as a vast experimental resource for the government." And the *Washington Post* made much the same point when it observed, "There is always a lofty goal in the research work of medicine but too often in the past it has been the bodies of the poor . . . on whom the unholy testing is done."[30]

The problems of poor people in the rural South during the Great Depression troubled the editor of the *Los Angeles Times,* who charged that the men had been "trapped into the program by poverty and ignorance." After all, the incentives for cooperation were meager—physical examinations, hot lunches, and burial stipends. "For such inducements to be attractive, their lives must have been savagely harsh," the editor observed, adding: "This in itself, aside from the experiment, is an affront to decency." Thus, quite apart from the questions it raised about human experimentation, the Tuskegee Study served as a poignant reminder of the plight of the poor.[31]

Yet poverty alone could not explain why the men would cooperate with a study that gave them so little in return for the frightening risks to which it exposed them. A more complete explanation was that the men did not understand what the experiment was about or the dangers to which it exposed them. Many Americans probably agreed with the *Washington Post's* argument that experiments "on human beings are ethically sound if the guinea pigs are fully informed of the facts and danger." But despite the assurances of PHS spokesmen that informed consent had been obtained, the Tuskegee Study precipitated accusations that somehow the men had either been tricked into cooperating or were incapable of giving informed consent.[32]

An Alabama newspaper, the *Birmingham News,* was not impressed by the claim that the participants were all volunteers, stating that "the majority of them were no better than semi-literate and probably didn't know what was really going on." The real reason they had been chosen, a Colorado journalist argued, was that they were "poor, illiterate, and completely at the mercy of the 'benevolent' Public Health Service." And a North Carolina editor denounced "the practice of coercing or tricking human beings into taking part in such experiments."[33]

The ultimate lesson that many Americans saw in the Tuskegee Study was the need to protect society from scientific pursuits that ignored human values. The most eloquent expression of this view appeared in the *Atlanta Constitution.* "Sometimes, with the best of intentions, scientists and public officials and others involved in working for the benefit of us all, forget that people are people," began the editor. "They concentrate so totally on plans and programs, experiments, statistics—on abstractions—that people become objects, symbols on paper, figures in a mathematical formula, or impersonal 'subjects' in a scientific study." This was the scientific blindspot to ethical issues that was responsible for the Tuskegee Study—what the *Constitution* called "a moral astigmatism that saw these black sufferers simply as 'subjects' in a study, not as human beings." Scientific investigators had to learn that "moral judgment should always be a part of any human endeavor," including "the dispassionate scientific search for knowledge."[34]

## Notes

1. *New York Times,* July 26, 1972, pp. 1, 8.
2. Because of the high rate of geographic mobility among the men, estimates of the mortality rate were confusing, even in the published articles. PHS spokesmen in 1972 were reluctant to be pinned down on an exact figure. An excellent example is the Interview of Dr. David Sencer by J. Andrew Liscomb and Bobby Doctor for the U.S. Commission on Civil Rights, Alabama State Advisory Committee, September 22, 1972, unpublished manuscript, p. 9. For the calculations behind the figures used here, see *Atlanta Constitution,* September 12, 1972, p. 2A.
3. During this primary stage the infected person often remains seronegative: A blood test will not reveal the disease. But chancres can be differentiated from other ulcers by a dark field examination, a laboratory test in which a microscope equipped with a special indirect lighting attachment can view the silvery spirochetes moving against a dark background.
4. At the secondary stage a blood test is an effective diagnostic tool.
5. Dr. Donald W. Prinz quoted in *Atlanta Journal,* July 27, 1972, p. 2; *Birmingham News,* July 27, 1972, p. 2.
6. *New York Times,* July 27, 1972, p. 18.
7. Dr. Ralph Henderson quoted in ibid.; *Tuskegee News,* July 27, 1972, p. 1.
8. *New York Times,* July 27, 1972, p. 2.
9. Eunice Rivers, Stanley Schuman, Lloyd Simpson, Sidney Olansky, "Twenty Years of Followup Experience in a Long-Range Medical Study," *Public Health Reports* 68 (April 1953): 391–95. (Hereafter Rivers et al.)
10. Ibid., p. 393.
11. Dr. John D. Millar quoted in *Birmingham News,* July 27, 1972, pp. 1, 4; *Atlanta Journal,* July 27, 1972, p. 2.

12. Prinz quoted in *Atlanta Journal,* July 27, 1972, p. 2.
13. Millar quoted in *Montgomery Advertiser,* July 26, 1972, p. 1.
14. Ibid.; Prinz quoted in *Atlanta Journal,* July 27, 1972, p. 2.
15. Millar quoted in *Montgomery Advertiser,* July 26, 1972, p. 1; *New York Times,* July 28, 1972, p. 29.
16. Dr. Edward Lammons quoted in *Tuskegee News,* August 3, 1972, p. 1.
17. Prinz quoted in *Atlanta Journal,* July 27, 1972, p. 2; Millar quoted in *Montgomery Advertiser,* July 26, 1972, p. 1.
18. *St. Louis Dispatch,* July 30, 1972, p. 2D.
19. *Time,* August 7, 1972, p. 54; *Chicago Sun Times,* July 29, 1972, p. 23.
20. *News and Observer,* Raleigh, North Carolina, August 1, 1972, p. 4; ABC Evening News, August 1, 1972.
21. Their reactions can be captured at a glance by citing a few of the legends that introduced newspaper articles and editorials that appeared on the experiment. The *Houston Chronicle* called it "A Violation of Human Dignity" (August 5, 1972, Section I, p. 12); *St. Louis Post-Dispatch,* "An Immoral Study" (July 30, 1972, p. 2D); *Oregonian*, an "Inhuman Experiment" (Portland, Oregon, July 31, 1972, p. 16); *Chattanooga Times,* a "Blot of Inhumanity" (July 28, 1972, p. 16); *South Bend Tribune,* a "Cruel Experiment" (July 29, 1972, p. 6); *New Haven Register,* "A Shocking Medical Experiment" (July 29, 1972, p. 14); and Virginia's *Richmond Times Dispatch* thought that "appalling" was the best adjective to describe an experiment that had used "Humans as Guinea Pigs" (August 6, 1972, p. 6H). To the *Los Angeles Times* the study represented "Official Inhumanity" (July 27, 1972, Part II, p. 6); to the *Providence Sunday Journal,* a "Horror Story" (July 30, 1972, p. 2G); and to the *News and Observer* in Raleigh, North Carolina, a "Nightmare Experiment" (July 28, 1972, p. 4). The *St. Petersburg Times* in Florida voiced cynicism, entitling its editorial, "Health Service?" (July 27, 1972, p. 24), while the *Milwaukee Journal* made its point more directly by introducing its article with the legend "They Helped Men Die" (July 27, 1972, p. 15).
22. R.H. Kampmeir, "The Tuskegee Study of Untreated Syphilis," *Southern Medical Journal* 65 (1972): 1247–51.
23. Ibid., p. 1250.
24. *Philadelphia Inquirer,* July 30, 1972, p. 4H; *Montgomery Advertiser,* August 12, 1972, p. 13; letter to the editor signed A.B., *Evening Star,* Washington, D.C., August 10, 1972, 18A; for examples of a similar reaction, see the *Gazette,* Charleston, West Virginia, July 30, 1972, p. 2D, and Salley E. Clapp to Dr. Merlin K. Duval, July 26, 1972, Tuskegee Files, Center for Disease Control, Atlanta, Georgia. (Hereafter TF-CDC).
25. *Providence Sunday Journal,* July 30, 1972, p. 2G; for the same view, see *Evening Sun,* Baltimore, Maryland, July 26, 1972, p. 26A.
26. Roderick Clark Posey to Millar, July 27, 1972, TF-CDC; *Daily News,* July 27, 1972, p. 63; see also *Milwaukee Journal,* July 27, 1972, p. 15; *Oregonian,* July 31, 1972, p. 16; and Jack Slater, "Condemned to Die for Science," *Ebony* 28 (November 1972), p. 180.
27. *Atlanta Journal,* July 27, 1972, p. 2; *Campus Digest,* October 6, 1972, p. 4.
28. *Afro-American,* August 12, 1972, p. 4. For extended discussions of the race issue, see Slater, "Condemned to Die," p. 191, and the three-part series by Warren Brown in *Jet* 43, "The Tuskegee Study," November 9, 1972, pp. 12–17, November 16, 1972, pp. 20–26, and, especially, November 23, 1972, pp. 26–31.
29. *Los Angeles Times,* July 27, 1972, Part II, p. 6; *New Courier* also stated, "No other minority group in this country would have been used as 'Human Guinea Pigs,'" and explained, "because those who are responsible knew that they could do this to Negroes and nothing would be done to them if it became known," August 19, 1972, p. 6.
30. *Greensboro Daily News,* August 2, 1972, p. 6; *Gazette-Telegraph,* Colorado Springs,

August 3, 1972, p. 8A; *Washington Post,* July 31, 1972, p. 20A. See also *Arkansas Gazette,* July 29, 1972, p. 4A.

31. *Los Angeles Times,* July 27, 1972, p. 20A.
32. *Washington Post,* July 31, 1972, p. 20A.
33. *Birmingham News,* July 28, 1972, p. 12; *Gazette-Telegraph,* August 3, 1972, p. 8A; *Greensboro Daily News,* August 2, 1972, p. 6A.
34. *Atlanta Constitution,* July 27, 1972, p. 4A.

# The Politics of Cancer

*Samuel S. Epstein*

With over 900,000 new cases and 450,000 deaths last year in the United States alone, cancer has now reached epidemic proportions. Cancer strikes one in three people and kills one in four. It is now the only major killing disease in the industrialized world whose rates are sharply rising.

Analysis of overall cancer rates standardized for age, sex and ethnicity, has demonstrated steady increases since the 1930s, with more recent sharp annual increases in incidence rates by some 2 percent and in mortality rates by some 1 percent. Striking confirmation of these recent increases comes from estimates of the lifetime probability of getting cancer for people born at different times. For white males born between 1975 to 1985 for instance, the probability of developing cancer has risen from 30 to 36 percent and from 19 to 23 percent for dying from cancer. Such increases in overall cancer rates are also reflected in increasing rates for cancers of organs including lung, breast, colon, prostate, testis, urinary bladder, kidneys and skin, malignant melanoma and lymphatic/hematopoietic malignancies including non-Hodgkin's lymphoma. Lung cancer is responsible for about one-third of the overall recent increase in incidence rates. Some 75 percent of all cancer deaths occur in people over 55 years, and recent increases are largely restricted to these ages.

## Static Cure Rates

The overall cancer "cure rate," as measured by survival for over five years following diagnosis, is currently 50 percent for whites but only 38 percent for blacks. There is no evidence of substantial improvements in treatment over the last few decades, during which five year survival and age-adjusted mortality rates for the major cancer killers—lung, breast and colon—have remained essentially unchanged. The only improvements have been for cancer of the cervix, and for relatively rare cancers, such as testicular seminomas, Hodgkin's disease and childhood leukemias treated with radiation and/or chemotherapy. Apart from immediate toxicity, such treatment, while effective, can increase the subsequent risk of developing a second cancer by up to 100 times.

---

Samuel S. Epstein, "The Politics of Cancer." This article is reprinted from the *Multinational Monitor* 9 (March 1988), pp. 6–13. *Multinational Monitor* is a monthly newsmagazine published by Essential Information, Inc., P.O. Box 19405, Washington, D.C. 20036. $22 individual.

---

See Statistical Appendix Table A–20.

## Increasing Carcinogenic Exposures

Cancer is an age-old and ubiquitous group of diseases. Its recognized causes and influences are multifactorial and include natural environmental carcinogens (such as aflatoxin and sunlight), lifestyle factors, genetic susceptibility, and more recently, industrial chemicals. Apart from modern lifestyle factors, particularly smoking, increasing cancer rates reflect exposure to industrial chemicals and run-away modern technologies whose explosive growth has clearly out paced the ability of society to control them. In addition to pervasive changes in patterns of living and diet, these poorly controlled technologies have induced profound environmental degradation, resulting in the contamination of air, water, food and workplaces with toxic and carcinogenic chemicals. This has led to involuntary exposures.

With the dawn of the petrochemical era in the early 1940s, technologies such as fractional distillation of petroleum, catalytic and thermal cracking and molecular splicing became commercially established. The annual U.S. production of synthetic organic chemicals at the time was about one billion pounds. By the 1950s, this had reached 30 billion pounds annually, and by the 1980s over 400 million pounds annually. The overwhelming majority of these industrial chemicals has never been adequately, if at all, tested for chronic toxic, carcinogenic, mutagenic and teratogenic effects, let alone for ecological effects. And much of the available industrial data is at best suspect.

Occupational exposure to industrial carcinogens has clearly emerged as a major risk factor for cancer. The National Institute for Occupational Safety and Health (NIOSH) estimates that some 10 million workers are now exposed to 11 high-volume carcinogens. Five to 10-fold increases in cancer rates have been demonstrated in some occupations. Also persuasive are British data on cancer mortality by socioeconomic class, largely defined by occupation, which show that the lowest class, particularly among males, has approximately twice the cancer mortality rate of the highest class.

Living near petrochemical and certain other industries in highly urbanized communities increases cancer risks, as evidenced by clustering of excess cancer rates; high levels of toxic and carcinogenic chemicals are deliberately discharged into the air of surrounding communities by a wide range of industries. Fall-out from such toxic air pollutants is an important source of contamination of surface waters, particularly the Great Lakes. While there still are no regulatory requirements for reporting and monitoring these emissions, unpublished government estimates indicate that they are in excess of 3 billion pounds annually.

Another result of run-away technologies is the hazardous waste crisis. The disposal of hazardous waste has increased from less than one million tons of hazardous waste in 1940 to well over 300 million tons annually in the 1980s—more than one ton per person per year. The industries involved—fossil fuel, metal mining and processing, nuclear, and petrochemical—have littered the entire land mass of the United States with some 50,000 toxic waste landfills, 20,000 of which are recognized as potentially hazardous, 170,000 industrial impoundments (ponds, pits, and lagoons),

7,000 under ground injection wells, not to mention some 2.5 million underground gasoline tanks, many of which are leaking. Not surprisingly, an increasing number of rural and urban communities have found themselves located on or near hazardous waste sites, or downstream, down-gradient, or downwind from one. Particularly alarming is growing evidence of contamination of ground water from such sites, contamination which poses grave and difficult to reverse hazards for centuries to come.

Environmental contamination with highly potent carcinogenic pesticides has reached alarming and pervasive proportions. Apart from the high level exposure of workers in manufacturing, formulating and applicating industries, contamination of ground and surface waters has become commonplace. While the exact numbers are uncertain, it is probable that tens of millions of homes nationwide are contaminated with varying levels of chlordane/heptachlor, pesticides still registered by EPA for termite treatment. Yet, in extensive hearings some 15 years ago the Agency concluded that exposure to such pesticides posed an ''imminent hazard'' because of carcinogenic as well as chronic toxic effects and they were subsequently banned for agricultural use.

Much cancer today reflects events and exposures in the 1950s and 60s. Production, uses and disposal of synthetic organic and other industrial carcinogens were then minuscule compared to current levels, which will determine future generations' cancer rates. There is every reason to anticipate that even todays' high cancer rates will be exceeded in the coming decades.

While most concern has understandably focused on increasing cancer rates, these substantially underestimate the extent and scope of the public health effects of environmental pollutants. Only a small proportion of the tens of thousands of petrochemicals in commerce, well under 500, are carcinogenic. However, many of these, together with other non-carcinogenic petrochemicals, can induce other chronic toxic effects, including neurological, respiratory, reproductive, hepatic and probably immunological diseases, whose true causation is generally not suspected let alone investigated.

## Who's to Blame

### Industry

Twentieth century industry has aggressively pursued short-term economic goals, uncaring or unmindful of harm to workers, local communities and the environment. So far, industry has shifted the responsibility for such costs and harm to society-at-large. Belated governmental efforts to control polluting industries have generally been neutralized by well-organized and well-financed opposition. Excepting special purpose legislation for drugs, food additives and pesticides, there were no regulatory requirements for pre-testing industrial chemicals until the 1976 Toxic Substance Control Act. This legislation, which industry had stalled for years, is now honored more in the breach than in the observance.

Apart from the failure to pre-test most chemicals, key in industry's anti-regulatory strategy has been the generation of self-serving and misleading data on toxicology and epidemiology, regulatory costs and cost-benefit analyses. The track record of such unreliable and often fraudulent data is so extensive and well documented as to justify the presumption that much industry data must be treated as suspect until proven otherwise.

Attempts by the Carter administration to develop comprehensive, "generic," regulation of occupational carcinogens, later reversed by the Reagan administration, were attacked by the Manufacturing Chemists Association, which created the American Industrial Health Council to organize opposition. Such reactions generally reflect reflex ideology and short-sighted preoccupation with perceived self-interest rather than with efficiency and economy. The virtual uniformity of industry opposition to regulation is in marked contrast to the heterogeneity of size and interests of the industries involved. Regulation has, in fact, generally resulted in substantial improvements in industrial efficiency and economy, particularly in large industries, by forcing development of technologies for recovery and recycling of valuable resources. A deplorable result of regulation, however, has been and continues to be the export of the restricted product or process to less developed countries.

Apart from well-documented evidence on control and manipulation of health and environmental information, industry has used various strategies to con the public into complacency and divert attention from their own recklessness and responsibility for the cancer epidemic. Key among these is the "blame-the-victim" theory of cancer causation, developed by industry scientists and consultants and a group of conservative pro-industry academics, and tacitly supported by the "cancer establishment." This theory emphasizes the faulty lifestyle—smoking, a fatty diet, sun bathing, and genetic susceptibility, as the major causes of preventable cancer. And at the same time it trivializes the role of involuntary exposures to occupational and environmental carcinogens. Another misleading diversion is their claim that there is no evidence of recently increasing cancer rates other than lung cancer, for which smoking is given the exclusive credit. While the role of lifestyle is obviously important and cannot be ignored, the scientific and exclusionary basis of this theory is as unsound as it is self-serving. Certainly, smoking is a major, but not the only, cause of lung cancer. Evidence such as the following clearly incriminates the additional role of exposure to occupational carcinogens and carcinogenic community air pollutants: some 20 percent of lung cancers occur in non-smokers; there have been major recent increases in lung cancer rates in non-smokers; an increasing percentage of lung cancer is of a histological type (adenocarcinoma) not usually associated with smoking; high lung cancer rates are found with certain occupational exposures independent of smoking; and excess lung cancer rates are found in communities where certain major industries are located. The chemical industry clearly uses tobacco as a smoke screen to divert attention from the role of carcinogenic chemicals in inducing lung cancer as well as other cancers.

When it comes to diet, the much touted role of high fat consumption, while clearly linked to heart disease, is based on tenuous and contradictory evidence with regard to breast and colon cancers. The evidence certainly does not justify the wild claims by lifestyle theorists that some 30 to 40 percent of all cancers are due to faulty diet. For instance, a 1982 National Academy of Sciences report concluded that "in the only human studies in which the total fiber consumption was quantified, no association was found between total fiber consumption and colon cancer." Similarly, a large scale 1987 study, based on the eating habits of nearly 90,000 nurses, concluded that "there is no association between dietary fat and breast cancer." Another illustration of grossly misleading strategies relates to the identification of chemical carcinogens. When a particular chemical or product is threatened with regulation on the basis of animal carcinogenicity tests the industry invariably challenges the significance of these tests, while routinely using negative test results as proof of safety. At the same time industry insists on the need for long-term prospective epidemiological investigations to obtain definitive human evidence. To test this apparent reliance on direct human evidence, researchers at Mt. Sinai Hospital in New York compiled a list of some 100 chemicals accepted as carcinogenic on the basis of animal tests, but for which no epidemiological information is available, and sent this list to 80 major chemical industries. Respondents were asked whether any of the listed carcinogens were in use and, if so, whether epidemiological studies had been conducted, whether they were being conducted, or whether they intended to conduct them in the future, and if not, why not. The responses were revealing. The great majority of those industries using particular carcinogens replied that they had done no epidemiological studies, were not doing any, and didn't intend to do any for various reasons, including alleged difficulty, impracticality, expense, or because of their belief that these chemicals could not possibly be carcinogenic to humans. A perfect catch-22. Knock the animal tests and insist on human studies, but make sure that the human studies are never done.

Industry positions are vigorously advocated by trade associations, such as the Chemical Manufacturers Association, public relations firms, such as Hill and Knowlton, and front organizations, such as the American Council on Science and Health (the contributions of whose director, Elizabeth Whelan, have been aptly characterized as "voodoo science"). Disturbingly, another major source of support for anti-regulatory strategies is a stable of academic consultants who advance the industry position in arenas including the scientific literature, federal advisory committees, and regulatory and congressional hearings.

## Government

Presidents play a powerful role in setting national public health priorities, not unnaturally reflecting their own political agendas. Reagan, however, is unique in having run for office on an ideological anti-regulatory platform, and in having then systematically used his office to implement this ideology, often in contravention to the spirit and letter of the law. Reagan has thus neutralized legislative mandates on controls of toxic and carcinogenic exposure by frontal assaults on regulatory agencies. Strategies employed include: staffing senior positions with unqualified, ideologically selected staff hostile to their agency mandates; budget cutting; insisting on formal cost-benefit analyses which focus on industry costs with little or biased consideration of costs of failure to regulate and which effectively stall the regulatory process; illegal, behind closed doors meetings with industry; and making regulations dependent on the Office of Management and Budget with its subservience to the White House. An informative example is the White House decision to block the $1.3 million 1984 request by the National Institute for Occupational Safety and Health (NIOSH) to notify some 200,000 workers of risks from previously undisclosed exposure to workplace carcinogens, as identified in some 60 government studies, in order to enable medical follow-up and early diagnosis of cancer. The reason for this refusal of modest funding seems to have been a desire to shield corporations from possible legal claims. Such a track record justifies the conclusions of a 1984 Congressional Study Group report that "efforts to protect public health and the environment from the dangers of toxic pollution have ground to a standstill under the Reagan administration."

The U.S. Congress has become sensitized to public health and environmental concerns, as exemplified in a plethora of legislation in recent decades. Such legislation has evolved fragmentarily, reflecting particular interests and priorities. New laws have focused on air, water, food or the workplace, or on individual classes of products or contaminants, such as pesticides or air pollutants, with little or no consideration of the need for more comprehensive and integrated approaches. Furthermore, legislative language traditionally has been ambiguous thus giving maximal regulatory discretion to bureaucracies which in some instances have then become closely associated with or even "captured" by the regulated industries. A noteworthy exception is the 1958 Delaney Amendment to the Federal Food, Drug and Cosmetic Act, with its absolute prohibition against the deliberate introduction of any level of carcinogen into the food supply. Even so, the Reagan FDA is redefining the Delaney Amendment to allow carcinogenic food additives at levels alleged to be devoid of significant risk.

Congress has also tended to abdicate decision-making to scientific authority—or perceived authority—rather than questioning its basis in the open political arena. Of particular importance was passage of the 1971 Cancer Act in response to orchestrated pressures from the "cancer establishment," the National Cancer Institute (NCI), American Cancer Society (ACS), and the clinicians aggressively pushing chemotherapy as a primary cancer treatment. The cancer-establishment misled Congress into the unfounded and simplistic view that the cure for cancer was just around the corner, provided that Congress made available massive funding for cancer treatment research. The Act did just this, while failing to emphasize the need for cancer prevention. It also gave the NCI virtual autonomy from the parent National Institutes of Health, establishing a direct chain of command between the NCI and the White House. Some 16 years and billions of dollars later, Congress still has not recognized that the poorly informed special interests of the cancer establishment have minimized the importance of and failed to adequately support critically needed cancer prevention efforts. Nor has Congress recognized the long overdue need for oversight of the NCI. Given the heterogeneity of congressional interests, the complexity of the problem involved, the heavy industry lobbying, the indifference of the general scientific community and the well-orchestrated pressures of the cancer establishment, it is not surprising that Congress has still to realize that we are losing the war against cancer.

Until recently, state governments have largely deferred to federal authority, exercising relatively minor roles in cancer prevention. Reagan's federal de-regulatory efforts have begun to reverse this relationship. Regulatory actions against carcinogens are now emerging at the state level, such as the banning of chlordane/heptachlor and aldrin/dieldrin for termite treatment by Massachusetts and New York, the banning of daminozide (Alar) for apple ripening and tough restrictions on ethylene dibromide food tolerances by Massachusetts, and informative occupational labeling laws by various states, such as the "right to know" workplace legislation of New Jersey. Some such state initiatives have evoked federal preemption by restricting regulations, such as the 1983 Hazard Communication Standard of the Occupational Safety and Health Administration. In striking paradox to Reagan's new federalism which claims to have popular support in its efforts to get big government off the backs of the people, in February 1987, a coalition of labor and citizen organizations asked the U.S. Court of Appeals to enforce its 18 month-old order directing OSHA to expand coverage of its communication standard from manufacturing to all workers. In an apparent about face, the Chemical Manufacturers Association is supporting the expansion in conformity with regulations developed for various states.

## The Cancer Establishment

The cancer establishment continues to mislead the public and Congress into believing that "we are winning the war against cancer," with "victory" possible only with more time and money. The NCI and ACS also insist that there have been major advances in treatment and in cures, and that there has been no increase in cancer rates (with the exception of lung cancer which is exclusively attributed to smoking). Yet, the facts show just the contrary.

The cancer establishment periodically beats the drum to announce the latest "cancer cure" and dramatic "breakthrough." These announcements reflect optimism and wishful thinking, rather than reality. The extravagant and counterproductive claims for interferon as the magic cancer bullet of the late 70s have been followed by the unpublicized recognition of its limited role in cancer treatment. The latest NCI "breakthrough" claims for interleukin-2 as a cancer cure are grossly inflated and rest on questionable data. These claims fail to reflect the devastating toxicity and lethality of this drug, and gloss over the high treatment costs, which can run into six figures. Equally questionable are claims by the NCI and ACS that overall cancer survival rates have improved dramatically in recent years. These claims, based on "rubber numbers" according to one prominent critic, ignore factors such as "lead-time bias," earlier diagnosis of cancer resulting in apparently prolonged survival even in the absence of any treatment, and the "over diagnosis" of essentially benign tumors, particularly of the prostate, breast, and thyroid, as malignant. Revealing is the recent finger-pointing by the director of the NCI, Vincent DeVita at community physicians for using inadequate doses of chemotherapy drugs as the "real" reason why cancer cure rates are no better than they are.

The NCI misrepresentations are well reflected in budgetary priorities which are largely and disproportionately directed to cancer treatment research, to the neglect of cancer prevention. Even the very modest funding of cancer prevention is largely directed to endorsing industry's "blame-the-victim" concept of cancer causation. Thus the NCI exaggerates the role of tobacco for a wide range of cancers besides lung, and treats as fact the slim and contradictory evidence relating diet to colon, breast, and other cancers. Apparently still oblivious to mounting criticism, the NCI continues to vigorously propagate these misrepresentations. A 1986 NCI document on cancer control objectives, the executive summary of which fails to even mention environmental and occupational exposures to carcinogens and focuses on diet and tobacco as the major causes of cancer, rashly promises that annual cancer mortality rates could be reduced by 50 percent by the year 2,000.

More disturbing than indifference to cancer prevention is evidence uncovered in September 1982 by Rep. Dave Obey, D-Wisc., that the NCI has pressured the International Agency for Research on Cancer (IARC), funded in part by the NCI, to downplay the carcinogenicity of benzene and also formaldehyde in IARC monographs which review and rank the carcinogenicity data on industrial and other chemicals. Such evidence is noteworthy since, contrary to the scientific literature and its own explicit guidelines, IARC has also downgraded the carcinogenicity of other carcinogenic industrial chemicals, such as the pesticides aldrin/dieldrin and chlordane/heptachlor, and the solvents trichloroethylene and perchloroethylene.

Following nearly a decade of fruitless discussions with the ACS, at a February 1987 press conference, a national coalition of major public interest and labor groups headed by the Center for Science in the Public Interest and supported by some 24 independent scientists, charged that the ACS "is doing virtually nothing to help reduce the public exposure to cancer causing chemicals. Despite its promises to the public to do everything to 'wipe out cancer in your lifetime,' the ACS fails to make its voice heard in Congress and the regulatory arena, where it could be a powerful influence to help reduce public exposure to carcinogens." More specific criticisms included the following:

- ACS fails to support, and at times has been hostile to, critical legislation that seeks to reduce or eliminate exposure to environmental and occupational carcinogens. For example, ACS refused to join a coalition of major organizations, including the March of Dimes, American Heart Association, and American Lung Association, to support the Clean Air Act. ACS has rejected requests from congressional subcommittees, unions, and environmental organizations to support their efforts to ban or regulate a wide range of occupational and environmental carcinogens. Giant corporations, which profit handsomely while they pollute the air, water and food with cancer causing chemicals, must be greatly comforted by the ACS's silence.

- ACS's approach to cancer prevention largely reflects a "blame the victim" philosophy, which emphasizes faulty lifestyles, rather than workplace or environmental carcinogens. For instance, ACS blames the higher incidence of cancer among blacks primarily on their diet and smoking habits, which diverts attention from the fact that blacks work in the dirtiest, most hazardous jobs, and live in the most polluted communities.
- A few days after the press conference, ACS announced a "new set of policies," passing resolutions for improved regulation of such chemicals as asbestos and benzene, and for cleanup of toxic waste sites. However, there has been no evidence of any real change of heart in the ACS since then.

## The Lifestyle Academics

The lifestyle academics are a group of conservative scientists including Richard Doll, warden and director of the industry financed Green College, Oxford, his protege R. Peto, a statistician also from Oxford, and more recently Bruce Ames, a California geneticist. The puristic pretentions of the lifestylers for critical objectivity are only exceeded by their apparent indifference to or rejection of a steadily accumulating body of information on permeation of the environment and workplace with industrial carcinogens, and the impact of such involuntary exposures on human cancer. Consciously or subconsciously, these academics have become the mouthpiece for industry interests, urging regulatory inaction and public complacency. Among the more noteworthy contributions of these academics is a series of publications claiming that smoking and fatty diet are each responsible for 30–40 percent of all cancers, that sunlight, drugs and personal susceptibility account for another 10 percent, leaving only a few percent unaccounted for which, just for want of any better reason, are then ascribed to occupation. According to the lifestylers, this then proves that occupation is an unimportant cause of cancer and does not warrant much regulatory concern. Apart from circularly referencing each other as authority for these wild guesses, the lifestylers have never attempted to develop any estimates of how many workers are exposed to defined levels of specific carcinogens. Without such estimates there is no way of attempting to determine just how much cancer is due to occupation.

The lifestyle theory was further advocated in a 1981 report dealing with the causes of cancer in the United States by Doll and Peto. In the report, they denied evidence of increasing cancer rates other than for lung cancer, which was largely ascribed to tobacco without adequate consideration of the importance of carcinogenic community and occupational exposures. To reach their misleading conclusions on static cancer rates, Doll and Peto excluded from analysis people over the age of 65 and blacks, the groups where cancer mortality rates are already the highest and are increasing. They claimed that occupation was only responsible for some 4 percent of all cancers, without apparent consideration of a wide range of recent studies dealing with the carcinogenic effects of such exposures. This wild 4 percent guess was matched by "guesstimates" that diet was determinant in some 35 percent of all cancers. To trivialize the significance of animal carcinogenicity data on industrial chemicals, Doll and Peto minimized the predictive value of these tests, while emphasizing the epidemiological data as the basis of regulation.

Doll is prompt to side with industry in downplaying evidence on carcinogenicity of industrial chemicals. He recently lent enthusiastic support to the Australian Agent Orange Royal Commission in their dismissal of the experimental and epidemiological carcinogenicity data on the herbicides 2,4-D and 2,4,5-T.

Ames is a geneticist who, in the 1970s, developed bacterial assays for mutagenicity which he advocated as short-term tests for carcinogens. He then published a series of articles warning of increasing cancer rates and of the need for tough regulation of industrial carcinogens, such as the fire retardant Tris and the fumigant ethylene dibromide. By the 1980s, however, Ames did an unexplained 180 degree switch, now claiming just the opposite, that overall cancer rates are not increasing, that industrial carcinogens are unimportant causes of cancer which do not need regulating, and that the real causes of cancer are natural dietary carcinogens, largely because mutagens can be found in a variety of foods.

## What To Do About It

The cancer epidemic poses a grave and growing crisis of enormous cost to health, life and economy for the nation. *The Politics of Cancer* (Sierra Club Books, Samuel Epstein, M.D., 1978) concluded with the following specific recommendations designed to reduce the toll of preventable cancer:

- Cancer must be regarded as an essentially preventable disease.
- The hidden political and economic factors which have blocked and continue to block attempts to prevent cancer must be recognized.
- The ineffective past track record of government in cancer prevention must be recognized.
- The critical roles in cancer prevention that public interest groups and informed labor leadership have exercised must be recognized and their further efforts fully encouraged and supported.
- Congress must resolve the major inconsistencies in a wide range of legislation on environmental and occupational carcinogens.
- Substantially higher federal priorities for the prevention of cancer must be developed.
- Policies of the various federal agencies with responsibilities in cancer prevention must be effectively integrated and coordinated.
- Top business management must recognize the essential similarities between their long-term interests and goals and those of society. Prevention of occupa-

tional cancer and cancer in the community-at-large is of primary importance to both.

- The American Cancer Society must be influenced to balance its preoccupation with treatment with activist programs designed to prevent cancer.
- The medical and scientific community must accept a higher degree of responsibility and involvement in the prevention of cancer by actions on both the professional and political levels.
- Medical schools and schools of public health must be persuaded to massively reorient their educational and training programs from the diagnosis and treatment of disease and cancer to prevention.
- Chemicals in consumer products and in the workplace must be clearly and simply identified and labeled.
- Additional new approaches must be developed for obtaining and for retaining honest and scientifically reliable data on the carcinogenicity and toxicity of new chemicals already in commerce; such data must be made accessible to public scrutiny. Maximum legal penalties should be directed against all those responsible, directly and indirectly, for distortion or manipulation of toxicological and epidemiological data on the basis of which decisions on human safety and risk are based.
- Apart from actions on a political level, there are limited personal options. To some extent, it may be possible to reduce the chances of developing cancer by making informed changes in lifestyle, use of consumer products and work.
- The major determinants of preventable cancer are political and economic, rather than scientific, and as such must be addressed in the open political arena. Cancer prevention must be made, at least, to rank with inflation on the next local, state and national political tickets.

A decade later, these goals still stand as valid, but none have been achieved while cancer rates have steadily risen. To prevent similar conclusions a decade from now, the cancer prevention rhetoric must be translated into reality.

To compete with the well-financed propaganda of industry that is tacitly supported by the cancer establishment and lifestyle academics, an educational offensive must be mounted to inform the public and develop grassroots pressures for a cancer prevention campaign. The cutting edge for such campaigns can be provided by the major public interest organizations, including the Natural Resources Defense Council, Sierra Club, Environmental Defense Fund, Public Citizen's Health Research Group, Environmental Action, Consumer Federation of America, National Campaign Against the Misuse of Pesticides, the National Campaign Against Toxic Hazards, Greenpeace, the Rachel Carson Council, and the Center for Science in the Public Interest. Equally critical will be involvement of the Industrial Union Department, AFL/CIO, and key unions, such as the United Steel Workers of America, United Rubber Workers, Linoleum and Plastic Workers of America, International Association of Machinists, Oil Chemical and Atomic Workers, Amalgamated Clothing and Textile Workers, and the United Auto Workers. Many of these organizations have well informed professional staff, and some have played major roles in whatever limited legislative and regulatory successes have been achieved over the last two decades.

Active support at the local level is being provided by activist citizen and labor groups that have formed in response to community or regional concerns such as hazardous waste dumps, contaminated drinking water or lawn care chemicals; the motto of such groups is "Think globally, act locally." Further support can be provided by a small network of independent and government scientists, whose thinning ranks, however, have been recently boosted by the welcome involvement of professional organizations such as the American Public Health Association and the American Lung Association.

A potential source of cancer prevention funding is the multi-million dollar budget of the American Cancer Society (ACS) raised by voluntary public contributions. An economic boycott of the ACS is now well overdue. Funding inappropriately used by the Society should be diverted to public interest organizations and labor. Other potential funding sources include certification to participate by designation in the United Way and Combined Federal Campaign.

Public interest and labor organizations should develop coalitions with initially limited objectives, focused around specific areas of cancer prevention of local concern. These could be subsequently expanded into wider rainbow coalitions with more comprehensive goals. The Congress, revitalized by the defeat of the Reagan revolution and by a democratic renaissance, is now more likely to be receptive to such initiatives. This receptiveness should be directed into increasing governmental concern for cancer prevention and restoring the fragmented regulatory apparatus. Key congressional members should be galvanized into making cancer prevention a major political priority and presidential candidates should be brought into the debate.

Equally important are initiatives at the state level, which offer encouraging precedents. These include the banning of chlordane and heptachlor for termite treatment by Massachusetts in 1985 and New York in 1986, largely at the impetus of a citizen group, People Against Chlordane (PAC), passage of a $1.5 billion hazardous waste cleanup bond by New York, the Environmental Quality Bond Act of 1986, and passage of Proposition 65, the Safe Drinking Water and Toxic Enforcement Act of 1986, by California. Proposition 65, masterminded by the Sierra Club and Environmental Defense Fund and supported by a coalition of California public interest citizen and labor groups, is a sophisticated referendum which imposes tough financial penalties on industries knowingly discharging carcinogens into drinking water supplies. The Proposition mandates full public disclosure of such discharges by industry and state officials. However, Governer Deukmejian, responsive to special interest lobbying, has recently neutralized the scope of the new legislation by restricting it to only epidemiologically confirmed carcinogens. This restriction is now under legal challenge. Irrespective of the outcome of this challenge, Proposition 65 has excited national interest and is being used as a model for similar regional initiatives.

Among early congressional priorities should be the enactment of comprehensive white collar crime legislation. This would impose tough sanctions on individual executives, managers and professionals of industries found guilty of willful "non-disclosure" of information on hazards to workers, local communities and the nation. White collar crime legislation should also be extended to U.S. and multinational corporations which export carcinogenic products or processes which have been banned or regulated in the United States to less developed countries, especially in the absence of full disclosure of hazards to the ultimate users and consumers. Attention should also be directed to developing comprehensive new "cradle-to-the-grave" legislative approaches to the regulation of toxic and carcinogenic chemicals. Such legislation can be designed to complement regulation by the judicious application of marketplace pressures, in the form of financial incentives and disincentives designed to wean industry from unsafe practices, and to insure that responsible industry is not penalized and subject to unfair competition. At present, other than the prospect of toxic tort litigation, there are virtually no incentives for industry to develop safer new products and processes. Legislation is needed to develop federal R&D funding to promote such benign technologies and also to ensure that they are closely coordinated with environmental, energy and resource policies.

A critical legislative priority is amendment of the National Cancer Act to give the highest possible priority to cancer prevention, to redress the historic imbalance existing in the NCI between cancer prevention and research, diagnosis, treatment and the basic sciences, and also to insulate the NCI from direct presidential influence. In addition to replacing NCI's director DeVita who, in spite of his contrary protestations, has been indifferent if not hostile to cancer prevention efforts and has played a major role in perpetrating the myth that we are winning the war against cancer, senior NCI staff should be restructured and boosted by a critical mass of professionals competent in environmental and occupational cancer and committed to cancer prevention. The National Cancer Advisory Board should be reconstituted with a balanced mix of independent cancer prevention professionals, representatives of public interest and labor organizations and concerned citizens, and should be subject to close congressional oversight. Such oversight should insure that the institutional resources are largely directed to cancer prevention, that grants and contracts reflect this priority and that NCI staff play a key role in providing the supporting scientific basis for legislative and regulatory cancer prevention efforts at the national and state levels.

Cancer is essentially a preventable disease. Given high national priority, this goal will be achieved.

# The Reagan Domestic Legacy: Greater Inequality and Destabilization

*D. Stanley Eitzen and Maxine Baca Zinn*

Ronald Reagan's Administration has been touted by some observers as a domestic triumph. Through a combination of a consistently applied ideology, a more or less compliant Congress, and luck, the President has achieved a reduction in the inflation and interest rates, a significant lowering of marginal tax rates for individuals and corporations, a strengthening of the defense establishment, and a freeing of the business sector from many of the constraints of government.

This essay examines and assesses the domestic program of the Reagan presidency. The analysis is selective, with critical attention centered on the consequences of Reagan's policies for the three major structures of domination—class, race, and gender. The discussion is divided into four parts: (1) the Reagan rhetoric and reality; (2) widening inequality under Reagan; (3) the Reagan project; and (4) the Reagan legacy.

## The Reagan Rhetoric and Reality

Reagan's consistent theme, packaged in images invoking God, flag, and country, is that the system is working. The picture is rosy and if his proposals are implemented, it will be even rosier. All of us benefit, he contends, because the economy is robust, millions of jobs are being created, unemployment is down, and inflation is down. There is no talk of malaise in his speeches, only talk of the great American comeback; this is morning in America, and we can be proud to be Americans. What he paints for us is a Norman Rockwell painting of America that omits its "dark side." The system is clearly not working for many people, and those who think that they are benefiting from the system are in for some surprises if present trends continue. The downside that Reagan clearly ignores includes:

- Farmers are experiencing the worst depression since the Great Depression. Some 50,000 family farms went under in 1987. There are severe economic

---

D. Stanley Eitzen and Maxine Baca Zinn, "The Reagan Domestic Legacy: Greater Inequality and Destabilization," original essay.

---

See Statistical Appendix Tables A-1, A-2, A-3, A-4, A-6, A-8, A-10, A-11, A-12, A-13, A-14, A-15, A-16, A-17, A-18, and A-20.

problems in other economic sectors as well, including oil, timber, mining, and manufacturing.

- The number of individual and business bankruptcies, as well as bank failures, are higher than at any time since the Great Depression. From 1940 to 1980 some 360 banks failed—the same number that failed in 1986 and 1987 (Weil, 1988). Put another way, there were 138 bank failures in 1986 compared to an average of 10 a year through the 1970s (Nash, 1987). Also in fiscal 1986, there were 568,942 individual bankruptcies and 100,000 businesses went bankrupt.
- The federal debt, at more than $2 trillion and growing at $200 billion or so a year, is sapping the treasury. In 1980 one dollar of each ten that the federal government spent was to pay interest on the national debt. By 1985 interest consumed one dollar of each seven (Fallows, 1985:22). Put into perspective, the interest payments in 1985 were double the amount spent on Medicare, four times the amount spent on education, and five times that spent on agriculture (Kotz, 1987). Examined another way, when Reagan began his presidency the interest on the national debt was $1,200 per family; it is expected to be $3,200 per family when Reagan leaves office (Zuckerman, 1987).
- The changing economy, the shift from an industrial economy to a service/information one, is creating two major social problems—structural unemployment and the pauperization of work. There were 5.1 million displaced workers (i.e., workers with at least three years experience) who had lost their jobs between 1979 and 1983 because of plant closings, relocations, or the cancellations of positions or shifts (Flaim and Schgal, 1985). President Reagan is fond of pointing out that many new jobs are being created in the new economic climate (10.6 million from 1979 to the end of 1985). The problem, however, is that the new jobs are for the most part in the low wage service sector (clerks, janitors, fast foods, recreation, and security guards) and often they are part-time. Economists Bluestone and Harrison have found that between 1973 and 1979 about one in five net additional jobs paid as little as $7,000 (in 1984 dollars), while from 1979 to 1984 that fraction has risen to nearly six in ten (1986:5). The negative implications of this trend are significant: (1) a declining middle class (Kuttner, 1983); (2) new manifestations of class, race, and gender inequality; (3) a suffering economy resulting from individuals and families having less discretionary income (Harrington, 1987); and (4) declining government revenues from income and sales taxes, exacerbating the fiscal crisis at federal, state, and local levels.
- While the official unemployment rate for March 1987 was 6.5 percent, the rate for blacks was 13.9 percent and 9 percent for Hispanics. These government rates, of course, are misleading because they count as employed those 5.5 million who work part-time because they cannot find full-time jobs and they do not count as unemployed the 1.17 million discouraged workers who have given up their search for work (Hershey, 1987).
- The National Coalition for the Homeless estimates that there may be as many as 3 million homeless (Associated Press, 1986). A survey of 25 cities by the

U.S. Conference of Mayors found that the fastest-growing segment of the homeless were families (28 percent of the urban homeless) and that the number of families seeking emergency shelter increased 22 percent from 1985 to 1986 (*Newsweek,* 1987).

- There are 32.5 million Americans—1 out of 7—who were living below the government's poverty line in 1987.
- The Physician Task Force on Hunger in America estimates that some 20 million Americans are seriously hungry at least some period of time each month and that serious malnutrition impacts about 500,000 children (1985:8–9).

## Widening Inequality Under Reagan

Reagan's public rhetoric does not address these problems. What is especially significant about the very problems Reagan chooses to ignore is that they have in many important ways been exacerbated by his administration and a passive Congress. Let us illustrate this by examining three fundamental structures of domination in American society: class, race, and gender. Our thesis is that for all of Reagan's rhetoric calling for patriotism and other forms of unity, he has reduced social cohesiveness in society. In short, American society has become more unequal during his watch.

### Class

The gap between the rich and poor has widened during the Reagan years because of a shift in taxing and spending priorities. For example, from 1970 to 1986 the income share of the highest quintile rose from 43.3 percent to 46.1 percent, while the bottom one-fifth fell from 4.1 percent to 3.8 percent of all income (Pear, 1987). Put another way, "between 1977 and 1988 some $129 billion in income will have been shifted from the lower 90 percent of families to the top 10 percent" (Faux, 1988:129). This continuing transfer of wealth, while a long term trend, has increased markedly in the Reagan years because of six policies (*Dollars & Sense,* 1987):

1. The Kemp-Roth tax cut bill of 1981 slashed taxes for corporations and wealthy households. Because of a simultaneous rise in Social Security taxes, for 80 percent of the population taxes actually rose. Taxes decreased for those with incomes exceeding $100,000.

2. The rising federal debt redistributed income to the wealthy because they owned the Treasury bills and other government securities. In 1985 these interest payments were second only to Social Security disbursements. They were double Medicare spending and four times the amount spent on education (Kotz, 1987).

3. Reagan's Economic Recovery Tax Act of 1981 slashed significantly the federal estate tax—the only tax designed to reduce the concentration of wealth. By 1987 this tax was further reduced so that all estates up to $600,000 were exempt from federal death taxes. The tax now applies only to the top 0.3 percent of all estates and the rates for these estates have been lowered.

4. The Tax Reform Act of 1986 was a huge boon to the very rich because it reduced significantly their marginal tax rates and the principle of the progressive income tax. To the bill's credit, it did remove 6 million of the poorest from the tax rolls.

5. Each of the Reagan budgets has lowered programs that helped the needy in society. Over the years he has cut a total of $12 billion, for example, from programs providing nutrition assistance. He proclaimed that Americans are hungry only because they lack the knowledge of how they might qualify for existing programs. As a footnote to this, he abolished the very government program that would provide the information about nutrition programs to these targeted groups. The 1988 Reagan budget proposal illustrates his bias against programs to assist the poor and the marginal. A few examples make this case (*The New York Times,* 1987a):

- While middle class entitlements such as Social Security go untouched, the proposal requested a cut of $6 billion from programs to help the poor.
- Cut Medicaid—the Federal–State health insurance program for the poor—by $1 billion.
- Withdrew federal funds from construction of low-cost housing.
- Reduced child nutrition programs by another $415 million.
- Reduced Pell grants for needy college students by $1.1 billion for 1988 and another $700 million for 1989, and eliminated the low-interest National Direct Student Loans.
- Eliminated the Work Incentive Program and the Legal Services Corporation.
- Proposed to ban the states from collecting federal aid for providing rooms in hotels and other emergency housing for more than 30 days. Mayor Ed Koch of New York City, whose city stood to lose $85 million a year to aid the homeless, called the proposal "heartless" (cited in Barbanel, 1988:B3).

6. The cutbacks in human services since Reagan's election have produced severe hardships for women and children. Since 1980, the cuts in programs affecting family services have been dramatic. In 1983, family planning was cut by 24 percent. Birth control services and family planning education for poor women were also reduced. Aid to Families with Dependent Children has been slashed a total of $2 billion. In 1979, 88 percent of all poor families were receiving AFDC. In 1983, 62.9 percent of all poor families were receiving AFDC (Sidel, 1986).

## Race

The present Administration's policies, and in some cases its inaction, have exacerbated racial inequities and even racial animosities. First, data supplied by the National Urban League contrasts the economic situation of blacks in the 5 pre-Reagan years with that of the first five Reagan years (Swinton, 1987):

Per capita income in constant 1985 dollars:

-for blacks it slipped from 58.8% of white income to 57.2%.

-median family income for blacks dipped from 58.1% of white income to 56.7%.

Percent of blacks below the government's poverty line:

-31.3% in the 5 pre-Reagan years; 34.1% in the first 5 Reagan years.

Median weekly earnings of full-time black workers in constant 1985 dollars:

-Black males decreased from $342 to $311 and black females dipped from $250 to $245.

In the aggregate black workers lost earnings of $10.1 billion per year during each of the first four Reagan years.

These data show that blacks are less well-off under President Reagan than they were before. Discussions of race should also recognize the changing demographics of poverty. Certain categories of Hispanics are also disproportionately poor. While the median family income for blacks is still below that of Hispanics, per person income for Hispanics is actually lower because Hispanics tend to have larger families. By 1990 Hispanics are expected to replace blacks as the racial minority with the highest poverty rate in the United States (*U.S. News & World Report,* 1986). In 1987, the poverty rate for blacks was 33.1 percent, for Hispanics, 28.3 percent, and for whites, 10.5 percent.

These high poverty rates for blacks and Hispanics are due in part to Reagan's policies, but it is more the result of racism in the labor market and educational systems that consign blacks and Hispanics to dead end, marginal jobs in our segmented labor market structure. Most important, the lowering of their economic status is the consequence of the structural transformation of the economy. Economic changes such as the mechanization of agriculture in the South and the contraction of the manufacturing sector especially in the North have negatively impacted many workers, especially minorities. Bluestone and Harrison have found that minorities tend to be concentrated in those industries most affected by plant closings and capital flight (1982:54–55). In effect, then, these racial minorities are the victims of structural racism. The result is a dramatic shift downward in black and Hispanic male employment in the past few decades and this pace has accelerated under President Reagan. The Reagan Administration recognizes the high unemployment rate for blacks and other racial minorities, but it interprets this as a consequence of their maladaptive culture and not as a result of the structural changes affecting work, the location of jobs, and the types of jobs. Clearly, the adoption of such an explanation "blames the victim," justifies government inaction, and perpetuates misery.

Finally, let us examine Reagan's overt decisions regarding race. First, he has appointed people to key positions who share his views on race. Most significant, he appointed Edwin Meese as Attorney General and Bradford Reynolds as head of the Civil Rights wing of the Justice Department. These Reagan appointees have led the charge against Affirmative Action, opposed bills to enforce voting rights, abandoned mandatory pupil reassignment—allowing school segregation to continue, and been virtually inactive in prosecuting cases charging discrimination in housing (in 1986 the Justice Department only filed 12 cases in court from the over 5,000 complaints charging discrimination in housing). The Justice Department has also argued before the Supreme Court that segregated academies should be entitled to tax-exempt status.

Perhaps most telling of President Reagan's fundamental hostility to the civil rights laws that protect Americans who have been historic victims of discrimination was his veto of the Civil Rights Restoration Act in 1988. This measure insisted that colleges and other institutions which receive federal funds must not discriminate on the basis of sex, race, age, or physical handicap (Reagan's veto was overridden by Congress).

## Gender

Unlike other forms of inequality, sexism in the Reagan years has not become more intense, but rather has taken new forms. Women have continued to move from the private sphere (family) to public arenas, albeit under the conditions of labor market discrimination that have always plagued women. The new forms of sexism under Reagan are summarized by the Center for Popular Economics:

> Ironically, an administration which campaigned on the platform of getting the government off the backs of the American people and out of the economy has also attempted to legislate the most private aspect of people's lives. The conservative attack on abortion, homosexuality, and family planning is directed at legislating people's—especially women's—sexual decisions (1986:70).

Prominent among President Reagan's policy goals has been restricted access to abortion. He has spoken out against the Supreme Court decision in *Roe* v. *Wade,* where abortion was legalized. He has nominated Robert Bork, also a foe of the *Roe* v. *Wade* decision, for the Supreme Court, and he has sought to repeal Title X of the Public Health Service Act, which established the government's family-planning services. Recently, Reagan has sought to ban federal funds to clinics that offer abortion counseling. If this is enacted, it would

> neatly tie together both elements of the President's longstanding opposition to family-planning and sex-education programs: Don't tell them how they get pregnant; and when they do, don't tell them how to get unpregnant (Kramer, 1987:14).

The Reagan Administration has also marshalled its resources to oppose pay equity and Affirmative Action. Title IX, which has led to extraordinary changes toward equity in schools, has not only lost momentum, but it has also lost ground during the Reagan years. Public policies of special interest to women such as equality before the law, reproductive rights, equal pay for equal work, desegregating the labor force by sex, and government subsidized day care have been either ignored or opposed by the Reagan Administration. To illustrate the unfairness of the workplace for women, full-time working females make 70 cents for each dollar that a full-time working male receives. The case is worse for women of color, where black women make 56 cents and Hispanic women make 53 cents for each dollar made by men.

## The Reagan Project

Most of us, friends and foes alike, have sometimes found President Reagan to be uninformed, wrong, and confused. He occasionally makes horrible goofs that his staff must quickly try to mend (Green, 1987). But despite these shortcomings, an analysis of Reagan's proposals and policies reveals a coherent plan. There is a Reagan project and its intent is to redirect America in a particular direction.

A central part of this plan is to reduce the role of the federal government, especially its welfare functions. This Reagan has done by cutting tax revenues about $100 billion a year, while vastly increasing military spending, thus creating a $2 trillion deficit (double the amount when he took office). The deficit is no despised orphan. It is President Reagan's child, and secretly, he loves it. According to his former director of the budget, David Stockman, the deficit rigorously discourages any idea of spending another dime for welfare (*The New York Times,* 1987b). In short, this manufactured economic crisis has been used to coerce the Congress into accepting the conservative agenda for crippling, if not destroying, certain government social, regulatory, and environmental programs. Given the crisis, there is ample reason to cut social programs, reduce the government bureaucracy, and sell government assets to the private sector.

President Reagan's policies have clearly reduced governmental interference on the business sector. Government regulations and the number of inspections concerning pollution, consumer protection (Pertschuk, 1982), and workplace safety have been reduced significantly (ABC News, 1987). Corporations have been relatively free to merge, to move overseas, to dump dangerous products in the Third World, and to do whatever else is dictated by profits.

The business sector has also benefited from Reagan's efforts to reduce its labor costs. Labor unions have been weakened in a number of ways (e.g., the government's handling of the air controller's strike, the stacking of the National Labor Relations Board with pro-business partisans, the decline of the basic industries, and the threat of corporations to move overseas or to the South where labor is cheap). The costs of labor have also been kept at a minimum by the government's efforts to attack Affirmative Action and comparable worth.

President Reagan's "trickle down" economics and the resulting inequality gap have presented a critical dilemma to the Administration—how to minimize or dissolve the threat of discontent among the have-nots. The dissolution of this threat has been accomplished in several ways:

1. By keeping the Cold War "hot." The Russian menace helps to unify all Americans.

2. By creating false hopes; by promoting the fantasy that anyone who has the will can be successful.
3. By promoting false consciousness among the working and lower classes through active support of programs such as prayer in the schools, patriotism, anti-abortion, anti-homosexual rights, and support of the traditional family.
4. By dividing those who have similar economic interests. He has promoted policies and issues that divide fundamentalists and main line church members; that antagonize men against women; and that increase the tensions among the races. Racial and ethnic tensions, for example, easily divert people who should be coalition partners into enemies.

Although we have outlined what we believe to be the Reagan project, we should remember that the policies of this administration, while extreme and we believe, dangerous, are really only an extension of what the United States has always stood for, whichever party was in power and whichever personality sat as president. We have always had policies that supported:

- an upside down society where the few benefit at the expense of the many.
- the belief that what is good for business is good for the entire society.
- the protection of privilege and the privileged.
- the belief in growth at the expense of the powerless (domestically and internationally).
- the ethnocentric notion that there is only one way—our way.

## Summary: The Reagan Legacy

The sins of omission and commission by the Reagan Administration will have, in our judgment, several serious negative consequences:

1. The welfare state will have been weakened and replaced with a warfare state.

2. The huge deficit, the negative balance of payments, and the pockets of economic depression that already exist will result in a serious economic depression for us all.

3. The increasing magnitude of inequality will likely result in even more misery for an increasing proportion of the population (homelessness, poverty, malnutrition, and inadequate health care). Moreover, it will mean an increased likelihood of political instability, a higher rate of street crime, lower economic productivity because of lowered demand, increased class and racial hostility, and very serious dislocations in our cities.

4. The failure to understand and address the implications of the structural transformation of the economy will result, in our view, in immense societal, regional, community, and personal dislocations. The Reagan answer of letting the marketplace decide courts serious disaster.

5. Clearly we do not "sit tall in the saddle," nor is "dawn is breaking" in Amer-

ica as President Reagan proclaims. The U.S. is not the showcase for democracy and capitalism that Reagan, his California kitchen cabinet, and the Heritage Foundation envision. The misery index is rising. Compared to other industrial societies we rank quite unfavorably in education, infant mortality, incarceration rates, the magnitude of inequality, and other indices of progress. Most important, the lasting legacy of Ronald Reagan's presidency will be that he divided America rather than uniting it. As economist Robert Lekachman has put it, "He has divided our society between winners and losers, particularly, in a way that is very damaging to our functioning as a reasonable, decent society" (1987:47; see also Kopkind, 1984). His policies will have led to the destabilization of society.

6. Perhaps there is one part of the Reagan legacy that is positive. Perhaps Americans will have learned from this experience that *feeling good* about ourselves, our economy, and our society is not enough. Perhaps we will realize that we have serious social problems that have either been ignored by this Administration or have been enhanced by flawed policies. The next president and Congress, and we, must confront these problems with progressive policies that address the needs of all Americans—not just those of the already privileged. Failure to do this, in other words, to continue the Reagan project, would be the least patriotic thing we could do.

## References


ABC News. (1987). "Government Oversight Over Business Done During Reagan Years," (April 28).

Associated Press. (1986). "Major Cities Report Increase in Homeless," Associated Press Release (December 18).

Barbanel, Josh. (1988). "Officials Oppose U.S. Cuts In Aid to Homeless Families," *The New York Times* (March 29):B3.

Bluestone, Barry and Bennett Harrison. (1982). *The Deindustrialization of America.* New York: Basic Books.

Bluestone, Barry and Bennett Harrison. (1986). "The Great American Job Machine: The Proliferation of Low Wage Employment in the U.S. Economy," a study prepared for the Joint Economic Committee, U.S. Congress (December).

Center for Popular Economics. (1986). *Economic Report of the People.* Boston: South End Press.

*Dollars & Sense.* (1987). "Reaganomics Report Card," *Dollars & Sense No. 126* (May):6–8.

Fallows, James. (1985). "The Three Fiscal Crises," *The Atlantic Monthly 256* (September):18–28.

Faux, Jeff. (1988). "The Party's Over, But Who Pays?" *The Nation* (January 30):128–130.

Flaim, Paul O. and Ellen Schgal. (1985). "Displaced Workers of 1979–1983: How Well Have They Fared?" *Monthly Labor Review 108* (6):3–16.

Graham, Fred. (1987). "The Administration's Strategy Boomeranged," *USA Today* (March 31):8A.

Green, Mark. (1987). "Amiable Dunce or Chronic Liar?" *Mother Jones 12* (June/July): 9–17.

Harrington, Michael. (1987). *The Next Left: The History of a Future.* New York: Henry Holt.

Harrison, Bennett, Chris Tilly, and Barry Bluestone. (1986). "Wage Inequality Takes a Great U-Turn," *Challenge 29* (March–April):26–32.

Hershey, Robert D. (1987). "Jobless Rate Down but Growth of Jobs Also Falls," *The New York Times* (April 4):7.

Kopkind, Andrew. (1984). "The Age of Reaganism," *The Nation* (November 3):433; 448–51.

Kotz, David M. (1987). "What to do about the Budget Deficit?" *In These Times* (January 28–February 3):17.

Kramer, Michael. (1987). "Reagan's Backdoor War on Abortion," *U.S. News & World Report* (August 17):14.

Kuttner, Bob. (1983). "The Declining Middle," *The Atlantic Monthly 252* (July):60–72.

Lekachman, Robert. (1987). "America's Morning After Reagan," *Challenge 30* (March/April):34–44.

Nash, Nathaniel C. (1987). "Bank Failures Rose 20% in '86," *The New York Times* (January 5):20.

*Newsweek*. (1987). "A Family Down and Out," *Newsweek* (January 12):44–46.

*The New York Times*. (1987a). "The Poverty Budget, More or Less," *The New York Times* (January 7):26.

*The New York Times*. (1987b). "The State of the President," *The New York Times* (January 25):E22.

Pear, Robert. (1987). "Poverty Rate Dips as the Median Family Income Rises," *The New York Times* (July 31):8.

Pertschuk, Michael. (1982). "Reaganism is Harmful to Your Health," *The Nation* (July 24-31):*65,* 83–84.

Physician Task Force on Hunger in America. (1985). *Hunger in America: The Growing Epidemic.* Middletown, Conn.: Wesleyan University Press.

Sidel, Ruth. (1988). *Women and Children Last: The Plight of Poor Women in Affluent America.* New York: Viking.

Swenton, David. (1987). "Economic Status of Blacks," *The State of Black America 1987.* New York: National Urban League, pp. 49–73.

*U.S. News & World Report*. (1986). "Progress and Poverty," (September 8):8.

Weil, Ken. (1988). "Bleak Times for World Economy," *Denver Post* (March 15):B7.

Zuckerman, Mortimer B. (1987). "Rich People, Poorer Country," *U.S. News & World Report* (July 20):66.

# Part 2
# STRUCTURED INEQUALITY

The three major hierarchies of stratification—class, race, and gender—are the foci of this section. These hierarchies ''place'' groups, families, and individuals in society. The crucial consequence of this placement is that the rewards and resources of society such as wealth, power, and privilege are unequally distributed. The differential access to these societal resources and rewards produces different life experiences and different life chances. Life chances are critical because they refer to what money can buy (education, medical care, a comfortable existence, safety, and expert service). In a stratified society some people and their children have wonderful life chances, while others do not. Those who do not are likely to live miserable lives, ultimately dying earlier than if they had had adequate resources.

The topic of Chapter 3 is poverty. Michael Harrington, the leading social science expert on poverty since the 1950s, leads off with a discussion of the myths about poverty and welfare. The next two selections focus on two growing problems associated with poverty in the United States—hunger and homelessness. The final essay provides a set of solutions to the problem of hunger by the Physician Task Force on Hunger.

The first three articles in Chapter 4 deal with racial stratification focusing on blacks, Chicanos, and Asian Americans, respectively. The final article from William Julius Wilson's influential book, *The Truly Diasdvantaged,* proposes some policies that would help to alleviate the problem of the ghetto underclass.

Chapter 5 provides three essays on how women are disadvantaged by the structure of American society. Nancy Barrett's essay focuses on how the economy and the workplace disadvantage women. Barbara Ehrenreich's essay and the one by the Center for Popular Economics concentrate on the relatively high probability of single women and their children being economically deprived and the reasons for this.

# Chapter 3
# POVERTY

## Myths about Poverty and Welfare

*Michael Harrington*

What follows is a statistical detective story.

There are two facts in American society which are as palpable as the nudity of the emperor in the famous legend and just as scrupulously ignored. Between the poor and the nonpoor, who gets the most from social spending? . . . The answer: The nonpoor get much more than the poor. We will now fill in some of the important details. And there is the second, related issue: Among the poor themselves, who gets the most from Washington? Not the welfare poor, but the aging poor.

The stereotype that is directly contrary to these facts—that the United States devotes the lion's share of its social spending to the lazy, dependent poor—is one of the chief ideological defenses of our complacent callousness. It is an utter falsification, as will be seen when we deal with the most astounding conservative discovery of the 1970s: Poverty has disappeared and no one noticed.

The central thesis in this stunning revelation can be stated simply enough. The official poverty definition only counts cash income. It does not include the money value of the in-kind income received by the poor—food stamps, housing subsidies, and, above all, medical care—and therefore, it is argued, systematically overstates the extent of poverty in the United States. When one does compute the worth of the in-kind income and adds it to the cash income, poverty is either drastically reduced or even abolished. The extent of this statistical triumph depends upon precisely what measure one uses to translate the in-kind goods and services into an equivalent cash sum.

One of the first statements of this theme came from Edgar K. Browning in a 1974 article in *The Public Interest,* the theoretical journal of all those who develop sophisticated arguments for turning the nation's back upon the poor. Browning's article was titled "How Much More Equality Can We Afford?"—which provides a rather obvious

---



---

See Statistical Appendix Tables A-6, A-10, A-11, A-12, A-13, A-14, A-15, A-16, A-17, and A-18.

clue as to his political bias. By using the argument about uncounted in-kind benefits, Browning concluded that "there is practically no poverty—statistically speaking—in the United States today and indeed there has not been for several years." In 1976, Gerald Ford's Council of Economic Advisors took up this theme, announcing that it had serious doubts about the poverty statistics because they did not calculate the cash value of the in-kind goods and services.

In the mid-seventies, "informed opinion" was ready to take any hypothesis that reduced the number of the poor, and to treat it as a fact. So it was that this highly questionable—indeed, erroneous—theory began to appear in the media as an unvarnished statement about reality. Harry Schwartz of *The New York Times* quoted these speculations and then chided the government for publishing "misleading" figures about poverty. Schwartz and others like him did not notice the extremely fancy statistical footwork required to reach the new conclusions. One analysis, for instance, declared that the nonworking poor—mainly the old and the young, the ill and single parents keeping house—were "voluntarily" unemployed, and went on to count the "potential additional earnings" they would receive for giving up some of their leisure as part of their real income.

Then, in 1977, the Congressional Budget Office, under the direction of a certified liberal, Alice Rivlin, took up the *Public Interest* thesis. By taking the "market value" of the in-kind goods and services, the CBO reduced the poverty population by 47 percent. The next year, Martin Anderson of the Hoover Institution—later to be an advisor to President Reagan—published a book-length statement on the new nonpoverty. In *The Political Economy of Welfare Reform in the United States,* Anderson wrote, "The 'war on poverty' that began in 1964 has been won. The growth of jobs and income in the private economy, combined with an explosive increase in government spending for welfare and income transfer programs, has virtually eliminated poverty in the United States."

To be fair, the political attitudes involved in all of these sweeping redefinitions were complex. Some—the CBO, for instance—argued that the revisions were necessary to show the public that liberal programs had actually worked, which was an interesting rationalization of conservative analysis. Others, like Browning and Anderson, were straightforward in their conservatism. A third conservative tendency took the opposite tack from Browning and Anderson: The federal efforts, it said, had not achieved, but blocked, the elimination of poverty . . . But whether liberal, optimistically conservative, or pessimistically conservative, all of these thinkers pointed in the same political direction: No more money for antipoverty efforts. The latter had either succeeded too brilliantly or failed too abysmally to justify any further funds.

There were, however, some interesting admissions made along the way. The Congressional Budget Office, for instance, discovered that the normal outcome of the American economy left 25 percent of the people poor. The only reason that appalling percentage did not constitute a menace was that government transfer programs did away with roughly 80 percent of that poverty. Similarly, one of the most determined of the conservative pessimists, Charles Murphy, came up with the concept of "latent poverty": those who were poor before cash and in-kind programs saved them. He concluded that latent poverty had actually increased during the seventies (from 19 percent in 1972 to 22 percent in 1980), and charged, contrary to both the CBO and Anderson, that all that federal spending had been wasted on a treadmill.

By the early eighties, then, the statistical abolition of poverty had turned into an academic cottage industry in the United States. In late 1983, David Stockman testified on behalf of the administration that despite the impression that there had been an enormous increase in poverty—indeed, despite the testimony to that effect by the conservative director of the CBO a month earlier—the numbers of poor were actually declining, with even better days foreseen ahead. Small wonder that *New York Times* thinkers and editorialists around the country had begun to take complex and questionable theories as statements of observed fact. To be sure, they might have taken a tour of the South Bronx in New York, as almost every Presidential candidate did, and the acres of rubble and the milling unemployed people in the middle of the day might have suggested that all was not yet quite well. Most, however, avoided that exertion.

Then, in 1982, the Bureau of the Census published a formidable technical paper on "Alternative Methods for Valuing Selected In-Kind Transfer Benefits and Measuring Their Effect on Poverty." There was a flurry of newspaper reports, but they had to tell of a complexity, not of a stunning simplicity like the secret abolition of poverty. There were, the Census said, serious difficulties in "cashing in" the in-kind benefits. Indeed, one plausible measure reduced the number of the poor by a mere 12.2 percent rather than by 42.3 percent (these are 1979 numbers; i.e., they predate an increase of more than five million people in the officially defined poverty population). Corrections in the United States, particularly intricate statistical corrections, rarely have the media impact of the initial—wrong—revelations. Small wonder, then, that by 1983 so many people had concluded that the poor were either nonexistent or undeserving.

We will attempt to sort out the truth about those in-kind benefits shortly. But there is an important prelude to that task. All of the intellectual effort since 1974 has been devoted to exploring the possibility that we have overestimated the poor. Thus, even the most serious and careful count made by the Bureau of the Census reduces the dimensions of poverty. It should be made clear at this point that I, too, want the figures to be as exact and realistic as possible. After all, I want the most accurate data to guide the formulation of policy in a new war on poverty. So part of my objection to these various revisions has to do with means, not with ends. I think they have done a careless job in carrying out investigations that are quite relevant in themselves. That will be explored in a moment.

But there is a second objection, and it is the subject of my prelude. Why has so much attention been devoted to documenting the overestimation of the poor—and so little to exploring the underestimation of them? In two areas, involving millions of poor people, there is evidence of an undercount. It is a well-kept secret in the United States.

The first area has to do with the definition of poverty in terms of cash income.

All of the critics of an overcount take that definition as a starting point, even as they charge that it is utterly inadequate. After they have made their computations about the value of the in-kind benefits, they add them to the official poverty line in order to establish a new poverty (or nonpoverty) line. So, strange as it may seem, they implicitly acknowledge the authority of the very definition they want to replace.

Under the circumstances, one might think it would be a matter of some moment that the person who originally elaborated that cash-income definition of poverty has thought for some time that it underestimates the problem. In 1974 (a year when the official poverty rate went up), Mollie Orshansky argued that the "line" was $3,000 below what it should be and that the poor therefore numbered 55.4 million—not, as in the official count, 23.4 million. In a complex argument presented to the American Statistical Association in 1979, Orshansky (along with C. Fendler) asserted that in 1977—a "good" year for the poor—the official measure understated poverty by a factor of 54 percent, i.e., *it overlooked 25 million people.*

The central (but not the only) factor in Orshansky's revisions had to do with the relation between food cost and the total budget of the poor. In 1954, when the definition was first developed, it was assumed that this ratio was 3-to-1, as shown in a 1955 USDA survey of American food consumption patterns. But in 1965, another USDA analysis concluded that the percentage spent on food was actually less than in 1955. Adjusting the definition of poverty to conform to this empirical pattern meant that the multiplier had to be increased from 3 to 3.45. That change, along with some other technical amendments, resulted in Orshansky's conclusion that there had been a significant undercount.

The Bureau of the Census took note of this challenge, though the news did not get through to the media pundits. This procedure, Census said, tended to relativize poverty, and such updating could mask significant reductions in poverty. But, as we have already seen, there is, and must be, a relative component in any definition of the poor. Were 1955 food patterns, which were the base for the original definition of poverty, absolute? If so, in that year there was no poverty at all, compared to diets in Europe in 1755 or in much of India today. And, as Townsend emphasized, one must look at the poor in terms of their participation—in food and everything else—in *their* society, a concept that, as we have seen, has empirical grounding in those careful studies of the poverty threshold in the United Kingdom. Finally, Orshansky's method does not make it as impossible to eliminate poverty as a Barry Goldwater might think; if the seventies had merely been as good as the sixties in this area, her 1977 computation would have been set much lower, even if it were still higher than the official poverty line.

Let me be fair. Decent and serious analysts can reject Orshansky's methodology without being prejudiced against the poor. I am not saying that her measure is the only plausible one. But her case cannot be ignored, because she is one of the most widely recognized and authoritative researchers in the field. But the fact is that those who want to revise the poverty problem downward—who make their 50-percent reductions in the number of the poor—get incomparably more attention than one who presents a very reasonable case for revising upward. It is therefore at least possible that the United States is now undercounting poverty by a factor of much more than 25 million people (I say "much more than" because the poor, by any measure, have significantly increased since 1977).

The second area in which the poor are undercounted is not a creation of the statistical method used, but a fact. The only question is, how many people does it contain? It is well known that there are many undocumented families in the United States, and it is equally well known that a majority of them are poor . . . This is the reason why the sweatshop has made a dramatic return to the United States of the seventies and the eighties. The estimates of the size of this undocumented population vary from five to ten million people. Assuming that 80 percent of them are poor, there might be four to eight million impoverished humans in this society who have never achieved the dignity of being a statistic.

In the spring of 1983, the Reagan administration unwittingly lent its authority to my point. The White House said that there were 6.25 million undocumented people in the country and that if the Simpson-Mazzoli immigration bill, which would "legalize" some of them, passed, 1.7 million would become eligible for naturalization. In the Senate version of the bill, the aliens who came to the United States before January 1, 1977, would become permanent residents, while those who entered prior to January 1, 1980, would become temporary residents. That, the Office of Management and Budget said, could mean $9.3 billion in additional welfare costs over a period of four years. Obviously, there is no doubt in the Reagan administration that there are millions of predominantly poor undocumented workers in the United States. No doubt, that is, until it comes to counting the poor, when these people are most conveniently forgotten.

But there are also social realities that point in the other direction. There is an important "underground economy" in the United States, with billions of dollars in unreported income. One of its sectors has nothing to do with the poor: the professionals and skilled workers who barter their services or else provide them, in whole or in part, off the books. Another sector does harbor people who are poor in terms of their reported income, but not in terms of their real income: the world of crime and drugs. But we know . . . that class distinctions hold even in the underworld, and that the most successful lawbreakers tend to be white and better educated than the petty criminals. The latter also spend a disproportionate amount of time in one of the major institutions of American poverty, the prison system.

But even taking into account the probability that there is a certain amount of undeclared income that abolishes the poverty of the underworld poor, still the undocumented workers, and the people counted if one accepts Orshansky's revised definition, are potentially more numerous than *all* those now officially declared to be poor. We are talking about an undercount that could total more than thirty million rather miserable human beings. Even if one were to accept the conservative theories about an overcount in their most extreme version, it is probable that far more people in America are poor than we now recognize officially.

In fact, most of the revisions are sweeping and excessive. Let us now look at how they compute the cash value of in-kind goods and services and see why.

To begin with, the statistical conservatives mix apples and oranges in their calculations. On the one hand, they still use the cash-income definition of poverty; on the other hand, they change it radically. Consider an analogous case. Suppose that the U.S. government were suddenly to announce that it was going to tax the cash value of public schools, including colleges and universities, which would be tacked onto the income of all those with children when they computed their income tax. The insurance value of all employee medical plans would be counted as taxable income, and so would the worth of all business perks, such as food and transportation. It is not, I think, hard to imagine the anguished outcry that would result.

Part of the complaint would be that tax rates which had been decided in terms of cash income, and which were set at a certain level for precisely that reason, were now being applied to noncash income. But that is exactly what the statistical revisionists are doing to the poor. For when the poverty line is adjusted, or when certain in-kind benefits are computed in determining eligibility for a social program, that is not just a matter of theory. It has to do with how much money people get—just as the income tax does.

In two significant areas, then—the technical question of how the poverty line is fixed, and the fact that there is a huge and uncounted population of the undocumented poor—there is evidence of an undercount. As a result, even if the new [statisticians] were right in their calculations of the overcount, the number of the impoverished is higher than the official statistics indicate, not lower. But—and we return here to our detective story—those new estimates about how we exaggerated poverty are not accurate. Rather they overgeneralize a single, rarely stated fact: The aging poor receive a disproportionate share of the in-kind benefits. To treat their benefits as if they go to the poverty population as a whole is obviously wrong.

This fact about the aging is, we will see later on, a subordinate aspect of a larger truth, i.e., that the welfare state in the United States is primarily for people over sixty-five, most of whom are not now, and for a long time have not been, poor. Obviously I do not say these things because I propose to take benefits away from the aging or to argue that they have been given too much assistance. Quite the opposite. But I do want to point out that there are very special problems in evaluating these benefits—above all in assigning a cash value to nursing home and/or terminal health care—that makes it dubious to attribute them to the poor as a group.

There are three methods that have been devised for computing the cash value of in-kind benefits. The market-method estimates the dollar worth of the benefit in terms of its purchase price in a private market. This is the approach that yields the highest estimates of an overcount and accomplishes the greatest reduction in the number of the poor. It is, as one might guess, favored by conservatives, and was also used by the Congressional Budget Office. When it is employed by conservatives, a considerable irony surfaces. These normally implacable critics of government waste assume that all in-kind goods and services are provided to the poor with 100-percent efficiency, that the public sector is every bit as good as the private sector. Needless to say, such assumptions, so convenient in the argument against any further poverty expenditures, are quickly forgotten when it comes to other areas of social policy.

The second method values the goods and services in terms of their worth to the recipient. What is the cash amount for which the recipients would be willing to trade their right to the in-kind transfer, given their current incomes? Perhaps a poor person does not share that extraordinary conservative assumption that every good and service is provided in just the right proportion and with total efficiency. He or she might want less, or more, of certain benefits than the omniscient bureaucracy posited by trusting the conservatives' decrees. One way of figuring the cash value for the recipient is to look at how much other people, similar in most respects but not getting the in-kind benefit, actually do pay for it.

The third method is called the "poverty budget share value" approach. It deals, among other things, with a central problem in this whole exercise: How does one evaluate the worth of medical care that goes mainly to the aging poor? The Bureau of the Census gives an excellent case in point. In 1979, the market value of Medicaid coverage for an elderly person in New York State was estimated at $4,430. But this was almost $1,000 more than the poverty line for that person ($3,472). Clearly this $4,430 is "income" in a very special sense, since it cannot be spent on food, housing, or any other need (and is indeed most unwelcome "income" since one has to be ill to get it). If one were to take that $4,430 at face value, then a person could enter the middle class, or even the upper middle class, by virtue of having a long, expensive, subsidized terminal illness. So the "poverty share" method limits the value of medical care (or any other in-kind benefit) to its share in the definition of the poverty budget. Anything over that sum is not really additional disposable income but, more often than not, too much of a good thing.

There are many complications in each of these methods, but they need not concern us here. Taking the extreme case—the one in which each approach yields the highest "reduction" in poverty—the differences are striking. In 1979 terms, market value eliminates almost 13 million people, or 42.3 percent of the total; recipient value cuts out a mere 9,305,000 human beings, or 26.7 percent; and poverty budget shares drop out 7,757,000 of the poor, or "only" 20.1 percent. Remember, once again, that the highest computation of the overcount—13 million—is not even equal to one-half of the possible undercount already documented (30 million or more).

Moreover, the bulk of the downward revisions mainly comes from looking at the in-kind benefits of one group among the poor—the 15 percent who are over sixty-five years of age—and then equating them with benefits received by the entire population. This point requires us to focus on the fact that antipoverty measures in the United States are primarily for the aging. It also utterly subverts Martin Anderson's assertion that "an explosive increase in government spending for welfare and income transfer programs" was a major reason for the famous disappearance of poverty in America.

Between 1975 and 1980, according to census figures, the real buying power of cash public assistance transfers ("welfare") did not explode but declined. There was one area that might have seemed to be an exception: Washington increased its outlays for medical care from $28 billion in 1975 to $58.545 billion in 1980. That more than 100-percent increase was, however, fictitious to a considerable degree, since it primarily represented an inflation of medical costs of around 75 percent, not an increase in medical services. Moreover, slightly more than half of that rise is attributable to Medicare, a program for the aging only, 85 percent of whose recipients are not poor. Even if one adds in the 15 percent of the people over sixty-five who might have been poor were it not for Medicare, it is hardly a poverty program.

That leaves Medicaid, which is indeed a means-tested program for the poor alone. Not so incidentally, it accounts for about two-thirds of the in-kind benefits so critical to the statistical triumph over poverty. But then, when one looks a little more closely, it turns out that 46 percent of all Medicaid funds go for nursing homes and other forms of institutional care. To qualify for that, the elderly, blind, or disabled have to forfeit their social security or supplemental social security income. In short, the largest single portion of in-kind income goes to people waiting to die or utterly unable to care for themselves and without any cash income. Whether this constitutes the advance in well-being predicted by the conservatives and the Congressional Budget Office is, I think, at least open to question.

Let us look at the *reductio ad absurdum* of all these figures. In 1979, the medical care benefits for a single aging person were equal to 85.9 percent of the poverty line; for two persons they were 136.7 percent of the line. This latter family, it will be noted, turned a handsome profit on being sick. I do not, let me repeat, begrudge the elderly their benefits, and I opposed their reduction in the social security reform of 1983. But I most strenuously object to assigning those benefits—which are a very special kind of income for a very particular group of the poor—to the poverty population as a whole.

In short, a great deal, but not all, of the reduction of poverty by giving cash value to in-kind benefits is the result of statistical smoke and mirrors. Moreover, even the critique I have made of these tricky numbers somewhat understates the dimensions of poverty. Almost all of the figures used come from the late seventies or from 1980. That is because our calculations obviously always lag somewhat behind the reality they quantify. In this case, that is of great significance, because 1981–1983 was a period in which poverty was on the increase, first of all among those working people described in the last chapter, and, second, among those aging poor whose "one-time" loss of the indexing of their social security benefits in 1983 will affect the base of their payments for the rest of their lives.

How many poor people are there? Honest analysts can sincerely differ on the definition, but the reasons given for the alleged great decrease in the number of the poor in recent years are simply not persuasive. I would suggest that there are in the range of forty to fifty million Americans who live in poverty. That is roughly the same number I suggested more than twenty years ago, but, since the population has increased during those decades, it represents an exceedingly modest decline in the percentage of the poor.

It is also, if I may take off my stifling statistical mask and speak in a human voice, an unambiguous outrage.

As we toured the mathematical maze it became apparent that, relatively speaking, the aging poor get better care than anyone else under the poverty line. But that is only one point in a larger case, which may be stated as follows: The entire welfare state in the United States is primarily for people over sixty-five, most of whom are not poor; and this welfare state is the cheapest in the Western world.

Non-defense spending in the 1981 budget was $497.4 billion. Of that, interest payments—which benefited the rich disproportionately, but also helped the federal retirees—accounted for $82.5 billion. Indeed, as we shall see in a moment, more was paid to the recipients of interest than to the poor, which says something about our values. Payments to individuals (mainly social security checks) amounted to $316.6 billion, and roughly $60 billion of that total went to Medicare and Medicaid. As we have seen, 85 percent of the former and at least half of the latter went to people over sixty-five. Various retirement funds (social security, federal employee, railroad retirement, etc.) came to about $256 billion. Most of those monies went to people who were not poor. Indeed, if one looks at the funds directly assigned to the income security of those at the bottom of the society in 1981, they amount to a little less than $43 billion.

Anything that can be remotely called "welfare," then, is about 13 percent of the total federal payments to individuals. Put a little more dramatically, approximately 87 percent of the checks that Washington sends out goes to people who are not poor, not a few of whom spend a good deal of time complaining about welfare cheats. This truth was discovered by Peter Peterson, the former Secretary of Commerce, in a *New York Times* article in early 1982 and presented to the public as something of a revelation. We cannot, Peterson said, balance the budget by taking the poor off welfare, because we don't pay the welfare poor that much in the first place. Therefore, he concluded, we have to turn to social security, which is where the real money is. Peterson's proportions were correct; his policy proposals were, of course, reactionary.

James R. Storey, in a scholarly analysis of the same basic fact for the Urban Institute, concluded that the percentage of public money devoted to need-related programs (the poor) "has actually been less since 1965 than before. About 25 percent of total benefits was spent on aid to the needy before 1965, but this proportion has since ranged between 15 and 20 percent." The aging nonpoor, then, were the ones who made the greatest gains in recent years. They deserved them, and more, but this does not mean that the poor made similar progress.

But isn't this point a statistical trick of my own? It may well be, someone could argue, that the share of the public pie going to the impoverished has gone down, but hasn't the pie itself become much, much larger? If so, the relative decline in the poverty share of social spending disguises an absolute increase.

There are a number of problems with this thesis. We have already seen how a nominal doubling of outlays for health care between 1975 and 1980 amounted to a three-quarters inflation in costs and only a one-quarter increase in actual service. Ronald Reagan delights in citing soaring increases in spending, and almost always uses figures uncorrected for inflation to make his charge more compelling (needless to say, he always corrects for inflation when talking about defense spending), and quite often uses infinitesimal baselines in order to get huge percentage increases. If, however, we are serious about understanding the trends in federal spending, we obviously have to deal with constant dollars. This is particularly important, since many of the things the government buys—medical care, above all—have rates of inflation much higher than the Consumer Price Index.

Second, interest payments have been a growing factor in the budget, not the least because of the power of monetarist ideas in the White House and at the Federal Reserve Bank. Moreover, the interest cost does not represent current outlays on new goods and services, but rather reflects payments for past outlays. So it makes sense, if we want to compute what federal policy is doing in the present, to prescind from the latest component of the budget, which pays for the priorities of the past.

Third, a portion of federal expenditures is the result not of policy choices, but of the business cycle. For instance, Reagan's Council of Economic Advisors conceded in its 1983 report that a one-percent increase in unemployment results in lost revenues and increased costs (unemployment compensation, food stamps, welfare) of $25 billion. I agree with trade-union economists and others that the figure is more likely $30 billion, but there is no need to dispute a mere $5 billion here. The unemployment rate was 7.5 percent when Ronald Reagan took office in January 1981, and 10.8 percent in December 1982. That 3.3-percent increase meant, if one uses the Reagan figure, more than $80 billion in additional expenditures, and about $100 billion if the higher estimate is used. In short, increased unemployment accounted for about half of the federal deficit in 1982. In 1983, when the deficit remained at stratospheric levels even though joblessness was coming down, that factor was clearly not as important. Still, in any given year, one has to differentiate between the spending imposed upon an administration in Washington by the business cycle and the spending (or cuts) decided as a matter of policy. In 1982, for instance, if the unemployment rate had simply been at the official "target" of the early sixties, the budget would have been in surplus.

If we make all of these quite realistic corrections (adjusting for inflation and unemployment, subtracting interest), there is a rather startling result. Total federal outlays as a percentage of the GNP in 1956 under Eisenhower were 17.6 percent and—after all of those presumed "explosions" of the sixties and seventies—were 18.9 percent in 1981. The vast increase in the size of the public economic pie, in terms of GNP, was then 1.3 percent. And two-thirds of that quite modest rise occurred *after* Kennedy and Johnson, under the Presidencies of Richard Nixon and Gerald Ford. So the liberals were responsible for a 0.4-percent increase in real federal spending relative to gross national product. This is not to deny that there was a significant internal shift in the composition of that spending, as the defense portion went down and the social sector increased in the decade 1969–1979. But that shift, as we have seen, channeled money primarily to the nonpoor.

In all of this, the poor made some modest, and absolute, gains in their living standards during the sixties when gross national product was on the rise, and at least some of the new programs helped those who were impoverished but not aging. In the seventies and early eighties, GNP rose and fell, social meanness was up, and social programs were down. There was a relative and absolute decline in the conditions of life in the other America. For the fact is that, contrary to our stereotypes, the welfare state in this country is only incidentally for the poor and is primarily oriented toward people over sixty-five years of age, not toward people living under the poverty line.

That welfare state is also the cheapest in the advanced capitalist world.

If one looks at the percentage of the GNP spent on social programs in the mid- to late seventies, as Robert Reich and Ira Magaziner did in their book, *Minding America's Business,* there is a marked contrast between this country and all the other (relatively) rich nations. The United States spent around 14 percent of GNP on such functions, the West Germans more than twice that, and even the Japanese spent 17 percent. I say "even" the Japanese, because many programs that are in the public sector in the West are carried out privately there; e.g., male workers in major corporations are not laid off and given unemployment compensation, but are kept on by their employers even though there is no work for them. Still, the official Japanese outlays as a percentage of GNP are higher than in the United States.

The low percentage of GNP spent on social programs in the United States is reflected in the fact that this country is one of the least taxed in the Western world. In 1980, according to the OECD, American tax receipts were 30.7 percent of the gross domestic product, which meant that we lagged behind thirteen European nations. In that year, Sweden, under a conservative government, collected 49.9 percent of GDP in taxes; the Netherlands, 46.2 percent; West Germany, 37.2 percent; and Canada, 32.8 percent. Indeed, the United States's relative position actually declined in the years between 1955 and 1980. We ranked eleventh in 1955 and sixteenth in 1980. Thus, in international comparative terms, the American feeling that this is a highly taxed country with an elaborate welfare state contradicts the facts.

I do not want to suggest that all is well with the European welfare state. They, too, devote more funds to the nonpoor than to the poor in their social programs (by a ratio of three to one in the mid-seventies, according to *Le Monde*). And they are in deep trouble because of the economic crisis of the eighties. Indeed, their problems are in some ways even more formidable than those in this country, because they all have national health systems that cover the entire population, and medical costs in Europe are also soaring. I do not wish, then, to contrast a European utopia with an American social slum.

I do, however, want to attack one conservative argument on the basis of the contrast between the European and American welfare states. People like Ronald Reagan and William Simon say that this country fell behind in productivity and competitiveness in the 1970s because it lavished so much money on the unproductive poor and thereby starved private investment. Leave aside the fact that the data of the seventies simply do not support that thesis. The fact is that the Europeans in the postwar period spent much more on social programs *and* had lower rates of unemployment and inflation *and* high levels of investment. West Germany, whose economic performance significantly outclassed that of the United States in every one of these areas, spent twice as high a percentage of its GNP on social programs.

If, in short, social meanness were the key to productivity, America would, on the record of the past twenty years, be the most productive nation on the face of the earth.

But when will we recognize these truths? There are, as this [essay] asserts, many more people who are poor than we recognize, not fewer; there is a welfare state that is stingy to those most in need, and second-class by comparison with Europe. When will America open its eyes?

# Homeless Families

*Jonathan Kozol*

Since 1980 homelessness has changed its character. What was once a theater of the grotesque (bag ladies in Grand Central Station, winos sleeping in the dusty sun outside the Greyhound station in El Paso) has grown into the common misery of millions.

"This is a new population," said a homeless advocate in Massachusetts. "Many are people who were working all their lives. When they lose their jobs they lose their homes. When they lose their homes they start to lose their families too."

Even in New York City, with its permanent population of the long-term unemployed, 50 percent of individuals served at city shelters during 1984 were there for the first time. The same percentage holds throughout the nation.

The chilling fact, from any point of view, is that small children have become the fastest-growing sector of the homeless. At the time of writing there are 28,000 homeless people in emergency shelters in the city of New York. An additional 40,000 are believed to be unsheltered citywide. Of those who are sheltered, about 10,000 are homeless individuals. The remaining 18,000 are parents and children in almost 5,000 families. The average homeless family includes a parent with two or three children. The average child is six years old, the average parent twenty-seven.

In Massachusetts, three fourths of all homeless people are now children and their parents. In certain parts of Massachusetts (Plymouth, Attleboro, and Northampton) 90 to 95 percent of those who have no homes are families with children.

Homeless people are poor people. Four out of ten poor people in America are children, though children make up only one fourth of our population. The number of children living in poverty has grown to 14 million—an increase of 3 million over 1968—while welfare benefits to families with children have declined one third.

Seven hundred thousand poor children, of whom 100,000 have no health insurance, live in New York City. Approximately 20 percent of New York City's children lived in poverty in 1970, 33 percent in 1980, over 40 percent by 1982.

---



---

See Statistical Appendix Table A-23.

*Where are these people?*

We have seen that they are in midtown Manhattan. They are also in the streets of Phoenix, Salt Lake City, Philadelphia, San Antonio, Miami, and St. Paul. They are in the Steel Belt. They are in the Sun Belt. They are in Kansas City and Seattle. They are in the heartland of America.

In Denver, where evictions rose 800 percent in 1982, hundreds of families were locked on waiting lists for public housing. Many were forced to live in shelters or the streets. In Cleveland, in one classic situation, the loss of a home precipitated by the layoffs in a nearby plant led to the dissolution of a family: the adolescent daughter put in foster care, the wife and younger children ending up on welfare, the husband landing in a public shelter when he wasn't sleeping underneath a bridge. Cleveland was obliged to open shelters and soup kitchens in blue-collar neighborhoods that housed traditional white ethnic populations.

The *Milwaukee Journal* wrote: "The homeless in our midst are no longer mainly urban hobos and bag ladies. In recent months, joblessness has pushed heretofore self-reliant families into this subculture." In Michigan, in 1982, the loss of jobs in heavy industry forced Governor Milliken to declare "a state of human emergency"—a declaration other governors may be forced to contemplate by 1988.

As an easterner, I had at first assumed that most of these families must be urban, nonwhite, unemployable—perhaps a great deal like the ghetto families I have worked with for much of my life. In 1985, however, I was given an opportunity to visit in over 50 cities and in almost every region of the nation. My hosts were governors and other local politicians, leaders of industry, organizers of the working poor, leaders and advocates of those who recently had joined the unemployed, teachers, school board members, farmers, bankers, owners of local stores. Often they were people who had never met each other and had never even been in the same room with one another, even though they lived in the same towns and cities. They had come together now out of their shared concern over the growth of poverty, the transformation of the labor market, and the rising numbers of those people who no longer could find work at all.

I was invited, in most cases, to address the problems of the public schools. Often, however, education issues became overshadowed by more pressing matters. For many poorly educated people, literacy problems proved of little urgency when they were threatened with the loss of work and loss of home. In a depressed industrial town in Pennsylvania, Lutheran church leaders spoke of the loss of several hundred jobs as truck and auto manufacture left the area and families saw their savings dwindle and their unemployment benefits and pensions disappear while rents rose, food prices climbed, and federal benefits declined.

"Yes, there are new jobs," a minister said. "There's a new McDonald's and a Burger King. You can take home $450 in a month from jobs like that. That might barely pay the rent. What do you do if somebody gets sick? What do you do for food and clothes? These may be good jobs for a teenager. Can you ask a thirty-year-old man who's worked for G.M. since he was eighteen to keep his wife and kids alive on jobs like that? There are jobs cleaning rooms in the hotel you're staying at. Can you expect a single mother with three kids to hold her life together with that kind of work? All you hear about these days are so-called service jobs—it makes me wonder where America is going. If we aren't producing anything of value, will we keep our nation going on hamburger stands? Who is all this 'service' for, if no one's got a real job making something of real worth?''

In Oklahoma, Arkansas and Texas I met heads of families who had been, only a year or two before, owners of farms, employees of petroleum firms, shopkeepers who supplied the farmers and the oil workers. They had lost their farms, their jobs, their stores. Bankers in Oklahoma City spoke about the rising number of foreclosures. ''Oil and agriculture—those are everything for people here. Both are dying. Where will these people go after their farms are boarded and their restaurants and barbershops and hardware stores have been shut down?''

The answers were seen in Phoenix and Los Angeles, where the shelters overflowed and people slept in huge encampments on the edges of the seamy areas of town. In one city homeless families lived in caves. I went out to visit. I had never seen a family living in a cave before.

In Portland, Oregon, the governor told me of some counties in which unemployment caused by the declining lumber industry had climbed above 30 percent. Where did the lumber workers go? I met some of them the same night in a homeless shelter by the Burnside Bridge. A pregnant woman and her husband spoke to me while waiting for the soup line to be formed. ''We had good work until last year. Since then we've had no home. Our kids were put in foster care.'' They had been sleeping on a plywood plank supported by the girders of the bridge. The traffic was two feet above their heads.

''The sound of the trucks puts me to sleep at night,'' she said. I learned that even makeshift housing space under the bridge was growing scarce.

In San Antonio I met a father with two boys who had been sleeping for four months next to the highway not far from the Hyatt Regency Hotel. He sold blood plasma twice a week to buy food for his kids. ''They draw my blood, put it in a centrifuge, take the white cells, and inject the red cells back into my arm.'' If he showed up four weeks straight he got a bonus. In a good month he made $100. ''The blood places,'' he told me, ''poor people call them 'stab labs.' They're all over.'' He showed me a card he carried listing stab labs, with phone numbers and addresses, in a dozen cities. He had been an auto worker in Detroit. When he lost his job his wife became depressed and since was hospitalized. He had developed crippling asthma—''from the panic and the tension, I believe.'' He had thought mistakenly that San Antonio might offer health and labor and cheap housing that were not available in Michigan.

In Miami I met a woman, thirty-five years old, from Boston. She had attended Girls' Latin, the same high school that my mother had attended. After graduation she had gone to college and had worked for many years until she was the victim of a throat disease that led to complications that wiped out her savings, forced her to lose her home, ended her marriage, and at last compelled her to give up her kids.

She'd moved to Miami hoping it would help her health but couldn't cope with illness, loss of family, loss of home—and now was sleeping on Miami Beach.

She had a tube in her stomach to bypass her damaged throat. At a shelter run by Catholic brothers she would pulverize the food, mix it with water, and inject the liquid mix into her tube.

In New York I spoke with Robert Hayes, counsel to the National Coalition for the Homeless. Hayes and his co-workers said that three fourths of the newly homeless in America are families with children.

In Washington, D.C., in late September 1986, I spent an afternoon with the director of a shelter, Sandy Brawders, one of those saints and martyrs of whom Robert Hayes has said, only half-jokingly, the homeless movement is primarily composed. ("There are the saints," he says, "and then there are the martyrs who have to put up with the saints.") Sandy told me that the homeless population was exploding in the District; the largest growth in numbers was among young children and their parents.

Four months later, the *Washington Post* reported that the number of homeless families in the District had increased 500 percent in just one year and that there were 12,000 people on a waiting list for public housing, with a waiting period of more than seven years.

Home in New England in a small town north of Boston, I shared some of these stories with a woman who works at the counter of a local grocery. "You didn't have to go to San Antonio and Florida," she said. "There's hundreds of homeless families just a couple miles from here." When I asked here where, she said: "In Ipswich, Gloucester, Haverhill . . . There are families who are living in the basement of my church." After a moment's pause she told me this: "After my husband lost his job—we had some troubles then, I was divorced . . . I had to bring my family to the church . . . Well, we're still there."

*How many are homeless in America?*

The U.S. Department of Health and Human Services (HHS), relying on groups that represent the homeless, suggested a figure of 2 million people in late 1983. Diminished numbers of low-income dwelling units and diminished welfare grants during the four years since may give credence to a current estimate, accepted by the Coalition for the Homeless, of 3 to 4 million people.

There is much debate about the numbers; the debate has a dreamlike quality for me because it parallels exactly the debates about the numbers of illiterate Americans. Government agencies again appear to contradict each other and attempt to peg the numbers low enough to justify inaction—or, in this case, negative action in the form of federal cuts.

Officials in the U.S. Department of Housing and Urban Development (HUD) puzzled congressional leaders during hearings held in 1984 by proposing a low estimate of 250,000 to 350,000 homeless people nationwide. The study from which

HUD's estimate was drawn had contemplated as many as 586,000 people, but this number was discredited in its report.

A House subcommittee revealed serious flaws in the HUD study. Subsequent investigations indicated HUD had "pressured its consultants to keep the estimates low." HUD's researchers, for example, suggested a "reliable" low estimate of 12,000 homeless persons in New York City on a given night in January 1984. Yet, on the night in question, over 16,000 people had been given shelter in New York; and this, of course, does not include the larger number in the streets who had received no shelter. U.S. Representative Henry Gonzalez termed HUD's study intentionally deceptive.

Estimates made by shelter operators in twenty-one selected cities in October 1986 total about 230,000 people. This sampling does not include Chicago, San Francisco, Houston, Cleveland, Philadelphia, Baltimore, Atlanta, Pittsburgh, St. Paul, San Diego, or Detroit. With estimates from these and other major cities added, the total would exceed 400,000.

Even this excludes the metropolitan areas around these cities and excludes those middle-sized cities—Lawrence, Lowell, Worcester, Brockton, Attleboro, for example, all in Massachusetts—in which the loss of industrial jobs has marginalized hundreds of thousands of the working poor. Though technically not unemployed, most of these families live in economic situations so precarious that they cannot meet the basic costs of life, particularly rent, which in all these cities has skyrocketed. Nor does this include the rural areas of the Midwest and the Plains states, the oil towns of the Southwest, the southern states from which assembly plants and textile industries have fled, lumber counties such as those in Oregon and their New England counterparts in northern Maine. The homeless in these areas alone, if added to the major-city totals, would bring a cautious national count above 1.5 million.

We would be wise, however, to avoid the numbers game. Any search for the "right number" carries the assumption that we may at last arrive at an acceptable number. There is no acceptable number. Whether the number is 1 million or 4 million or the administration's estimate of less than a million, there are too many homeless people in America.*

Homeless people are, of course, impossible to count because they are so difficult to find. That is intrinsic to their plight. They have no address beyond a shelter bed, room number, tent or cave . . . My own sense [is] that the number is between 2 and 3 million. If we include those people housing organizers call the "hidden homeless"—families doubled up illegally with other families, with the consequent danger that both families may be arbitrarily evicted—we are speaking of much larger numbers.

---

*One reason for discrepancies in estimates derives from various ways of counting. Homeless advocates believe that all who ask for shelter during any extended period of time ought to be termed homeless. The government asks: "How many seek shelter on a given day?" If the HUD study, cited above, had considered those who asked for shelter in the course of one full year, its upper estimate would have exceeded 1.7 million.

In 1983, 17,000 families were doubled up illegally in public housing in New York City. The number jumped to 35,000 by spring of 1986. Including private as well as public housing, the number had risen above 100,000 by November 1986. If we accept the New York City estimate of three to four family members in each low-income household, the total number of people (as opposed to families) doubled up in public and private housing in New York is now above 300,000.

The line from "doubling up" to homelessness is made explicit in a study by Manhattan's borough president: At least 50 percent of families entering New York City shelters (1986) were previously doubled up. Nationwide, more than 3 million families now are living doubled up.

It is, however, not only families doubled up or tripled up who are in danger of eviction. Any poor family paying rent or mortgage that exceeds one half of monthly income is in serious danger. Over 6 million American households pay half or more of income for their rent. Of these, 4.7 million pay 60 percent or more. Of mortgaged homeowners, 2 million pay half or more of income for their housing. Combining these households with those who are doubled up, it appears that well above 10 million families may be living near the edge of homelessness in the United States.

*Why are they without homes?*

Unreflective answers might retreat to explanations with which readers are familiar: "family breakdown," "drugs," "culture of poverty," "teen pregnancies," "the underclass," etc. While these are precipitating factors for some people, they are not the cause of homelessness. *The cause of homelessness is lack of housing.*

Half a million units of low-income housing are lost every year to condominium conversion, abandonment, arson, demolition. Between 1978 and 1980, median rents climbed 30 percent for those in the lowest income sector. Half these people paid nearly three quarters of their income for their housing. Forced to choose between housing and food, many of these families soon were driven to the streets. That was only a beginning. After 1980, rents rose at even faster rates. In Boston, between 1982 and 1984, over 80 percent of housing units renting below $300 disappeared, while the number of units renting above $600 more than doubled.

Hard numbers, in this instance, may be of more help than social theory in explaining why so many of our neighbors end up in the streets. By the end of 1983, vacancies averaged 1 to 2 percent in San Francisco, Boston and New York. Vacancies in *low-income* rental units averaged less than 1 percent in New York City by 1987. In Boston they averaged .5 percent. Landlords saw this seller's market as an invitation to raise rents. Evictions grew. In New York City, with a total of nearly 2 million rental units, there were half a million legal actions for eviction during 1983.* Half of these actions were against people on welfare, four fifths of whom were paying rents above the maximum allowed by welfare. Rent ceilings established by

*Half a million families, of course, were not evicted in one year. Many of these legal actions are "repeats." Others are unsuccessful. Still others are settled with payment of back rent.

welfare in New York were frozen for a decade at the levels set in 1975. They were increased by 25 percent in 1984; but rents meanwhile had nearly doubled.

During these years the White House cut virtually all federal funds to build or rehabilitate low-income housing. Federal support for low-income housing dropped from $28 billion to $9 billion between 1981 and 1986. "We're getting out of the housing business. Period," said a HUD deputy assistant secretary in 1985.

The consequences now are seen in every city of America.

*What distinguishes housing from other basic needs of life? Why, of many essentials, is it the first to go?*

Housing has some unique characteristics, as urban planning specialist Chester Hartman has observed. One pays for housing well in advance. The entire month's rent must be paid on the first day of any rental period. One pays for food only a few days before it is consumed, and one always has the option of delaying food expenditures until just prior to eating. Housing is a nondivisible and not easily adjustable expenditure. "One cannot pay less rent for the next few months by not using the living room," Hartman observes. By contrast, one can rapidly and drastically adjust one's food consumption: for example, by buying less expensive food, eating less, or skipping meals. "At least in the short run," Hartman notes, "the consequences of doing so are not severe." The cost of losing housing and then paying for re-entry to the housing system, on the other hand, is very high, involving utility and rent deposits equal sometimes to twice or three times the cost of one month's rent. For these reasons, one may make a seemingly "rational" decision to allocate scarce funds to food, clothing, health care, transportation, or the search for jobs—only to discover that one cannot pay the rent. "Some two and a half million people are displaced annually from their homes," writes Hartman. While some find other homes and others move in with their friends or relatives, the genesis of epidemic and increasing homelessness is there.

*Is this a temporary crisis?*

As families are compelled to choose between feeding their children or paying their rent, homelessness has taken on the characteristics of a captive state. Economic recovery has not relieved this crisis. Adults whose skills are obsolete have no role in a revived free market. "The new poor," according to the U.S. Conference of Mayors, "are not being recalled to their former jobs, because their former plants are not being reopened. . . . Their temporary layoffs are from dying industries."

Two million jobs in steel, textiles, and other industries, according to the AFL-CIO, have disappeared each year since 1979. Nearly half of all new jobs created from 1979 to 1985 pay poverty-level wages.

Increased prosperity among the affluent, meanwhile, raises the profit motive for conversion of low-income properties to upscale dwellings. The Conference of Mayors reported in January 1986 that central-city renewal has accelerated homelessness by dispossession of the poor. The illusion of recovery, therefore, has the ironic consequence of worsening the status of the homeless and near-homeless, while diluting explanations for their presence and removing explanations for their indigence.

But it is not enough to say that this is not a "temporary" crisis: Congressional research indicates that it is likely to grow worse. The House Committee on Government Operations noted in April 1985 that, due to the long advance-time needed for a federally assisted housing program to be terminated, the United States has yet to experience the full impact of federal cuts in housing aid. "The committee believes that current federal housing policies, combined with the continuing erosion of the private inventory of low-income housing, will add to the growth of homelessness. . . . " The "harshest consequences," the committee said, are "yet to come."

# Hunger in America: Findings and Conclusions

*Physician Task Force on Hunger in America*

## Major Findings and Conclusions

***Hunger is a problem of epidemic proportions across the nation.***

Hunger in America is a serious and widespread problem. It is in fact so widespread and obvious that its existence has been documented by fifteen national studies, and even more state-level studies, during the past few years.

While no one knows the precise number of hungry Americans, available evidence indicates that up to 20,000,000 citizens may be hungry at least some period of time each month. In the 1960s, before the expansion of federal nutrition programs, hunger was a daily problem for millions of citizens. Today, evidence indicates that weaknesses in these same programs leave millions of citizens hungry several days each month, and often more.

***Hunger in America is getting worse, not better.***

Evidence from the states and regions of the nation indicates that hunger continues to grow. Reported improvements in the economy appear to be having little, if any, impact on the problem of hunger.

Almost without exception, emergency food programs across the nation report significant increases in the number of hungry people. Accordingly, the pounds of food provided to alleviate this growing problem are, themselves, increasing at a steady rate. It appears that most Americans who are "recovering" economically were never hungry, and those who are hungry are not recovering.

***Malnutrition and ill-health are associated with hunger.***

Hunger and poverty are frequently associated with malnutrition and other forms of ill-health. Today, compelling evidence indicates that members of vulnerable population groups, particularly children and the elderly, are at increased risk of adverse health outcomes due to hunger.

Malnutrition is a problem which impacts somewhere in the vicinity of a half mil-

---



---

See Statistical Appendix Tables A–10, A–11, A–12, A–13, and A–14.

lion American children. Growth failure, low birth-weights, and other outcomes associated with inadequate nutrition are serious among low-income pediatric populations, and health problems and chronic diseases associated with undernutrition are serious among the elderly poor.

***Hunger is the result of federal government policies.***

Hunger in America is the result of a series of governmental policies, some within the past few years and others of longer duration.

Hunger does not just happen in a nation with more than enough food to feed itself and a good part of the world. Hunger occurs because policies either produce it or fail to prevent it. Today our leaders have permitted poverty in this nation to reach record levels and then cut back on programs which help our citizens endure economic hardship. As a result, America has become a "soup kitchen society," a spectre unmatched since the bread lines of the Great Depression.

***Present policies are not alleviating hunger in America.***

Hunger is getting worse, and no evidence indicates that it will lessen as a problem.

Poverty in the country is at the highest rate in twenty years, and purchasing power for the poorest forty percent of the population is lower than it was in 1980. It is unlikely that economic changes helping the better-off will assist those who are hungry.

The bottom line is that policies which supposedly were to help the poor have not done so.

We believe that our political leaders must end their laissez-faire attitude toward hunger. Millions of Americans are hungry now, and political leadership—Republican and Democratic—is required to address their plight. Even if things do improve in the future, our job is to make sure that all of our citizens have the opportunity to reap the rewards of democracy today.

# Eliminating Hunger in America

## *Physician Task Force on Hunger in America*

As a body of doctors and health care professionals, we believe it is time to end hunger in America.

It is our judgment that hunger and related ill-health have no place in a democratic society, especially one with the resources of the United States.

This nation has the resources and ability to end hunger. We have heard no one deny that this is true. America is not a poverty-stricken Third World nation caught between the pincers of a poor economy and inadequate food supply. To the contrary, we produce enough food to feed our people probably several times over. Our nation's warehouses bulge with food, so much food that each year thousands of tons are wasted or destroyed. Clearly lack of food is not the cause of hunger in America.

Neither do we lack the financial resources to end hunger in this land. Ours is perhaps the strongest economy in the world. We cannot maintain that we lack the resources to end hunger when numerous other industrialized nations have done so. That is illogical. In fact, by increasing annual federal food programs just by the amount we spend on two CVN Nuclear Attack Carriers, we could probably eliminate hunger in the nation. No, lack of money is not the cause of hunger in America.

Neither do we have hunger because we don't know how to end it. Through very recent experience, we are certain that we can end hunger if we wish to do so. Hunger and malnutrition were serious problems in this country in 1968. Then as today, national organizations, church groups, and universities investigated and found hunger. Government agencies, as today, found hunger. And as today, doctors went into regions of the country and reported that it was a widespread and serious problem.

The nation responded to that problem. In the decade between 1970 and 1980 we extended the food stamp program from the 2 million poor Americans which it covered at the time to some 20 million people. While this did not cover all Americans living in poverty, other nutrition programs provided assistance. We expanded the free school lunch and breakfast programs. We established elderly feeding programs (congregate meal sites and Meals-on-Wheels for shut-ins) to insure that our senior

---



---

See Statistical Appendix Table A–16.

citizens did not go hungry. And we established the Women, Infants, and Children (WIC) program to insure adequate nourishment for low-income pregnant women and their infants.

These programs were established in response to hunger among American people, and they worked. Teams of doctors in 1977 retraced the routes they had covered the previous decade when they found serious hunger and malnutrition. Summarizing their findings, the medical teams stated:[1]

> Our first and overwhelming impression is that there are far fewer grossly malnourished people in this country today than there were ten years ago . . . many poor people now have food and look better off. This does not appear to be due to an overall improvement in living standards. In fact, the facts of life for Americans living in poverty remain as dark or darker than they were ten years ago.
>
> But in the area of food there is a difference. The food stamp program, the nutritional component of Head Start, school lunch and breakfast programs, and to a lesser extent the Women, Infants, and Children (WIC) program have made the difference.

In a few years this nation basically eliminated hunger as a problem. The success was relatively swift and not difficult to see. So, clearly, we do not lack the experience or the knowhow to end hunger in America. We have enough food to end hunger in this land. We have enough wealth to end hunger. And we have recent experience upon which to rely. All that remains is the political will.

## Immediate Steps to End Hunger

Today we have a public health crisis which threatens a significant segment of our population. We must respond to it as we would any other problem of epidemic proportions.

We would not permit other health crises to become so widespread before acting. Yet hunger afflicts more of our citizens than do AIDS or Legionnaires Disease. In fact it constitutes one of the more serious problems imperiling the health and well-being of our people today.

But while hunger is a health epidemic, it cannot be ended by those in the medical profession. Like most public health problems it must be addressed in the political and public policy arena. In short, our political leaders must be responsible for ending hunger. The essence of political leadership is to lead—to respond to problems. That, in part, is why we have government. Today, we need leadership from our political leaders. It is time to end the contrived befuddlement of some who wring their hands wondering what to do about hunger.

---

[1]Nick Kotz, *Hunger in America: The Federal Response* (New York: The Field Foundation, 1979).

It is time to stop responding to hunger by cutting children's school lunches. It is time to show more compassion for hungry families than by reducing their food stamps even as they become poorer. And it is time to set aside compassionate platitudes and political rhetoric about how loving a people we are.

Let us feed the hungry of our nation.

***We call upon Republicans and Democrats in the United States Congress to take immediate action to feed the hungry.***

We ask that the leadership of the House and Senate, on a bipartisan basis, announce that it will prepare an emergency legislative package to respond to the hunger crisis. The components of the plan should include:

- *Strengthening the food stamp program*

*Increase food stamp benefits* to American families and individuals by a minimum of 25%, to the level of the USDA low-cost food plan.

*Remove restrictive food stamp measures* which eliminated the "new poor" and working poor from the program; families with gross incomes of up to 150% of poverty, but whose disposable income is below poverty, should be assisted.

*Alter asset restrictions* so families experiencing temporary economic hardship are not driven further into poverty as a condition for getting food stamps.

*Alter restrictive deductions* such as those for shelter, child care, and residency requirements in the food stamp program.

*Take immediate legislative action* (similar to that enacted recently for Social Security Disability Insurance) to terminate administrative policies which harass and otherwise prevent needy eligible citizens from receiving food stamp assistance.

- *Strengthening school and other meals programs for children*

*Restore eligibility* for free and reduced-price meals for children recently removed from the programs.

*Increase the federal subsidy* for free and reduced-price meals to enable more children from families living on the economic margins to participate in the program.

*Restore the child care, milk, and summer feeding programs* for children whose family incomes previously permitted them to participate.

- *Utilizing the WIC and Medicaid programs more fully to protect high-risk children*

*Expand the WIC* (Women, Infants, and Children Supplemental Feeding Program) to cover all currently eligible mothers who wish to participate.

*Extend Medicaid benefits* to all pregnant women and children under 18 living below the federal poverty level, to insure better health care and birth outcomes.

- *Expanding elderly meals programs to be certain that all low-income elderly have access to congregate meals or the Meals-on-Wheels program*
- *Protecting families by strengthening income support programs*

*Expand unemployment benefits* for unemployed families left without work so that the two-thirds of the unemployed now with no benefits are covered by the program.

*Expand AFDC assistance* by federal legislation to bring children above the poverty level; this should include coverage for the unborn child to insure adequate nutrition, and should include mandatory coverage in all states for fathers in the home so that federal and state policy no longer forces families to break apart to become eligible for help.

***Congress should pass legislation to create a permanent and independent body to monitor the nutritional status of the population.***

Our nation should have on-going access to current data on the nutritional status of its people, particulary high-risk populations such as children, pregnant women, and the elderly. This proposal was made by the 1969 White House Conference on Food, Nutrition, and Health convened by President Nixon. It should be established without further delay.

***We ask that appropriate Congressional committees direct responsible administrative agencies to report on a quarterly basis progress made in eliminating hunger, until such time as it has been ended in America.***

We believe that, based on past experience and the fact that we have the programmatic vehicles still in place, our nation can eliminate hunger within six months. Such a time frame, however, will require continuing oversight by appropriate Congressional committees to be certain that administrative departments and agencies are carrying out the will of the Congress.

## Longer-Term Steps to Prevent the Return of Hunger

If the Congress agrees to undertake the above plan of action, it will end the present hunger crisis. But the proposed plan alone may be insufficient to end poverty in America.

The fact that hunger, once nearly ended in the nation, returned as such a serious problem clearly points to the need to undertake more serious and far-reaching policies to eliminate the poverty which underlies hunger. We would do well to address this more fundamental problem.

***We ask the United States Congress to establish a Bipartisan Study Commission to recommend legislative changes to protect all our citizens from the ravages of poverty and its attendant ills in the future.***

As a body of physicians and other health professionals, we believe it is unwise to permit hunger and malnutrition to exist in this nation. We believe not only that these problems must be eradicated, but that our country can and should address the underlying poverty which victimizes so many of our citizens.

We would not tell sick patients that they might improve without medical treatment if we have the means to treat them and limit their present pain and discomfort. Neither should our political leaders hope that hungry Americans will one day be less hungry when our nation now has the means to respond to their suffering and its underlying cause.

# Chapter 4
# RACE

## Black America, 1987: An Overview

*John E. Jacob*

Black Americans, like their fellow-citizens, closed 1987 beset by economic uncertainties that were not dispelled by the superficial glow of an arms control treaty or the hoopla of a presidential election campaign moving into high gear.

When the stock market crashed in October, it raised the specter of economic turmoil and greater fiscal austerity, along with growing fears of worldwide economic depression and accelerated racially-based disadvantage.

In the wake of the market's crash, it became popular to say that the long bull market prosperity and economic recovery era of the 1980s was ended—"the party's over."

But when parties end, bills become due. And the nation's "party" of deficit-driven prosperity will have to be paid for. The big question is: who will pay?

The pundits foresee an extended period of belt-tightening, spending cuts, and "sacrifices" to pay for the binge of the 1980s. Such statements are usually accompanied by token promises to screen the poor from the effects of the necessary fiscal adjustments.

But we heard that before—when President Reagan came to office with his plans for a party of tax cuts and increased military spending while preserving the safety net for the "truly needy."

We all know what happened: the party roared on, but the safety net for the poor was shredded. So assurances that the poor will be protected carry little weight today. The poor were shut out of the party, and now that the bills are due, those who had the most fun should pick up the check.

The poor and moderate-income families were the most obvious victims of recent policies. The numbers of the poor increased by four million in the 1980s. The real income of the lowest fifth of the population, adjusted for inflation, *declined* between 1979 and 1986 by $663 per family. Meanwhile, the top fifth of the population *gained* $12,218 in real income during those years.

---

John E. Jacob, "Black America, 1987: An Overview," *The State of Black America 1988* (New York: National Urban League, 1988), pp. 1–6. 

---

See Statistical Appendix Tables A–5, A–9, A–11, A–12, A–17, A–19, A–21, A–23, and A–24.

Black people, too, were not at the party. The 1980s were a time of increasing black hardship, with inner-city communities decimated by crack and crime, and national policies of withdrawal from efforts to increase opportunities for blacks.

Programs that benefited the black poor the most were cut the most. Between 1981 and 1987 the federal government slashed subsidized housing programs by 79 percent, training and employment programs by 70 percent, the Work Incentive Program by 71 percent, compensatory education programs for poor children by 12 percent, and community development block grants and community services block grants by well over a third.

Black youth weren't at the party either. Even as their high school graduation rates increased, black college attendance rates plummeted throughout the 1980s, helped in part by a shift in federal college aid programs from direct assistance to loans.

Black youth unemployment remained high, and the economic deterioration experienced by young black males is directly responsible for the tragic weakening of the black family. As the Children's Defense Fund pointed out in a 1987 study, the majority of young black males in 1973 earned enough to keep a three-person family out of poverty. Now, less than half do. Young men aged 20 to 24 who earn enough to stay above the poverty line marry at rates three to four times higher than young men with below-poverty line earnings. Constricted opportunities for young men have cut their marriage rates in half over the past 15 years and have led to the alarming rise in single female-headed households.

Many of the elderly weren't at the party, either, but some want them to pay the tab through a Social Security cost-of-living-adjustment (COLA) freeze. But over 20 percent of the elderly live on incomes below 125 percent of the poverty line—a higher percentage than all Americans do—and the majority of the elderly rely on Social Security for over 70 percent of their incomes. Restricting COLA payments would mean increased hardship for the non-affluent elderly and for most black older citizens.

Children weren't at the party, but the coming austerity targets include domestic programs such as education, training, nutrition and other essential social services that benefit youth.

A fifth of all children grow up poor and a majority of black children are in poverty. The Reagan administration's spending binge did not include efforts to draw those youngsters into the mainstream, to help their families, or to create opportunities for them.

The unemployed and the homeless weren't at the party, either. Black unemployment has improved slowly to the point where it now stands at recession-levels of about 12 percent. But counting discouraged workers, and part-timers who want full-time work, the true black unemployment rate hovers around the 20-percent mark—after five years of economic recovery.

In fact, the Reagan boom was a false prosperity era, a period in which gains were concentrated on a relatively small portion of the population while large segments of the citizenry saw a real deterioration in their living standards. It was a period marked by growing homelessness, and the homeless population included a far higher portion of families and children than ever before.

The major task for 1988 will be to reverse that ugly trend, and to assure that those who were brutally excluded from the prosperity party of the 1980s will not be forced to pay its bills.

Whether sound economic policy dictates higher taxes or lower spending or both, the nation must make investments in its people necessry to create the infrastructure of human capital without which future prosperity will be impossible.

Education is one such investment. The demographics suggest that a third of America's work force will be minority, but most will come from poverty backgrounds. They have high dropout rates and few of the skills needed in a high-tech society. It is in the national interest to invest in educating at-risk children, as numerous studies and private sector groups have urged. In 1987, the prestigious business group, the Committee for Economic Development, published a report "Children in Need" that documented the urgency of such investments.

With less than one of five eligible children in Head Start and less than half of the eligible children in compensatory education programs, and with nutrition, medical, and other programs reaching too few of the children in poverty, it is essential that such programs be funded at levels sufficient to reach all eligible children and families.

The emerging consensus on a welfare reform program that encourages work, education, and training should be implemented through legislation that retains strict federal controls, establishes inflation-adjusted benefit levels above the poverty line, provides universal coverage of all the poor, and assures child care, transportation, counseling, and other services that enable people to get training and to work.

The refusal to invest in the nation's physical infrastructure also acts as a brake on future growth while constricting job opportunities. Long-overdue investments in affordable housing, roads, and bridges must be made. In the process, jobs can be created and skills learned.

Such investments lay the groundwork for future prosperity that is shared by all, generate tax revenues, and actually save federal resources. A dollar invested in immunization or in nutrition programs pays for itself many times over through lower medical costs. Similarly, a dollar spent on education or on training is repaid with rich dividends through future tax payments and reduced social welfare benefit costs. Even in times of fiscal austerity, we have to take a long view of social investments that increase society's fairness and enable it to become more competitive and productive.

And as America totters near the brink of recession, we must understand that the thin line separating us from economic hardship is the purchasing power of masses of people who spend their paychecks, their Social Security checks, and their transfer payments on goods and services that keep the economy afloat. An austerity that punishes those who were excluded from the party will result in a decline in consumer spending and a fast slide into recession, while raising taxes for the affluent will merely impinge on sales of luxury items.

The view that social programs are actually investments in human capabilities that pay off in the future is confirmed by the rise of the black middle class. A series of articles in *The Washington Post* in late November highlighted blacks' entrance into the mainstream, but a less-noted follow-up article by the author of the series made a point neglected in the articles themselves: that in an extraordinary number of instances, the members of that emerging middle class were enabled to escape from poverty through the intervention of federal social programs—whether Title One compensatory education, a federal training program, or a minority contractor program.

The writer, Joel Garreau, identifies himself as "a true believer in the forces of the market place," but he also realizes the value of some Great Society programs: "Despite the views of those who would rewrite history for ideological reasons, not all that money went down the drain."

Indeed, those programs proved far more efficient and cost-effective than the Pentagon expenditures and federal subsidy programs to the affluent. They unleashed the energies of people who were enabled by government's helping hand to contribute to our society. Their success proves that fairness and compassion must be an integral part of the nation's policies as we move into the difficult period ahead.

The focus in 1988 will be on government's role because our fate will be decided by national economic policies and because it is a presidential election year.

But that does not mean private sector responsibilities should be ignored. In fact, the private sector which had most of the fun at the Reagan-era party, failed to pay its entrance fee in full. The president slashed social welfare programs partly on the premise that voluntarism and the private sector would fill the gaps left by government. In fact, despite increased voluntarism and a higher level of interest by corporate America, those gaps were not filled. And in recent years the wave of mergers and a new spirit of austerity among many companies threaten to leave widening gaps.

In 1988, the private sector needs to reassess its role in helping to solve national problems, and I am hopeful that reassessment will lead to expanded participation in the solutions to those problems. The most enlightened companies understand that their future work force needs and their need for social stability will be threatened unless new opportunities can be created, and unless people have opportunities to escape from the bitterness of deep poverty.

Within the black community, 1987 was a year of expanded efforts to do what can be done to overcome our disadvantages. Prime among these efforts was the Urban League's Education Initiative.

After a year of planning, community mobilization, and coalition-building, most Urban League affiliates are moving their local education initiatives into the operational phase, with several already making significant contributions to black student achievement. In Harrisburg, Pennsylvania, for example, students participating in the League's academic support program have raised their scholastic aptitude test scores in math, science, and language skills by 70 to 100 points.

Other national and local black community-based organizations are also deeply involved in programs to make our schools work for our kids. The black community is making a long-term commitment to do what is necessary to ensure that our children's educational achievement levels equal and *exceed* those of others.

Black underachievement is intolerable and unacceptable. Ending that underachievement requires systemic changes the help our kids to fulfill their potential.

Too often, discussions of urban school problems center on the kids, with claims that their home environment, their supposed cultural failings, and similar stereotypical excuses are to blame for the schools' failure to educate students.

But minority youngsters aren't the problem—the problem is the inferior education they're getting.

We can no longer allow our kids to be processed for failure—we have to start training them for success, and an active, concerned black community can make it happen.

In 1988, the black community will also have to direct its energies to assuring that its needs are addressed by the presidential candidates and their parties. We must recognize that blacks come to the political table, not as supplicants, but as sharers of power. Today, minority political clout has to be widened, for the presidential election of 1988 will be a major turning point.

There can be no more urgent task in the coming months than to register as many black voters as possible. Every black community organization must do its part in national voter registration efforts. We need black and minority citizens in both parties and in *every* candidate's camp. We've seen what happens when blacks are frozen out and we can't let that happen again. Exercising black voting power can influence policies that bring opportunities to poor people.

A 1987 Census Bureau report found that for the first time in history, young blacks registered and voted at rates higher than those for young whites.

This trend to increased political participation is especially important for black people—who don't have economic power. The black population has a far higher percentage of young adults than the general population. Using that potential political clout can pay off in more responsive government policies that help the poor and open doors of opportunity.

For both parties, the road to the White House leads through Houston's Third Ward, through Watts, through Harlem, through Chicago's South Side. The major parties are in peril if they ignore that fact.

They certainly should have understood that it was the power of the black vote that defeated Judge Robert Bork's Supreme Court nomination.

The White House thought it could win a Senate showdown by keeping the Republican minority in line and adding enough southern Democrats to put Judge Bork on the Supreme Court. But when those southern senators looked at his record, they found enough to make them leery of routinely backing the president's candidate. The decisive factor, however, was their reliance on black votes. That hard political reality determined the outcome of the Bork nomination.

Exercising our constitutional right to vote is the surest means of preserving black rights. And it is the appropriate means of paying tribute to the generations of blacks who sacrificed to secure those rights despite blatant oppression.

We were reminded of that in 1987 by Supreme Court Justice Thurgood Marshall, who brought badly needed perspective to the mindless hype surrounding the celebrations of the 200th anniversary of the framing of the Constitution.

Justice Marshall eloquently pointed out that the famous first three words of the Constitution, "We The People," did not include women, who were denied the right to vote, or blacks, who were enslaved. They also excluded poor whites, who could not meet the property test qualifications for voting. He also pointed out that the document itself was seriously flawed—caught in the contradiction between guaranteeing liberty and justice to all and denying both to blacks. It took a century of struggle before slavery was ended and before the Constitution was amended to guarantee rights to all and to assure the equal protection of the laws.

Justice Marshall's message needed to be said—and it needed to be said now, when the Attorney General and a group of newly-appointed federal judges seem to think that constitutional issues can best be resolved by going back to determine the intent of the framers.

By calling the nation's attention to the fact that intent of the framers included preserving slavery for blacks and second-class status for women, Justice Marshall helped us see that the "original intent" school of argument is not to be taken seriously.

The Founders created a flawed structure, a structure that became democratic through the pain of civil war and reconstuction, and in the fitful, periodic drives to reform and renew our society.

We may be nearing another one of those cycles of renewal, a period in which Americans will once again recover the spirit that fights the racism and poverty that stain our democracy.

In 1988, we must work to lay the foundations for a Great Awakening that brings our society to a higher stage of fulfillment of the potential of all our people.

# Chicano Votes Don't Count: Patron Politics in McAllen, Texas

*David C. Kibbe and Kenneth Bain*

Last spring, when Henry Cisneros surprised Texas and the nation by easily and peacefully winning the mayoral election in San Antonio, thus becoming the only Mexican-American leader of a major U.S. city, things were quite different 250 miles to the south in the city of McAllen. There, the victor in the race for mayor was a representative of the Anglo establishment, incumbent Othal Brand. The election was marked by charges of racism, police brutality and labor-baiting, and by allegations that "outside influences" were trying to take over the government, and it left deep scars in the body politic of this normally tranquil border community of 65,000 inhabitants. The election may have set the tone for future area clashes between Anglo and Mexican-American voters, and the tactics employed by the winner underscore the need for the renewal of the Voting Rights Act of 1965.

The campaign was a no-holds-barred contest between McAllen's Anglo elite and a populist coalition of the city's Mexican-American professionals, small-business men and poverty-stricken farm laborers. The leading figure in the political drama was 61-year-old Mayor Brand, a Baptist conservative who likes to refer to himself as the "Onion King of the World." Brand came to the isolated but fertile Rio Grande Valley from Georgia forty years ago, when McAllen's population was one-fifth what it is today. He has since become a multimillionaire on the profits from his forty-five vegetable growing, packing and shipping operations throughout the Valley, Mexico, Canada and Europe. A high school dropout with a keen eye for business and political opportunity, Brand's aggressive style matches his large stature (he once punched a fellow school board member in the face during a meeting). An avowed union-hater who has said he would give up his lucrative vegetable business and go into ranching rather than sign a contract with a farm workers' union, Brand has been known to wave his pistol in the faces of striking laborers in his fields. He counts among his friends Texas Governor Bill Clements, Dallas computer magnate H. Ross Perot and conservative radio and TV commentator Paul Harvey.

Brand's major opponent was Dr. Ramiro Casso, a 58-year-old general practitioner whose popularity stems from thirty years of service to Mexican-Americans in some of McAllen's poorest neighborhoods. Fifteen years ago, Casso established a clinic to provide free medical care to migrant farm workers. He has been a member

---

of the school board, the board of trustees of McAllen's hospital and the board of directors of one of the area's largest banks. A soft-spoken man with a wry sense of humor, Casso holds a mechanical engineering degree from Texas A&M University, a master's degree in chemistry from Baylor and a medical degree from the University of Texas Southwestern Medical School in Dallas.

A longtime opponent of Brand's, Casso decided to challenge him for mayor several months after successfully organizing a campaign to block him and the City Commission from selling McAllen's municipal hospital to the Hospital Corporation of America (H.C.A.), a private, for-profit chain of hospitals. . . . According to Casso, "Mr. Brand tried to make a deal which would have shut the hospital doors to our city's poor, without even notifying the citizens of the plan. Apparently he hadn't bothered to look at the city charter." Casso and his supporters forced a referendum, which narrowly decided the issue against selling the hospital to H.C.A. A subsequent referendum almost unanimously approved the sale of the hospital to Methodist Hospitals of Dallas, known for its commitment to community interests.

Another person whose opposition to the mayor's administration was important in the campaign was James C. Harrington, the American Civil Liberties Union lawyer who had filed seven police brutality suits against the city and individual police officers dating back to 1976. Because many of the incidents of police mistreatment of prisoners occurred during Brand's first term, the coalition backing Casso hoped to make a political issue of the Mayor's apparent unwillingness to discipline the officers involved. But the rumors of beatings did not excite the electorate—that is, not until videotapes were released that showed policemen routinely punching, kicking and verbally abusing Mexican-American prisoners, all of them handcuffed and most of them intoxicated. The videotapes were made by a camera located directly behind the booking desk. The camera had been placed there with the intent of protecting policemen from false charges of mistreatment; instead, it recorded the midnight rampages of officers, who called themselves the "C-shift animals," slamming heads on the booking desk and dragging prisoners to their cells by their hair.

In an ironic twist, Brand and the McAllen City Attorney were responsible for the release of the videotapes to the press just weeks before the election. In an attempt to defuse the police brutality issue, the city agreed to an out-of-court settlement in a class-action suit brought by Harrington on behalf of fifteen victims of the beatings. The agreement was overseen by Federal District Judge James De Anda in Brownsville, Texas, and included payment of $250,000 by the city to the claimants as well as the city's promise to make structural reforms within the Police Department, among them a citizen review board and additional training for police officers.

When the city immediately reneged on that part of the agreement dealing with structural reforms, Harrington filed a new suit on behalf of another beaten citizen; this time, the parties went to trial. Judge De Anda ruled that the videotapes could become public evidence (the city had tried to persuade the judge to view them privately in his chambers), and shock waves spread throughout the Valley and the country when the sadistic treatment of prisoners at the hands of the McAllen police was aired on CBS national news.

Testimony during the trial implicated Brand, who has been mayor since 1977, in a scheme to destroy the tapes in defiance of a protective court order in effect since 1976. It is a charge that Brand vehemently denies, saying that he took steps to halt the abuse as soon as he learned of it in 1978. Brand claims that his order to erase tapes referred only to those that, for reasons that are still not known, were made of his telephone conversations with members of the Police Department. The Mayor has been hard pressed to explain, however, why he did not know of the incidents of brutality earlier, and why, if he had "thoroughly looked into the matter," as he claims to have done in 1978, the beatings continued until at least 1979.

Enraged by the city's obvious abuse of power, Casso made Brand's style of leadership and his mishandling of the brutality cases a major issue in his appeal to the voters. Urging them to "throw off the iron fist" of the Brand administration, Casso charged that the mayor ruled the city like an "ayatollah." In any previous campaign, direct attacks by a Hispanic on an incumbent mayor would have been unthinkable, if not suicidal, but Casso was able to count on the support of some 4,300 newly registered voters, the product of one of the strongest voter registration drives ever made in Texas. The drive signed up 14,000 Hispanic voters in Hidalgo County in the winter of 1980–81 under the leadership and financial backing of the Southwest Voter Registration and Education Project (S.V.R.E.P.) in San Antonio. According to Willie Velasquez, the project's executive director, the drive brought the total number of Hispanic voters to a thin majority in McAllen, an estimated 15,600 of the city's 27,917 registered voters.

Brand, for his part, countered with allegations of "widespread voter fraud" involving the Casso campaign. Just before the election, Brand announced that he was asking Governor Clements to send officials from the Secretary of State's office to monitor the election in order to prevent the "fraud" from going any further, that is, to stop any illegally registered voters from participating. Finally, he announced plans to have the ballots impounded.

Brand was actually attempting to frighten Mexican-American voters away from the polls. Although they are a large numerical majority in McAllen and throughout the Valley, political participation has come slowly for the region's Mexican-Americans, many of whom do not speak English. In Hidalgo County, close to half the residents earn less than $6,000 a year, below the Federal poverty line, and fully 80 percent of them are Mexican-American. While the Anglo rich and the emerging Mexican-American middle class live in exclusive neighborhoods on the north and east sides of McAllen, the poor, mostly unskilled migrant agricultural workers subject to high seasonal unemployment, live in barrios south of the railroad tracks and in *colonias,* makeshift settlements where many of the streets are unpaved and sanitary facilities consist of outdoor privies. Under such conditions, many eligible Mexican-American voters do not feel that they have much at stake in the political process. With rumors circulating in the barrios that Brand had brought in state officials to watch how they would vote, these people, naturally suspicious of the authorities, stayed away from the polls.

Yet, on April 4, in the first round of the election, Casso led the field by 869 votes.

Brand was second. Mike Frost, a businessman, garnered only 2,071 of the 12,788 votes cast, but that was enough to force a runoff. Less than four hours after the polling stations closed, Frost appeared arm-in-arm with Brand on the local evening news to offer his warm support and that of his backers.

After the election, in preparation for testimony on the Voting Rights Act before the House Judiciary Committee, S.V.R.E.P. conducted a study of the election-fraud allegations raised by Brand. The study concluded, as did the Texas Secretary of State's office, that no fraud had been committed. There were 629 double-registered citizens of *all* ethnic backgrounds who had been purged from the voter lists by Hidalgo County voter registrar Frank Champion—only 2.5 percent of the total number of persons registered, a figure that compared favorably to other areas of Texas (in Bexar County, for example, the last purge removed 4.85 percent of the registered voters for duplicate registration, change of address and death). As S.V.R.E.P.'s Velasquez summed up:

> The vast weight of data leads us to the inevitable conclusion that Mayor Brand's allegations are a shameful attempt to appeal to the worst elements in Texas politics. The allegations and hysteria raised by Othal Brand are clearly designed to intimidate Mexican-American voters from participating in the electoral process. For that reason, we have asked the Department of Justice to send Federal observers to McAllen to insure the integrity of the vote in the May 9, 1981, run-off election.

The Federal monitors never came. The only voting irregularities that occurred were committed by the city officials running the election. Judges and clerks in some precincts consistently displayed prejudice against Hispanic voters. Brand was allowed to enter the polling stations, where he engaged in electioneering and antagonized Casso's poll watchers. During the two-week period allowed for absentee voting prior to the runoff, more than fifty sworn affidavits were signed by Hispanic voters, most of them elderly, who either had been turned away from the polls with no effort made to search the voting lists for their names or had been discouraged from voting by judges unnecessarily demanding identification papers and belittling them for not speaking English. It was discovered that people entering and leaving the absentee voting station were being videotaped by Brand's campaign workers with a camera hidden in a house across the street—a revelation that the latter may have encouraged. Brand justified the action as a ''necessary precaution'' to prevent illegal voting, but it was clearly another example of his high-handed tactics of intimidation.

Brand spent $133,000 during the first campaign to win a post that pays $50 a year, and he was to spend another $69,000 to insure his victory in the runoff. The ''Stop Casso'' campaign moved into high gear in the weeks before the second election, as rhetoric escalated on both sides and a concerted effort was begun to label Casso as bent on a ''Mexican takeover'' of McAllen's government. It was rumored that Casso, if elected, would fire all Anglos on the city staff (twenty-one of whom had quit their jobs during Brand's term). Some of the stories that spread throughout the north-side coffee shops and beauty salons were so absurd as to be humorous, to say nothing of the catch phrase, "Remember: Fidel Castro was a doctor, too!"

In order to stir up fears in the Anglo community, Brand accused Casso of being a racist. It wasn't easy. Casso and his running mates for the City Commission, educator George Gonzalez and engineer Richard Salinas, had run advertisements before the first election requesting that both sides in the contest refrain from using ethnic references. Casso never gave the ethnic issue any importance in his speeches or advertisements. At one point, he privately commented, "What's all this talk about racial differences? I was under the impression we were both Caucasians." He did, however, call Brand "cruel and inhumane" in spots played over Spanish-speaking radio stations. This gave Brand the opportunity he had been seeking. After mistranslating the word *bárbaro,* which as an adjective means cruel or savage, a local TV announcer said that Casso had called Brand "a barbarian." During a follow-up interview, Brand off-handedly remarked that his opponent's comment was "a typical racist slur from a racist campaign," evidence of the attempts by Casso's supporters to divide the city. From that point on, Brand's standard rejoinder to any criticism was to accuse its maker of racism.

Meanwhile, in newspaper advertisements and a massive letter-writing campaign, the Brand team pulled out its trump card: the accusation that Casso was a front man for the United Farm Workers. Valley Texans ought to have known better than to believe it. The United Farm Workers in Texas is a union in name only. It has yet to sign a contract with a single grower, and its primary goals have been to provide much-needed legal and social services to its small membership. In fact, labor organization is almost nonexistent in the Valley. Of the light industries that have recently moved into the area and expanded the region's economy from its agricultural base, none are unionized. But the mere threat of a union incursion was enough to frighten many Anglos, whose only associations with organized labor hark back to the socialism of the 1930s.

Self-proclaimed champion of the moral minority's right to maintain the status quo against a racist hoard of Mexican-American unionists, Brand limped to victory with a narrow margin of 882 votes. Casso actually led by a similar margin until the 4,901 absentee votes were counted, many of them cast by "winter Texans," who live in trailer parks in the Valley during the winter months and return to their homes in Michigan, Wisconsin and other northern states in the spring. Their participation added the final irony to the Mayor's charges of "outsider" influence in the election.

A Federal grand jury is investigating charges of civil rights violations by the city in connection with the police beatings, and the famous videotapes are being reviewed in Washington by the Justice Department. The question posed by the irregularities is, Why did the department refuse to send marshals to monitor the election? As an editorial in *The Wall Street Journal* pointed out, here was an election that raised issues concerning the protection of minority groups' voting rights, yet, on the eve of the McAllen runoff, Justice Department officials were in Mobile, Alabama, attempting to reopen a case there. We agree with *The Journal* that debate about the renewal of the Voting Rights Act of 1965 must focus on protecting against abuses at the voting booth. McAllen would have been the perfect place for the Justice Department to renew enforcement of the original intentions of the act. In the absence of such an effort, George Powell of Texas Rural Legal Aid has filed a class-action suit, on behalf of McAllen's Mexican-Americans, against Brand and the city, accusing them of having violated the Voting Rights Act and the Constitution during the elections.

As for Mayor Brand, he and the *patrón* system he epitomizes may be on their way out. The Mayor faces a divided city and an aroused Mexican-American populace that will forge a stronger political organization in the years ahead. A bid by Brand's own *patrón,* Governor Clements, to give him statewide political recognition was recently quashed. Despite—or was it because of?—the police-brutality scandal in McAllen, Clements nominated Brand to the State Board of Corrections. The Texas Senate rejected the nomination in deference to the Senator representing McAllen, Hector Uribe.

# The Triumphs of Asian Americans

*David A. Bell*

It is the year 2019. In the heart of downtown Los Angeles, massive electronic billboards feature a model in a kimono hawking products labeled in Japanese. In the streets below, figures clad in traditional East Asian peasant garb hurry by, speaking to each other in an English made unrecognizable by the addition of hundreds of Spanish and Asian words. A rough-mannered policeman leaves an incongruously graceful calling card on a doorstep: a delicate orgami paper sculpture.

This is, of course, a scene from a science-fiction movie, Ridley Scott's 1982 *Blade Runner.* It is also a vision that Asian-Americans dislike intensely. Hysterical warnings of an imminent Asian "takeover" of the United States stained a whole century of their 140-year history in this country, providing the backdrop for racial violence, legal segregation, and the internment of 110,000 Japanese-Americans in concentration camps during World War II. Today integration into American society, not transformation of American society, is the goal of an overwhelming majority. So why did the critics praise *Blade Runner* for its "realism"? The answer is easy to see.

## A Population Explosion

The Asian-American population is exploding. According to the Census Bureau, it grew an astounding 125 percent between 1970 and 1980, and now stands at 4.1 million, or 1.8 percent of all Americans. Most of the increase is the result of immigration, which accounted for 1.8 million people between 1973 and 1983, the last year for which the Immigration and Naturalization Service has accurate figures (710,000 of these arrived as refugees from Southeast Asia). And the wave shows little sign of subsiding. Ever since the Immigration Act of 1965 permitted large-scale immigration by Asians, they have made up over 40 percent of all newcomers to the United States. Indeed, the arbitrary quota of 20,000 immigrants per country per year established by the act has produced huge backlogs of future Asian-Americans in several countries, including 120,000 in South Korea and 336,000 in the Philippines, some of whom, according to the State Department, have been waiting for their visas since 1970.

The numbers are astonishing. But even more astonishing is the extent to which Asian-Americans have become prominent out of all proportion to their share of the

---

population. It now seems likely that their influx will have as important an effect on American society as the migrations from Europe of 100 years ago. Most remarkable of all, it is taking place with relatively little trouble.

The new immigration from Asia is a radical development in several ways. First, it has not simply enlarged an existing Asian-American community, but created an entirely new one. Before 1965, and the passage of the Immigration Act, the term "Oriental-American" (which was then the vogue) generally denoted people living on the West Coast, in Hawaii, or in the Chinatowns of a few large cities. Generally they traced their ancestry either to one small part of China, the Toishan district of Kwantung province, or to a small number of communities in Japan (one of the largest of which, ironically, was Hiroshima). Today more than a third of all Asian-Americans live outside Chinatowns in the East, South, and Midwest, and their origins are as diverse as those of "European-Americans." The term "Asian-American" now refers to over 900,000 Chinese from all parts of China and also Vietnam, 800,000 Filipinos, 700,000 Japanese 500,000 Koreans, 400,000 East Indians, and a huge assortment of everything else from Moslem Cambodians to Catholic Hawaiians. It can mean an illiterate Hmong tribesman or a fully assimilated graduate of the Harvard Business School.

Asian-Americans have also attracted attention by their new prominence in several professions and trades. In New York City, for example, where the Asian-American population jumped from 94,500 in 1970 to 231,500 in 1980, Korean-Americans run an estimated 900 of the city's 1,600 corner grocery stores. Filipino doctors—who outnumber black doctors—have become general practitioners in thousands of rural communities that previously lacked physicians. East Indian-Americans own 800 of California's 6,000 motels. And in parts of Texas, Vietnamese-Americans now control 85 percent of the shrimp-fishing industry, though they only reached this position after considerable strife (now the subject of a film, *Alamo Bay*).

Individual Asian-Americans have become quite prominent as well. I. M. Pei and Minoru Yamasaki have helped transform American architecture. Seiji Ozawa and Yo Yo Ma are giant figures in American music. An Wang created one of the nation's largest computer firms, and Rocky Aoki founded one of its largest restaurant chains (Benihana). Samuel C. C. Ting won a Nobel prize in physics.

## College Enrollments

Most spectacular of all, and most significant for the future, is the entry of Asian-Americans into the universities. At Harvard, for example, Asian-Americans ten years ago made up barely three percent of the freshman class. The figure is now ten percent—five times their share of the population. At Brown, Asian-American applications more than tripled over the same period, and at Berkeley they increased from 3,408 in 1982 to 4,235 only three years later. The Berkeley student body is now 22 percent Asian-American, UCLA's is 21 percent, and MIT's 19 percent. The Julliard School of Music in New York is currently 30 percent Asian-American.

American medical schools had only 571 Asian-American students in 1970, but in 1980 they had 1,924, and last year 3,763, of 5.6 percent of total enrollment. What is more, nearly all of these figures are certain to increase. In the current, largely foreign-born Asian-American community, 32.9 percent of people over 25 graduated from college (as opposed to 16.2 percent in the general population). For third-generation Japanese-Americans, the figure is 88 percent.

By any measure these Asian-American students are outstanding. In California only the top 12.5 percent of high school students qualify for admission to the uppermost tier of the state university system, but 39 percent of Asian-American high school students do. On the SATs, Asian-Americans score an average of 519 in math, surpassing whites, the next highest group, by 32 points. Among Japanese-Americans, the most heavily native-born Asian-American group, 68 percent of those taking the math SAT scored above 600—high enough to qualify for admission to almost any university in the country. The Westinghouse Science Talent search, which each year identifies forty top high school science students, picked twelve Asian-Americans in 1983, nine last year, and seven this year. And at Harvard the Phi Beta Kappa chapter last April named as its elite "Junior Twelve" students five Asian-Americans and seven Jews.

Faced with these statistics, the understandable reflex of many non-Asian-Americans is adulation. President Reagan has called Asian-Americans "our exemplars of hope and inspiration." *Parade* magazine recently featured an article on Asian-Americans titled "The Promise of America," and *Time* and *Newsweek* stories have boasted headlines like "A Formula for Success," "The Drive to Excel," and "A 'Model Minority.'" However, not all of these stories come to grips with the fact that Asian-Americans, like all immigrants, have to deal with a great many problems of adjustment, ranging from the absurd to the deadly serious.

Who would think, for example, that there is a connection between Asian-American immigration and the decimation of California's black bear population? But Los Angeles, whose Korean population grew by 100,000 in the past decade, now has more than 300 licensed herbal-acupuncture shops. And a key ingredient in traditional Korean herbal medicine is *ungdam,* bear gallbladder. The result is widespread illegal hunting and what *Audubon* magazine soberly calls "a booming trade in bear parts."

As Mark R. Thompson recently pointed out in *The Wall Street Journal,* the clash of cultures produced by Asian immigration can also have vexing legal results. Take the case of Fumiko Kimura, a Japanese-American woman who tried to drown herself and her two children in the Pacific. She survived but the children did not, and she is now on trial for their murder. As a defense, her lawyers are arguing that parent-child suicide is a common occurrence in Japan. In Fresno, California, meanwhile, 30,000 newly arrived Hmong cause a different problem. "Anthropologists call the custom 'marriage by capture,'" Mr. Thompson writes. "Fresno police and prosecutors call it 'rape.'"

A much more serious problem for Asian-Americans is racial violence. In 1982 two unemployed whites in Detroit beat to death a Chinese-American named Vincent

Chin, claiming that they wanted revenge on the Japanese for hurting the automobile industry. After pleading guilty to manslaughter, they paid a $3,000 fine and were released. More recently, groups of Cambodians and Vietnamese in Boston were beaten by white youths, and there have been incidents in New York and Los Angeles as well.

Is this violence an aberration, or does it reflect the persistence of anti-Asian prejudice in America? By at least one indicator, it seems hard to believe that Asian-Americans suffer greatly from discrimination. Their median family income, according to the 1980 census, was $22,713, compared to only $19,917 for whites. True, Asians live almost exclusively in urban areas (where incomes are higher), and generally have more people working in each family. They are also better educated than whites. Irene Natividad, a Filipino-American active in the Democratic party's Asian caucus, states bluntly that "we are underpaid for the high level of education we have achieved." However, because of language difficulties and differing professional standards in the United States, many new Asian immigrants initially work in jobs for which they are greatly overqualified.

Ironically, charges of discrimination today arise most frequently in the universities, the setting generally cited as the best evidence of Asian-American achievement. For several years Asian student associations at Ivy League universities have cited figures showing that a smaller percentage of Asian-American students than others are accepted. At Harvard this year, 12.5 percent of Asian-American applicants were admitted, as opposed to 16 percent of all applicants; at Princeton, the figures were 14 to 17 percent. Recently a Princeton professor, Uwe Reinhardt, told a *New York Times* reporter that Princeton has an unofficial quota for Asian-American applicants.

The question of university discrimination is a subtle one. For one thing, it only arises at the most prestigious schools, where admissions are the most subjective. At universities like UCLA, where applicants are judged largely by their grades and SAT scores, Asian-Americans have a higher admission rate than other students (80 percent versus 70 percent for all applicants). And at schools that emphasize science, like MIT, the general excellence of Asian-Americans in the field also produces a higher admission rate.

Why are things different at the Ivy League schools? One reason, according to a recent study done at Princeton, is that very few Asian-Americans are alumni children. The children of alumni are accepted at a rate of about 50 percent, and so raise the overall admissions figure. Athletes have a better chance of admission as well, and few Asian-Americans play varsity sports. These arguments, however, leave out another admissions factor: affirmative action. The fact is that if alumni children have a special advantage, at least some Asians do too, because of their race. At Harvard, for instance, partly in response to complaints from the Asian student organization, the admissions office in the late 1970s began to recruit vigorously among two categories of Asian-Americans: the poor, often living in Chinatown; and recent immigrants. Today, according to the dean of admissions, L. Fred Jewett, roughly a third of Harvard's Asian-American applicants come from these groups, and are included in the university's "affirmative action" efforts. Like black students, who have a 27 percent admission rate, they find it easier to get in. And this means that the *other* Asian-Americans, the ones with no language problem or economic disadvantage, find things correspondingly tougher. Harvard has no statistics on the two groups. But if we assume the first group has an admissions rate of only 20 percent (very low for affirmative action candidates), the second one still slips down to slightly less than nine percent, or roughly half the overall admissions rate.

Dean Jewett offers two explanations for this phenomenon. First, he says, "family pressure makes more marginal students apply." In other words, many Asian students apply regardless of their qualifications, because of the university's prestige. And second, "a terribly high proportion of the Asian students are heading toward the sciences." In the interests of diversity, then, more of them must be left out.

## Clashing Cultural Standards

It is true that more Asian-Americans go into the sciences. In Harvard's class of 1985, 57 percent of them did (as opposed to 29 percent of all students) and 71 percent went into either the sciences or economics. It is also true that a great many of Harvard's Asian-American applicants have little on their records except scientific excellence. But there are good reasons for this. In the sciences, complete mastery of English is less important than in other fields, an important fact for immigrants and children of immigrants. And scientific careers allow Asian-Americans to avoid the sort of large, hierarchical organization where their unfamiliarity with America, and management's resistance to putting them into highly visible positions, could hinder their advancement. And so the admissions problem comes down to a problem of clashing cultural standards. Since the values of Asian-American applicants differ from the universities' own, many of those applicants appear narrowly focused and dull. As Linda Matthews, an alumni recruiter for Harvard in Los Angeles, says with regret, "We hold them to the standards of white suburban kids. We want them to be cheerleaders and class presidents and all the rest."

The universities, however, consider their idea of the academic community to be liberal and sound. They are understandably hesitant to change it because of a demographic shift in the admissions pool. So how can they resolve this difficult problem? It is hard to say, except to suggest humility, and to recall that this sort of thing has come up before. At Harvard, the admissions office might do well to remember a memorandum Walter Lippman prepared for the university in 1922. "I am fully prepared to accept the judgment of the Harvard authorities that a concentration of Jews in excess of fifteen per cent will produce a segregation of cultures rather than a fusion," wrote Lippmann, himself a Jew and a Harvard graduate. "They hand on unconsciously and uncritically from one generation to another many distressing personal and social habits. . . ."

The debate over admissions is abstruse. But for Asian-Americans, it has become an extremely sensitive issue. The universities, after all, represent their route to complete integration in American society, and to an equal chance at the advantages that enticed them and their parents to immigrate in the first place. At the same time, discrimination, even very slight discrimination, recalls the bitter prejudice and discrimination that Asian-Americans suffered for their first hundred years in this country.

Few white Americans today realize just how pervasive legal anti-Asian discrimination was before 1945. The tens of thousands of Chinese laborers who arrived in California in the 1850s and 1860s to work in the goldfields and build the Central Pacific Railroad often lived in virtual slavery (the words ku-li, now part of the English language, mean ''bitter labor''). Far from having the chance to organize, they were seized on as scapegoats by labor unions, particularly Samuel Gompers' AFL, and often ended up working as strikebreakers instead, thus inviting violent attacks. In 1870 Congress barred Asian immigrants from citizenship, and in 1882 it passed the Chinese Exclusion Act, which summarily prohibited more Chinese from entering the country. Since it did this at a time when 100,600 male Chinese-Americans had the company of only 4,800 females, it effectively sentenced the Chinese community to rapid decline. From 1854 to 1874, California had in effect a law preventing Asian-Americans from testifying in court, leaving them without the protection of the law.

Little changed in the late 19th and early 20th centuries, as large numbers of Japanese and smaller contingents from Korea and the Philippines began to arrive on the West Coast. In 1906 San Francisco made a brief attempt to segregate its school system. In 1910 a California law went so far as to prohibit marriage between Caucasians and ''Mongolians,'' in flagrant defiance of the Fourteenth Amendment. Two Alien Land Acts in 1913 and 1920 prevented noncitizens in California (in other words, all alien immigrants) from owning or leasing land. These laws, and the Chinese Exclusion Act, remained in effect until the 1940s. And of course during the Second World War, President Franklin Roosevelt signed an Executive Order sending 110,000 ethnic Japanese on the West Coast, 64 percent of whom were American citizens, to internment camps. Estimates of the monetary damage to the Japanese-American community from this action range as high as $400,000,000, and Japanese-American political activists have made reparations one of their most important goals. Only in Hawaii, where Japanese-Americans already outnumbered whites 61,000 to 29,000 at the turn of the century, was discrimination relatively less important. (Indeed, 157,000 Japanese-Americans in Hawaii at the start of the war were *not* interned, although they posed a greater possible threat to the war effort than their cousins in California.)

## Self-Sufficiency

In light of this history, the current problems of the Asian-American community seem relatively minor, and its success appears even more remarkable. Social scientists wonder just how this success was possible, and how Asian-Americans have managed to avoid the "second-class citizenship" that has trapped so many blacks and Hispanics. There is no single answer, but all the various explanations of the Asian-Americans' success do tend to fall into one category: self-sufficiency.

The first element of this self-sufficiency is family. Conservative [economist] Thomas Sowell writes that "strong stable families have been characteristic of . . . successful minorities," and calls Chinese-Americans and Japanese-Americans the most stable he has encountered. This quality contributes to success in at least three ways. First and most obviously, it provides a secure environment for children. Second, it pushes those children to do better than their parents. As former Ohio state demographer William Petersen, author of *Japanese-Americans* (1971), says, "They're like the Jews in that they have the whole family and the whole community pushing them to make the best of themselves." And finally, it is a significant financial advantage. Traditionally, Asian-Americans have headed into family businesses, with all the family members pitching in long hours to make them a success. For the Chinese, it was restaurants and laundries (as late as 1940, half of the Chinese-American labor force worked in one or the other), for the Japanese, groceries and truck farming, and for the Koreans, groceries. Today the proportion of Koreans working without pay in family businesses is nearly three times as high as any other group. A recent *New York* magazine profile of one typical Korean grocery in New York showed that several of the family members running it consistently worked fifteen to eighteen hours a day. Thomas Sowell points out that in 1970, although Chinese median family income already exceeded white median family income by a third, their median personal income was only ten percent higher, indicating much greater participation per family.

Also contributing to Asian-American self-sufficiency are powerful community organizations. From the beginning of Chinese-American settlement in California, clan organizations, mutual aid societies, and rotating credit associations gave many Japanese-Americans a start in business, at a time when most banks would only lend to whites. Throughout the first half of this century, the strength of community organizations was an important reason why Asian-Americans tended to live in small, closed communities rather than spreading out among the general population. And during the Depression years, they proved vital. In the early 1930s, when nine percent of the population of New York City subsisted on public relief, only one percent of Chinese-Americans did so. The community structure has also helped keep Asian-American crime rates the lowest in the nation, despite recently increasing gang violence among new Chinese and Vietnamese immigrants. According to the 1980 census, the proportion of Asian-Americans in prison is one-fourth that of the general population.

The more recent immigrants have also developed close communities. In the Washington, D.C., suburb of Arlington, Virginia, there is now a "Little Saigon." Koreans also take advantage of the "ethnic resources" provided by a small community. As Ivan Light writes in an essay in Nathan Glazer's new book, *Clamor at the Gates,* "They help one another with business skills, information, and purchase of ethnic commodities; cluster in particular industries; combine easily in restraint of trade; or utilize rotating credit associations.'' Light cities a study showing that 34 percent of Korean grocery store owners in Chicago had received financial help from within the Korean community. The immigrants in these communities are self-sufficient in another way as well. Unlike the immigrants of the 19th century, most new Asian-Americans come to the United States with professional skills. Or they come to obtain those skills, and then stay on. Of 16,000 Taiwanese who came to the U.S. as students in the 1960s, only three percent returned to Taiwan.

So what does the future hold for Asian-Americans? With the removal of most discrimination, and with the massive Asian-American influx in the universities, the importance of tightly knit communities is sure to wane. Indeed, among the older Asian-American groups it already has: since the war, fewer and fewer native-born Chinese-Americans have come to live in Chinatowns. But will complete assimilation follow? One study, at least, seems to indicate that it will, if one can look to the well-established Japanese-Americans for hints as to the future of other Asian groups. According to Professor Harry Kitano of UCLA, 63 percent of Japanese now intermarry.

But can all Asian-Americans follow the prosperous, assimilationist Japanese example? For some, it may not be easy. Hmong tribesmen, for instance, arrived in the United States with little money, few valuable skills, and extreme cultural disorientation. After five years here, they are still heavily dependent on welfare. (When the state of Oregon cut its assistance to refugees, 90 percent of the Hmong there moved to California.) Filipinos, although now the second-largest Asian-American group, make up less than ten percent of the Asian-American population at Harvard, and are the only Asian-Americans to benefit from affirmative action programs at the University of California. Do figures like these point to the emergence of a disadvantaged Asian-American underclass? It is still too early to tell, but the question is not receiving much attention either. As Nathan Glazer says of Asian-Americans, ''When they're already above average, it's very hard to pay much attention to those who fall below.'' Ross Harano, a Chicago businessman active in the Democratic party's Asian caucus, argues that the label of ''model minority'' earned by the most conspicuous Asian-Americans hurts less successful groups. ''We need money to help people who can't assimilate as fast as the superstars,'' he says.

Harano also points out that the stragglers find little help in traditional minority politics. ''When blacks talk about a minority agenda, they don't include us,'' he says. ''Most Asians are viewed by blacks as whites.'' Indeed, in cities with large numbers of Asians and blacks, relations between the communities are tense. In September 1984, for example, *The Los Angeles Sentinel,* a prominent black newspaper, ran a four-part series condemning Koreans for their ''takeover'' of black businesses, provoking a strong reaction from Asian-American groups. In Harlem some blacks have organized a boycott of Asian-American stores.

Another barrier to complete integration lies in the tendency of many Asian-American students to crowd into a small number of careers, mainly in the sciences. Professor Ronn Takaki of Berkeley is a strong critic of this ''maldistribution,'' and says that universities should make efforts to correct it. The extent of these efforts, he told *The Boston Globe* last December, "will determine whether we have our poets, sociologists, historians, and journalists. If we are all tracked into becoming computer technicians and scientists, this need will not be fulfilled."

Yet it is not clear that the "maldistribution" problem will extend to the next generation. The children of the current immigrants will not share their parents' language difficulties. Nor will they worry as much about joining large institutions where subtle racism might once have barred them from advancement. William Petersen argues, "As the discrimination disappears, as it mostly has already, the self-selection will disappear as well. . . . There's nothing in Chinese or Japanese culture pushing them toward these fields." Professor Kitano of UCLA is not so sure. "The submerging of the individual to the group is another basic Japanese tradition," he wrote in an article for *The Harvard Encyclopedia of American Ethnic Groups.* It is a tradition that causes problems for Japanese-Americans who wish to avoid current career patterns: "It may only be a matter of time before some break out of these middleman jobs, but the structural and cultural restraints may prove difficult to overcome."

## Looking Toward Politics

In short, Asian-Americans face undeniable problems of integration. Still, it takes a very narrow mind not to realize that these problems are the envy of every other American racial minority, and of a good number of white ethnic groups as well. Like the Jews, who experienced a similar pattern of discrimination and quotas, and who first crowded into a small range of professions, Asian-Americans have shown an ability to overcome large obstacles in spectacular fashion. In particular, they have done so by taking full advantage of America's greatest civic resource, its schools and universities, just as the Jews did fifty years ago. Now they seem poised to burst out upon American society.

The clearest indication of this course is in politics, a sphere that Asian-Americans traditionally avoided. Now this is changing. And importantly, it is *not* changing just because Asian-Americans want government to solve their particular problems. Yes, there are "Asian" issues: the loosening of immigration restrictions, reparations for the wartime internment, equal opportunity for the Asian disadvantaged. Asian-American Democrats are at present incensed over the way the Democratic National Committee has stripped their caucus of "official" status. But even the most vehement activists on these points still insist that the most important thing for Asian-Americans is not any particular combination of issues, but simply "being part of the process." Unlike blacks or Hispanics, Asian-American politicians have the luxury of not having to devote the bulk of their time to an "Asian-American agenda," and thus escape becoming prisoners of such an agenda. Who thinks of Senator Daniel Inouye or former senator S. I. Hayakawa primarily in terms of his race? In June a young Chinese-American named Michael Woo won a seat on the Los Angeles City Council, running in a district that is only five percent Asian. According to *The*

*Washington Post,* he attributed his victory to his "links to his fellow young American professionals." This is not typical minority-group politics.

Since Asian-Americans have the luxury of not having to behave like other minority groups, it seems only a matter of time before they, like the Jews, lose their "minority" status altogether, both legally and in the public's perception. And when this occurs, Asian-Americans will have to face the danger not of discrimination but of losing their cultural identity. It is a problem that every immigrant group must eventually come to terms with.

For Americans in general, however, the success of Asian-Americans poses no problems at all. On the contrary, their triumph has done nothing but enrich the United States. Asian-Americans improve every field they enter, for the simple reason that in a free society, a group succeeds by doing something better than it had been done before: Korean grocery stores provide fresher vegetables; Filipino doctors provide better rural health care; Asian science students raise the quality of science in the universities, and go on to provide better medicine, engineering, computer technology, and so on. And by a peculiarly American miracle, the Asian-Americans' success has not been balanced by anyone else's failure. Indeed, as successive waves of immigrants have shown, each new ethnic and racial group adds far more to American society than it takes away. This Fourth of July, that is cause for hope and celebration.

# American Social Policy and the Ghetto Underclass

*William Julius Wilson*

Why have the social conditions of the ghetto underclass deteriorated so rapidly in recent years? Racial discrimination is the most frequently invoked explanation, and it is undeniable that discrimination continues to aggravate the social and economic problems of poor blacks. But is discrimination really greater today than it was in 1948, when black unemployment was less than half of what it is now, and when the gap between black and white jobless rates was narrower?

As for the poor black family, it apparently began to fall apart not before but after the mid-twentieth century. Until publication in 1976 of Herbert Gutman's *The Black Family in Slavery and Freedom,* most scholars had believed otherwise. Stimulated by the acrimonious debate over the Moynihan report, Gutman produced data demonstrating that the black family was not significantly disrupted during slavery or even during the early years of the first migration to the urban North, beginning after the turn of the century. The problems of the modern black family, he implied, were associated with modern forces.

Those who cite discrimination as the root cause of poverty often fail to make a distinction between the effects of *historic* discrimination (i.e., discrimination prior to the mid-twentieth century) and the effects of *contemporary* discrimination. Thus they find it hard to explain why the economic position of the black underclass started to worsen soon after Congress enacted, and the White House began to enforce, the most sweeping civil rights legislation since Reconstruction.

The point to be emphasized is that historic discrimination is more important than contemporary discrimination in understanding the plight of the ghetto underclass—that, in any event, there is more to the story than discrimination (of whichever kind). Historic discrimination certainly helped to create an impoverished urban black community in the first place. In *A Piece of the Pie: Black and White Immigrants Since 1880,* Stanley Lieberson shows how, in many areas of life, including the labor market, black newcomers from the rural South were far more severely discriminated against in northern cities than were the new white immigrants from southern,

---

William Julius Wilson, "American Social Policy and the Ghetto Underclass." From *The Truly Disadvantaged* by William Julius Wilson.  (pp. 140–163)

---

See Statistical Appendix Tables A–1, A–7, A–9, A–15, and A–17.

central, and eastern Europe. Skin color was part of the problem but it was not all of it.

In addition to the problem of historic discrimination, the black migration to New York, Philadelphia, Chicago, and other northern cities—the continued replenishment of black populations there by poor newcomers—predictably skewed the age profile of the urban black community and kept it relatively young.

Age correlates with many things. For example, the higher the median age of a group, the higher its income; the lower the median age, the higher the unemployment rate and the higher the crime rate (more than half of those arrested in 1980 for violent and property crimes in American cities were under twenty-one). The younger a woman is, the more likely she is to bear a child out of wedlock, head up a new household, and depend on welfare. In short, part of what had gone awry in the ghetto was due to the sheer increase in the number of black youths.

The population explosion among minority youths occurred at a time when changes in the economy were beginning to pose serious problems for unskilled workers. Urban minorities have been particularly vulnerable to the structural economic changes of the past two decades: the shift from goods-producing to service-producing industries, the increasing polarization of the labor market into low-wage and high-wage sectors, innovations in technology, and the relocation of manufacturing industries out of the central cities.

Most unemployed blacks in the United States reside within the central cities. Their situation, already more difficult than that of any other major ethnic group in the country, continues to worsen. Not only are there more blacks without jobs every year; men, especially young males, are dropping out of the labor force in record proportions. Also, more and more black youths, including many who are no longer in school, are obtaining no job experience at all.

However, the growing problem of joblessness in the inner city exacerbates and is in turn partly created by the changing social composition of inner-city neighborhoods. These areas have undergone a major social transformation in the last several years as reflected not only in their increasing rates of social dislocation but also in the changing class structure of ghetto neighborhoods. In the 1940s, 1950s, and even the 1960s, lower-class, working-class, and middle-class black urban families all resided more or less in the same ghetto areas, albeit on different streets. Although black middle-class professionals today tend to be employed in mainstream occupations outside the black community and neither live nor frequently interact with ghetto residents, the black middle-class professionals of the 1940s and 1950s (doctors, lawyers, teachers, social workers, etc.), resided in the higher-income areas of the inner city, and serviced the ghetto community. The exodus of black middle-class professionals from the inner city has been increasingly accompanied by a movement of stable working-class blacks to higher-income neighborhoods in other parts of the city and to the suburbs. Confined by restrictive covenants to communities also inhabited by the urban black lower classes, the black working and middle classes in earlier years provided stability to inner-city neighborhoods and perpetuated and reinforced societal norms and values. In short, their very presence enhanced the social organization of ghetto communities. If strong norms and sanctions against aberrant behavior, a sense of community, and positive neighborhood identification are the essential features of social organization in urban areas, inner-city neighborhoods today suffer from a severe lack of social organization.

In contrast to previous years, today's ghetto residents represent almost exclusively the most disadvantaged segments of the urban black community—including those families who have experienced long-term spells of poverty and/or welfare dependency, individuals who lack training and skills and have either experienced periods of persistent unemployment or have dropped out of the labor force altogether, and individuals who are frequently involved in street criminal activity.

The significance of changes embodied in the social transformation of the inner city is perhaps best captured by the concepts "concentration effects" and "social buffer." The former refers to the constraints and opportunities associated with living in a neighborhood in which the population is overwhelmingly socially disadvantaged—constraints and opportunities that include the kinds of ecological niches that the residents of these communities occupy in terms of access to jobs, availability of marriageable partners, and exposure to conventional role models. The latter refers to the presence of a sufficient number of working- and middle-class professional families to absorb the shock or cushion the effect of uneven economic growth and periodic recessions on inner-city neighborhoods. The basic thesis is not that ghetto culture went unchecked following the removal of the higher-income family in the inner city, but that the removal of these families made it more difficult to sustain the basic institutions in the inner city (including churches, stores, schools, recreational facilities, etc.) in the face of prolonged joblessness. And as the basic institutions declined, the social organization of inner-city neighborhoods (defined here to include a sense of community, positive neighborhood identification, and explicit norms and sanctions against aberrant behavior) likewise declined.

In underlining joblessness as an important aspect of inner-city social transformations, we are reminded that in the 1960s scholars readily attributed poor-black-family deterioration to problems of employment. Nonetheless, in the last several years, in the face of the overwhelming attention given to welfare as the major source of black-family breakup, concerns about the importance of joblessness have diminished, despite the existence of evidence strongly suggesting the need for renewed scholarly and public-policy attention to the relationship between the disintegration of poor black families and black male labor market experiences.

Although changing social and cultural trends have often been said to explain some of the dynamic shifts in the structure of the family, they appear to have more relevance for changes in family structure among whites. And, contrary to popular opinion, there is little evidence to support the argument that welfare is the primary cause of family out-of-wedlock births, break-ups, and female-headed households. Welfare does seem to have a modest effect on separation and divorce, particularly for white women, but recent evidence indicates that its total effect on the proportion of all female householders is small.

By contrast, the evidence for the influence of joblessness on family structure is much more conclusive. Research has demonstrated, for example, a connection between an encouraging economic situation and the early marriage of young people. In this connection, black women are more likely to delay marriage and less likely to remarry. Although black and white teenagers expect to become parents at about the same ages, black teenagers expect to marry at later ages. The black delay in marriage and the lower rate of remarriage, each associated with high percentages of out-of-wedlock births and female-headed households, can be directly tied to the employment status of black males. Indeed, black women, especially young black women, are confronting a shrinking pool of "marriageable" (that is, economically stable) men.

White women are not experiencing this problem. Our "male marriageable pool index" shows that the number of employed white men per 100 white women in different age categories has either remained roughly the same or has only slightly increased in the last two decades. There is little reason, therefore, to assume a connection between the recent growth of female-headed white families and patterns of white male employment. That the pool of "marriageable" white men has not decreased over the years is perhaps reflected in the earlier age of first marriage and the higher rate of remarriage among white women. It is therefore reasonable to hypothesize that the rise in rates of separation and divorce among whites is due mainly to the increased economic independence of white women and related social and cultural factors embodied in the feminist movement.

The argument that the decline in the incidence of intact marriages among blacks is associated with the declining economic status of black men is further supported by an analysis of regional data on female headship and the "male marriageable pool." Whereas changes in the ratios of employed men to women among whites have been minimal for all regions of the country regardless of age from 1960 to 1980, the ratios among blacks have declined significantly in all regions except the West, with the greatest declines in the northeast and north-central regions of the country. On the basis of these trends, it would be expected that the growth in numbers of black female-headed households would occur most rapidly in the northern regions followed by the South and the West. Regional data on the "male marriageable pool index" support this conclusion, except for the larger than expected increase in black female-headed families in the West—a function of patterns of selective black migration to the West.

The sharp decline in the black "male marriageable pool" in the northeast and north–central regions is related to recent changes in the basic economic organization of American society. In the two northern regions, the shift in economic activity from goods production to services has been associated with changes in the location of production, including an interregional movement of industry from the North to the South and West and, more important, a movement of certain industries out of the older central cities where blacks are concentrated. Moreover, the shrinkage of the male marriageable pool for ages sixteen to twenty-four in the South from 1960 to 1980 is related to the mechanization of agriculture, which lowered substantially the demand for low-skilled agricultural labor, especially during the 1960s. For all these reasons, it is often necessary to go beyond the specific issue of current racial discrimination to understand factors that contribute directly to poor black joblessness and indirectly to related social problems such as family instability in the inner city. But this point has not been readily grasped by policymakers and civil rights leaders.

## The Limits of Race-Specific Public Policy

In the early 1960s there was no comprehensive civil rights bill and Jim Crow segregation was still widespread in parts of the nation, particularly in the deep South. With the passage of the 1964 Civil Rights Bill there was considerable optimism that racial progress would ensue and that the principle of equality or individual rights (namely, that candidates for positions stratified in terms of prestige, power, or other social criteria ought to be judged solely on individual merit and therefore should not be discriminated against on the basis of racial origin) would be upheld.

Programs based solely on this principle are inadequate, however, to deal with the complex problems of race in America because they are not designed to address the substantive inequality that exists at the time discrimination is eliminated.

On the other hand, the competitive resources developed by the *advantaged minority members*—resources that flow directly from the family stability, schooling, income, and peer groups that their parents have been able to provide—result in their benefiting disproportionately from policies that promote the rights of minority individuals by removing artificial barriers to valued positions.

Nevertheless, since 1970, government policy has tended to focus on formal programs designed and created both to prevent discrimination and to ensure that minorities are sufficiently represented in certain positions. This has resulted in a shift from the simple formal investigation and adjudication of complaints of racial discrimination to government-mandated affirmative action programs to increase minority representation in public programs, employment, and education.

However, if minority members from the most advantaged families profit disproportionately from policies based on the principle of equality of individual opportunity, they also reap disproportionate benefits from policies of affirmative action based solely on their group membership. This is because advantaged minority members are likely to be disproportionately represented among those of their racial group most qualified for valued positions, such as college admissions, higher paying jobs, and promotions. Thus, if policies of preferential treatment for such positions are developed in terms of racial group membership rather than the real disadvantages suffered by individuals, then these policies will further improve the opportunities of the advantaged without necessarily addressing the problems of the truly disadvantaged such as the ghetto underclass.[1] The problems of the truly disadvantaged may require *nonracial* solutions such as full employment, balanced economic growth, and manpower training and education (tied to—not isolated from—these two economic conditions).

It would be ideal if problems of the ghetto underclass could be adequately addressed by the combination of macroeconomic policy, labor market strategies, and manpower training programs. However, in the foreseeable future employment alone will not necessarily lift a family out of poverty. Many families would still require income support and/or social service such as child care. A program of welfare reform is needed, therefore, to address the current problems of public assistance, including lack of provisions for poor two-parent families, inadequate levels of support, inequities between different states, and work disincentives. A national AFDC benefit standard adjusted yearly for inflation is the most minimal required change. We might also give serious consideration to programs such as the Child Support Assurance Program developed by Irwin Garfinkel and colleagues at the Institute for Research on Poverty at the University of Wisconsin, Madison.[2] This program, parts of which are currently in operation as a demonstration project in the state of Wisconsin, provides a guaranteed minimum benefit per child to single-parent families regardless of the income of the custodial parent. The state collects from the absent parent through wage withholding a sum of money at a fixed rate and then makes regular payments to the custodial parent. If the absent parent is jobless or if his or her payment from withholdings is less than the minimum, the state makes up the difference. Since all absent parents regardless of income are required to participate in this program, it is far less stigmatizing than, say, public assistance. Moreover, preliminary evidence from Wisconsin suggests that this program carries little or no additional cost to the state.

Neither the Child Support Assurance Program under demonstration in Wisconsin nor the European family allowances program is means-tested; that is, they are not targeted at a particular income group and therefore do not suffer the degree of stigmatization that plagues public assistance programs such as AFDC. More important, such universal programs tend to draw more political support from the general public because they are available not only to the poor but to the working- and middle-class segments as well. Finally, the question of child care has to be addressed in any program designed to improve the employment prospects of women and men.

If the truly disadvantaged reaped disproportionate benefits from a child support enforcement, child allowance program, and child care strategy, they would also benefit disproportionately from a program of balanced economic growth and tight labor-market policies because of their greater vulnerability to swings in the business cycle and changes in economic organization, including the relocation of plants and the use of labor-saving technology. It would be shortsighted to conclude, therefore, that universal programs (i.e., programs not targeted at any particular group) are not designed to help address in a fundamental way some of the problems of the truly disadvantaged such as the ghetto underclass.

By emphasizing universal programs as an effective way to address problems in the inner city created by historic racial subjugation, I am recommending a fundamental shift from the traditional race-specific approach of addressing such problems. It is true that problems of joblessness and related woes such as poverty, teenage pregnancies, out-of-wedlock births, female-headed families, and welfare dependency are, for reasons of historic racial oppression, disproportionately concentrated in the black community. And it is important to recognize the racial differences in rates of social dislocation so as not to obscure problems currently gripping the ghetto underclass. However, as discussed above, race-specific policies are often not designed to address fundamentally problems of the truly disadvantaged. Moreover, as also discussed above, both race-specific and targeted programs based on the principle of equality of life chances (often identified with a minority constituency) have difficulty sustaining widespread public support.

Does this mean that targeted programs of any kind would be necessarily excluded from a package highlighting universal programs of reform? On the contrary, as long as a racial division of labor exists and racial minorities are disproportionately concentrated in low-paying positions, antidiscrimination and affirmative action programs will be needed even though they tend to benefit the more advantaged minority members. Moreover, as long as certain groups lack the training, skills, and education to compete effectively on the job market or move into newly created jobs, manpower training and education programs targeted at these groups will also be needed, even under a tight labor-market situation. For example, a program of adult education and training may be necessary for some ghetto underclass males before they can either become oriented to or move into an expanded labor market. Finally, as long as some poor families are unable to work because of physical or other disabilities, public assistance would be needed even if the government adopted a program of welfare reform that included child support enforcement and family allowance provisions.

For all these reasons, a comprehensive program of economic and social reform (highlighting macroeconomic policies to promote balanced economic growth and create a tight labor-market situation, a nationally oriented labor-market strategy, a child support assurance program, a child care strategy, and a family allowance program) would have to include targeted programs, both means-tested and race-specific. However, the latter would be considered an offshoot of and indeed secondary to the universal programs. The important goal is to construct an economic-social reform program in such a way that the universal programs are seen as the dominant and most visible aspects by the general public. As the universal programs draw support from a wider population, the targeted programs included in the comprehensive reform package would be indirectly supported and protected. Accordingly, *the hidden agenda for liberal policymakers is to improve the life chances of truly disadvantaged groups such as the ghetto underclass by emphasizing programs to which the more advantaged groups of all races and class backgrounds can positively relate.*

I am reminded of Bayard Rustin's plea during the early 1960s that blacks ought to recognize the importance of fundamental economic reform (including a system of national economic planning along with new education, manpower, and public works programs to help reach full employment) and the need for a broad-based political coalition to achieve it. And since an effective coalition will in part depend upon how the issues are defined, it is imperative that the political message underline the need for economic and social reforms that benefit all groups in the United States, not just poor minorities.

However, at this point, a program of economic reform is not one of the items currently under serious discussion in the national political arena. Indeed, discussions of reform seem to be limited to debates over the need for workfare programs for welfare recipients. In the 1970s the term "workfare" was narrowly used to capture the idea that welfare recipients should be required to work, even make-work if necessary, in exchange for receiving benefits. This idea was generally rejected by liberals and those in the welfare establishment. And no workfare program, even Governor Reagan's 1971 program, really got off the ground. However, by 1981 President Ronald Reagan was able to get congressional approval to include a provision in the 1981 budget allowing states to experiment with new employment approaches to welfare reform. These approaches represent the "new-style workfare." More specifically, whereas workfare in the 1970s was narrowly construed as "working off" one's welfare grant, the new-style workfare "takes the form of obligational state programs that involve an array of employment and training services and activities—job search, job training, education programs, and also community work experience."[3]

According to Richard Nathan, "We make our greatest progress on social reform in the United States when liberals and conservatives find common ground. New-style workfare embodies both the caring commitment of liberals and the themes identified with conservative writers like Charles Murray, George Gilder, and Lawrence Mead." On the one hand, liberals can relate to new-style workfare because it creates short-term, entry-level positions very similar to the "CETA public service jobs we thought we had abolished in 1981"; it provides a convenient "political rationale and support for increased funding for education and training programs"; and it targets these programs at the most disadvantaged, thereby correcting the problem of "creaming" that is associated with other employment and training programs. On the other hand, conservatives can relate to new-style workfare because "it involves a strong commitment to reducing welfare dependency on the premise that dependency is bad for people, that it undermines their motivation to self-support and isolates and stigmatizes welfare recipients in a way that over a long period feeds into and accentuates the underclass mindset and condition."[4]

The combining of liberal and conservative approaches does not, of course, change the fact that the new-style workfare programs hardly represent a fundamental shift from the traditional approaches to poverty in America. Once again the focus is exclusively on individual characteristics—whether they are construed in terms of lack of training, of skills, or of education; or whether they are seen in terms of lack of motivation or other subjective traits. And once again the consequences of certain economic arrangements on disadvantaged populations in the United States are not considered in the formulation and implementation of social policy. Although new-style workfare is better than having no strategy at all to enhance employment experiences, it should be emphasized that the effectiveness of such programs ultimately depends upon the availability of jobs in a given area. Perhaps Robert D. Reischauer put it best when he stated:

> As long as the unemployment rate remains high in many regions of the country, members of the underclass are going to have a very difficult time competing successfully for the jobs that are available. No amount of remedial education, training, wage subsidy, or other embellishment will make them more attractive to prospective employers than experienced unemployed workers.[5]

As Reischauer also appropriately emphasizes, with a weak economy "even if the workfare program seems to be placing its clients successfully, these participants may simply be taking jobs away from others who are nearly as disadvantaged. A game of musical underclass will ensue as one group is temporarily helped, while another is pushed down into the underclass."[6]

If new-style workfare will indeed represent a major policy thrust in the immediate future, I see little prospect for substantially alleviating inequality among poor minorities if it is not part of a more comprehensive program of economic and social reform that recognizes the dynamic interplay between societal organization and the behavior and life chances of individuals and groups—a program, in other words, that is designed both to enhance human capital traits of poor minorities and to open up the opportunity structure in the broader society and economy to facilitate social mobility. The combination of economic and social welfare policies discussed in the previous section represents, from my point of view, such a program.

## A Comprehensive Program

The problems of the ghetto underclass can be most meaningfully addressed by a comprehensive program that combines employment policies with social welfare policies and that features universal as opposed to race- or group-specific strategies. On the one hand, this program highlights macroeconomic policy to generate a tight labor market and economic growth; fiscal and monetary policy not only to stimulate noninflationary growth, but also to increase the competitiveness of American goods on both the domestic and international markets; and a national labor-market strategy to make the labor force more adaptable to changing economic opportunities. On the other hand, it highlights a child support assurance program, a family allowance program, and a child care strategy.

I emphasize that although this program also would include targeted strategies—both means-tested and race-specific—they would be considered secondary to the universal programs so that the latter are seen as the most visible and dominant aspects in the eyes of the general public. To the extent that the universal programs draw support from a wider population, the less visible targeted programs would be indirectly supported and protected. The hidden agenda for liberal policymakers is to enhance the chances in life for the ghetto underclass by emphasizing programs to which the more advantaged groups of all class and racial backgrounds can positively relate.

Before such programs can be seriously considered, however, the question of cost has to be addressed. The cost of programs to expand social and economic opportunity will be great, but it must be weighed against the economic and social costs of a do-nothing policy. As Levitan and Johnson have pointed out, "the most recent recession cost the nation an estimated $300 billion in lost income and production, and direct outlays for unemployment compensation totaled $30 billion in a single year. A policy that ignores the losses associated with slack labor markets and forced idleness inevitably will underinvest in the nation's labor force and future economic growth." Furthermore, the problem of annual budget deficits of almost $200 billion dollars (driven mainly by the peacetime military buildup and the Reagan administration's tax cuts), and the need for restoring the federal tax base and adopting a more balanced set of budget priorities have to be tackled if we are to achieve significant progress on expanding opportunities.[7]

In the final analysis, the pursuit of economic and social reform ultimately involves the question of political strategy. As the history of social provision so clearly demonstrates, universalistic political alliances, cemented by policies that provide benefits directly to wide segments of the population, are needed to work successfully for major reform.[8] The recognition among minority leaders and liberal policymakers of the need to expand the War on Poverty and race relations visions to confront the growing problems of inner-city social dislocations will provide, I believe, an important first step toward creating such as alliance.

## Notes

1. James Fishkin covers much of this ground very convincingly. See his *Justice, Equal Opportunity and the Family* (New Haven: Yale University Press, 1983).
2. Irwin Garfinkel and Sara S. McLanahan, *Single Mothers and Their Children: A New American Dilemma* (Washington, D.C.: Urban Institute Press, 1986).
3. Richard Nathan, "The Underclass—Will It Always Be With Us?" Paper presented at a symposium on the underclass, New School for Social Research, New York, N.Y., November 14, 1986.
4. Ibid.
5. Robert D. Reischauer, "America's Underclass: Four Unanswered Questions," paper presented at the City Club, Portland, Oregon, January 30, 1987.
6. Reischauer, "Policy Responses to the Underclass," paper prepared for a symposium at the New School for Social Research, November 14, 1986.
7. Sar A. Levitan and Clifford M. Johnson, *Beyond the Safety Net: Reviving the Promising Opportunity in America* (Cambridge, Mass.: Ballinger Publishing Co., 1984), pp. 169–170.
8. Theda Skocpol, "Brother Can You Spare a Job? Work and Welfare in the United States," paper presented at the Annual Meeting of the American Sociological Association, Washington, D.C., August 17, 1985.

# Chapter 5
# GENDER

## Women and the Economy

*Nancy Barrett*

### Highlights

The increase in women's labor force participation over the last 25 years has brought with it questions of equal employment opportunity, pay equity, and family services that were less frequently raised when the paid labor force comprised largely males and single women, and child care and other household duties were managed by full-time homemakers.

- The number of women working or looking for work has increased by roughly 28 million over the past 25 years.
- The huge shift of labor resources out of the household economy and into other sectors such as manufacturing and services is not due to an influx of new workers, but to women who are remaining in the workforce rather than dropping out upon marriage or a first pregnancy.
- The most dramatic increase in labor force participation has been among middle-class, well-educated women who formerly would have dropped out of the labor force during their childrearing years.
- In 1960, fewer than 20 percent of married women with pre-school-age children were working outside the home, compared with more than 50 percent today.
- Seventy percent of married women with college degrees were either employed or looking for work in 1981, compared with 50 percent in 1971.
- The percentage of women pursuing advanced professional degrees has increased substantially. From 1970 to 1979, the percentage of graduates earning degrees in

---



---

See Statistical Appendix Tables A–4, A–7, and A–8.

law who were women jumped from 5.4 to 28.5 percent, and in medicine from 8.4 to 23.0 percent.

- Despite advances made in women's educational attainment and employment opportunities, women remain overwhelmingly concentrated in low-paying female occupations.
- In 1985, 70 percent of all full-time employed women were working in occupations in which over three-quarters of the employees were females.
- Over one-third of all employed women work in clerical jobs.
- Women tend to be employed in low-paying jobs with no on-the-job training and little security, and thus they are often among the first fired.
- In almost all areas of employment, women are overrepresented at the bottom and underrepresented at the top.
- The average female worker is gaining in experience and should be progressing more rapidly up the job ladder than is actually the case.
- Women college graduates who work full time, year round, have earnings roughly on a par with male high school dropouts.
- The concentration of women in low-paying occupations, their ghettoization within male-dominated professions, and their lack of upward mobility translates into a lower average wage for women than for men.
- The median earnings for women working full time, year round, in 1985 were 68 percent of men's earnings, up from 61 percent in 1978.
- The slight improvement in the wage gap is not due to women moving into higher-paying jobs but to a recession that has had a disproportionately negative effect on the high-wage, male-dominated sectors of the economy.
- The wage gap between men and women increases with age. Younger workers of both sexes enter the labor force in the lowest pay categories, but men are more likely to advance in earnings while women remain behind. A 45- to 55-year-old woman makes approximately the same wage as a woman of 25.
- During the 1970s, adult women experienced higher unemployment rates than adult men: 6.0 percent for women compared to 4.5 percent for men.
- In the 1980s, the average unemployment rates for both women and men rose and were virtually identical at 7.2 and 7.1 percent, respectively. Between 1980 and 1985, 6.9 million new jobs were created in the female-dominated sectors of sales and services, while 500,000 jobs were lost in the male-dominated sectors of manufacturing, mining, construction, and transportation.
- The decline of full-time homemaking as the predominant occupation for married women has been accompanied by a rapid increase in the number of women seeking part-time jobs. Roughly one-third of the shift out of homemaking has been into part-time employment.
- About three-quarters of women working part time are in the low-paying sales, clerical, and service occupations.
- Women workers' low part-time pay is accompanied by the virtual absence of fringe benefits or opportunity for advancement.
- Female jobs have traditionally been and remain undervalued because of their

association with unpaid work in the home and because women are not seen as important economic providers.

- Although women, on average, earn less than men, their contributions to the economic resources of families are substantial.
- For all families, and especially for black families, a second paycheck makes a significant difference in living standards and substantially reduces the incidence of poverty.
- Women with paid jobs still bear most of the responsibility for housework. The shift to paid employment has not meant an offsetting decline in the number of hours most women spend in the household economy. Thus, women now contribute more total hours to the economy (both paid and unpaid) than they did before the shift. . . .

## The Earnings Gap and Pay Equity Strategies for Women

Since the passage of the Equal Pay Act of 1963, there has been legislative support for eliminating wage disparities based on sex. At that time, median earnings for women working full time, year round were about 60 percent of men's earnings. That ratio held remarkably constant throughout the 1960s and 1970s, despite the rapid change in women's work roles associated with the household-sector transformation and the passage of an impressive body of legislation mandating equal employment opportunity. Although there has been a barrage of anecdotal reporting about upwardly mobile women, the statistical evidence shows that despite radical changes in women's work and family roles, there has not been a substantial narrowing of the pay gap between men and women.

The previous description of women's employment patterns provides a foundation for understanding why the pay gap persists. The pay gap is inextricably bound up with the sex-based division of labor that characterizes our economy. The concentration of women in low-paying occupations, their ghettoization within male-dominated professions, and their lack of upward mobility all translate into a lower average wage for women than for men. This means that the pay gap cannot be closed simply by enacting a law. Rather, pay equity will require a radical realignment of the occupational profiles of men and women, or alternatively, a major restructuring of the pay scales in men's and women's jobs. Egalitarian views of social justice may favor pay equity for women, yet there is a conflict with the deeply entrenched social expectations regarding differences in men's and women's work roles. It is important to face this dilemma squarely in seeking policy remedies.

### The Role of Occupational Segregation

The persistence of the wage gap despite the Equal Pay Act demonstrated that pay equity for women could not be achieved simply by mandating equal pay for equal work. In a labor market segregated by sex, equal pay for equal work, however important to establish in principle, is not the main issue.

Female-dominated occupations and industries are the lowest paying. A recent study by the Bureau of Labor Statistics shows a strong inverse relationship between the percent of an industry's employees that is female and the level of average hourly earnings (Norwood, 1982:2). A ranking of 52 industries in July 1982 shows that the apparel and textile products industry had the highest percentage of women workers (81.9 percent), and ranked 50th in average hourly earnings. The bituminous coal and lignite mining industry, on the other hand, ranked 52nd in percentage of women employees (5.1 percent) and first in average hourly earnings.

Roughly one-third of all women work in clerical occupations, where median weekly earnings in 1985 were $286 for full-time workers of both sexes. This compares unfavorably with a median weekly wage for all full-time male workers of $406, but is roughly equivalent to the median of $277 for full-time female workers.

Table 1 shows earnings for groups of predominantly female and predominantly

**Table 1** Earnings[1] in Selected Occupations, 1985

| | Percent female | Median weekly wage (in dollars) |
|---|---|---|
| *Predominantly female occupations* | | |
| Secretary/typist | 97.7 | 276 |
| Receptionist | 97.6 | 225 |
| Licensed practical nurse | 96.9 | 294 |
| Private household | 96.2 | 132 |
| Child care worker | 96.1 | 169 |
| Registered nurse | 95.1 | 434 |
| Teacher's aide | 93.6 | 196 |
| Bookkeeper | 91.5 | 272 |
| Bank teller | 93.0 | 219 |
| Data entry keyer | 90.7 | 277 |
| Textile sewing machine operator | 90.8 | 178 |
| Health service worker | 89.9 | 210 |
| Librarian | 87.0 | 391 |
| Elementary school teacher | 84.0 | 412 |
| Cashier | 83.1 | 178 |
| *Predominantly male occupations* | | |
| Extractive occupations | 1.1 | 501 |
| Fire fighting/prevention | 1.4 | 436 |
| Truck driver | 2.1 | 363 |
| Construction trades | 2.0 | 393 |
| Airplane pilot/navigator | 2.6 | 738 |
| Construction laborer | 3.1 | 276 |
| Material-moving equipment operator | 3.2 | 360 |
| Furnace operator | 3.6 | 406 |
| Welder | 4.8 | 371 |
| Engineer | 6.7 | 661 |
| Lathe operator | 9.6 | 339 |
| Police officer and detective | 10.1 | 424 |
| Architect | 11.3 | 488 |

[1]Usual weekly earnings of full-time workers.

*Source:* U.S. Bureau of Labor Statistics, unpublished tabulations.

male occupations. Forty percent of all adult women employees hold jobs in the female-dominated categories listed. (Men are not similarly concentrated in a few job categories.) While these jobs vary considerably in terms of the education, skill requirements, and responsibility involved, women's jobs are generally lower-paying than men's jobs. For instance, a licensed practical nurse averages $294 per week, compared with $363 for a truck driver and $406 for a furnace operator. A child care worker averages $169, and a bank teller $219, compared with $276 for an unskilled construction laborer.

Recognition that the pay gap is largely the result of occupational differences between men and women led to a focus on providing equal employment opportunity (EEO) in higher-paying, male-dominated job categories as the best way to achieve pay equity for women. Title VII of the Civil Rights Act of 1964 was the legislative basis of the EEO mandate, and this was followed by a series of court decisions and executive orders that shifted the policy focus from merely prohibiting employment discrimination to actually promoting improved representation of women in higher-paying occupations and industries. The motive behind these efforts was not necessarily to integrate occupations as an end in itself (although many proponents of equality for women support occupational integration as a way to eliminate stereotypes), but rather to reduce the pay gap.

But women have made only modest inroads into the high-paying sectors of the economy. And, as noted earlier, where women have been successful in penetrating nontraditional occupations, they are ghettoized into lower-paying, female enclaves within them, or concentrated on the lower rungs of the seniority ladder. The result is that the pay gap between men and women is often greater in male-dominated occupations than in female-dominated ones.

Because women are generally located at the bottom of the job hierarchy and men at the top, there is a considerable difference in how the level of their earnings is distributed within the same category of work. In 1982, 16.2 percent of women managers and administrators earned less than $200 per week, compared with only 3.2 percent of men. On the other hand, only 14.9 percent of those women earned more than $500 per week compared with 51.3 percent of the men. Among craft workers, 28.4 percent of the women and only 7.0 percent of the men earned less than $200 per week, while 7.7 percent of the women and 23.9 percent of the men earned more than $500. Similar patterns were also found in the specific occupations within these general categories (Mellor, 1984: 24).

The concentration of women at the bottom of the distribution of earnings results in a wage gap that increases with age, as shown in Table 2. Young workers of both sexes enter the labor market in the lowest pay categories, but the men are more likely to advance in earnings while the women remain behind. This is either because women are in occupations without opportunities for upward mobility, or because they are denied access to the opportunities that are available to men.

Another way of looking at the problem is to examine the age-earnings profile. Male earnings advance rapidly between ages 25 and 35, with men between 35 and 55 typically earning more than double that of younger men. Women's earnings, as a rule, rise modestly between ages 16 and 25 and then remain virtually flat. A 45- to

**Table 2** The Ratio of Female to Male Earnings by Age Group among Full-Time, Year-Round Workers, 1975 and 1984

| Age group | 1975 | 1984 |
|---|---|---|
| All ages | 59.5 | 68.2 |
| 16–24 | 75.9 | 87.5 |
| 25–34 | 64.7 | 74.3 |
| 35–44 | 51.9 | 63.2 |
| 45–54 | 52.5 | 60.4 |
| 55–64 | 55.0 | 60.8 |
| 65+ | 55.9 | 65.9 |

*Source:* U.S. Bureau of the Census, Current Population Reports, Series P-60, No. 105, *Money Income in 1975 of Families and Persons in the United States,* and Series P-60, No. 149, *Money Income and Poverty Status of Families and Persons in the United States: 1984* (Washington, D.C.: U.S. Government Printing Office, 1977 and 1985).

55-year-old woman makes approximately the same wage as a woman of 25, reflecting the fact that the vast majority of women are in dead-end jobs. Men, on the other hand, seem to experience considerable upward mobility.

Occupational segregation, ghettoization, and lack of upward mobility deserve great emphasis, but other factors contribute to the pay gap as well. For instance, women work fewer hours per week than men, and despite gains among younger women, have slightly less education than men on the average. However, differences in education and hours worked account for a relatively small part of the pay gap. Together, in 1982, they contributed 3.7 percentage points to a pay gap of 35 percentage points (Mellor, 1984: 26).

Lack of work experience and intermittent labor force activity of women are sometimes thought to contribute significantly to their lower earnings. However, a recent study by the Bureau of the Census reports that work interruptions explain only a small part of the earnings disparity between women and men. The bureau found that even if women's education, experience, and interruptions were the same as men's, the earnings gap would be reduced by only about five percentage points (U.S. Department of Labor, Women's Bureau, 1985).

## Pay Equity Strategies

Implementation of the laws and executive orders that followed the passage of Title VII focused on moving women into higher-paying, male-dominated occupations, either by eliminating barriers to women's entry or by encouraging women to seek these careers. It was increasingly recognized that the distinction between institutional and attitudinal barriers is to some extent a false dichotomy, since attitudes as well as social and economic institutions are the products of a history of sexual stratification.

During the 1970s, attention turned to the question of upward mobility for women, and the practice of "tracking" women and men, ostensibly in the same occupation, through different internal labor markets of firms or promotions systems of trades and professions (Bergmann, 1976). For instance, a firm may hire male and female economists with bachelors' degrees at the same pay rate, but after a time provide management opportunities for male economists while assigning the women to be research assistants. After a few years, the men are promoted and earning considerably more than the women, who are found to be "not qualified" for the higher positions because they lack management experience.

Equal employment opportunity only at the entry level will not eliminate the wage gap if men are later provided superior job opportunities within the firm. Unfortunately, it is more difficult to monitor internal pay and promotion practices than the entry-level offers that are publicly advertised. Although firms may be forced to demonstrate that they have not discriminated in hiring, they are not under similar public scrutiny when it comes to promotions, unless they are monitored by their own employees.

## Comparable Worth

The persistence of occupational segregation has led to the advocacy of a more direct approach to pay equity for women, namely equal pay for work of comparable value. This means compensation on the basis of the skill and responsibility entailed in the job, and not on the sex of the person performing it. Female jobs have traditionally been and remain undervalued because of their association with unpaid work in the home and because women are not seen as important economic providers. It was shown earlier, for instance, that an average child care worker earns far less than an unskilled construction laborer and a licensed practical nurse averages less than a truck driver. Jobs done predominantly by women tend to be low-paid, regardless of the skill and responsibility they require.

Because societal expectations condition the career patterns of many women, it is unrealistic to expect a rapid elimination of their occupational segregation. More than 60 percent of women (or men) would have had to change jobs in 1981 in order for the occupational distribution of the sexes to be the same (Blau and Ferber, 1986: 166–68). Most women apparently find no alternative to accepting the low pay offered in traditionally female occupations. In turn, because female labor is relatively cheap, employers have little incentive to structure women's jobs efficiently and to provide on-the-job training and opportunities for professional development. An effective comparable worth pay strategy that raises women's earnings could force a reevaluation of job quality in traditional female occupations.

While redress of the inequities caused by the undervaluation of work traditionally done by women is vital, continued progress in reducing occupational segregation of women is also important to weaken stereotypes regarding women's work. Improving women's access to male-dominated occupations and establishing comparable worth compensation in female-dominated occupations are important ways to reduce the pay gap.

## Education

Women and men at the same level of educational attainment still experience substantial differences in earnings, as shown in Table 3. Women college graduates who work full time, year round have earnings roughly on a par with male high school dropouts. This suggests that simply providing women with more education will not, by itself, eliminate the pay gap, although it may be an important element of employment strategy for low-income women.

## Recent Trends in the Pay Gap

After several decades of virtual stagnation, the pay gap has narrowed slightly. In 1978, the earnings ratio was 61 percent; by 1985, it was 68 percent. Most of this "improvement," however, was not the result of women moving into better-paying jobs. Rather, as noted earlier, there was a deep recession that had a disproportionate effect on the high-wage, male-dominated sectors of the economy. The same factors that caused men's unemployment rates to rise caused their real earnings to fall. Thus, the appearance of greater equality between men and women is actually the result of a deterioration in labor market conditions facing male workers rather than an absolute gain for women.

While women's earnings have barely kept pace with inflation, men's have fallen behind. In 1985, women's median weekly earnings of $283 would have purchased $172 in 1978 dollars, or about the same as their actual 1978 earnings of $166. Men's 1985 median weekly earnings of $410 would have purchased $249 in 1978 dollars, substantially less than their actual 1978 earnings of $271.

As the economy adapts to lower oil prices and an exchange value of the dollar more favorable to exports, it is likely that the goods-producing sectors will once again expand. It will be important to monitor progress on the pay equity front as the growth of these high-paying employment opportunities occurs. Without further reduction of occupational segregation, or progress in achieving comparable worth pay increases for women in traditional jobs, the pay gap could once again widen as job opportunities for male workers improve.

**Table 3** Yearly Earnings by Sex and Educational Attainment of Full-Time, Year-Round Workers, 1984 (in dollars)

| Educational attainment | Female earnings | Male earnings |
|---|---|---|
| Fewer than 8 years | 9,828 | 14,624 |
| 1–3 years high school | 11,843 | 19,120 |
| High school graduate | 14,569 | 23,269 |
| 1–3 years college | 17,007 | 25,831 |
| College graduate | 20,257 | 31,487 |
| 1 or more years postgraduate | 25,076 | 36,836 |

*Source:* U.S. Bureau of the Census, Current Population Reports, Series P-60, No. 149, *Money Income and Poverty Status of Families and Persons in the United States: 1984* (Washington, D.C.: U.S. Government Printing Office, 1985), Table 7.

## References

Blau, Francine and Marianne A. Ferber. *The Economics of Women, Men, and Work*. Englewood Cliffs, NJ: Prentice-Hall, 1986.

Mellor, Earl F. "Investigating Differences in Weekly Earnings of Women and Men." *Monthly Labor Review* 107 (June 1984):17–28.

Norwood, Janet L. *The Female-Male Earnings Gap: A Review of Employment and Earnings Issues*. Report 673. Washington, D.C.: U.S. Government Printing Office, September 1982.

U.S. Department of Labor, Women's Bureau. *Facts on U.S. Working Women*. Fact Sheet No. 85-7. Washington, D.C.: U.S. Department of Labor, Women's Bureau, July 1985.

# What Makes Women Poor?

*Barbara Ehrenreich*

One morning, Brenda C. woke up crying. "I couldn't take it anymore," she explained. My welfare check and food stamps were cut and I had to choose between paying the rent or buying food and school clothes for my growing kids—my oldest son's shoe size went from an eight to an eleven over one summer! Things had to be bought. What could I do?"

What Brenda did came as a shock to herself and her two sons, Kenny, thirteen, and Tony, eight. "I went down and enlisted in the army," she said. "It's my last chance to try and support my family. I don't know any other way." Soon afterwards, Brenda left for basic training, leaving Kenny and Tony in the care of a friend until she returned.

Brenda is black, a single parent in her thirties, and like many welfare recipients, she worked whenever she could. Her last job as a Volunteers in Service to America (VISTA) worker, organizing community food and nutrition programs, was eliminated when the Reagan administration revamped VISTA. The string of low-paid jobs that Brenda held never paid enough to support her family without public assistance. And when she wasn't working, welfare payments alone barely covered rent, household items, and school supplies. Often the food stamps didn't last through the end of the month. Brenda and her children managed by doing without almost everything but the essentials. Once their income shrank, however, even the essentials were not affordable.

Avis Parke joined the ranks of the American poor after her divorce from a middle-class husband, a minister. Avis, in her early fifties, is white and college educated. Like many other "displaced homemakers," she found a cold greeting in the job market.

*Parke* v. *Parke* was a classic case of a middle-aged man leaving for a younger woman; and when the marriage dissolved, so did Avis' middle-class life-style. Now, Avis and her three youngest children (the oldest three live on their own) have made an unheated New England summer cottage their year-round home. Avis survives on a tenuous combination of welfare, food stamps, child support, and a lot of thriftiness.

---



---

See Statistical Appendix Tables A–8, A–12, A–18, A–20, A–21, A–23, and A–24.

Avis and Brenda are among the more than 32 million Americans who live below the official poverty level: $9,287 for a nonfarm family of four in 1981. Today, one out of seven Americans is poor according to official measures. Many people know that poverty is on the rise. What many do not know is that more and more of the poor are women and their dependent children.

## The Increasing Impoverishment of Women

Two out of three poor adults in this country are women, and one out of five children is poor. Women head half of all poor families, and more than half the children in female-headed households are poor: 50 percent of white children, 68 percent of black and Latino children.[1] A woman over sixty is almost twice as likely as her male counterpart to be impoverished. One fifth of all elderly women are poor. For elderly black women, the poverty rate in 1981 was 43.5 percent; for elderly Latina women, 27.4 percent. Among black women over sixty-five living alone the 1982 poverty rate was about 82 percent.[2]

While the "feminization of poverty" isn't yet a household phrase, for growing numbers of women and their dependent children, it is an everyday reality. According to sociologist Diana Pearce, who tagged the trend in a 1978 study, 100,000 additional women with children fell below the poverty line each year from 1969 to 1978. In 1979, the number surged to 150,000, which was matched in 1980.[3] Households headed by women—now 15 percent of all American households—are the fastest growing type of family in the country.[4]

So clear is the spiraling pattern of women's impoverishment that the President's National Advisory Council on Economic Opportunity observed in September 1981: "All other things being equal, if the proportion of the poor in female-householder families were to continue to increase at the same rate as it did from 1967 to 1978, the poverty population would be composed solely of women and their children before the year 2000."

"All other things," of course, are not equal. Poverty is disproportionately borne by people of color, and with continued racial discrimination and high unemployment there will be many poor men in the year 2000. Yet, however many impoverished men there will be, there will still be many more poor women. Women are increasingly likely to carry primary responsibility for supporting themselves and their children as a result of rising divorce rates and nonmarital childbirths. At the same time, most women remain locked into dead-end jobs with wages too low to support themselves, let alone sustain a family. In 1980, the median income of a female household head, with no husband present, was $10,408; for black women it was $7,425 and for Latina women $7,031.

A 1977 government study found that if working women were paid what similarly qualified men earned, the number of poor families would decrease by half.[5] In 1980, the median income of a full-time, year-round working woman was $11,590—versus $19,172 for her male counterpart. In short, there is a fundamental difference between male and female poverty: for men, poverty is often the consequence of unemployment, and a job is generally an effective remedy, while female poverty often exists even when a woman works full-time.

Virtually all women are vulnerable—a divorce or widowhood is all it takes to throw many middle-class women into poverty. Yet as Sally Michaels (not her real name), a divorced mother of three, points out, "There is a lot of denial among women. It's like how people are about seat belts. They don't want to wear them because they don't want to face the fact that they're in danger."

## Decline of the Breadwinner Ethic

According to popular wisdom, it was women, and especially feminists, who brought about the "breakdown of the family."[6] What has gone almost unnoticed is that men, too, have changed and in a way that directly threatens the traditional family centered on the male breadwinner. In fact, in the last three decades, men have come to see themselves less and less as breadwinners and have ceased to measure their masculinity through their success as husbands and providers.

Yet, this drastic change in men, and in our cultural expectations of them, has been ignored, down-played, or else buried under the rubric of "changing sex roles." True, our expectations of adult womanhood have also altered dramatically in the last thirty years. The old feminine ideal—the full-time housewife with station wagon and suburban ranch house—has been largely replaced by the career woman with skirted suit and attaché case. Partly because the changes in the woman's role were given conscious articulation by the feminist movement, changes in men (and in the behavior expected of them) are usually believed to be derivative of, or merely reactive to, the changes in women. Yet what we could call "the male revolt" began well before the revival of feminism and stemmed from dissatisfactions every bit as deep, if not as idealistically expressed, as those that motivated the "second-wave" feminists.

Signs of male discontent began to emerge in the 1950s, a time when the media celebrated American "togetherness" and all men were expected to grow up only in order to settle down. To do anything else was less than grown-up, and the man who willfully deviated was judged, in both expert and popular opinion, to be "less than a man," someone about whom "you had to wonder." Yet, at the same time, middle-class men anguished over "conformity," which was covertly understood as acquiescence to the burdens of job and family. *Playboy* appeared, in 1953, as the first manifesto of open rebellion, describing wives as "parasites" and "gold diggers" that the free-spirited male eluded for life. By the end of the decade, the medical profession offered would-be male rebels a more respectable rationale than *Playboy's* hedonism: the responsibility of breadwinning (combined with cholesterol) was what drove men to early deaths from heart disease. Soon after, psychology, the erstwhile champion of male heterosexual conformity, did an about-face, reclassifying responsibility as "guilt" and guilt as a psychic "toxin." By the end of the 1970s, the old ideological props for the male breadwinner ethic had crumbled. Today the man who postpones marriage and avoids women who are likely to become financial dependents is considered not deviant but healthy.

The greater prosperity men gained from the decline of the breadwinner ethic has not, however, been shared by women. A consequence of the changed economic relationship between the sexes has been the feminization of poverty. Indeed, for an increasing number of single mothers, there is only one thing left of the family-wage system, the fact that women, on the average, are paid less than a family (at current urban rents, less than a very small family) requires for a moderate standard of living.

## The Goals of Feminism

If public policy cannot restore the breadwinner ethic and the male-centered family-wage system, then public policy can at least acknowledge their demise. To do so would require, for a start, a commitment to implementing some of the most elementary goals of feminism.

First, women should have the opportunity and the right to earn living wages, in fact, family wages, for many of them must support a family as well as themselves. This means the occupational segregation that locks 80 percent of women workers into low-paid "women's jobs" must be ended. It also means there must be greater financial recognition for those occupations that have come to be considered "women's work"—clerical, sales, light assembly, and service jobs. There must be an end to all forms of discrimination, subtle and otherwise, that have kept women out of men's higher-paid crafts and professions; and those who choose a "woman's job" such as nursing or clerical work, should receive pay equal to what men receive for jobs requiring comparable levels of skill and effort.

Nevertheless, the goal of financial independence for women, however elementary in the sense of having broad feminist support, is more radical than it may once have appeared. It is clear in the 1980s, if it was not in the more prosperous 1960s, that anti-discriminatory measures such as the Equal Rights Amendment are not enough to guarantee women's economic well-being. It will not help women to break out of their occupational ghetto if there are fewer and fewer well-paying jobs outside of it and it is hard to insist on higher pay from employers who are busily disinvesting, fleeing overseas, or replacing human labor with robots and microcomputers. For women (as well as for a growing number of men) the achievement of a family wage will require both a major redistribution of wealth and an economy planned to generate well-paying, useful employment—in short, an economic approach that is considerably to the left of anything in the current realm of American political discourse.

Second on the list of elementary goals, women need a variety of social supports before they will be able to enter the labor market on an equal footing with men. The most obvious and desperately needed service, both for women who are married and joint breadwinners and for those who are sole breadwinners, is reliable, high-quality child care. Job-training programs are another necessity, if only because so many of us, in all social classes, were educated for dependency and were never offered the skills that might sustain us through long stretches of financial independence, if not for a life-time. Finally we must recognize that at least for the foreseeable future, many women will find themselves unable to enter the labor market at all, either because they have small children to care for or because they cannot find jobs that pay enough for material subsistence. This means there must be a government program of adequate income support, something far more generous and dignified than our present system of welfare. It is worth recalling that even before the recent wave of budget cutbacks, there was no state where the combined benefits of Aid to Families with Dependent Children (AFDC), the major form of public assistance, and food stamps were enough to bring a family up to the official poverty level. For women supporting families, unemployment means destitution, and a minimum-wage job is not much of an improvement.

## The Need for Social Welfare

Feminists have demanded and fought for expanded social welfare programs from the beginning of our movement in the 1960s, a time when such a policy seemed reasonable and even inevitable, to a time when any expansion of government spending, other than military, is viewed as subversive to economic stability. Yet I believe that we need to push this set of demands even further. The collapse of the family-wage system requires nothing less than the creation of a welfare state, that is, a state committed to the welfare of its citizens and prepared to meet their needs—for financial assistance, medical care, education, child care, etc.—when they are unable to meet those needs themselves.

Those who believe that the country can no longer collectively afford such services should consider two obvious sources of revenue for social purposes: (1) increased corporate income taxes (corporate taxes have been declining steadily as a share of federal revenue since the 1950s while the burden of financing government activities has been shifted to individuals) and (2) drastically reduced military expenditures. As more and more people are coming to realize, our present stock of missiles and countermissiles does not constitute a "defense" but a standing invitation to annihilation. The kind of defense program we most urgently need is a program of defense against the mounting domestic dangers of poverty, unemployment, disease, and ignorance—that is, we need a welfare state.

If that phrase, "welfare state," has been made to sound morally distasteful by our current policy makers, we should recall that the family-wage system was itself a kind of private-sector welfare system, in which a woman's only "entitlement" was her share of her husband's wage. Those who believe that it is somehow more honorable to rely on an individual man than on agencies created by public wealth are simply clinging to an idealized memory of male paternalism. The breadwinner ethic never had the strength of law or even the transient support of public policy. If men cannot be held responsible as individuals—and there is no way consistent with democracy to do so—then we must all become more responsible collectively.

There are those who will argue that a welfare state only substitutes one sort of paternalism for another. The conservative analysis of the social welfare programs of the 1960s is that they failed, and that they failed because they engendered dependency and helplessness in their beneficiaries. (This, at least, is George Gilder's argument; others on the right argue that there is no need for further social welfare spending because the programs of the 1960s succeeded.) I am more impressed by the analysis of scholars such as Frances Fox Piven and Richard Cloward that the social welfare programs introduced in the 1960s, limited as they were, succeeded not only in lifting many of their direct beneficiaries out of poverty but in enabling working people in the "near poor" category, which includes so many women, to struggle for wage and benefit gains from their employers.

Not, as Piven and Cloward would agree, that those programs are in any way adequate models for the future. In fact, one of the most important feminist criticisms of the programs that constituted President Lyndon Johnson's Great Society is that they tended to assume a society of male breadwinners and female dependents. Thus, for example, Aid to Families with Dependent Children, whose beneficiaries are primarily single mothers and their children, continues to be based on the premise that the mere presence of a male in the household is a cure for poverty and a sufficient reason to suspend or reduce benefits. Job training programs such as the Comprehensive Employment and Training Act (CETA) have been faulted for tracking women toward low-wage service employment and away from potentially well-paying technical jobs. As Diana Pearce argues, social services must be based on the "acknowledgement that more and more women are financially on their own; that the female headed household is here to stay." Otherwise, government programs pepetuate the myth of male paternalism and the reality of female financial dependence.

Nor is there any reason why social welfare programs have to be intrinsically paternalistic. Frank Riessman, Alan Gartner, and many others have made a convincing case over the past ten years that publicly sponsored services do not have to be bureaucratically or professionally dominated but can actually generate participatory citizenship and self-help initiatives. For example, instead of funding programs like Medicaid, which has served as a bountiful subsidy to the medical profession and associated industries, government health-care initiatives could focus on the direct provision of care, on preventive measures, and on environmental improvement. And surely financial assistance does not have to carry the stigma associated with welfare. Consider the contrast between unemployment insurance, which is collected by both men and women, and welfare, which is primarily collected by women. There is no reason why the institutions of an American welfare state could not be democratic, accountable, decentralized, and respectful of individual dignity—and there is no reason why liberals and feminists should abandon this as a goal.

I do not propose an expanded welfare state as an ultimate social goal but as a pragmatic step that circumstances have forced upon us. My utopian visions are far more socialistic, more democratic at every level of dialogue and decision making, more "disorderly," as Paul Goodman would have said, than anything that would ordinarily be described as a welfare state. Yet women like Brenda C. and Avis Parke have very few immediate alternatives. If they had won equality and economic independence before the collapse of the family-wage system, they might have been able to step right into the liberal feminist vision of an androgynous and fully capitalist society. But the collapse of the family-wage system came first, before either the economy or the culture was ready to admit the female breadwinner on equal terms. The result is that for an increasing number of women and children, the services that an adequate welfare state should provide have become essential to survival.

## Relations With Men

But what about the men? For there is, of course, more at stake here than their wages. The collapse of the breadwinner ethic, and with it the notion of long-term emotional responsibility toward women, affects not only the homemaker who could be cut loose into poverty but the financially self-sufficient working woman, not to mention the children of either. For better or worse, most of us grew up expecting that our lives would be shared with those of the men in our generation; that we would marry or, in the modern vernacular, that we would have "long-term committed relationships." Only within those relationships could we imagine having children (and not only because of the financial consequences of motherhood) or finding the emotional support to do what we increasingly identified as our own things. Yet we—and the "we" here includes not only the educated urban women, feminists and others, whom conservatives might dismiss as members of marginal groups—face the prospect of briefer "relationships," punctuated by emotional dislocations and seldom offering the kind of loyalty that might extend into middle age. If we accept the male revolt as a fait accompli and begin to act on its economic consequences for women, are we not in some way giving up on men? Are we aquiescing to a future in which men will always be transients in the lives of women and never fully members of the human family?

To an extent, that is what women are beginning to do: look for emotional support and loyalty from other women, while remaining, in most instances, sexually inclined toward men. A neighbor, abandoned by her husband two years ago, still hopes to meet "a nice, reliable guy," but her daily needs for intimacy and companionship are met by a local women's group. An acquaintance, single and successful in her career, plans to have a baby with the help of women friends who are committed to serving as "co-parents." Two divorced women in their fifties decide that it will be both cheaper and less lonely to share the suburban house that one of them inherited from her marriage. According to Howard University professor Harriette McAdoo, there has always been a strong tradition of mutual support among urban black women, and a similar pattern is now emerging among the growing number of single women in the suburbs. That aid may involve practical help, like the exchange of babysitting or the loan of a credit card, and it usually involves affectionate support—friends to call in a moment of depression or to share a holiday meal. These are small steps, improvisations, but they grow out of a clear-headed recognition that there is no male breadwinner to lean on and probably not much use in waiting for one to appear.

Yet I would like to think that a reconciliation between the sexes is still possible. In fact, so long as we have sons as well as daughters, it will have to happen. "Grown-up", for men, should have some meaning for a boy other than "gone away"; and adulthood should mean more than moral vagrancy. If we cannot have—and do not want—a binding pact between the sexes, we still must have one between the generations, and that means there must be a renewal of loyalty and trust between adult men and women. But what would be the terms of such a reconciliation? We have seen the instability, and the indignity, of a bond based on a man's earnings and a woman's dependence. We cannot go back to a world where maturity meant "settling," often in stifled desperation, for a life perceived as a "role." Nor can we accept the nightmare anomie of the pop psychologists' vision: a world where other people are objects of consumption, a world of chance encounters of a "self" propelled by impulse alone.

I can see no other ethical basis for a reconciliation than the feminist principle often repeated—that women are also persons, with the same need for respect, for satisfying work, for love, and for pleasure as men. As it is, male culture seems to have abandoned the breadwinner role without overcoming the sexist attitudes that role has perpetuated: on the one hand, the expectation of female nurturance and submissive service as a matter of right; on the other hand, a misogynist contempt for women as "parasites" and entrappers of men. In a "world without a father," that is, without the private system of paternalism built into the family-wage system, we will have to learn to be brothers and sisters.

Finally, I would hope that we might meet as rebels together—not against one another but against a social order that condemns so many of us to meaningless or degrading work in return for a glimpse of commodified pleasures and condemns all of us to the prospect of mass annihilation. If we can do this, if we can make a common commitment to ourselves and future generations, then it may also be possible to rebuild the notion of personal commitment and to give new strength and meaning to the words we have lost—responsibility, maturity, and even, perhaps, manliness.

## Notes

1. See U.S. Department of Commerce, Bureau of the Census, "A Statistical Portrait of Women in the U.S.," *Current Population Reports,* Special Study, Series P-23, no. 56, 1976 and "Characteristics of the Population Below the Poverty Level," *Current Population Reports,* 1978, cited by Harriette McAdoo and Diana Pearce in "Women and Children: Alone and in Poverty," in National Advisory Council on Economic Opportunity, *Final Report* (National Advisory Council on Economic Opportunity, 1981); and *Current Population Survey* cited by the Children's Defense Fund, *A Children's Defense Budget: An Analysis of the President's Budget and Children* (Washington, D.C.: Children's Defense Fund, 1982).

2. *New York Times,* 19 December 1982; Alexander Cockburn and James Ridgeway, *Village Voice,* 1 March 1983, pp. 10–11.
3. Diana Pearce, "The Feminization of Poverty: Women, Work and Welfare," *Urban and Social Change Review,* February 1978; Statistics from an interview with Pearce, March 1982.
4. See Bureau of the Census, "Profile of the United States: 1981, *Current Population Reports,* Series P-20, no. 374 and "Families Maintained by Female Headed Householders 1970–79," *Current Population Reports,* Series P-23, no. 107 (Washington, D.C.: Government Printing Office, 1980).
5. Patricia C. Sexton, *Women and Work,* Research and Development Monograph no. 46 (Washington, D.C.: U.S. Department of Labor, Employment and Training Administration, 1977), cited in the National Advisory Council on Economic Opportunity, *Final Report* (Washington, D.C.: National Advisory Council on Economic Opportunity, 1981).
6. Barbara Ehrenreich, "The Male Revolt: After the Breadwinner Vanishes," *The Nation,* 26 February 1983, pp. 225, 240–42.

# Women and Children Last

## *Center for Popular Economics*

Conservative economics has brought some bad news for women, as well as some not-so-bad news. The not-so-bad news is that the availability of paid employment (albeit in segregated occupations at low wages) and of government income support programs (however inadequate) has meant that women's access to income is no longer restricted to that which is redistributed to them through marriage. The bad news is that women with children but without male breadwinners are more likely to be poor.

Three quarters of the 6.2 million new jobs which opened up between 1979 and 1984 went to women. But women have not succeeded in closing the gender gap in living standards. Despite dramatic increases in the number of employed women, women's average income—obtained either from wages, the government, and/or husbands—relative to men's income did not improve over these years.[1] Almost a million more families headed by women fell below the official poverty line between 1979 and 1984 . . .[2]

The increased employment of women relative to men in the labor market was offset, on the one hand, by cuts in the public programs on which women's—and children's—living standards depend; and on the other hand, by the continuing increase in the number of women whose household income is not augmented by a male paycheck. Just short of half of all adult women now live in such households.[3]

Yet conservative economic policies are not the only thing working against women and their families. There is also a distinct conservative social "gender agenda" that aims to restore the male-headed, nuclear family—which they call *the* family—to its former prominence. The Reverend Jerry Falwell writes:

> The strength and stability of families determine the vitality and moral life of society. The most important function performed by the family is the rearing and character formation of children, a function it was uniquely designed to perform, and for which no remotely adequate substitute has been found. The family is the best and most efficient "department of health, education and welfare."[4]

---



---

See Statistical Appendix Tables A–8, A–12, A–13, A–18, A–21, and A–23.

Cutbacks in government health, education and welfare programs—especially those which support unmarried women with children—are welcomed as a crucial strategic victory in what fundamentalist Tim LaHaye calls "The Battle for the Family."[5]

Does the agenda of patriarchal fundamentalism dovetail with other programs of the new economic orthodoxy—an overvalued dollar, high interest rates, and the attack on organized labor? The answer, ironically, is no. These national economic policies decimated the predominantly male manufacturing, mining, and construction sectors, and pushed many women into a depressed labor market. This is hardly what Reverend Falwell had in mind.

The conservative social and economic agenda has been a response not only to the structural crisis of the capitalist economy, but to the crisis of the traditional family as well. Much of the support for the conservative agenda over the past decade has come not from the businessman's concern with the long-term decline in profits or from the bankers' project to restore the Almighty Dollar; rather, it springs from an attempt to buttress a traditional concept of what it means to be a man and a woman in our society. Ironically, by drawing more women into the labor force, the economic policies of the right have done as much to challenge as to support their preferred form of "the family."

Thus the implicit industrial policy of conservative economics—to shift labor out of well-paid manufacturing and into lower-wage services—is on a collision course with the overt family policy of the right—to accept no substitutes for the patriarchal family. Women and children are caught in the middle.

## Women Hold Up Half the Economy (at Less Than Half the Price)

Many women have entered the labor market over the past two decades (see Figure 1). Why has their standard of living relative to men not improved?

Important changes in women's economic status have occurred over the past two decades, in both access to earned income and to governmental transfers and in-kind services. But the relative earnings of full-time female workers have shown little improvement. In 1970, women earned 62.3% of what men did. By 1983, the figure inched up to 66.5%, then dipped in 1984 to 64.8% (see Figure 2).

Many have pointed out the disappointingly slow pace of improvement. Responding to 1984 projections of further gradual improvements, Sandra Farha, President of the California National Organization of Women said:

> I hear them saying to women, "Hey, its getting better. You're increasing your earning power. Don't feel bad if you're only making 59 cents. You'll be making 74 cents soon."[6]

At the rate of improvement between 1970 and 1984, the 74 cent figure would be attained in the year 2031—by our granddaughters.

Conservatives point to the increased visibility of professional women as evidence of economic progress. While the percentage of women in law, medical and manage-

**Figure 1.** Women Enter the Labor Market

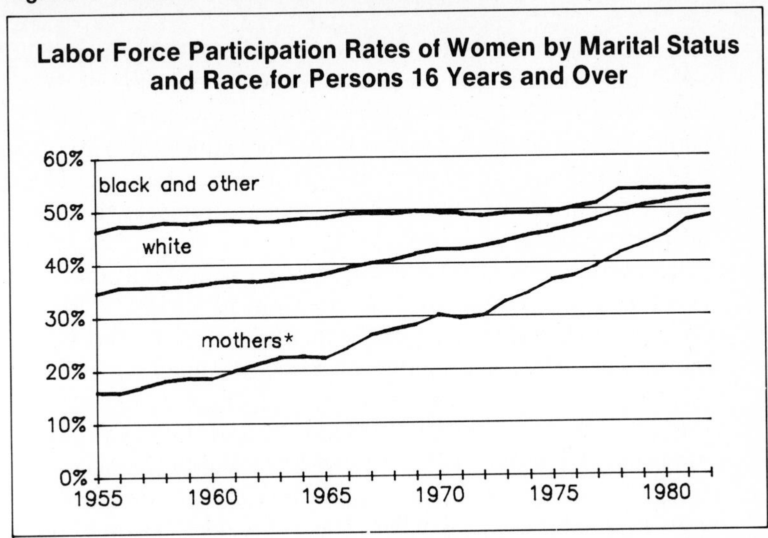


*Source:* U.S. Department of Labor Handbook of Labor Statistics, 1985 Table 5, pp. 18–19, 22.
*Mothers refers to married women with children under 6.

**Figure 2.** Women Run Hard to Stay in Place (Ratio of Female to Male Median Weekly Earnings for Full-Time Wage and Salary Workers, 1974–1984)

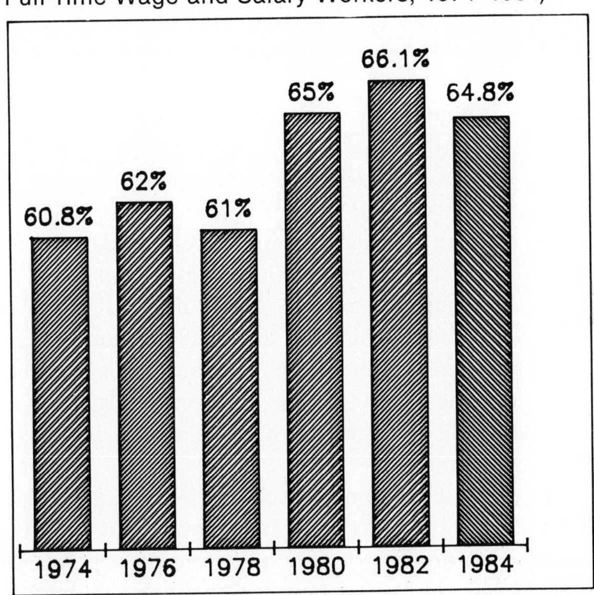


*Source:* For 1984 figures: Employment and Earnings, January 1985, p. 210; for all other years, various Statistical Abstracts of the United States.

ment professions increased between 1979 and 1984, most women remain in low-paid, "pink-collar" job ghettos. Changes in the federal classification of occupational categories in 1983 make long-term comparisons difficult.[7] But a look at some detailed occupational categories shows that close to 50% of all women are employed in 20 occupations out of over 200 possible occupations. The top 10 occupations, which account for one-third of all women employees, changed little between 1980 and 1984.

Between 1979 and 1983, the ratio of year-round full-time female to male workers' income improved for women, moving from 59% to 64%. But this "improved" ratio was based on a descending target—men's income. During this four-year period, the real income of men fell a crushing $1483. Women's real income increased by less than $24 over the entire four-year period.[8] The average women's earning power was stuck on a treadmill, barely keeping up with inflation.

Furthermore, a slight rise in women's recorded income and the entry of a few women into professional and managerial positions does not spell generally improving living standards for women. This is because "income" measures only earnings and government transfers, and not transfers from other household earners, particularly husbands. The amount of money women actually receive in their households simply does not appear in income statistics. Changes in the real economic picture of women, therefore, cannot be accurately assessed in earned income figures alone.

To gain a more comprehensive picture, we have estimated a measure of the relative standard of living of women which takes account of all sources of livelihood: spouse and other family members, government transfers, and wage and other income. Of course, we do not know how income is actually shared by the members of a household. Our measure must therefore be an approximation. We measure the per capita income of all households with women and compare that to the per capita income of all households with men. We thus measure the average access to livelihood (measured in dollars) of women compared to men on the assumption that income is equally shared within households. We term our measure the *P*er capita *A*ccess to *R*esources or PAR (see Figure 3).[9]

Taking account of sharing within households, the per capita income of women in 1983 was 87% of the per capita income of men. We term the difference between men's and women's income 13 points under PAR. Since 1967, the first year for which we were able to calculate the index, the amount by which women were under PAR gradually increased through the late 1970s, and has remained constant since. Between 1967 and 1983, the gap between men's and women's income has doubled almost exactly, despite the fact that the ratio of female to male incomes of full-time workers was rising.

Much of the decline in the relative living standards of women stems from the rapid increase in the percentage of women living in households with no adult male. This change in family structure has been made possible in part by changing social attitudes and legal practices concerning divorce. It has also been facilitated by women's reduced economic dependence on men, caused by the expansion of jobs avail-

**Figure 3.** The Gender Gap in Income Widens*

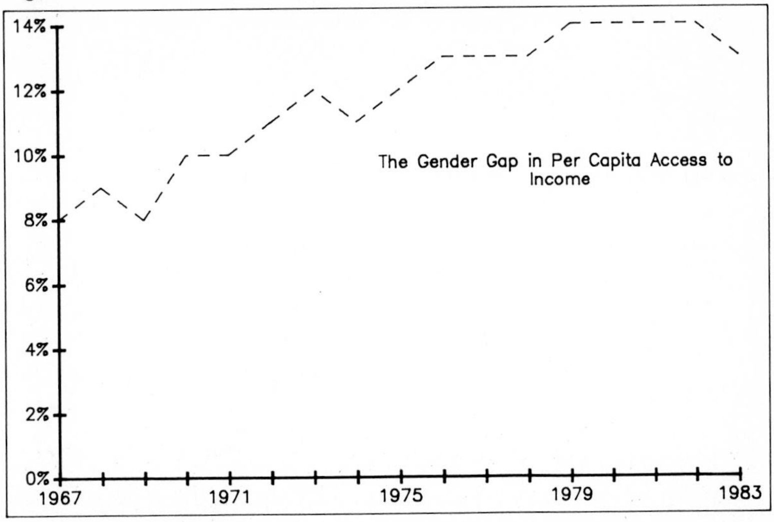

14%
12%
10%
8%
6%
4%
2%
0%
1967 1971 1975 1979 1983
The Gender Gap in Per Capita Access to Income

*One minus the PAR index** measures the gap between gender equality (PAR equals one) and the actual situation.

****Measuring the PAR Index.** The PAR index is an estimate of the average per capita income of women relative to men. To construct it, we made the hypothetical assumption that income is shared equally by household members.

We first calculated the total income of married women by multiplying the number of married couple households by their per capita income. We then calculated the income of unmarried women and other female headed households (these include married women with husband absent, divorced women, single women, and widows) by multiplying the number of such households by their per capita incomes. We added the two incomes together and then divided the sum by the total number of households with women in them to get the numerator of the ratio. Performing the same operation for men yields the denominator.

able to women and some sources of income support through AFDC, Food Stamps, and other government programs.

Reduced economic dependence on men is a major gain for many women, but the monetary costs of being without a man are still high. Well over a third of female-headed households live below the poverty line, and the fraction is rising. . . . Indeed, per capita household income varies greatly with marital status. By comparison, with married-couple households, the per capita income of divorced men is 57% greater; divorced women are 26% poorer; men with wife absent are 27% richer; and women with husband absent are 56% poorer.[10]

According to the logic of conservative economics, what the market does not provide, the family will. But the market has provided women with jobs in unprecedented numbers and partly as a result, the male-centered single-earner family of conservative lore is a fast-fading myth. Many of the budgetary decisions and policy and legislative initiatives of the current administration can be understood as an attempt to offset the increase in women's autonomy that the growing demand for labor has afforded.

## Government Off Whose Backs?

Triggered by the dissolution of the male breadwinning family and the "ghettoization" of women into low-paying jobs, women's under-PAR income has been exacerbated by changes in the role and philosophy of government under the reign of the new right. Conservatives not only identify the government as the source of all evil in the economy; they also decry government "intervention" in the family.

Embracing a political philosophy that goes beyond the New Federalism, Reagan has publicly stated his admiration for family traditionalist George Gilder, author of *Wealth and Poverty.* In his book, Gilder argues it is the government—in the form of the welfare state—which is responsible for the collapse of the family, as well as the stagnation of the economy.

According to Gilder, income-support programs for poor and unemployed women undermine the breadwinning role of the father. As a result, men have lost the incentive to work and labor productivity has suffered. Furthermore, Gilder claims, the high taxes required to support the welfare state have caused family after-tax income to fall, driving women out of their homes and into the labor force. The male-headed nuclear family has been the casualty.

The policy prescriptions that emerge from these views are clear: cut personal income taxes and slash public income support for unmarried women and their children. The advantage of such a strategy, based on unleashing the "free" market, is that the same policies implicitly double as prescriptions for the economy and for the family.

The stated objectives of Reagan's conservative economic policies, however, have obscured their implications for women and for family structure. Under the rubric of getting government "off our backs," conservatives have advocated not only cuts in public support specifically for women but generally in domestic government spending.

But since militarism is one of the planks of the conservative economic approach, defense spending is exempt from conservative budget-cutting scissors. Instead, income-support and human development programs have been the primary target of conservative proposals to cut government spending. Congress and public opinion have curtailed the possibility of severe cuts in Social Security programs which support the elderly, leaving unemployed and poor families to bear the brunt of the budget cuts. . . . While programs for low-income families constitute less than 10% of federal expenditures, they sustained 30% of all budget cuts between 1981 and 1985.[11]

Because women and children comprise a large and increasing proportion of the poor, the primary recipients of public income-support programs are women. Indeed, the number of poor persons in female-headed households rose by 100,000 a year between the mid-1960s and the mid-1970s. According to feminist analysts Barbara Ehrenreich and Frances Piven, two of three adults living below the poverty level in 1980 were women; more than half of poor families were headed by women.[12]

Because of the increasing "feminization of poverty," the cuts in income-support and other social programs which began in 1981 disproportionately affected women.[13] A study by the Coalition on Women and the Budget found that 94% of all families who receive AFDC (Aid to Families with Dependent Children) payments were maintained by women (as of March 1979); 63% of all SSI recipients (Supplemental Security Income) were women (as of December 1981). Moreover, Medicaid and Food Stamp recipients in 1983 were 60% and 85% female, respectively, while legal services clients were 67% female.[14] Women of color have been particularly hard-hit. In 1980, black female-headed families comprised 27.7% of all female-headed families but 43.4% of all families that are poor.[15]

The effects of the social spending cuts on women's living standards were worsened by the 1980–1982 recession, which generated the highest rates of unemployment since the 1930s. Prior to the conservative strategy of cutting the federal budget when the economy is contracting, income-support programs functioned precisely in reverse: to provide counter-cyclical assistance to people hurt by an economic downturn.

Cutting public support precisely at the moment when the market curtails economic opportunity, however, is the "stick" approach of conservative economics. The elimination of social welfare as a source of support "frees" large numbers of women workers for the expanding low-wage service economy.[16]

Besides the threat of poverty, there is an added twist when the stick approach is applied to women. Like men, they are subject to the "discipline of the market"; unlike men, they are also subject to the discipline of the family. Reduced options, either in the labor market or in social support programs, may force women into dependence on men. Once there, if they become victims of domestic violence, they will find battered women's shelters underfunded. Even before the Reagan budget cuts, battered women's shelters across the country were forced to turn away three times the number of people they served.[17]

## Women and Children Last

A favorite target of conservative cuts in social spending programs is the AFDC program. Leading the attacks is Charles Murray. In his book *Losing Ground: American Social Policy 1950–1980,* Murray argues that AFDC reduces the poor's incentive to work. Perhaps more than any other social program, AFDC represents an alternative—however meager—to the male-headed nuclear family for women with children.

Conservative policies rest on the assumption that childbearing and childrearing are private, not social, responsibilities. But the costs of raising children—in labor and material resources—are disproportionately borne by women.[18]

Furthermore, it is unlikely that the long-term trend toward nonmarriage will be reversed. An increasing number of children, therefore, will be part of female-headed households. Given that children take shares out of female income which is at poverty level or below, it is not surprising that the economic welfare of such households depends primarily on the age and number of children within them. Economist Nancy Folbre had termed this phenomenon "the pauperization of motherhood."[19]

Like public support to the elderly, public intergenerational transfers of income to children comprise part of government responsibility in most other industrialized countries. Indeed, according to a recent study, the United States does less to relieve the private costs of rearing children than any of the other industrialized countries.[20]

Government income support for raising children, which often takes the form of child welfare allowance, reflects the reality that child-rearing is not only work but work that is important to the long-term health of the economy. Indeed, child-rearing might be considered the most important of all long-term economic investments. Yet, it is labor which is unpaid.

Recent data on the amount of unpaid work performed in the home by women and men are difficult to obtain, but there is no evidence that men are participating substantially more. The available information suggests that the amount of time women spend doing unpaid work is falling, but that their total work week (waged and unwaged work) is rising. The bulk of necessary work at home is still left up to women. Victor Fuchs estimated that women performed 70% of "non-market" work in 1979.[21]

Women provide 30–40% of all wage work and 70% of all unwaged work; yet the ratio of average income of women with income relative to that of men with income in 1983 was 42%.[22] In other words, it is likely that women do over half of all the work that gets done in this country and continue to make less than half of what men do.

## The New Double Standard

Our contention that conservative economics is about family policy as well as economic policy helps to explain aspects of it that otherwise appear to be contradictory. The 1985 *Economic Report of the President,* for example, emphasized a reduced role for the federal government in all aspects of the economy. In particular, it supported deregulation, competition and free choice. In other statements, Reagan administration officials have objected to government interference in the "free" labor market to overcome sexual and racial discrimination by mandating that all work of comparable value to the employer is paid equally. Indeed, Clarence Pendleton, head of the Civil Rights Commission, called comparable worth the "looniest idea since looney tunes."[23]

According to a report in *Business Week,* if women today earned even three quarters of what men did, the country's total wage bill would be an additional $100 billion.[24] That means that discrimination cost every employed woman $2,123.38 in 1984.[25] It is clear that what is meant by the "market solution" is the continuation of depressed wages for women because discrimination is part of the marketplace.

Furthermore, so committed are conservatives to the workings of the existing "free" market they have reduced government support for programs that help women compete in the market. The Women's Educational Equity Act, funded at $10 million in 1981, was cut to $5.8 million in 1984, and was slated to receive no funds at all in the proposed FY1986 budget.[26]

Similarly, Title IV of the Civil Rights Act of 1964, which provides school districts with technical assistance to comply with federal anti-discrimination laws, received $37 million in 1981, $24 million in 1984, and zero requested dollars in FY1986. Provisions of the Vocational Education Act (which mirrors the occupational distribution) have been proposed for elimination.[27]

According to a recent report in *The New York Times,* the Reagan administration has begun a review of regulations that, in the words of Vice President Bush, are perceived to be "burdensome, unnecessary or counterproductive." Among those guidelines under review are the sexual harassment guidelines of the Equal Opportunity Commission ("terms such as unwelcome sexual advances and verbal sexual conduct . . . rely greatly on individual perception") and those that prohibit a job selection process "that disproportionately excludes members of a race, sex or ethnic group." Title IX policies which require equal expenditures on male and female athletic programs are also slated for review.[28]

The President, who campaigned against the Equal Rights Amendment on the grounds that adequate legislation against sex discrimination already exists, has curtailed enforcement of those laws. Reagan's Justice Department has also changed the standard by which discrimination can be said to exist. According to an Urban Institute Report, court decisions in the years prior to 1981 have held that the effects of apparent discrimination, e.g. underrepresentation of women in a particular firm's pattern of promotion, was sufficient cause to order a remedy. The current Justice Department standard requires instead the more stringent proof of *intent* to discriminate.[29] As a result, the Equal Employment Opportunity Commission (EEOC) failed to find violations in 40% of all new charges filed with it in 1984. The figure for 1981 was 23%.[30] Federal outlays for enforcement of equal opportunity statutes have also declined. Between FY1981 and FY1983 the EEOC saw its budget cut by 10% in real terms and its staff by 12%. The EEOC is authorized to initiate litigation against discriminators. Between 1981 and 1983 there was a 60% decline in lawsuits filed by the Commission.[31]

Ironically, an administration which campaigned on the platform of getting the government off the backs of the American people and out of the economy has also attempted to legislate the most private aspect of people's lives. The conservative attack on abortion, homosexuality, and family planning is directed at legislating people's—especially women's—sexual decisions. Restricting access to abortion is prominent among President Reagan's social policy goals.[32] Conservatives have gone so far as to support a so-called Human Life Amendment to the U.S. Constitution. And the New Right aims to overturn the *Roe* vs. *Wade* Supreme Court decision (1973) which ruled that a woman's decision to end a pregnancy was a fundamental right to privacy protected by the 14th Amendment.

## Conclusion

The changing relationship of family, economy, and government in the U.S. today has not opened up new vistas of economic opportunity and personal choice to women: it has closed them down. Continuing labor market discrimination and cutbacks in income support programs leave many women with little choice but to endure unwanted marriages, exchanging their autonomy for their livelihood.

To improve women's—and children's—living standards and to make individual choice about family structure a reality, public policy must move in three directions: (1) it must increase women's employment opportunities and remuneration; (2) it must provide adequate public support for the work of child-rearing; and (3) it must provide adequate income support programs. As long as child-raising is devalued and unpaid, and as long as discrimination persists in labor markets, women will continue to share unequally in social income and their personal liberty will be constrained.

Establishing greater social responsibility for children and their caretakers through government is a high-priority step for reducing women's and children's poverty, involving a major reorientation of the relationship between state and family. By way of comparison, an enormous transformation of the relationship between government and the private economy was necessary to address the record levels of unemployment in the Great Depression. After the end of World War II, tremendous headway was made in reducing unemployment because the government made a commitment to moderate the effect of the business cycle. Likewise, poverty among the elderly was reduced because the government committed itself to transfers through the Social Security system. Something of the same order is now necessary to contend with the social challenge of female-headed families.

Women and men are increasingly choosing non-traditional family structures: many are single, many will pass through one or more marriages, many live in collectives, many live in lesbian and gay couples. Allowing a wide and broadening range of family choices must be a central tenet of any society which calls itself democratic. Neither the market nor the traditional family—the two pillars of conservative thought and social policy—will secure this liberty; indeed, we have suggested that they constitute obstacles to broadening the range of choices facing women and men.

Without active government intervention in markets to combat discrimination; without the recognition of child-raising as socially valued work worthy of social remuneration; and without the establishment of an adequate income floor, the freedom to choose will remain a mirage for most—and for many, an impoverished freedom.

## Footnotes

1. See Figure 3 which presents our calculations of women's income relative to men's.
2. U.S. Census Bureau, Current Population Survey, P-60 Series, 1985.
3. Thirty-two percent in 1983, up from 30% in 1979 and 22% in 1967, U.S. Census Bureau, Current Population Survey, *Money Income of Families, Households and Persons in the United States,* P-60 Series, 1985.
4. Reverend Jerry Falwell, *The Fundamentalist Phenomenon: The Resurgence of Conservative Christianity,* Doubleday, New York, 1981, p. 206.
5. Tim LaHaye, *The Battle for the Family,* Fleming H. Revell Company.
6. *The New York Times,* October 31, 1984.
7. Nancy F. Rytina and Suzanne M. Bianchi document those changes in *Monthly Labor Review,* March, 1984, Vol. 107, No. 3, pp. 11–17.
8. *Economic Report of the President,* 1985, p. 264. The figures are in 1983 dollars.
9. The measure does not take account of taxes, or of in-kind transfers of any sort.
10. The data are from U.S. Census Bureau, Current Population Survey 1983. Elaine McCrate has measured the changing "cost of non-marriage" over the post-war period. While it has declined in the 1980s due to falling male incomes, it rose substantially in the 1960s and 1970s. Elaine McCrate, "The Growth of Non-Marriage Among U.S. Women," Ph.D. Dissertation, University of Massachusetts, Amherst, 1985.
11. Center on Budget and Policy Priorities, *End Results: The Impact of Federal Policies Since 1980 on Low Income Americans,* Washington, D.C., 1984.
12. Barbara Ehrenreich and Frances Piven, "The Feminization of Poverty: When the Family Wage System Breaks Down," *Dissent,* Spring 1984, p. 162.
13. Diana Pearce coined the term in "Women, Work and Welfare: The Feminization of Poverty," in Karen Wolk Feinstein, Ed., *Working Women and Their Families,* Sage Publications, London, 1979.
14. Coalition for Women and the Budget, *Inequality of Sacrifice,* National Women's Law Center, Washington, D.C., 1984. Food stamp recipients include women and children combined. Women also constitute more than 50% of Social Security recipients. This program, however, was not severely trimmed back.
15. Catherine L. Hammond, "Not Always 'Just a Husband Away From Poverty': Race, Class, and the Feminization of Poverty," Mimeo, University of Massachusetts, Amherst, 1982, p. 25.
16. Frances F. Piven, and Richard A. Cloward, *The New Class War: Reagan's Attack on the Welfare State and Its Consequences,* Pantheon, New York, 1982.
17. Coalition on Women and the Budget, *op. cit.*
18. Nancy Folbre, "The Pauperization of Motherhood: Patriarchy and Public Policy in the U.S.," *Review of Radical Political Economics,* Vol. 16, No. 4, 1985. While social conservatives like Gilder suggest that women shoulder the burden because welfare payments have undermined the traditional family, there is evidence that even within male-headed families, the time costs of bearing and rearing children fall disproportionately on women.
19. *Ibid.*
20. Alfred J. Kayn and Sheila B. Kamerman, "Income Maintenance, Wages, and Family Income," *Public Welfare,* Fall 1983.
21. Victor Fuchs, "His and Hers: Gender Differences in Work and Income, 1959–1979," Working Paper No. 1501, National Bureau of Economic Research, New York, 1984.
22. *Economic Report of the President,* 1985, Table B-27, p. 264.
23. *The New York Times,* November 17, 1984, p. A15.
24. *Business Week,* January 28, 1985, p. 81.
25. Calculated from a total female labor force of

47,095,000 in 1982. See *Statistical Abstract of the United States 1984,* p. 413.
26. Coalition on Women and the Budget, *op. cit.*
27. *Ibid.*
28. *The New York Times,* August 12, 1984.
29. John L. Palmer, and Isabel V. Sawhill, Ed. *The Reagan Record,* Urban Institute, Washington, D.C., 1984, p. 206.
30. *Coalition on Women and the Budget, op. cit.,* p. 51.
31. Palmer and Sawhill, *op. cit.*
32. *The New York Times,* July 21, 1985.

# Part 3
# INSTITUTIONAL PROBLEMS

This section addresses social problems specific to six institutional areas. Chapter 6 examines three family-related problems. Martin O'Connell and David Bloom focus on a major problem of contemporary families—child care. Over 50 percent of American mothers with children under six are in the work force, yet American society has the poorest child care arrangements of any industrialized nation. Joyce Ladner's essay addresses the major problem of black teenage pregnancy, looking at the sources and consequences, as well as pointing to some possible solutions. The final essay, by the editors of *Dollars & Sense,* shows how government policies, even those by a so-called pro-family administration, negatively impact family life.

Chapter 7 is devoted to issues surrounding work. The first essay, by Warner Woodworth, describes how the monetary rewards of work are so unequal. The next three articles examine various manifestations of the transformation of the economy from one based on manufacturing to one based on providing services. The editors of *Dollars & Sense* examine the problems generated by the new service economy. Eileen Boris then focuses on a special form of worker exploitation, those who work in their homes. Finally, John Kasarda shows the negative impact of the changing economy on cities and certain populations within cities.

The topic of Chapter 8 is the way society is structured to care for the health of society's members. The first two articles—by Michael Millenson and Mimi Abramovitz—show how health care delivery depends on money rather than need. Peter Taylor's article moves to a different health area—government policies that not only permit, but promote the sale of tobacco, an acknowledged unhealthy substance. Peter Conrad then tackles society's response to the AIDS crisis. Finally, Rashi Fein offers some solutions to providing equal health care to all in society.

The media disseminate information in society. Chapter 9 begins with a description by media expert Ben Bagdikian of the concentration of power among the media giants. The next two articles focus on the effects of the media on consumers. William Fore examines the extent of violence portrayed in the media and its consequences, and Susan Pearson describes how the toy industry uses the media to influence children.

A major function of the polity is to define and control criminality. Chapter 10 examines this in several ways. Elliott Currie's essay compares violent crime in American society with that in other industrialized societies. His finding that American society is considerably more violent than its peers leads to some interesting speculations as to why this is true. The next two articles look at the punishment of criminals in the criminal justice system. Of special interest is the piece by Amnesty International, which documents racial discrimination with respect to carrying out the death penalty. The final selection, by Jeffrey Reiman, provides some possible solutions for rehabilitating the criminal justice system.

The subject of Chapter 11 is national security, another major function of the polity. The first selection, by Ruth Leger Sivard, compares America's military ranking with its ranking on various social indicators. Clearly, the United States ranks high in military might, but is woefully lacking in spending to alleviate social problems. This raises the question as to exactly what is military security. The following two articles, the first by Joan Anderson and Dwight Lee, and the second by Amitai Etzioni, look at the problem of waste and inefficiency in the military sector. The final selection, by Lester Brown, looks at ways that the leading nations of the world might work to defuse the tensions throughout the world. To accomplish this would diminish the ultimate social problem—war and mutual annihilation.

# Chapter 6
# THE FAMILY

## Juggling Jobs and Babies: America's Child Care Challenge

*Martin O'Connell and David E. Bloom*

The past three decades have seen profound changes in the labor market activity of American women. The 53 million women in the labor force in 1986, 44 percent of the civilian work force, were over three times the number working just after World War II. But the most remarkable aspect of the feminization of the American work force has been the growing involvement of women with preschool-age children. Barely one out of every eight married women with a child under age 6 was working in 1950; this statistic skyrocketed to more than one of every two women by 1985. This trend, showing few signs of abating in the near future, has catapulted the child care concerns of American families out of the home and into the economic and political arena of employers, government policymakers, and local regulatory agencies governing the operations of child care centers.

Increases in the number and proportion of children living with single mothers—whether separated, divorced, widowed, or never married—raise numerous issues for employers and policymakers on how to accommodate the child care needs of these mothers. In 1985, one-fourth of all working mothers with dependent children were not currently married. One-fourth of these women failed to receive child support payments owed by the child's father, and 40 percent were not awarded any child support payments at all.[1] There is a great deal of pressure on an unmarried mother to work: she is usually the principal breadwinner for her family.

---

Martin O'Connell and David E. Bloom, "Juggling Jobs and Babies: America's Child Care Challenge," *Population Trends and Public Policy* Report No. 12 (Washington, D.C.: Population Reference Bureau, 1987). (pp. 2–16). Reprinted with permission.

---

See Statistical Appendix Tables A–21 and A–23.

## Why More Women are Working

There is no simple explanation for the skyrocketing labor force participation rates* of women. Rather, it appears that these trends arise from a complex set of factors. First, labor shortages experienced during World War II drew record numbers of women into the job market. Most of these women left their jobs at the war's end when returning veterans sought jobs and America entered the Baby Boom. However, many women stayed in the labor force after the war, contributing to the social acceptability of women working outside of the home.

A second critical factor which favored women entering the work force was the introduction of the contraceptive pill in the late 1960s. Widespread use of this first really convenient and effective contraceptive enabled women to choose if and when to have children. This newfound freedom led many women to postpone childbearing to continue their education and begin a career. Also, with marriage rates declining and divorce rates increasing, many women faced the need to be economically independent.

A third factor of some importance is the economic problems faced by the Baby Boom cohorts when they reached working ages. The 76 million Baby Boomers, born between 1946 and 1964, overwhelmed the labor market because there were not enough new jobs. They earned relatively low wages and suffered from high unemployment rates.[2] Two incomes, especially during a long period of inflation, became necessary for many couples to attain a desirable standard of living.

Many other factors, such as the growth of traditionally female jobs in the service sector, operated to lure women into the paying work force. It is equally significant that these factors operated against the backdrop of social revolution in the 1960s and 1970s which facilitated the rejection of old values. One of the major casualties was the prestige of the American housewife who was often viewed as a servant to children and husband.

## Documenting the Trends

In 1950, only one in three females aged 16 and over were either at work or looking for work. But the 1960s marked a turning point in the demographic composition of the labor force and the emergence of the current trend among women to enter and stay in the labor force (see Figure 1). This trend coincided with a sharp decline in the birth rate from an average of 3.7 children per woman during the peak of the Baby Boom in 1957 to 1.8 children by 1975, where it has remained during the 1980s. As expected, fewer children and delayed childbearing prompted more women to enter the labor force, but the rate for women with dependent children increased even more sharply than for all women. By 1985, 54 percent of the women with children under age 6 were

---

*The **labor force** includes persons over age 15 who are working or looking for work. The **labor force participation rate** is the ratio of the number of persons in the labor force to the total number of persons over age 15 in the population.

**Figure 1.** Labor force participation for all women and women with preschool children and total fertility rate,* 1950–1985

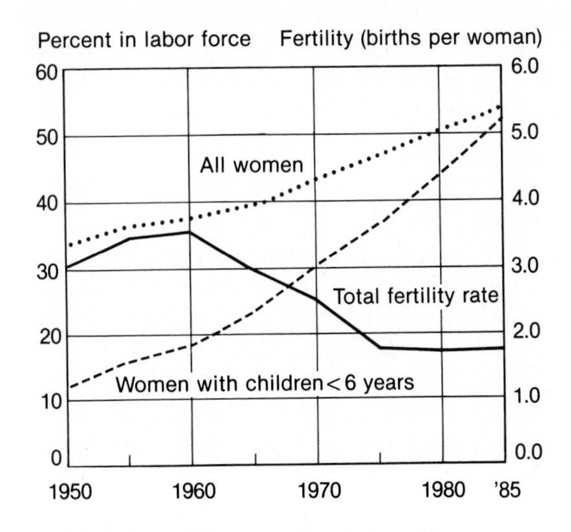


*Average number of children per woman
*Source:* ref. 1

working, only 1 percentage point below the rate for all women. Even more remarkable was the increase in the rate for women with newborn children, from 31 to 48 percent between 1976 and 1985.[3]

There has also been some change in the types of jobs women do. However, with some exceptions, the segregation of women in certain types of jobs continues. Women still predominate in schoolteaching, secretarial positions, and nursing. Few women work as firefighters, construction workers, or engineers, although their representation in non-traditional jobs is increasing.

More women are entering the male-dominated professions. While 20 percent of lawyers and 18 percent of medical doctors were women in 1986, in 1970 women accounted for only 5 and 10 percent of these professions. In fact, as of February 1986, women made up a majority of all professional workers, including teachers, in the United States.[4]

But most American women work in less prestigious jobs. . . . In 1985, 45 percent of the mothers of newborn children worked in clerical and sales jobs, 31 percent in service and blue collar jobs, and only 24 percent in higher paying professional and managerial positions.

A new and somewhat surprising trend is the growing number of female entrepreneurs. From 1976 to 1986, the share of small businesses owned by women soared from 5 to 25 percent. Small Business Administration projections show that 50 percent of small businesses will be woman-owned by the end of this century.[5]

A variety of factors underlie this trend, including the growing number of two-paycheck families in which capital for starting a business may be easily available. The establishment of federal equal credit laws have made it easier for women to borrow money. Some women entrepreneurs report that they began their own business to escape employment hierarchies that discriminated against women; many others say that they wanted more flexible hours, making child care much easier.

## Combining Family and Jobs

A new norm has emerged in the past decade: that most women will work, regardless of their short-term plans for childbearing. In the 1950s and 1960s, women normally held jobs outside the home only before starting a family and after their children were old enough to care for themselves. Labor force participation rates by age for these years show a "double humped" profile (Figure 2), reflecting high rates in the early twenties and after age 35, but low rates between ages 25 and 35, the ages when most women are raising children. By 1985, the valley between the two humps had almost disappeared; women were not leaving the labor force during those prime childbearing years.

**Figure 2.** Labor force participation for women by age: 1950–1985

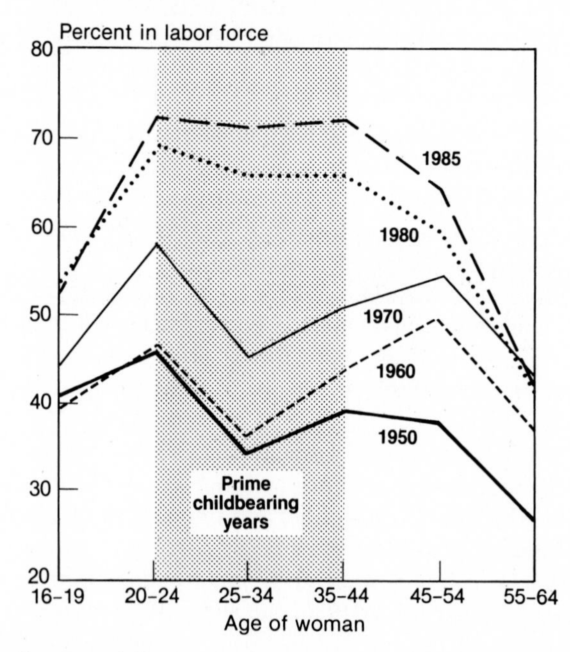


*Source:* ref. 3

Part of the changed pattern of labor force activity can be explained by more women delaying childbearing or remaining childless, but it is also because women are more willing and able to intertwine jobs and family creation. In 1976, only one-third of the mothers of newborn children who wanted another child in the next five years were in the labor force, compared with nearly one-half of women who expected no future births. Clearly, these mothers were conforming to the traditional norm by staying home until completing their families.

Comparable data for 1983 show that women expecting at least one additional child within five years were just as likely to be working as mothers with no immediate plans for more children. About one-half of both groups were working.[6]

## Balancing Personal and Professional Lives

The growing number of women working raises a number of very difficult issues for them and their families. Indeed, most working women face a tremendous personal struggle in trying to balance their personal and professional lives.

Thirty years ago, the life course of a typical woman involved her graduating from high school, marrying, having children, and staying at home to care for her family. Some married women worked, but few actively planned their careers the way men did.

Today, while many still follow the old patterns, a growing number of women are establishing a new pattern in which they delay, or ultimately forego, marriage and childbearing to establish themselves in a career. Among those women who eventually do marry and have children, many interrupt their careers for just a short time to care for their children. They may switch from full-time to part-time work for a few years to maintain their jobs and keep their skills from depreciating. Only a small number of women leave their jobs permanently to concentrate on raising a family.

Many women find it extremely difficult to decide whether they are mothers who happen to work, or workers who happen to be mothers. They lack role models, facing dilemmas their mothers and grandmothers never had to confront. Their simultaneous involvement in career and mothering entangles many women in exhausting lifestyles. About one-third of working women ease this burden by hiring domestic help, although most housekeepers do less than half the necessary housework. Husbands are not much help either. A recent *Newsweek* survey found that "only 14 percent of husbands in two-earner families perform as much as half the housework, and 60 percent do less than one-quarter."

The amount of pure leisure time available to women has declined by about 20 minutes per day over the past quarter century[7] because the increase in the number of hours working for pay has not been associated with a similar decrease in the time spent on housework and child care. Leisure time is a scarce resource for working women. Working women fuel market demand for goods and services that help organize their time, such as microwave ovens, VCRs, home computers, and automated bank tellers. But the purchase of child care services is the primary way working mothers of all income levels balance the competing demands of the workplace and family life.[8]

## Caring for Children at Work

Some women are able to satisfy work and child care duties simultaneously. Table 1 shows that in 1982, 9 percent of employed mothers with preschool children cared for their youngest child while at work. About one-third of these mothers actually worked out of their homes; over one-half worked part-time.

Self-employed women have the best chance of looking after a child while at work. In 1982, one-half of the self-employed mothers of preschoolers cared for their children while at work. But 90 percent of all working mothers of preschool-age children are government or private employees where, constrained by office or factory environments, only 5 percent manage to combine child care with their jobs.

Projections of future trends in the number of mothers caring for children while at work depend upon the future structure of the workplace. Due mainly to the computer revolution, more jobs are expected to be located at home in the future. While only selected occupations could realistically be relocated to an employee's home, likely candidates include many traditional female jobs such as typing and bookkeeping.

## Which Mothers Are Working: Four Profiles

The most remarkable growth in the female labor force in the postwar period has been among women with very young children. Between 1976 and 1985, especially large increases were experienced by mothers with newborns who were (1) 30 to 44 years old; (2) white; (3) divorced, separated or widowed; and (4) who had completed

**Table 1** Employed Mothers Caring for a Preschool Child while Working, 1982

| | | Percent caring for own child | | |
|---|---|---|---|---|
| | | | Place of work | |
| | Number of mothers (thousands) | Total | Home | Outside home |
| All mothers | 5,087 | 9% | 3% | 6% |
| Full-time | 3,263 | 6 | 2 | 4 |
| Part-time | 1,824 | 14 | 5 | 9 |
| Employer | | | | |
| Private | 3,821 | 5 | 2 | 3 |
| Government | 791 | 2 | 1 | 1 |
| Self-employed | 391 | 51 | 12 | 39 |
| Works without pay | 84 | 51 | 23 | 28 |

*Source:* ref. 4

a year or more of college. Conversely, black women, high school dropouts, and young, unwed mothers had modest gains in labor force participation.

Some of this change can be summarized in the four profiles of American mothers presented below, which compare labor force participation rates in 1976 and 1985, based on a statistical analysis of survey data on mothers with newborn babies (see Figure 3):

**1. The Young Mother:** A young married white woman, whose first child was born before she was 24 years old. Her formal education stopped with high school graduation. The chance of her returning to work within a year of the birth of her child was 34 percent in 1976; in 1985, it was 54 percent, a substantial increase.

**2. The Delayed Childbearer:** A married white woman whose first child was born after age 24 and who completed some years of college. Forty-four percent of the women in this category worked in 1976. By 1985, this percentage had risen to 64 percent.

**3. The Unmarried Mother:** A white woman, aged 25 to 44, from the growing ranks of the formerly married. A high school graduate with two or more children, her chances of working within a year of the birth of her last child doubled in the past decade from 27 to 54 percent.

**4. The Young Single Mother:** A black woman, 18 to 24 years old, with two or more children. She has not married, nor has she finished high school. Her chances of working have actually decreased over the past decade, from 34 to 31 percent, and in relative terms, she has lost ground to her contemporaries. While less common than the other women profiled here, she is not atypical of a growing percentage of women with out-of-wedlock births.

**Figure 3.** Labor force participation among mothers with newborn children, 1976 and 1985

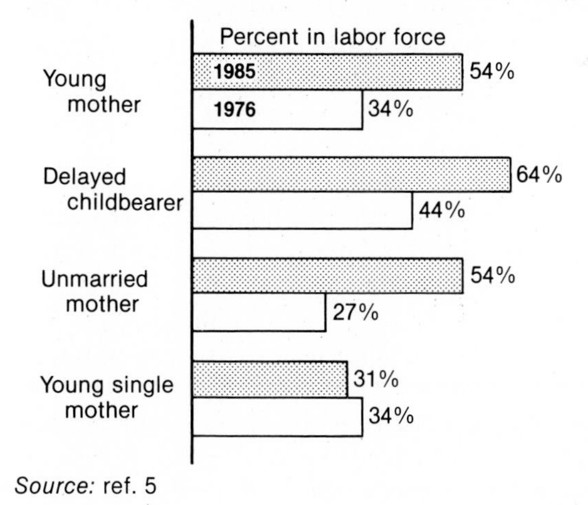


*Source:* ref. 5

In general the profile of the mother most likely to return to work before her baby's first birthday conforms to the human capital theories of labor force behavior: the greater the investment of time and money in education, the more rapid the return to work after childbirth to minimize losses in earnings and depreciation of job skills. In addition, an investment in schooling may indicate a great personal commitment to a career. And women who have spent many years in school may have delayed marriage and would, on average, have fewer children than less-educated women.

But it is not only potential earning power which encourages women to work, but potential wages in relation to the costs of working. For mothers of small children, child care is usually the greatest expense. The primary reason for the leveling off of labor force activity among black women and high school dropouts, who earn lower average salaries than other women, may well be a lack of affordable child care.

## Child Care Problems a Major Constraint

In a special 1982 Census Bureau survey, non-working mothers with preschool children were asked if they would look for work if child care were available to them at a "reasonable cost." Their responses, combined with actual labor force data, can be used to estimate the potential percentage of women who would seek jobs if child care were cheaper and more widely available.

The survey found that considerably more mothers of young children would work if they had access to reasonably priced child care. This is especially true for unmarried women, black women, women who never finished high school, and for women from low-income families (Figure 4). These are the same groups of women whose entrance into the labor force slowed during the past decade.

About 13 percent of women with preschoolers said they would look for work if child care were available at a reasonable cost. This figure contributes to a "potential" rate of 62 percent for women with preschool children in 1982 (i.e., the sum of the 48.1 percent already working and the 13.4 percent who said they would look for work). Child care is a greater obstacle for single than for married women. The percentage of single mothers in the labor force could increase by 24 points with more accessible child care.

The biggest gaps between actual and potential labor force rates are by educational achievement. Only 36 percent of high school dropouts with preschool children were in the labor force in 1982, 20 percentage points less than the rate for college educated women. When nonworking high school dropouts were asked if they would look for work if they had reasonably priced child care, just over one-third said they would, resulting in a potential labor force participation rate of 59 percent, almost equal to the potential rate of 63 percent for the college educated.

While these "potential participation rates" are projections that might never be realized, even if "reasonably priced" child care were available, the evidence suggests that many more mothers would work if child care services were expanded,[9] and that

**Figure 4.** Potential increases in 1982 labor force rates if child care were more accessible

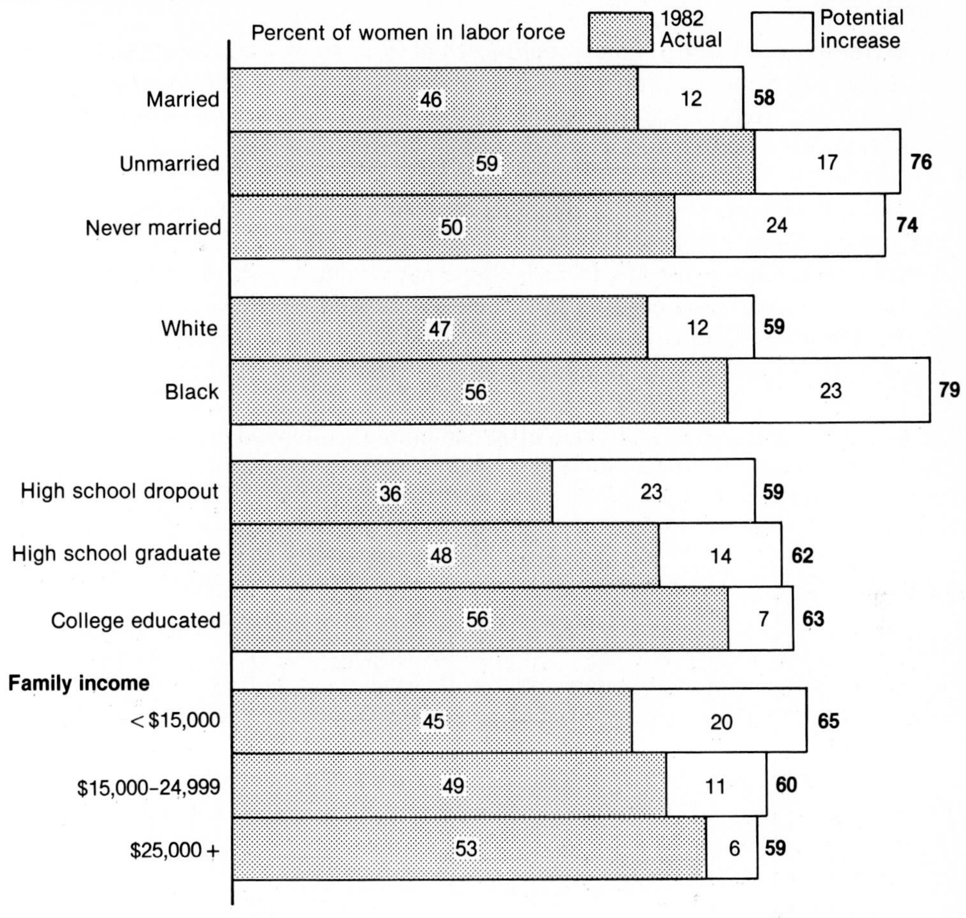


*Source:* ref. 4

some of the differences in whether women work may be due to their access to child care. Indeed, Sweden, which has perhaps the world's most advanced national system of child care, also has the world's highest rate of female labor force participation.[10]

## Actual Child Care Choices

How do working women care for their young children? College educated women tend to transport their children to day care centers and babysitters' homes. In contrast, less-educated women rely on relatives and neighbors for child care, as shown in Figure 5. The type of care also depends upon the age of the child. Infants are typically cared for in a "home environment," their own or a babysitter's, but older children are frequently placed in group care centers or nursery schools. Women with several small children often use multiple child care arrangements since many nursery schools accept only children ages 3 to 5 and relatives may only be willing to care for infants. Considering the logistics of daily commuting for these women, it is no wonder that women with two or more children are less likely to work at all.

To a large extent, the type of child care a woman chooses reflects her ability to pay for outside care and the availability of relatives and neighbors willing to babysit. Typical child care costs in four major metropolitan areas . . . indicate that families hiring a babysitter to come to their home pay as much as $200 to $300 per week, including salaries and benefits. But for most families, in-home care is provided by grandmothers or other relatives at little or no monetary cost to the mother.

**Figure 5.** Percent distribution of child care arrangements of employed mothers for youngest child under 5 years old, by mother's education, 1982

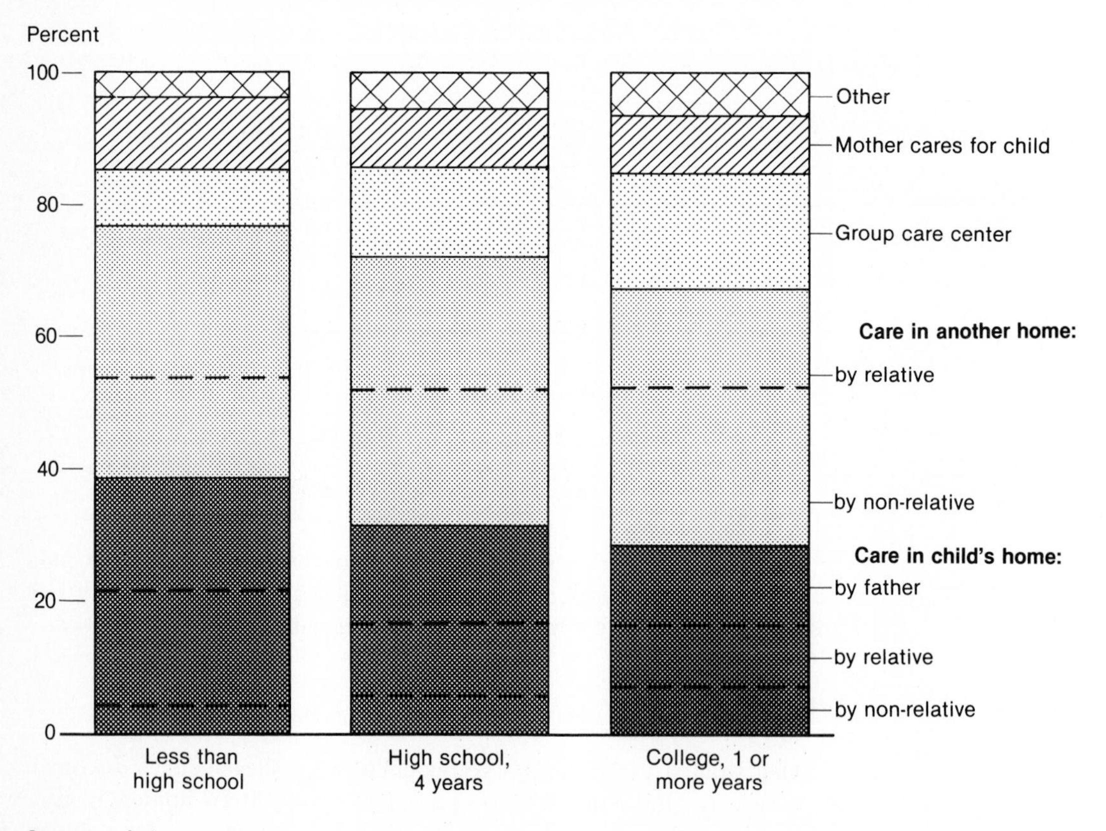


*Source:* ref. 4

Child care away from home, in group care centers or a babysitter's own house, costs about $50 to $100 per child weekly. Since it is less expensive than paying for in-home care, this is the option chosen by about two-thirds of the working mothers with preschoolers. Unless mothers have access to free babysitting by relatives, their annual child care costs constitute one of the largest household budget items, comparable to housing and taxes.

## Demand Increasing

Several demographic trends point toward a continued demand for child care services in the future. First, women are having children at older ages, which means that they accumulate substantial work experience before becoming mothers. With greater job experience, they earn higher salaries and are more willing and able to pay for child care. Women's salaries will also be boosted by the tightening of U.S. labor markets in the 1990s when the relatively small "baby bust" cohorts reach working age.

Second, delayed childbearing is associated with fewer children per woman, increasing the odds that a substantial number of mothers will return to work shortly after a child's birth. However, even at the current U.S. average of only 1.8 lifetime births per woman, there will be a steady future supply of children requiring care. The Census Bureau projects about 19 million children under age 5 by 1990. Given current labor force trends, more than one-half of these children will have mothers in the labor force.

Third, women are acquiring more education—more than four out of ten women have attended college—and are developing values which deemphasize the role of the traditional housewife. Finally, the high divorce rate and high rate of births to unmarried mothers suggest that the number of unmarried women with children—a source of strong demand for child care—will continue to grow.

Taken together, these trends point to increasing demand for child care services. The future supply of in-home care by friends and relatives is limited, partly because these potential babysitters will also be holding a paying job. We can expect to see more and more families placing the daily care of their preschool-age children in the hands of non-family members.

## The Child Care Industry

The child care industry is a small but growing segment of the service sector of the American economy. Child care businesses are defined as establishments primarily engaged in the care of infants or children or in providing prekindergarten education. In 1982, there were 30,762 establishments classified as child care businesses, up 24 percent since 1977.

Child care businesses are categorized as being either for-profit (therefore subject to federal income tax) or not-for-profit (tax-exempt). Child care businesses made up 9 percent of all tax-exempt service industry businesses in 1982 and constitute the second largest tax-exempt service industry. But the child care industry is dominated by the for-profit sector. In 1982, about 18,000 child care businesses operated on a for-profit basis—an increase of 28 percent over the 1977 figure. Not-for-profit businesses grew by 19 percent between 1977 and 1982.

Equally impressive gains occurred in the number of persons employed as child care workers. The 1980 census recorded 727,000 persons primarily employed as child care workers, up 84 percent since 1970 (Figure 6). The location of child care employment changed dramatically during this period. In 1970, over half of all child care workers were employed as private household workers. By 1980, only 20 percent were employed in private households, while 80 percent cared for children in another setting, such as their own homes or in a group care center. This shift reflects the general movement of child care services out of the child's home during this period.

Most child care workers are women, 94 percent in 1980. Over 50 percent work just part-time. They earn low salaries; in 1980, the average pay for women working in group centers was only $3.13 per hour. Women who work in residential homes may earn even less and many receive no employee benefits.[11]

## Public Policy Issues

The complex struggle that many women face in trying to combine careers and childbearing raises a number of issues for employers and public policymakers. Indeed, as Secretary of Labor William Brock said in 1986, "It's just incredible that we have seen the feminization of the work force with no more adaptation than we have had. . . . It is a problem of sufficient magnitude that everybody is going to have to play a role: families, individuals, businesses, [and] government."

*Flexible Work Schedules.* Many employers are experimenting with policies designed to make it easier for women with young children to work. One option is

**Figure 6.** Child care workers by place of work, 1970 and 1980

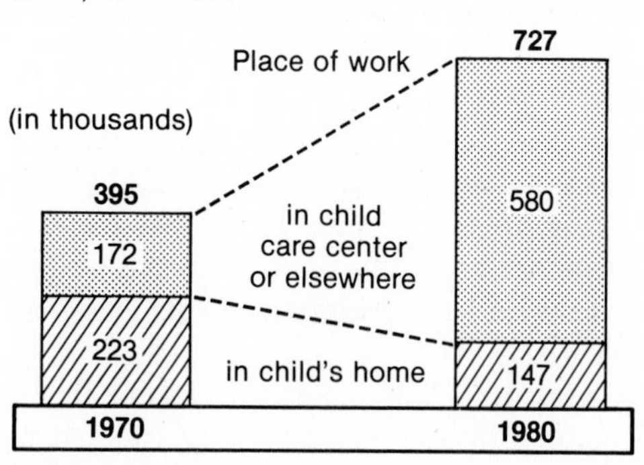


*Source:* ref. 7

flexible scheduling, which encompasses such arrangements as flexitime and block scheduling. Flexitime typically allows an employee to choose his own work schedule within specified limits. For example, an employee may choose to work from 7 am to 3 pm or from 10 am to 6 pm. Block scheduling allows an employee to compress a full work week into three or four days instead of five. Flexitime and block scheduling enable women to juggle family and job responsibilities to the benefit of both employers and families. An estimated 12 percent of all full-time workers were on flexible work schedules in the early 1980s (almost 8 million employees), up from under 5 percent in 1974.

The most extensive experiment to date with flexible scheduling was conducted by the federal government, which established alternative work schedule arrangements for 325,000 federal employees over a three-year period. A 1981 government report evaluating the success of the program concluded that flexible scheduling "allows employees workable alternatives to enhance the quality of family relationships and child care." Ninety-three percent of employees said that the ability to determine their own schedules was "somewhat important" to "very important." Eighty-three percent of single parents said it was "very important."

*Employer-Sponsored Child Care.* A second option available to employers involves the provision of child care. Between 1970 and 1986, the number of employers providing child care facilities for the children of their employees increased from under 50 to about 2,000. But a large percentage of these new facilities are located in California and within firms in the health care industry. They represent few of the nation's 6 million employers or the 44,000 companies of 100 or more workers. About 9 percent of all employed women use day care centers as their principal child care arrangement. Only 9 percent of these women use centers in the workplace, while 91 percent rely on centers situated elsewhere. In 1985, only 1 percent of employees in medium and large firms were *eligible* for even partial defrayment of the costs associated with day care for their children. The corresponding figure for professional and administrative employees in these same firms was a mere 2 percent.[12]

There are several reasons why child care is seldom offered as a fringe benefit. The primary reason may be the employers' belief that child care is an expensive benefit that will only be used by a small fraction of their workers. According to a 1984 report issued by the Bureau of National Affairs, "an average of less than four percent of a firm's employees appear to use the [child care] service" when it is available. In addition, an on-site child care facility can mean a great deal of traveling for young children. Relying on employers for child care can complicate parents' decisions about changing jobs. Finally, to the extent that providing convenient child care might encourage employees to become pregnant, it may not seem desirable to employers. In small and medium-size businesses, employee needs for child care will fluctuate from year to year, making operation of a child care service complicated. Nonetheless, most firms that operate or pay for child care facilities for employees' children report reduced rates of lateness, absenteeism, and turnover, and improved employee satisfaction and productivity.

*Flexible Benefits Plans.* There are other types of child care assistance employers may offer. For example, child care information and referral services are being established by a growing number of employers. These services provide general information on the various types of care available. They may also help employees to set up arrangements.

In all likelihood, child care will be included in many of the flexible fringe benefits plans which are becoming popular. One such plan involves the establishment of "flexible spending accounts." These accounts are maintained by employers on behalf of individual employees to pay for specific benefits such as child care. Funds for the account are deducted from employee paychecks and are not subject to income tax. This lets employees avoid the payment of federal income taxes on the income they intend to spend on child care, giving them a kind of deduction on the cost. The only possible snag relates to an IRS rule that salary reductions not spent for the specific benefit at the end of each year must be forfeited by the employee. However, since child care expenses are relatively easy to project (easier, say, than expenses for medical care), they fit well into these types of benefits plans. Moreover, Congress and the IRS have recently resolved most issues involving the tax and legal status of flexible benefits plans, paving the way for a major surge in their utilization and in the provision of child care as an employee benefit.[13]

A third set of policies that directly affect child care issues are those governing the use of employee leave. At the present time, most medium and large firms (i.e., firms with at least 100 to 250 employees) provide some form of maternity leave, although few provide paternity leave.[14] However, there is wide variation in whether maternity leave is paid or unpaid, whether other fringe benefits continue while employees are away from work, and whether employees have the right to their old jobs when they return to work. Another important issue involves the use of paid sick leave to stay home and care for ill children. Since most schools and day care centers require parents to keep children home if they show signs of illness, a mother (or less often, father) forfeits salary or annual leave if she cannot use her earned sick leave to care for her ill child. A small but growing number of firms permit employees to use their paid sick leave in this way.

*Federal Policies Affecting Child Care.* Public policymakers are beginning to respond to the need for relief from the serious financial burden imposed by child care. In 1976, the federal tax code was amended to permit working parents with a dependent child to take a tax credit on child care costs. At the present time, the tax code allows a tax credit of 20 to 30 percent of child care expenses incurred by working parents, depending on income. In 1986, the maximum credit was up to $720 for one dependent child, $1,440 for two or more under age 15. But the total cost of child care remains high, and tax credits offer minimal relief for low-income parents who pay little tax anyway.

Nonetheless, as an employer, the federal government itself has a long way to go in the child care arena. A recent General Accounting Office report estimates that only 1,500 preschool children of federal employees are enrolled in the 28 existing federal on-site day care centers. This represents just 0.2 percent of the estimated 700,000 preschool-age children of federal employees.

Federal involvement in child care was severely curtailed in 1981 when the Title XX program, which provided child care funds for low and moderate income families, was made a block grant program. The funds targeted for child care were cut by $200 million as a result, and the number of children served under the program actually declined in 32 states between 1981 and 1983.

The Child Care Opportunities for Families Act of 1985 contained a provision to restore these cuts but this section failed to pass Congress. However, the 1985 act does provide funds for the training and accreditation of child care workers and for financial assistance to both public and private child care centers. The act also helps disadvantaged mothers to continue their education by authorizing $10 million to colleges and universities for the purchase of slots in licensed child care centers for the children of low-income students.

Despite the federal government's somewhat inconsistent record to date, future federal initiative in these areas seems likely. For example, although it was not voted on, a "maternity/paternity leave" bill was introduced in the House of Representatives in early 1986, under which a working mother or father would be permitted to take up to 18 weeks of unpaid leave to care for a newborn or newly adopted child or for a dependent child who falls seriously ill. Moreover, the bill would have guaranteed them the same or a similar job upon their return to work. The bill's fate may be aided by a landmark U.S. Supreme Court decision in January 1987. In *California Federal Savings and Loan Association* v. *Guerra* the court upheld a California law requiring most employers to grant pregnant women four months of unpaid disability leave and the right to return to their same jobs.

*Learning from Sweden's Experience.* Since the end of World War II, Sweden has been faced with chronic labor shortages. The government has eased this shortage by encouraging women to work through, among other measures, the establishment of an extensive network of successful government-sponsored day care centers. The government has also legislated a variety of other financial incentives and legal guarantees designed to make it easier for women to start a family and continue working. These policies provide for up to nine months of maternity or paternity leave (at 90 percent of full pay) with a guaranteed job upon returning to work, as well as a guarantee that a parent can receive full-time pay for working six-hour days until the child's eighth birthday.[15]

*State and Local Government Actions.* State and local governments throughout the U.S. are starting to form policies with implications for mothers of small children. Working mothers in five states—California, Hawaii, New Jersey, New York, and Rhode Island—are entitled to paid maternity leave under their short-term disability insurance. In Massachusetts, an experimental program has been established to provide low-interest loans of up to one-quarter million dollars to companies who establish their own child care centers. Two states (New York and California) actively sponsor child care programs for state workers, and four states (Arizona, California,

Connecticut, and Florida) provide tax benefits to employers that offer child care assistance. In 1986, Fairfax County, Virginia, created an Employer Child Care Development Council to help arrange corporate child care services. This is among the first such efforts in the nation. Finally, an ordinance passed by the City of San Francisco in October 1985 requires downtown office building developers to either include space for child care facilities in their buildings or to contribute one dollar per square foot of office space to a city fund to finance the construction of inner-city child care facilities.

Some public and private schools provide before and after school care for students, eliminating the need by working mothers to transport their children from school to a babysitter or day care center. As of 1984, however, only 100 of the nation's 15,000 public school systems offered this service.

## Outlook for the Future

In the future, tight labor markets will make it harder to replace experienced female employees who leave work to start a family. Employers will have an incentive to cater to the special needs of working mothers. As discussed above, such practices include flexible work schedules, the provision of day care assistance, the establishment of maternity and paternity leave, and the use of employee sick leave to care for sick children. Another possibility is job-sharing, in which two or more part-time employees share one full-time job.

Over the next decade, at least 75 percent of all new jobs are expected to be in the service-producing industries. This rapid growth of service sector jobs, with relatively flexible time requirements, should favor the development of new personnel practices. We can also expect to see more women starting their own businesses and more women and men working at home so they can personally care for their children. Continued low marriage and fertility rates and high divorce rates will also serve to keep women in the labor force.

Most experts agree that women are permanent members of the American labor force. This "feminized work force" can be expected to demand better child care services and seek ways to lessen child care expenses. However, one factor that injects some uncertainty into the future is the Tax Reform Act of 1986, passed by Congress and signed by President Reagan. Designed to relieve some of the tax burden on families, it increases the amount of the income deduction for a dependent child from the 1986 level of $1,080 to $1,900 per child in 1987, with minor increases thereafter.

The new law also makes it less cost effective for some wives to work by eliminating the deduction for married couples when both work. This reinstates the "marriage penalty" by which two-earner couples pay more tax on their combined incomes than they would if they were single and filing separately. Indeed, in signing the tax bill President Reagan said, "We're going to make it economical to raise children again,'' hoping perhaps for a return to the 1950s era family with one male breadwinner. This could dampen the expected increase in the demand for child care, depending, of course, on how women actually respond to the new tax provisions. Labor force participation by single and low-income mothers is not likely to be affected by these tax changes because, first, they tend to pay less tax anyway, and second, the mother is often the primary breadwinner for her family.

One effect of the ''feminization'' of the U.S. labor force may be to accelerate change in American personnel practices through enactment of laws favoring working mothers and through direct pressure on employers. Existing evidence suggests that businesses owned or managed by women are more likely than those run by men to adopt innovative personnel policies, especially policies important to women. As more women enter the highest levels of American business and as ''old-girl'' networks achieve more clout in organizational power structures, the many factors that hinder women's abilities to combine careers and families may well subside.

Overall, the increased entry of women into the labor force has altered the American labor system irrevocably in terms of the work that gets done, the profile of the workers, and the terms and conditions under which they do it. Rising wages and innovative personnel practices should help to relieve both the financial burden and complex logistics of child care arrangements. While gender will probably never completely disappear as an important labor market variable, its significance will almost certainly be eroded. But for mothers of young children, adequate child care will always remain paramount in their ability to compete for jobs on an equal basis with men.

## Footnotes

1. U.S. Bureau of the Census, ''Child Support and Alimony: 1983,'' *Current Population Reports,* Special Studies, Series P-23, No. 141 (July 1986).
2. David E. Bloom and Richard B. Freeman, ''The Youth Problem: Age or Generational Crowding,'' Harvard Institute of Economic Research Working Paper No. 1223 (April 1986).
3. U.S. Bureau of the Census, ''Fertility of American Women: June 1985,'' *Current Population Reports,* Series P-20, No. 406, June 1986.
4. U.S. Bureau of Labor Statistics, *Employment and Earnings,* Vol. 33, No. 3 (March 1986).
5. ''Women Entrepreneurs Thrive,'' *The New York Times,* August 18, 1986.
6. Data from the June 1976 and June 1983 Current Population Surveys, U.S. Bureau of the Census.
7. Victor R. Fuchs, ''Sex Differences in Economic Well-Being,'' *Science,* Vol. 232 (April 25, 1986), pp. 459–464.
8. Marjorie Lueck, Ann C. Orr, and Martin O'Connell, ''Trends in Child Care Arrangements of Working Mothers,'' *Current Population Reports,* Special Studies, Series P-23, No. 117 (June 1982).
9. Harriet Presser and Wendy Baldwin, ''Child Care as a Constraint on Employment: Prevalence, Correlates, and Bearing on the Work and Fertility Nexus,'' *American Journal of Sociology,* Vol. 85, No. 5 (1980), pp. 1202–1213.
10. Patrick J. McMahon, ''An International

Comparison of Labor Force Participation, 1977–84," *Monthly Labor Review,* Vol. 109, No. 5 (May 1986), pp. 3–12.

11. U.S. Bureau of the Census, "Earnings by Occupation and Education," *1980 Census of Population,* PC80-2-8B, *Special Subject Reports* (Washington, D.C.: May 1984).
12. U.S. Bureau of Labor Statistics, *Employee Benefits in Medium and Large Firms, 1985,* Bulletin 2262 (July 1986).
13. David E. Bloom and Jane T. Trahan, *Flexible Benefits and Employee Choice* (New York: Pergamon Press, 1986).
14. William J. Wiatrowski, "Employee Income Protection Against Short-Term Disabilities," *Monthly Labor Review,* Vol. 108, No. 2 (February 1985), pp. 32–38.
15. Lueck, Orr, and O'Connell, 1982.

## References

1. U.S. Bureau of Labor Statistics, *Handbook of Labor Statistics,* Bulletin 2217 (Washington, D.C.: 1985); Howard Hayghe, "Rise in mothers' labor force activity includes those with infants," *Monthly Labor Review,* Vol. 109, No. 2 (February 1986), pp. 43–45; National Center for Health Statistics, *Vital Statistics of the United States, 1981, Volume 1, Natality* (Washington, D.C.: 1985), and "Advance Report of Final Natality Statistics, 1984," *Monthly Vital Statistics Report,* Vol. 35, No. 4, Supplement, July 18, 1986; and unpublished estimates.
2. U.S. Bureau of the Census, "Fertility of American Women: June 1985," *Current Population Reports,* Series P-20, No. 406, June 1986.
3. U.S. Bureau of Labor Statistics, *Handbook of Labor Statistics* (1985) and *Employment and Earnings,* Vol. 33, No. 1 (January 1986).
4. Data from the June 1982 Current Population Survey, U.S. Bureau of the Census.
5. Data from the June 1976 and June 1985 Current Population Surveys, U.S. Bureau of the Census.
6. Dana Friedman, "Corporate Financial Assistance for Child Care," The Conference Board Research Bulletin No. 117 (New York: 1985).
7. U.S. Bureau of the Census, *1980 Census of Population,* PC80-1-D1-A, *United States Summary* (Washington, D.C.: March 1984).

# Black Teenage Pregnancy: A Challenge for Educators

*Joyce A. Ladner*

## Introduction

No social problem affecting youths has received as much attention in recent times as adolescent pregnancy. Its causes, consequences, and solutions have been debated in the private and public arenas by legislators, policy advocates, social scientists, child welfare experts, educators, and, notably, in the mass media.

The purpose of this article is to analyze the impact of teen pregnancy on the education of black adolescents. The scope of the problem, the social context of black teen pregnancy and the consequences will be examined. Several effective approaches to teenage pregnancy prevention, including sex/family life education, school-based health clinics, life skills, school retention, and self-esteem enhancement, will be discussed.

## Overview of the Problem

In 1983, 1.1 million teenagers (of all races) became pregnant; almost 500,000 of them gave birth. Black teens accounted for 142,105, or 24.2 percent of all births. Roughly one-fifth of all births are to teens.[1] The births to teenagers rose when the baby boom generation entered the teen years, and has since declined. The number of births to married teens has also decreased. The major change has occurred in the increase in out-of-wedlock births to teens. At present, a majority of births to teenagers are out-of-wedlock. Minority youths constitute 27 percent of the teen population in the United States, but they have roughly 40 percent of the adolescent births and 57 percent of births to unmarried teens. In 1982, white teens had 362,101 births,

[1]U.S. Department of Health and Human Services, National Center for Health Statistics, "Advance Report of Final Natality Statistics, 1983," *Monthly Vital Statistics* (Washington, D.C.: U.S. Government Printing Office, 1985).

Joyce A. Ladner, "Black Teenage Pregnancy: A Challenge for Educators," *Journal of Negro Education* 56 (Winter 1987), pp. 53–63. Reprinted with permission.

See Statistical Appendix Tables A–22 and A–23.

38 percent of which were out-of-wedlock; black teens had 125,929 births, 87 percent of which were out-of-wedlock. By their eighteenth birthday, 22 percent of black females and 8 percent of white females have become mothers. By the time they are twenty, 41 percent of black females and 19 percent of white females have become mothers.[2] Furthermore, an estimated 90 percent of black teens who give birth keep their babies rather than surrender them for adoption.

## Causal Explanations

Various explanations have been advanced as to the causes of teen pregnancy. These include an attempt to fulfill emotional needs by having someone to love and call one's own[3] and a feeling of hopelessness and despair toward the future which stems from economic deprivation. In such cases, early childbearing is not necessarily regarded by the pregnant teens as a major obstacle to achievement,[4] because these youths experience a severe limitation of achievement opportunities. Teen pregnancy is also thought to result from cultural transmission among some blacks who regard the bearing of children as a symbol of having achieved womanhood and manhood, especially in the absence of more traditional and acceptable methods for achieving success.[5]

Teen pregnancy may be symptomatic of widespread alienation from and rebellion against traditional societal norms. According to a study by the Education Commission of the States, by conservative estimates there are 1,250,000 white, 750,000 black, and 375,000 Hispanic 16-to-19-year-olds who are at risk to become "disconnected" from the wider society. These are alienated and economically disadvantaged youths who will not be prepared to participate in the workforce unless programs are developed to provide education and jobs for them. Since 1960, teen pregnancy in this age group has increased by 109 percent for whites and 10 percent for nonwhites.[6]

The causes of teen pregnancy are sufficiently complex to defy single factor explanations. The restriction of opportunities to acquire education and training and to have access to necessary resources is a major cause of too-early childbearing. For black teen parents, most of whom are poor, economic causation offers the best explanation for the increase in the magnitude of the problem. As blacks have faced greater economic scarcity, the black family has experienced increased fragmentation

---

[2]Kristin Moore, comp., "Fact Sheet (on Teenage Pregnancy)" (Washington, D.C.: Child Trends, Inc., 1985).

[3]Thomas J. Silber, "Adolescent Pregnancy Programs: A Perspective for the Future," *Journal of Sex Education and Therapy,* 8 (1982), 48–50.

[4]Joyce A. Ladner, "Teenage Pregnancy: Implications for Black Americans," in *The State of Black America,* ed. James Williams (New York: National Urban League, 1986), 65–84.

[5]Joyce A. Ladner, *Tomorrow's Tomorrow: The Black Woman* (New York: Doubleday, 1971).

[6]Education Commission of the States, "Reconnecting Youth" (Washington, D.C.: Education Commission of the States, 1985).

which has led to a rapid increase in female-headed households, most of which are at the poverty level. A large percentage of households are headed by women who were teenage mothers. In less than twenty-five years, black female-headed households more than doubled, increasing from 21 percent in 1960 to 48 percent in 1984. The problem is compounded by the weakening of the extended family. Traditionally, this resource was an indispensable support system to its members, providing child care when needed for the teen mother to complete her education.

## Socio-Historical Context of Black Teen Pregnancy

Teen pregnancy among blacks must be placed within the context of changing sexual norms in the American society. For over twenty years, since the so-called "sexual revolution," the society has experienced a major transformation of sexual mores which has had an influence on every sector of the population. Teenagers of all races are now experiencing the residual effects of this major shift in cultural values—a shift from the premarital double standard, abstinence, and stigma for out-of-wedlock births to the abolition of the double standard, premarital sexual permissiveness, and a lessening of stigma for out-of-wedlock births. There are now few punitive social sanctions leveled against females who have out-of-wedlock births or their children. The decline of marriage as a means to legitimize birth is a result of this lessening of stigma.

It is important that the socio-cultural context of pregnancy of black teenagers is explored. Historically, blacks have expressed greater tolerance and acceptance of teen pregnancy than have whites. Out-of-wedlock pregnancies were expected to result in early marriage in order to legitimize the child's birth and to form an intact family. Usually, the welfare of the child from such a union was very important. Historical accounts of blacks' attitudes on this subject reflect a consistent and uniform theme.[7] Invariably, the out-of-wedlock birth was regarded as a mistake made by the female, for which she could be rehabilitated. Early marriage was a major method of rehabilitation. If marriage did not occur, blacks were generally more tolerant in accepting the teen mother, and assisting her in efforts to reorganize her life in a productive manner. Failure on her part to utilize the assistance made available by the extended family, including child care, assistance in completing her education, and obtaining employment, resulted in the isolation of the female from the respectable community. The literature is consistent in regard to the treatment of children born into the out-of-wedlock status. These children, for the most part, were not assigned negative labels and inferior treatment since they were regarded as innocent and, therefore, were not held responsible for their own birth status.[8]

---

[7]W. E. B. Du Bois, *Efforts for Social Betterment among Negro Americans* (New York: Russell and Russell, 1969); Charles S. Johnson, *Shadow of the Plantation* (Chicago: University of Chicago Press, 1934); and Hortense Powdermaker, *After Freedom: A Cultural Study in the Deep South* (New York: Viking Press, 1939).

[8]Ladner, *Tomorrow's Tomorrow.*

Another equally compelling and unique feature of teen pregnancy from an historical perspective is that blacks rarely surrendered their children to agencies for adoption.[9] While the practice of informal adoption occurred with frequency, it almost always involved the rearing of the child by one or more members of the extended family, or by other individuals known to and accepted by the mother. It was a practice referred to as "giving the child" to persons who were expected, because of personal familiarity, to provide adequately for the child. This practice was not one of first choice, but often resulted when it was difficult or impossible for the teen parent(s) to marry, or to provide for the child. Agency adoptions were rarely practiced because they catered to a white middle-class clientele and did not place significant numbers of black children in families. Today, a small minority of black teenagers place their children for adoption despite the fact that a majority of black teens who become pregnant are also poor and have little of the economic support necessary to provide for their children. A widespread sentiment among black teen parents is that the economic and other hardships encountered due to the birth of the child are unavoidable realities of life over which they have little control. Indeed, it is a fatalistic attitude engendered by a lifetime of economic deprivation and a sense of powerlessness to exercise control over their lives. The expectation, enforced by cultural and religious standards among the black poor, is that out-of-wedlock children are not to be placed in adoption agencies, but are to be kept in the family and community regardless of the hardships.

The most serious consequence for too-early childbearing is the truncation of educational attainment, without which teen parents are unable to fulfill adequately the parenting role. It is estimated that at least 50 percent of teen mothers drop out of school because of pregnancy. In some cities, the rates are much higher. A study by Card and Wise based on a national sample found that mothers who had given birth before they reached eighteen years of age were half as likely to have graduated from high school as those who postponed childbearing until after their twentieth birthday. They also found that adolescent males who became fathers before age eighteen were 40 percent less likely to have graduated from high school than those who waited.[10]

Youths who already have a low level of school performance are more likely than those with high performance to become teen parents.[11] Low levels of aspiration and performance place them at greater risk to have children. Early parenthood may

---

[9]Andrew Billingsley and Jeanne Giovanonni, *Children of the Storm: Black Children and American Child Welfare* (New York: Macmillan, 1972); and Joyce A. Ladner, *Mixed Families: Adopting Across Racial Boundaries* (New York: Doubleday, 1977).

[10]J. J. Card and L. L. Wise, "Teenage Mothers and Teenage Fathers: The Impact of Early Childbearing on the Parents' Personal and Professional Lives," *Family Planning Perspectives,* 10 (1978), 199–205.

[11]Jerald G. Bachman, S. Green and I. Wirtanen, *Youth in Transition,* Vol. 3, *Dropping Out—Problem or Symptom?* (Ann Arbor: University of Michigan, Institute for Social Research, 1971); I. Berkowitz, "Improving the Relevance of Secondary Education for Adolescent Developmental Needs," in *Adolescent Parenthood,* ed. Max Sugar (New York: S. P. Medical and Scientific Books, 1980); Frank Furstenburg, *Unplanned Parenthood: The Social Consequences of Teenage Childbearing* (New York: The Free Press, 1976).

symbolize, for many, the ability to achieve in at least one area deemed to be important by their peers, even if all others are obstructed. To have a child remains an ancient rite of passage into womanhood and manhood for many of this nation's poor youths. It may also enhance self-esteem, albeit temporarily, and some teens have reported increased popularity in their peer group. Moreover, poor school performance frequently represents the inability of the youth, due to a variety of internal and external factors, to conceptualize and plan for the future. Teenagers who cannot conceptualize the future are unlikely to acquire the necessary skills to prepare for future jobs and careers. To be able to conceptualize the future requires that the individual have positive role models, resources, and a basic understanding of the how and where to acquire the skills to achieve goals.

Youths who are at-risk educationally are not only more likely to become parents, but they are also at-risk to become unemployed if they drop out of school. In 1985, the unemployment rates for black teenagers were 41.4 percent for males and 37.9 percent for females.[12] An obvious repercussion for teen mothers is that at any given time, 60 percent rely on Aid to Families of Dependent Children (AFDC) for their livelihood. In 1985, the cost of AFDC, Medicaid, and food stamps for teen parents and their children was $18.5 billion.[13]

## Issues and Approaches to Teen Pregnancy Prevention

There is a greater understanding of the causes and consequences of teen pregnancy than of solutions to prevent its occurrence. The society has failed to adopt a prevention model to counter the consequences of early, unprotected sexual activity by youths. The traditional approach to solving social problems in this country has been the adoption of the short-term, stop-gap (residual) method of intervention. It has also included the adoption of a services-delivery model designed to assist individuals in need on a temporary basis with the objective of providing rehabilitation, *after the fact*. The more effective and rarely used alternative approach is the long-term, or institutional, model that attempts to identify and eradicate root causes. This comprehensive approach emphasizes prevention.[14]

The Alan Guttmacher Institute found that the United States has the highest teen pregnancy rate of any Western nation and is the only major Western country that fails to provide teens with adequate information on family planning. In all other countries surveyed, contraceptives were much more readily available to teens with-

---

[12] "The Employment Situation—Current Population Survey" (Washington, D.C.: U.S. Bureau of Labor Statistics, 1985). USDC 85-471.

[13] M. Burt, *Estimates of Public Costs for Teenage Childbearing* (Washington, D.C.: Center for Population Options, 1986).

[14] Elizabeth Huttman, *Introduction to Social Policy* (New York: Macmillan, 1981); Alfred Kahn, *Social Policy and Social Services* (New York: Random House, 1979); and Thomas Meenaghan and Robert O. Washington, *Social Policy and Social Welfare* (New York: Free Press, 1980).

out the traditionally punitive sanctions and double standards practiced here.[15] Another barrier to the adoption of the institutional/prevention model is the reluctance of many adults to sanction contraceptive programs for teens because they feel such designs encourage youths to become sexually active. There is no data to substantiate such a claim.

The most effective approaches to teen pregnancy prevention are those that emphasize a variety of strategies, including education and training, jobs, sex/family life education, life-skills training, peer counseling, and male responsibility counseling with equal emphasis on the needs of females and males. There have been some effective programs implemented in educational settings. The Teen Outreach Program and the Choices and Challenges curriculum, which are described below, are examples of what is being done in the schools.

## Life Skills Training

An innovative teen pregnancy prevention program is the Teen Outreach Program that was started in St. Louis in 1977 by the Danforth Foundation, the Junior League, and the St. Louis Public Schools. Teen Outreach, which now exists at twenty-four sites in several cities, is an after-school program that works with male and female at-risk youths in middle and high school to reduce teen pregnancy and encourage the completion of high school. The program is conducted by facilitators who instruct the participants in a curriculum on such life management skills as sexuality, self-esteem building, career planning, substance abuse, child abuse, and teen suicide. The program also requires that each participant, all of whom are self-selected, volunteer for services in the community. By helping others, they are able to derive a stronger sense of self-worth and a sense of mastery over their environment. The Teen Outreach Program was evaluated in 1985 with the use of a comparison group and participants were found to be less likely to get pregnant or to fail courses than were subjects in the control group.[16]

Another program of interest to educators is the Choices and Challenges curriculum developed by Girls Club of America to assist preadolescent and adolescent males and females to plan their futures and to acquire a more realistic understanding of the social, economic, and emotional implications of teen parenthood. It is a very popular course designed to take the participants through the maze of experiences they are likely to encounter as adults in a variety of typical situations. The participants get a more realistic picture of what to expect, and they acquire coping skills to meet many of these expectations. After completion of the Choices and Challenges course, students are less likely to romanticize about becoming parents because they

---

[15]Elise Jones et al., "Teenage Pregnancy in Developed Countries: Determinism and Policy Implications," *Family Planning Perspectives,* 17 (1985), 53–63.

[16]Karen Pittman, *Model Programs Preventing Adolescent Pregnancy and Building Youth Self-Sufficiency* (Washington, D.C.: Children's Defense Fund, 1986).

will have acquired a concrete understanding of the demands parenthood will impose on their lives.[17]

## Sex Education and School-Based Clinics

Contradictory views about teen sexuality are demonstrated in the considerable opposition launched against sex/family life education in the schools and school-based clinics that offer family planning services. Critical issues are related to what is appropriate sex education, what are acceptable boundaries (for example, should courses include contraceptives, abortions, decision making, population issues, and so forth), who should have control over the curriculum, and at what age (or grade) should youths take sex education classes. There is little unanimity on this range of concerns. In a study conducted by Allen and Bender[18] it was found that responses varied widely on what was the appropriate forum in which sex education should be taught. The family, school, and church were regarded as the appropriate institutions to teach sex education.

Sex education in the schools is an especially controversial issue today because of the political conservatives' advocacy of the view that parents have the exclusive right to determine the proper forum in which their offspring should receive such information. This presents a serious barrier for youths who come from families where the parents cannot capably discuss sex. Parents may lack an understanding of basic sex education, or they may be reluctant to mention the subject for fear of stimulating the child's interest in it.

Sex/family life education programs in schools vary according to curriculum design, staff, resources, and the extent to which they are regarded as a priority by the school system, parents, and the community. For example, Washington, D.C., is one of only three areas in the nation which have mandated sex/family life education for grades kindergarten through twelve (Maryland and New Jersey are the other two). Yet, even here there is no systematic implementation of the curriculum nor are there effective teacher training and coordination.[19] In an evaluation of fourteen sex education programs in schools and operated by community-based organizations, Kirby found that the most effective programs were those affiliated with a school-based health clinic and those that attempted to facilitate positive parent-child interaction and communication.[20] Unfortunately, most students do not take a sex education

---

[17] *Choices: A Teen Woman's Journal for Self-Awareness and Personal Planning* (Santa Barbara: Girls Club of America, 1983); and *Challenges: A Young Man's Journal for Self-Awareness and Personal Planning* (Santa Barbara: Girls Club of America, 1984).

[18] James E. Allen and Deborah Bender, *Managing Teenage Pregnancy: Access to Abortion, Contraception, and Sex Education* (New York: Praeger Special Studies, 1980).

[19] *Preventing Children from Having Children* (Washington, D.C.: District of Columbia Department of Human Services, 1985).

[20] Douglas Kirby, *Sexuality Education: An Evaluation of Programs and Their Effects* (Santa Cruse: Network Publications, 1984).

course until high school, long after they may have become sexually active. The more innovative curriculum designs propose teaching sex/family life education in elementary school on a level consistent with the learning environment of young children.

The type of education and support that schools are able to provide to the prospective teen mother and father is critical to their success. Until recently, efforts were not made to maintain the pregnant girl in school on a consistent basis. Title IX of the 1972 Education Amendments prohibits the expulsion of pregnant students, and requires that they be provided instruction either in the school or elsewhere. Whether the expectant teen mother will remain in school usually depends on the availability of child care, a service most teen parents cannot afford. Grandmothers, who previously provided this service, are more likely to be in the workforce or still in their childbearing years, and thus have less time to take care of grandchildren while their daughters return to school.[21] A few schools offer child care for teen parents, which can be especially effective in promoting secondary prevention (i.e., prevention of repeat pregnancies) and providing parent education and quality child care. A recently completed longitudinal study found that teen mothers who had day-care service were more likely to complete high school, to obtain post-secondary training, and to become self-supporting. The children benefitted intellectually from the programs, scoring significantly higher than controls on a general cognitive index.[22]

## School-Based Comprehensive Health Clinics

An education-related innovation in teen pregnancy prevention are the school-based health clinics which started in St. Paul, Minnesota twelve years ago. Since the introduction of the clinics in two St. Paul high schools, there has been a 56 percent reduction in birthrates and a 35 percent reduction in the school drop-out rate among teen mothers.[23] There are now over seventy clinics nation-wide, with over one hundred more in the planning stages. School-based clinics are thought to be very effective because they provide comprehensive health services to a highly underserved population within close proximity to the one institution with which the teenager has the most consistent and sustained involvement outside the family. Clinics are staffed by health practitioners and social service workers, known to the teenagers, who provide basic quality services at minimal or no cost. They provide broad and comprehensive health care to teens, including physical examinations for sports, screening for undiagnosed health problems, family planning counseling, counseling and treatment for sexually transmitted diseases, and other basic health services that teens frequently do not get.

---

[21] Joyce A. Ladner and R. M. Gordine, "Intergenerational Teenage Motherhood: Some Preliminary Findings," *SAGE: A Scholarly Journal on Black Women,* 1 (1984), 22–24.

[22] Frances A. Campbell, Bonnie Breitmayer and Craig T. Ramey, "Disadvantaged Single Teenage Mothers and Their Children: Consequences of Free Educational Day Care," *Family Relations,* 35 (1986), 63–68.

[23] Douglas Kirby, *School-Based Health Clinics: An Emerging Approach to Improving Adolescent Health and Addressing Teenage Pregnancy* (Washington, D.C.: Center for Population Options, 1985).

A widely held myth is that the clinics' only function is to provide contraceptives to teenagers. Critics overlook the fact that this is only one of the many services these facilities provide. In a speech before the Education Writers of America in which he criticized school-based clinics, Secretary of Education William Bennett stated that "clinics legitimate sexual activity and cause an 'abdication of moral authority'."[24] A widely publicized controversy arose at the DuSable High School in Chicago when protesters picketed the school because a clinic was slated to be introduced in the school. However, parents of DuSable students supported the clinic, and it opened in spring of 1986. The following fall, a group of local black ministers filed suit to have the clinic closed. As of this writing, the case is in litigation. Most clinics have not been so controversial, as evidenced by their rapid growth in school districts across the country. They promise to continue to be a highly effective method of educating teens on primary health care concerns and for preventing too-early child-bearing.

## Concluding Comment

The author recognizes that teen pregnancy is a national problem that transcends racial and class boundaries; however, it takes a far greater toll on the lives of blacks and the poor than on other groups. Over the past fifteen years, the most vulnerable black families have become severely fractured. The impact of a worsened economy has produced the highest rates of chronic male unemployment in history, leading to a drastic increase in the number of female-headed households. As noted, 48 percent of black families are headed by women and 46.5 percent of black children live in poverty. Such households are under great amounts of stress in almost every area of functioning.

In 1971, the writer published a study of the impact of race and poverty on the psychosocial development of black female adolescents in a St. Louis housing project.[25] Although these youths were acutely sensitive to racial and class discrimination, they were optimistic about their futures and felt they could overcome the handicaps of race and poverty. The quality of their lives was substantially better than the quality of life experienced by many black adolescents with similar backgrounds today. Another striking qualitative difference between the two groups is the lack of optimism about the future that one observes in today's black youths. A generation ago, the typical pregnant teenager did not suffer what is often the multiple exposures experienced by many pregnant teens today. In addition to pregnancy, today's pregnant teens are more likely to have health problems, inadequate or nonexistent child care, become school drop-outs, and lack job skills and employment opportunities. The erosion of many of the stable institutions in black communities has created a more pervasive configuration of multiple exposures (e.g., crime, drugs, and poverty)

---

[24]Joyce A. Ladner, "The Most Basic Health Care," *Washington Post,* April 27, 1986, p. C8.

[25]Ladner, *Tomorrow's Tomorrow.*

to which children and youths are subjected. Hence, the most troubled families are more distressed than ever before, and there has been an increase in the incidence and severity of the problems affecting the poor.

While the problem of adolescent pregnancy for blacks is now receiving widespread attention, there are still far too few effective educational programs to curtail the high incidence. The recent decrease in federal spending for social programs is an indication of the government's lack of commitment to primary prevention. There is, however, an increase in programs undertaken by black organizations, including those sponsored by fraternities; sororities; and civil-rights, advocacy, policy, social welfare, and religious groups. It is clear that blacks, recognizing the magnitude of the problem, have seized the opportunity to provide much of the leadership needed to bring about solutions.

# It's All in the Family: How Government Influences Family Life

*Dollars & Sense*

Ever since the premiere of "Leave it to Beaver" and "Father Knows Best," TV families have tried to convince us that the pursuit of individual happiness begins at home. These days, the range of family-oriented sitcoms—from "The Cosby Show" and "The Jeffersons" to "Growing Up Pains" and "Kate and Allie"—have expanded the 1950s definition of the family to include blacks and single mothers.

Still, the images they portray are far from realistic: husbands and wives easily surmount the temporary conflicts of married life, and parents and children maintain remarkable friendships despite the challenges of parenting and the traumas of adolescence. On TV, the nuclear family reigns, and no one ever has to deal seriously with the difficulties of poverty, racism, or homophobia, much less question accepted notions of who's supposed to be in love with whom.

It's almost as if the television producers have set out to prove the numbers wrong. For example, only 11% of all households can afford to have just one parent working. For most married couples, a living wage requires that both partners work for pay. But the number of households that contain a married couple fell to under 60% in 1984. Meanwhile, that same year, the proportion of families headed by women reached just over 11%.

The last 30 years have seen a major transformation in household composition. U.S. families don't fit any single model. Yet the popular media—and conservative rhetoric—make it sound as if they do. As a result, family policies, those social and economic programs that affect the kinds of households people form and the ways we share resources, barely accommodate actual family needs.

## What is Family Policy?

In some countries, there are laws that specifically address families. Family policy in the United States, however, has always been implicit, rather than explicit. Government policies that affect family life fit into three major arenas: income transfers to

"It's All in the Family: How Government Influences Family Life." Reprinted by permission from *Dollars & Sense,* No. 124 (March 1987), pp. 6–9. (Dollars & Sense, One Summer Street, Somerville, MA 02143)

See Statistical Appendix Table A–18.

families who do not make enough to support themselves; employment policies, which determine whether or not parents can manage to raise children and support a family; and child-care policies, which help determine which family members leave the home to work for wages.

Current U.S. family policy perpetuates the notion that all households should delegate responsibilities so that a father earns a wage and a mother stays at home to clean, cook, and diaper the baby. While many white, middle-class families fit this description at the turn of the 20th century, a significant number of families never did. Nevertheless, this conventional notion of the family remains the socially accepted norm.

The nuclear family is a relatively new concept in this country. Until the 19th century, most families lived and worked on farms. To improve productivity, members of the extended family and non-blood relatives often joined the household. While women still were responsible for the bulk of child care, they worked with men in the fields.

As factory wage labor became more common in the late 19th century, family arrangements changed, as did individual members' access to paid work. Men were expected to become wage laborers. Many women, who were already expected to raise children and do other domestic chores, were cut off from paid work.

Rapid industrialization during the progressive era of the 1920s introduced vast changes in U.S. life. The sweeping reforms in government policy that were meant to accommodate that process reinforced sexual divisions of labor. The Mother's Pension Program, instituted in Illinois in 1911, was a transfer plan that provided a limited form of child support. (It was intended primarily as a health measure since single mothers were thought to be unfit to raise children.) To become eligible, mothers had to prove they were without husband or property. Mothers who received transfer income were generally widows and almost exclusively white. Because of the social stigma attached to government support, many women turned to other relatives and neighbors before asking for state subsidies.

Employment policies, particularly protective legislation (enacted to "protect" mothers from work), also sanctified the role of women as mothers. Although many women had to work because their husbands' wages were so low, these laws made it more difficult. By 1917, only nine states did not have provisions limiting women's working hours. Protective legislation also systematized occupational segregation and kept wages down for women who did work. In fact, given the insufficient earnings of their husbands, many women simply could not opt for leisure.

## Historical Neglect

Little has changed since the progressive era regarding the U.S. government's approach to child care, welfare, or employment policies. During the Great Depression, for example, the Work Projects Administration (WPA) set up child-care centers. The program's stated purpose, however, was not to provide mothers with child care—and thus with the opportunity to work for wages—but to address the urgent need for jobs.

During the height of World War II, thousands of housewives (and other older relatives who ordinarily were responsible for child care) answered their patriotic call to duty by taking on paid employment. Men had gone to battlefields abroad and that, together with the booming economy, made job opportunities plentiful. In a momentary change of the national mindset, states and the federal government spent over $75 million to establish 3,102 centers for 600,000 children. These centers, set up through the 1942 Community Facilities Act, were poorly run and underutilized. At the end of the war, the centers were immediately dismantled and "Rosie the Riveter" was forced back into the kitchen.

In terms of family policy, the 1950s and early 1960s essentially took women a step backward. They joined the labor force in steadily increasing numbers, but images of model housewives—like June Cleaver and later Donna Reed—prevailed.

The 1970s did not bring much of an improvement. Although Congress approved the Family Assistance Plan, a program that would have required the federal government to finance child care, President Nixon vetoed it. Today, the only such provision by the federal government is a child-care tax credit, instituted a few years ago. The 1986 Tax Reform, however, restricts the maximum credit to $700 per year.

The absence of a comprehensive child-care policy limits the options families have for juggling work and children. Many parents have no alternative but to provide their own child care at home. Others who are able to pay for child care have nowhere else to turn but the inequities of the marketplace. Post-World War II demand for child care has outstripped the supply, making the service a scarce—and therefore expensive—resource. The spiraling costs of insurance have pushed child-care fees upward. As a result, only the well-paid can afford to both work and pay for child care.

This situation is not likely to change. Because child-care centers for working-class people tend not to be particularly profitable, the supply remains low. Recently, businesses have become concerned with the child care needs of their employees. Despite such trends in the private sector, in the future the need for child care will far exceed the number of available slots.

Like child-care policies, welfare policies historically have failed to meet family needs. Although welfare payments were extended and liberalized in the 1960s, they still do not provide economic stability for families. Furthermore, AFDC (Aid to Families with Dependent Children) benefits do not even allow families to climb over the poverty line. For example, in Massachusetts' highly publicized "Up to Poverty" campaign, the state Department of Human Services determined that AFDC mothers need $926 per month to cross the poverty line. They only receive $491. In 1986, AFDC families in more than 30 other states were unable to reach the poverty level.

Conservatives and neoliberals alike often harp on the notion that poverty is caused by welfare and dependency. Welfare payments have soared, they argue, because poor people prefer the "free ride." In fact, the government has had to raise the *absolute* sum it spends on welfare. But much of that increase occurred because so many new households have become eligible for aid. In fact, since welfare payments are not indexed for inflation, the amount recipients can buy with their checks has steadily fallen.

Instead of trying to make it on welfare, one obvious alternative for a single mother would be to work. But a mother of three children would have to make $5.30 per hour at a full-time, year-round job—nearly $2 more than the minimum wage—to reach the 1985 poverty level of $10,989. (The average income for all women in 1985 was $10,173.) What makes that option even less feasible is that full-time work leaves little time to raise children; part-time work gives women time but very little income. For a single mother, working her way off the welfare rolls can be next to impossible.

Nevertheless, more and more women, married and single, now work for pay. Trends in the post-war economy have both pushed and pulled women into the labor force. The pull, beginning in the 1950s, came from the rapid growth in the economy and the corresponding demand for workers, particularly low-wage women workers for service sector jobs. The push, starting in the late 1960s and continuing throughout the inflationary 1970s, resulted from a need in many households for a second earner. In 1985, 54.7% of all women were in the labor force. Of all married women, 53.9% actually had jobs.

This phenomenon has affected families in two major ways. First, the increase in the number of two-income families represents an irreversible trend in household structures. Second, the diversity of family types has increased. Marriage is no longer the only way for women to obtain financial stability. Nevertheless, unlike most men, many self-supporting women are still poor.

Some changes in family structure have political, not economic, roots and represent a greater, not lesser, freedom of choice. Feminists, gays, and lesbians have raised important questions about the traditional nuclear family. In so doing, they have paved the way for alternative living arrangements.

## Crisis in Morality?

With support from the Moral Majority, the Reagan administration depicts the dramatic change in household structures as a crisis: the nation's moral fiber is deteriorating. They claim that the country has suffered because feminists are greedy, people of color are undisciplined, and gays and lesbians are unspeakable.

But this response is not original; 20 years ago, Daniel Moynihan blamed the "black matriarchy" for high rates of poverty among blacks. Fifteen years before that, black sociologist Franklin Frazier voiced a similar view. Gearing up for the liberals' next push for welfare reform, Moynihan recently published a book entitled *Nation and Family* that extols his earlier work, claiming his arguments retain relevance today.

A recent report by the Reagan administration's Working Group on the Family, laying the ground work for the welfare reform debate, calls for a concrete set of measures that will improve "family life." According to the report, a strong economy promotes strong families. To strengthen the economy, they mean to keep tax rates and inflation low and wages even lower—although the link between the strength of the family and the strength of the economy is dubious at best. The group also suggests that the federal government stay out of the business of legislating and adjudicating family rights and responsibilities. Their stated preference is for a laissez-faire approach that makes family affairs "private" affairs.

There are better policies for families than this, and they need to be part of the debate in Washington and in local communities. For starters, these policies would include: a national effort to provide accessible, affordable, and accountable day care; employment policies that ensure livable wages; and a welfare system that guarantees housing and health care rights for those who cannot work because they are too old, too young, busy raising children full time, or disabled.

The change in family structure *has* precipitated a crisis, but it is decidedly not one of working peoples' moral values. Instead, this is a crisis among economic policymakers who refuse to recognize, much less promote, the diversity of household structures. If nothing else, their policy is consistent: in all cases, those without access to adequate income have fewer choices about how they can live their lives. What is desperately needed is a set of economic policies that enhances those choices.

---

*Sources:* U.S. Bureau of the Census, Current Population Reports, Series P-60, No. 151, *Money Income of Households, Families, and Persons in the United States: 1984.*

# Chapter 7
# WORK

## The Scandalous Pay of the Corporate Elite

*Warner Woodworth*

Lee Iacocca's $20.5 million compensation for 1986 heavily overshadowed the $11.4 million he received the previous year. The difference is a whopping 180 percent increase, while Chrysler's performance dropped considerably. The case suggests an inverse relationship between executive pay and company results.

The Chrysler chairman is no innovator in grabbing an exorbitant salary while his company languishes. Hundreds of other top managers have pulled the same trick over the past several years. In 1985, for instance, while Inland Steel suffered a net loss of $41 million, Frank Levessen chairman and CEO, enjoyed a 24 percent salary and bonus boost. In a classic case of strategic error, Coca-Cola's new taste flopped while Chairman Robert Goizveta was "rewarded" a hefty $6.4 million in long-term compensation because of his "courage" in trying a new product.

### Executive Bloat

Among the most dramatic contradictions between pay and performance in 1986 are the following:

- John Nevin of Firestone received $6,355,000, a 71 percent surge, while his company's return on common equity was under one percent, sales dropped by 7.6 percent, and earnings per share declined by 85.2 percent. In recent years, Nevin cut the work force from 107,000 to 55,000, closed eight of seventeen North American plants, and still presided over a revenue decline from $5.3 billion to $3.5 billion in 1986. Claiming the company needed wage concessions, he wrestled wages in some plants down $3.65 an hour and then pocketed some of the savings as his own reward.

---

Warner Woodworth, "The Scandalous Pay of the Corporate Elite," *Business and Society Review* 61 (Spring 1987), pp. 22–26. 

---

See Statistical Appendix Tables A-1, A-4, A-6, and A-7.

- Robert Hunsucker, head of Panhandle Eastern, a Houston pipeline company, took over $2 million in compensation during the past three years as the firm lost $542 million last year alone, the worst in its fifty-eight year existence.
- Victor Posner collected $8.4 million while his holding company, DWG, lost over $8 million on revenues of $1.1 billion. The Miami Beach industrialist was recently convicted of evading over $1 million in taxes, but that doesn't seem to impact his wealth significantly.
- William Schreyer, chairman of Merrill Lynch, picked up an 81 percent pay hike in 1986, $2.9 million, and the firm's president, Daniel Tully, got an increase of 92 percent ($2.5 million). The company's return on equity grew only 17 percent, a fifth of the top officer's increase. Now, in the spring of 1987, they woefully announced that the company has suffered a $250 million trading loss, the worse debacle in its history.
- David Jones who heads the hospital chain, Humana, has benefited from a personal income of $17.7 million over the past three years while his shareholders lost 3 percent on their investment. Company earnings dropped 74.8 percent in 1986, earning a mere $54 million on revenues of $3.4 billion.
- Robert Mercer, Goodyear's chairman, extracted a total of $4,226,000 over the past three years, a period in which the company's return on equity dropped 62 percent.
- Tom Murphy, chairman of Capital Cities/ABC, got a hefty $4,076,000, and President Daniel Burke picked up $3,781,000. Meanwhile, the television side of the business remained stuck at the bottom of the ratings heap and the company's return on equity has declined 46.8 percent in recent years.
- Rand Araskog, chairman of ITT, was paid $4,255,000, a 66 percent raise over 1985, while sales in 1985 declined 14.2 percent and earnings per share dropped 9.7 percent. During recent years, ITT's ROE has decreased by 32 percent while Araskog's personal fortune rose.

Moderate-size firms followed the 1986 lead of the "heavies." American Motors President Joseph Cappy got a 33 percent pay raise while his company lost $91.3 million during the same period, forcing a sale of the firm to Chrysler in order to survive. Texas Instruments CEO, J.R. Junkins, picked up $614,000 in compensation, a 32 percent hike, although the high-tech firm suffered a mere 1.6 percent return on equity. And while Fluor Corporation lost $694 million in the last two years, its chairman, D.S. Tappon, received $590,000.

## Taken to the Cleaners

Other executives took their companies to the cleaners, not in spite of a bad performance but under other questionable conditions. For instance, Alan Greenberg, chairman of Bear Sterns, a financial services firm, took the enterprise public in the middle of 1986. For his "efforts" during the last six months of the year, his bounty totaled $4,078,000. Who knows how much he piled up the first half of the year?

At Salomon, the Wall Street firm, Chairman John Gutfreund's 1986 booty was $3,637,000, while his Executive Vice President Richard Schmeelk, did even better, taking $3,870,000 home. While these top two officials extracted over $7 million, company profits dropped 7 percent.

The evidence is that executives of firms engaging in unethical or unlawful practices "make out like bandits" when it comes to the end of the year. In a classic case, Robert Fomon, head of E.F. Hutton, the once prestigious stock brokerage, took it on the chin for his company overdrafting as much as $250 million per day, bilking tens of millions from over 400 banks. Under hard evidence, the firm eventually pled guilty to 2,000 counts of federal mail and wire fraud, agreeing to pay $2 million in fines. The result of all these shenanigans? While company earnings dropped 17.1 percent, cash compensation to Fomon grew 23 percent in 1986, to $1.2 million. He also netted 12,000 shares of stock. In May 1987, Fomon agreed to retire and was given a $4 million paycheck, his regular pension, and a supplemental pension. In addition he signed a seven-year retainer clause as a consultant.

Indeed, corporate misconduct in many cases seems tied to heightened executive rewards rather than to negative sanctions. General Dynamics, with 99,000 employees and sales of $6 billion a year, is the company that created a certain notoriety for its unethical pricing policies. For instance, it marked up the price of an antenna hexagonal wrench, which normally sells for $0.12 at hardware stores, some 80,000 percent. As a radar tool for use in F-16 fighters, the U.S. Air Force paid $9,609 for that $0.12 item. The company maintained two sets of books in order to defraud the U.S. government out of some $75 million, including personal travel, country-club fees, and other "necessities." Although the legal struggle has gone on for three years, Stanley C. Pace, the chairman and CEO, picked up $725,000 in 1986. That's a 33 percent increase over the previous year, while the company's return on equity dropped by 5 percent.

Not to be outdone, William E. Brown at Bank of Boston presided over a scheme to allow the shipment of $1.2 billion in cash from overseas institutions. Accused of allowing reputed organized crime families to launder millions of dollars in dirty money through bank offices, Brown pled guilty for the bank and paid a $500,000 fine. After all these ethical and legal abuses, Brown was rewarded last year with $755,000, a 40 percent pay hike.

Of course, in 1986 Wall Street executives undoubtedly cornered the market on corporate crime. It all started with Dennis B. Levine, of Drexel Burnham Lambert, who determined his $1 million-a-year income was not adequate. So he started a complex scheme several years ago of making big profits using illegal insider trading techniques, purchasing shares of stock involved in mergers, funneling profits to a Swiss bank in the Bahamas. He pocketed an extra $12.6 million in fifty-four illicit deals before getting caught. He finally admitted to securities fraud, tax evasion, and perjury. Now serving two years in a federal penitentiary in Pennsylvania, Levine got off easy because he agreed to report on others.

The biggest catch so far is Ivan Boesky, who ripped off perhaps as much as $200 million, making Levine look like an innocent babe in arms. This "Dean of Wall

Street Arbitraguers," as he was known, was so busy making deals that he needed 160 different telephone lines and was much envied by the business community and the press. When caught, he agreed to provide $100 million in restitution for a Securities and Exchange Commission civil action. He currently faces up to five years in prison for a felony count. Boesky's views of capitalism became transparent two years earlier when he spoke at Berkeley's business school graduation ceremonies: "Greed in business is all right. Greed is healthy. You can be greedy and still feel good about yourself."

Other prominent swindlers have joined the parade in cheating shareholders, customers, and the public. They include a number of lawyers, investment bankers, and Yuppie defendants, mostly in their late 20s who held high-paying, promising jobs in New York's most prestigious firms.

Old-guard businessmen have also been caught. Aldo Gucci, head of the family's designer fashions, is currently completing a one-year sentence in a halfway house for tax evasion; commodities trader Marc Rich is now exiled in Switzerland, allegedly having evaded $48 million in U.S. taxes; Paul Thayer, former chairman of LTV, has served nearly two years for insider trading abuses; Martin Siegel, a specialist in corporate mergers, recently pled guilty to felony charges; and Boyd Jefferies, 56, president of an innovative Los Angeles brokerage firm with a twenty-five year history of success, has left the company and admitted he kept false records and manipulated stocks.

## Another Day, Another $121,000

The incomes of these business officials, regardless of malfeasance, pale in comparison to the nation's top financiers. If one really wants to feed from the economic trough, then hustling deals is the job to have—managing money, trading, leveraging, hedging. The top fifteen buck makers in this line of work grossed over $700 million in 1986, an average of $44 million per person. This translates into a weekly paycheck of $850,000, or $121,000 a day including weekends and holidays. Assuming these are hardworking souls who put in a solid eight hours on the job each day, this breaks down to an amazing $15,125 an hour.

Among the highest paid in the group are George Soros, who made $90 million last year, Michael Milken of Drexel Burnham Lambert who is riding the tide of junk bond fame of $60 million annually; William Simon and Raymond Chambers, both of Wesray Corporation, each receiving $50 million; Jerome Kohlberg, Jr., Henry Kravis, and George Roberts, all of Kohlberg Kravis Roberts and Company, divided $150 million equally between them. Who says life at the top isn't a comfortable living?

In other firms, incompetent executives were eventually pushed out after considerable damage was done, but the costs in doing so were high. Samuel Armacost's role as head of BankAmerica is instructive of the problem. According to a recent story in *Fortune*, since Armacost took over in 1981, B of A fell from being the largest and most profitable bank in the United States to history's biggest disaster—losing $4.1 billion and holding $4.6 billion in bad debt. The bank's own stock plummeted from $25 a share to $9.50. *Fortune* ranked B of A 299 out of 300 major corporations, reporting it was the "least admired" of all for its "quality of management." After six years of the bank's hemorrhaging, Armacost was finally kicked out in 1986, but not without a price. Instead of paying reparations for the damage done, he was awarded $1.7 million in severance pay and stock worth $1.8 million.

A number of chief officers exacted heavier tolls to leave their corporations. The biggest golden parachute for 1986 was the bounty given to Thomas Macioce of Allied Department Stores. When the firm was taken over by Campeau, Macioce got $13.6 million. Elsewhere, Gerald Office, Jr., Chairman of Ponderosa, obtained $8.3 million to leave when Asher Edelman bought the company. Upon Sperry's merger with Burroughs, CEO Gerald Probst picked up a tidy $6.67 million. All told, the ten largest parachutes for last year totaled $69,832,000—simply to exit big companies. All this is a strange reversal of managerial opposition to the idea of severance pay for workers, a concept resisted for years. Now that executives have applied the notion of compensation for jobless managers, it's become a million-dollar necessity.

This spring, while many CBS news staffers were fired in a move to "economize," the network's departing chairman enjoyed a $4.3 million settlement, plus salary of $1.1 million. So much for the plight of executives caught in corporate layoffs to reduce costs!

These parachutes seem like small potatoes when compared with the actions of the largest corporation in America, General Motors. Chairman Roger Smith paid a staggering $700 million to Ross Perot as "hush money" if he would leave GM's board of directors and cease his criticism of the automaker's weaknesses and the need for more effective management. Rather than invest in new equipment and products, Smith was paranoid about Perot's outspoken style and paid dearly for the ouster. The ransom fee to rescue GM, incidently, was approximately $200 million more than the entire amount of venture capital spent in 1986 as seed money to launch new high-tech entrepreneurial ventures. Perhaps the Smith/Perot package will start a new trend—executive compensation for a "golden muzzle."

Of course, Smith himself didn't do too badly. He has presided over a $60 billion plan which began in the late 1970s to invest in new plants and equipment. The effort has been a dismal failure, as the giant firm has fallen behind in production and the bottom line. GM's share of the automobile market has eroded during the 1980s from 48 percent to 40 percent. Although 1986 profits were down by 28 percent, Smith grabbed a cool 15 percent pay hike, $1,368,000.

## Economic Contradictions

*Business Week's* annual executive compensation scoreboard reports data from 317 major corporations. Most managers averaged a pay increase of 6 percent. But top executives enjoy average salary and bonus increase of 17.9 percent to $829,887, double the 1985 average CEO raise of 9 percent. Last year, top officials also reaped a whopping 56 percent raise in long-term compensation, pushing one's total package of salary, bonus, and long-term pay 29 percent higher, to an average $1.2 million. Some 220 executives made over $1 million in 1986, dramatically up from only four in 1981.

What *Business Week* neglects to mention is that inflation last year was under 2 percent, meaning these top honchos made a killing in their personal lifestyles. In contrast, the Bureau of Labor Statistics reports that collective bargaining agreements for unionized workers in 1986 averaged a minuscule 1.9 percent wage increase, the lowest percent observed since this data began to be tracked decades ago. The median wage in America during 1986 was $18,616. Translated, while U.S. employees skimp along, today's chief executives receive roughly sixty times the wages of an average worker.

All this must make Adam Smith turn over in his grave. The author of *The Wealth of Nations* emphasized that capitalism was predicated on human virtues of sympathy, prudence, and benevolence. Instead, today there has risen an executive elite obsessed primarily with self-preservation. Top managers enjoy discretionary authority to pursue personal interests regardless of what might be best for the company.

The economic contradiction is that while top executives fatten their purse, rank-and-file workers are sacrificed in the name of profits. Today's corporate strategies emphasize downsizing, demassing, chapter 11 bankruptcy, and the runaway factory. Rather than launching innovative products, generating new wealth, and fostering the creation of decent jobs, the priority is on cutting out the heart of the organization, leaving the head intact. Such actions not only deserve the stern criticism of ethics, but they raise questions about financial judgement as well.

## Glimmers of Hope?

Despite rhetoric to the contrary, research continues to grow which suggests there is no correlation between company performance and executive pay. Michael Jensen, a professor at the University of Rochester, concludes from an analysis of 2,000 executives' pay between 1974–1984 that "we've got a pay system that is out of whack . . . designed for bureaucrats. . . . Executives tend to be overpaid for bad performance."

The business establishment supports this rise of corporate robbery as the necessary and appropriate status quo. Says Lee Isgur, an analyst for Paine Webber, Inc.: "If a guy ends up giving you a home run with the bases loaded, why complain?" Isgur ignores the rest of the analogy based on the numerous cases of huge personnel increases amidst declining corporate performance. Many American executives are not exactly hitting home runs. Instead, they are taking the ball and bat, rounding up the bases, and hauling off everything of value, leaving the shareholders in the left-field bleachers with empty pockets and no more game.

Iaccoca justifies his $20 million very simply: "That's the American way. If the kids don't aspire to make money like I did, what the hell good is this country? You gotta give them a role model, right?''

Are there any signs of sanity in all this? A few faint hopes point to the slight possibility that justice will yet prevail. Some greedy executives are now behind bars. A few even lost their jobs because of performance. Frank Borman, for example, has left Eastern after years of running the airline into the ground. Finally, in desperate straits, he turned the company over to arch-rival Texas Air and agreed to resign.

In some cases, outside interests have forced a more rational approach to pay and performance. For instance, the Federal Home Loan Bank Board was outraged at the 1985 compensation paid to Thomas Spiegel, president of Columbia Savings and Loan—a hefty $9 million. Last year, the FHLB pressured Columbia's directors to strip Spiegel to his base salary, a pittance of $960,000. Spiegel fought back, however, and eventually wrested a 1986 package of $3.9 million. Admittedly straining it, on the bright side, one could say that Spiegel's pay was cut by approximately 75 percent.

Elsewhere, some companies are weary of the trouble and tension caused by executive bonuses. GM, as a case in point, has come under intense pressure from its unions and the public after it first declared it would not pay profit-sharing dollars to its half million workers because of a poor company bottom line. Then it promptly announced the firm would spread $169 million around the executive suite for management bonuses. As the outcry has subsided, GM determined to create a new system which ties executive bonuses to the company's long-term strategic objectives, hopefully minimizing the furor which erupts so frequently.

In a truly exceptional illustration of integrity, at least one executive in the United States took the initiative in keeping his own paycheck from rising in the midst of a dismal corporate record in 1986. Kenneth Lay, chairman of Enron Corporation in Texas, actually turned down a $187,000 bonus he was scheduled to receive because of the firm's lackadaisical performance in the hard hit natural gas pipeline industry. Without the bonus, Lay's base salary consisted of a miniscule $650,973!

The bottom line of all this is that chief executives of too many corporations are not managing plants, equipment, and people. They aren't representing the stockholders' interest. They seem interested and skilled in primarily one thing—managing their personal portfolios.

# The New Service Economy

*Dollars & Sense*

In a comment about the massive growth in the service sector over the past two decades, economist Lester Thurow queried whether the United States is becoming a nation of people who just do each other's dirty laundry. A more relevant question might be whether we are becoming a nation of people who advertise and sell shirts, finance their distribution, quibble over contracts and breaches of contracts, and otherwise split the profit from their sales.

Since the mid-1960s, activities that don't directly produce goods—like automobiles, corn, or coal—have increasingly dominated the U.S. economy. To a large extent, this shift away from manufacturing and other goods production has been *relative*. As the proportion of output and employment in the goods-producing industries gradually declined, the share of output and jobs accounted for by other sectors naturally has increased.

Between 1969 and 1984, the proportion of total output or GNP in goods-production—agriculture, mining, construction, and manufacturing—declined from 38% to 33%. During that time the share of output from the so-called service or non-goods-producing sectors—which include such industries as finance, insurance, real estate, health, education, and government—expanded from 62% to 67%.

Although the economy has been moving away from goods production for several decades, in the mid-1980s this trend accelerated. According to the Bureau of Labor Statistics, about 72% of all jobs in the United States today are in services. Despite the magnitude of the shift, its effect on the workforce or the overall economy will depend on the composition of the service sector itself. Services comprise a vague and broad category—with nearly three-fourths of all jobs categorized as services, the sector clearly is anything but well defined.

## Losses on the Line

While job opportunities have been declining in the goods-producing industries over the last 20 years, until the mid-1980s, most of the drop was in agriculture, mining, and construction rather than manufacturing. Individual industries such as steel, leather, and tires declined steadily in employment until the late 1970s, but the abso-

"The New Service Economy." Reprinted by permission from *Dollars & Sense*, No. 120 (October 1986), pp. 6–8. (Dollars & Sense, One Summer Street, Somerville, MA 02143).

See Statistical Appendix Tables A-2, A-3, A-6, and A-7.

lute number of manufacturing jobs continued to grow, although more slowly than the rest of the economy. During the 1970s, almost one million net new factory jobs were created. Even as some smokestack industries lost their steam, new high-tech industries seemed to be rising to take their place.

Manufacturing reached its peak in 1979, when 21 million people worked in factories. Since then, it has lost much of its resiliency: over 10 million net new jobs have been added to the economy overall, while manufacturing alone has lost almost two million jobs. Eleven out of 20 major manufacturing industries have fewer employees today than they did at the bottom of the 1982 recession. This summer, factory employment reached its lowest level in almost three years, having dropped by 200,000 over the past year and by 120,000 since January. Output also has declined, and manufacturing essentially has experienced no growth for two years.

The losses have been uneven. Some of the big losers are the obvious ones: steel, textiles, autos, and apparel, all of which are pressed by import competition; oil companies, hit by the fall in oil prices; and heavy industry, which provided equipment for manufacturing. But some of the so-called high-tech saviors have also turned out to have clay feet. The instrument industry (which brings us sophisticated electronics and health instruments) added only 7,000 jobs, growing by just 1%. Since 1985, 7,000 out of 200,000 Massachusetts high-tech workers have been laid

**Figure 1.** Employment gains and losses by industry (between fourth quarter 1984 and 1985)

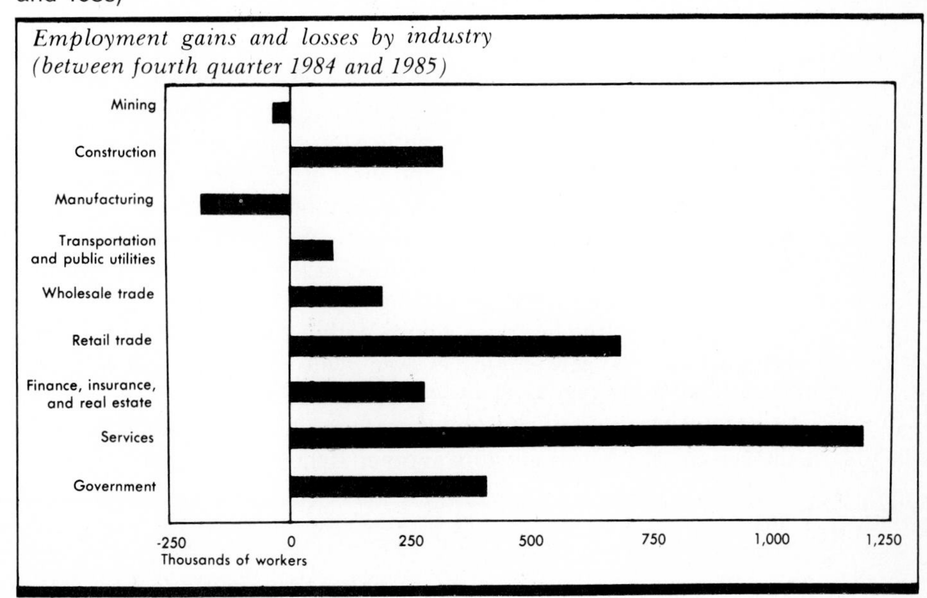


*Source:* Monthly Labor Review, February 1986

off, and another 15,000 have lost income due to furloughs and wage cuts. In California's Silicon Valley, employment in electronics dropped from 215,000 in September 1984 to 199,500 this spring.

Those industries that continue to grow or at least hold their own are primarily linked with defense spending and construction. Not surprisingly, the military buildup led to new jobs making missiles, aircraft, communication equipment, and ammunition. Driven by the recent real estate and construction boom in parts of the country, employment grew in the lumber, furniture, and cement industries. Between 1982 and 1986, printing and publishing also added 175,000 new jobs, growing by 14%. But although the high-tech and information industries continue to grow, they aren't expanding fast enough to make up for the lost jobs.

While manufacturing employment has been falling, the number of jobs in the economy has been rising by 200,000 per month—all in sectors that produce services, not goods. . . . The term "services" includes distributive services, like transportation, communications, utilities, and wholesale; the rapidly expanding producer services, like finance, insurance, real estate, and advertising; retail sales; the nonprofits, including health and education; and government. Until recently, the definition of the services primarily included consumer services, such as hotels and auto repair services. To some extent, therefore, old and new figures referring to services are not directly comparable.

The category "services" is also dubious for other reasons. Defining economic activities as producing either goods or services does not account for "goods" like repaired cars, films, or hamburgers and french fries: auto repair shops, Hollywood movie studios, and fast-food restaurants are all considered part of the non-goods-producing sector.

This approach also divides the economy by industries, rather than occupations. Using occupations to analyze productive activity, as the Department of Labor does, leads to a different view of the economy. Industrial categories place secretaries or data entry clerks who work for General Motors, for example, in the manufacturing sector, regardless of their job descriptions. On the other hand, people who do identical work but are hired by GM from a temporary agency are officially counted as part of the service sector.

Employment in all industries included in the service sector, without exception, expanded over the past few years. The retail trade industry grew the most, adding 700,000 jobs over the last year alone. Within this category, for example, clothing stores hired 50,000 new employees even while employment at U.S. clothing manufacturers fell by 16,000. In the last year finance, insurance, and real estate together added 300,000 workers. Consumer services like hotels swelled by 1,100,000 jobs, and even social services grew by another 100,000 jobs.

## Shifting Sands

The shift from manufacturing to services has happened in tandem with other important changes in the U.S. economy. After World War II—when the movement to a service-based economy began—national consumer markets started to develop in a new way. Local and regional barriers to distribution broke down, leading to the development of national networks of distribution and retailing for most consumer goods and services. In the late 1960s, corporations began to create multiple products for what had been single "product niches," developing new versions of clothes, cosmetics, cars, and other consumer goods, each one only slightly different from the others of its ilk.

This product differentiation brought the boost to such services as engineering and design needed to create that nth brand of breakfast cereal, detergent, or jeans. At the same time, services like advertising, marketing, and sales grew, their sole purpose being to make individual firms more competitive by creating a demand for these proliferating products. Finally, the expansion of corporations created a further need for such producer services as legal help and finance to help them function on an international scale.

Even more significantly, in the decades after World War II, the U.S. economy became sensitive to pressures from the international economy. Since 1971, the United States has imported more goods from other countries than it exported, creating a net trade deficit. Early trade deficits in the 1970s were linked to rising oil prices, but since 1982, they have instead reflected competition from foreign goods in domestic markets and a failure of U.S. firms to increase exports abroad. The international debt crisis, especially in Latin America, has lowered U.S. exports to those countries. The parts of the economy that have felt the squeeze the most are agriculture, and manufacturing, which is particularly susceptible to disinflation, high interest rates, low consumer demand, and other weaknesses in the economy.

On the other side of the coin, the situation that hurt manufacturing in part helped the growth of the services. Some service industries, like health care and education, are less vulnerable to competition from imports, simply because it's more difficult to export services than manufactured goods. In addition, as the goods producers increasingly felt the effects of import competition and faced lower profit rates, they turned to advertising, marketing, and other distribution ploys to help them compete.

The service sectors were able to expand as much and as quickly as they did because of another change in the economy—the availability of women workers. Since 1970, both single and married women have moved into the paid labor force (outside of domestic labor) in large numbers, motivated by changing opportunities, social forces—and numerous service sector jobs. They also have sought paid labor because shrinking real wages have pushed many families to earn two incomes instead of just one. With fewer women working at home, there was a greater demand for services that women traditionally had provided for free—like quick meals, clean laundry, and home-typed manuscripts.

The service sector found the labor it needed largely because women were and continue to be forced to take low-paying jobs—often the only ones the economy offers them. It's important to recognize that the availability of relatively cheap, inexperienced labor didn't *cause* the shift from manufacturing to services—but it did *enable* those changes to take place. Between 1970 and 1980, women filled nearly

86% of all new private sector jobs in the service industries. While it might seem reasonable that new members of the labor force should take jobs that didn't previously exist, women *disproportionately* filled service sector jobs.

## The Bottom Line

As long as there are enough jobs for everyone who wants to work, does it make a difference which sectors of the economy are growing? The categories "goods-producing" and "non-goods-producing" mask a great diversity of jobs. In terms of quality of work, for example, it's difficult to determine whether noisy, high-pressure assembly-line work provides a better quality of worklife than isolated high-pressure word processing.

What can be contrasted, however, are figures for work hours, turnover rates, wages, and benefits. Jobs in the services tend to turn over rapidly and more often are part time or temporary: according to the Bureau of Labor Statistics, between 1982 and 1984, the number of temporary workers in all sectors soared a whopping 70%. But more important, they are not unionized and, unlike manufacturing, have no tradition of unionization. Manufacturing wages and benefits are relatively high because of past labor struggles. In 1985 the average weekly earnings for a production worker in manufacturing was $385. Higher wages for workers in manufacturing helped fuel past economic growth by increasing consumer demand, including demand for a number of services.

Service sector jobs, on the other hand, do not all pay poorly. In categories like finance, for example, professionals tend to bring home higher wages than workers in retail or fast-food jobs. Nevertheless, on average the wages don't measure up to those in manufacturing. In 1986 the average weekly wage was $303 in the financial sector, $270 in the service industries, and $176 in retail trade. The figure for retail in part reflects the fact that many of these jobs are part time, but it's also lower because retail workers bring home a low hourly wage.

These numbers do not tell the whole story. The gap between manufacturing wages and the rest of the economy has been widening. Over the last year, average weekly earnings in manufacturing rose $13 to $393 (a 3.3% increase). By contrast, the comparable increases were $6 (1.8%) for wholesale trade, $.23 (.13%) for retail trade, $10 (3.9%) for services, and $14 (3.1%) for transportation. The finance, insurance, and real estate industry came close with a $13 (4.6%) rise, but in no service industry was there a long-term narrowing of the wage gap with manufacturing.

The net results of the shifting economy will be good or bad depending on what types of jobs are created. Service sector jobs don't by default have to be poorly paid—although the only way to prevent this may be to change union organizing strategies to target non-manufacturing jobs. If service industries do end up offering well-paying jobs, then the job growth would benefit the majority of the U.S. workforce. But if the service industries continue in the direction they're headed, the bulk of employment will remain in low-paid jobs where people have little bargaining power. In the 1950s and 1960s, higher wages and good benefits boosted the economy by shoring up the buying power of its workers. In the late 1980s and 1990s, inadequate working conditions could drag the U.S. economy down.

---

*Sources:* Bureau of Labor Statistics, *Employment and Earnings*, February 1982 and February 1986; Ronald E. Kutscher and Valeria A. Personick, "Deindustrialization and the Shift to Services," *Monthly Labor Review*, June 1986; Susan E. Shank and Patricia M. Getz, "Employment and Unemployment: Developments in 1985," *Monthly Labor Review*, February 1986; Thierry J. Noyelle, "Work in a World of High Technology," unpublished paper, Columbia University.

# The Exploitation of Industrial Workers in Their Homes

*Eileen Boris*

Does the Department of Labor (DOL) really care about enforcing labor standards for home workers or will it succumb to New Right political pressure? That question is being asked in Washington. Secretary of Labor William Brock has delayed issuing final rules which would lift the prohibition of home work in the six remaining garment-related industries (knitted outerwear was rescinded in late 1985). Internal scrutiny by the DOL itself has suggested that the proposed certification program, modeled after the one in effect for knitted outerwear, has failed and the woefully understaffed Wage and Hour Division will be unable to enforce the proposed rules, thus invalidating the rule change.

According to columnist Warren Brookes in the *Washington Times*, one senior official in the Department of the Justice admitted, "There was simply no way that the ruling, as prepared by Labor, could have survived a court challenge." Though later denied, this statement appears to explain what now seems like an endless process by which a combination of deregulators (like the U.S. Chamber of Commerce), antiunion "right to work" legal foundations, New Right politicians (e.g., Sen. Orrin Hatch (R-Utah) and Sen. Jesse Helms (R-N.C.), and rural working mothers have sought to overturn an over-forty-year-old ruling under the Fair Labor Standards Act (FLSA) that banned home work for undermining wage and hour standards. Some estimate it will take another three to six months before DOL comes up with rules that may withstand the expected court challenge by the International Ladies Garment Workers' Union (ILGWU); others feel that political pressure from the White House might lead to the promulgation of the existing rule, even if it is thrown out in court. After all, the days of the Reagan Administration are numbered and a Democratic presidency would be unlikely to end the home-work bans.

On August 21, 1986, the DOL proposed new regulations for home work in women's apparel, jewelry, handkerchiefs, belts and buttons, embroidery, and gloves. As with the rule for knitted outerwear, which went into effect only after a lengthy court battle with the ILGWU, the proposed rule would rescind outright prohibition and institute a certification program. Employers who requested and received certificates would be able to give out work to individuals in their homes, provided they abided by the minimum wage, maximum hour, overtime, recordkeeping, and child labor

---

Eileen Boris. "The Exploitation of Industrial Workers in Their Homes," *Business and Society Review*, No. 62 (Summer 1987), pp. 27–30. 

provisions of FLSA. During the extended public comment period that ended last December 4, DOL received 19,000 comments, of which 11,000 opposed and 8,000 supported the changes.

The question of home work has polarized the nation. The number working as employees from their home—as opposed to entrepreneurs or the truly self-employed, independent contractors—is small, with even the best estimates only ballpark figures (8,500 to 122,000 for the six questioned industries in 1987; 180,000 clerical home workers as of 1980, but 20,000 to 30,000 garment home workers in New York City alone in 1986). Yet home work has become a symbolic issue: for its defenders, it promises to unleash free enterprise, heighten competitiveness, and bring back rugged individualism while reviving "the American cottage industry" and solving the problem of day care for working mothers. Opponents, like ILGWU President Jay Mazur, predict "back to the sweatshop" because "sweatshops and home work have almost always gone hand in hand in the apparel industry." Feminists suggest that home work offers a false solution to the problem of the working mother because it pushes both parts of the double day into the home without relieving women of childcare or housework.

What about the home workers themselves? The latest attempt to rescind rules began in early 1986, when a group of North Carolina women stitching gloves at home for the Tom Thumb Glove Company of Wilkesboro, North Carolina complained of job loss to their Sen. Jesse Helms after the DOL cited their employer for home-work violations. To point out presumed irrationalities in the rules, they sent a box of home-worked items to the President: men's boxer shorts were legal to make at home, but not ladies' panties; athletic gloves, but not work gloves; buttons for upholstery but not for women's garments. Their senator allegedly put pressure on Secretary Brock to move on rescinding all the home-work bans, as called for in the 1984 Republican Party National Platform.

## Historic Roots

These prohibitions had their roots in the historic differences between the more rationalized and standardized men's garment industry and the more highly competitive hand labor women's garment industry. Whatever the reasons for the rules in the first place, the glovemakers' lawyers from the Center on National Labor Policy (also counsel to the Vermont knitters, whose protests sparked the initial reevaluation of home work in the early 1980s) have argued for deregulation because women can stay home with their families and still work. As Virginia Deal, one of the glovemakers, testified before Congress, her rural town "provides limited opportunities for women to go into the workplace but for many of us, our homes and families take precedence and we want to be allowed to stay where we are, working in the comfort of our homes." Claiming to earn more than the minimum wage, she saved the costs of transportation, babysitters, clothes, and meals, determined her own hours, and could care for her family while earning needed income.

## Low Wages

Deal's story contrasts with that of Connie Jorgensen, a former sewer of appliqued sweatsuits for Bordeaux, Inc. of Clarinda, Iowa. She also described her experiences before Congress last year: "I estimate that I earned at most $1.80 to $1.85 per hour. Plus, my husband and my eight-year-old daughter often had to help me finish my work. Many times I sewed until 2 or 4 A.M. to finish pieces for the owners to take to market. This was after I had worked in the store for eight hours that day. Several times the owners brought me new pieces at 11 P.M. or midnight to be finished by 6 A.M. But I received no overtime pay or extra benefits for my time; I was paid the straight piece rate pay per item." Jorgensen developed an allergy to fleece dust and had to wear a surgical mask for nearly a year while working, but her employers provided no medical coverage or benefits. Initially even the long drive for home work seemed attractive because any cash could aid her plight. However, sewing for Bordeaux failed to provide a living wage and meant additional expenses for transportation, electricity, and the sewing machines themselves. Although the DOL learned of Bordeaux's violations of FLSA the day prior to issuing the proposed new home work rules, they did not file suit against the company for nearly $750,000 in back pay until the day before the end of the comment period, thus avoiding negative publicity but losing $1,000 a day in compensation under a statute-of-limitation clause. The case against Bordeaux is still pending.

## Minority Workers

The typical home worker in the needle trades, however, is not a native-born white citizen of rural Iowa or North Carolina; she is not a Vermont knitter watching her toddler and stoking her fireplace while running her knitting machine. She is more likely to be nonwhite, urban, and an immigrant, both documented and undocumented, from the Americas or Asia. Perhaps she must take work home in the evening in order to keep her job at a sweatshop by day. One Mexican woman in Chicago told the House Subcommittee on Labor Standards: "She [her employer] had a lot of work and instead of hiring new workers or giving us overtime, she gave us all home work to do. We were paid by the piece—seven cents for a woman's tie. I usually could sew about fifty ties in three hours, for a grand total of $3.50 in three hours. At home, I was doing the exact same work as in the shop, but being paid much, much less."

Can we end such exploitation while respecting the desires of women who need income but want to remain in the home? The DOL claimed last August: "The experience under the knitted outerwear program has demonstrated that this program is an acceptable alternative to a total ban on the use of home workers in promoting FLSA compliance." This claim was a serious overstatement; DOL itself, prompted by the ILGWU's analysis of its enforcement, has found its program lacking in the four areas that historically have impeded home-work enforcement.

While certified employers have given the DOL the names of their competitors to reduce the competitive advantages of noncompliers, there is still no firm idea of the size of the universe of home-work employers or employees. Identifying and locating home workers remain problematic because employers may not be listing all workers (to avoid exposing violations with FLSA or other laws like immigration, FICA, or OSHA), they may be falsely identifying workers as independent contractors to avoid the regulations, or they may not know who is actually working on their goods. Home work, after all, is unsupervised, and the pressure of piece rates and deadlines has encouraged the principal home worker to seek aid from family or friends, even though only the principal is paid and recorded as having done the work.

Determining hours worked is particularly complex in garment and related industries because of wide style variation. Time studies outside a factory setting also often fail to capture actual working conditions, especially the interrupted nature of home labor. Moreover, interviews with employees may not provide accurate or enough information to reconstruct hours. The labor process and home setting themselves preclude keeping good records, and employees have ample reasons to hide violations. They fear jeopardizing their livelihood, even if meager, by exposing their employer to back-wage assessments that would force bankruptcy, or they fear employer retaliation. Underreporting of hours is common among slower workers, who feel they will be fired unless they appear to be making the minimum wage.

The certification program over the last year and a half also has not solved the difficulty of remedying those FLSA violations that could be identified. The ILGWU, based on the DOL's own records, has cited a considerably worse rate of compliance (instead of 14 percent in monetary violation, it appears that 71 percent of certified employers are) and a larger amount of back wages due than DOL has listed. Compliance officers had submitted incomplete reports and neglected to use all possible measuring devices, increasing the difficulty of remedial action. Finally, DOL continues to lack sufficient numbers to enforce FLSA for home work, not to speak of the other laws administered by the Wage and Hour Division. Staff years dropped during the first Reagan term from 587 to 474, and budget cutting hardly promises to make up for this loss.

## Labor Initiatives

Are there initiatives that labor could take to regulate home work in the interest of home workers? It could put some bite into the rules by assessing civil monetary penalties to violators and it would place the burden of documentation on employees as well as on employers (which would be less burdensome than rules that took work away from workers). Additional penalties could come to those who fail to request certification if they are later identified as using home workers. Better trained and more numerous compliance officers could not hurt. Such initiatives would prove the certification program, but they probably would not transform the abusive nature of home work. Those employers whose profits depend on shifting overhead onto employees, maintaining labor flexibility, and underpaying workers will continue to bypass the rules.

Most significantly, home work as it currently exists is the symptom, not the cause, of economic exploitation. It belongs to the restructuring of the economy which would, in many cases, increase U.S. competitiveness by bringing Third World labor standards home. Like temporary work, part-time work, and other aspects of a growing contingent work force, home work is a device that severs benefits from jobs, lowering the overall wage bill. Moreover, its appeal to many women comes from the difficulties faced by working mothers (or those who care for dependent family members). Until we take social responsibility for parenting—through family allowances, parental leaves, and adequate child care—until women's wages match men's, some women will see home work as their only option to pink-collar jobs that are not worth leaving their children poorly supervised for. Some women may prefer mother care, but we must create a society that no longer associates women with mothers and mothers with the home, where all women need not be caretakers. Only when home work is no longer women's work, low paid because it is done by mothers, only when employers use home-based labor for reasons other than cost cutting on the backs of their employees, only when such work reflects acceptable labor standards, could a certification program end the exploitative nature of the century-old home-work system. Only then would the "choice" to work at home become meaningful. My bet is that the Reagan Administration, given its different agenda, won't be willing to wait that long before attempting to lift all the home-work bans.

# Caught in the Web of Change

*John D. Kasarda*

Two fundamental, yet conflicting, transformations mark the recent history and near-term prospects of our older, larger cities. First is a *functional* change: these cities are becoming administration, information, and higher-order service centers, rather than centers for producing and distributing material goods. Secondly, there is *demographic* change: the residents are no longer predominantly whites of European heritage, but are predominantly blacks, Hispanics, and members of other minority groups.

Concomitant with the functional transformation of these cities have been changes both in the composition and the size of their overall employment bases. During the past two decades, most older, larger cities have experienced substantial job growth in occupations associated with knowledge-intensive service industries. However, selective job growth in these high-skill, predominantly white-collar industries has not nearly compensated for post–World War II employment declines in manufacturing, wholesale trade, and other predominantly blue-collar industries, which once constituted the urban economic backbone. As a result, the total number of jobs available in most of these cities has shrunk considerably over the past three decades.

Analogously, concomitant with the ethnic and racial transformations, there have been substantial changes in the socioeconomic composition and total size of the cities' residential populations. As predominantly white, middle-income groups have dispersed (initially to the suburbs and now increasingly to nonmetropolitan areas), they have been only partially replaced by predominantly lower-income minority groups. The result has been dramatic declines both in the aggregate sizes and the aggregate personal-income levels of the cities' resident populations, while concentrations of the economically disadvantaged continue to expand.

The simultaneous transformation and selective decline of the employment and residential bases of the cities have contributed to a number of serious problems, including a widening gap between urban job-opportunity structures and the skill levels of disadvantaged residents (with correspondingly high rates of structural unemployment), spatial isolation of low-income minorities, and intractably high levels of urban poverty. Accompanying these problems have been a plethora of social and institutional ills further aggravating the predicament of people and places in distress:

---



---

See Statistical Appendix Table A-2.

rising crime, poor public schools, and the decay of once-vibrant residential and commercial subareas.

Responsive to the hardships confronting cities and their inhabitants, the federal government has introduced a variety of urban programs over the past fifteen years. Unfortunately, these programs have had little effect in stemming urban decline or improving long-term employment prospects for the underprivileged. Indeed, mounting evidence suggests that the plight of economically distressed cities and their underprivileged residents is worse than before America's urban programs began.

The poor track record of these federal urban programs is attributable primarily to the failure of our policy-makers to appreciate fully the technological and economic dynamics underlying industry's locational choices, on the one hand, and an inadequate consideration of the changing roles of older cities in an advanced service economy, on the other. I will focus on these dynamics and transformations, especially as they have altered the capacity of America's older cities to offer employment opportunities and social mobility for disadvantaged resident groups.

## Socioeconomic Springboards

Cities always have and always will perform valuable social and economic functions, but changing technological and industrial conditions (both national and international) alter such functions over time. Apropos of the assimilation and socioeconomic upgrading of masses of disadvantaged persons historically, it must be remembered that cities performed these functions most effectively during an industrial and transportation age now gone.

During the late nineteenth and early twentieth centuries, America's industrial revolution fostered dramatic national economic development, creating millions of low-skill jobs. Most of this economic development and employment growth occurred in the cities, which possessed comparative advantages over other locations. For firms concentrating in the cities, costs were substantially reduced and efficiency was increased. Among the advantages were superior long-distance transportation and "break in bulk" terminal facilities; abundant and ambitious immigrant labor, willing to work for extremely low wages; essential complementary businesses; and private and public municipal services, such as police and fire protection, sewage systems, and running water.

Territorially restricting transportation technologies and the burgeoning manpower needs of a labor-intensive manufacturing economy generated unprecedentedly high urban concentration. Because the transit and terminal costs of coal were high, manufacturers sought to minimize expenses by clustering together around rail or water terminal sites and sharing bulk carriage costs. Since the main terminal was also where most other raw materials used in the production process were received, and where finished products were shipped, additional cost advantages accrued to factories concentrating near terminal points.

The lack of efficient short-distance transportation technology likewise acted to confine the sites of complementary businesses as well as the residences of the urban labor force. Wholesale establishments, warehouses handling finished goods, and ancillary businesses that serviced the factories or used their by-products reduced costs by locating close to the factories. Similarly, most workers employed by the factories and related business establishments, unable to afford commuting, were clustered within walking distance of their place of employment. Indeed, as late as 1899, the average commuting distance of workers in New York City was approximately two blocks.

Our industrial cities thus evolved in the late nineteenth century as compact agglomerations of production and distribution facilities and as places where millions of unskilled or semiskilled migrants both lived and worked. Spatially circumscribed by prevailing transportation technologies, industrial development and concentrative migration occurred together, generating explosive urban growth. Chicago, for example, which was incorporated in 1833 with a population of 4,100 grew to be a city of more than 2 million residents by 1910, the vast majority of whom lived and worked within a three-mile radius of the city's center.

Spurring the dramatic growth of our industrial cities were a rapidly advancing western resource frontier and burgeoning commercial markets. A powerful entrepreneurial spirit held that individualism, competition, the pursuit of profit, and economic growth were uniformly positive and beneficial. In this political-economic climate, urban industrial development surged, catapulting the entire country into a period of enormous economic expansion. By the dawn of the twentieth century, the output of America's industrial cities had surpassed the *combined* total industrial output of Britain, France, and Germany, the world's leaders in 1860.

It cannot be overemphasized that the employment bases of our early industrial cities were characterized by entry-level job surpluses; today, entry-level job deficits characterize urban employment bases. It was these job surpluses, with few requisites for entry, that attracted the waves of migrants and offered them a foothold in the urban economy. In turn, the rapidly expanding job base that accompanied national economic growth provided ladders of opportunity and social mobility for the migrants, most of whom were escaping areas of economic distress.

Access to opportunity and social mobility was obtained at significant human cost, however. Prejudice, discrimination, hostility, and (frequently) physical violence greeted the new arrivals. Lacking financial resources, unaccustomed to city ways, and often without English language skills, immigrants were given the lowest status and were segregated in overcrowded dwellings in the least desirable areas. A polluted, unsanitary physical environment contributed to high morbidity and mortality, as did the hazardous working conditions found in the factories. Political corruption and exploitation were common, working hours were long, and there was no such thing as a minimum wage. Virtually all immigrants held so-called dead-end jobs.

Nonetheless, there was an abundance of jobs for which the only requisites were a person's desire and physical ability to work. Overall economic growth and this surplus of low-skill jobs gave our older industrial cities a unique historical role as developers of manpower and springboards for social mobility.

During the first half of the twentieth century, numerous advances occurred in transportation, communication, and production-distribution technologies. These served to reduce markedly the previous locational advantages that our older, compactly structured cities had held for manufacturing and warehousing and made uncongested suburban sites more cost-effective. Among these advances were the shift from rail and barge transport to trucking, the spread of peripheral highways and public utilities, and automated assembly-line techniques. By 1960, further advances in transportation and communication technologies, together with growing industrial competition from nonmetropolitan areas and abroad, made our larger, older cities all but obsolete with respect to manufacturing and warehousing. A massive exodus of blue-collar jobs began—an exodus that accelerated during the past decade.

Exacerbating blue-collar job losses in the cities has been the post–World War II flight of retail trade and consumer services, which followed their traditional middle- and upper-income patrons to the suburbs and exurbs. Between 1954 and 1978, more than 15,000 shopping centers and malls were constructed to serve expanding suburban and exurban populations. By 1975, these shopping centers and malls produced more than one-half of the United States' annual retail sales. As a consequence, central cities have suffered marked job losses in standard retail and consumer-service industries.

Significant countertrends, however, are under way in certain retail and service sectors, as businesses and institutions offering highly specialized goods and services continue to be attracted to downtown areas. The specialized nature of these establishments often makes it advantageous to locate at centralized nodes that maximize accessibility to people and firms in the metropolitan area. Advertising agencies; brokerage houses; consulting firms; financial institutions; luxury goods shops; legal, accounting, and professional complexes—these have been accumulating in the central business districts. Traditional department stores and other establishments—unable to compete effectively or unable to afford the skyrocketing rents—are being replaced.

The past two decades have also witnessed a remarkable growth of high-rise administrative offices in the central business districts of our largest cities. Even with major advances in telecommunications technology, many administrative headquarters still rely on a complement of legal, financial, public relations, and other specialized services that are most readily available in the central business districts. Unlike manufacturing, wholesale trade, and retail trade—which typically have large space-per-employee requirements—most managerial, clerical, professional, and business-service functions are space-intensive. In addition, persons performing these service functions can be "stacked" vertically, layer after layer, in downtown high-rises without losing any productivity. Indeed, office proximity often enhances the productivity of those whose activities entail extensive, nonroutinized, face-to-face interaction. The result has been an office-building boom in the central business districts.

## Employment-Demographic Disarticulations

The growth of administrative, financial, professional, and similar "knowledge class" jobs in the central business districts of our large cities, together with substantial losses of blue-collar jobs, has altered the important role the cities once played as opportunity ladders for the disadvantaged. Aggravating the problems engendered by the deterioration of historical blue-collar job bases has been the flight of middle-income population and traditional retail-trade and consumer-service establishments elsewhere in the city. Further, these movements have combined to erode city tax bases, damage secondary labor markets, and isolate many disadvantaged persons in economically distressed subareas where the opportunities for employment are minimal.

Particularly hard hit by post–World War II declines of middle-income population and blue-collar jobs are our larger, older cities in the northern industrial belt. Unfortunately, it is many of these same cities that have experienced the largest postwar migration inflows of persons whose educational backgrounds and skills are ill-suited for the information-processing jobs which have partially replaced the lost blue-collar jobs. Consequently, inner-city unemployment rates are well above the national average and are inordinately high among educationally disadvantaged minorities, whose numbers continue to grow in our urban centers.

Data presented in Table 1 for our four largest northern cities illustrate the scope of urban employment decline in the postwar period. New York City and Chicago, for example, have each lost more than 300,000 manufacturing jobs since 1947, with the most pronounced employment losses occurring after 1967. Also ravaged have been Philadelphia and Detroit.

Wholesale and retail trade employment in all these cities likewise deteriorated considerably. However, there are temporal differences. Whereas most retail-

**Table 1** Employment Changes in Major Northern Cities

| | Manufacturing | Wholesale | Retail | Selected Services | Total |
|---|---|---|---|---|---|
| **New York** | | | | | |
| 1948–77 | −330,535 | −122,071 | −208,595 | 153,250 | −507,951 |
| 1967–77 | −285,600 | −82,925 | −94,053 | 30,992 | −431,586 |
| **Chicago** | | | | | |
| 1948–77 | −301,407 | −51,827 | −100,803 | 57,874 | −396,163 |
| 1967–77 | −180,900 | −41,023 | −49,829 | 45,246 | −226,506 |
| **Philadelphia** | | | | | |
| 1948–77 | −171,130 | −26,573 | −63,263 | 15,263 | −245,703 |
| 1967–77 | −106,400 | −19,328 | −23,743 | 2,242 | −147,229 |
| **Detroit** | | | | | |
| 1948–77 | −185,073 | −21,980 | −78,804 | −4,484 | −290,341 |
| 1967–77 | −56,400 | −20,617 | −32,632 | −10,706 | −120,355 |

*Source:* Censuses of Manufacturing and Censuses of Business.

employment losses occurred before 1967, wholesale-employment declines (like those in manufacturing) accelerated after 1967, during which more than two-thirds of the total 1947–77 job declines occurred. The accelerating pace of central-city job losses in the manufacturing and wholesale sectors reflects the technological forces discussed above as well as the growing diseconomies of central-city locations for production and warehousing activities.

The selective nature of job declines in the twelve large cities noted above is indicated by employment-change data for their service industries. Only Detroit showed a net loss in service-industry jobs between 1947 and 1977, and this loss is entirely accountable by service-industry job losses since 1967. Chicago and New York City, on the other hand, have shown substantial vitality in their service industries since World War II. Even in these cities, though, service-industry job growth was overwhelmed by employment declines in manufacturing, wholesale trade, and retail trade. Overall, Chicago lost nearly 400,000 jobs between 1947 and 1977; during the same time period, New York City lost more than 500,000 jobs. In each case, the vast majority of overall job losses are attributable to blue-collar employment declines. Moreover, detailed analysis of sectoral employment change demonstrates that all of the net increase in service employment in New York City, Chicago, and Philadelphia has been in knowledge-intensive industries (e.g., finance, health and legal services, colleges and universities, engineering firms, and such business services as accounting, advertising, data processing, management consulting, and R&D). Conversely, service-sector employment opportunities with lower educational requirements (e.g., in hotels, personal services, and a full range of such consumer services as auto repair) have declined markedly.

Thus, a rather clear picture emerges. Central-city employment in those industries which traditionally sustained large numbers of less-skilled persons has declined precipitously. These employment losses have been partially replaced by newer service industries, which typically have high educational requisites for entry. The dissonant expansion in large northern cities of population groups whose educational backgrounds place them at a serious disadvantage deserves attention.

Obtaining an accurate account of each city's changing demographic composition (by race and ethnicity) is not without its complications. Because Hispanics (most of whom are classified as whites in the census) are typically considered a racial-ethnic minority, one cannot determine actual minority compositional changes in the cities without separating this group from whites, blacks, and others. Published census data do not permit one to do this. However, the 1970 fourth-count summary computer tapes and the 1980 system's File-1A computer tapes both contain information on how the Hispanic/Spanish-origin population was allocated for each city across "white," "black," and "other." With this information, it is possible to reconstruct each city's 1970 and 1980 non-Hispanic white population, non-Hispanic black population, and non-Hispanic "other" (primarily Asian) population in addition to its Hispanic population. These adjustments permit refined analysis of each city's racial-ethnic residential compositional changes and their actual minority demographic transformation. (See Table 2.)

**Table 2** Demographic Changes in Major Northern Cities

| | Total Population | Non-Hispanic Whites | Non-Hispanic Blacks | Non-Hispanic Other* | Hispanic Population* | Percent Minority |
|---|---|---|---|---|---|---|
| **New York** | | | | | | |
| 1980 | 7,071,639 | 3,668,945 | 1,694,127 | 302,543 | 1,406,024 | 48 |
| 1970 | 7,894,851 | 5,061,663 | 1,517,967 | 112,940 | 1,202,281 | 36 |
| CHANGE | −823,212 | −1,393,718 | 176,160 | 189,603 | 203,743 | |
| **Chicago** | | | | | | |
| 1980 | 3,005,072 | 1,299,557 | 1,187,905 | 95,547 | 422,063 | 57 |
| 1970 | 3,362,825 | 1,998,914 | 1,076,483 | 39,571 | 247,857 | 41 |
| CHANGE | −357,753 | −699,357 | 111,422 | 55,976 | 174,206 | |
| **Philadelphia** | | | | | | |
| 1980 | 1,688,210 | 963,469 | 633,485 | 27,686 | 63,570 | 43 |
| 1970 | 1,948,609 | 1,246,940 | 646,015 | 10,975 | 44,679 | 36 |
| CHANGE | −260,399 | −283,471 | −12,530 | 16,711 | 18,891 | |
| **Detroit** | | | | | | |
| 1980 | 1,203,339 | 402,077 | 754,274 | 18,018 | 28,970 | 67 |
| 1970 | 1,511,336 | 820,181 | 651,847 | 9,254 | 30,054 | 46 |
| CHANGE | −307,997 | −418,104 | 102,427 | 8,764 | −1,084 | |
| **Total Change 1970–80** | −1,749,361 | −2,793,650 | 377,479 | 271,054 | 395,756 | |

*The term "Hispanic" is used for all those classified as Hispanic or Spanish origin. "Non-Hispanic Other" is used for those classified as Asians, American Indians, and Pacific Islanders.

New York City, which experienced an overall population decline of 823,212 during the 1970–80 decade, lost 1,392,718 non-Hispanic whites. Thus, in just ten years, New York's non-Hispanic white population (i.e., its nonminority population) dropped by an amount larger than the *total* population of any other U.S. city with the exception of Los Angeles, Chicago, Philadelphia, and Houston. Approximately 25 percent of the loss of non-Hispanic whites in New York City was replaced by an infusion of more than 200,000 Hispanics during the 1970s and, to a somewhat lesser extent, by the growth of non-Hispanic "others" and non-Hispanic blacks. The transition to minority residential dominance of our nation's largest city seems all but assured.

Chicago's demographic experience during the 1970s was similar to New York City's, but at about one-half the scale. Registering a net population drop of 357,753 residents between 1970 and 1980, Chicago's non-Hispanic white population declined by 699,357, whereas the city's minority population (non-Hispanic blacks, non-Hispanic "others," plus Hispanics) grew by 341,604. More than 50 percent of Chicago's minority population increase during the decade consisted of Hispanics (174,206). By 1980, 57 percent of Chicago's resident population was composed of minorities.

Among the four largest northern cities in the United States (New York, Chicago, Philadelphia, and Detroit), the City of Brotherly Love had the smallest aggregate population decline, losing slightly over a quarter of a million residents during the

1970s. Both the number of non-Hispanic whites and non-Hispanic blacks declined in Philadelphia between 1970 and 1980, while other, non-Hispanic minorities and Hispanics increased. Philadelphia's substantial decline in non-Hispanic whites (283,471) together with its net increase of 23,072 minority residents during the 1970s raised its minority proportion to 43 percent in 1980.

Detroit experienced the highest rate of non-Hispanic-white residential decline of any major city in the country. Between 1970 and 1980, Detroit lost more than one-half of its non-Hispanic white residents (from 820,181 to 402,777). Concurrently, Detroit had the fourth-largest absolute increase of non-Hispanic blacks of any city in the country (102,427), falling just behind Chicago in black population increase. Combined with modest increases in Hispanics and other minorities, Detroit's large increase in black residents and precipitous drop in non-Hispanic white residents transformed the city's residential base from 46 percent minority in 1970 to 67 percent minority in 1980.

Between 1970 and 1980, our four largest northern cities suffered an aggregate loss of 2,793,650 non-Hispanic whites, while their Hispanic residential bases increased by nearly 400,000. Added to the Hispanic increase during the 1970s were substantial cumulative increases of non-Hispanic blacks (377,479) and other non-Hispanic minorities (271,054), resulting in a total increase of more than 1,040,000 minority residents in the four cities. These compositional changes have further implications.

## Consequences of Mismatch

It has been noted that job opportunities matching the educational backgrounds and skills of many minorities have disappeared from major northern cities. Concurrently, as higher-income white-collar workers moved to the suburbs and exurbs, white-collar jobs increased substantially in the central city. One consequence of the residence–job opportunity mismatch is increased commuting in both directions between central cities and outlying nodes. This mismatch manifests itself each weekday morning on the radial urban expressways, where one observes heavy streams of white-collar workers commuting into the central business districts from their suburban residences; simultaneously, in the opposite lanes, streams of inner-city residents are commuting to their blue-collar jobs in outlying areas.

The job opportunity–residential composition mismatch has had especially deleterious consequences for minorities and blue-collar ethnic whites left behind in the inner city. As blue-collar industries have deconcentrated, they have become scattered among suburban, exurban, and nonmetropolitan sites. Their dispersed nature makes public transportation from central-city neighborhoods to most outlying locations impractical, requiring virtually all city residents who work outside the central city to commute by private automobile. The high and increasing costs of inner-city automobile ownership, insurance, and maintenance imposes a heavy financial burden on these people. Moreover, a large portion of inner-city residents, particularly low-income minorities, can afford neither the luxury nor the employment necessity of owning an automobile. In Chicago, for example, four out of five inner-city blacks do not own automobiles. The result is rising rates of urban structural unemployment, especially among disadvantaged minorities who traditionally had found employment in those industries which have relocated in the suburbs, nonmetropolitan areas, and abroad.

In our four largest northern cities, unemployment rates among minorities have risen dramatically. (See Table 3.) With the exception of industrially crippled Detroit, the rise in unemployment rates among whites in these cities between 1971 and 1980 corresponded very closely with the rise in the national unemployment rate. The moderate rise in youth unemployment among whites also echoed national trends. Black and other minority unemployment rates, however, soared. Worst hit was Detroit, where adult-male minority unemployment rates rose to nearly 30 percent in 1980. Recall that Detroit also experienced a major increase in black residents between 1970 and 1980. Youth minority unemployment rates for Detroit, already high in 1971 (44.4 percent), rose to 52.1 percent in 1980.

New York City, with its huge white outmigration, experienced negligible growth in adult white-male unemployment between 1971 and 1980. But unemployment rates for adult black males nearly doubled during the decade, and rates for black youth unemployment rose from 26.3 percent to 40 percent. Chicago lost a much larger proportion of its jobs than New York City during the 1970s and registered significant increases both in its white and black resident-unemployment rates. By 1980, adult black-male unemployment reached 14.3 percent, and black youth unemployment had climbed to 55 percent—nearly triple the unemployment rate for white youths.

The picture in Philadelphia is no brighter, with adult male minority-unemployment rates reaching nearly 20 percent and minority youth unemployment rates exceeding 46 percent in 1980. Diverging from the pattern in other major northern cities, unemployment rates for adult minority women increased *fourfold* in Philadelphia between 1971 and 1980.

**Table 3** Changing Unemployment Rates in Major Northern Cities

| Race, Sex, and Age | New York | | Chicago | | Philadelphia | | Detroit | |
|---|---|---|---|---|---|---|---|---|
| | 1971 | 1980 | 1971 | 1980 | 1971 | 1980 | 1971 | 1980 |
| **White** | | | | | | | | |
| Men, 20+ | 5.8 | 6.6 | 4.0 | 8.6 | 3.4 | 7.0 | 6.5 | 18.2 |
| Women, 20+ | 5.5 | 7.1 | 3.7 | 6.9 | 4.4 | 6.3 | 5.3 | 11.8 |
| Both sexes, 16–19 | 20.4 | 23.8 | 14.2 | 21.0 | 14.2 | 19.4 | 17.5 | 22.2 |
| **Black and other** | | | | | | | | |
| Men, 20+ | 6.2 | 11.0 | 6.4 | 14.3 | 7.7 | 19.4 | 10.4 | 29.3 |
| Women, 20+ | 7.4 | 7.7 | 7.1 | 11.5 | 3.5 | 15.7 | 13.6 | 19.8 |
| Both sexes, 16–19 | 26.3 | 40.0 | 36.3 | 55.0 | 22.7 | 46.4 | 44.4 | 52.1 |

*Source:* Current Population Surveys and Geographic Profiles of Employment and Unemployment, 1971 and 1980.

The extent of unemployment in these four cities is not fully captured by the rates just cited, for they refer only to those jobless persons actively seeking employment during the month before the survey was taken. Thus these figures exclude workers who have given up searching and others who have dropped out of the labor force but who would work if presented with an opportunity. If such persons were included in the unemployment statistics, central-city jobless rates would, no doubt, be much higher.

## What Next?

It is certain that chronically high unemployment will plague large portions of the urban underclass so long as the demographic and job-opportunity structures of the cities move in conflicting directions. Despite a variety of public policy efforts to slow the departure of blue-collar jobs from our cities, the exodus continues apace. Government subsidies, tax incentives, and regulatory relief contained in existing and proposed urban programs are not nearly sufficient to overcome the technological and market-driven forces that are redistributing jobs and shaping the economies of our major cities.

Cities that can exploit their emerging service-sector roles may well experience renewed economic vitality and net job increases in the years ahead. However, it is doubtful that those on the bottom rungs of the socioeconomic ladder will benefit, since they lack the appropriate skills for advanced service-sector jobs. Indeed, their employment prospects could further deteriorate. New York City, for instance, capitalizing on its strength as an international financial and administrative center, experienced a net increase of 167,000 jobs between 1977 and 1981. Yet, while the city's overall employment base was expanding, its minority unemployment rates continued to climb. This is because virtually all of New York's employment expansion during the four-year period was concentrated in white-collar service industries, whereas manufacturing employment dropped by 55,000 jobs and wholesale and retail-trade employment declined by an additional 9,000 jobs. These figures, together with the other data for New York City presented above, provide dramatic testimony that the urban residence–job opportunity mismatch and corresponding minority unemployment rates can worsen even under conditions of overall central-city employment gains.

The seemingly dysfunctional growth of underprivileged populations in our urban centers at a time when these centers are experiencing serious contractions in lower-skill jobs raises a number of interrelated questions: What is it that continues to attract and hold underprivileged persons in inner-city areas of distress? How are the underprivileged able to stay economically afloat? What, in short, has replaced traditional urban jobs as a means of economic subsistence for the underclass?

Answers to these questions may be found in the dramatic rise since 1960 of two alternative economies that increasingly dominate the livelihood of the urban underclass: the *welfare economy* (public housing, food stamps, aid to families with dependent children, etc.) and the *underground economy* (illegal activities and unreported cash and barter transactions). These alternative economies have mushroomed in our cities, functioning as institutionalized surrogates for the declining production economies that once attracted and sustained large numbers of disadvantaged residents.

Yet, while the burgeoning production economies of our urban past provided substantial numbers of the disadvantaged with a means of entry into the mainstream economy as well as with opportunities for mobility, today's urban welfare and underground economies often have the opposite effects—limiting options and reinforcing the urban concentration of those without access to the economic mainstream. Most urban welfare programs, for example, have been specifically targeted to inner-city areas of greatest distress, thereby providing the subsistence infrastructure that keeps disadvantaged people there. Dependent on place-oriented public housing, nutritional assistance, health care, income maintenance and other such programs, large segments of the urban underclass have become anchored in areas of severe employment decline. Racial discrimination and insufficient low-cost housing in areas of employment growth further obstruct mobility and job acquisition by the underclass, as do deficiencies in the technical and interpersonal skills so necessary to obtain and hold jobs. The upshot is that increasing numbers of potentially productive persons find themselves socially, economically, and spatially isolated in segregated inner-city wastelands, where they subsist on a combination of government handouts and their own informal economies. Such isolation, dependency, and blocked mobility, breed hopelessness, despair, and alienation which, in turn, foster drug abuse, family dissolution, and other social malaise disproportionately afflicting the urban underclass.

My comments here should not be interpreted as implying that government aid to people and places in distress is unnecessary or without merit. Most urban welfare programs have had important palliative effects, temporarily relieving some very painful symptoms associated with the departure of blue-collar jobs—poor housing, inadequate nutritional and health care, and so on. Still, while some success has been achieved in relieving these pains, underlying structural disarticulations are growing worse. These disarticulations, to reiterate, are rooted in conflicting demographic and functional transformations in our cities, resulting in a widening gap between their residents' skill levels and new job-opportunity structures.

# Chapter 8
# HEALTH CARE AND DELIVERY

## The Unhealthy Medical Care for the Poor

*Michael Millenson*

For years, physicians and hospitals have financed care for those who couldn't pay by upping the bills of those who could. This implicit but universally-accepted "charity tax" was made possible by a generous reimbursement system that essentially paid providers whatever they claimed was "reasonable."

Today, that arrangement is being destroyed. The old system's generosity led too many patients, physicians, and hospitals to regard medical insurance as the equivalent of a credit card whose bill never came due. When health-care costs soared above even the high general rate of inflation, those who *did* have to pay the tab—the government and private businesses—finally took the credit card away.

The clearest symbol of this change was Medicare's decision in 1983 to begin paying hospitals set fees for each of 468 diagnosis-related groups (DRGs) rather than reimbursing hospitals based on their individual costs. On average, Medicare accounts for about 40 percent of a hospital's revenues. In a like manner, most private insurers are vowing to pay only for what *they* believe is reasonable, just as in any other business transaction.

A number of hospitals have established limits on free care. Some have also limited care for Medicaid patients. (Medicaid is a joint federal-state program that covers some of the poor. Payments vary by state, but reimbursement is usually much less than private insurance or Medicare.) The limits are often informal, but they are real and widespread, and they show up repeatedly in interviews with physicians and with hospital managers.

"From the perspective of paying patients, the newly emerging buyer's market in health care will be a delight," says Prof. Uwe E. Reinhardt, James Madison Professor of Political Economy at Princeton University. "[However,] the American public must be prepared to pay explicitly for the health care of poor fellow citizens or let the latter wither on the vine." Adds Reinhardt, "We are now firmly embarked on a march toward two-class medicine."

---

Michael Millenson, "The Unhealthy Medical Care for the Poor," *Business and Society Review*, No. 61 (Spring 1987), pp. 40–43. 

See Statistical Appendix Table A-20.

Research being done by Northwestern University's Center for Health Services and Policy Research is among the first to show clear evidence of this splintering. The center is analyzing actual patient data provided by hospitals as part of a three-year national study of hospital strategies.

The data shows that "competition has had a positive effect on the number of services offered" the middleclass, says Prof. Stephen Shortell, the principal investigator for the study. For the poor, though, competition means hospitals "are less likely to offer charity care."

However, Carol McCarthy, president of the American Hospital Association, insists, "There has not been any stepping away from the indigent care issue on the part of hospitals."

## Dumping Epidemic

Perhaps, but what then of the epidemic of "dumping" highlighted by medical reports during the first half of 1985? Private hospitals were repeatedly caught transferring uninsured patients to public hospitals in circumstances that can only be described as barbaric.

For example, a 21-year-old in critical condition was denied entry to the burn unit of a university hospital in Nashville. A pregnant woman in Wyoming, diagnosed as having complications, bled internally for a month as she and her husband scraped up the $500 down payment an investor-owned hospital demanded before surgery. A Dallas woman was transferred in the middle of labor after mentioning she had no insurance. A stabbing victim in San Francisco was refused care at several private hospitals before dying at the public one. And the list goes on. Comments Elliot C. Roberts, administrator of New Orleans's Charity Hospital: "To be medically indigent in a competitive system . . . is tantamount to being an outcast."

There is some evidence that dumping has abated, though it certainly hasn't disappeared. No one knows for sure, however, because no one is tracking "dumping" nationally. If dumping has declined, credit must go to publicity, lawsuits, and new federal legislation prohibiting transfers of unstable patients. Dallas's Parkland Memorial Hospital has tracked the problem for itself and reports that dumping appears to have lessened after passage of a Texas law regulating emergency transfers.

On the other hand, Parkland's neighboring hospitals may simply have been discouraged by the reputation of Parkland's president, Dr. Ron Anderson. Anderson was a major backer of the anti-dumping measure. He helped prod the state legislature into action by cooperating with *60 Minutes* in an episode featuring tapes of doctors telling Parkland they were transferring critically ill patients because they lacked insurance.

The pain and discomfort routinely visited on patients like car accident victim John Thompson, the Cook County patient who was transferred with "stable" compression fractures of the spine, has sparked no public outcry. Both private and public hospitals say the publics are in existence to take these patients. Ignored in this cozy arrangement is the fact that the Joint Commission on Accreditation of Hospitals prohibits *any* transfer of patients for an economic reason. There is no record, however, of any hospital losing its accreditation because of a transfer.

Parkland's Anderson explains the lack of a public outcry by saying, "I don't think the American people are ready to see people die on the streets and walk over them. [But] as long as public hospitals keep them out of sight, it's not on their conscience."

## The Uninsured

There are more and more people to keep out of sight. In 1984, almost one in six Americans—or a little over 35 million people—had no medical insurance, according to the Census Bureau. That's up 22 percent from five years before. An estimated 65 percent of those without medical coverage were working or were the wives, husbands and children of workers. Many small businesses and service businesses do not provide health insurance.

Charles Gilmore, 32, works for a window cleaning company that employs thirty to forty people. "No one that I know [at work] has health insurance," says Gilmore, who has come to Cook County Hospital's outpatient clinic after three days of a cough and cold. Gilmore is fortunate—he waited only three and a half hours to be seen after arriving at 5:30 in the morning. A five-hour wait is not uncommon.

Mary Allen, 47, seeing a doctor about chest pains, usually comes to the hospital's emergency room at 5 or 6 in the morning to keep the wait down to about two hours. Allen has a temporary job filling orders for a large cosmetics firm. Like a growing number of companies, hers employs part-time workers to keep costs down. Allen has no health insurance.

For the working poor, Medicaid gives little medical aid. In fact, Reagan budget pressures helped reduce the percentage of poor people covered by Medicaid from a high of 63 percent in 1975 to about 46 percent in 1985.

Suffering the most may be victims of chronic conditions. Those "dying in the streets," after all, command attention. Not so the sufferer from high blood pressure, diabetes, or sickle-cell anemia. At big public hospitals, a visit with a doctor is rationed by waiting. At Cook County, officials estimated that 8 to 10 percent of the patients simply get up and leave.

"People just grow to accept it as part of the process," says Dr. Ted Brockett, the attending physician running Cook County's ambulatory screening clinic one evening. "It's strictly patch up and send 'em out."

Community health clinics are similarly overwhelmed. At Los Barrios Unidos Community Clinic in western Dallas, Dr. Kathy Simon, acknowledges, "We turn away lots of people." The clinic has two doctors and a nurse practitioner; it has neither the funds nor the staff to remain open long hours. So, except for emergencies, it's first come, first served for twenty-five people in the morning and twenty-five people in the afternoon.

Unfortunately, says Simon, "a lot of problems that are really medical emergencies that shouldn't wait a few days are not picked up by a receptionist." For instance, says Simon, "I've had at least three diabetics with foot ulcers" who failed to convince a receptionist of the seriousness of the problem. After losing several days at work because of immobility, the patients finally got treatment.

Dr. Ron Anderson sums up the dilemma of the new medicine this way: "Never in human history has economic competition resulted in the just distribution of scarce and life-sustaining resources."

Anderson should know. To defray costs of the uninsured, Parkland is competing for paying patients with a special floor featuring a few more amenities and better nursing service. And to appease the university physicians on whom it depends for staff, Parkland is helping to build a private hospital next door that will give its staff a chance to have private patients, too. Other public hospitals have also taken steps to attract paying customers to offset some of the cost of the medically indigent.

## Who's to Blame?

If there are clear villains here, they are hard to find. Should hospitals, especially tax-free ones, be more responsive to the uninsured? Probably. But as the nun who heads a large Catholic chain puts it, "There's no mission without a margin." (That's profit margin, of course.) Naturally, doctors can't be expected to provide their services for free, either.

Should insurers, HMOs, and businesses be condemned for driving a hard bargain on medical prices? Perhaps, except consumers don't expect to pay a higher hotel bill as a way of funding the homeless or a steeper restaurant tab in order to feed the hungry. The government is an obvious bad guy. But the government, of course, is elected by all of us.

Any number of solutions to the indigent-care problem have been proposed, including various special funds and reforms of Medicaid and Medicare. None will go anywhere until the middle class remembers that the extra medical services and conveniences that competition is bringing them are in part resulting in services and conveniences being taken away from others.

"The social contract is not a set of promises or laws. It is a process," writes Emily Friedman, a longtime activist in the indigent-care arena. "We all seek protection from the random violence of life. . . . We have to protect each other because we don't know who's next.

# Privatizing Health Care: The Bottom Line Is Society Loses

*Mimi Abramovitz*

The Reagan Administration wants private enterprise to operate more of the welfare state. It has encouraged the development of private, for-profit prisons, contracted with small firms rather than nonprofit agencies for social service programs, expressed interest in selling public housing projects to tenants, supported tuition tax credits that foster the use of private schools and considered replacing the Social Security program with individual retirement accounts and private life insurance plans.

Welfare state privatization is most advanced in health care. For years, Federal policies have subsidized health care providers, but more recently they have encouraged greater "competition" and more "cost sharing," arguing that market strategies make social welfare programs less costly and more efficient as well as improving the quality of care. Tax incentives for the development of health maintenance organizations and preferred-provider organizations were designed to make health care more competitive, as were those that encouraged employers to offer workers a choice of health care plans. On the assumption that "cost sharing"—through higher out-of-pocket costs—induces consumers to use services more selectively, the Reagan Administration more than once has raised Medicare deductibles and co-insurance charges; added new Medicaid user fees and copayments for home health care; and proposed that employer-paid health insurance premiums be taxed as income to workers. Similarly, public housing tenants now pay more of their income in rent; agencies consider the monetary value of food stamps when calculating income for those applying for benefits for public housing and Aid to Families with Dependent Children; and student loan requirements are more stringent. The power of competition and user fees to reduce program costs has not been firmly established, but they do decrease the use of services, particularly preventive services and especially by the poor. They also reinforce the inequalities between those who can and cannot pay.

The entry of corporations into the health care system has accelerated its privatization, transforming it from a competitive mix of municipal, small nonprofit and

---



---

See Statistical Appendix Table A–20.

physician-owned for-profit hospitals into a monopolistic sector characterized by large investor-owned, multihospital chains. Individually owned proprietary hospitals have existed for decades, but their number fell relative to public and nonprofit hospitals from the late 1920s to the early 1970s, when new government policies changed the dynamics of the health care market. Although there still are fewer for-profit than public and nonprofit hospitals, the number of for-profits in investor-owned chains jumped from 378, or just 6 percent of the nation's hospitals, in 1975 to 878, or 13 percent of the total, in 1984. A 1980 survey found 176 chains owning or managing 294,199 beds; another reported 245 multihospital systems with 301,894 beds. Corporate chains also own, lease or manage many for-profit nursing homes and about 85 percent of all proprietary psychiatric beds. Organizations such as Kaiser, Blue Cross and Prudential have developed into chains themselves, consisting primarily of alternative health-care delivery systems. Industry analysts ranging from critic Arnold Ralman, editor of *The New England Journal of Medicine*, to the American College of Hospital Administrators, predict that for-profit chains will control from 30 to 60 percent of all U.S. hospitals and 50 percent of all nursing homes by the mid-1990s.

The system quickly became highly concentrated. The number of hospital consolidations jumped from five a year in 1961 to fifty a year in the early 1970s, as investor-owned corporations purchased small, often failing, for-profit and nonprofit hospitals. The ten largest chains own, operate or manage more than 11 percent of all U.S. hospitals and more than 70 percent of the for-profits. By 1981 the top three among the chains, Humana, the Hospital Corporation of American (H.C.A.) and American Medical International (A.M.I.), accounted for 75 percent of hospital chains' beds and the top four owned nearly half the nation's 1,000 proprietary hospitals.

Government policies have played a significant role in corporatizing health care. Although privatization may not have been the immediate or the only goal, the Federal government has regularly brought private enterprise into the delivery of health services. As far back as 1935, to stem the flow of New Deal dollars into the deteriorating public poor-houses, it restricted old-age assistance payments to small, profit-making convalescent facilities, laying the foundation for today's private nursing home industry. The defeat of numerous efforts to enact a national health insurance program in the late 1940s resulted in the development of an extensive system of private health insurance offered to workers as a fringe benefit. In the 1950s, welfare agencies began to pay private medical personnel to treat public-assistance recipients. In 1965 Congress created Medicaid and Medicare to reimburse those who provided health care to the aged and the poor, two groups whose high incidence of illness kept private insurers away. By 1985 the government funded more than 40 percent of all medical costs; private insurance paid for 30 percent, with individuals covering the remainder. Drug, hospital supply and insurance companies as well as private hospitals and physicians benefited from the public subsidy, which undercut the development of a more universal national health insurance program, not to mention a national health service. The availability of public and private insurance, combined with a projected surplus of doctors and a decline in the incidence of solo practices, paved the way for the emergence of profit-making hospital chains in the late 1960s.

In the 1970s new corporate tax breaks and the exemption of health care institutions from antitrust provisions created additional incentives for investor-owned chains to enter the health care business. So did the growing number of financially troubled hospitals and nursing homes ripe for takeover due to government anti-inflation cost-control regulations and cuts in domestic programs. More recently, the Reagan Administration's attempt to regulate hospital costs using diagnostic-related groups and other measures has created strong incentives for for-profit facilities to promote outpatient services, psychiatric care and new equipment, on which there is less Federal regulation and more opportunity to pass costs on to the consumer.

For-profit hospitals make lots of money. By the early 1980s the thirty-eight major investor-owned chains grossed over $12 billion in revenues, with profit margins ranging from 15 to 30 percent. The after-tax profits of H.C.A. rose 55 percent in 1982 and 41 percent in 1983; from 1983 to 1985, the company retained earnings of $878 million. National Medical Enterprises (N.M.E.) earned $93 million in profits in 1983 and $149 million in 1985, while A.M.I.'s profits jumped 29 percent between 1982 and 1983. Advocates of privatization attribute these gains to economies of scale, diversification of holdings and efficient management practices, but the evidence increasingly suggests that large profits derive more from higher prices, lower labor costs and less service for the poor.

Several recent studies have found that, contrary to the claims of their supporters, for-profit hospitals provided more costly care than did voluntary or public hospitals. A major study conducted by the Institute of Medicine, a branch of the National Academy of Medicine, concluded in 1985 that for-profit hospitals charge, on average, 10 percent more than nonprofits; that per diem charges in those owned by corporations exceed those of other hospitals by 29 percent and that by avoiding physician training and clinical research on new treatments and medications, the for-profits "freeload" on the entire medical care system. A 1981 study found that for-profit and nonprofit hospitals charged similar amounts for routine items like room and board, but that the for-profits sharply marked up ancillary services like providing drugs and supplies. The for-profits also reported 13 percent higher administrative and general service costs. The chains themselves concede that patient charges often increase dramatically when they take over a public hospital. When A.M.I. bought a Texas county hospital, patient fees rose by 20 percent, the hospital's first significant increase in several years.

For-profit hospitals use staff cutbacks, unionbusting and computerization to bring down labor costs. To maximize its 1980 profits, the Humana hospital in Louisville lowered its full-time employee-to-patient ratio from 5.5 to 1 to 4.2 to 1. When N.M.E. contracted to manage the St. Louis city hospital and clinics in 1984, it discharged the entire work force to cancel all accrued benefits, eliminate jobs and break the union. Elsewhere in the United States, N.M.E. institutions cut the number of registered nurses on staff from 40 to 25 percent and hired lower-paid aides and other unlicensed medical workers in their place. Gateway Medical Systems, which specializes in taking over private, inner-city hospitals, typically slashes the payroll by half. Nor do hospital chains hesitate to close service units or entire hospitals if they do not yield adequate returns. In June 1986 hard times led N.M.E. to announce plans to sell up to eighteen of its fifty hospitals. Growing fiscal pressure for quick discharges and the increased use of computers caused total hospital employment to drop by 73,000, or 2.3 percent, in 1984. In 1985 Gerald McEntee, president of the American Federation of State, County and Municipal Employees (AFSCME), stated that hospital takeovers have cost his union thousands of jobs.

By treating health care as a commodity, privatization has diminished the quality of services and made them less available to those less able to pay. The for-profit chains may provide quality care for some patients, but the poor, whose complex medical problems often require more expensive care, typically lose out. That is because for-profit hospitals gravitate to suburban communities and prosperous regions, where the expanding population tends to be well off, young and healthy, and where unions are generally weak. The chains also effectively select whom they will serve by placing surgical and ancillary operations above medical and routine care; favoring "new services" such as "wellness clinics" and sports medicine over more comprehensive and long-term care; and shrinking unprofitable services such as ophthalmology, therapeutic radiology, call-in emergency psychiatric services and home care for psychiatric patients. They prefer to treat insured patients with uncomplicated diagnoses, requiring frequently used but expensive diagnostic tests, services and drugs over those with costly chronic illnesses requiring long-term, labor-intensive care or rarely used, highly specialized equipment. For-profit hospitals often are built without the emergency rooms on which the poor rely for routine care, due to shortages of doctors and clinics in their neighborhoods.

By law, for-profit hospitals can turn away the medically indigent and uninsured—including the 12 million people living below the poverty line who do not have Medicaid; the 30 million with inadequate private health insurance; and the 37 million with no coverage at all. Such patients are "dumped" onto a declining number of small nonprofit hospitals willing to serve the poor, or onto overcrowded municipal hospitals. Despite contrary claims, an epidemic of such dumping has occurred in some places in recent years. Indeed, between 1983 and 1985 the number of transfers from private hospitals to Cook County hospitals in Chicago jumped tenfold due to economic cutbacks at private hospitals. Significant numbers of patients across the country have been transferred, in unstable condition, from private to public hospitals, resulting in some deaths. The problem has been compounded by the rise of Medicaid mills as well as by the development of profit-making subsidiaries, multihospital chains and stringent cost-saving practices by nonprofit hospitals, which are no longer obliged as recipients of government hospital construction funds to provide community services. Research suggests that both nonprofit and for-profit hospitals now spend only 3.5 to 4 percent a year of their gross revenues on the care of indigents.

It is increasingly clear that profit-making business practices do not necessarily generate responsive health care service. An official of a firm that operates mental health and drug abuse clinics stated, "My job is not a whole lot different from Lee Iacocca's. You need to have quality products, know how to sell them and know how to control costs." The chair of a major hospital chain stated that when the interests of society and those of business conflict, the latter must prevail. "You cut down on people, cut down on space, cut down wherever you can," he said. "If you still can't solve the problem you try to find out if there are abuses. You let some doctors go; if you feel you're doing too much indigent care you just put a cap on the level of indigent care you will accept."

Actually, public subsidy of nonprofit services began in colonial times, when officials contracted out the care of the poor and the sick to the lowest town bidder. By the late nineteenth century private asylums, hospitals and charitable societies received sizable government grants and dominated the social welfare establishment until the economic collapse of the 1930s. From the New Deal to the Great Society, the Federal government became more directly involved in the operation of social welfare programs. The welfare state expanded as the Depression, postwar prosperity and grassroots political pressures led the government to provide income maintenance and social services to workers and the poor, to subsidize hospital construction, to build low-income public housing and to develop health and mental health services under its own auspices.

In the relatively prosperous but turbulent decade from 1965 to 1975, privatization replaced direct government programming. In response to demands made by women, minorities, workers and the poor for a greater share of the economic pie, the Federal government continued to expand the welfare state, causing state spending on income maintenance and social services to soar from $77 billion in 1965 to $290 billion in 1975. But mounting opposition to its enlarged role led the government to transfer some of its more marketable programs to private nonprofit groups and to extend publicly supported services to segments of the middle class. Perceiving the wider availability of public subsidies and middle-class clients, some for-profit firms regarded social welfare programs as a new investment opportunity. Then, in the recession of the mid-1970s, social welfare spending slowed. While lower taxes, wage concessions and cuts in social programs contracted the welfare state, privatization intensified. Government incentives, particularly in the 1980s, encouraged for-profit firms, even more than they did nonprofit social agencies, to play a larger role in the scaled-down welfare state.

Both Republicans and Democrats are likely to continue their support of austerity and privatization in the social welfare system. Even Senator Edward Kennedy, a longtime advocate of a national health insurance system and critic of earlier business health care proposals, recently called for businesses rather than government to pay the health care bill for their employees. The evidence, however, does not support the view that the private sector delivers the best health care at the lowest cost. It shows that profit-making doctors, hospitals and insurance companies keep their eye on the bottom line at the expense of sound and equitable patient care. The failure of many employers to insure their workers, the loss of health care coverage by the unemployed, the emergence of health insurance as a key issue in the welfare reform debate and employers' dissatisfaction with the rising cost of health care benefits has recently led the state of Massachusetts to consider legislation that requires all employers to provide health insurance coverage to workers, with the state insuring those without jobs. This approach, which ameliorates the plight of the uninsured, inevitably creates a two-class health care system, with private insurance and services for society's healthier and wealthier groups and unpopular, less-well-funded government programs for the unemployed and the poor. But the development in Massachusetts also suggests that the injustices of the current health care system themselves have created pressures for change. Rather than leave the solution to private enterprise, progressive forces might draw on this momentum to expose the limits of privatization, re-examine the national health care systems in Canada and Western Europe and mobilize Americans once again to insist that quality health care is not a privilege but a right.

# The Politics of Tobacco

*Peter Taylor*

. . . In the United States, government was even less interested in taking political action. Tobacco is part of American history. It helped the early Jamestown colony to survive and financed the American Revolution by serving as collateral for the loans received from France. George Washington grew it and Thomas Jefferson had it engraved on the pillars inside the Capitol building. To attack tobacco is, in the eyes of its defenders, to attack the foundation of America itself. Tobacco is still one of America's most important cash crops, and part of the economic fabric of the country, giving employment to tens of thousands of families in eighteen tobacco-growing states mainly in the southeastern United States. It is not surprising that in 1962 the young President John F. Kennedy was in no hurry to face the political implications of a problem so close to home, following the publication of the Royal College of Physicians's report on the other side of the Atlantic. Kennedy had defeated Richard Nixon in the presidential election of 1960 by the narrowest margin in seventy-six years—0.1 percent of the popular vote. Kennedy himself admitted his victory was "a miracle."[1] Without the support he had received from the South, largely through his choice of the Texan Lyndon Johnson as his running mate, Kennedy would never have made it to the White House. The last thing the new President could afford to do was to attack tobacco and antagonize the powerful southern politicians who dominated the committees in the Congress and with whom he would have to do business in the years that lay ahead. But the new President could not afford to be seen to be doing nothing. At a press conference on May 23rd, 1962, shortly after the publication of the Royal College of Physicians's report in Britain, President Kennedy was asked:

> Mr. President, there is another health problem that seems to be causing growing concern here and abroad, and I think this is largely being provoked by a series of independent scientific investigations, which have concluded that cigarette smoking and certain types of cancer and heart disease have a causal connection.
>
> I have two questions. Do you and your health advisers agree or disagree with these findings, and secondly, what, if anything, should or can the federal Government do in the circumstances?

The President chose his words carefully:

---

> That matter is sensitive enough, and the stock market is in sufficient difficulty without my giving you an answer which is not based on complete information, which I don't have, and, therefore, perhaps I will be glad to respond to that question in more detail next week.

Five days later the *Wall Street Journal* predicted that Dr. Luther Terry, the U.S. Surgeon General (who had already been sent a copy of the Royal College report by Britain's Chief Medical Officer, Sir George Godber, with the exhortation to act) would convene a committee to do what the Royal College of Physicians had done, observing that the move would serve "the tactical purpose of gaining time" and would take "public pressure off government officials."[2]

Kennedy had already been under pressure from the American medical establishment and had taken steps to defuse the issue. The previous year, at the instigation of the Surgeon General, Dr. Luther Terry, the Presidents of the American Heart Association, the Lung Association, the American Cancer Society and the Public Health Association had written a joint letter to the President, asking him to set up a special presidential commission. The President summoned his Surgeon General and told him to get on with the job, with the assurance that there would be no political interference. "Of course he knew there might be interference," Dr. Terry told me. "There was politics written all over it." The *Wall Street Journal* speculation was correct. Three days later the Surgeon General announced the formation of his committee of experts "to study all evidence and make whatever recommendations are necessary."[3]

From the beginning, Dr. Terry consulted the tobacco industry on the formation of his committee. He took the precaution of ensuring that the industry did not turn around and reject the committee's findings because it did not agree with its composition. He sent the industry a list of 150 "outstanding medical scientists in the United States" and asked them to strike out any names it found unacceptable. He remembers "three or four" names being crossed off from his original list. In the end, eleven scientists were chosen whose names were acceptable to all the parties concerned. Five of them happened to be smokers.[4] The prerequisite of membership was that none of them should have taken a public position on the issue. There was an early casualty. The scientist from the National Cancer Institute, Dr. Herman Kraybill, who was named as the committee's executive director, was forced to step down when he told a reporter back home that he believed the evidence "definitely suggests that tobacco is a health hazard."[5] The tobacco industry was not to be allowed to blame the messenger when the news arrived. The Surgeon General's advisory committee was given a whole block in the sub-basement of the new National Library of Medicine in Bethesda, Maryland, in which to carry out its work. "We knew there were going to be attempts by the press and the tobacco industry to break our wall of confidentiality and get advance information, but there wasn't a leak," Dr. Terry told me. "I still don't know how we did it. When the report was at the government printers, it was given the same security classification as military and state secrets." The committee sat for over a year, analyzing the now vast corpus of information on smoking and health, running to some 6,000 articles in 1,200 publications. "The industry did submit their view," said Dr. Terry, "but it didn't convince the committee that they were right and others were wrong." Security was maintained to the last. Even senior government officials, who wanted to know what lay in store so they could prepare themselves for when the report was published, were told they would have to wait like everyone else. The report was launched on a Saturday for maximum impact, although the more cynical said it was because the stock exchange was closed. The State Department auditorium was borrowed as neutral and prestigious ground on which to hold a press conference. At nine A.M. journalists were given their first sight of the historic report and an hour in which to digest it before questioning the committee. The press conference over, they rushed to the telephones. "It was like flushing ducks off a pond," remembers Dr. Terry. The report confirmed the tobacco industry's worst fears. It said that cigarette smoking was causally related to lung cancer, was the most important cause of chronic bronchitis and increased the risk of dying from the disease and emphysema as well; and that it was prudent to assume from the public health viewpoint that cigarette smoking caused coronary disease. It summed up its judgment in a brief sentence: Cigarette smoking is a health hazard of sufficient importance in the United States to warrant appropriate remedial action.[6]

In America the Surgeon General's report had the same immediate impact on sales as the Royal College of Physicians's report had done in Britain, two years earlier. In 1963, the year before publication, 510 billion cigarettes were sold in America. In the year of publication they fell to 495 billion.[7] The year after, again following the British pattern, they picked up again, and more than made up for the loss by soaring to 518 billion. However short smokers' memories, or however unshakable their addiction, the tobacco industry knew it was in trouble. Looking back on the period, one of their scientists told me, "We were far more concerned about the Surgeon General's report. We'd vetted the names on the Committee. We agreed before it started work that it was sound and had given the Surgeon-General our commitment that we were happy with its composition. We couldn't turn around and say, 'These people aren't experts.'"

If the industry feared that these reports from the U.S. Surgeon General and the British Royal College of Physicians in the early 1960s would change the political perspective on tobacco and drive governments out of the Smoke Ring, there was little to worry about. The worse "blows" the industry suffered were having cigarette advertisements banned from television in Britain in 1965, and in America in 1970 (the companies simply replied by switching the millions they saved into other media); and being forced to put health warnings on packets in 1965 in America ("Caution: Cigarette smoking may be hazardous to your health") but not until 1971 in Britain ("Warning By HM Government: Smoking Can Damage Your Health"). These health warnings were even privately welcomed in some quarters of the industry on the grounds that if consumers, particularly in America, were to sue for damages, they could not claim ignorance. (Consumers did sue. By the end of the 1970s these "product liability" claims totalled over $40 million.[8] To date no suit has been successful.) These measures enabled politicians to satisfy the public's desire for action without seriously damaging the industry's wealth and the economic benefits which government derived from it.

The industry's main concern in response to the medical evidence was to make sure that consumers carried on smoking. It had already met their growing awareness of the medical problem in the 1950s by introducing filter cigarettes, although the original reason for their design was vanity, not health; filters were meant to attract female smokers by offering them a cigarette whose end didn't go soggy. The tobacco companies had also taken steps to protect themselves by starting to diversify in case governments and consumers did desert the Smoke Ring once the case against cigarettes was proven. The industry's main problem was to *reassure* smokers. This it sought to do by publicly refusing to accept the medical evidence, while commercially developing cigarettes which were lower in "tar" and therefore less hazardous. The industry met the obvious contradiction by insisting that they were developing "low-tar" cigarettes in response to consumer demand, not because they accepted the medical evidence. For tobacco companies to have admitted that cigarettes were harmful would not only have laid them open to economic ruin in an avalanche of successful product liability suits, but might have triggered mass defections amongst smokers, which would have had the same economic effect. To admit responsibility would risk destroying the Smoke Ring. The industry had no intention of committing suicide. Guided by the advice of its scientists and public relations experts, it constructed a defense in the 1960s to which it has clung ever since. The commercial defense was that the tobacco companies were selling a legal product; they were not doctors, and if governments believed what their medical experts told them, it was up to them to act and not expect the industry to cut its own throat. The medical defense was that the case against cigarettes was not proven; the evidence was purely statistical; the precise causal mechanism by which cigarettes were alleged to produce cancer had never been identified; that no one knows the root cause of cancer and only unbiased scientific inquiry will provide the answers. This defense became known within the industry as the "tightrope" policy and was most widely propagated by the Tobacco Institute in Washington, D.C., the industry-financed propaganda organization which lobbied on its behalf. The Tobacco Institute insisted: "Years of scientific research have failed to provide conclusive evidence that smoking causes disease."[9]

This was not a view with which the industry's own scientists necessarily agreed, having done years of research themselves. In the late 1950s and early 1960s when the industry first realized it had what it referred to as a "problem," many of these scientists left their jobs in the research departments of other industries, such as food, pharmaceuticals, atomic energy and textiles, to join the tobacco industry's growing research teams. Many were attracted by the scientific challenge of either disproving the evidence or, if that proved impossible, of developing less hazardous cigarettes. Some who joined in the early days found that code names were used instead of the word "cancer": that medical journals like *The Lancet* which contained learned papers on the disease were sent around in locked correspondence boxes for the eyes of senior executives only; that rumors abounded such as the one about the director of one tobacco company who suggested closing down and giving the shareholders their money back if the case were ever proven. "They'd never met anything like this," one scientist told me. "They didn't know how to handle it. I remember saying to them, 'Look, you have a problem which would shake a pharmaceutical company to its foundations and yet you've no background in research. There isn't anybody on the board who's even got a good working knowledge in chemistry.'"

One of the new research recruits told his employer that if he had $280 million to spend on the problem, he would spend $225 million diversifying and most of what was left on public relations: he believed that any organic material which was burned was bound to produce carcinogens and was not prepared to put his money on a research solution.

The industry spent millions on research. It set up its own laboratories to examine the chemical constituents of cigarette smoke and its biological activity. Less hazardous cigarettes could only be developed once the existing hazards in "tar" were identified and modified. To do this required technical analysis and animal experiments on a huge scale. Much of this pioneering work was done in Britain in the 1960s. The industry opened its own laboratories in Harrogate, with a staff of 120 and an annual budget of $6 million. As far as the scientists were concerned, the animal experiments which had been conducted in the 1950s were perfectly valid but lacked any statistical significance because there were not enough of them. At the Harrogate laboratories experiments were conducted on over 100,000 mice. The researchers took the fact that cigarettes caused cancer as a working hypothesis. "If they don't," one of them told me, "we don't have a problem. If they do, we'll solve it." Most of the work consisted of "lump counting," analyzing the tumors which appeared on the skin of mice when painted with cigarette "tar." "We confirmed with our massive experiments all that smaller experiments had claimed before: that cigarette tar caused skin cancer on mice and that there was a dose–response relationship [the cancer produced was related to the tar painted on the skin]," said one of the scientists closely associated with the work at the Harrogate laboratories. "There's absolutely no doubt, and there's no one in the world who knows anything about it could say differently, that cigarette tar is carcinogenic." The work at Harrogate continued for ten years and provided much of the scientific basis for the development of low-tar cigarettes. When the work was finished, which confirmed the scientists' working hypothesis that cigarettes caused cancer, the laboratories were closed down and sold to an American company for over $2.5 million.

Despite the fact that many of their own researchers confirmed the scientific evidence, the industry maintained its "tightrope" policy on the health issue. Tobacco company spokesmen, when asked questions on smoking and health, retreated behind the slogan, "We are not doctors." One scientist told me he couldn't understand "why somebody never said, 'Well, get some bloody doctors.'" Impatience grew. In the early 1970s, the industry was told by one of its scientists:

> I believe it will not be possible to maintain indefinitely the rather hollow "we are not doctors" stance. In due course we shall have to come up in public with

> a rather more positive approach to cigarette safety. In my view it would be best to be in a position to say in public what we believe in private.[10]

The advice went unheeded. The industry stuck to its view that the case against cigarettes was not proven, because the precise causal mechanism by which cigarettes "are alleged" to cause lung cancer had never been demonstrated. The British Royal College of Physicians had answered this charge in 1962 when it noted that political action in the face of the great cholera epidemics of the nineteenth century had not been dependent upon the identification of the precise mechanism by which the disease was caused:

> . . . the great sanitary movement in the mid nineteenth century began to bring infective diseases such as cholera and typhoid under control long before the germs that caused these diseases were discovered. The movement was based on observations such as that drinking polluted water was associated with the disease. If the provision of clean water had had to await the discovery of bacteria, preventable deaths, numbered in thousands, would have continued to occur for many years.[11]

At least one industry scientist dismissed the insistence on the identification of the causal mechanism as "rubbish." He believed that in demanding the "billiard ball" proof of cause and effect, the industry was applying the mechanistic principles of the nineteenth century to twentieth-century science when they were no longer applicable. "In my view," he said, "the case that cigarettes cause lung cancer is proven. The fact that lower smoke deliveries [lower tar cigarettes] produce lower risk is a clincher for causality. If people stop smoking or smoke less, then lung cancer in the population is reduced." At one stage he informed the industry that as long as it stood by this nineteenth-century definition of "proof," its position would be impregnable as there was no way the standard could be met: but he also pointed out that no twentieth-century scientist would ever seek to apply it and, although it might be convenient, it was irrelevant. "There is no controversy on smoking and health," he concluded, "it's an invention of the tobacco industry."

This creation of the illusion of controversy is a vital part of the industry's strategy to keep smokers on its side. The Tobacco Institute is their champion:

> The "war against cancer" . . . degenerated into a war against cigarettes. . . . Now it has further degenerated into a war against smokers, waged through vilification, banishment from public places, denial of employment and repressive taxation. No one really knows whether this personalized warfare against tens of millions of Americans will prevent a single case of lung cancer or heart disease. . . .
>
> Many people do look for a "scapegoat" when they feel threatened. In this case it is smoking. We are on the brink of paranoia. . . . In the meantime, the quest for knowledge about disease is prejudiced. . . . The smoking controversy must be resolved by scientific research.[12]

The industry has made a great contribution to that research. Although the tobacco companies do not carry out medical research themselves, they have made over $70 million available over the years[13] to enable other bodies to do so. This research which they have sponsored has not undermined the medical evidence. The longest, most detailed and most expensive program the industry financed only confirmed what the U.S. Surgeon General had said in 1964. The study *Tobacco and Health* was carried out by the American Medical Association, took nearly fifteen years to complete, and was financed by the tobacco industry to the tune of $10 million. The AMA announced the proposed study and the industry's financial commitment to it in January 1964, the month the U.S. Surgeon General issued his report. The study was published fourteen years later in 1978. The committee's brief was to commission *new* research in the field of smoking and health, as the reports of the U.S. Surgeon General and the British Royal College of Physicians had been based on *existing* scientific evidence. The purpose was to examine:

> Human ailments that may be caused or aggravated by smoking, the particular element or elements that may be the causal or aggravating agents and the mechanisms of their action.[14]

A massive amount of research was commissioned. Eight hundred and forty-four research scientists from America and overseas produced 795 new papers on tobacco and health.[15] In a progress report, five years into the study, the AMA announced that it "had not altered the conclusions of the . . . report of the Surgeon General." When *Tobacco and Health* was finally published a decade later, it concluded:

> The committee believes that the bulk of research sponsored by this project supports the contention that cigarette smoking plays an important role in the development of chronic obstructive pulmonary diseases and constitutes a grave danger to individuals with pre-existing diseases of the coronary arteries.

The AMA was not ungrateful for the tobacco industry's support. Throughout this time, it kept $1.4 million[16] worth of shares* in the R.J. Reynolds and Philip Morris companies in its pension fund and continued to give political support to the federal government's annual subsidy of $50 million to America's 500,000 farm families who grow tobacco.[17]

There was certainly no shortage of the research which the industry kept insisting was the only solution to the problem. But scientists involved in tobacco-funded research did not always find that it was free from political considerations, especially when carried out in the heart of tobacco country or in the industry's own laboratories. In 1970 the state of Kentucky, America's second biggest tobacco producer, established its own Tobacco and Health Research Institute, which was financed by a half-cent tax placed on every packet of cigarettes sold in the state.[18] In twelve years

---

*The AMA finally disposed of these shares following pressure from some of its members, in 1981.

the institute cost Kentucky smokers nearly $35 million. The purpose was to "prove or disprove" the health hazards of cigarette smoking and to "preserve and strengthen" Kentucky's tobacco industry. The chairman of the institute's advisory board, Tom Harris, a Kentucky tobacco farmer, declared:

> It is incumbent on us to find if there is something wrong health-wise with tobacco. If it's so, alright, let's find out what it is and take it out. If it isn't so, let's prove them to be liars and get them off our backs.[19]

The institute was plagued with internal problems, mainly the result of the inevitable political conflict between tobacco and health in a state where tobacco is worth over $600 million a year, employs nearly 120,000 people, and raises nearly $10 billion in state and local taxes.[20] In its twelve years the institute went through six directors. One who left after sixteen months said:

> The program was created by politicians for political reasons. As such, scientific objectives were secondary. The tobacco industry needed . . . an Institute as a symbol to their commitment to tobacco and health research. Some in this state even have indicated that it did not matter that the research was not good, as long as there was visible image of research on tobacco and health.[21]

I contacted one of the scientists who had worked at the institute. He said some good work had been done, but "they were very reluctant to face the issue of lung cancer": when he wrote a grant application he had to be circumspect, wording it so as not to appear that he was really looking at cancer. "Kentucky is very economically dependent on the tobacco industry," he said, "the state legislature did the funding of research. They had to approve it. If people came down hard on the problem of lung cancer, the state legislature would say, 'Why are we spending money to kill our main industry?' You can see why people were circumspect." I asked him if he thought cigarettes caused lung cancer. He said of course he did.

Scientists working in the tobacco industry's world-famous research laboratories in Hamburg, West Germany, also encountered political problems. The work of its team of scientists under the institute's director, Professor W. Dontenwill, was internationally renowned and featured prominently in all the world's major reports on smoking and health. Hamburg carried on the experiments with animals where Harrogate left off, improving inhalation techniques to study the effect of cigarette smoke on the respiratory system. Using Syrian golden hamsters, they produced for the first time cancer in the larynx of an animal. The 1982 U.S. Surgeon General's report, *Cancer*, pointed out that carefully controlled animal experiments such as these were sufficient to allow "clear experimental demonstration of causality," adding:

> The application of these rigid laboratory techniques for establishing causality to the study of cancer in humans is clearly impossible. The idea of exposing human subjects to potentially cancer-producing agents in order to establish causality is morally and ethically unacceptable.[22]

Having succeeded in inducing cancers in the larynx of golden hamsters, the team then began experiments with pigs, whose respiratory system and arterial linings are most akin to those of a human being. These experiments, which opened up a completely new field in smoking and health research, were designed to examine changes in the vascular tissues which lead to coronary disease and to arteriosclerosis (hardening of the arteries) in particular. One member of the team told me that their preliminary experiments showed that there appeared to be a connection between the inhalation of carbon monoxide, the injection of nicotine and arteriosclerosis. Given time, the team thought they could prove the connection between smoking and arterial disease. (Diseases of the heart and arteries claim far more victims than lung cancer.) But it never got the chance. Suddenly, in 1976, the institute was closed down. An official statement was issued which said that the institute did not have the resources for new research and the director, Professor Dontenwill, was ill. The scientist I spoke to said the news came "like a flash of lightning out of the sky."[23] I asked him if the Professor was ill. He said he was not and had joked about how "ill" he felt when they had talked about the official announcement. What did he and his colleagues think had happened? "We suppose that the institute was closed down because of the results we were getting from our experiments into arteriosclerosis," he said. "If a connection between smoking and vascular disease was established, the cigarette industry would be pushed even more into the firing line." The industry closed down its laboratories and rented them to the Hamburg health authorities for twenty years at a nominal charge of one Deutschmark a year. Redundancy payments were generous. Professor Dontenwill received nearly half a million pounds (1.6 million Deutschmarks) to cover his salary until he was sixty. When I contacted the Professor and asked him about his research, he said he was no longer involved, had forgotten it, and had no wish to give an interview on smoking and health.[24]

Above all, the industry needs to convince its own employees of its case. Attracting and keeping high-quality recruits is not easy. One former employee of an American cigarette company told me of his experience. He had stopped smoking some time before he applied for the job. At the interview, a packet of the company's latest brand was pushed across the table for him to try. He did not refuse because he wanted the job. When he went for the company physical examination to an outside doctor whom the company retained, he was asked if he smoked. He said he had just stopped. The doctor told him not to start again. He pointed out that he was going to work for a tobacco company. "It doesn't matter," the doctor said, "you still shouldn't smoke." But once inside the company, the social pressure was stronger than the doctor's advice. "They say there are lots of people in the industry who don't smoke," he said. "I never found any of them." The only advice on smoking he was given was by a more experienced colleague who warned that if he smoked a competitor's brand, he should make sure he put it in one of his own company's packs. As part of his apprenticeship, he was enrolled as a student in the tobacco industry's "college of knowledge," a seat of learning in a Washington hotel which the industry used to hire for a week of indoctrination. There were lectures by doctors who said that cigarettes were good because they helped you relax and who assured their audience that the case against cigarettes was not proven. I asked whether anyone in his class ever raised questions about the years of research. He said they didn't. "We were all preselected and in the company's judgment ready, willing and able to go out and tell the story. It was preaching to the choir." Graduation day came at the end of the week, when students were presented with scrolls to certify that they were now graduates of the "tobacco college of knowledge." But the reluctant cigarette executive found it increasingly difficult to remain one of the true believers. "One has to have some moral compass to even feel the pressure in the first place," he said. "It becomes pretty intense after a time. If others had moral compasses, they shut them off. I sometimes sat down over dinner with friends and talked of how ludicrous it was to be fighting a battle which was essentially wrong. Some of my colleagues felt the same. It was tough. You either suffer or you leave." In the end he left and paid out $300 for a SmokeEnders (*sic*) course to help him stop smoking all over again.

The only person out of step on the issue of smoking and health is the tobacco industry itself, which stands like King Canute, (the ancient British King who believed he could defy the power of the sea) denying the rising tide of medical evidence. Even many of its staunchest political allies, the politicians in Washington, D.C. who represent the great tobacco-growing states of America, accept the medical evidence. The senior aide to a North Carolina congressman assured me that tobacco politicians would have no credibility on Capitol Hill if they took the industry line on the health issue. He explained that their defense of tobacco was purely economic. "Our Congressman thinks that cigarettes can kill you," he said. "Most of the tobacco state guys do. Sure, cigarettes cause cancer, but so do lots of other things. You've got the tobacco industry out there saying, 'There isn't any proof. There's no causal relationship,' You can't carry that line through Congress. You're not productive or effective doing that. You can't kid our guys. They're brighter than that." I asked him how he thought senior executives he knew in the tobacco industry really felt about the health issue. He said they were concerned about corporate profits, not the health of America: that was the government's job. In Britain a blunter view of the industry's position is taken by Sir George Godber who, as Chief Medical Officer for Health from 1960 to 1972, was one of the industry's most bitter opponents. "I just don't believe that anybody could be unconvinced who's really taken the trouble to look at the evidence," he told me. "They know they're selling death now. They're not stupid. They just don't choose to admit it. I think they're an enormous, wealthy industry in which the major decision-makers can distance themselves sufficiently far from the outcome of the use of their product to ignore it."

## Notes

1. Theodore C. Sorensen, *Kennedy*, p. 249, Bantam Books, 1965.
2. Maurine B. Neuberger, *Smoke Screen: Tobacco and the Public Welfare*, p. 62, Prentice-Hall, Inc., 1963.
3. *Ibid.*, p. 63.
4. Maurice Corina, *Trust in Tobacco*. London: Michael Joseph, 1975, p. 233.
5. *Smoke Screen, op. cit.*, p. 65.
6. 'Smoking and Health', a Report of the Advi-

sory Committee to the Surgeon-General, 1964, *op. cit.*, p. 33.
7. *Business Week*, December 12th, 1964; December 11th, 1965.
8. BBC TV *Panorama*, 'A Dying Industry?', April 14th, 1980.
9. 'The Smoking Controversy; a Perspective', a statement by the Tobacco Institute, December 1978.
10. BBC TV *Panorama, op. cit.*
11. 'Smoking and Health', a Report of the Royal College of Physicians, 1962, *op. cit.*, p. 26.
12. 'The Smoking Controversy; a Perspective', *op. cit.*
13. R. J. Reynolds, *Smoking and Health*, Pride in Tobacco series of booklets.
14. 'Tobacco and Health', compiled by the AMA-ERF Committee for Research on Tobacco and Health, American Medical Association Education and Research Foundation, 1978.
15. *Ibid.*
16. Philip J. Hills, *Washington Post*, June 11th and 12th, 1981.
17. 'Tobacco in the United States', US Department of Agriculture, February 1979.
18. *Sunday Herald-Leader* (Lexington, Kentucky), 'Up in Smoke', an Investigation by Gary Cohn, March 14th, 1982.
19. *Ibid.*
20. 'A Study of the US Tobacco Industry's Economic Contribution to the Nation, its Fifty States and the District of Columbia', pp. 29 ff., the Wharton School, Applied Research Center, University of Pennsylvania, 1979.
21. *Sunday Herald-Leader*, Special Report: 'The Tobacco Institute', Gary Cohn, November 15th, 1981.
22. 'The Health Consequences of Smoking. Cancer', a Report of the Surgeon-General, 1982, *op. cit.*, p. 16.
23. BBC TV *Panorama, op. cit.*
24. *Ibid.*

# The Social Meaning of AIDS

*Peter Conrad*

Disease and illness can be examined on different levels. Disease is understood best as a biophysiological phenomenon, a process or state that affects the body. Illness, by contrast, has more to do with the social and psychological phenomena that surround the disease. The world of illness is the subjective world of meaning and interpretation; how a culture defines an illness and how individuals experience their disorder.

In this article I am going to examine the social and cultural meanings of Acquired Immunodeficiency Syndrome or AIDS as it is manifested in late-20th-century America and relate these meanings to the social reaction that it has engendered. When I talk about the social meaning of AIDS, I am including what Susan Sontag has termed the metaphorical aspects of illness: those meanings of diseases that are used to reflect back on some morally suspect element of society.[1] As Sontag suggests, metaphorical aspects of illness are especially prevalent with dread diseases that have great unknowns about them. We need to look at AIDS not only as a biomedical entity, but as an illness that has a socially constructed image and engages particular attitudes. The social meanings of AIDS are simultaneously alarmingly simple and bafflingly complex, but are key to understanding the social reaction to AIDS.

## The Social Reaction to AIDS

Five years ago virtually no one had heard of AIDS. In the past five years, however, AIDS has become a household term and a feared intruder in the society.

The medical reality of AIDS, as we know it, remains puzzling but is becoming clearer. AIDS is a disease caused by a virus that breaks down the immune system and leaves the body unprotected against "opportunistic infections" that nearly invariably lead to death. The number of AIDS cases is growing dramatically and AIDS is considered an epidemic in the society. Over 19,000 cases have been diagnosed, with four or five times that many people having a chronic disorder called AIDS-Related Complex (ARC) and perhaps over a million individuals having an antibody-positive response to HTLV-III, the virus believed to cause AIDS. It is estimated that 5 to 20 percent of this exposed group will contract AIDS, but no one knows who they will be.

Over 90 percent of AIDS victims come from two risk groups: homosexual or

Peter Conrad, "The Social Meaning of AIDS," *Social Policy* 17 (Summer 1986), pp. 51–56. 

bisexual men and intravenous drug users. (Hemophiliacs and others requiring frequent blood transfusions and infants born to mothers with AIDS are also considered risk groups.) The evidence is clear that the AIDS virus is transmitted through the direct exchange of bodily fluids, semen and blood; the most common mode of transmission is anal intercourse among male homosexuals and unsterile needle-sharing among intravenous drug users. There is virtually *no* evidence that the virus can be transmitted by everyday "casual contact," including kissing or shaking hands, or exposure to food, air, water, or whatever.[2] With the exception of very specific modes of semen or blood-related transmission, it does not appear that the AIDS virus is very easy to "catch."

Yet the public reaction to AIDS has bordered on hysteria. Below are a few examples of the reactions to AIDS or AIDS victims.

- 11,000 children were kept out of school in Queens, New York, as parents protested the decision to allow a 7-year-old girl with AIDS to attend second grade (despite no evidence of transmission by school children).
- Hospital workers in San Francisco refused to enter the room of an AIDS patient. When ordered to attend the patient, they appeared wearing masks, gowns, and goggles.
- A Baltimore policeman refused to enter the office of a patient with AIDS to investigate a death threat and donned rubber gloves to handle the evidence.
- A local school district in New Jersey tried to exclude a healthy 9-year-old boy whose sister has ARC (despite no sign of sibling transmission).
- An Amarillo, Texas, hospital fired a cafeteria worker who participated in a blood drive. This worker showed no signs of being ill or unable to perform his duties, but his blood had registered seropositive.
- In early 1985, Delta Airlines proposed a rule (later dropped) forbidding the carrying of AIDS patients.
- In New York, undertakers refused to embalm AIDS victims, householders fired their Haitian help, and subway riders wore gloves, all from fear of contracting AIDS.
- One child, hospitalized with AIDS, had a "do not touch" sign on her bed and was isolated from all physical contact with her parents.
- *The New York Times* reported cases of dentists who refused to treat gay patients (not just confirmed AIDS cases).
- In Dallas, a small group of doctors and dentists formed Dallas Doctors Against AIDS and began a campaign to reinstate Texas' sodomy laws.
- In a Boston corporation, employees threatened to quit en masse if the company forced them to work with an AIDS patient.
- Dade County, Florida, voted to require the county's 80,000 food workers to carry cards certifying they are free of communicable diseases, including AIDS, despite no known cases of AIDS transmitted through food and even though public health officials opposed this policy.
- The U.S. military is beginning to screen all new recruits for AIDS antibodies,

with the likely result of declaring those who test seropositive ineligible for service.

- Several major life insurance companies are requiring certain applicants (young, single, male, living in certain areas) to undergo an HTLV-III antibody test.
- Public health officials in Texas passed a measure allowing quarantine of certain AIDS patients. A candidate with a platform calling for the quarantining of all people with AIDS won the Democratic party's nomination for lieutenant governor in Illinois.

The list could go on. There is clearly a great fear engendered by the spectre of AIDS, a fear that has led to an overreaction to the actual problem. This is in no way to say that AIDS is not a terrible and devastating disease—it is—or to infer that it is not a serious public health concern. What we are seeing is an overblown, often irrational, and pointless reaction to AIDS that makes the disease more difficult for those who have it and diverts attention from the real public health concerns.

## The Social and Cultural Meanings of AIDS

To better understand the reaction to AIDS, it is necessary to examine particular social features of the disease: 1) the effect of marginal and stigmatized "risk groups"; 2) sexually-related transmission; 3) the role of contagion; and 4) the deadly nature of the disease.

*The effect of marginal and stigmatized "risk groups."* There are some illnesses that carry with them a certain moral devaluation, a stigma. Leprosy, epilepsy, mental disorder, venereal disease, and by some accounts, cancer, all reflect moral shame on the individuals who had the ill luck to contract them. Stigmatized illnesses are usually diseases that in some fashion are connected to deviant behavior: either they are deemed to produce it as with epilepsy or are produced by it, as in the case of VD.

The effect of the early connection of AIDS to homosexual conduct cannot be underestimated in examining its stigmatized image. The early designation of the disorder was Gay Related Immune Deficiency Syndrome (GRID) and was publicly proclaimed as a "gay plague." It was first thought to be caused by the use of "poppers" (amylnitrate) and later by promiscuity.[3] Something those fast-track gays were doing was breaking down their immune system. However, AIDS is not and never was specifically related to homosexual conditions; viruses don't know homosexuals from heterosexuals.

Within a short time, other "risk" groups were identified for what was now called AIDS—intravenous drug users, Haitians, and hemophiliacs. With the exception of hemophiliacs (who made up less than two percent of the cases), AIDS' image in the public eye was intimately connected with marginal populations. It was a disease of "those deviants," considered by some a deserved punishment for their activities. In

1983 Patrick J. Buchanan, who later became a White House staffer, wrote: "Those poor homosexuals. They have declared war on nature, and nature is exacting an awful retribution."[4] It is certain that fear of AIDS was amplified by the widespread and deeply rooted "homophobia" in American society.

*Sexually-related transmission.* The dominant vector of transmission of AIDS is through sexual activity, particularly anal intercourse of male homosexuals. Although scientifically AIDS is better seen as a "blood disease" (since contact with blood is necessary for transmission), this common form of transmission has contributed to its image as a sexually transmitted disease.

Venereal diseases are by nature also stigmatized. They are deemed to be the fault of the victims and would not occur had people behaved better. As Allen Brandt points out, venereal diseases have become a symbol of pollution and contamination: "Venereal disease, the palpable evidence of unrestrained sexuality became a symbol for social disorder and moral decay—a metaphor of evil."[5]

AIDS, with its connection to multiple sex encounters and once-forbidden "sodomy," touches deep Puritanical concerns and revives alarms of promiscuity and "sexual permissiveness" that have become more muted in recent decades. The connection of AIDS to "sexual irresponsibility" has been made repeatedly.

Now that it appears AIDS can be transmitted through heterosexual intercourse as well, although apparently not as efficiently and rapidly, there is increasing concern among sexually active people that they may be betrayed in their most intimate moments. This connection with intimacy and sexuality amplifies our anxieties and creates fears that one sexual act may bring a lifetime of pollution and ultimately death.

*The role of contagion.* We have almost come to believe that large-scale deadly epidemics were a thing of the past. The polio panics of the early 1950s have receded far into our collective memory, and the wrath of tuberculosis, cholera, or diptheria have become, in American society at least, artifacts of the past. Everyday models for contagion are more limited to the likes of herpes, chicken pox, and hepatitis. When we encounter AIDS, which is contagious but apparently in a very specific way, our fear of contagion erupts almost without limits. When little is known about a disease's transmission, one could expect widespread apprehensions about contagion. But a great deal is known about AIDS' transmission—it appears only to be transmitted through the exchange of bodily fluids and in *no* cases through any type of casual contact. In fact, compared to other contagious diseases it has a relatively low infectivity. Yet the fear of contagion fuels the reaction to AIDS.

Given our extant medical knowledge, what are the sources of fear? We live in a society where medicine is expected to protect us from deadly contagious diseases, if not by vaccine, then by public health intervention. And when medicine does not do this, we feel we must rely on our own devices to protect ourselves and our loved ones. Contagion, even of minor disorders, can engender irrational responses. Several months ago my 5-year-old daughter was exposed to a playmate who came down with chicken pox. A good friend of mine, who happens to be a pediatrician, did not want his 4-year-old to ride in the car with my daughter to gymnastics class, even though he knew medically that she could not yet be infectious. He just did not want to take any chances. And so it is with us, our reactions to contagion are not always rational.

With AIDS, of course, the situation is much worse. When we read in the newspapers that the AIDS virus has been found in saliva or tears, though only occasionally, we imagine in our commonsense germ-theory models of contagion that we could "catch AIDS" in this manner. Reports that no transmission has ever occurred in this fashion become secondary. The public attitudes seem to be that exposure to the AIDS virus condemns one to the disease.

While AIDS is contagious, so is the fear and stigma. The fear of AIDS has outstripped the actual social impact of the disease. But, more importantly for families of people who suffer from AIDS, the stigma of AIDS becomes contagious. They develop what Erving Goffman has called a courtesy stigma, a taint that has spread from the stigmatized to his or her close connections.[6] Family members of people with AIDS are shunned and isolated by former friends and colleagues, for fear that they too might bring contagion.

*A deadly disease.* AIDS is a devastating and deadly disease. It is virtually 100 percent lethal: 75 percent of people with AIDS die within two years. There are few other diseases that, like AIDS, attack and kill people who are just reaching the prime of their lives. Currently, AIDS is incurable; since there are no treatments for it, to contract AIDS in the 1980s is to be served with a death warrant. Many sufferers waste away from Kaposi's sarcoma or some rare form of chronic pneumonia.

As various researchers have shown, caretakers and family alike tend to distance themselves from sufferers who are terminally ill with diseases that waste away their bodies.[7] The pain of suffering and the pollution of dying are difficult for many people to encounter directly in a society that has largely removed and isolated death from everyday life.

Taken together, these features form a cultural image of AIDS that is socially as well as medically devastating. It might even be said that AIDS is an illness with a triple stigma: it is connected to stigmatized groups (homosexuals and drug users); it is sexually transmitted; and, like cancer, it is a terminal, wasting disease. It would be difficult to imagine a scenario for a more stigmatizing disease, short of one that also makes those infected obviously visible.

## The Effects of AIDS

The social meaning affects the consequences of AIDS, especially for AIDS sufferers and their families and the gay community but also for medicine and the public as well.

The greatest consequences of AIDS are of course for AIDS sufferers. They must contend with a ravaging disease and the stigmatized social response that can only make coping with it more difficult. In a time when social support is most needed, it may become least available. And in the context of the paucity of available medical treatments, those with AIDS must face the prospect of early death with little hope of survival.

People with ARC or those who test antibody-positive must live with the uncertainty of not knowing what the progression of their disorder will be. And living with this uncertainty, they must also live with the fear and stigma produced by the social meanings of AIDS. This may mean subtle disenfranchisement, overt discrimination, outright exclusion, or even total shunning. The talk of quarantine raises the anxiety of "why me?" Those symptomless seropositive individuals, who experts suggest have a 5 to 20 percent chance of developing full-blown AIDS, must live with the inner conflict of who to tell or not to tell, of how to manage their sexual and work lives, and the question of whether and how they might infect others. The social meanings of AIDS make this burden more difficult.

Families and lovers of people with AIDS, ARC, or an antibody-positive test are placed in an uncomfortable limbo status. Many live in constant fear that they might contract the AIDS virus, and thus limit their contact with the infected individual. Others wonder whether they too might be or become infectious. As mentioned earlier, families often share the AIDS stigma, as others see them as tainted, cease visiting their home, or even sever all contact with them. In one recent study of screening for AIDS among blood donors, the researchers noted they "have interviewed people in the pilot phase of [their] notification program who have been left by their spouses or significant others after telling them about their blood test results."[8]

The gay community has been profoundly affected by AIDS. The late 1960s and 1970s were an exciting and positive period of the American gay community. Thousands of gay men and women came "out of the closet" and proclaimed in a variety of ways that "gay is good." Many laws forbidding gay sexual activity were removed from the books. Gay people developed their own community institutions and more openly experimented and practiced alternative lifestyles. Although the celebration of anonymous sex among some gay males resulted in high rates of sexually-transmitted diseases and hepatitis B, the social atmosphere in the gay community remained overwhelmingly positive. While the attitudes toward homosexuality never became totally accepting, public moral opprobrium toward gays was perceptably reduced.[9]

And along came AIDS. With its image as a "gay disease" related to a fast-track gay male lifestyle, the fear of AIDS tapped into a reservoir of existing moral fear of homosexuals. It was a catalyst to the reemergence of a latent "homophobia" that had never really disappeared. Now there was a new reason to discriminate against gays. Thus AIDS has led to a restigmatization of homosexuality. Every avowed male homosexual is a suspected carrier of AIDS and deemed potentially dangerous. This, of course, has pushed many gay men back into the closet, living their lives with new fears and anxieties. It is clear that AIDS threatens two decades of social advances for the gay community.

Concern about AIDS has also become the overriding social and political concern of the gay community, consuming energy that previously went toward other types of social and political work. The gay community was the first to bring the AIDS problem into the public arena and to urge the media, medicine, and government to take action. Action groups in the gay community have engaged in extensive AIDS educational campaigns. This was done out of concern, but not without a fear of government surveillance and invasion of privacy. There was also apprehension that the images of "bad blood" and depictions of gays as health risks might lead to new exclusions of gays.[10]

The scourge of AIDS in the gay community has led, on the one hand, to divisions among gays (e.g., should bath houses be closed) and, on the other, to unprecedented changes in sexual behavior (e.g., witness the dramatic drop in the number of sex partners and types of sexual encounters reported in several studies and indexed by the large decrease in new cases of rectal gonorrhea).[11]

There is also a great emotional toll from the AIDS epidemic in the gay community. Nearly everyone in the community has friends or acquaintances who have died from the disease. As one gay activist recently put it, many people in the gay community were suffering a "grief-overload" as a result of the losses from AIDS.[12]

The social image of AIDS has affected medical care and scientific research as well. In general, the medical voice concerning AIDS, at least in terms of describing it to the public and outlining its perils, has on the whole been cautious and even-handed. The tenor of information has been factual and not unduly emotional. The Center for Disease Control (CDC) has again and again declared that AIDS is not transmitted by casual contact and, although it is a major epidemic and a public health threat, it is one with specific risk groups.

However, some medical scientists have placed the dangers of AIDS in a highly negative light either to raise the public's concern or to elicit private or governmental research funds. For example, "Dr. Alvin Friedman-Kein, an AIDS researcher who saw the first cases, said that AIDS will probably be the plague of the century."[13] Dr. Mathilde Krim was quoted in *The New York Post* last September as saying that "it is only a matter of time before it afflicts heterosexuals on a large scale" while presenting no evidence or data to support the claim.[14] The media, of course, picks up these assertions, often highlighting them in headlines, which reinforces the public fear.

The stigma of AIDS in a few cases has affected medical practice. There have been some reports of doctors, health workers, or hospitals who have refused to treat AIDS patients. But fortunately, these extreme examples are rare and, for the most part, AIDS sufferers seem to have received at least adequate care from most medical facilities. But a mistrust of the ramifications of the public attitudes toward AIDS may well keep some "high risk" individuals from seeking medical diagnosis or care. The fear of being found seropositive and becoming a social pariah might well keep carriers of the AIDS virus from medical attention.

Finally, stigmatized attitudes toward a disease can constrain medical progress. As Allen Brandt points out, the negative social meanings attached to VD actually obstructed medical efforts. He noted that research funding was somewhat limited because the issue was thought to be best dealt with behaviorally. Among many VD researchers the discovery of penicillin was treated with ambivalence, since they were afraid a cure of syphilis would promote promiscuity.[15]

While medical scientists have recently gained a great deal of knowledge about AIDS, including isolating the virus, describing the modes of transmission, and developing a test for screening HTLV-III antibodies in blood (although it is imperfect for screening people[16]), the stigma AIDS presents has probably limited public funding for AIDS research and deterred some types of community research on AIDS natural history. Several commentators have noted that federal funding for research and prevention of AIDS was slow in emerging because AIDS was seen as a "gay disease." It was only when it threatened blood transfusions and blood products that public consciousness was aroused and federal support was forthcoming. Unfortunately, this increased support for research and education was "misinterpreted as an indicator that AIDS was a universal threat destined to work its way inexorably through all segments of society."[17]

One of the most striking aspects about the social reaction to AIDS is how fear and stigma have led to a resistance to information about AIDS. While at times the media has sensationalized AIDS, there has also been a great deal of information communicated concerning AIDS, its characteristics, and its modes of transmission. Yet study after study finds a small but substantial and consistent proportion of the population that exhibits profound misinformation about AIDS. An October, 1985, Harris Poll reported that 50 percent of those asked believed one could get AIDS from living in the same house with someone who had it or from "casual contact," and one-third of the respondents thought that one can catch it from "going to a party where someone with AIDS is."[18]

Another study of high school students in San Francisco found that 41.9 percent believed you could get AIDS if kissed by someone with the disease; 17.1 percent thought if you touched someone with the disease you could get AIDS; 15.3 percent believed just being around someone with AIDS can give you the disease; and 11.6 percent thought all gay men have AIDS.[19] In a study of adolescents in Ohio, fully 60 percent believed that touching or coming near a person with AIDS might transmit the disease.[20] These authors contend that low knowledge of AIDS is correlated with high perceived susceptibility.

In a survey in San Francisco, New York, and London, the researchers found that "more knowledge was significantly negatively correlated with general fear of AIDS and with anti-gay attitudes among risk groups."[21] It appears that rather than low knowledge creating fear, the social meaning of AIDS creates resistance and barriers to taking in accurate information about AIDS.

Such misinformation is also prevalent among health-care providers. In a Massachusetts study of the effect of AIDS educational programs on health-care providers, the researchers reported that before the program, "20.5 percent of providers thought AIDS could be transmitted by shaking hands and 17.2 percent thought it could be acquired simply by being in the same room with a patient."[22] Many of these beliefs seem resistant to change. In the Massachusetts study, "after the [educational] programs, 15 percent of the providers still thought AIDS could be transmitted by sneezing or coughing, and 11.3 percent thought it could be transmitted by shaking hands. [In addition] after the . . . programs, the majority (66.2 percent) still thought that gowns were always necessary and a substantial minority (46.3 percent) still considered quarantine necessary.''[23] While the educational programs affected some change in knowledge about AIDS, the researchers found a strong resistance to changing knowledge and attitudes among a substantial minority of health-care providers. Such misinformation among health-care providers can only have negative effects on AIDS patients.

One of the social tragedies of the fear and stigma is that it has constrained compassion for AIDS sufferers. In our culture, we generally show caring and compassion for severely and terminally ill patients. The social meaning of AIDS mutes this compassion in families, among health-care providers, and with the public at large. It is a shame that a victim of any disease in our society must suffer the plight of Robert Doyle of Baltimore. After discovering he had pneumonia brought on by AIDS, no nursing home or hospice would take him. His family rejected him and his lover demanded that he move out of the apartment. With only months to live, he had no support, resources, or place to die. He finally rented a room in a rundown hotel, where the staff refused to enter the room and left food for him in the hallway. After a newspaper story, a stranger took him into her home, only to ask him to leave in a few days; next an elderly couple took him in, until threatening phone calls and vandalism forced him to move again. He finally found a home with three other adults, one also an AIDS victim. Soon he was returned to the hospital where he died.[24] The fear of AIDS turned this sick and dying man into a social outcast.

## Conclusion

The social meaning of AIDS has added to the victim-blaming response common to sexually and behaviorally-related diseases a powerful victim-fearing component. This has engendered an overreaction to the perils of AIDS and fueled the public fears of the disease. Some dangers and threats are, of course, very real, but the triple stigma of AIDS presents a frightening picture to the public, which leads to misguided attempts at ''protection'' and to resistance to contrary information. This only makes managing life more difficult for the sufferers and does not make the world ''safer'' from AIDS.

Since a medical cure or prevention for AIDS in the near future is unlikely, it is important that efforts be made to reduce the ''hysteria'' and overreaction surrounding this disease. We need to redouble our efforts to diffuse the unwarranted aspects of the fear of AIDS and to reduce its stigma. There are several strategies for attempting to accomplish this.

AIDS appears to be ''out of control.'' If some type of medical intervention emerged that could limit the spread and/or symptoms of the disease, this sense of lack of control might be decreased and the public expectations of medicine's protective function might be somewhat restored. But given the historical examples of epilepsy and syphilis, available and efficacious medical treatments do not in themselves alter the image of a disorder. The stigma of these diseases, while perhaps reduced, are still prevalent in our society.

Activists, policymakers, and medical personnel must directly attempt to change the image of the disease. Sometimes a disease's stigmatized image is reinforced by incorrect information. A classic example is the notion that leprosy was highly contagious and sufferers needed to be placed in isolated colonies. We know now that leprosy is not easily communicable. With epilepsy, myths developed that both emerged from and sustained the stigma, including notions like epilepsy is an inherited disease or it causes crime. These myths often gained professional support and led to misguided public policies such as forbidding marriage or immigration.[25] Such incorrect information and mythology must be unmasked and not be allowed to become the basis for social policies.

Another strategy to reduce stigma is to "normalize" the illness; that is, to demonstrate that not only "deviants" get the disease. It is important to show that conventional people can suffer the disease and, to the extent possible, lead normal lives. For example, Rock Hudson's belated public disclosure of his AIDS was an important symbol. He was identified as a solid, clean-cut American man, almost an ideal. He was also a movie hero with whom many people had made some kind of vicarious relationship. To a certain extent Rock Hudson helped bring AIDS out of the closet. An important public policy strategy should be to "normalize" AIDS as much as possible—to present exemplars of people who still can live relatively normal, if difficult, lives, with positive antibodies, ARC, or even AIDS. The media has done this to a degree with children—depicted as innocent victims of the disease—but we need to bring other AIDS sufferers back into our world and recreate our compassion for them.

We need to develop policies that focus on changing the image of AIDS and confront directly the stigma, resistance to information, and the unnecessary fears of the disease. Given the social meaning of AIDS, this won't be easy. While studies have shown us how difficult it is to change public attitudes toward illnesses,[26] images of diseases like leprosy (Hanson's disease) and, to a lesser degree, epilepsy have changed. We must develop the professional and public resolve to change the social meanings and response to AIDS and make this a high priority, along with the control, treatment, and eventual eradication of the disease. It is incumbent upon us to reduce the social as well as the physical suffering from AIDS.

## Notes


1. Susan Sontag, *Illness as Metaphor* (New York: Farrar, Straus and Giroux, 1978).
2. Merle A. Sande, "The Transmission of AIDS: The Case Against Casual Contagion," *New England Journal of Medicine*, vol. 314 (1986), pp. 380–82. See also, June E. Osborn, "The AIDS Epidemic: An Overview of the Science," *Issues in Science and Technology* (Winter, 1986), pp. 40–55.
3 Jacques Liebowitch, *A Strange Virus of Unknown Origin* (New York: Ballantine, 1985), pp. 3–4.
4. Cited in Matt Clark et al., "AIDS," *Newsweek* (October 12, 1984), pp. 20–24, 26–27.

5. Allen M. Brandt, *No Magic Bullet* (New York: Oxford University Press, 1985), p. 92.
6. Erving Goffman, *Stigma* (Englewood Cliffs, NJ: Prentice-Hall, 1963), pp. 30–31.
7. Sontag, 1978. See also, Anselm Strauss and Barney Glaser, *Awareness of Dying* (Chicago: Aldine, 1965).
8. Paul D. Cleary et al. "Theoretical Issues in Health Education about AIDS Risk." Unpublished paper, Department of Social Medicine and Health Policy, Harvard Medical School, 1986.
9. Peter Conrad and Joseph W. Schneider, *Deviance and Medicalization: From Badness to Sickness* (St. Louis: C. V. Mosby, 1980).
10. Ronald Bayer, "AIDS and The Gay Community: Between the Specter and the Promise of Medicine," *Social Research* (Autumn, 1985), pp. 581–606.
11. Donald E. Riesenberg, "AIDS-Prompted Behavior Changes Reported," *Journal of the American Medical Association* (January 10, 1986), pp. 171–72; Ronald Stall, "The Behavioral Epidemiology of AIDS: A Call for Anthropological Contributions," *Medical Anthropology Quarterly* (February, 1986), pp. 36–37; Jonathan Lieberson, "The Reality of AIDS," *New York Review of Books* (January 16, 1986), p. 47.
12. Christopher Collins, "Homosexuals and AIDS: An Inside View." Paper presented to the American Society of Law and Medicine conference on "AIDS: A Modern Plague?" Boston, April, 1986.
13. Lieberson, 1986, p. 45.
14. Ibid., p. 46.
15. Brandt, 1985, p. 137.
16. Carol Levine and Ronald Bayer, "Screening Blood: Public Health and Medical Uncertainty," *Hastings Center Report* (August, 1985), pp. 8–11.
17. George F. Grady, "A Practitioner's Guide to AIDS," *Massachusetts Medicine* (January/February, 1986), pp. 44–50. See also, Kenneth W. Payne and Stephen J. Risch, "The Politics of AIDS," *Science for the People* (September/October, 1984), pp. 17–24.
18. Cited in Lieberson, 1986, p. 44.
19. Ralph J. DiClemente, Jim Zorn, and Lydia Temoshok, "A Large-Scale Survey of Adolescents' Knowledge, Attitudes, and Beliefs About AIDS in San Francisco: A Needs Assessment." Paper presented at the meetings of the Society for Behavioral Medicine, March, 1986.
20. Cited in Ibid., p. 4.
21. Lydia Temoshok, David M. Sweet, and Jane Zich, "A Cross-Cultural Analysis of Reactions to the AIDS Epidemic." Paper presented at the meetings of the Society for Behavioral Medicine, March, 1986.
22. Dorothy C. Wertz et al., "Research on the Educational Programs of the AIDS Action Committee of the Fenway Community Health Center: Final Report." Submitted to the Massachusetts Department of Public Health, AIDS Research Program, 1985, p. 11.
23. Ibid., p. 12.
24. Jean Seligman and Nikki Fink Greenberg, "Only Months to Live and No Place to Die," *Newsweek* (August 12, 1985), p. 26.
25. Joseph W. Schneider and Peter Conrad, *Having Epilepsy: The Experience and Control of Illness* (Philadelphia: Temple University Press, 1983), pp. 22–46.
26. Elaine Cumming and John Cumming, *Closed Ranks* (Cambridge, Harvard University Press, 1957).

# Toward Adequate Health Care

*Rashi Fein*

Each year more Americans face an uncertain health future with inadequate or no insurance to help pay for medical care. National efforts to control and contain medical expenditures, which are endangering the quality of care, have met with few successes. Advances in biomedical science, though welcome, will add to costs and will further strain government and private budgets. We can expect additional pressure to restrict existing health insurance policies, to increase patient "cost-sharing," and to cut benefits. More and more of us will be forced into health plans and patterns of care we now reject. It will become harder to pay for the care we need. Inevitably, this will be doubly difficult for those not covered by employer group health plans. Insurers, concerned about future costs, will reject self-selected individual subscribers. Decisions will be made for us and for physicians by cost accountants; attaché case and three-piece suit will replace stethoscope and white coat.

This article focuses on the way we finance health care and its implications for equity and expenditure control. I shall briefly review our recent record, examine the genesis of our present situation, and describe the characteristics of a responsible comprehensive and universal health insurance program. I suggest that we view health care as part of a general set of issues concerning the nature of the American community and our social well-being.

As I write, the Hundredth Congress is considering some form of catastrophic health insurance of Medicare beneficiaries. Medicare, however, is only one item on the health policy agenda. Whatever the outcome of this debate, we need to encourage our representatives and those who seek the presidency to address the larger health problems that remain: the inequities in access to care and the ever-increasing expenditures for care.

## Some Progress, Many Gaps

Progress has been made over the last two decades. Between 1960 and 1980, life expectancy at birth increased by a full four years. Put differently, but no less dramatically, the age-adjusted death rate—that is, the number of deaths per 100,000 population adjusted for the changing age of that population—declined from 760 in 1960 to 585 in 1980.

Though there are large variations between subgroups of the population, on the

---

Rashi Fein, "Toward Adequate Health Care," *Dissent* 35 (Winter 1988), pp. 98–104. 

whole we live longer and with less impairment. In a word, we are healthier. But that is not all we find on our report card. Other entries are disconcerting:

First: the percentage of Americans under age 65 without any public or private health insurance has been growing—up by over five million persons since 1980. Thirty-seven million individuals, one out of every six Americans, have *no* health insurance whatsoever and millions more have inadequate coverage. Expansion of the service sector, which traditionally has not provided health insurance for its employees, will increase these numbers.

Second: in the two-year period 1982–1984 fully half of America's major corporations increased employee premiums and deductibles and one-third increased co-insurance and co-payments, or the amount that the insured must pay for each service. In 1981, 84 percent of a sample of corporate medical-insurance plans paid all hospital room and board charges incurred by employees or their dependents. By 1986, this was true of only 38 percent of the very same plans. Fewer Americans have insurance and those that do, have less of it.

Third: Medicare, the federal health-financing program for the aged and disabled, has become more expensive. Premiums for physicians' services have increased and the hospital deductible rose from $400 in 1985 to $520 in 1987. *Medicare now pays for less than half of the health care costs of the elderly.*

Fourth: Medicaid, the federal-state health-financing program for the poor (more correctly: for some of the poor), now assists only 40 percent of America's poor and only half of America's poor children. *Between 1977 and 1983 the number of Americans in poverty grew by 10.5 million while the number of Medicaid recipients declined by 1.3 million.*

Fifth: the health sector is becoming more commercialized. For-profit firms have been legitimized. Their "bottom-line" mentality has led to denial of care to those patients who will not be "profitable" or who cannot pay.

There is another issue. In spite of the fact that many of us have less protection and receive less care than we require, American health expenditures continue to grow rapidly. In 1986 these totaled $458 billion, an increase of 8.4 percent over 1985. A larger and larger proportion of our income and total production goes for medical care. The percent of the Gross National Product allocated to the health care sector has expanded from 5.9 percent in 1965 and 8.3 percent in 1975 to 10.9 percent in 1986. More resources for medical care means fewer resources for capital investment, education, parks, housing, or consumer goods.

Let us dispose of myths. There is a myth that the uninsured are shiftless, lazy, and unwilling to work. Not so. Most of those without insurance are employed (or dependents of people with jobs). The enterprises they work for do not provide the "fringe benefit" of nontaxable health insurance, do not organize group enrollment at lower premiums, and do not pay wages sufficient to enable individual purchase of policies.

Another myth: the uninsured generally get care anyway, paid for by Medicaid or given free. That is only partially the case. Medicaid covers less than one-half of America's poor. Though many providers take care of people who can't pay, the uninsured—who tend to be poorer and sicker—receive half the hospital care and two-thirds the physician care that others do.

A final myth: because America spends more on health care than other nations, our health indices lead the world. We do spend more for care. Yet, in 1983, sixteen countries around the world had lower infant mortality rates (a traditional health measure) than we. Our infant mortality rate is 23 percent higher than that of our neighbor, Canada. It's not that we lack medical technology or expertise; it's not a question of survival rates for low-weight babies. In large measure our problem derives from inadequate prenatal care, often due to lack of access.

## The Choices We Made

The progress we once made (as well as the slippage in the recent past) was neither preordained nor accidental. Although personal behavior in regard to smoking, diet, and life-style played a role in improving health indices, the record we achieved was largely the result of collective rather than individual and independent action.

These actions were stimulated, implemented, and financed by the most important instruments through which we undertake collective action: the various levels of government. In 1965, in the wake of Lyndon Johnson's landslide victory over Barry Goldwater, Congress enacted Medicare and Medicaid. The Office of Economic Opportunity helped organize and fund neighborhood health centers. Support for nutrition programs and maternal and child health activities expanded. The civil rights movement and consequent federal legislation helped remove segregation barriers in hospitals. Research activities supported by the National Institutes of Health expanded, as did the number of medical schools and students. The guarantee of funding through public payment stimulated the renovation and expansion of American hospitals and the addition of sophisticated technology. Disparities in access were reduced. It was a golden age for American medicine.

Rising incomes and full employment (for part of the period) and increases in Social Security also made significant contributions to improvement in America's health indices. Important as medical care is for the achievement of higher health status, so also is an increase in living standards.

In recent years, however, many federal health programs have been cut back. Where the economic gains of the 1960s were widely shared and poverty rates declined, recent advances have been smaller and have not been distributed as widely. Income disparities have widened. So, too, have disparities in access to care and in health indices.

That, too, is not an accident. It reflects the difference in the attitudes we hold, and the social and economic policies we have chosen to pursue.

In the early 1970s our social outlook and attitudes were different. One should not succumb to nostalgia—not for Vietnam, the oil crisis of 1973, Watergate, or rapid inflation. Yet we should recall that in spite of those difficulties, we were seriously examining important social issues. There were efforts at welfare reform. President Nixon even proposed a national health insurance program.

The assumption in the early 1970s—and it was a reasonable assumption—was that national health insurance would soon be enacted. That did not happen, but the fact that leaders of Congress and the president debated specific health insurance proposals showed a willingness to address issues of social policy—specifically that millions of Americans did not have any insurance to protect them against rapidly increasing costs of medical care.

That debate assumed that Medicare, the largest public health-financing program, was working well. Social insurance was acceptable and accepted. Indeed, in 1972, Medicare was liberalized to include the disabled and those suffering from renal failure (it was suggested, sardonically to be sure, that we might get comprehensive national health insurance ''organ by organ'').

It's also worth noting how different were our attitudes toward reliance on government's helping hand. In contrast to today, when many Americans ''mistrust'' government, in the mid-1960s we did turn—with ambivalence, but turn nevertheless—to government to lead the war on poverty and to provide the social insurance of Medicare. Perhaps one of the reasons we were willing to do so was that the issue of distributional equity was raised at the highest level of government. We did not think it unreasonable for the president to tell us that decent medical care should be available to all and that government could solve domestic social problems. Our record was not as good as that to which we aspired, but we did make significant progress.

Out attitudes changed. We grew cynical (and there was much to be cynical about). We were buffeted by inflation (low by European Standards but high by American ones and alien to our experience). New leaders told us we couldn't solve problems by throwing money at them—quite as if money didn't matter. We were lectured that there were no simple answers—almost as if complex ones were un-American. We were encouraged to think that hope lay only in free-enterprise markets. We hunkered down and, beset by problems, looked inward and tried to protect our individual selves. Something important happened to the sense of community. Of great significance for the longer run, and tied to the decline in the sense of community, is the coming apart of arrangements by which one group of consumers assists another (sometimes, to be sure, without knowing it and as a consequence of regulation). Such systems of cross-subsidy existed in airline and telephone service as well as in health insurance.

Many of us still remember the days when Blue Cross used ''community rating''—a system of voluntary cross-subsidy—to set premiums. It charged the same premium to all subscribers even though, as a function of age and health status, some individuals predictably would use more and others would use fewer services.

That system collapsed in the face of competition from commercial insurers whose ''experience rating'' premium structure reflected the health experience and projected use of health care services of particular groups narrowly defined. Since most group insurance was employment-related, employed individuals who were younger could get a lower premium than called for by the Blue Cross/Blue Shield community rate (which included the retired elderly). The consequence was clear: the young and healthy opted for lower premiums and dissociated themselves from those who were older and likely to need more care. By 1965 most of the population age 65 and over had no private health insurance because the unsubsidized rates they faced had increased beyond their ability to pay. The enactment of Medicare, a compulsory collective effort to help the aged, was the inevitable consequence of the collapse of the earlier voluntary system of sharing costs.

The age (and, in the case of airline and telephone service, residence) distinctions on which cross-subsidies are based are poor proxies for distinctions based on income. If we seek equity, we should be troubled by situations in which low-income young persons subsidize the health care of more affluent older individuals. Income provides a more acceptable way to assess whether we are being "fair"; compulsory taxation is a more refined tool to achieve equitable redistribution.

Nevertheless, cross-subsidies do help in the "average" case. Thus, if we give up voluntary cross-subsidies we must be prepared to replace them—as in the case of Medicare—with collective and compulsory redistribution programs. But that runs counter to what we have heard for seven years from an administration that has been telling us that we should do privately what we had been doing communally through government. Welcome as increased private effort might be, private charity cannot substitute for government programs, nor can individual priority-setting substitute for communal determination of needs. Solutions for the disparities in our income distribution will not be found in privatization, competition, or the free market. Indeed, it is in the context of the free market that our major corporations indicate their unwillingness to continue to pay the higher premiums that once provided funds to cover the costs incurred by the uninsured.

Our health care financing system has two unfortunate characteristics: (1) private insurance is employment-related rather than universally available; (2) public and private payment systems have no control mechanism, no way of arriving at a decision concerning the appropriate level of total expenditures. The existing insurance systems have not furthered equity and have encouraged the expansion of the health sector without consideration of real costs, alternative ways that medical care could be produced, and other social priorities.

Expenditures are high. None of us is certain we are getting value for money. Liberals and conservatives agree that we need a control mechanism (liberals would say "an equitable control mechanism"), a process by which to determine how much society will spend. But there is disagreement about whether government or the free market is the appropriate mechanism. The resolution of that issue remains on our agenda. To understand what is at stake requires a redefinition of the "right to medical care."

## What Are our Health Care Rights?

When medical care could do less and was less costly, we spoke as if every American should have a right to all the care that he or she might benefit from, however marginal that benefit might be and however large the cost. Today we are increasingly aware, if only because of advances in medical science, that no society can make that definition operational. We must be more specific when we speak of "the right to care."

That requires a recognition that the right is composed of two parts. The first is the right of citizens to expect that the dollars and resources allocated to medical care will be consistent with their collective perception of the benefits that care confers and the alternative benefits that might be generated were the dollars and resources used in other ways. That right is similar to our expectations in areas such as national defense, highways, education, etc.

The second right is the individual's right to an equitable share of those total health resources, where equitable means that the distribution of care reflects medical needs and the costs and benefits of care rather than individual income, wealth, political power, or social status. This right is similar to our expectations in areas such as access to education, parks, and a basic level of sustenance. (It, too, is a concept with which we are familiar.)

This two-part definition is the antithesis of one that calls for private decision-making through the marketplace. The marketplace determines what we spend on fine brandy, vacations in Acapulco, sun-dried tomatoes, yachts, and other less exotic consumer products. But this level of expenditure does not represent the collective perception of all the citizenry. Rather it is the sum of the individual perceptions of those who have the dollars. It is *not* the way we decide how much to spend on education or other public goods in which public benefits exceed private ones.

If, as I suggest, both rights are necessary, we require a structure that can determine the citizenry's perceptions and that enables us to translate them into an effective program. Such a structure exists and operates at various levels. It is called government. Of course, it does not function as well as it might. It is cumbersome (though the "invisible hand" of the free market can be "all thumbs") nor is it always wise or beneficent. It is influenced by small but powerful groups—though we may all enjoy free speech, some use loudspeakers while others can only whisper. Even so, in the political realm each of us has no more or fewer votes than the next person, whereas in the marketplace each of us votes with dollars and that means that some have far more votes than others. There is little reason to believe that the two voting systems would yield the same result; there is much reason to believe that the democratic method, though imperfect and in need of repair, could more appropriately reflect the health needs of the total population.

In contrast, the free-market solution to America's health problems is replete with problems. It assumes competition, but, in fact, the market characteristics necessary to make competition work (e.g., many buyers and sellers, ease of entry, access to information) do not prevail. Furthermore, competition is likely to lead to segmentation of the market and to inequities. There is profit to be made by enrolling healthier patients into an insurance or delivery program. But if each insurer or delivery system competes for healthy patients, who will protect or take care of those who are sicker and "bad risks"? This issue has already arisen: insurers do not want to enroll individuals at risk of contracting AIDS. Given advances in medical science that will permit assessment of the future risk of heart attack, diabetes, and other ailments, the temptation to segment the market and exclude some (many?) individuals will prove irresistible to firms playing by the rules of the marketplace and trying to maximize profits.

## Defining a Universal Health Insurance Plan

The two-part formulation of rights has an operational counterpart: a universal health insurance program with budget control. It does not require that government produce medical care, but it does require that government be concerned with how much care will be produced. It does not require that government run the delivery system, but it does require that those who run it be held accountable. It does not require that government make clinical decisions, but it does require that government set appropriate incentives and a framework for those decisions so that they more adequately reflect medical and social needs.

In constructing a universal health insurance system with budget controls, it will not do to present the national health insurance plans that were debated in the 1910s or 1920s or 1930s. Harry Truman's plan of the late 1940s is not appropriate today and neither are the ideas put forward in the 1960s and 1970s. We must take account of recent changes in the health sector and in the American economy. Even the best program will not operate perfectly, for the design will have to compromise between our various goals. But given the fact that, except for the United States (and South Africa), every industrialized nation has some form of national health insurance, it is clear that the obstacle to such a program is ideological rather than technical.

What characteristics might a national health program have? The first issue is the appropriate level of administration and on that, as on other matters, we would do well to learn from Canada. For some time it has been assumed that NHI would be a federal program administered from Washington. I would suggest a different approach: administration by the individual states (Canada uses provincial administration). The federal government would have the responsibility to define the benefit structure (the list of covered services), to monitor compliance, review quality, assure nondiscriminatory behavior, enforce portability of benefits across state boundaries, and set standards for enrollment. It would also provide financial assistance to help the individual states enroll their total population in the insurance program (the goal is an insurance program, not a pool of funds to pay for "uncompensated care"). But the development of appropriate health-care budgets, payment mechanisms, enrollment options, and ways to raise and pool dollars would be state responsibilities.

The various states could develop different mechanisms to discharge those responsibilities. One desirable approach would require that states set up "authorities" into which all funds would flow (including all subsidies) and from which "premiums" would be disbursed, in response to the insured individual's choice, to insurers acting as fiscal intermediaries or to organized delivery systems. This arrangement would enable public funds to be mixed with private funds and still allow individuals to select from among providers and reimbursement agents.

As in Canada, we would have state programs meeting basic federal requirements, but each would be administered in ways that more adequately reflected local priorities. The Canadian system works effectively: Canada's universal and comprehensive insurance system is less expensive than our patchwork quilt, yet its health indices equal (and in some cases, exceed) ours. One reason the Canadian system costs less is that administrative costs are lower. If we adopt a similar system, we could use part of the savings on administration to offset the increased costs associated with increased access. We could spend our money on health care rather than on enrollment, marketing, claim forms, and bookkeeping.

The United States, of course, if not Canada. Our history, tradition, and attitudes are different. So too, our size, population, and economic structure. It would not do to adopt the Canadian health insurance program, but we can adapt it. I opt for state-administered programs, even knowing that there will be disparities between the states, for what I believe are powerful and persuasive reasons. The fact is that at present many of our states have greater capacity for effective administration than does the federal civil service, which has been decimated in recent years. A number of our states have worked at cost-containment issues and have developed expertise that can be built upon. Given the freedom to act (federal legislation now prevents that) and some part of the necessary funds, they are likely to move with vigor.

Furthermore, our health care delivery system is far more heterogeneous than in earlier days. Health Maintenance Organizations are far more prevalent in some parts of the nation than in others. What makes sense in St. Paul may not fit Des Moines' needs or be responsive to its population's desires. There is reason, particularly with a set of services as personal as health care, to bring decision-making about the allocation of resources closer to the citizenry. Perhaps that was not as necessary during periods of rapid expansion. But it would be beneficial if we are trying to contain costs and are engaged in political battles about health budgets, appropriate levels of spending, and necessary trade-offs.

There are arguments against relying on state administration. I do not find them compelling. The first is that the states are not likely to develop social-insurance-based enrollment programs. Most states will mandate employers to provide insurance for their employees (with state assistance to meet the premium costs) and will develop special enrollment programs to cover remaining parts of the population. But it is important to recognize that for the last fifteen years that has been the very kind of program that many liberal members of Congress (who in earlier years supported a social-insurance program) have favored at the federal level. They have not been enamored of the kind of program that would increase the federal budget and raise taxes. They prefer to build upon existing employment-based insurance, believing that employers view premiums differently than taxes. Therefore, it is not clear that we lose anything by going the state route. Indeed, there is the possibility that some state legislatures would be more daring than the Congress and opt for more broadly based enrollment mechanisms supported by state taxes.

A second argument against state administration is that it would inhibit equalization between the various states. Though the federal government could (and should) take account of income differences and provide funds for equalization purposes, there is the possibility that residents in some localities would have more and better health care than if they lived elsewhere. That remains the case even in Great Britain, which has a National Health Service, and in the U.S. under Medicare. Disparities will only be erased over a long period of time. It is not clear that a purely federal program will achieve more rapid equalization. What is may do is erect a façade of legislation that pretends to equality even as the reality is otherwise.

A third argument stems from the fact that not all the states have equal administrative ability or commitment. Although the federal government can use the power of purse to "induce" states to participate (for example, denial of business deductions for health insurance premiums in states that fail to set up an approved program), federal authorities should assess performance and be prepared to administer the program in any state that fails to discharge its responsibilities. Nevertheless, all states should be given the opportunity to implement an insurance program.

It is time to develop the detailed specifications for a federal-state national health insurance program that explicitly recognizes which macro-health-care decisions are essentially political and invite more active participation by the electorate. Over the years countless polls have shown that the American people support national health insurance. A future president could articulate a vision of a more equitable and responsible health care system.

# Chapter 9
# THE MEDIA

## The Media Brokers: Concentration and Ownership of the Press

*Ben Bagdikian*

If all major media in the United States—every daily newspaper, magazine, broadcasting station, book publishing house, and motion picture studio—were controlled by one "czar," the American public would have reason to fear for its democracy.

The danger is not that this single controller would necessarily be evil, though this kind of extravagant power has a grim history. Whether evil or benevolent, centralized control over information, whether governmental or private, is incompatible with freedom. Modern democracies need a choice of politics and ideas, and that choice requires access to truly diverse and competing sources of news, literature, entertainment, and popular culture.

Fortunately, no single corporation controls all the mass media in the United States. But something is happening that points in that direction. If mergers and acquisitions by large corporations continue at the present rate, one massive firm will be in virtual control of all major media by the 1990s. Given the complexities of social and economic trends, that is not inevitable. It is, however, quite possible—and serious corporate leaders predict—that by the 1990s a half-dozen large corporations will own all the most powerful media outlets in the United States.

The predictions are not groundless. They are based on extraordinary changes in recent years. At the end of World War II, for example, more than 80 percent of the daily newspapers in the United States were independently owned, but by 1987 the proportion was almost reversed: 72 percent were owned by outside corporations and 15 of those corporations had most of the business. The pace of takeovers by large national and multinational corporations is increasing. In 1981 twenty corporations controlled most of the business of the country's 11,000 magazines, but only five years later that number had shrunk to six corporations.

Today, despite 25,000 media outlets in the United States, 29 corporations control

---

Ben Bagdikian, "The Media Brokers: Concentration and Ownership of the Press." This article is reprinted from the *Multinational Monitor* 8 (September 1987), pp. 7–12. *Multinational Monitor* is a monthly newsmagazine published by Essential Information, Inc. P.O. Box 19405 Washington D.C. 20036 $22 individual.

**Table 1** Media Moguls

The dominant 29 corporations are:

- Bertelsmann, A.G. (books)
- Capital Cities/ABC (newspapers, television)
- CBS, Inc. (television)
- Central Newspapers
- Coca-Cola (motion pictures)
- Cox Communications (newspapers)
- Dow Jones & Co. (newspapers)
- Encyclopedia Britannica (books)
- Freedom Newspapers
- Gannett Co. (newspapers)
- General Electric Co. (television)
- Gulf + Western (books, motion pictures)
- Harcourt Brace Jovanovich
- Hearst Corp. (newspapers, magazines)
- International Thomson Org. (newspapers, magazines, books)
- Knight-Ridder (newspapers)
- Macmillan (books)
- McGraw-Hill (magazines, books)
- New York Times Co. (newspapers)
- Newhouse (newspapers, magazines, books)
- News America (newspapers)
- Reader's Digest Assn. (books)
- Scripps Howard (newspapers)
- Time, Inc. (magazines, books)
- Times Mirror Co. (newspapers)
- Triangle Publications (magazines)
- Tribune Co. (newspapers)
- Universal-MCA (motion pictures)
- Warner Communications (motion pictures)

most of the business in daily newspapers, magazines, television, books, and motion pictures.

Few investors believe that the process of tightening control will stop soon. An investment banker, Christopher Shaw, chairman of Henry Ansbacher, Inc., has negotiated more than 120 media acquisitions. When asked where it will all stop, Shaw likes to quote a client, saying that by the year 2000 all U.S. media may be in the hands of six conglomerates. Robert Maxwell, a British publisher, said in 1984, "In ten years' time, there will be only ten global corporations of communications. I . . . would expect to be one of them."

But there is something strange about leaders of the media acquisition drive. Most would agree that one "czar" in control would be disastrous for democracy, yet they praise the march toward that unhealthy end. The media they control take every opportunity to report the beauties of corporate bigness. And while there is much news and commentary about media mergers and acquisitions, it is reported almost exclusively as a financial game without social consequences. The general public is told almost nothing of the dangers.

If executives of dominant media corporations are personally silent about the dangers of concentrated ownership, it is not surprising: the process benefits them. But the media they control also are silent. The silence is not convincing evidence that the media never reflect the corporate and political interests of their owners.

On the other hand, it is unrealistic to expect media leaders to do otherwise. The answer is not a futile plea asking controllers of power to criticize their own power. The answer is to prevent dangerous concentration of power in the first place or, having failed that, to diversify that power.

Compounding the trend has been the practice of companies already dominant in one medium, like newspapers, investing in a formerly competitive medium, like television. In the past, each medium used to act like a watchdog over the behavior of its competing media. The newspaper industry watched magazines and both kept a public eye on the broadcasting industry. Each was vigilant against the other industries' lobbying for unfair government concessions or against questionable business practices. But now the watchdogs have been cross-bred into an amiable hybrid.

Not surprisingly, the giants universally insist that they improve the media they buy. But even if, in an unreal world, all corporate owners universally improved their acquisitions, even if they all made their properties totally open to conflicting news and views, concentrated media ownership would still damage democracy in the United States: concentrated power over public information is inherently antidemocratic.

Today, the chief executive officers of the 29 corporations that control most of what Americans read and see can fit into an ordinary living room. Almost without exception they are conservative Republicans. They can, if they wish, use control of their newspapers, broadcast stations, magazines, books and movies to promote their own corporate values to the exclusion of others. Most say that they would never use that power. But even if sincere, they ignore human nature and they ignore history: when central interests are at stake, available power will always be used.

In a democracy, the answer to great power is accountability to the public. Accountability in business life in some cases requires government regulations to prevent monopoly or to make natural monopolies meet public service standards. But for most commerce, accountability is self-induced because there is enough diversity and competition so that consumers have real choices.

In the media, "real choices" means a rich variety of political and social content in news, entertainment, and other public information, and enough competition in content and prices so that the average consumer has genuine alternatives. It means equitable distribution of economic power in the marketplace so that a few dominant leaders cannot prevent true competition or the reasonable entry of new enterprises. Today the country is losing diversity and competition among its major media and with it, thanks to monopoly and oligopoly, losing not only a variety of political voices but the economic accountability of the marketplace.

Though the media controlled by the dominant corporations do not alert the public to such problems, they do claim that the process is improving the country's media outlets. Their principal claims are that they bring greater resources to improve their new acquisitions, that they have more sophisticated business management skills, that their size makes it easier to fend off government incursions on freedom of expression and improper advertiser influence, and, finally, that if they were tempted to use their power to the disadvantage of the public, the public would not stand for it.

In thousands of media transactions of recent years, some of these claims have been realized some of the time. But at best the record is mixed; most of the time the record is unimpressive or worse.

A few newspaper chains, for example, improved independent papers they acquired, notably Knight-Ridder, Times Mirror, the New York Times Company, and Dow Jones's Ottoway subsidiary. Most have not. In the hundreds of small and medium-sized communities whose fate does not reach commentators in New York and Washington, acquisition of the local paper or television station by a large firm more often is followed by drastic cutbacks in staffs, either in brutal instant firings or more subtly by forced retirements and resignations that are not replaced. Editorial content is cheapened.

Corporations do not purchase local newspapers and broadcast stations for sentimental reasons. They buy them as investments that will yield a maximum return as quickly as possible. When they buy a local monopoly, which is typical of newspapers, or an assured share of the market, typical of television, few investors can resist the spectacular profits that can be made by cutting quality and raising prices. Christopher Shaw, the merger expert, for example, speaking at a session of potential media investors in October 1986, said that a daily monopoly newspaper with a 15 percent annual operating profit, can, within two years of purchase, be making a 40 percent profit by cutting costs and raising advertising and subscription prices.

Shaw's prescription has, in fact, been the history of media acquisitions in hundreds of communities during the past 20 years. It is why, with one exception (Knight-Ridder's *Philadelphia Inquirer*), no contemporary newspaper chain has ever created a distinguished American daily paper. Every other outstanding paper was originally created by an independent, noncorporate owner committed to long-term quality and strength.

The claim that large corporations can better resist incursions of government into freedom of the press can be true. Some—not all—have done so. They can also better afford to fight large libel actions brought for political purposes, though by being large they tend to attract larger lawsuits. Many of the larger media companies—the New York Times, Washington Post, and Gannett, for example—have spent money and energy working for more open meetings of public bodies and resisting White House efforts to weaken the Freedom of Information Act. But when large media corporations have to choose between, on the one hand, candidates who will give governmental favors in corporate taxes and relaxed business regulation, or, on the other hand, candidates who support freedom of the press, the record is not encouraging. The history of relations between big government and big corporations is more of accommodation than of confrontation. Richard Nixon and Ronald Reagan, in their first terms in the White House, made the most severe attacks in this century on freedom of the press, but both made extraordinary moves to support corporate expansion in the media; newspaper publishers overwhelmingly endorsed both Nixon and Reagan for reelection.

The claim by corporate owners of greater resistance to advertiser pressures has mixed validity. Greater public sophistication and professional journalistic standards have made ineffective past clumsy interjection of ads into editorial content, though it still exists in many places. But alteration of the basic form and content in newspapers, magazines, and television programs—creating editorial content not for the needs and interests of the audience but to enhance advertising—has become far more intense under corporate ownership.

It is a favorite axiom of large media operators that while they have great power, if they abuse it the public will reject their product. But public choice is inoperative where there is monopoly, which is the case in 98 percent of cities with a daily newspaper, or market dominance by the few, which is the case with television. New corporate owners of newspapers and television stations, for example, commonly reduce staff and news space. Neither newspapers nor broadcasters tell their audience about their staffing and investment in content, except in self-serving promotional terms. If the audience senses a new thinness, they seldom have an alternative.

Large media corporations are the primary shapers of American public opinion, and through that, they are a major influence on government. Whether politicians are elected or reelected and whether their issues are publicized, depends on their treatment in the news. Consequently, government leaders tend to be extraordinarily attentive to the corporate wishes of the media.

(It is not accidental that one factor stimulating the growth of newspaper chains was a favorable government tax ruling. A company's accumulated annual profits enjoy a forgiving tax rate if the profits are for "a necessary cost of doing business," usually assumed to mean contingencies for future problems. But the Internal Revenue Service decided that a newspaper using its accumulated profits to buy another newspaper is "a necessary cost of doing business.")

Media outlets can be purchased to pursue the political promotion of the owner when the owner lusts after high office. Hearst wanted to be president. James M. Cox, publisher of a paper in Ohio, became Democratic candidate for president in 1920, only to be defeated for the presidency by another Ohio newspaper publisher, Warren Gamaliel Harding.

Today, the primary political advantage of concentrated media power is no longer to gain high political office for the media executive. The primary danger of excessive media power is not promoting candidacies of the anonymous men and women who run corporations, but of promoting the politics and economics of the corporate world.

The desire of most corporate leaders is not to become president of the United States, but to influence the U.S. president.

The desire for governmental favors is not limited to large media corporations. That was just as true of independent local owners. The difference is in the magnitude of desire and the magnitude of power. Many media owners are substantial defense contractors and are affected by success or failure of disarmament, by the size of defense budgets, by public versus private sector spending, by the level of social programs, by involvement of the United States in foreign countries where American corporations have heavy investments—all the components of a force changing the shape of American society that President Eisenhower called "the military-industrial complex." The potential conflicts of interest in the new corporate domination of the mass media involve the essence of the country's public policy.

The new media-industrial corporations also want quite specific actions from government, such as government contracts, relaxed application of antitrust laws, deregulation of business, elimination of limits on corporate profits, and corporate tax loopholes.

For example, when General Electric bought RCA in 1986 (and with it NBC news), it combined its media power with its other industrial and financial interests. General Electric is a major defense contractor, it manufactures and sells electronic, electrical and nuclear systems worldwide, produces aircraft and spacecraft components, and is in the insurance and banking business, with sales exceeding $28 billion a year. Its multinational operations are sensitive to both domestic and foreign policy.

In 1986, the Wall Street acquisition expert, Christopher Shaw, listed for the benefit of potential media buyers the reasons one should buy newspapers, magazines, broadcast stations, or book publishing firms. The first reason was "profitability," the next reason was "influence."

It is possible that large corporations are gaining control of the American media because the public wants it that way. But there is another possibility: the public, almost totally dependent on the media to alert them to public problems, has seldom seen in their standard newspapers, magazines, or broadcasts anything to suggest the political and economic dangers of concentrated corporate control. On the contrary, for years, the media have treated mergers and acquisitions as an exciting game that poses no threat to the national pattern of news and information.

It is also possible that the public image of owners' selfish use of their media power is obsolete, based on the historical notoriety of the crudities of nineteenth-century "yellow journalism."

Most owners and editors no longer brutalize the news with the heavy hand dramatized in movies like "Citizen Kane" or "The Front Page." More common is something more subtle, more professionally respectable, and, in some respects, more effective: the power to treat some subjects accurately but briefly, to treat other subjects accurately but in depth, or in the conventional options every medium has of taking its own initiatives, carefully avoiding some subjects and enthusiastically pursuing others.

Other evidence of the welcome departure of the large-scale shrillness of a century ago and of the newer subtleties is the appearance in the standard media, every day, of news that does not reflect owners' private values and may be offensive to them. With few exceptions, major media owners are conservative Republicans but they still carry the news when liberal Democrats are elected and when legislatures impose environmental regulations on reluctant industries. Most of the time, professional journalistic standards and public sophistication are high enough to make gross suppression of dramatic developments ineffective.

But there are two kinds of impact on public opinion, one brief and superficial, the other prolonged and deep. The first is the single, isolated item, one of dozens reported on any given day in newspapers, radio, and television. That item and its other daily companions are followed the next day with dozens of new ones, each day tending to obliterate the impact of what went before.

Far more effective in creating public opinion is the pursuit of events or ideas until they are displayed in depth over a period of time, until they form a coherent picture and become integrated into public thinking. It is this continuous repetition and emphasis that creates high priorities among the general public and in government. It is in that power—to treat some subjects briefly and obscurely but others repetitively and in depth, or to take initiatives unrelated to external events—where ownership interests most effectively influence the news.

Because these discriminations are normal and necessary, it is difficult for the public (and often for individual journalism professionals) to detect when ownership interests become a problem. Ownership biases usually are not obvious because they are part of normal daily rapid decision-making and rarely is the owner personally present.

Fifty years ago, executive editors spoke openly to their staffs about owners' sensibilities. Today most editors do not. It is ironic confirmation of raised professional standards that today it is too embarrassing. When protection of owner interests intrudes into news decisions, other professionally acceptable reasons are given. And in most news organizations, there is no absolute barrier against all developments that will embarrass the owner. Over time, with some kinds of items entering the news easily and others with difficulty, the total news picture of society is skewed in favor of corporate interests. The special values of the owning corporation, along with professionally respectable ones, flow quietly and anonymously into the convention of what is "news."

There are 15 dominant companies that have half or more of the daily newspaper business, six in magazines, three in television, 10 in book publishing, and four in motion picture production, making a total of 38 firms. But some corporations are dominant in more than one medium. For example, Newhouse and Thomson are dominant in newspapers, magazines, and books; Time Inc. and McGraw-Hill in magazines and books; Capital Cities/ABC in newspapers and television; and Gulf + Western in books and motion pictures. Because of the multiple dominance of some firms, the total number of corporations dominating all major media is 29.

In 1981, there were 46 corporations that controlled most of the business in daily newspapers, magazines, television, books and motion pictures. Five years later the number had shrunk to 29.

Like other large media companies, General Electric presents yet another complication that differs from small, local companies: it has, through its board of directors, interlocks with still other major industrial and financial sectors of the American economy, in wood products, textiles, automotive supplies, department store chains, and banking.

Under law, the director of a company is obliged to act in the interests of his own company. An unanswered dilemma is what happens when an officer of Corporation A who sits as a director on the board of Corporation B has to choose between acting in the best interests of his own company or of the one on whose board he sits.

What is the proper behavior of a banker who is a director of General Electric, owner of NBC, if he hears that the network is about to produce a documentary highly embarrassing to the banking industry? It could be in the best interests of NBC News to attract an audience with a documentary on what could be a compelling public issue. Yet such a documentary might not be perceived as being in the best interests of the banks.

The emergence of major national and multinational corporations as controllers of most of the country's media has enormously complicated the potential conflicts of interest in, among other things, interlocked boards of directors.

A study by Peter Dreier and Steven Weinberg in 1979 found interlocked directorates in major newspaper chains, for example. Gannett shared directors with Merrill Lynch (stockbrokers), Standard Oil of Ohio, 20th Century Fox, Kerr-McGee (oil, gas, nuclear power and aerospace), McDonnell Douglas Aircraft, McGraw-Hill, Eastern Airlines, Phillips Petroleum, Kellogg Company, and New York Telephone Company.

The most influential paper in America, the *New York Times,* interlocked with Merck, Morgan Guaranty Trust, Bristol Myers, Charter Oil, Johns Manville, American Express, Bethlehem Steel, IBM, Scott Paper, Sun Oil, and First Boston Corporation.

Time, Inc. has so many interlocks they almost represented a plenary board of directors of U.S. business and finance, including Mobil Oil, AT&T, American Express, Firestone Tire & Rubber Company, Mellon National Corporation, Atlantic Richfield, Xerox, General Dynamics, and most of the major international banks.

Louis Brandeis, before joining the Supreme Court, called this linkage "the endless chain." He wrote: "This practice of interlocking directorates is the root of many evils. It offends laws human and divine . . . It tends to disloyalty and violation of the fundamental law that no man can serve two masters . . . It is undemocratic, for it rejects the platform: A fair field and no more favors."

As media conglomerates have become larger, they have integrated into the higher levels of American banking and industrial life as subsidiaries and interlocks within their boards of directors. Half the dominant firms are members of the Fortune 500 largest corporations in the country. They are heavy investors in, among other things, agribusiness, airlines, coal and oil, banking, insurance, defense contracts, automobile sales, rocket engineering, nuclear power, and nuclear weapons. Many have heavy foreign investments affected by American foreign policy.

It is normal for all large businesses to make serious efforts to influence the news, to avoid embarrassing publicity, and to maximize sympathetic public opinion and government policies. Now they own most of the news media that they wish to influence.

**Table 2** Motion Pictures

The motion picture industry has always been volatile in its corporate convolutions, but through it all the major studios, in one incarnation or another, have remained dominant. A welcome development has been the growth of independent producers with a parallel increase in films of more than routine quality and interest. But the independents most often work through the major studios and other associated agencies, with the result that though the top studios differ in ranking from year to year, depending on how their films do at the box office, the major companies are still familiar names.

In 1985, in terms of box-office grosses for their films, there were four firms with the most business.

- Warner Communications (Warner Brothers)
- Gulf + Western (Paramount Pictures)
- Universal-MCA
- Coca-Cola (Columbia Pictures)

**Table 3** Newspapers

The 15 corporations that dominate the daily newspaper industry have all become larger in the last five years. The largest company, Gannett, increased from 88 papers to 93, its total circulation rose from 3,751,000 to 6,101,000. Though in those five years total national circulation for all 1,676 papers has risen slightly from 61 million to 62.8 million, the number of dominant corporations has shrunk from 20 to 15, and the number of daily papers in the country continued to diminish.

The 15 at the end of 1986, in order of their total daily circulation were:

- Gannett Company, *USA Today* and 92 other dailies
- Knight-Ridder, Inc., *Philadelphia Inquirer, Miami Herald* and others
- Newhouse newspapers, *Staten Island Advance, Portland Oregonian,* and other papers (Newhouse, a private firm, also owns Conde Nast magazines and Random House book publishing)
- Times Mirror, *Los Angeles Times* and others
- Tribune Company, *Chicago Tribune, New York Daily News,* and others
- Dow Jones & Company, *Wall Street Journal* and Ottoway newspapers
- New York Times, *New York Times* and others
- Scripps Howard, *Pittsburgh Press* and others
- Thomson, 77 dailies
- Cox, *Atlanta Journal* and others
- News America (Murdoch), *New York Post* and others
- Hearst, *San Francisco Examiner* and others
- Capital Cities/ABC, *Ft. Worth Star-Telegram* and others
- Freedom Newspapers, *Santa Ana Register* and others
- Central Newspapers, *Indianapolis Star* and others

**Table 4** Magazines

Tightening concentration was most dramatic in magazines, which from 1981 to 1986 went from 20 dominant corporations to six. The chief cause was further enlargement of Time, Inc. which, despite some failed attempts at starting new magazines, acquired other magazine groups to give it 40 percent of all U.S. magazine revenues.

The six dominant corporations, in order of annual revenues, are:

- Time, Inc., *Time, People, Sports Illustrated, Fortune,* and others
- Newhouse, *New Yorker, Glamour, Vogue,* and others
- McGraw-Hill, *Business Week, Byte,* and others
- Triangle, *TV Guide, Seventeen,* and others
- Hearst, *Good Housekeeping, Cosmopolitan,* and others
- International Thomson, *Medical Economics* and others

**Table 5** Book Publishing

Book publishing, less profitable than newspapers and broadcasting, and less driven by the commanding force of mass advertising on which newspapers, magazines, and broadcasting depend, is still highly concentrated, given the large number of individual publishers. The 2,500 companies that issue one or more books a year are dominated in revenues by 10 corporations that grossed more than half of the almost $10 billion in book revenues in 1985.

In books, as in other media, there is a growing presence of corporations that dominate in other media. Of the 10 dominant firms in publishing, five are in other media where they also are among companies with half or more of the business. The other five are highly active in other fields but are not top leaders.

The ten companies are:

- Gulf + Western (Simon & Schuster, Ginn & Company, and others)
- Time-Life Books (Little Brown, Scott, Foresman, and others)
- Bertelsman, A.G. (Doubleday, Bantam books, and others)
- Reader's Digest Association (Condensed books and others)
- McGraw-Hill (Standard & Poor's and others)
- Macmillan (Macmillan, Scribners, and others)
- Harcourt Brace Jovanovich (former CBS publishing group and others)
- Newhouse (Advance Publications, Random House, and others)
- Encyclopedia Britannica (G & C Merriam and others)
- International Thomson (South-Western and others)

**Table 6** Television

The three networks—Capital Cities/ABC, CBS, NBC—despite mergers, attempted takeovers, extreme corporate turbulence, and declining prime-time viewing, still dominate the field. Cable and home ownership of VCRs has grown, but the three networks still have three-quarters of the prime time market.

Powerful as the networks have always been, they, too, felt the forces of merger and consolidation. Right-wing ideologues, led by Senator Jesse Helms, attempted to take over CBS; they failed, and a newcomer to network television, Ted Turner, made a largely paper attack that also failed. Though CBS fought off the hostile takeovers, the financial battle led to heavy debt and an internal power struggle. The result was draconian cost-cutting, decimation of staffs in every network and their wholly owned stations, including CBS documentary and news operations, which for decades had been the best in broadcasting.

Capital Cities/ABC and NBC also went through drastic cost-cutting and managerial changes in an attempt to increase profits. ABC was bought by Capital Cities, a rich but undistinguished newspaper chain. General Electric, the tenth largest corporation and a major defense contractor, bought RCA, owner of the National Broadcasting Company (NBC). NBC's purchase by General Electric was the latest acquisition of a major news medium by a global corporation that has always had highly political overtones. The purchase price was also a reminder of the escalation of financial stakes in the media. In 1979 when Gannett Company bought Combined Communication Corporation (billboards, newspapers, and broadcasting) it was the largest amount of money ever involved in a media acquisition at that time—$340 million. Seven years later General Electric bought RCA for $6.3 billion.

# Media Violence: Hazardous to Our Health

*William F. Fore*

Of all the people in industrialized nations, Americans are the most prone to violence. Between 1963 and 1973, when the war in Vietnam took 46,212 lives, firearms in America killed 84,644 civilians. In the past 50 years the per capita rape rate in the United States has increased by 700 per cent. During the past 30 years our per capita homicide rate has almost doubled. In 1980 there were eight reported handgun murders in England and 10,012 in the United States (Jervis Anderson, "An Extraordinary People," *New Yorker,* November 12, 1984], p. 128). And the U.S. Bureau of the Census reported that between 1974 and 1983, the number of aggravated assaults has increased by 6 per cent, forcible rape by 26 per cent, robbery by 2 per cent and child abuse by 48 per cent (*Statistical Abstract of the United States 1985,* pp. 166, 172, 183).

For years people have wondered whether the amount of violence portrayed on American movie and TV screens has any correlation with the growing violence in our streets and homes. For 20 years, the evidence has been slowly accumulating. Now the verdict is as clear as the evidence that links smoking to cancer: Violence in media *is* causing violence in the society.

As early as the 1950s Congress held hearings on the effects of television. When senators expressed concern over television's role in increasing juvenile delinquency and crime, industry representatives immediately promised to reduce violence (while denying any evidence of harmful effects). Yet during that same period—in the mid-50s to mid-60s—television programming shifted noticeably toward action-adventure formats, and TV violence increased markedly.

As programming became more violent, research became more decisive. The National Commission on the Causes and Prevention of Violence, headed by Milton S. Eisenhower, focused on the relationship between violence and television in 1969 and concluded that "violence on television encourages violent forms of behavior and fosters moral and social values about violence in daily life which are unacceptable in a civilized society."

Noting that advertisers were spending $2 billion each year in the belief that television does influence human behavior, the commission declared, "Television entertainment based on violence may be effective merchandising, but it is an appalling way to serve the 'public interest, convenience and necessity.'"

---

Three years later, U.S. Surgeon General Jesse Steinfeld testified at a Senate hearing that a study, ordered by Congress, had unearthed "sufficient data" to establish a causal relationship between watching television violence and aggressive behavior. "Broadcasters should be put on notice," he said, "that television violence, indeed, does have an adverse effect on certain members of our society" (*Broadcasting,* March 27, 1972, p. 25).

The broadcasting industry, however, resisted the conclusions of both studies, and research by George Gerbner, dean of the University of Pennsylvania's Annenberg School of Communication, shows that the level of violence on television during the '70s did not change significantly.

The broadcasting industry challenged Gerbner's violence profile. Writing in the *Journal of Broadcasting,* David M. Blank contended that Gerbner's study defined violence too broadly by including cartoons and slapstick violence and that it counted some single acts of violence as multiple (Summer 1977, pp. 273–79). The Annenberg School countered in the same issue of the journal that comic content (such as cartoons) is a highly effective form of conveying serious lessons, and that when a new person or agent enters a scene, a "single" violent episode becomes "multiple" (pp. 280–86).

Broadcasters continued to insist in the face of such evidence that the research was still inconclusive. Gene Mater, a CBS spokesperson, told a congressional hearing that "our figures, our studies, and lots of other studies [show] that there is no unanimity." Mr. Mater cautioned against making television a scapegoat when seeking solutions to the problem of violence. He argued that "with this single focus we ignore many of the root causes of societal ills," thus neglecting elements other than media that influence our lives: the home, school, church and peer groups.

In a memorandum, "Research on Television Violence: The Fact of Dissent," prepared for the hearings, CBS quoted Eli Rubenstein, who had been vice-chairman of the original surgeon general's report, as saying that "opinions are more sharply divided than they were [in 1969]. Paradoxically, the hundreds of studies done in the past decade have apparently served to support diametrically opposing conclusions" (p. 50).

But research continued, and in May 1982 the National Institute for Mental Health released the findings of a ten-year followup on the surgeon general's study, "Television and Behavior," conducted by David Pearl. "After ten more years of research," the report said, "the consensus among most of the research community is that violence on television does lead to aggressive behavior by children and teenagers who watch the programs."

The report noted that "not all children become aggressive, of course," but that "the correlations between violence and aggression are positive," indeed as strong as "any other variable behavior that has been measured." Conversely, the study found that "children can learn to be altruistic, friendly and self-controlled by looking at television programs depicting such behavior patterns."

Earlier this year Pearl released another report in which he maintained that the NIMH report demonstrated that television has four effects on violent behavior: direct imitation of observed violence; "triggering" of violence that otherwise might be inhibited; desensitization to the occurrence of violence; and viewer fearfulness. "Consider the situation if even only one out of a thousand viewing children or youth were effected (there may well be a higher rate)," Dr. Pearl wrote. "Consider also the cumulative effects for viewers who watch such programs throughout the year. Even if only a small number of antisocial incidents were precipitated in any community, these often may be sufficient to be disruptive and to impair the quality of life for citizens of that community" (p. 6).

After completing the most thorough and most conclusive overview of research on television violence to date, George Comstock—who, only four years earlier, was quoted by the broadcasting industry as saying that the evidence was not yet conclusive—declared that "a very large majority of studies report a positive association between exposure to media violence and aggressiveness" ("Media Influences on Aggression," in A. Goldstein (editor), *Prevention and Control of Aggression* [Pergamon, 1983]).

Despite these decisive conclusions, the level of violence does not appear to be diminishing. Dean Gerbner's Violence Profile, which has traced television's performance annually since 1966, indicated that in the 1982–83 season, violence on television had not diminished but was approximately at its 17-year average. However, violence in children's weekend programs reached a record *high,* with a rate of 30.3 violent incidents per hour against a 17-year average of 20. In a paper prepared for the National Council of Churches of Christ, Gerbner said:

> For the past 17 years, at least, our children grew up and we all lived with a steady diet of about 16 entertaining acts of violence (2 of them lethal) in prime time alone every night, and probably dozens if not hundreds more for our children every weekend. We have been immersed in a tide of violent representations that is historically unprecedented and shows no real sign of receding ["Gratuitous Violence and Exploitative Sex: What Are the Lessons?," pp. 2–3].

Dr. Gerbner went on to explain television's role in creating a "mean and violent world" in the minds of many viewers, particularly heavy viewers:

> Symbolic violence . . . is a show of force and demonstration of power. It is the quickest and most dramatic demonstration of who can get away with what against whom. . . .
>
> Violence as a scenario of social relationships reflects the structure of power in society and tends to cultivate acceptance of that structure. . . . It is clear that women, young and old people, and some minorities rank as the most vulnerable to victimization on television. . . .
>
> Most heavy viewers in every education, age, income, sex, newspaper reading and neighborhood category express a greater sense of insecurity and apprehension than do light viewers. . . . Fearful people are most dependent, more easily manipulated and controlled. . . . They may accept and even welcome repression if it promises to relieve their insecurities. That is the deeper problem of violence-laden television [pp. 5–6].

Violence on television—as well as on cable, in movies and on videocassettes—is lowering our quality of life. Whether or not we personally watch the excessive amounts of TV violence, enough people *do* see the violence, which, in the end, causes more crime, more abuse, more injuries and more deaths in our society.

Of course, television can—and never should—be "sanitized" to the point that it contains no violence at all. Such a depiction of life would be dishonest in a different way. The problem is gratuitous and excessive violence—an identifiable phenomenon that we created and that, if we wish, we can correct.

Some observers have said that we are faced with pollution of our mental environment that is just as dangerous as pollution of our physical environment. But how does a free society combat mental pollution? The First Amendment guarantees each of us the freedom to speak whatever we wish, since one person's truth is another person's heresy. The media industries hide behind this freedom, to the injury of us all. On the other end of the spectrum lurk those True Believers who, knowing the truth, are anxious to impose it on us by censoring all other perspectives. Somewhere between these two poles there must be a middle way which enables society to curb harmful violence without curbing freedom of speech.

Before we can do anything to confront the problem of violence in the media, I suspect that we must first decide what kind of society we really want. At that point the solution will become more apparent. In the meantime, at least we now know the facts about the effects of violence in the media, and our ignorance can no longer be blissful—or even a valid excuse for inaction.

# Babes in the Marketplace: The Toy Industry Takes Over Saturday Morning Cartoons

*Susan Pearson*

First there was Strawberry Shortcake, then came a family of squeezable bears known as Care Bears, and finally there was He-Man—the strongest man in the universe.

Together these trademarked characters and their manufacturers have transformed Saturday morning cartoons and children's after-school programs into a sales bazaar. Once the most regulated of television's time slots, children's television has been cut wide open by the Reagan administration and the toy industry has moved in to take advantage of the windfall.

Increasingly, major toy companies are joining forces with production houses and television stations to give their latest toys starring roles in television series. Eight of the 20 top selling toys for June, 1987, are toy lines which were developed simultaneously with or prior to their corresponding television specials or series. They include G.I. Joe, Alf, Transformers, Cabbage Patch Kids, Silverhawks and Pound Puppies.

These shows, a more subtle marketing technique than the traditional one-minute commercial, are prompting a new wave of prime time children's shows and increasing the competition in the already competitive $12.5 billion toy industry.

At first glance this type of programming appears relatively harmless; the animated "Real American Heroes" extol the virtues of good triumphing over evil and the "Cabbage Patch Kids" promote wholesome, if syrupy, behavior.

But the shows, called program-length commercials by their detractors, have raised the ire of both parents and those concerned with the quality of children's television.

It is like replacing all the children's books in public libraries with toy catalogs, says Peggy Charren, president of Action for Children's Television (ACT).

"This is a major abuse of the public interest standard," says Dr. William Dietz, a pediatrician at the New England Medical Center and an associate of the American Academy of Pediatrics. "Television for children, more than [for] anybody else, is designed to market products and not enrich their lives."

Children's rights groups, including ACT, the American Academy of Pediatrics and the National Coalition for Television Violence, are heading up the opposition.

---

Susan Pearson, "Babes in the Marketplace: The Toy Industry Takes Over Saturday Morning Cartoons." This article is reprinted from the *Multinational Monitor* 8 (September 1987), pp. 18–20. *Multinational Monitor* is a monthly newsmagazine published by Essential Information, Inc. P.O. Box 19405 Washington, D.C. 20036. $22 individual.

Together, they have launched a campaign to protect small children from the barrage of commercialized programming brought about by broadcasting deregulation.

"This country's broadcasters and the Federal Communications Commission (FCC) should be ashamed of themselves for exploiting children in this fashion," said Charren, in testimony before a congressional hearing on children's programming in July.

But the toy industry maintains that the line between ads and programs is clear, or at least as clear as it ever was. After all, Mickey Mouse products were derived from the "Mickey Mouse Club." The industry claims that its latest foray into the world of children's television is an attempt at diversifying not advertising. Says Jim Pisors of Tonka Toys, "We are moving into the entertainment industry."

Although Jodi Levin of the Toy Manufacturers Association says basing shows on toys "is a very effective marketing technique," spokespeople from Mattel and Tonka deny any connection between a manufacturer's profits and the popularity of "kidvid," as children's programming is often called.

Critics say no matter what they are called, the bottom line is the same. "A commercial is a production designed to sell," says Dr. Dietz. "A program about a toy is designed to sell the toy and [is] therefore a commercial."

Indeed, in their own trade publications, toy manufacturers tout the important connections between marketing the toy and marketing the program. An ad in *Toy & Hobby World* for Pound Puppies by Tonka Toys reads "Every one irresistible. And every one backed by major promotions, a Saturday morning network series and the premiere of a major motion picture." Tonka doesn't stop here. Another ad for Maple Town toys reads "To show our commitment, we're giving it unprecedented support, including its own 65-part syndicated series and a blockbuster national promotion campaign."

Another ad in *Toy & Hobby* about Mattel's He-Man sums it all up: "In fact, what you're about to see in 1987 is going to make He-Man the man of the hour. And Masters of the Universe the brand to watch."

The ad continues "And our daily television show will keep He-Man running strong." In summary: "It's all a simple show business formula. You create a fabulous cast of characters starring 'the most powerful man in the universe,' a timeless story of good versus evil, support them with a strong marketing program, and you don't have to be on Broadway to know this 'show' is a hit."

Although toy manufacturers say the difference between shows designated as legitimate entertainment and those designated as program-length commercials is subtle, critics say when advertising or marketing expenditures include provisions for television programs, the shows are being designed to sell toys. Some of the most familiar examples of these connections include "G.I. Joe: A Real American Hero" produced by Sunbow Productions, a wholly-owned subsidiary of Hasbro's ad agency, Griffin Bacal, and "Captain Power and the Soldiers of the Future" distributed by Mattel Television Syndication, which is owned by Mattel Corporation.

Freda Thyden of the FCC defends the move by the Commission to deregulate children's television to allow program-length commercials, on the grounds that the distinction between shows where the toy is the basis for the show and programs where the show spurs the development of toys is too arbitrary.

"It's no different if the show is entertaining to the child," she says. "If the show is entertaining the Commission is not concerned [if the toy came first or second]."

In true Reaganese, Thyden says the marketplace will have to determine "the set up of children's programming." Thyden says parents concerned about the over-commercialization of children's programming should be mini-regulators. "Remove the TV from your house or keep on top of your kids," she advises.

The FCC's prescription for dealing with interactive toys, an extension of program-length commercials, is less bold. Interactive toys are held by the viewer and a "game" is played in conjunction with a designated segment of a program. The premise of the interactive toy is similar to a video game; the significant difference is that when these high-priced toys are pointed at the television screen they in essence use the airwaves to score points.

So far, although several toy companies are moving to market such shows, interactive toys have not received the outright approval that regular program-length commercials have received from the FCC.

Both Mattel and World Events, which have interactive children's shows set to make their U.S. debut this fall, plan to market their interactive products and shows to a worldwide market. "Satellite and cable," says Charren, "have made this an international problem."

Mattel will market "Captain Power and the Soldier of the Future" mainly to Japan and Western Europe. While World Events' "Saber Rider and the Star Sheriffs" will be marketed to at least 20 Third World countries. And Susan Kalishman of World Events said they sell the show to Hong Kong, Malaysia, Brunei, Taiwan, Thailand, Philippines, Turkey, Botswana, and in Central and South American countries. Producers acknowledge, of course, that orders for the show's high-priced interactive toys may be low in some countries.

Until Reagan came to power, children's television, though containing its bothersome share of one-minute commercials, was considered somewhat sheltered from the ad man's machinations. In 1969, in a landmark case on children's television, the sanctity of Saturday morning fare seemed assured. A complaint was filed against ABC for airing the infamous "Hot Wheels" program based on Mattel's toy line. As the first example of a program based on a toy, the "Hot Wheels" show was designated by the FCC as a 30-minute commercial and not a children's program; the ruling reinforced the public interest responsibility of broadcasters and dashed the hopes of those who saw "Hot Wheels" as the wave of the future.

In 1974 the FCC's "Children's Television Policy Statement and Report" designated children as a special audience with programming needs different from adults. Guidelines for commercial time were also established. During prime-time slots 9.5 minutes of commercial time was permitted and non-prime time slots were allowed a maximum of 12 minutes of commercial time. Broadcasters were required to show a clear separation between program content and commercial messages. Television for the most vulnerable segment of society was to teach counting, the alphabet, and other basic skills, but not become the vehicle for product promotion.

Then in 1980, Ronald Reagan was elected. He appointed Mark Fowler to head the FCC and a furious deregulation campaign began. Fowler did not support the "Hot Wheels" ruling and toy companies responded by testing the waters with program-length commercials.

In 1984, the FCC eliminated commercial guidelines for children's television, ending the last barriers to program-length commercials. "We will rescind our policy banning program length commercials," stated the report. "We believe that the existing regulatory scheme is no longer necessary to assure operation in the public interest."

Since the 1984 report did not mention children's television, the National Association of Broadcasters (NAB) asked for clarification and ACT asked for a reconsideration. The FCC denied ACT's request but responded to the NAB's request for clarification by stating that:

"Elimination of the policy is consistent with [the] Commission's general de-emphasis regarding quantitative guidelines engendered in the [1984] Report and Order. Moreover, the Commission has consistently noted the importance of advertising as a support mechanism for the presentation of children's programming."

A dissenting member of the FCC staff says confidentially that "as long as [toy manufacturers and producers of children's television shows] can make a claim with a straight face that they put out the show for the purpose of entertainment or information and not for exploitation [or] profit-making," the programs can be broadcast as shows and not advertisements.

All hope is not lost though. A surprising development in the Reagan era occurred on June 26, 1987, when a U.S. Court of Appeals acted on an ACT lawsuit and ordered the FCC to review its 1984 decision. "[W]ithout explanation the Commission has suddenly embraced an unthinkable bureaucratic conclusion that the market did in fact operate to restrain the commercial content of children's television," noted the decision. The court then mandated the Commission to explain its sudden change of heart.

If the FCC reinstates commercial limits, a regeneration of children's television may be in sight, but toy companies say they aren't worried about the possibility of having to change marketing strategies in mid-stream. With Reagan at the helm, they say, shows based on toys are a safe bet.

## Addendum: Profits in Toyland

The three basic methods that are used to get shows on the air, says Jodi Levin of the Toy Manufacturers Association, are:

### Profit-Sharing

The most controversial arrangement is profit-sharing. Under this arrangement the toy company offers a television station that airs its show a cut in the profits from licensed products based on characters in the show. The most widely publicized case of profit sharing was when Telepictures offered to share in the profits of licensing agreements from ThunderCats to independent stations in 1983. Although some stations considered the arrangement unethical, approximately 45 agreed to the terms.

According to Freda Thyden of the Federal Communications Commission, profit-sharing is a "mechanism to get more kidvid on TV." It is a "way to encourage broadcasters to take a chance on a new program," she says.

There have been very few cases of direct profit-sharing documented, many agreements allow both stations and toy companies to profit from hit shows that spur toy sales. ABC/Capital Cities developed a special called "The Kingdom Chums" and put the Adrienne Weiss Corporation on retainer to create and license products based on the characters of the show. But Adrienne Weiss of Adrienne Weiss Corporation said it technically wasn't profit-sharing since it wasn't a toy company soliciting a broadcaster but a broadcaster soliciting a company to license products. "Profits are a very specific word in the industry," she said.

## Barter Agreements

Another way these shows are introduced is by arranging bartering time with stations. A station receives a show free of charge and the distributor, syndicator or toy company receives free advertising time to sell or to use. Some toy companies won't advertise the product portrayed in the program in commercial spots within the program because of ethical considerations. John Weems, vice president of Mattel Entertainment, says it "is a corporate policy that they don't advertise the same character toys that are in a show or adjacent to it." According to Edmund Rosenthal of *Television/Radio Age,* in 1986 $80 million of advertising money was at stake for those who sold time in the children's television bartering business.

## Pay and Play

A station can also pay for the show and then sell advertising time during the show. Sometimes the toy company is willing to pay a production house to produce the show and distribute it. Then production or distribution houses can sell the show.

# Chapter 10
# CRIME AND JUSTICE

## Rethinking Criminal Violence

*Elliott Currie*

This . . . is about why there is so much crime in America and what we can do about it. No one living in a major American city needs much convincing that despite more than a decade of ever-"tougher" policies against crime, the United States remains wracked by violence and fear. Criminal violence is woven deeply into our social fabric—a brutal and appalling affront to any reasonable conception of civilized social life.

In recent months, these incidents took place in the United States: In Illinois, armed marauders attacked travelers on an interstate highway, robbing the occupants of two cars and killing a twelve-year-old boy. In Florida, a passing motorist's intervention barely saved a young woman from attack by a crowd of nearly a hundred men. In New York, gangs of youths robbed and beat participants in a charity walkathon in Central Park. In Fort Lauderdale, Florida, a bandit held up an entire church congregation during an evening service. Not far away, near Pompano Beach, two intrepid men broke *into* a prison and robbed two inmates. A United States senator and his companion, on their way to dinner with the mayor of New York, were mugged by two men just down the street from the mayor's mansion. In Los Angeles, eleven people died in a single weekend in episodes of youth-gang violence, while the home of the chief of the Los Angeles Police Department was burglarized—twice.

The public response to criminal violence has become correspondingly bitter and even desperate. Three-fifths of the American public expressed their support for a self-styled vigilante who shot down four young black men after they asked him for five dollars in a New York subway; respected commentators urge people living in cities to "adopt the tough attitudes of an embattled population."

To live in the urban United States in the 1980s is to feel that the elementary bonds of society are badly frayed. The sense of social disintegration is so pervasive that it is easy to forget that things are not the same elsewhere. Violence on the American level comes to seem like a fact of life, an inevitable feature of modern society. It is not. Most of us are aware that we are worse off, in this respect, than other advanced countries. How *much* worse, however, is truly startling.

---

Criminal statistics are notoriously tricky, and comparisons of one country's statistics with another's even more so. But the differences in national crime rates—at least for serious crimes of violence, which we rightly fear the most—are large enough to transcend the limitations of the data. In recent years, Americans have faced roughly seven to ten times the risk of death by homicide as the residents of most European countries and Japan. Our closest European competitor in homicide rates is Finland, and we murder one another at more than three times the rate the Finns do.

These differences are sometimes explained as the result of America's "frontier" ethos or its abundance of firearms. Both of these are important, but neither even begins to explain the dimensions of these international differences. With similar frontier traditions, Australia and Canada have murder rates that are, respectively, less than a fourth and less than a third of ours. Though their numbers are roughly the same, Californians are murdered almost six times as often as Canadians. Nor does this simply reflect the relative ease with which Americans can obtain handguns: more Californians are killed with knives alone than Canadians are by *all* means put together. And Canada ranks fairly high, internationally, in homicide rates.

What holds for homicide also holds for other serious crimes of violence. Here the comparisons are more chancy, because of greater problems of definition and measurement. But careful research reveals that Americans are more than three times as likely to be raped than West Germans, and six times as likely to be robbed. These rates were derived from police statistics, which are known to be subject to strong biases. But similar results come from "victimization" studies, which calculate crime rates by asking people whether, and how often, they have been the victims of crime.

In the first English study of this kind, the British Home Office (using a sample of eleven thousand respondents) estimated that the British robbery rate in 1981 was about twenty for every ten thousand people over age sixteen in 1981. In the same year, a comparable American survey by the Bureau of Justice Statistics estimated a robbery rate nearly four times higher. The British study turned up not one rape and only a single attempted rape: the American survey estimated an overall rape rate of about ten per ten thousand (three completed, seven attempted). And Britain is by no means one of the most tranquil of European countries: rates of serious criminal violence in Denmark, Norway, Switzerland, and the Netherlands are lower still.

In the severity of its crime rates, the United States more closely resembles some of the most volatile countries of the Third World than other developed Western societies; and we won't begin to understand the problem of criminal violence in the United States without taking that stark difference as our point of departure. Its consequences are enormous. If we were blessed with the moderately low homicide rate of Sweden, we would suffer well under three thousand homicide deaths a year, thereby saving close to sixteen thousand American lives—nearly three times as many as were lost in battle annually, on average, during the height of the Vietnam War.

The magnitude of the contrast between the United States and most other developed societies is often ignored as we scrutinize the fluctuations in our own crime rates from year to year. We watch the state of the public safety, like that of the economy, with a kind of desperate hopefulness. Just as the economy has "recovered'' several times in recent years, so we have periodically ''turned the corner on crime.'' And indeed, by the mid-1980s, the level of violent crime had fallen off from the disastrous peak it had reached at the start of the decade. That respite was certainly welcome; but it should not obscure the more troubling general upward trend since the sixties. From 1969 through 1983, the rate of violent crime—as measured by police reports—rose nationwide by 61 percent. Rape went up 82 percent, robbery 44 percent, and homicide 14 percent (the first two figures are almost certainly inflated because of changes in reporting, the third probably not). Measured this way, the more recent declines have only returned us to the already horrendous levels of the late 1970s, just before we suffered one of the sharpest *increases* in criminal violence in American history. Still more disturbingly, reported rapes and aggravated assaults *rose* again in 1984—at the fastest pace since 1980. Criminal victimization surveys offer a somewhat different but scarcely more encouraging picture, indicating virtually no change in crimes of violence for the past decade, with a slight decline in many violent crimes in 1983—but a slight *rise* in others in 1984.

The recent dip in crime, moreover, has been ominously uneven. Between 1982 and 1983, the murder rate in the economically depressed states of Illinois and Michigan rose by 10 percent; reported rapes shot up by 20 percent in Michigan and 27 percent in Wisconsin. Detroit's murder rate jumped 17 percent from 1981 to 1983; that of East St. Louis, Illinois, by an astonishing 96 percent. Drug-related gang wars helped boost the homicide rate in Oakland, California, by 17 percent between 1983 and 1984. The national crime rate, in short, may have improved—but the situation in some of America's inner cities was worsening.

What makes all this so troubling is that our high crime rates have resisted the most extraordinary efforts to reduce them. Since 1973, we have more than doubled the national incarceration rate—the proportion of the population locked up in state and federal prisons and in local jails. By 1983, the prison inmates alone would have filled a city the size of Atlanta, Georgia; including the inmates of local jails (a number that jumped by more than a *third* between 1978 and 1982 alone) would have swollen the ''city'' to the size of Washington, D.C. And this number doesn't include those confined in juvenile detention facilities, military prisons, and psychiatric facilities for the criminally insane.

Nor is this all. We have not only put a record number of offenders behind bars; we have also drastically changed our daily behavior and escalated the level of social resources we devote to defending ourselves against crime. In 1969, the National Commission on the Causes and Prevention of Violence made a gloomy prediction of what urban life would be like if America did not take immediate and fundamental measures to attack the root causes of crime. Central business districts would be surrounded by zones of ''accelerated deterioration,'' largely deserted at night except for police patrols. The affluent would huddle together in what the commission called ''fortified cells,'' high-rise apartment houses and residential compounds protected by increasingly elaborate security devices and private guards. Homes would be ''fortified by an array of devices from window grilles to electronic surveillance equipment,'' and the affluent would speed from these fortified homes to their fortified offices along heavily patrolled expressways that the commission, in a revealingly military euphemism called "sanitized corridors." People with business in the central cities would require access to indoor garages or valet parking; schools and other public facilities would be patrolled by armed guards. The ghetto slums would be "places of terror" that might be out of police control altogether after dark.

The commission, writing in a more hopeful time, found this prospect of a society in which the haves were forced to defend themselves ever more vigilantly against the have-nots foreign to the American experience and abhorrent to American values. Yet what is striking is that, in the eighties, much of the commission's indignant vision seems almost old-hat. Most of the changes they feared have taken place, and though their scenario doesn't accurately describe *every* American city, it does describe many. Virtually every big-city police department now possesses a sophisticated armory—from the ubiquitous police helicopter to the armored personnel carrier recently acquired by the Los Angeles police. More generally, we have changed the way we live and go about our daily business in ways that would have seemed appalling and unacceptable in the sunnier sixties. In 1984, a New York Appellate Court justice, speaking for an association of judges calling for still more severe prison sentences in that state, declared that the climate of fear suffusing New York "would have been unthinkable" a generation before. "If then someone had said that in 1984 hundreds of thousands of apartment windows in New York City would be covered with metal gates," said Justice Francis T. Murphy, Jr., "and that private security guards would patrol the lobbies, hallways, and rooftops of apartment buildings, we would have thought him insane." Like the unprecedented increase in incarceration, this new defensiveness might have been expected to do something substantial about the crime rate. With the possible exception of declines in burglary resulting from more elaborate "hardware," it did not.

Our devastating levels of criminal violence, moreover, have also proved to be remarkably resistant to the effects of a benign demographic change. The frightening rise in violent crime in the late 1970s and early 1980s came just when the most volatile segment of the population—young adult and teenaged men—was growing smaller relative to the population as a whole. Between 1975 and 1982, the proportion of young men aged fourteen to twenty-one in the population fell by 10 percent. Other things being equal, as many criminologists argued, this should have brought down the crime rate. But other things weren't equal, for though the decline in the youth population may have kept the crime rate lower than it would have been otherwise, other forces were clearly keeping it up.

What progress we've made against our uniquely high crime rate seems disturbingly small given our massive attempts to control it. The disparity between effort and results tells us that something is clearly wrong with the way we have approached the problem of violent crime in America, and few are happy with the results. But there is no consensus on how we might do better.

To be sure, there is no lack of prescriptions, ranging from the merely silly to the bizarre and the brutal. Within the last few years, some established scholars have solemnly proposed that we "restore" regular corporal punishment in the schools and home; others, that we revive the practice of sending criminals to penal colonies, perhaps on distant islands. Some have urged that we devise elaborate physiological tests to weed out those children who, on the basis of irregular encephalograms or insufficiently sweaty palms, seem likely to be the robbers and killers of the future. Others wistfully hope for a revival of the movements of temperance and "moral uplift" of the nineteenth century. Many of these proposals seem barely serious; some are a little frightening. All of them reflect a sense of social and intellectual desperation.

More often, our social policies toward crime and punishment have simply lost a sense of direction or definable vision. In a 1981 cover story, *Newsweek* deplored what it described as an "epidemic" of violent crime, but also declared that we were apparently helpless to deal with it. We had lost, the magazine lamented, "the old optimism proclaiming that we know what the problems are and that we have the solutions at hand." For the indefinite future, we would have to learn not to "expect too much." In the same year, the Reagan administration's Task Force on Violent Crime, departing sharply from a long line of more ambitious commissions, refused even to take on the task of investigating the causes of crime in America, on the ground that intervention at that level wasn't the government's job. "We are not convinced," they wrote, "that a government, by the invention of new programs or the management of existing institutions, can by itself recreate those familial and neighborhood conditions, those social opportunities, and those personal values that in all likelihood are the prerequisites of tranquil communities." The passivity that began to infect scholarly thinking about crime during the seventies had become enshrined as a fundamental principle of government policy.

How did we arrive at this impasse?

As with many other issues of social policy in the eighties, there is a pervasive sense that older ways of thinking about crime have lost their usefulness and credibility; but no convincing alternatives have come forward to take their place. It is painfully apparent that the decade-long conservative experiment in crime control has failed to live up to its promises. That experiment, launched with high hopes and much self-righteous certainty, was based on the alluringly simple premise that crime was pervasive in the United States because we were too lenient with criminals; in the economic jargon fashionable during the seventies, the "costs" of crime had fallen too low. The reverse side of the argument was that other ways of dealing with crime—through "rehabilitating" offenders or improving social conditions—at best didn't work and at worst had made the streets more dangerous. But the policies that resulted from these premises have left us with both the world's highest rate of incarceration for "street" crimes *and* the highest levels of criminal violence outside of some developing countries. We have created an overstuffed and volatile penal system of overwhelming barbarity, yet we endure levels of violence significantly higher than in the more "permissive" sixties.

To be sure, it is likely that some part of the recent dip in the crime rate is a result of the huge increases in incarceration in the past several years; after all, it would be remarkable if they had had *no* effect on crime. But the hard fact is that violent crime is worse in America today than before the "prison boom" of the seventies and eighties began, and indeed was highest just when our rate of incarceration was increasing the fastest. At best, very little has been accomplished, at great social cost. To borrow a medical analogy, it's plausible to argue that a series of drastic and unpleasant treatments has relieved some of the symptoms of the disease; it is not plausible to argue that the patient is well, or even demonstrably recovering. And as we shall see, there is little ground for hope that the same strategies can accomplish much more in the future, short of draconian measures on a scale that would transform our criminal-justice system—and American society as a whole—beyond recognition.

It could, of course, be argued that this strategy *would* have worked, if it had only gone far enough—but that it was undermined by the leniency and obstinacy of officials and the public, especially the unwillingness of legislators to vote for more prisons. If the streets are still unsafe despite the swelling of the prisons, blame it on the failure to build enough new prison cells and the consequent vacillation of judges hesitant to pack still more criminals into the time-bombs that our prisons have mainly become. In 1984, for example, the Federation of New York Judges declared that the streets had become "lawless marches of robbers, rapists, and felons of every kind," and called for more prisons, on the ground that "swift and severe punishment is the only defense against predators." Appellate Justice Murphy even went so far as to argue that without a greater investment in punishment "we will live in the sickly twilight of a soulless people too weak to drive predators out of their own house." Justice Murphy and his colleagues were apparently unfazed by the fact that criminals had "taken the city" despite the doubling of New York's incarceration rate during the previous decade.

So proponents of this "get-even-tougher" approach are confronted with a formidable job of persuasion. It is difficult to think of any social experiment in recent years whose central ideas have been so thoroughly and consistently carried out. The number of people we have put behind bars, for ever-longer terms, is unprecedented in American history. And unlike most such experiments, which are usually undertaken with minimal funding and on a limited scale, this one has been both massively financed and carried out on a grand scale in nearly every state of the union. If it has failed to work in the way its promoters expected, they have fewer excuses than most applied social theorists.

We have become a country in which it is possible to be sentenced to a year behind bars for stealing six dollars' worth of meat from a supermarket, but we are still by far the most dangerous society in the developed world. That paradox has deeply undercut the credibility of the conservative strategy of crime control in the eighties. No one today seriously disagrees that we need a strong and effective criminal-justice system; that is no longer a matter for real debate. But that is a far cry from believing that we can rely on the prisons to solve the crime problem. Clearly, we need more creative approaches to crime—and we need them urgently.

But I do not think that the earlier perspective, which for want of a more precise term I will call "liberal criminology," can, by itself, offer a sufficiently compelling alternative. It is risky to generalize about that perspective, because it included several diverse—and not always compatible—lines of thought and practice. But there were common themes. Most liberal criminology linked crime to the pressures of social and economic inequality and deprivation, and assumed that a combination of rehabilitation for offenders, better opportunities for the disadvantaged, and a more humane, less intrusive criminal-justice system would reduce crime, if not end it. By the end of the sixties, that vision was a shambles, undermined by the apparent "paradox" of rising crime rates in the face of the Great Society's social programs, the general improvement in the American standard of living, and the reduction of unemployment. Conservatives made much of the fact that American society seemed to be becoming more dangerous just when it was also becoming both more affluent and more committed to action against poverty, inequality, and racial subordination.

That "paradox," as I'll argue in some detail in a later chapter, was highly exaggerated. And indeed, the vision of the liberal criminology of the sixties has been unfairly maligned and often misunderstood. Much of what it had to say about the roots of crime and about the potentials of the criminal-justice system remains both remarkably fresh and, more important, correct. It rested on several crucial perceptions that have stood up well under the test of time and experience. One was that crime could not be dealt with through the criminal-justice system alone, and that the system is likely to crack if we load it with that burden. Another was that if we wanted to deal with crime in America in other than marginal ways, we would have to move beyond the level of merely patching up, punishing, or quarantining individuals who had gone wrong to confront a range of deep and long-standing social and economic problems. Both of these principles fell out of fashion during the seventies, but both were right—and both must be a part of any credible analysis of crime in the future.

But the liberalism of the sixties had important limitations as well. At times, it seemed to say that crime wasn't really as much of a problem as the public naïvely thought it was—a position that won few friends outside the relatively tranquil preserves of the academic world. Most other Americans were afraid of crime, or enraged by it, and they had good reason to be. It didn't help to imply, as some liberal and radical criminologists did, that worrying overmuch about being mugged or raped was a sign of incipient racism or an authoritarian character. Likewise, it didn't help when liberals, pressed for answers to the problem of violent street crime, responded by insisting that the crimes of white-collar people and corporate executives were *also* costly and vicious. That was certainly true, but it simply sidestepped the question at hand.

More generally, liberals were often reluctant to acknowledge the depth and seriousness of the human damage that violent crime both caused and reflected. The brutality of some youth crime, for example, suggested that something was deeply wrong with the way some children were being brought up in America. But liberal criminologists sometimes argued that any concern with the family life of delinquents was an expression of middle-class bias. The ferocity of urban crime likewise underscored the need for more intensive approaches to the problems of violent offenders than the minimal efforts typically offered as "rehabilitation." But some liberal criminologists instead adopted an extreme posture of "nonintervention": the less we did with criminals, the better.

There were good reasons for this position. A great deal of abusive and inhumane treatment had been meted out under the guise of rehabilitation, much of it cloaked in high-sounding language and humane intentions. And most students of crime believed—rightly . . . —that the experience of being processed through the courts and prisons, even if it was done in the name of rehabilitation, often made criminals worse rather than better, particularly if they were young and relatively unspoiled when they first encountered the criminal-justice system.

The noninterventionist approach led to many overdue reforms designed to get less dangerous offenders out of the justice system, and especially out of closed penal institutions. But noninterventionists sometimes went too far. In particular, they were often vague about what should be done about serious crimes of violence and the more hardened or disturbed people who committed them. A hands-off attitude was justifiable when applied to juvenile runaways or marijuana smokers, but less than adequate as an approach to armed robbers or repeat rapists.

At the same time, other liberals adopted the quite different view that crime, like many other social problems, could best be attacked through the twin mechanisms of big money and high technology. There is nothing wrong with spending money to solve social problems, and I think it is naïve to believe that we can affect crime very much without spending any. But some liberal criminologists simply opted for throwing money at the criminal-justice system on the one hand and at the inner cities on the other, in a kind of scattershot approach that sometimes substituted for hard thinking.

Thus, in 1969, the National Commission on the Causes and Prevention of Violence proposed that we "double our investment" in the criminal-justice system, but it was remarkably unspecific about what the money would be spent for, and equally unclear about how that proposal fit with its several hundred pages of analysis of the roots of violence in America. For nothing in that analysis really supported the idea that the problem existed because the justice system was starved for money.

This was one illustration of a bigger problem. The liberal criminology of the sixties was often long on ameliorative rhetoric but short on more concrete ideas for social action—especially ones that were clearly linked with its theoretical understanding of the causes of crime. The President's Commission on Law Enforcement and the Administration of Justice set the rhetorical tone of the Great Society's anti-crime efforts in 1967 when it declared, in a much-quoted passage, that "warring on poverty and inadequate housing" was "warring on crime," that money for schools was money against crime, that "every effort to improve life in America's inner cities is an effort against crime." Although this was a worthy sentiment and not a bad starting-place for social policy, it was also quite vague. Would *every* effort to improve life in the inner cities be equally helpful in reducing crime? And which of the many possible measures we might use to "war" on the inner city's problems—higher welfare benefits, community economic development, summer jobs for kids—would bring the biggest payoff in the fight against crime? Like much liberal urban policy at the time, the commission's approach put most of its stock in fiscal solutions to the cities' problems. But was there really much evidence that money for public housing would by itself reduce crime? And were we so certain that the *main* problem with the urban schools was sheer lack of money—or that we knew exactly what we would spend the money *for*?

The failure of liberal criminology to follow through on some of its most important perceptions gave it an oddly disjointed character, for its programs were frequently at odds with its theory. A fundamental liberal theme, for example, was that economic inequality and stunted opportunities were fertile breeding grounds for serious crime. Yet with few exceptions, most liberal anticrime programs did not directly address those problems. Instead, they tried to equip individuals to make better use of the limited opportunities already available to them. They were designed to increase what economists call the "human capital" of high-risk people, through job training, vocational counseling, and remedial education. These programs were often worthwhile; but they fit uneasily with theories whose central point was that there were not enough jobs for all of the poor at respectable wages. Confronting the problem of creating jobs, of course, is much more difficult than funding another program to increase the "employability" of ghetto teenagers. But by avoiding that issue, liberal anticrime programs often got the not entirely undeserved reputation of being token responses to tough problems that cried out for deeper intervention.

The same confusion undermined the liberal commitment to the "rehabilitation" of offenders. That commitment was, for the most part, principled and humane, and it originated in a sense of social responsibility that was far more civilized than the glorification of punishment for its own sake that has dominated public policy in more recent years. But liberal practice failed to carry its understanding of crime to its logical conclusions—and, in the process, helped undercut the credibility of the idea of rehabilitation itself. If, as most liberal criminologists believed, crime was ultimately a *social* problem rooted in economic and racial disadvantage and the erosion of communal and familial institutions, the rehabilitation of individual offenders, even if it was successful in the short term, was sure to be overwhelmed if they were simply returned to the deprived and shattered communities from which they had come. But instead of insisting that rehabilitation couldn't work well unless it was firmly linked to larger social interventions, many liberals simply adopted the staple conservative platitude that rehabilitation didn't work. This default encouraged the sense that there were no practical alternatives to simply warehousing offenders in the prisons, and helped speed the demise of both the rehabilitative impulse and the social vision that lay behind it.

If we are to build a society that is less dangerous, less fearful, and less torn by violence, we will have to move beyond *both* perspectives—liberal and conservative. Can we do so? I think we can . . .

My approach . . . is bound to disappoint both those who believe that nothing much can be done about serious crime and those who hunger for immediate solutions. Both views are deeply embedded in the public culture in America; but both are terribly misleading. We will not eliminate criminal violence from American life overnight; but there is much we can do to reduce it. Doing so, however, will require hard choices and a serious commitment of social and economic resources. In a society traditionally drawn to the quick fix, many people, at all points on the political spectrum, want to know what will stop crime next month, and are impatient with the idea that we are in for a long haul. But the hard truth is that there are no magic buttons to push, no program waiting just around the corner to reform the courts or strengthen the police or organize the neighborhood that will make criminal violence disappear tomorrow. There are, however, steps we can take now that can begin to make a difference in the safety of our streets and homes—and to reverse the tragic waste of lives that criminal violence involves.

Many of those steps are based on evidence that has been available for years. It was often said during the seventies that we knew very little about the causes of crime. That was not true then, and it is even less true now, after several more years of research and experience. We do not know as much as we would like, but we are not groping in the dark, either. To agree that more research needs to be done is not the same as saying that we don't know enough to start.

If we know as much about crime as I think we do, why haven't we already acted on that knowledge more consistently and more constructively? Part of the answer has to do with the relative obscurity of much of the best and most serious research and writing in criminology. It is scattered through several social science disciplines whose practitioners sometimes have trouble communicating with each other, let alone with a wider audience; it is frequently buried in specialized journals and, especially in the last several years, often couched in numbing jargon and a forbiddingly arcane and mathematical style. It isn't often that anyone tries to make this material accessible or understandable beyond limited academic and professional circles. The result is that policies toward crime are often created in a near-vacuum.

Another reason for inaction is the tendency to compartmentalize social problems along bureaucratic lines. We take it for granted that it is the business of the criminal-justice system to deal with crime, but someone else's to deal with the social, economic, or familial problems that foster it. As a result, the more important causes of crime are nearly always regarded as someone else's problem. Policy-makers rarely consider how their decisions may increase the risks of criminal violence, whether the decisions involve shutting down a factory, tightening the money supply to slow the economy, eliminating jobs through technological change, or cutting off funds for family planning. All of these actions may affect the crime rate; but it is nevertheless unthinkingly assumed that crime should be exclusively the province of police, lawyers, and judges, who are rarely in a position to influence those decisions. The failure to make these necessary connections between causes and consequences stifles the development of intelligent policies to prevent criminal violence, and burdens the criminal-justice system with the impossible job of picking up the pieces after broader social policies have done their damage.

But there is another, still more important reason for our failure to come to grips with criminal violence. It is not lack of knowledge or technical prowess that keeps us from launching an honest and serious fight against crime; the obstacles are much more often ideological and political. What seem on the surface to be technical arguments about what we can and cannot do about crime often turn out, on closer inspection, to be moral or political arguments about what we should or should not do; and these in turn are rooted in larger disagreements about what sort of society we want for ourselves and our children. If we are serious about rethinking the problem of crime, we need to engage the issues on that higher level of moral and political values. It is always easier, as R. H. Tawney once observed, to "set up a new department, and appoint new officials, and invent a new name to express their resolution" to do things differently. "But unless they will take the pains," Tawney cautioned, "not only to act, but to reflect, they end by effecting nothing."

All societies suffer from predatory and brutal behavior. But not many of them, and no other advanced industrial societies (except perhaps South Africa, a revealing but not inspiring example)—suffer it to the extent we do in America. This tells us that the unusual dangerousness of American life is not simply the result of fate or of human nature, but of forces which, within broad limits, are subject to social action and control. We have the level of criminal violence we do because we have arranged our social and economic life in certain ways rather than others. The brutality and violence of American life are a signal—and a particularly compelling one—that there are profound social costs to maintaining those arrangements. But by the same token, altering them also has a price; and if we continue to tolerate the conditions that have made us the most violent of industrial societies, it is not because the problem is overwhelmingly mysterious or because we do not know what to do, but because we have decided that the benefits of changing those conditions aren't worth the costs.

Not all of those changes will be easy. To be sure, some of them are much less difficult than we have lately been led to believe. But others involve reversing institutional patterns whose origins lie far back in our history. I am not suggesting that this could be a simple task, but I hope to show that it is within our means to build a society that is less brutal, less fearful, and more cohesive. Whether we do so is up to us.

# Who's Punishing Whom?

*Richard Greene*

Picture a lovely spring day and Ivan Boesky, wealthy arbitrager and convicted inside trader, leaving his pleasant Manhattan apartment.

"Cab, sir?" inquires a doorman.

"No, thanks."

Boesky, dressed in coveralls and work boots, is picked up by a small yellow van, which transports him, three car thieves and two pickpockets to Central Park, where the six felons spend the next eight hours scrubbing graffiti off statues and grooming the bridle path. When Boesky arrives home that night, an electronic device around his ankle transmits that fact to a central computer. If he sneaks out before the next morning, the computer will immediately call an officer of the court.

Boesky, in fact, got three years in a minimum security prison, due to start on Mar. 24. But was that a sensible fate? More and more states are now facing up to the fact that prison cells are too scarce and expensive a resource to be devoted, indiscriminately, to everyone who happens to break a law. Forcing lawbreakers to do menial labor is only one possible way to cope with the now staggering price society pays to keep wrongdoers in prison. Here's an update on the costs and the search for alternatives.

Keeping an inmate in a state or federal prison typically runs between $12,000 and $24,000 a year. For that kind of money you can send a kid to Harvard. Maximum security prisons in some places, like New York, can run far higher—sometimes $30,000 to $35,000 a year. Now we're talking about sending the kid for summer study and travel in Europe as well. As Orville Pung, commissioner of Minnesota's correctional system, says ironically, "Prison is the ultimate welfare state."

Prisons have become the fastest-growing major user of state revenues. In Ohio the state's general budget grew by only 4% for 1988, while the corrections budget ballooned by 16.5%. Texas' general budget grew by 6.8%, its corrections budget by 33.8%. Texas, Florida, Michigan and Ohio now spend around $400 million a year operating their prisons. California and New York spend about $1 billion a year.

Staff salaries are responsible for the biggest chunk of this expense, and guards' salaries, as low as $11,000 a year in some states, are heading inexorably upward. But the biggest cause of the prison crunch is an avalanche of prisoners. There are about 550,000 men and women in the nation's prisons—500,000 in state facilities

---

and another 50,000 in federal prisons. One of every 450 Americans is in prison—the highest rate in the Western World.

The burden will get heavier. We're adding a net total of 35,000 to 40,000 inmates a year—the equivalent of a new prison every four days. In the meantime, we're exhausting even short-term fixes in coping with the crush—the practice, for example, of keeping prisoners at county jails instead of transferring them to state and federal prisons. These jails, now holding about 300,000 nationwide, have grown overcrowded and unmanageable themselves. Witness the recent riots on New York City's Rikers Island, in which much-needed space for 600 prisoners was temporarily lost.

Until recently the crush was partly managed by jamming two or three inmates into 6-by-8-foot cells intended for one. "You can save a lot of money that way—until you get sued," says Randall Guynes, president of a research firm that deals with prison-related issues. Indeed, 36 states are now under court orders to make their overcrowded prisons conform to more humane occupancy standards.

A new prison typically costs between $15 million and $60 million, and virtually every state is building more. In Michigan alone, 19 new prisons are under construction, another 7 are on the drawing board and 4 are being refurbished. "There's no bigger growth industry in the last two years in Michigan than the corrections department," says State Senator Jack Welborn. The Edna McConnell Clark Foundation, which provides funds for criminal justice research, reckons the nation's total tab for prison construction will run over $2 billion next year and around $70 billion over the next 30 years, not counting inflation.

Is the need for this huge outlay the result of some ghastly spike in the crime rate? Not at all. Rates of frequency for many crimes—including murder, robbery and burglary—have come down since 1982. But in the same time the U.S. prison population has grown nearly 40%.

The avalanche of new prisoners is attributable to higher conviction rates and longer sentences—for criminals of all types generally, for drug and sex offenders in particular. Until now, such get-tough policies have made good politics. "No judge has ever been thrown out of office for being too harsh on sentencing," notes William Kime, deputy director of research in Michigan's department of corrections. But given the need for new prisons, the old problem of cost has new weight. The public generally cheers when a bad person is packed off to jail, but will they still cheer when prison bond issues come up at the rate of $2 billion and more a year?

Further complicating that question is another vexing problem: Do incarceration rates have anything to do with crime rates? Throwing people into prison may make the average citizen feel better, many penologists have long maintained, but it doesn't make him safer.* The average prison sentence for armed robbery in Louisiana is

*If it is still debatable whether prisons deter crime, it is beyond dispute that they don't rehabilitate. Says David Ward, head of the sociology department at the University of Minnesota, "No one can argue that people are better off for the experience of having gone to prison."

16.7 years, nearly double the national average. But Louisiana has the tenth-highest rate of armed robbery in the country.

The one thing prisons unarguably do well is punish and keep lawbreakers off the streets for a while. But given their cost, prisons will always be a scarce resource, to be allocated with far more care than has been the custom in the U.S. That, looking at the problem another way, means taking sensible risks in deciding how some lawbreakers might be effectively punished some other way.

Hopeful alternatives do exist, but jobbing out inmates to commercially run prisons is not likely to be one of them. That may make the prisons we have more efficiently run, but it won't significantly stem the total cost of a growing prison population.

More to the point are those alternatives that actually get people—many of them nonviolent criminals who do not need to be kept off the streets—out of prison. Evidence is building that drunk drivers, hit-and-run drivers, burglars, white-collar criminals, forgers, fences, car thieves, even some sex offenders can all be punished effectively without spending $50 to $100 a day and more per inmate to keep them behind bars.

Electronically monitored home detention is one such strategy. In use in a number of states, including California, Florida, Kentucky, Utah, Oregon and Delaware, it allows nonviolent criminals to be incarcerated in their homes for periods that are often the equivalent of prison sentences. Such prisoners generally are allowed to go to work or look for a job during the day. If they leave their houses without permission at any other time, electronic anklets or bracelets can report that fact to the authorities. The bracelets can even be programmed to detect the use of drugs or alcohol.

Intensive supervision programs that keep lawbreakers under scrutiny, out of prison, for up to a year are another strategy. In Georgia, where such a program has been particularly successful, offenders meet with a probation officer at least five times a week, have frequent unannounced drug or alcohol tests, must hold a job—often doing community service—and are often subject to curfews. This costs the state about $1,700 per year, compared with a conservative estimate of $12,000 a year for incarceration.

Nowhere in the country is there a more sensible approach to the prison problem than in Washington State. Judges there determine a sentence guided by a grid that coordinates a specific offense with the felon's record. First-degree arson, for instance, will get you two years if you have no record. A burglar with four offenses will spend 13 months in prison.

The Washington experiment rests on pioneering work in Minnesota, where the system has been successful. But Washington, a larger state and one with a higher crime rate, is a more crucial test.

"We made the decision in Washington that prisons are made primarily to punish," says Chase Riveland, the 45-year-old, 6-foot-2 chief of Washington's correctional department. "We want to have longer terms for violent criminals and shorter terms for nonviolent property offenders."

Net result: About 1,700 fewer people were incarcerated over the last couple of years, with no noticeable effect on the crime rate. "If we had been operating under the old law," says Riveland, "I would have had to build at least three new facilities to hold those people, at a cost of $100 million, with $15 million a year operating costs." The state even rents cells to the federal government for $27 million a year.

What is Washington doing with the people it has chosen not to imprison? First- or second-time property offenders mostly, they generally find themselves doing community service. Their tasks vary from sweeping up National Guard armories to helping fight forest fires. Is community service—also in use in many other states—sufficient punishment? "It's still a limitation on freedom," says Riveland. "It's a different degree of punishment, hopefully in proportion to the crime."

Such alternatives, paradoxically, can have the effect of strengthening get-tough policies aimed at more dangerous felons already in jail. For those who wind up in a Washington prison, there are no quick paroles after a few years. A prisoner's sentence can be cut by a maximum of only one-third for good behavior. "One of the few things that seem to have impact on criminals is the certainty of something happening," says Riveland. "Not the degree but the certainty."

The greatest single benefit of Washington's program, however, is that it allows the state legislature to make intelligent decisions about criminal justice with their costs in mind. If a legislator wants to wow the crime-fearing folks back home by doubling the mandated sentence for burglary, say, he's going to have to listen to Chase Riveland tell him exactly how much that's going to cost. "We can predict what the need in funds is going to be from a certain decision six years out or more," says Riveland. "That has resulted in the legislature's being very cautious and very frugal."

Despite the huge cost of the U.S. penal system, that way of thinking is still rare. Says Michigan's Kime: "The size of prisons is determined by the courts, because the courts decide how many go to prison and for how long. But the courts don't have to appropriate the money to build them."

Alternatives to incarceration won't be accepted overnight. Judges are justifiably fearful of public outcry at a perceived "softness" on crime. Equally important are yet-to-be-answered questions about the Constitutional authority for some alternatives.

But the prospect of building new prisons at the rate of $2 billion a year seems certain to raise voter consciousness everywhere. It will surely embolden hard-pressed legislators and penologists to push harder for promising alternatives.

# Racial Discrimination and the Death Penalty

*Amnesty International*

There [is] considerable evidence of racial discrimination in the application of the death penalty before 1967—especially in the southern states. [There are] apparent continuing racial disparities in charging decisions in some states, and the under-representation of blacks or other minorities on juries in capital trials. In fact, there is evidence to suggest that the death penalty continues to be applied in a way which systematically discriminates on racial grounds, although disparities based on race of offender alone appear to have diminished under the present statutes.

Some 48 per cent of the nation's death row population in 1985 were blacks or members of other minorities, although they made up only 12 per cent of the population.[1] The proportion of blacks on death row is much higher in some individual states. However, statistics on race of offender alone do not necessarily indicate bias, given that roughly 50 per cent of all those arrested for murder are black.

Nevertheless, wide disparities are revealed when considering the race of the victim in cases where the death penalty has been imposed. Although blacks and whites are also the victims of homicide in almost equal numbers, the large majority of offenders sentenced to death have been convicted of murdering whites. Forty-six (92 per cent) of the 50 prisoners executed between 1977 and 1985, for example, had been convicted of killing whites, as had 77 per cent of the prisoners on death row nationally in 1985.

Furthermore, blacks who kill whites have been found more likely to be sentenced to death than any other category of offender; whites, on the other hand, have rarely been sentenced to death for killing blacks.

State governments have maintained that these disparities are due entirely to differences in the types of crime committed by or against members of different racial groups. This is likely to account for some of the racial disparities in sentencing,

---

[1]The racial breakdown of the US death row population in May 1986 was as follows (percentages): Black—41.25; White—50.82; Hispanic—5.83; Native American—1.34; Asian—0.35; Unknown—0.41. (Figures published by the NAACP Legal Defense and Educational Fund Inc.) The proportion of blacks on death row was much higher in some states. In Alabama, for example, 67 per cent of death row inmates in 1986 were black (55 out of 82 prisoners). Over 50 per cent of death row inmates in Georgia, Illinois, Mississippi, North Carolina, South Carolina and Pennsylvania were black. In California and Texas a relatively high proportion of death row inmates were Hispanics, reflecting the relatively high proportion of the minority population in these states.

---

"Racial Discrimination and the Death Penalty." From *United States of America: The Death Penalty,* published in London, 1987 by Amnesty International Publications (ISBN 0 86210 114x). (pp. 54–64).

especially as regards the victim's race. National crime reporting data suggest, for example, that whites may constitute a greater proportion of felony-murder victims (the types of homicide for which death sentences are most frequently imposed) than other racial groups. Blacks, who are generally poorer and have a higher unemployment rate, are less likely to be the victims of murders which occur in circumstances for which the death penalty is available (such as murder during the commission of a robbery, or murder for pecuniary gain).

However, a number of research studies have isolated race as a factor in death sentencing, after allowing for differences in the types of homicide. The findings of some of these studies are summarized below.

## Recent Studies on Racial Disparities in Death Sentencing

In the late 1970s William J. Bowers and Glenn L. Pierce, Director and Assistant Director, respectively, of the Center for Applied Social Research at Northeastern University, Boston, compared statistics on all criminal homicides and death sentences imposed in Florida, Georgia, Texas and Ohio from the dates their respective post-*Furman* statutes came into effect (between 1973 and 1974) up to December 1977.[2] Death sentences in these four states accounted for 70 per cent of all death sentences imposed nationally at this time. Bowers and Pierce found that, as in other states, the large majority of homicides were "intra-racial", committed within the same racial group. Although there was a high homicide rate among both whites and blacks in all four states examined, far more killers of whites than killers of blacks were sentenced to death. They also found that, although most killers of whites were white, blacks killing whites were proportionately more likely to receive a death sentence.

In Florida and Texas, for example, blacks who killed whites were, respectively, five and six times more likely to be sentenced to death than whites who had killed whites. Among black offenders in Florida, those who had killed whites were 40 times more likely to get the death penalty than those who had killed blacks. No white offender in Florida had ever been sentenced to death for killing a black person during the period studied.[3] The findings were similar in the other two states.

Researchers Samuel Gross and Robert Mauro also looked at later figures for the race of victims in criminal homicide cases in eight states from 1976 to 1980: Arkan-

---

[2]William Bowers and Glenn Pierce: "Arbitrariness and Discrimination under Post-*Furman* Capital Statutes", in *Crime and Delinquency,* vol. 26, No. 4, October 1980, pp. 563–635; also reproduced in *Legal Homicide: Death as a Punishment in America 1864–1982,* by William Bowers, Northeastern University Press, 1984. Although the death penalty statutes in Florida, Georgia and Texas were not ruled constitutional until the US Supreme Court decision in 1976 (*Gregg* v. *Georgia*), the statutes themselves pre-dated this ruling, having been introduced as follows: Florida, December 1972; Georgia, March 1973; Texas, June 1973; Ohio, January 1974 (ruled unconstitutional in 1978 and amended in 1981).

[3]A white man sentenced to death in Florida in 1980 for killing a black woman was the first white person in the state's history to be sentenced to death for killing a black victim only.

sas, Florida, Georgia, Illinois, Mississippi, North Carolina, Oklahoma and Virginia. They found that homicides and white victims resulted in death sentences from 2.3 to nearly nine times more often than in cases with black victims.[4]

As mentioned above, state prosecuting authorities have argued that these disparities result from differences in the types of homicide committed by blacks and because cases with white victims are more likely to be capital crimes. It has also been argued that, in non-felony cases, murders committed across racial lines (in which statistically more blacks kill whites than whites kill blacks), usually involving strangers, are likely to be more aggravated than those within racial groups.

The Attorney General of Florida used some of the above arguments in a case brought before the federal courts in September 1977. The petitioner was John Spenkelink (later executed) who, as a white who had killed a white, argued that more than 90 per cent of prisoners on Florida's death row at that time had killed whites, demonstrating that the application of the post-*Furman* Florida statute was discriminatory. The Attorney General argued that black murders were qualitatively different, and more likely to result from "family quarrels, lovers' quarrels, liquor quarrels and bar-room brawls".[5] The former Fifth Circuit Court of Appeals denied Spenkelink's discrimination claim, stating that the data produced by the NAACP Legal Defense Fund (LDF) in support of his case was insufficient to demonstrate intent to discriminate in an individual case.

However, several studies have since attempted to measure racial factors in otherwise similar capital crimes. The study conducted by the Northeastern University team cited above went on to compare race-of-victim/race-of-offender ratios in felony-murders only, in Texas, Florida and Georgia. They found that significant disparities in the rate of death sentencing based on the victim's race persisted.

These results were consistent with the findings of a Florida study conducted in 1981 by Michael Radelet, Professor of Sociology at the University of Florida, Gainesville. He examined all homicide indictments in 20 Florida counties in 1976 and 1977, focussing only on those cases involving what he termed "non-primary" homicides (killings of strangers, usually felony-related): 326 cases. Of these "non-primary" homicides, 5.4 per cent of cases with black victims resulted in death sentences, compared to 14 per cent of cases with white victims. He also found that 53.6 per cent of cases with black victims resulted in first-degree murder indictments, compared to 85 per cent of cases with white victims.[6]

Hans Zeisel, Professor of Law at the University of Chicago Law School, also looked at arrests in Florida for felony-murders only, comparing them with the num-

---

[4]Samuel R. Gross and Robert Mauro: *Patterns of Death: an Analysis of Racial Disparities in Capital Sentencing and Homicide Victimization,* 37 Stanford Law Review, 1984.

[5]*Spinkellink* v. *Wainwright* 578 F.2d 582 (Fifth Circuit 1978). The court's spelling of the petitioner's name is incorrect; the correct spelling, as given elsewhere in this report, is "Spenkelink". (The federal judicial circuits have since been changed and Florida now falls under the Eleventh Circuit.)

[6]Michael Radelet, "Racial Characteristics and the Imposition of the Death Penalty", 46 *American Society Review* 918 (1981).

ber of prisoners on death row in September 1977 (at the time of the Spenkelink appeal). He found that at that time 47 per cent of black defendants and only 24 per cent of white defendants arrested for murdering whites in a felony circumstance ended up on death row.[7]

## Georgia Study

Studies of the operation of Georgia's capital sentencing system, conducted in the early 1980s by Professor David Baldus, Professor of Law at the University of Iowa, provided the most detailed analysis of racial disparities in death sentencing at the time of writing. Professor Baldus, in collaboration with two colleagues, Dr. George Woodworth and Professor Charles Pulaski,[8] aimed to discover why killers of white victims in Georgia during the 1970s had received the death penalty approximately 11 times more often than killers of blacks, taking into account the possibility that different levels of aggravation within potentially capital murders could explain the difference in sentencing.

Professor Baldus and his associates examined data on all homicide cases in Georgia from 1973 to 1979 from indictment to sentencing.[9] In an effort to assess whether race played an independent role in sentencing, they subjected each case to a series of rigorous tests, matching the known facts against all possible factors which might play a role in determining sentence. More than 230 control factors were identified, including statutory and non-statutory aggravating and mitigating circumstances, weight of evidence, the defendant's background and prior record, race of defendant and victim, geographical area, and chance.[10]

The team started with a pool of more than 2,000 cases, which they divided into groups according to rising levels of aggravation. They found that most fell into

---

[7]Hans Zeisel, "Race Bias in the Administration of the Death Penalty: The Florida Experience", 95 *Harvard Law Review* 456 (1981).

[8]At the time of writing Dr. Woodworth was Associate Professor of Statistics, University of Iowa, and Professor Pulaski was Professor of Criminal Law, Arizona State University.

[9]Baldus and his associates first measured for racial disparities in sentencing in the cases of all defendants convicted of murder from March 1973 to July 1978. (The Georgia statute has no degrees of murder and anyone tried on a murder charge may face the death penalty, provided aggravating factors are present.) The study was then expanded to cover all homicide cases resulting in murder or manslaughter convictions from 1973 to 1979, and included information on prosecutors' plea bargaining decisions as well as jury guilt and sentencing determinations. From an initial pool of 2,484 cases, the team drew a sample of 1,066 cases, which they subjected to the most rigorous series of tests. This sample comprised all cases where defendants were convicted of murder and sentenced to death or life imprisonment after a penalty hearing; 41 per cent of cases where convicted murderers received automatic life sentences without a penalty hearing, and 35 per cent of cases resulting in voluntary manslaughter convictions (some of which were originally charged as murder).

[10]The data included information from official records of the Georgia Supreme Court, the Georgia Department of Offender Rehabilitation, the Department of Probations and Paroles, the Georgia Bureau of Vital Statistics, all other relevant court records and detailed attorney questionnaires.

categories involving levels of aggravation so low that almost no one received the death penalty: in these cases no significant racial impact could therefore be deduced.

However, the team identified some 400 aggravated homicide cases, each of which involved potentially capital circumstances. They found that no significant racial disparities in sentencing appeared in the most highly aggravated cases (a relatively small number of homicides involving three or more statutory aggravating circumstances, such as a serious additional felony, multiple victims and torture). Although most of the victims in such cases were white, the severity of the crime at this level of aggravation was more important than the victim's race. These were also cases in which the death penalty was most frequently imposed.

However, the team identified a mid-range of cases with intermediate levels of aggravation, in which death sentences were also imposed. These cases—in which there was most room for discretion—comprised the bulk of the 400 potentially capital cases. In this range of cases Professor Baldus found that offenders with white victims were 20 per cent more likely to receive death sentences than those with black victims, at similar levels of aggravation. In fact, the victim's race at this level was more important than several of Georgia's 10 statutory aggravating circumstances. The team also found at this level that black defendants were more likely to receive a death sentence than similar white defendants.

Professor Baldus then examined the outcome of homicide cases at each stage after arrest to see at what procedural points the racial disparities manifested themselves.

He observed that the proportion of white-victim murder cases rose sharply as the cases advanced through the system, from 39 per cent at indictment to 84 per cent at death sentencing. The proportion of black-offender/white-victim cases rose even faster from nine per cent at indictment to 39 per cent at death sentencing. He found that the two most significant points affecting the likelihood of an eventual death sentence were prosecutors' decisions on (1) whether or not to permit pleas to voluntary manslaughter, and (2) whether to seek a penalty hearing in cases where defendants were convicted of murder. Thus, racial disparities manifested themselves at every stage of the judicial process, from indictment to sentencing, with black-victim cases being more likely to result in pleas to manslaughter or life sentences on conviction of murder, than cases with white victims; black defendants with white victims were less likely than others to have their charges reduced and more likely, on conviction of murder, to receive death sentences.

In his earlier review of Georgia's Supreme Court decisions . . . Professor Baldus had noted that Georgia prosecutors had sought the death penalty in only 40 per cent of cases where defendants were convicted of a capital crime: the others received automatic life sentences without a penalty hearing. He found that, although cases with white victims tended to be more aggravated in general, the levels of aggravation in crimes involving black victims had to be substantially higher before the prosecutors sought the death penalty and a penalty hearing. Overall disparities in death sentencing were thus due more to prosecutors' charging and sentencing recommendations than to jury sentencing decisions.

## Appeal to the Federal Courts on Racial Discrimination

The Georgia findings were used in support of an appeal to the Eleventh Circuit Federal Court of Appeals brought by the LDF on behalf of Warren McCleskey, a black man sentenced to death for killing a white Atlanta police officer. Warren McCleskey claimed that the discriminatory application of Georgia's death penalty statute violated both the Eighth Amendment's prohibition of cruel and unusual punishment and his Fourteenth Amendment right to equal protection of the law.[11] In a nine-to-three decision given in January 1985, the appeals court rejected the claim that Georgia had unconstitutionally discriminated against the petitioner on account of race.

The court, which reviewed the Georgia study in some detail, did not dispute its findings, stating: "the statistics show there is a race-of-the-victim relationship with the imposition of the death sentence *discernible enough in cases to be statistically significant in the system as a whole*", but "the magnitude cannot be called determinative *in any given case*" (emphasis added). The court held that, because there was no proof that the state had *intentionally* discriminated against the defendant, there could be no constitutional violation of his rights.

The appeals court acknowledged that direct proof of discriminatory intent by the state might not be required if the statistical evidence was "so strong as to permit no other inference than that the results are the product of a racially discriminatory intent or purpose". However, it said that: "The key to the problem lies in the principle that the proof, no matter how strong, of some disparity is alone insufficient." It concluded that the 20 per cent racial disparity in sentencing among similar offenders in the mid-range of aggravated homicides was insufficient to find that the operation of the Georgia death penalty statute as a whole was unconstitutional.

Indeed, the court went on to say that:

> "The marginal disparity based on race of victim tends to support the state's contention that the system is working far differently from the one which *Furman* condemned. In pre-*Furman* days, there was no rhyme or reason as to who got the death penalty and who did not. But now, in the vast majority of cases, the reasons for a difference are well-documented."[12]

Three judges, Judges Johnson, Hatchett and Clark, filed separate dissenting opinions in which they expressed the view that the evidence of discrimination among the mid-range of aggravated homicide cases was sufficient to show that the Georgia

---

[11]A study by Professor Baldus of similar cases in Fulton County, where Warren McCleskey was tried, was also used in the appeal. This showed that 17 other Fulton County defendants had been charged with the homicide of a police officer between 1973 and 1979. Only two of these defendants even went to a penalty hearing: one, whose police victim was black, received a life sentence, the other, whose victim was white, got a death sentence.

[12]The 1972 US Supreme Court *Furman* decision ruled that most state death penalty laws then were unconstitutional (see Chapter 1).

statute operated unconstitutionally. As Judge Clark pointed out, race had no effect in the large majority of cases because "the facts are so mitigated that the death penalty is not even considered as a possible punishment". Judge Hatchett found that the 20 per cent racial disparity among the middle range of cases, in which "decision on the proper sentence is most difficult and the imposition of the death penalty most questionable" was "intolerable". He said:

> "To allow this system to stand is to concede that in a certain number of cases the consideration of race will be a factor in the decision whether to impose the death penalty. The Equal Protection Clause of the Fourteenth Amendment does not allow this result."

Judge Johnson, who wrote the longest dissent, addressed the question of discriminatory intent, expressing the view that a finding of intent was not necessary to show an Eighth Amendment violation. However, he said that, even if this were necessary ". . . under any reasonable definition of intent, the Baldus study provides sufficient proof. The majority ignores the fact that McCleskey has shown discriminatory intent at work in the sentencing system even though he has not pointed to any specific act or actor responsible for discriminating against him." He added that the study showed:

> ". . . a clear pattern of sentencing that can only be explained in terms of race and it does so in a context where direct evidence of intent is practically impossible to obtain. It strains the imagination to believe that the significant influence on sentencing left unexplained by 230 alternative factors is random rather than racial, especially in a state with an established history of racial discrimination."

Warren McCleskey appealed to the US Supreme Court against the decision in May 1985. More than a year later, in July 1986, the Supreme Court announced that it would hear the appeal. Among the issues the Supreme Court agreed to review were whether proof of specific intent was necessary to sustain a constitutional claim of racial discrimination; whether a "proven disparity" in death sentencing was unconstitutional "irrespective of magnitude" and whether—as Warren McCleskey's lawyers argued—the 20 per cent disparity "among that class of cases in which a death sentence is a serious possibility" so undermined the fairness of Georgia's capital sentencing system as to "violate the Eighth or Fourteenth Amendment rights of a death-sentenced black defendant in that class of cases."[13]

The Supreme Court's ruling on these questions—which was not expected to be given until at least the end of 1986—will have an important bearing on the cases of many prisoners under sentence of death who have raised racial discrimination claims. Several prisoners in Georgia and other states whose execution dates were imminent when the Supreme Court granted *certiorari* in *McCleskey* were granted stays pending the decision.

[13]Warren McCleskey's own case was found to fall within the mid-range of aggravated homicide cases.

## Summary and Comment

The findings of research conducted in a number of different US states since 1979 are consistent in showing that homicides with white victims are far more likely to result in death sentences than those with black victims. Although some of this disparity may be explained by higher levels of aggravation in homicides committed against whites, researchers have found that an independent racial factor remains in cases that are otherwise similar. Differential treatment was found to occur throughout the judicial process, especially at the indictment stage. Black defendants with white victims were also found to be more likely to receive death sentences than white defendants in similar situations.

There are a number of problems in providing statistical proof of discrimination, especially when this may occur through discretionary decisions taken early in the judicial process. Prosecutors' decisions to permit guilty pleas to non-capital offences (or to charge an offender with a lesser offence such as manslaughter or second-degree murder) may involve the removal of additional felonies from the charge sheet, for example. Also, in some states (for instance, Florida) aggravating circumstances accompanying a potentially capital charge need not be listed on the indictment and may be raised at the time of trial only if the prosecutor decides to seek the death penalty. Thus, the true level of differential treatment may not be readily apparent in the trial record. . . . Several Florida researchers have tried to match initial police records with later court charging decisions. However, such research requires exhaustive investigation of all possible circumstances that may lead to the imposition of capital or non-capital charges.

The difficulties in trying to obtain complete data on the disposition of potentially capital cases are illustrated by an order issued by a California judge on 26 June 1986. In investigating a *habeas corpus* claim that the California death penalty law discriminated against a defendant on racial grounds (in the case of Earl Lloyd Jackson) the judge ordered the state Attorney General to provide the court with a record of all cases involving potentially capital circumstances which were disposed of through plea bargains or convictions for non-capital offences since the enactment of the state death penalty law in 1977. The order asked the Attorney General and the Los Angeles District Attorney to turn over the name, case number and county where charges were brought in all cases: where a defendant was convicted of first- or second-degree murder or manslaughter after having originally been accused of murder with special circumstances; where a defendant was convicted of first- or second-degree murder or manslaughter where additional felonies were involved; and where defendants convicted of first-degree murder had prior murder convictions.[14] The Attorney General appealed against the order on the grounds that it would be too difficult and costly an operation, involving the compilation of data on more

[14]All these cases involved circumstances which made the homicides eligible for the death penalty under the California statute.

than 10,000 cases in numerous state counties. A motion against the order was denied by the court and the Attorney General given until May 1986 to comply. The outcome of the order and the appeal were still pending at the time of writing.

The Georgia study has tried to measure for such circumstances by obtaining data from the widest possible sources. Detailed information relating to the crime, defendant and victim was obtained, for example, from the Georgia Department of Pardons and Paroles, which keeps a record of more information than that necessarily given in the court records. Additional supplementary information was obtained from the Department of Offender Rehabilitation and the Georgia Bureau of Vital Statistics. The study, while limited to the state of Georgia, is by far the most comprehensive conducted so far.

Amnesty International finds it disturbing that the study's findings of racial disparities in the mid-range of aggravated homicide cases in Georgia were deemed by the Eleventh Circuit Court of Appeals to be of insufficient magnitude to cast doubt on the system as a whole. It is precisely in this range of cases—where prosecutors and juries have most room for discretion in their charging or sentencing decisions—that discrimination is most likely to occur. By using as a yardstick a system that was fundamentally irrational (as its reference to the pre-*Furman* statutes suggests), . . . the court appeared to tolerate a somewhat lower level of unfairness in the present system.

If the courts are unable to resolve the question of racial discrimination on the evidence presented so far, this should be the subject of urgent examination by the executive or legislative authorities at both state and federal level.

# Rehabilitating Criminal Justice in America

*Jeffrey Reiman*

The criminal justice system in America is morally indistinguishable from criminality because it exercises force and imposes suffering on human beings *while violating its own morally justifying ideals: protection and justice.* Once this is understood, the requirements for rehabilitating the system follow rather directly. The system must institute policies that make good on its claim to protect society and to do justice. In . . . this [essay] I will briefly suggest the outlines of a "treatment strategy" for *helping the system go straight.* It cannot be reiterated too frequently that these proposals are not offered as a means of *improving* the system. Nor am I under any illusion that these proposals will be easily adopted or implemented. They are presented as the necessary requirements for establishing the criminal justice system's moral difference from, and moral superiority to, *crime*; and, even if not implemented or not likely to be implemented, they stand as a measure against which this moral difference and superiority can be judged. The proposals fall under the headings of the two ideals that justify the existence of a criminal justice system. These ideals are that the criminal justice system protect us against the real dangers that threaten us and that it not be an accomplice to injustice in the larger society. In order to realize these ideals, it is necessary that the harms and injustices done by the criminal justice system itself be eliminated.

## Protecting Society

First, it must be acknowledged that every day that we refuse to implement those strategies that have a good chance of cutting down on the crimes people fear—the crimes on the FBI index—the system is an accomplice to these crimes and bears responsibility for the suffering they impose.

**We must enact and vigorously enforce stringent gun controls.**

Americans are armed to the teeth. The handgun is the most easily concealed, the most effective, and the deadliest weapon there is. Its ubiquity is a constant temptation to would-be crooks who lack the courage or skill to commit crimes without weapons or to chance hand-to-hand combat. Its ubiquity also means that any dis-

---

Jeffrey Reiman, "Rehabilitating Criminal Justice in America." Reprinted with permission of Macmillan Publishing Company from *The Rich Get Rich and the Poor Get Prison,* second edition, by Jeffrey Reiman. (New York: Macmillan 1984). (pp. 153–162)

pute may be transformed into a fatal conflict beyond the desires or expectations of the disputants. Trying to fight crime while allowing America to remain an armed camp is like trying to teach a child to walk and tripping him each time he stands up. In its most charitable light, it is hypocrisy. Less charitably, it is complicity in murder.[1]

**We must legalize the production and sale of heroin and treat addiction as a medical problem.**

Although most observers seem to agree that the British system of dispensing heroin to registered addicts is superior to our own punitive system, a number of experts have gone even further. Norval Morris and Gordon Hawkins urge that narcotics use be decriminalized and that drugs be sold in pharmacies by prescription. Arnold Trebach urges that doctors be permitted to prescribe heroin for the treatment of addicts and as a powerful painkiller. Philip Baridon recommends that pure heroin—clearly labeled as to contents, recommended dosage, and addictive potential—be sold at a low fixed price in pharmacies, without prescription, to anyone aged 18 or over.[2] I will not enter into debate about the various ways in which heroin can be decriminalized. I make the simple point that when heroin addicts cannot obtain heroin legally, they will obtain it illegally. And since those who sell it illegally have a captive market, they will charge high prices to make their own risks worthwhile. To pay the high prices, addicts must, will, and do resort to crime. Thus, every day in which we keep the acquisition of heroin a crime, we are using the law to protect the high profits of heroin black marketeers, *and* we are creating a situation in which large numbers of individuals are virtually physically compelled to commit theft. Since there is little evidence that heroin is dangerous beyond the fact of addiction itself, there can be little doubt that our present "cure" for narcotics use is more criminal (and criminogenic) than the narcotics themselves.

**We must develop correctional programs that promote rather than undermine personal responsibility, and we must offer ex-offenders real preparation and a real opportunity to make it as law-abiding citizens.**

The scandal of our prisons has been amply documented. Like our attitudes toward guns and heroin, they seem more calculated to produce than reduce crime. The enforced childhood of imprisonment may be the painful penalty offenders deserve, but if it undermines their capacity to go straight after release, we are cutting off our noses to spite our faces. People cannot learn to control themselves responsibly if they have spent years having every aspect of their lives—the hour they wake, the number of minutes they wash, the time and content of eating and working and exercising, the hour at which lights go out—regulated by someone else. Add to this the fact that convicts usually emerge with no marketable skill and little chance of getting a decent job with the stigma of a prison sentence hanging over them. The result is a system in which we never let criminals finish paying their debt to society and give them every incentive to return to crime.

If we are going to continue to punish people by depriving them of their liberty, we must do it in a way that prepares them for the life they will lead when their liberty is returned. Anything less than this is a violation of the Constitution's Eighth Amendment guarantee against "cruel and unusual punishment." Depriving a person of his or her liberty may be an acceptable punishment, but *depriving people of their dignity and a chance to live a law-abiding life when their punishment is supposed to be over is cruel and* (should be, but sadly is not) *unusual!*

Pursuant to the guarantee of the Eighth Amendment, every imprisoned person should have a right to training at a marketable skill as well as a right to compete equally with non-ex-convicts for a job once the punishment is over. This would require that it be illegal to discriminate against ex-convicts in hiring and illegal to require job applicants to state whether or not they had ever been arrested, convicted, and/or imprisoned for a crime. This requirement might have to be modified for particularly sensitive occupations, although on the whole I think it would be fairer and more effective in rehabilitating ex-cons to enact it across the board and to have the government finance or subsidize a fund to ensure against losses incurred as a result of ex-convicts. My hunch is that this would be much less costly than paying to support ex-cons in prison and their families on welfare when they return to crime for lack of a job. Beyond this, prison industries should pay inmates at prevailing wages; this money then could be used for restitution to victims and to purchase privileges and possibly increased privacy or freedom for the prisoners—all of which might tend to give them greater practice at controlling their own lives so that they will be prepared to do so after release.

But none of this will give us a criminal justice system worthy of the name, until we:

**Let the crime fit the harm and the punishment fit the crime.**

For the criminal justice system to justify its methods, it must make good on its claim to protect society. This requires that the criminal law be redrawn so that the list of crimes reflects the real dangers that individuals pose to society. Avoidable acts where the actor had reason to know that his or her acts were likely to lead to someone's death should be counted as forms of murder. Avoidable acts where the actor had reason to believe that his or her acts were likely to lead to someone's injury should be counted as forms of assault and battery. Acts that illegitimately deprive people of their money or possessions should be treated as forms of theft regardless of the color of the thief's collar. Crime in the suites should be prosecuted and punished as vigorously as crime in the streets.

The law must be drawn carefully so that individuals are not punished for harm they could not foresee or could not have avoided, or that others have freely consented to risk. The pursuit of security must not swamp the legitimate claims of liberty. However, within these guidelines, we must rid the law of the distinction between *one-on-one* harm and *indirect* harm *and treat all harm-producing acts in proportion to the actual harm they produce.*[3] *We must enact and implement punishments that fit the harmfulness of the crime without respect to the class of the criminal.* There is, for instance, general agreement that incarceration functions as an effective deterrent to corporate crime where the threat of imprisonment is believed.[4] And to be believed, it must be used.

The other side of this coin is the decriminalization of "victimless crimes," acts such as prostitution, homosexuality, gambling, vagrancy, drunkenness, and of course, drug use. As long as these acts only involve persons who have freely chosen to participate, they represent no threat to the liberty of any citizen. But this also means that there is generally no complainant for these crimes, no person who feels harmed by these acts and who is ready and able to press charges and testify against the wrongdoers. Therefore, police have to use a variety of shady tactics involving deception and bordering on entrapment, which undermine the public's respect for the police and the police officers' respect for themselves. In any event, the use of such low-visibility tactics increases the likelihood of corruption and arbitrariness in the enforcement of the law. Beyond this, since these acts produce no palpable, undeniable, tangible harm to others, laws against them appear to be no more than the imposition of some people's ideas of virtue on others, rather than laws that really protect society. To make good on its claim to protect society, the criminal justice system must not only treat the dangerous acts of business executives as crimes, but it must also decriminalize those acts that are not clearly dangerous.[5]

Over 100 years ago, John Stuart Mill formulated a guiding principle, still relevant in our time, for the design of legislation in a society committed to personal liberty:

> That principle is, that the sole end for which mankind are warranted, individually or collectively, in interfering with the liberty of action of any of their number, is self-protection. That the only purpose for which power can be rightfully exercised over any member of a civilized community, against his will, is to prevent harm to others.[6]

Although the principle has had to be modified in recognition of the ways in which individuals can cause future harm to themselves because of present injudicious choices, particularly in a complex modern society where people must deal with machines and chemicals beyond their understanding,[7] the heart of the principle is still widely accepted. This is the notion that a necessary condition of any justifiable legal prohibition is that it prohibit an act that does harm to someone, possibly the actor himself. Since priority should be given to freedom of action, this harm should be *demonstrable* (i.e., detectable by some widely agreed upon means, say, those used by medical science), and it should be of sufficient gravity to outweigh the value of the freedom that is to be legally prohibited.[8]

This principle should not only guide legislators and those engaged in revising and codifying criminal law, but it should be raised to the level of an implicit constitutional principle. The U.S. Supreme Court recognizes certain traditional principles of legality as constitutional requirements even though they are not explicitly written into the Constitution. For instance, some laws have been held unconstitutional because of their vagueness[9] and others because they penalized a condition (like being a drunk or an addict) rather than an action (like drinking or using drugs).[10] It strikes me that the entire tenor of the Bill of Rights is to enshrine and protect individual liberty from the encroachment of the state. But legal philosophers from Mill to the present have argued that to give priority to individual liberty, one must accept some version of the demonstrable harm requirement as a condition for acceptable laws. An act that threatens no harm is no threat to liberty, so a law that prohibits such an act is a limitation on liberty with no counterbalancing gain in liberty to justify it. In this light, it seems reasonable that the Supreme Court should strike down as *unconstitutional* any criminal law that prohibits an act that does not cause demonstrable harm, with the burden of proof lying with the state to demonstrate the palpable harm the law seeks to prevent.

Whether as a legislative or a judicial criterion, however, this principle would undoubtedly rid our law of the excrescences of our puritan moralism. It would bring our law more in line with a realistic view of what is harmful, and it would eliminate the forced induction into criminality of the individuals, mainly those of the lower class, who get arrested for "victimless crimes."

*These changes, taken together, would be likely to reduce dangerous crime and to bring us a legal order that actually punished (and, it is hoped, deterred) all and only those acts that really threaten our lives and possessions and punished them in proportion to the harm they really produce. Such a legal system could be truly said to protect society.*

## Promoting Justice

The changes recommended above would, in part, make the criminal justice system more just, since people would be punished in proportion to the seriousness of their antisocial acts, and the number of innocent persons victimized by those acts would be reduced. Much would still remain to be done to eliminate the disabilities of the poor caught up in the system.

A criminal justice system should arrest, charge, convict, and sentence individuals with an eye only to their crime, not to their class. Any evidence of more frequent arrest or harsher penalties for poor persons than for others accused of the same crime is a grave injustice that tends to undermine the legitimacy of the criminal justice system. Since many of the decisions that work to the disadvantage of the poor—police decisions to arrest, prosecutors' decisions to charge, and judges' decisions on how long to sentence—are exercises of discretion often out of public view, they are particularly resistant to control. Since, unlike prosecutors' or judges' decisions, the police officer's decision *not* to arrest is *not* a matter of record, it is the least visible exercise of discretion and the most difficult to control. Our best hope to make arrests by police more just lies in increased citizen awareness and education of police officers so that they at least become aware of the operation and impact of their own biases and are held more directly accountable to, and by, the public they serve and sometimes arrest.

As for prosecutorial and judicial discretion, two approaches seem potentially fruitful. First, our lawmakers ought to spell out the acceptable criteria that prosecutors may use in deciding whether or what to charge and the criteria that judges may use in deciding whether or what to sentence. The practice of multiple charging (e.g., charging an accused burglar with "the lesser included crimes" of breaking and entering, possession of burglar's tools, etc.) should be eliminated. It is used by prosecutors to "coax" accused persons into pleading guilty to one charge by threatening to press *all* charges. Of all the dubious features of our system of bargain justice, this seems most clearly without justification, since it works to coerce a plea of guilty that should be uncoerced if it is to be legally valid.[11] The law should also set out more specific sentencing ranges, since the present system leads to individuals receiving wildly different sentences for the same crimes—a practice that can only be viewed as arbitrary and capricious, that violates the principle that citizens should know in advance what is in store for them if they break a law, and that produces in convicts disrespect for the law rather than remorse for their violations. In addition to, and in conjunction with, these legislative changes, we ought to require prosecutors and judges to put in writing the reasons they have charged or sentenced in one way rather than another. And they should be required to give an account of their policies and practices to some truly representative body to show that they are fair and reasonable. However we achieve it, it is clear that to make the criminal justice system function justly:

**We must narrow the range in which police officers, prosecutors and judges exercise discretion, and we must develop procedures to hold them accountable to the public for the fairness and reasonableness of their decisions.**

But all these changes still leave standing what is probably the largest source of injustice to the poor in the system: *unequal access to quality legal counsel.* We know that, by and large, privately retained counsel will have more incentive to put in the time and effort to get their clients off the hook, and we know that this results in a situation in which *for equal crimes* those who can retain their own counsel are more likely to be acquitted than those who cannot. Note that as many as 70 percent of the inmates of our state correctional facilities could not afford to retain their own private counsel. The present system of allocating assigned counsel or public defenders to the poor, and privately retained lawyers to the affluent, is little more than a parody of the constitutional guarantee of a *right to counsel* and a clear violation of the constitutional guarantee of *equal protection under the law.*

There are simply no two ways about this. In our system, even though lawyers are assigned to the poor, justice has a price. Those who pay get the choicest cut—those who cannot, get the scraps. About a hundred years ago, before there were public police forces in every town and city, people got "police protection" by hiring private police officers or bodyguards if they could afford it. Protection was available for a price, and so those who had more money were better protected under the law. Today, we regard it as every citizen's right to have police protection, and we would find it outrageous if police protection were allocated to citizens on a fee-for-service basis. *But this is precisely where we stand with respect to the legal protection provided by lawyers*!

Legal protection is not only provided by the police. Attorneys are necessary to protect individuals from losing their freedom at the hands of the law before they have exhausted the legal defenses that are theirs by right. Both police officers and lawyers are essential to the individual's legal protection. It is sheer hypocrisy to acknowledge everyone's right to equal protection under the law by the police and then to allocate protection under the law by lawyers on the basis of what individuals can pay. As long as this continues, we cannot claim that there is anything like equal treatment before the law in the criminal justice system.

**We must transform the equal right to counsel into the right to equal counsel, as far as it is possible.**

Although this would appear to be a clear requirement of the "equal protection" and "due process" clauses of the Constitution, the Supreme Court has avoided it, perhaps because it poses massive practical problems. And surely it does. However, the creation of public police forces to protect everyone probably seemed to pose many practical problems in its time as well.

Certainly it would not be appropriate to use the police as a model for resolving the problem of equal counsel. To establish a governmental legal service for all—in effect to nationalize the legal profession—might make equal legal representation available to all. It would, however, undermine the adversary system by undercutting the independence of the defense attorney from the state. Some form of national legal insurance to enable all individuals to hire private attorneys of their own choice, however, could bring us closer to equal legal protection without compromising the adversarial relationship.

Such insurance would undoubtedly have to be subsidized by the government, as are the police, the courts, and prisons; but it would not necessarily have to be totally paid for out of taxes. People might rightly be expected to pay their legal bills up to some fraction of their income, if they have one. The rest would be paid for by a government subsidy that would pay the difference between what the accused could afford and the going rate for high-quality legal counsel. Nothing in the system need interfere with the freedom of the accused to select the lawyer of his or her choice (an option closer to the hearts of free enterprisers than the present public defender system allows) or interfere with the independence of the lawyer.

Undoubtedly, such a system would be costly. But our commitment to equal justice remains a sham until we are willing to pay this price. Americans have paid dearly to protect the value of liberty enshrined in the Constitution. Is it too much to ask that they pay to realize the ideal of justice enshrined there too?

One final recommendation remains to be made. I have already argued that the criminal justice system, by its very nature, embodies the prevailing economic relations in its laws. This means that it is an error to think of the criminal justice system as an entity that can be reformed in isolation from the larger social order. A criminal justice system is a means to protect that social order, and it can be no more just than the order it protects. A law against theft may be enforced with an even and just hand. But if it protects an unjust distribution of wealth and property, the result is *injustice evenly enforced.* A criminal justice system cannot hold individuals guilty of the injustice of breaking the law if the law itself supports and defends an unjust social order.

**We must establish a more just distribution of wealth and income and make equal opportunity a reality for all Americans.**

Without economic and social justice, the police officer in the ghetto is indeed an occupying soldier with no more legitimacy than his or her gun provides. Without economic and social justice the criminal justice system is the defender of injustice and is thus morally indistinguishable from the criminal. *A criminal justice system can be no more just than the society its laws protect.* Along with the other recommendations I have made . . . the achievement of economic and social justice is a necessary condition for establishing the criminal justice system's moral superiority to *crime.*

Every step toward domestic disarmament, toward decriminalization of heroin and "victimless crimes," toward criminalization of the dangerous acts of the affluent and vigorous prosecution of "white-collar" crimes; every step toward creating a correctional system that promotes human dignity, toward giving ex-offenders a real opportunity to go straight, toward making the exercise of power by police officers, prosecutors, and judges more reasonable and more just, toward giving all individuals accused of crime equal access to high-quality legal expertise in their defense; every step toward establishing economic and social justice is a step that moves us from a system of *criminal* justice to a system of criminal *justice.* The refusal to take those steps is a move in the opposite direction.

## NOTES

1. See the thoughtful recommendations for gun control and their rationale in Norval Morris and Gordon Hawkins, *The Honest Politician's Guide to Crime Control* (Chicago: University of Chicago Press, 1970), pp. 63–71.
2. Morris and Hawkins, pp. 3, and 8–10; Arnold S. Trebach, *The Heroin Solution* (New Haven: Yale University Press, 1982), pp. 267–270; and Philip C. Baridon, *Addiction, Crime, and Social Policy* (Lexington, Mass.: Lexington Books, 1976), p. 88.
3. For a convincing argument that there is no moral difference between directly caused and indirectly caused harm, see John Harris, "The Marxist Conception of Violence," *Philosophy & Public Affairs,* 3, No. 2 (Winter, 1974), pp. 192–220; and Jonathan Glover, *Causing Death and Saving Lives* (Hammondsworth, England: Penguin, 1977), pp. 92–112.

4. These are the words of a former director of the fraud division of the Department of Justice: "No one in direct contact with the living reality of business conduct in the United States is unaware of the effect the imprisonment of seven high officials in the Electrical Machinery Industry in 1960 had on the conspiratorial price fixing in many areas of our economy; similar sentences in a few cases each decade would almost completely cleanse our economy of the cancer of collusive price fixing and the mere prospect of such sentences is itself the strongest available deterrent to such activities." Gordon B. Spivak, "Antitrust Enforcement in the United States: A Primer," *Connecticut Bar Journal,* 37 (September, 1963), p. 382.
5. See Chapter One, "The Overreach of the Criminal Law," in Morris and Hawkins, pp. 1–28; Herbert Packer, *The Limits of the Criminal Sanction* (Stanford, Calif.: Stanford University Press, 1968); and Jeffrey H. Reiman, "Can We Avoid the Legislation of Morality?," in *Legality, Morality and Ethics in Criminal Justice,* eds., Nicholas N. Kittrie and Jackwell Susman (New York: Praeger, 1979), pp. 130–141.
6. John Stuart Mill, *On Liberty* (1859), (New York: Appleton-Century Crofts, 1973), p. 9.
7. See, for example, Gerald Dworkin, "Paternalism," in *Morality and the Law,* ed., Richard Wasserstrom (Belmont, Calif.: Wadsworth, 1971), pp. 107–126; and Joel Feinberg, "Legal Paternalism," in *Today's Moral Problems,* ed., Richard Wasserstrom (New York: Macmillan, 1975), pp. 33–50.
8. See, for instance, the excellent discussion of the principle in Peter T. Manicas, *The Death of the State* (New York: Putnam, 1974), Chapter V: "The Liberal Moral Ideal," pp. 194–241; and H. L. A. Hart, *Law, Liberty and Morality* (New York: Vintage Books, 1963).
9. The standard laid down in *Conally* v. *General Constr. Co.*, 269 U.S. 385, 391, 70 L. Ed. 322, 46 S. Ct. 126 (1926) is "whether or not the vagueness is of such a character 'that men of common intelligence must necessarily guess at its meaning.'" See also *Lanzetta et al.* v. *State of New Jersey, 306,* U.S. 451, 83 L. Ed. 888, 59 S. Ct. 618 (1939), where the Supreme Court struck down a New Jersey statute that made it a felony for anyone not engaged in any lawful occupation to be a member of a gang, etc., because the terms of the statute were "vague, indefinite and uncertain" and thus "repugnant to the due process clause of the Fourteenth Amendment." Both cases are cited and discussed in Jerome Hall, *General Principles of Criminal Law,* 2nd edition (New York: Bobbs-Merrill, 1960), pp. 36–48. For a constitutional and philosophical argument for treating Mill's harm principle as an implied constitutional principle, see David A. J. Richards, *Sex, Drugs, Death, and the Law: An Essay on Human Rights and Overcriminalization* (Totowa, N.J.: Rowman and Littlefield, 1982), pp. 1–34 *inter alia.*
10. See *Robinson* v. *California,* 370 U.S. 66 (1962), where the court held that a state law penalizing a person for a "status" such as addiction constitutes "cruel and unusual punishment" in violation of the Eighth Amendment. Cited and discussed in Nicholas N. Kittrie, *The Right to be Different: Deviance and Enforced Therapy* (Baltimore: The Johns Hopkins Press, 1971), pp. 35–36, *inter alia.*
11. I have already pointed out that the vast majority of persons convicted of crimes in the United States are not convicted by juries. They plead guilty as the result of a "bargain" with the prosecutor (underwritten by the judge), in which the prosecutor agrees to drop other charges in return for the guilty plea. Kenneth Kipnis argues that the entire system of bargain justice is a violation of the ideal of justice, since it amounts to coercing a guilty plea and often to punishing an offender for a crime other than the one he or she has committed. It is an argument worth considering. See Kenneth Kipnis, "Criminal Justice and the Negotiated Plea," *Ethics, 86,* No. 2 (January, 1976), pp. 93–106.

# Chapter 11
# NATIONAL SECURITY

## United States Military Costs and Consequences

*Ruth Leger Sivard*

In this lop-sided world, it is time that the public in every nation was given an official annual accounting of how its money is being spent, what choices had to be made, and why. No flim-flam, no obfuscation, just a straightforward report to the taxpayer that lays it all out.

Pending the real thing we must make do with pieces of the jigsaw puzzle. . . . Can a nation really afford to buy another aircraft carrier if it cannot feed all its people, or to spend generously on Star Wars research when it has so little to invest in research against the AIDS epidemic? If the decision-makers have the answers to such questions, why are they not on the public record?

Governments must continually make choices in the allocation of public funds. The decisions are seldom made in terms of a simple weighing of alternatives, particularly as between military defense and the public's welfare. But one purpose of a report of this nature is to give voice to the wealth of alternatives that nations do have in formulating budgets and, through them, national priorities.

Protection, for example, comes in various forms. At present one government in three spends more on weapons than on schools; two in three spend more to guard against external enemies than against all the threats to health and well-being that people face in their daily lives.

### Background

Before World War II annual government expenditures for education in the United States were two to three times military expenditures. During the war they dropped below military outlays and in the years since then they have not caught up. . . . Between 1940 and 1986 the rise in US military expenditures was more than double the rise in education expenditures. Currently 45 percent more public money goes to military defense than to the education of America's children.

---

**Table 1** Costs of Protection

| Weapons | | Dollars | | Other Options |
|---|---|---|---|---|
| 50 MX "Peace-keepers" | = | **$4,540,000,000**[a] | = | Year's cost of US health program for long-term home care of about 1 million chronically-ill children and elderly. |
| Research on Star Wars (*fiscal year 1988*) | = | **$3,900,000,000**[a] | = | An elementary school education for 1,400,000 children in Latin America. |
| 1 aircraft carrier (Nimitz class) | = | **$3,900,000,000**[a] | = | 1 solid meal a day for 6 months for the 20 million Americans who do not get enough to eat. |
| 1 Trident submarine | = | **$1,436,000,000**[a] | = | 5-year program for universal child immunization against 6 deadly diseases, preventing 1 million deaths a year. |
| 1 Trafalgar submarine | = | **$423,000,000**[b] | = | Cost to UK public of proposed fee of £10 for sight tests and £3 for dental tests, formerly paid by national health insurance. |
| 2 frigates (F 30) | = | **$280,000,000**[e] | = | Cost of campaign for global eradication of smallpox, which created annual savings 10 times the investment. |
| 1-year operating cost of anti-submarine warfare cruiser | = | **$59,400,000**[b] | = | Housing for 1 year for three-fourths of homeless families in London. |
| 2 fighter aircraft (JA 37) | = | **$45,000,000**[a] | = | Installation in Third World of 300,000 hand pumps to give villages access to safe water. |
| 1 tanker aircraft (VC 10) | = | **$26,300,000**[b] | = | 4 years of UK research on AIDS at current levels of government spending. |
| 1-year maintenance of 100 armored wheeled vehicles | = | **$16,700,000**[a] | = | Employment of 500 unemployed teachers in W. Germany to assist Third World education programs. |
| 1 nuclear weapon test | = | **$12,000,000**[a] | = | Training of 40,000 community health workers in the Third World. |
| 1 twin-engined attack helicopter | = | **$11,500,000**[a] | = | Insecticide spraying of housing for African population of 8 million. |
| 1 Leopard marine battle tank | = | **$2,800,000**[d] | = | 150–250 kms of protected bike lanes in W. Germany to reduce high death toll on highways. |
| 2 infantry combat vehicles | = | **$1,000,000**[e] | = | Year's supply of nutrition supplements for 5,000 pregnant women at risk. |
| 10 anti-tank missiles | = | **$135,000**[b] | = | Trained guide dogs for some of the 146,000 blind people in UK. |
| 1-hour operating cost of a B-1 bomber | = | **$21,000**[a] | = | Community-based maternal health care in 10 African villages to reduce maternal deaths by half in a decade. |
| 9mm personal defense weapon (military pistol) | = | **$212**[a] | = | Year's supply of vitamin A capsules for 1,000 pre-school children at risk. |

a United States b United Kingdom c Sweden d W. Germany e Spain

The sharp change in budget priorities is illustrative of the new role the US assumed in the post-war period as the world's preeminent military power. As the major foreign combatant in two big wars in Asia since the 1940's, a dynamic leader in nuclear and exotic weapons technology, and a heavy investor in a global navy and a world-wide network of military bases, the US has determinedly held its place as front-runner in the arms race, and volunteer policeman of world security.

The military role has been costly, even for a nation as richly endowed as the US. Since 1940 military expenditures in constant 1980 prices have amounted to $6.8 trillion, eating up 8.4 percent of the GNP created during these years. The military burden on the economy in terms of the ratio to GNP has increased six-fold compared with the first four decades of the century.

Put in historical context, the 1980's surge in the military budget can be seen as a war-equivalent mobilization. Although US forces are not actively engaged in hostilities, military outlays in constant 1980 prices now exceed the peak spending years of both the Korean and Vietnam wars. . . . Despite a precarious fiscal situation, 1987 has seen no reduction in US military expenditures. A heavy burden has been put on the domestic economy at a time when major structural changes underway in the global economy are impacting on the US. An erosion of the American economy's traditional manufacturing base has already occurred, and increasingly the US position in high technology production is also threatened.

The official emphasis on a war economy at a time of radical change in the global economic setting has impeded the necessary adjustment process. Rather than providing the leadership needed to stimulate vigorous and equitable domestic development in a new competitive situation, government policies emphasize geopolitical maneuvers and undercover military operations in the Third World that have very little to do with defense against the real threats to America today.

Two economic deficits, in foreign trade and in the government budget, are now in the headlines but another deficit, the cancer of social neglect growing out of an overindulgence in military power, attracts relatively little public or press attention. While the priorities of government continue to protect bloated military budgets, the erosion of social equity in America is a growing threat to domestic security and to the nation's place in the world community.

## Military Superpower

World War II propelled the US abruptly into a superstar military role. Between 1939 and the peak of the US war effort in 1945, the number of men in the armed forces rose from 334,000 to 12,123,000, and military expenditures skyrocketed from under $9 billion to $380 billion a year (constant 1980 prices). Rapid demobilization followed the big war but neither forces nor budgets ever returned to the levels of the prewar years.

In 1987 there are six times as many Americans under arms as there were before World War II and military expenditures in real terms are twenty-five times as large. Several factors account for this radical change in the military profile of the country.

In two major respects US post-war governments assumed military commitments which expanded its global role. One related to the containment of Soviet and Chinese expansionism in Europe and Asia; the other to activist anti-communist objectives in the Third World. A third influence, affecting both policy and the size of the budget, was the increased political power of the military-industrial complex. All three of these features, which are reviewed briefly below, are now receiving increasing public scrutiny.

Long arm of protection—Along with assistance for Europe's economic recovery after the World War, the US moved to provide protection against further Soviet territorial expansion westward. There may have been valid reasons for suspicion on both sides, but for America it was the communist takeover of Czechoslovakia in February 1948 and the blockade of Berlin in June 1948 which raised cold-war temperatures in the US and gave public support to a continuing American commitment to Europe's defense against communist encroachment. In April 1949 the US and Canada joined with western Europe in signing the North Atlantic Treaty which established the framework for a collective defense.

As a consequence, large US forces remained in Europe, and are there today. Demobilization at the end of the war had reduced their strength from 3,100,000 in 1945 to 391,000 in 1946. More than 40 years later, the number of American personnel on duty in the NATO area is still well over 300,000.

While the European NATO members themselves provide the bulk of the Alliance's armed forces in Europe, the US has from the earliest years carried the major share of the overall financial burden of NATO defense. Comparisons of military budgets and of GNP highlight the exceptionally large share of NATO defense costs still borne by the US. . . . In the late 1940's the US budget represented slightly over 70 percent of the NATO total; in 1986 it was 68 percent of the total. Since western Europe's economic recovery in the intervening years has been highly successful, and its combined income last year was close to the US income, the disproportionate share of the military burden borne by the US has moved to the fore as a political issue. This is also true of the US role in Asia and the Pacific.

US occupation forces remained in Japan after its defeat in 1945, and in South Korea after the end of the Korean War. Throughout the Pacific area the US created a vast network of anti-communist military alliances to contain China and North Korea, as well as the USSR, and in general to maintain the balance of power in the Far East.

Currently there are still 54,200 US forces stationed in Japan, 42,800 in South Korea, and at least 45,000 in other locations in the Pacific area. With Japan's spectacular growth of the last two decades, the gap between Japanese and American financial contributions to military defense has become particularly pronounced. In 1986 on a per capita basis Japan's military expenditures amounted to 11 percent of US expenditures and Japan's GNP to 68 percent of US GNP.

*Interventions.* An interventionist role is not new for the US, but in scope, variety, and in cost, the actions taken in recent decades are unprecedented. Earlier in the century, US marines occupied Haiti, the Dominican Republic, and on several occasions, Nicaragua, Mexico, and Panama. Since mid-century, interventions have been geographically more wide-ranging—among them, Lebanon (1958), Zaire (1962), Vietnam (1961–73). Indirect forms of intervention (interventions not involving US forces directly) have also become more common, and more of them are covert.

Although not always successful, such operations did succeed in overthrowing some popularly-elected but leftist governments, such as Guatemala (1954), Brazil (1964), and Chile (1973), governments which were then taken over by the armed forces. Under the Reagan Doctrine of supporting anti-communist insurgencies, current targets for destabilization are Angola, Afghanistan, Cambodia, Ethiopia, and Nicaragua, where governments under communist control are under attack by insurgents armed and in some cases recruited and trained by the US.

Public disclosures, including those related to the Iran-Contra arms deals, give a clue to the variety and range of US covert operations. An official investigation, made public in 1976, indicated that the CIA, which was originally established for the collection of intelligence information, by 1953 was conducting major covert operations in 48 countries. Of several thousand individual covert operations reportedly conducted between 1961 and 1976, about 900 were said to be paramilitary in nature. The CIA budget is believed to have increased substantially since that time; recent press estimates put it at about $25 billion in 1986. If roughly accurate that would make it as large as the total military budget of France or West Germany.

Foreign interventions that are hidden from public view are a triple threat to America's own security. It is a threat that goes well beyond the growing, uncontrollable drain on public funds. Since secrecy prevents public debate and oversight, these covert operations violate the very basis of democracy. They can also lead the country, unprepared and unwilling, into full-scale war.

*Military-Industrial Complex.* In addition to official policies emphasizing the global projection of military power, the US in the postwar period took on a new role as weapons supplier to the world. Aided by a strong increase in the government's investment in military research and development (R & D), the US vaulted to first place in the broadest range of weapons technology, including sophisticated conventional arms as well as nuclear weapons and their delivery systems. It also became the leading exporter of arms.

Private enterprise as well as the government was behind the push in weapons technology in the postwar period. Prior to the war, arms production had been a relatively small element in the US economy and largely centered in government arsenals and shipyards. This changed abruptly in the war years as private industry, especially aircraft and auto manufacturing, contributed to the miraculous increase in weapons production required to defeat the Axis powers. At war's end the military-industrial complex continued in a dynamic partnership. The government wanted high-tech arms and airpower and the weapons makers needed contracts to survive. The solution was a steadily-rising military budget to ensure continuing technological advance and "warm" (ever-ready) production lines in the event of more war.

The result was a tightly knit group of multi-billion-dollar corporations, with the labor and management skills needed for high-tech production, and research talent with a capacity to find ever new ways to improve the products. Since only big corporations could build the increasingly complex weaponry, the number of contractors was limited, as was the competition for contracts. And since more complex and expensive weapons were also more profitable, prices kept rising . . . as did profits and political power. As it became increasingly apparent that higher budgets were buying less hardware than planned, a GAO study in 1986 showed that defense contracting had been 120 percent more profitable than commercial manufacturing from 1980 to 1983.

## Economic-Social Deficits

The background on military trends is critical to an understanding of the US situation today in the non-military aspects of national security. The fact is that the US economy is ailing. The GNP growth rate has slowed, from 3.8 percent in the 1960's to 2.8 percent in the 1970's, and to 2.2 percent so far in the 1980's. The country's imports exceed its exports by a record amount, and its foreign indebtedness is high and rising rapidly. Workers' real earnings have dropped. Most of the economy's new jobs are in low-paying service industries; many are part-time and pay wages below the poverty level. The industrial base is shrinking, and manufacturing, traditionally the backbone of the economy, is of decreasing importance as a source of income.

*Economic Basics.* The sudden collapse of the stock market in October 1987 has helped to move these and other signs of economic malaise to center stage. The federal budget deficit is now a major focus of political as well as economic concern. At $221 billion in fiscal year (FY) 1986, the deficit was the largest ever recorded, having surged from $40 billion in 1979. One-time reductions in outlays caused it to shrink in 1987 but it is projected to swell again in 1988. . . .

The big culprit on the expenditure side has been the sharp rise in "national defense" budgets, which have actually increased more than the increase in the budget deficit. Between FY 1979 and 1988 defense outlays rose by $175 billion, the overall fiscal deficit by $143 billion.

As government borrowing to finance enormous deficits forced interest rates higher, the value of the dollar skyrocketed—and with it, the prices of US goods abroad. Between 1981 and 1987 the nation's position in world trade deteriorated rapidly. By 1987 the deficit on the merchandise account was six times greater than at the beginning of the 1980's . . . and America's foreign debt was close to $300 billion and rising.

In only five years, the military joyride, bought wholly on credit, had turned the world's largest net creditor into the world's largest debtor. The decline in America's international competitiveness had its beginnings years ago, but the abrupt growth of the trade deficit in the 1980's to a large degree can be laid at the door of excessive military expenditures. A few examples may help to illustrate the many ties between the loss of commercial markets and America's intense preoccupation with global military power.

- US government-supported research priorities, in their emphasis on weapons rather than commercial products, have been the exact opposite of policies pursued by America's major trading partners:

  In the US, 25 percent of the government research budget relates to products for the civilian market; in Europe, 70 percent is civilian.

  While the US under the Strategic Computing Initiative spends $600 million for such specialized military applications of supercomputers as battle-management programs, Japan spends $700 million on the commercial applications of supercomputers.

  In cutting-edge technologies (eg. lasers and artificial intelligence) defense projects in the US account for 70–80 percent of R & D expenditures.

- The highly specialized weapons technology which public funds have supported in the US plays a relatively small role in international trade. Weapons research accounts for 75 percent of government-funded research, but weapons exports are no more than 4 percent of US export trade.
- When US defense does result in technologies with potential commercial spinoffs, other countries are often ahead of the US in marketing them. For example, Japan now has the lead in small machine tools and in ceramics applications, technologies originally developed through US military research.
- In the competition for public finances, US education has taken second place to military programs, starving the resources needed to train and maintain a high-quality, skilled work force. Currently, US expenditures on education are barely three-fourths of military expenditures. West Germany, by comparison, spends 40 percent more on public education than on military defense, Japan five times more.

*The Public's Welfare.* Both the longer-term structural changes in the world economy and, more recently, the country's own fiscal and economic policies have operated against an equitable distribution of the fruits of progress in the US. Even during the years of solid economic expansion, the US poverty rate did not drop below 11 percent. In 1986, the last year for which data are available, 13.6 percent of the population, or 32.4 million Americans, lived below the poverty line. For all children under 6 years of age, the rate was 22 percent; for blacks under 6 years it was 45.6 percent.

The benefits of growth in recent years have gone disproportionately to the highest income group. The income shift, particularly in the period since 1980, is dramatically summarized in the annual surveys of the Bureau of the Census. . . . Beginning in the mid-1970's, the share of aggregate income going to the poorest fifth of the US population began to slip; by 1986 it was down to 4.6 percent, the lowest it had been since 1954. The second and third fifths of the population, representing the lower middle class, also dropped to the smallest shares on record, while the fourth held relatively steady. By contrast, the sharp gain in the 1980's by the richest fifth of the population set a new record for rapid change and also a new all-time high, with 43.7 percent of the country's income going to 20 percent of the population.

Available information on other economies suggests that the income gap between rich and poor in the US may now be larger than in any other advanced industrial society. Tax benefits to corporations and to higher incomes, along with budget cuts in social programs, were major factors in the early 1980's in the transfer of income from the poorer to the richer sector of the population. A study by the Congressional Budget Office (CBO) in 1984, for example, found that a typical family with income under $10,000 would lose $390 that year as a result of cuts in taxes and in social programs, while a family with income over $80,000 would gain $8,270.

While the comprehensive tax reform legislation enacted in 1986 is expected to make the income tax system somewhat more progressive, a CBO study this year shows that the poorer 10 percent of the taxpayers will see their total Federal tax liabilities (excise, Social Security, as well as income tax) rise by 20 percent in 1988 over 1987; the wealthiest 10 percent, however, will pay about 6 percent less.

Budget deficits incurred in the latest years now severely limit flexibility both in tax policy and in social legislation. With an enormous IOU overhanging the economy, budget choices to improve equity will be restricted, and politically very difficult unless public backing is strong.

Between FY 1980 and 1988, military expenditures grew from 5 percent of the GNP to an estimated 6.2 percent, while non-defense programs (excluding Social Security and interest) were squeezed down from 9.9 percent to an estimated 8.1 percent of the GNP. The country bought more military power at the direct cost of family welfare. In the absence of bold moves now to cut military spending, the chances of righting imbalances and moving toward more constructive goals for the future are not favorable. What happens next will depend on the readiness of the public to support the ideals of economic as well as political justice under which this democracy flourished.

# The Political Economy of Military Waste

*Joan B. Anderson and Dwight R. Lee*

The Reagan Administration's attempt to increase U.S. military might has been accompanied by enormous waste, a fact that is obvious to all. Who has not seen the reports of $200 ash trays, $640 toilet seats, and $6,000 coffee pots that the Pentagon has purchased for our defense? Unfortunately, these wildly reported examples of military waste are exceptional only in their lack of subtlety. They represent the tip of the iceberg of waste and inefficiency that is draining the country of billions of dollars of resources while providing little, if any, additional defense.

The natural reaction when confronted with the reality of military waste is to seek the identity of those members of the military-industrial complex who are responsible and to punish them with bad publicity, fines, and possibly imprisonment. In recent times, individuals within the military bureaucracy have been reprimanded for dereliction of duty. More notably, temporary sanctions have been imposed on the two major generals in the military establishment—General Dynamics and General Electric—for taking the offensive against the U.S. taxpayer.

There is justification for such reactions. Military waste is often the result of criminal behavior, and the punishment of this behavior is warranted on grounds of both deterrence and justice. It would be naive, however, to believe that military waste is primarily a function of criminal elements in the military-industrial complex. If fraud in military expenditures were eliminated, there would certainly be some reduction in the misallocation of funds, but the fundamental problem of wasteful military spending would remain.

The technical and secretive nature of the national defense service provided by the military makes it difficult for the public to exert control over its political agents who formulate defense policy. This difficulty creates a decision-making vacuum that readily is filled by those whose interests are tied directly to military appropriation. Many of the practices that have grown up around defense spending are understood best against the backdrop of special-interest control over national defense decisions—a special-interest control that leads to excessive defense budgets and wasteful allocations within those budgets.

In contrast to most goods, once national defense is provided for one individual in the country, it is provided for all. The fact that one U.S. citizen benefits from military protection in no way reduces the benefits available to other citizens. Goods

---

that have the characteristic of being nonrival in consumption commonly are referred to as public goods.

Unfortunately, the public-good nature of defense makes it difficult to transmit individual demands for military protection to potential suppliers. Were defense allocated through the marketplace, everyone would benefit, whether they contributed or not. Each individual would face the temptation to free ride on the contributions of others. This "free-rider" incentive works against funding public goods privately and justifies the government providing for the nation's defense, since it can require contributions through imposing taxes.

According to the standard analysis of public goods provision, in a democracy, citizens exert ultimate control over taxing and spending decisions through their choices at the polls. The standard assumption is that voting will reflect citizen demands rather accurately. As opposed to a decision to contribute to a public good in a market setting, the decision to support a public good at the ballot box will cost the voter nothing unless the vote obligates everyone to contribute to the good. So, citizens will support sensible national defense proposals if they are presented to them in a political setting, even though they would refuse to support the same proposals if offered in the market.

While this analysis of allocation of public goods contains elements of truth, it leaves out much that is important to understanding the problem of military waste. Despite the standard analysis, citizens' demands for the benefits provided by national defense are not easily transmitted politically. On the contrary, the political impetus for military spending comes primarily from those who supply national defense, not from the citizens who benefit from it. It is useful to consider in some detail the reasons for this supply-side influence and examine the implication it has for efficiency in military spending.

## General Interest vs. the Special Interests

Decisions on the size of the defense budget and the allocation of moneys within that budget are made under the interacting pressures exerted by four major interest groups: voters/consumers in whose names the expenditures are made; the suppliers—namely defense contractors; the customers, which consist of Pentagon and Defense Department officials and other military leaders; and politicians, acting as middlemen. This interacting pressure is driven by the private interests of these groups and their relative ability to push the growth and allocation of military appropriations in directions which serve these interests.

While voters/consumers are numerically the largest group as well as the group that pays the bill, their influence is far less than indicated by the standard view. The public votes only indirectly on military programs through its choice of candidates for political office. Each voter also realizes, at least at the subliminal level, that his or her single vote is extremely unlikely to determine the outcome of an election. There is no real incentive, then, for any individual voter to invest the time required to be well-informed. This "rational ignorance" that reduces the voter's ability to direct and monitor political decisions supposedly made on his behalf is especially pronounced in the case of defense spending. There are few, if any, other areas of public decision-making that involve as much technical complexity as decisions on defense. Further aggravating this problem is the shroud of secrecy (some justified, but much surely not) that surrounds political decisions on military expenditures.

In contrast to the weak, diffused, and largely uninformed effect of voters/consumers, defense contractors have strong incentives to exert influence. The Pentagon is the largest single purchaser of goods and services in the economy, with its purchases concentrated in a few industries. Each of these industries has an intense interest in all of the specifics of military spending decisions and in influencing these decisions. They develop the ability to exert influence by maintaining close contacts with the "customers" (the Pentagon), through the use of Political Action Committees (PAC's), and through careful geographical planning in awarding subcontracts. This builds political support at Congressional levels and at the grassroots level, among labor unions and workers.

Defense contractors also gain influence through this easy access to information. Advance information on the types of forthcoming programs not only can give established contractors a head start on securing contracts, but allows them to have input into the policy formation process. This two-way flow of information works to the advantage of the major defense contractors and is enhanced by the "government relations" offices that they maintain in Washington—offices well staffed by former Pentagon and/or Congressional personnel.

Military leaders, along with civilian Pentagon and Department of Defense (DOD) officials, strongly influence the decision-making on military spending. Pentagon and DOD officials are charged with developing military strategy and deciding on military needs. Their decision-making can not help but be influenced by their self-interests—interests that always are attached to the prospects of particular programs and spending proposals. Many Pentagon officials also appear to have personal incentives to accommodate defense contractors who may be former and/or future employers. This so-called "revolving door" has had frequent and extensive use.

The politicians play the role of middlemen in this process. While they are the representatives of the voters, money remains the "mother's milk" of politics. Politicians depend on heavy campaign contributions to survive in political office. Over time, the cost of campaigning, with the extensive use of media coverage, has escalated, making politicians increasingly sensitive to the needs of raising adequate campaign funds. The average voter, as suggested above, has only a marginal role and, hence, a marginal incentive to contribute. As a means of self-preservation, the politician must be sensitive to the desires of large contributors—*i.e.,* the organized interests on the receiving end of political appropriations.

The combination of ineffective consumers and tight cooperative arrangements between the suppliers and buyers of military equipment and the political middlemen who expedite the transactions ensures that the public's interest in efficiently providing an adequate defense has little influence on defense policy. In this regard, national defense presents more of a problem than most goods that the government provides. When the government provides goods that benefit a relatively small and politically organized group of voter/consumers, that constituency will exert political pressure for efficiency. This pressure is weak in the case of national defense because of the broad-based and intangible nature of the benefits provided.

The special interests that make up the defense contractor-Pentagon-Congress coalition possess broad latitude to pursue policies and fund programs that are more effective in promoting their private advantages than in enhancing national security. The result has been an excessively large military budget with a bias toward high-tech, high-profit weaponry instead of a less glamorous, and less profitable, emphasis on conventional weaponry and manpower.

## The Military Offensive

This failure in the political process, resulting in excessive and distorted military budgets, is being brought into focus in the current budget debate. An effective push for increased military expenditures beginning in 1979 had increased military spending from $116,300,000,000 in that year to $265,800,000,000 in 1986, with $282,200,000,000 requested in the fiscal year 1987 budget. The deficit rose from $40,200,000,000 in 1979 to $202,800,000,000 in 1986. In other words, military expenditures increased by $149,500,000,000, while the deficit increased by $162,600,000,000. Increases in military expenditures have been financed by borrowing (the path of least political resistance) so that, until now, the full costs of these expenditures have been postponed. Politically, it is easy to sell voters on more defense spending when the true costs are obscured.

With the advent of the Gramm-Rudman-Hollings bill, which requires decreases in the deficit, the real choices involved in this type of military build-up are forced. However, if the choices follow the pattern of recent years, the collective wills of the contractor-Pentagon forces will remain much stronger than those of the consumer/voters. For example, a Harris poll in June, 1985, found 69% of those questioned preferring to cut defense rather than aid to education. Notwithstanding, in the fiscal year 1986 budget, the share going to defense increased from 26.7% to 27.1%, while the share going to education remained a constant 3.1%. The trend has been to increase defense spending despite prevailing public opinion.

A major inefficiency created by the customer-supplier-political middleman interaction is reflected in the shift in resource allocation within the defense budget. While the share of the military budget going to personnel fell from 36.2% to 26.6% and the share for operations and maintenance fell from 31% to 27.9%, the share going for procurement increased from 17.9% to 29.1% between the fiscal years of 1976 and 1984. (Procurement is defined by the Department of Defense as "the acquisition of weapons, equipment, munitions, spares, and modification of existing equipment.")

This shift came in spite of the Joint Chiefs of Staff's call for a substantial build-up in conventional forces, which are said to be "dangerously" thin, given U.S. commitments abroad. Although current policy is aimed at rapid intervention into the world's trouble spots, military budgets emphasize the build-up of heavy, high-cost, limited-quantity weapon systems unsuited for this type of military action.

The reason for this misallocation is that technologically sophisticated weaponry is a very profitable business. It is highly capital-intensive, so labor costs are relatively low. Furthermore, since, under current arrangements, the government supplies a portion of the tools and facilities needed, capital requirements are relatively low. Risks are also low. Past history of government bailouts makes risk of failure remote. Furthermore, much of the contracting is done on a cost-plus basis, eliminating risks of loss. The result is a U.S. defense budget that is driven by a "technological imperative." It appears that special-interest pressures dictate a military strategy designed to maximize the use of exotic, high-tech weapons, rather than an efficient way to achieve security.

A recent illustration of designing strategy to fit a profitable high-tech system is the Strategic Defense Initiative (SDI), or "Star Wars." The program has the potential of being the first trillion-dollar weapons system. The Council on Economic Priorities has charged that the Pentagon is using its initial contracts to build political support, with 77% of the major contracts awarded to firms in states or districts represented by members of the armed services committees or defense appropriation panels. Defense contractors are calling it the business opportunity of the century, and several of the large contractors—including Lockheed and McDonnell Douglas—have set up special divisions to build political support and secure a share of the contracts.

SDI is the brainchild of physicist Edward Teller, the director of the Lawrence Livermore National Laboratories. Its promises of creating a "protective shield" against nuclear attack and eliminating the need for nuclear weapons are politically appealing. However, many scientists, including Nobel laureate physicist Hans Bethe, argue that it could provide at best a very porous umbrella. The goal of intercepting all incoming missiles is virtually impossible with our current and foreseeable levels of technology. For example, low-flying cruise missiles carrying nuclear warheads could fly under the shield. Bethe also argues that the system could be swamped by multiple warheads and decoys. Since the system works by attacking missiles in their burn phase, the Soviets also could foil the system by designing a missile with a faster burn phase.

Secretary of Defense Caspar Weinberger, in his *Annual Report to the Congress, Fiscal, 1987,* stated: "Even a thoroughly reliable shield against ballistic missiles would still leave us vulnerable to other modes of delivery, or perhaps to other devices of mass destruction." In other words, a successful SDI, as Bethe suggests, would force the Soviets to change their strategy and their mix of weapons. Is this worth a trillion dollars? Not according to former Secretary of State Dean Rusk, who (in private conversation with one of the authors) has said, "The movement of the arms race into outer space would be politically inflammatory, militarily futile, economically absurd, and aesthetically repulsive. Otherwise it may not be a bad idea.'' Nonetheless, the system is expanding, breathing new life into the Livermore Laboratories and bringing hope, along with research funds, to defense contractors.

Given the supply-determined nature of procurement decisions, once major weapon systems begin to be funded, they rarely are stopped, even after they become obsolete. One such example is the B-1 bomber. Scheduled to come into service in 1986, it is being displaced by a new advanced-technology, radar-evading bomber, the Stealth. Even though the B-1 is expected to be displaced within five years or less and its capabilities could be matched by an upgraded B-52 armed with cruise missiles (both of which also have been funded), it continues to be funded. In fiscal 1985, we spent $5,000,000,000 for procurement of 34 B-1 bombers plus $463,000,000 on additional development. In addition, $458,000,000 was spent to upgrade 90 B-52 bombers. From 1981 to 1988, $28,500,000,000 is expected to be spent on the B-1. It is not only ''old soldiers who never die,'' but also obsolete (and expensive) weapon systems.

Prominent military personnel have supported the view that the current military buildup in sophisticated weapon systems is not improving the defense system. For example, retired Adm. Noel Gayler, former Commander and Chief, U.S. Forces, Pacific and former director of the National Security Agency, wrote in an op-ed piece in *The Wall Street Journal,* March 7, 1984:

> The good news is that we can cut the defense budget significantly and improve our security. . . . The immediate way . . . is to cut out the useless, dangerous and inordinately expensive new nuclear-weapons programs. . . . There would be no loss of deterrence: We would still have the capability to devastate the U.S.S.R. even after being attacked. The TRIAD [land, sea and air forces] would still be in place; any leg alone could do the job many times over. . . . And there will be major military gains in focusing command attention and resources on our real military needs rather than on unusable weapons, or even magic.

Unfortunately, the ''major gains'' referred to would be spread over the general tax-paying public and, therefore, exert very little influence on the decisions that are made. It is sophisticated weaponry concentrating profits on the politically influential that wins support.

This misuse of military appropriations and abuse of U.S. taxpayers are the completely predictable consequences of the nexus of special interest control over military spending. Procurement policy reflects more the interests of suppliers than it does concerns of national security. The waste and inefficiency that have become the hallmark of the military-industrial complex are the expected outcome of the divergence that exists between private interests and the public interest when suppliers are not held accountable to the desires of consumers.

## Can Anything Be Done?

In an ideal political setting, the consumers of national defense would exert control over military spending. In such a setting, military spending would provide the maximum security for the amount spent, and the amount spent would reflect the consumers' collective willingness to make marginal tradeoffs between national security and other things of value. In other words, consumers would be able to transmit their preferences in such a way that suppliers served their private interests best by treating consumer preferences as their own. Obviously, real world imperfections will always stand between us and the realization of such an ideal. Even under the best of circumstances, suppliers will have some latitude within which they can promote their advantages at the expense of consumers. This latitude has taken on genuinely troublesome proportions, however, in the case of the national defense.

In view of political realities, what are the possibilities that the system can be changed? It is easy to be pessimistic. Any number of specific proposals come to mind that would force political decisions to be more accountable to the public desire for an adequate and efficiently supplied defense. In every case, however, these proposals would provide benefits to those who our analysis indicates are largely without political influence (the general public) and remove privileges from those with political influence (defense contractors and military brass). It would appear that we are trapped in a Catch 22 dilemma. We need reforms in military procedures for the very reason we are not likely to get them—*i.e.,* lack of public control over military decisions. Nonetheless, given the Heisenberg Principle (anything examined cannot remain unchanged), the recent public debate on the issue is a positive step. The effectiveness of special political influence depends on more than the exercises of political muscle—it is crucially dependent on the perception that the public interest is being served. Once the facade of public-interest rhetoric is pierced, the strength of private-interest influence is diminished.

In this regard, the recent publicity given spending excesses resulting from military procurement practices is useful. It is just such publicity that brings these practices clearly to the attention of the public and mobilizes public opinion against them in ways that politicians ignore at their own peril. There is already evidence that politicians are beginning to respond to the public's concern over military waste. The mounting publicity on outlandish prices paid for common items has caught the voters' attention and, therefore, also Congress' attention. At the same time, Gramm-Rudman-Hollings legislation is making politicians and consumer/voters face the painful choices between defense, other pet programs, and higher taxes. To the extent that Congress responds by institutionalizing more accountability in military procurement practices, like the proposed Pentagon reorganization plan [the Senate bill, "The Department of Defense Reorganization Act of 1986," sponsored by Senators Barry Goldwater (R.-Ariz.) and Sam Nunn (D.-Ga.), was approved by the Senate Armed Services Committee in March, 1986], the political process will be shifted to give more protection to the public interest against the special interests. Cuts in the military budget need not mean less defense if they can be made, as Rep. Les Aspin (D.-Wis.), chairman of the House Armed Services Committee, put it, "with a view from the mountain top of strategy instead of from the bottom of the pork barrel."

While we cannot hope for the elimination of all waste from the military budget or to achieve a completely rational defense policy, clear improvements are within the realm of political feasibility. Reform is possible, but only through an aroused public that exerts its collective will through the political process and shifts power back in favor of the taxpaying public.

# National Security: Mangled by Interest Groups

*Amitai Etzioni*

## Six Areas of Corruption

If there is an area in which one would expect the interest groups to restrain themselves, it is that of national security. Conversely, if this sector of public policy-making is found to be permeated by interest groups, one can hardly expect any other area to be immune. The evidence indicates that national security is mangled by special interests. These include major defense contractors (or industries with defense interests, such as aerospace), service associations (some of which mix retired service personnel with those on active duty, and with representatives of defense industries), thousands of smaller businesses and subcontractors, trade associations, labor unions, numerous local constituencies (in the areas in which defense generates jobs), and the armed services themselves, when they act as lobbies.

These various groups do not all pull together, working in cahoots with one another. There is no single, unified military-industrial complex which has captured the nation's public decision-making. Nor is private gain the only source of corrupting influence. Yet together, evidence shows, those interest groups have penetrated national-security decision-making to the point where independent or professional decision-making geared to national-security goals cannot prevail.

The undue role of private interests is evident in six major areas:

- A strong bias in favor of procurement of weapons, which contributes to a tendency to neglect the development of a security strategy and hinders efforts to ensure that the balance of various kinds of armed forces (infantry versus naval, for instance) will reflect a national strategy.
- The purchase of inferior weapons (weapons that fail to meet specifications, while superior ones are available), as well as the continued production of obsolete weapons.
- A bias in favor of costly ("big-ticket") items and complex technology over simpler, less costly items.
- A tendency to favor buying new items rather than properly maintaining those the military has already bought.

---

Amitai Etzioni, "National Security: Mangled by Interest Groups." Published by permission of Transaction Publishers, from *Capital Corruption: The New Attack on American Democracy* by Amitai Etzioni.  (pp. 102–119).

- A strong inclination to favor hardware over personnel, particularly dangerous in that it favors nuclear forces over conventional forces.
- An inflation of the total defense budget until it undercuts the economy, the social order, and its own effectiveness—and hence national security.

All these matters are surrounded by considerable controversy. For example, for each weapon a group of experts finds below specifications, there is a person or group who will champion it. Those who call for less reliance on technology are confronted by those who find high technology most effective, and so on. It is not my purpose to settle these arguments, but to show that they take place in a forum so invaded by special interests that it is difficult, if not impossible, to explore the issues and reach decisions on their merits.

Although the impact of special interests is quite evident, we shall see that the specific profile of private power is different in national security from that in other areas. True, PACs have been set up by defense industries just as by others, and are as busy in defense as elsewhere. However, because the older, pre-PAC forms of lobbying are particularly powerful in this area, PACs are an addition to the unwholesome brew, not the main ingredient. U.S. security has been hostage to special interests long before the age of PACs, and PACs largely serve to cement existing favored positions, forge additional links between defense manufacturers and members of Congress, and increase the awesome power of big defense corporations over smaller ones.

## Introducing the Main Interests

Before I report on the effects of special interests on the various facets of our defense, let me line them up, for brief inspection.

The *defense industry* is a rather concentrated business. While there are twenty-five thousand prime defense contractors, only thirty-three of these account for over half of the prime contracts. The largest defense contractors include General Dynamics ($3.5 billion from the Department of Defense [DOD] in 1980); McDonnell Douglas ($3.25 billion); Hughes Aircraft ($1.8 billion); Grumman ($1.3 billion); and Northrop ($1.2 billion).

The largest PACs in the defense area have been set up by the largest DOD contract recipients, and by some runners-up. Together, the PACs of the ten largest contractors shelled out more than $1.5 million to federal candidates in the 1982 election. These include the PACs of United Technologies, which gave $211,025; Lockheed, $183,330; General Dynamics, $176,990; Rockwell International, $175,233; General Electric, $149,125; McDonnell Douglas, $136,675; Hughes Aircraft, $136,265; Boeing, $128,400; Martin Marietta, $131,500; and Raytheon, $115,479.

True to form, defense PACs concentrated their dollars where they would count most. For instance, in 1982 McDonnell Douglas and Lockheed PACs favored with their dollar endorsement thirty-six of the thirty-nine members of the House Armed

Services Committee who were running for re-election, and all fourteen of the members of the Subcommittee on Procurement. PACs of Rockwell International, Raytheon, and Hughes Aircraft contributed handsomely to all ten of the members of the House Subcommittee on Defense Appropriations. The chairmen of the appropriate committees, Representative J. P. Addabbo (House Armed Services Committee) and Senator John Tower (Senate Armed Services Committee), did particularly well. These two names will come up again.

Typically, the argument is made that all defense PACs buy is access, not favor, as if special access were not a favor and as if that were all they paid for. Representative Norman D. Dicks of the House Subcommittee on Defense Appropriations claims: "You know who shows up at your fund-raiser. If people are helping you, you're certainly not going to turn them down if they want to come in and see you."

But others are either more blunt—or more carefree. "We actively support the candidacy of members who would further the interests of the McDonnell Douglas Corporation," said Thomas Gunn, head of McDonnell's Washington office.

Sometimes, it is reported, the White House gets involved. Professor William H. Lewis, director of George Washington University's Security Policy Studies program, was helping to set up the office of Under Secretary of State for Security Assistance during the transition from the Carter to the Reagan administration. He recalls receiving numerous phone calls from defense industry representatives concerned about their overseas programs. One was from a consultant to Northrop Industries, whose head, Thomas V. Jones, supported Reagan during the election. The consultant intoned: "The [new] President wants you to support the Northrop F-X." Lewis asked for written confirmation, which was not forthcoming. He further checked with the National Security Council staff. He was given the green light long before the new administration had a chance to review its defense policy and budget, let alone such important questions as which combat aircraft would be appropriate for sale to less-developed nations.

The *labor* defense parade is led by the International Association of Machinists and Aerospace Workers and the United Auto Workers. In other areas they may confront management or support liberal politicians. Here they tend to lobby closely with defense contractors. "We catch them [members of Congress] in crossfire," the head of an aircraft manufacturing corporation told me.

As might be expected, Gerry Whipple, representing the UAW in six Western states, is gung-ho on the B-1 and opposed to converting swords to plowshares.

> California has been built on food, defence and oil: you can't expect us to convert into industries for garbage disposal or cheap houses. There are some super-liberal congressmen with their heads in the clouds who dream of building houses instead of bombers: but workers can't have pride in making low-cost housing, when the low-income families just use them for putting garbage in the hall.

Because the amounts involved are staggering, because this is the only sector in which all the funds are public in source and hence subject to political decisions, and because all fifty states and most congressional districts are cut in in a big way—DOD money has been subject to logrolling and pork-barreling by members of Congress prodded by local interests since long before interest groups became PACed. The irrational way military bases are kept open to satisfy local political pressures is well known; it mirrors the considerations by which post offices used to be kept open.

A typical item in *The Wall Street Journal:*

> Perhaps the most common congressionally imposed cost in the defense budget is the expense of operating bases that the generals no longer want but that senators and representatives won't allow to close. One example: Congress has explicitly barred the military from moving a maintenance unit from New Cumberland, Pa., to Corpus Christi, Texas. Pentagon officials believe the change would save millions, but Pennsylvania's representatives don't want to see the jobs move out.

This 1983 report continues:

> Last year, as every year, Congress saddled the Pentagon with a long list of unrequested things to buy or build, plus others to avoid: The Army must buy milk and U.S. mined coal but mustn't recycle certain types of aluminum; an armory must be rebuilt in Buffalo, and a new parking apron built at a Michigan air base.

Senator J. Bennett Johnston, Jr., from Louisiana got the Senate Appropriations Committee in 1982 to split the army's purchasing of Multiple Launch Rocket Systems between the company the army wanted as sole supplier and companies in his district. The army estimated the additional cost at $93 to $105 million. Representative J. P. Addabbo demanded that the navy buy radar from a contractor near his district, Sperry Corporation. Waste: over $2 billion. Scores of other such incidents are on file and others can be traced practically daily.

*Congressional Quarterly* succeeded in quantifying some of the known items. It estimated that the House Armed Services Committee padded the 1983 defense budget by some $296 million—69 percent of which ended up in the districts represented by members of that committee.

When L. Mendel Rivers was chairman of the House Armed Services Committee, his district in Charleston, South Carolina, got itself a naval station, a shipyard, an air base, an army depot, a missile plant, and a mine-warfare center. Sixty percent of the industry in the district was reported to have become defense-based. A sign at a roadway in the district used to read, simply: "Rivers delivers." When Representative Carl Vinson became chairman of the same committee, he got so many defense projects for his Georgia district that an air-force general told him one day: "Sir, if you try to put one more base in Georgia, you will sink your state."

Although there are long lists of what has been pork-barreled each year, most items are not traceable, because

> In most instances, Congress's clubby rules make it difficult to pin down the individuals responsible. Deals are made in private; defense items are traded for favors elsewhere in the legislative agenda; and members push projects as favors for others, obscuring the true origins of an idea.

As a result, *"Congress votes itself [and the nation] regional or local defense programs instead of a national defense structure,"* stated Senator Barry Goldwater. When the cry in Congress was for lower defense spending in 1983, Senator John G. Tower asked his colleagues if any one of them was willing to accept a cut in defense spending in his own state. Senator Tower found very few takers. (Senator David H. Pryor of Arkansas would have done without nerve-gas production in his state.) More typical are coordinated drives by corporations, labor unions, and local community leaders in favor of their localities' share of the spoils. Thus, even Senator Alan Cranston from California, who has made peace his main presidential campaign issue, has been fighting for the B-1 bomber. The prime beneficiary of the $4-billion down payment involved, and the scores of billions to follow, is Rockwell International, headquartered in California. Lockheed got Atlanta's liberal Mayor Andrew Young to travel to Washington, D.C., to argue for the C-5B, production of which would bring eighty-five hundred new jobs to Georgia. These two will stand for hundreds of such accounts that can be listed.

When the President needs votes in Congress, defense expenditures are typically used as rewards. A recent example: "To win the votes of Long Island Congressmen last August [1982] for Reagan's tax increase, the White House promised to buy 20 more A-10s." The A-10 is built on Long Island.

*Service associations* are of and by civilians, but they act to promote the cause of one armed service or another. These include the Association of the U.S. Army, the Navy League, and the Air Force Association. Their membership runs into the hundred thousands of individuals. In the Army and Air Force associations, a high proportion are on active duty with their respective services. The service associations have corporate members, and these corporations pick up a sizable proportion of the associations' costs, including those of their annual dinners, "seminars," conventions, and so on. But a discussion of service associations' close links to defense industries will have to await an exploration of the details of lobbying.

And there are *trade associations,* groups of defense manufacturers such as the Aerospace Industries Association, the American Ordnance Association, and the National Security Industrial Association, among others.

The *armed services themselves* act as lobbies. Up to a point, their promotion of competing views of the nature of the Soviet danger, the kind of defenses the United States requires, and so on, is part of a wholesome and very American pluralistic way of deliberation and decision-making. But, we shall see, the armed services go much further, to absurd lengths, to advance *their own services,* adding to the cacophony of voices that render defense decision-making more a brawl of special interests than an orderly, rational process.

## Procurement "Drives" out Strategy

In a world free of special interests, defense experts and duly appointed defense authorities might draft a defense strategy, within guidelines laid down by the President and the National Security Council. This strategy might then be reviewed by the White House and the appropriate congressional committees, leading to requests for modification, clarification, and adaptation. After several reiterations of this process, a thoroughly worked-out strategy would result. It, in turn, would serve as the basis for guiding the armed services as to which mix of personnel they were to recruit and train, and which weapon systems to develop and purchase.

Such a strategy would reflect the nation's position, as articulated by duly vested authorities, on such questions as: Would the United States initiate a nuclear war even if attacked only by conventional forces? Should the United States be able to fight on several fronts simultaneously if attacked only on one front by the U.S.S.R. (and thus able to choose the theater most propitious for our counterattack)? Should the United States intervene in Third World countries in order to prevent Soviet takeover, even if indirect?

Once answers are formulated in that hypothetical world free of interest groups, "suitable" forces would then be tailored to the strategy. For instance, if we are not to be the first to start a nuclear war, and our most likely opponent, the U.S.S.R., has a large conventional force, we would need to be able to match that force (if not in numbers, then by a higher quality of personnel and of conventional weapons). If we plan a major Third World role, we might need sizable forward bases around the world and forces able to fight guerrillas, which would not be a high priority if we focus our efforts on countervailing the U.S.S.R. in Europe.

This is not, however, the way it is done. As incredible as it might seem, the fact is that the United States does not have an overall, worked-out military strategy. Louis J. Walinsky observed recently in the prestigious journal *Foreign Affairs* that "this country and its NATO allies have until now, incredibly, lacked a meaningful and coherent strategy of defense against the Soviet Union." Moreover, "military spending proposals have not clearly been related to specific threats to our national security or to a coherent defense strategy." He proceeds to cite a long list of defense experts who make the same point.

A position paper issued in 1983 by a Democratic think tank returns to a common criticism: "The United States lacks a coherent strategy for its military forces." It goes on to acknowledge that this "failing" of the Reagan administration is "not entirely its exclusive property."

In March 1983, six former members of various cabinets, of both parties, wrote jointly to President Reagan's National Security Adviser, William P. Clark, that they find U.S. defense outlays not linked to a strategy.

The record of the last decade suggests that to a large extent *procurement "drives" strategy, rather than serving it.* The Department of Defense repeatedly bought weapons systems because each was justified as a valuable technology, with little concern for an overall strategy and a mix of forces and weapons tailored to it. Interest groups are not the only reason the United States is weapons-happy and strategy-shy, but other factors need not concern us here; the role of interest groups is a sufficient threat in its own right. And they help push U.S. defense efforts away from strategic coherence.

Bill Keller, of the *Congressional Quarterly,* writes in an article entitled "In a Bull Market for Arms, Weapons Industry Lobbyists Push Products, Not Policy": "The arms lobby tends to avoid policy debates—such as the desirable size of defense spending overall or strategic arms limitations—but concentrates instead on marketing its own products."

A congressional expert on the research-and-development process attests: "Most of the defense programs are technology-driven rather than threat-driven." He adds: "It's more a matter of coming up with a new way of doing something and then working it in and adapting it to your warfare ideas."

Richard Sellers is a credible observer. He is the director of the Washington office of the American Security Council, a leading lobby for bigger defense budgets, with some twelve hundred corporate members. Not pacifistic or anti-industry, he says about the contractors: "They're so attuned to next week's allocation of government money they're not looking to the long-range national security interests of the country."

An extensive study of the influence of eight major aerospace firms' lobbying and campaign giving was sponsored by the Council on Economic Priorities, a liberal not-for-profit research group. Gordon Adams, the group's director of research on government relations, commented, "It is this network that makes it almost impossible to have a debate about alternative weapons systems, defense strategy or defense priorities."

Just as the tax code has special interests written into it—to the point where an overall tax concept is no longer visible—so our defense posture reflects the outcome of contractors' lobbying, service rivalry, and pork-barreling over C-5, B-1, F-18 production, rather than the reasoned analysis of a no-first-strike posture, or a hardened second-strike one, or any other coherent posture.

It might be said that little harm is inflicted thus, that it does not much matter whether a weapons system is built by Boeing in Washington or Lockheed in California or McDonnell Douglas in Missouri. Indeed, there is a certain virtue in distributing weapons purchasing so as to keep in business several major corporations that specialize in defense. However, one should not disregard the fact that not all corporations and districts are equally adept at producing whatever weapons system is being lobbied and pork-barreled at the time, and that the nation would benefit from having a weapons provider selected by merit, not political clout.

The pressures by special interests exacerbate an American tendency to avoid strategy, a tendency that has other sources. Strategies are inherently difficult to formulate. After all, we deal with hypothetical futures, under circumstances no one has ever faced, which are quite difficult to conceptualize. And we have a deeply ingrained national tendency, deeply rooted in our pragmatic, empiricist tradition, to concern ourselves with details and not with the whole picture. However, interest groups feed into, and on, these ingrained tendencies.

## Buying Inferior and Obsolete Weapons

Beyond the combination of a pro-procurement bias and neglect of strategy, interest-group pressures frequently result in the purchase of inappropriate weapons. That is, setting aside the question of how many and what general kind of weapons the U.S. defense requires, the decisions to buy *specific* weapons systems—a highly technical matter—are made under the undue pressure of special interests.

Senator William Proxmire of Wisconsin has pointed out that "the heaviest lobbying pressure—and the most potent with Congress—is to hold on to old weapons, keep old assembly lines rolling." Congress "primarily keeps things alive that ought to die" and increases production runs, according to Jacques S. Gansler, former deputy assistant Defense secretary for materials acquisition. "'Canceling an established program is extraordinarily difficult,' said William A. Long, the Deputy Under Secretary of Defense for acquisition policy, adding that each weapon developed a constituency in Congress, in its armed service, and in industry." Reports *The Wall Street Journal:* "History shows that once big weapons programs get rolling—generating jobs and business contracts—they are politically almost impossible to stop."

A few examples will serve to illustrate the role of pork-barreling and of defense contractors in the procurement of inferior weapons and in the continued production of obsolete weapons. A light attack aircraft used by both the navy and the air force, the A-7, saw extensive action in Vietnam. By the late seventies, however, it was considered so badly out of date that a Pentagon official described it as a "flying dump truck." The Pentagon stopped requesting money for the plane years ago, but year after year funds were appropriated by Congress. "It's [Senator] John Tower's project," explained an air-force officer, referring to the fact that General Dynamics builds the A-7 in Tower's home state of Texas. Despite the fact that the A-7 is "so out of date a lot just go into storage," Tower convinced the National Guard Association to "take his side and lobby for it."

It is often noted that defense contractors are successful in keeping an obsolete weapons system alive, and getting more orders for it than seems rational. To repeat: once a weapons system has emerged from the research-and-development system to a prototype stage, it has often acquired a "constituency" in industry and Congress which makes it very difficult to kill. Typically, *Forbes,* in an article concerned strictly with finding profitable stocks for its readers, recommends Rockwell, the producer of the B-1 bomber, with the following logic:

> The B-1 program has been a political football for many years, but the critical first-production unit was funded in the fiscal 1982 budget. Congressional appropriations on the fiscal 1983 budget should lock the B-1 program in place. Opposi-

> tion is likely to become less effective thereafter. This is true for two reasons: the program's momentum and the broadening use of political support as the prospects of jobs in Ohio, California, Texas, New York, Oklahoma, and Washington become more tangible.

Services acting as lobbies and service-related lobbies come a close second to contractors in lobbying for weapons systems suitable to their continued existence, rather than merely to national needs. There are many reports about interservice rivalries that result in highly irrational decision-making.

I gained a sense of the intensity of these rivalries through a trivial incident. Durign an off-the-record national-security seminar in Washington, D.C., a civilian suggested that the command of the rapid-deployment force be changed. He asked about a particular theater command post: ''Must the post have an *army* man?'' (Missions and posts were tightly divided among the services at a famous post–World War II meeting at Key West. Since then the division is usually fiercely upheld, even when technology and circumstances require adjustments.) A Pentagon man shouted from the back of the room: ''Does the Pope have to be Catholic?''

The services are repeatedly reported to act as if each of them is the only one entrusted with most if not all facets of U.S. military security. They fight one another with stories leaked to the press, self-serving information provided to the White House—and lobbying in Congress. At the least, their rivalry has resulted in enormous waste and overstocking of weapons. Harvard political scientist and hawk Samuel P. Huntington points out that conflicting services have continually developed similar weapons for the same mission. For instance, the army developed an intercontinental missile, Jupiter; the air force—Thor. Other examples include the army's Nike versus the navy's Talos; the army's Missile Master air defense control system versus the air force's SAGE.

It is reported that in Vietnam the impact of interservice rivalry was anything but trivial, costing many lives. The army could not provide close air cover, because it is not allowed to have ''fixed-wing'' aircraft that weigh more than 5,000 pounds—this military capability being reserved to the air force. To avoid an army incursion into air-force turf, an army field commander needing backup had to alert his HQ and so forth up the army chain of command; in turn, the message was relayed back down the air-force chain of command, until it reached the airplane circling above the field commander's head. To prevent direct communication, army and air force stuck to different frequencies. The resulting delays are reported to have caused numerous casualties.

For the same basic reasons, the army relied on helicopters, which it was permitted to buy because they do not have fixed wings, but lost many men because helicopters were more vulnerable to enemy fire than fighters. Even official estimates put the loss at forty-nine hundred helicopters. (There is no similar estimate of the number of lives lost when helicopters were shot down, or of the resulting defeats in various battles.) The lobbying pressures thus go beyond buying the wrong weapons; in combat, our soldiers are stuck with them, and our ability to win is undercut.

## High on Tech, But Low on People and Maintenance

The connection between lobbying and procurement is easy to see. But many of the effects of defense lobbying are much more subtle and indirect, and noticeable more in accumulation than individually. Nor, I am the first to acknowledge, can these links readily be indicated. The evidence is largely circumstantial; a major national study of the problem is very much needed. But bear with me as I first detail what many observers consider irrational decision-making before I point to those who seem to profit from it.

The U.S. military is often reported to accord much higher priority to buying complex technology than to buying simpler items; to buying new weapons of any kind than to maintaining old ones; and to investing in weapons than to investing in personnel. These tendencies were flagged in a study by Ret. Captain George W. S. Kuhn for the archconservative Heritage Foundation. They were pointed out by the congressional Military Reform Caucus, an ideologically mixed group including liberal Senator Gary Hart; conservative Senator Sam Nunn; Representative Jack Edwards, Republican from Alabama; and other members of Congress specializing in military oversight. The same tendencies were reported by the General Accounting Office, the auditing agency of considerable independence and expert standing that was established by Congress. They were indicated, albeit more indirectly, by several in-house Pentagon studies and by outside observers, including James Fallows in his book *National Defense.* This is not a consensus of all interested in the process. The Pentagon and the defense contractors, as well as several independent experts, do not agree.

Since these various criticisms of U.S. defense have been made frequently—and responded to—I will just review them quickly. To reiterate: my task is not to establish whether or not the criticisms are correct, but to point out that the issues cannot be explored in a professional, independent, even sensible manner because of intense pressures by special interests.

### How Much High Tech?

The military preoccupation with high tech is often discussed in terms of "quality versus quantity" of whatever the armed services are buying, be it anti-tank weapons or aircraft carriers. A bias is reported in favor of buying fewer items in order to be able to afford much more costly items which have more advanced capabilities. Critics point out that after a point, quantity makes up for quality, that it is more effective to have thousands of simple anti-tank weapons than a few score of very complex and "able" ones. They further maintain that high-tech items often malfunction, and that they require sophisticated soldiers, whereas many soldiers the United States is saddled with in the volunteer army are barely literate. Also, many of the professionals needed to maintain the equipment are hired away from the armed services by the private sector. (The military did better on both counts during the 1981–82 recession, but this advantage is expected to diminish quickly once better economic conditions prevail.)

The General Accounting Office concluded that military planners are mesmerized by high technology. Choice examples: The F-15 fighter plane is so dependent on sophisticated electronics that battlefield repairs require diagnostic computers, and these computers have numerous reliability problems of their own. To perform at all they must be kept air-conditioned. Electronic parts integral to the army's Cobra attack helicopter cause its anti-tank missile-firing system to fail on the average of once every hundred hours. The navy's MK86 weapons control system, at the heart of all the newest combat ships, has more than forty thousand parts and, during a period studied in 1979, was usable only 60 percent of the time.

A similar argument was made by John M. Collins, a retired army paratroop colonel and author of a major defense study, *U.S.-Soviet Military Balance.* He writes about the "seductiveness of high technology" that has led the United States to buy a wire-guided anti-tank weapon that works well only in open territory. It requires a soldier to stay in position until its slowly unwinding wire unfolds. And the ammunition costs so much that most U.S. teams would go into combat without ever having fired a live shot.

Pentagon analyst Franklin Spinney concluded his 1980 study of weapons systems with the statement: "Our strategy of pursuing ever increasing technical complexity and sophistication has made high-technology solutions and combat readiness mutually exclusive." This is reflected in a 90-percent *decrease* in tank production and a 95-percent drop in fighter-plane construction over thirty years (1950–80), which highlight the extremes of sacrificing quantity for hoped-for quality.

A panel of National Guard officers, in a report entitled *VISTA 1999,* points out that "the procurement of expensive, complex equipment to the exclusion of most other equipment has created a fundamental contradiction between what we have and what we need." The report laments the trend of buying the most complex weaponry available and argues, for example, in favor of developing an inexpensive tactical fighter to replace the A-10. (A-10s cost $10 to $12 million each; design studies indicate that a tactical plane of the kind needed would cost less than $3 million.)

The report states: "The national defense would be better served by providing the National Guard with lower cost weapons with proven 'here and now' effectiveness coupled with higher reliability, reduced maintenance problems, and procuring them in sufficient numbers to provide multiple battlefield coverage."

Captain Kuhn points out that the Department of Defense "has long committed most of its development resources and analysis to achieving the most complex battle tasks through technology. Tactics have been driven by technology and—to borrow a basketball analogy—hinge on low percentage mid- and full-court shots at the expense of less difficult and more effective lay-ups and twelve-footers." The results? Weapons with "markedly lower kill-rates in actual combat."

Sometimes high technology can produce a fair-size chuckle in what is otherwise a rather grim business. I owe to Curt Suplee the following account of a study of the DIVAD anti-aircraft cannon by Gregg Easterbrook:

> We're about to pay $5 billion for this mega-tech wingding festooned with multiple radars, laser range finders, infrared sights, firing computers and more com-

> puters to back up *those* computers. But, Easterbrook reports, the thing can't hit a maneuvering aircraft, won't work at night or in the rain, sends out a radar signal so strong that the enemy can pinpoint its position and aims less effectively than the human eye. And at a demonstration for top doggies last February, they switched on the electronic brain and "the gun immediately swung at full speed away from the target and toward the reviewing stand. . . . Brass flashed as the officers dove for cover. Then the gun slammed to a stop, but only because an interlock had been installed the night before to prevent it from pointing directly at the stands.

Not everyone agrees that the U.S. defense officials are obsessed with costly high tech. An air-force representative pointed out that while some high-technology systems have been poorly designed, "it is a myth that high technology is inherently less reliable." Others explain that high-technology items can do more. For instance, the navy's controversial F-18 Hornet doubles as both an interceptor and a strike-fighter, reducing the number of planes needed on a carrier. The success of American equipment adapted by the Israelis in the 1982 confrontation with Syrian forces armed with Soviet weapons (especially F-16 and F-15 fighters versus MIGs, and M-60A1 tanks versus Soviet T-72 tanks) is often mentioned as favoring the high-technology items under the toughest of tests: actual battle conditions.

It should be noted that those who question the preoccupation with high technology do not call for an army of foot soldiers, equipped with hand-operated anti-tank weapons and shoulder-carried anti-aircraft weapons, *but for a change in the mix.* They do not call for a low-tech system but for a more balanced high-tech/low-tech mix of items.

I do not claim to be able to judge which technological mix is the right one for the defense of the United States, although I must admit that the argument for a somewhat "lower" mix seems plausible. My main point is that the question cannot be explored on its merits in the context of interest groups fighting by and large for high tech, using not only technical data and briefs but all the instruments of lobbying as well, PACing included. Before I spell out this unfortunate parallelism between the directions in which interest groups push and weapons technology is bending, I will point to some other irrationalities that have been reported in our defense posture.

## Procurement Versus Personnel and Maintenance

During much of the seventies, the U.S. defense budget was being cut down on resources committed to people—salaries, training exercises, and maintenance of equipment it already has—to buy more and more hardware. The Reagan administration defense plans for the next years clearly accentuate these tendencies.

In 1982 the U.S. Army decided deliberately to stunt the growth of troops over the next five years to free funds for its biggest weapons-buying drive since World War II. The result is to be a force much smaller than the 870,000 called for by DOD plans. Critics have pointed out that the army is trying to introduce simultaneously

Figure 1

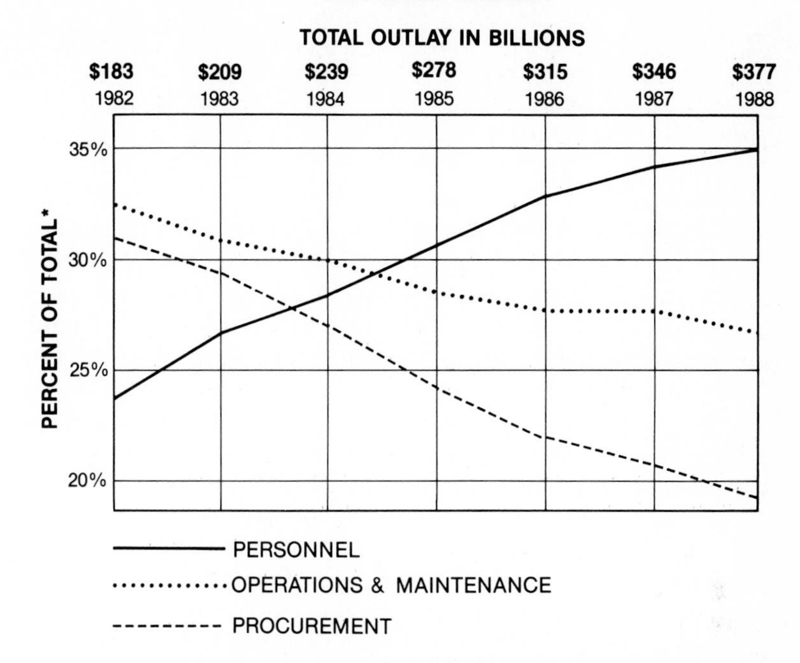


*Remaining percentage goes to research and development and other expenditures.

fourteen major weapons, which it will find difficult to absorb appropriately. The same holds for the defense budget in general, as highlighted in the following chart. The proportion of the defense budget dedicated to personnel is projected to drop sharply over the future years, while that of procurement is expected to rise sharply. This is a pivotal fact to keep in mind for the discussion to follow on which parts of the defense budget are more profitable to outside interests.

Captain Kuhn points out that the U.S. Army plans (*Army 90*) call for no increase in the number of divisions, a small increase in the size of each division (from seventeen or eighteen thousand men to twenty thousand or so), but much increase in the number of heavy artillery pieces per unit. Also, the use of a new tank is planned that will require twice the present daily fuel supplies. These changes, together with others that also favor hardware over people, will make the army, Kuhn argues, less maneuverable and more vulnerable to logistics snafus.

The Military Reform Caucus called for dedicating more resources "to attract and promote people who have the character, skill, and initiative to succeed in combat." This is compatible with the notion that it is impossible to match, gun by gun, tank by tank, the U.S.S.R.'s huge conventional capabilities in areas close to *its* borders, and that the United States will instead have to show more initiative, flexibility, and mobility, to use the advantage of the more individualistic entrepreneurial Americans versus the rigid, bureaucratic Russians. But to do this would require a greater investment in people.

In 1975, the U.S. Navy was ordered to send ships to the Gulf of Thailand when the *Mayaguez* was seized by Cambodian forces. But because of unmet maintenance needs, reports Representative Les Aspin, not a single ship could do so at full speed. Many air-force fighters were not "mission capable," and ground forces were short of spare parts, conventional ammunition, and training funds. The Carter administration began and the Reagan administration has accelerated efforts to correct these tendencies toward what General E. C. Meyer called a "hollow army." But two years into the Reagan administration, the old pressures for buying "big-ticket" weapons at the cost of maintenance reasserted themselves. One major reason is that corporations and services originally vastly underestimate the costs of a weapons system, and once it is being built, it must be paid for; the place to go for the additional funds, within a given budget, is the other items on that budget: maintenance and personnel.

Maintenance costs rise sharply with the complexity of the weapons system, yet the Department of Defense plans to increase complexity while reducing the funds available for maintenance. This is not entirely the result of outside pressure. In part it reflects a budgetary trap, sprung by the services. They secure funds for hardware now, on the assumption that such decisions are more difficult to reverse later, and that once the weapons systems are purchased, they will "justify" large maintenance expenditures. There is also a theory that maintenance can be simplified—for example, by replacing faulty parts rather than fixing them. But, we shall see, private interests accentuate this bias toward neglect of maintenance.

A misunderstanding to be avoided: suggesting that *proportionately* more and more funds are dedicated to weapons and fewer to personnel and maintenance is not to imply that the latter are not doing better under the accelerated defense buildup. So many new billions are being pumped into the Pentagon that even relatively neglected areas gain. Relatively speaking, however, personnel and maintenance are left behind the favored technology.

# Demilitarizing Our Planet

*Lester R. Brown*

For 40 years, the United States and the Soviet Union have been engaged in an arms race, an unremitting contest that has sapped the energies and resources of both countries. Each is determined to gain a strategic military advantage, regardless of cost. This competition has dominated not only relations between the two countries, but a generation of world affairs as well.

The U.S. decision to accelerate the arms race in the early 1980s has pushed military spending to a new level. Unwilling to raise taxes or cut other expenditures, the United States has run up massive fiscal deficits, causing the Treasury to compete with private firms for investment capital. This in turn has led to record-high real interest rates and contributed to a dollar that is overvalued against other currencies, making U.S. exports less competitive in world markets.

For the United States, declining competitiveness and higher capital costs are discouraging investment in new industrial capacity and contributing to industrial decline. The overvalued dollar reduced the ability of American farmers to compete in world markets, thus depressing commodity prices and reducing agricultural income. A portion of the farm debt—$213 billion at the end of 1985—will never be repaid.

In the Soviet Union, the arms race is exacting a heavy toll on living standards and diverting political energies from the sorely needed modernization. To maintain its position in the arms competition, the Soviet Union, with an economic output only half that of the United States, devotes twice as much of its national product to the military effort. Now the economy is in deep trouble.

For both superpowers, the costs of militarization are far higher than any fiscal reckoning would suggest. But the two superpowers that are perpetuating the arms race are not its only victims. Claims on the time of political leaders in Washington, Moscow, and elsewhere have been heavy, diverting them from other issues, including emerging new threats to security, such as the Third World debt that is weakening the international financial system and the ecological deterioration that is undermining the global economy.

## New Threats to Security

Since World War II, the concept of national security has been rooted in the assumption that the principal threat to security comes from other nations. Considerations

---

Lester R. Brown, *State of the World 1986,* © 1986. Reprinted with permission. (This selection, which was compiled from *State of the World 1986,* appeared in this form in *The Futurist,* 20 (July/August 1986), pp. 27–31.)

of military threats have become so dominant that new threats to the security of nations—threats with which military forces cannot cope—are being ignored.

The new sources of danger arise from oil depletion, soil erosion, land degradation, shrinking forests, deteriorating grasslands, and climate alteration. These developments will have great consequences over the long term, affecting the natural resources and systems on which the economy depends and thus threatening not only national economic and political security, but the stability of the international economy itself.

The extensive deterioration of natural support systems and declining economic conditions evident in much of the Third World will eventually translate into economic stresses with social and political dimensions: falling land productivity, falling per capita income, or rising external debt, to cite a few.

## The Debt Threat

The dramatic rise in the external debt in recent years is perhaps the most visible manifestation of this ecological and economic deterioration and the most worrisome new threat to security.

There is a remarkable parallel between countries crossing the sustainable yield threshold of their biological support systems and those crossing the sustainable debt threshold. Once the demand on a biological system exceeds its sustainable yield, further growth in demand is satisfied by consuming the basic resource stock. In such a situation, the deterioration begins to feed on itself.

So it is with external debt: As it grows faster than the economy, eventually a point is reached where servicing the debt, even if limited to interest payments, becomes such a drain on the economy that output is actually reduced, as has occurred, for instance, in Brazil and Mexico. When governments can no longer pay all the interest, then the debt begins to expand and the growth feeds on itself. Once these sustainable yield or debt-servicing thresholds are crossed, it is very difficult for countries to reverse the process.

In many Third World countries, the past three years have been a time of enforced austerity and sacrifice. Imports of consumer goods, including food, have been reduced; food subsidies have been eliminated; unemployment has risen. Belt-tightening has allowed Third World countries to maintain access to international credit and kept the lending banks solvent, but, because it has led to even greater debt, it has diminished the prospect of restoring a sustained improvement in living standards.

By the end of 1985, eleven countries were delinquent in their debt payments. For example, Bolivia—described in a U.S. government report as "in economic and political chaos"—did not make any payments during 1985. Morocco's external debt is now approaching the size of its annual gross national product, making it extremely difficult, if not impossible, to service.

Sudan, on the brink of famine in 1985, illustrates the complex relationship be-

**Table 1** Military Expenditures As Share of GNP, 1984

| Country | Share (percent) |
|---|---|
| **Industrial Countries** | |
| Japan | 1.0 |
| Canada | 2.1 |
| West Germany | 3.3 |
| United Kingdom | 5.4 |
| United States | 6.9 |
| Soviet Union | 14.0 |
| **Middle East** | |
| Egypt | 8.3 |
| Syria | 13.0 |
| Jordan | 14.9 |
| Saudi Arabia | 24.0 |
| Israel | 29.0 |
| **Asia** | |
| Sri Lanka | 1.5 |
| India | 3.5 |
| Pakistan | 5.4 |
| China | 8.0 |
| **Africa** | |
| Nigeria | 2.5 |
| South Africa | 4.3 |
| Ethiopia | 11.0 |
| Libya | 17.5 |
| **Latin America** | |
| Mexico | 0.6 |
| Brazil | 0.7 |
| Venezuela | 1.3 |
| El Salvador | 4.0 |
| Chile | 4.5 |
| Nicaragua | 10.2 |

Since 1960, global military expenditures have increased every year, regardless of economic downturns or of arms-control treaties between the United States and the Soviet Union. By 1985, global military expenditures reached $940 billion, surpassing the combined gross national products of China, India, and sub-Saharan Africa.

*Sources:* U.S. Arms Control and Disarmament Agency, *World Military Expenditures and Arms Transfers, 1985* (Washington, D.C.: 1985); Stockholm International Peace Research Institute Yearbook, *World Armaments and Disarmament* (London: Taylor and Francis, 1985).

tween ecological deterioration, declining per capita food production, and soaring external debt. As one of the 14 countries in which farmland productivity is lower today than it was a generation ago, mainly agrarian Sudan will obviously find it difficult to honor its external financial obligations, however well intentioned its leaders may be.

Peru, also facing a deteriorating domestic resource base, including the collapse of its anchovy fishery a decade ago and a heavy continuing loss of topsoil, has imposed a cap on debt servicing, limiting payments to 10% of export earnings. This action means Peru will probably not pay more than half the interest due, making it the largest debtor to refuse to pay all the interest on its debt.

More important, however, major debtor countries such as Mexico and Brazil are beginning to realize that the austerity and associated economic shrinkage that they agreed to in exchange for rescheduled loans are worsening economic and social conditions. Indeed, they are concerned that belt-tightening may eventually lead to political unrest, thus interfering with the very process of economic expansion required to service and repay the debt.

Assessments of Third World debt repayment prospects are grim, but they would be even grimmer if financial analysts understood what is happening to the environmental support systems underpinning most Third World economies. It is not a matter of an occasional country here or there experiencing deforestation, soil erosion, or land degradation. The great majority of Third World countries have crossed the sustainable yield thresholds of one or another of their basic biological support systems.

## Countries Reducing Arms Outlays

A few governments have begun to redefine national security, putting more emphasis on economic progress and less on buying arms. At a time when global military expenditures are rising, some countries are actually cutting military outlays. A handful are reducing them sharply, not only as a share of GNP, but in absolute terms as well. Among these are China, Argentina, and Peru.

As recently as 1972, China was spending 14% of its GNP for military purposes, one of the highest levels in the world at the time. Beginning in 1975, however, China began to systematically reduce its military expenditures, and, except for 1979, it has reduced them in each of the last eight years. By 1985, military spending had fallen to 7.5% of its gross national product.

Indications are that this trend may continue throughout the 1980s. In July 1985, Beijing announced a plan to invest $360 million over two years to retrain a million soldiers for return to civilian life. Such a move would cut the armed forces in China from 4.2 million in 1985 to 3.2 million in 1987—a drop of 24%. And worldwide, it would reduce the number of men and women under arms by some 4%.

In Argentina, the military government that was in office in the late 1970s and early 1980s increased military expenditures from the historical level of 1.5% of GNP to almost 4%. One of the first things that Raúl Alfonsín did as newly elected president in late 1983 was announce a plan to steadily lower this figure. By 1984, arms outlays had been cut to half the peak level of 1980, earning Alfonsín a well-deserved reputation for reordering priorities and shifting resources to social programs.

More recently, Peru has joined the ranks of those announcing plans to cut military expenditures. One of the first actions of President Alan García Pérez on taking office in the summer of 1985 was a call to halt the regional arms race. García is convinced of the need to reduce the 5% of Peru's GNP allotted to the military, a sum that consumed one-fourth of the federal budget. As an indication of his sincerity, the president announced that he was canceling half of the order for 26 French Mirage fighter planes.

## Economic Security

The overriding reason for cutting military expenditures in each of these three countries is economic. In effect, the three political leaders are defining security much more in economic terms. For the Chinese, the military sector was one place harboring the additional resources needed to achieve desired gains in living standards. Once the goal of rapidly improving living standards was adopted, the reduction of resources devoted to the military was inevitable.

In Argentina, the economic incentive was burgeoning public debt, inflation, and a huge external debt that threatened to become unmanageable. One source of Argentina's external debt was the taste for modern arms exhibited by Alfonsín's predecessors. In Peru, the challenge was to arrest the decline in living standards. At the time García took office, payments on the international debt were $475 million in arrears, and the government was threatened with a complete cutoff of all new sources of investment capital. García found that internal economic decline was leading to social deterioration and political violence.

Encouragingly, the reductions in military expenditures undertaken by these three governments were independent of any negotiated reductions in neighboring countries. China lowered its military outlays unilaterally, despite its 3,000-kilometer border with the Soviet Union, which has continued to increase its military might.

Over the next few years, as governments everywhere face difficulties in maintaining or improving living standards, others may also choose to reduce military expenditures. Quite apart from the positive momentum of the international peace movement in recent years, worsening economic conditions may become the key motivation for reversing the militarization of the past generation.

## The Challenge

The principal obstacle to Third World progress, one caused in part by ecological degradation, is mounting external debt. International financial institutions have been reluctant to recognize that scores of developing countries have crossed their debt-servicing thresholds. Private banks fear they will have to write off so many bad loans that it will greatly reduce their earnings and even threaten their solvency. Nonetheless, a substantial share of the $800 billion of the Third World's external debt will never be repaid.

At the moment, institutions such as the World Bank and the International Monetary Fund lack the lending capacity to restore the growth needed in Third World debtor countries. Private banks are unwilling to increase their lending, with the result that developing countries are unable to obtain the capital needed to sustain progress. The only acceptable resolution is one that leaves part of the interest payments in debtor countries, in order to get their economies moving again.

Many strategies have been proposed to resolve the mounting debt problem. One proposal, put forward by Robert Wesson of Stanford University's Hoover Institution, is to set up an investment trust within the countries with unpayable external debts. Under this system, international lending banks could use an agreed-upon portion of their interest repayments to buy shares in the trust. The trust, in turn, would invest in indigenous enterprises, providing the private sector with sorely needed capital. Such an approach would help restore investor confidence in Third World countries, and it would also give the private banks a long-term stake in these economies. For the lending institutions, the alternative may be to write off otherwise bad loans.

## Defusing New Threats

Continuing a "business as usual" approach to the Third World debt problem, with the deterioration in living standards that will result, is a recipe for political unrest at best and for social disintegration at worst. Fortunately, more and more Third World leaders and international lenders are coming to this conclusion.

Understanding the new threats to national security and economic progress will challenge the analytical skills of governments. But the decision-making apparatus in most governments is not organized to balance threats of a traditional military nature with those of ecological and economic origin.

Nonmilitary threats are much less clearly defined. They are the result of cumulative processes that ultimately lead to the collapse of biological systems. These processes are seldom given much thought until they pass a critical threshold and disaster strikes. Thus it is easier in the government councils of developing countries to justify expenditures for the latest-model jet fighters than for family planning to slow the population growth that is destroying the economy's environmental underpinnings.

The key to demilitarizing the world economy and shifting resources is a defusing of the arms race between the United States and the Soviet Union. Whether this can be achieved remains to be seen. But as the costs of maintaining the arms race multiply, both for the superpowers and for the world at large, the likelihood of reducing tensions may be improving.

In East Asia, traditional adversaries China and Japan appear to be in the process of establishing strong economic ties. In contrast to the United States, China appears to be abandoning military competition with the Soviet Union. With Japan showing little interest in becoming a military power, the stage is being set for peace in the region. Both countries have redefined security and reshaped their geopolitical strategies, accordingly setting aside any ideas of political domination in favor of pursuing mutually beneficial economic goals.

In Western Europe, France and Germany have battled each other periodically over the centuries, but armed conflict between these two countries now appears unlikely. And, in North America, the United States, Canada, and Mexico have lived peacefully for generations.

If ideology gives way to pragmatism, as it is doing in China, then the conflicts and insecurities bred by the ideological distinctions between East and West can soften. Indeed, this ideological softening appears to be coloring China's foreign policy, improving its relations with other countries and contributing to its reduction of military expenditures.

For the world as a whole, the past generation has seen an overwhelming movement toward militarization. Apart from the heavy claim on public resources, the East-West conflict contributes to a psychological climate of suspicion and distrust that makes the cooperative, international address of new threats to the security of nations next to impossible.

China and Argentina, which have already cut the military's share of their GNP in half, and Peru, which promises to do so, may provide the model for the future. If demilitarization could replace militarization, national governments would be free to reorder their priorities and could return to paths of sustained progress.

Ironically, for the United States and the Soviet Union, maintaining a position of leadership may now depend on reducing military expenditures to strengthen their faltering economies. Acting thus in their own interests, they could set the stage for demilitarizing the world economy. Once it starts, demilitarization—like militarization—could feed on itself.

# STATISTICAL APPENDIX

**Table A-1** Corporate Taxes as a Percentage of Profits

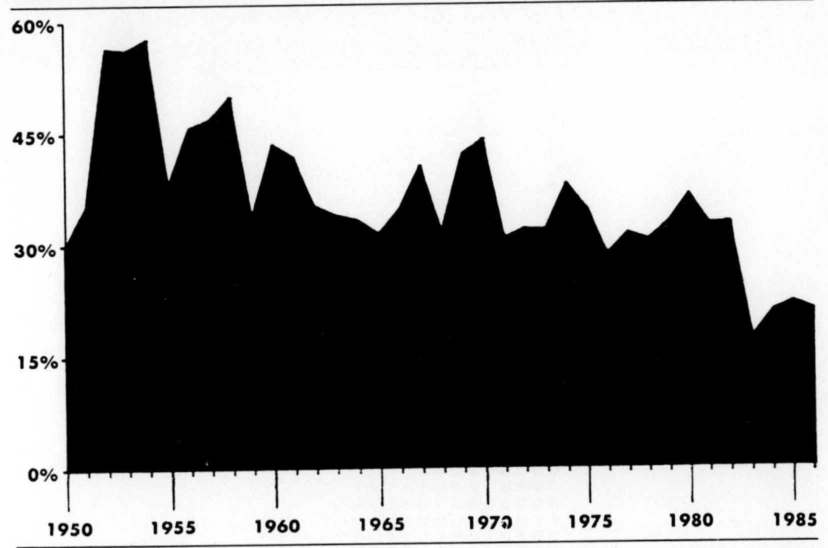


From *A Field Guide to the U.S. Economy* by Nancy Folbre (6.10). Copyright © 1987 by The Center for Popular Economics. Reprinted by permission of Pantheon Books, a Division of Random House, Inc.

**Table A-2** The Changing Industrial Composition of Employment

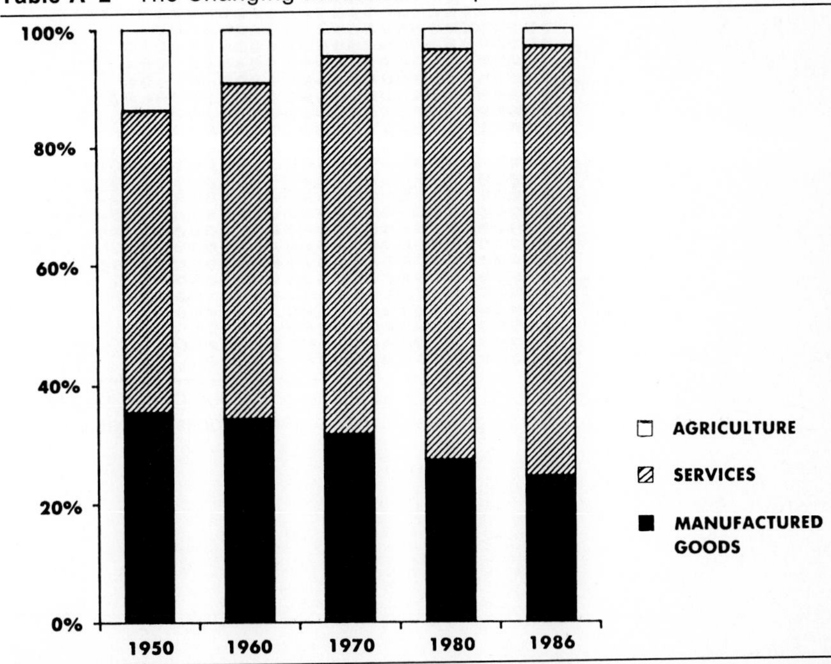


From *A Field Guide to the U.S. Economy* by Nancy Folbre (2.2). Copyright © 1987 by The Center for Popular Economics. Reprinted by permission of Pantheon Books, a Division of Random House, Inc.

**Table A-3** The Shrinking Middle Class: 1978–1986

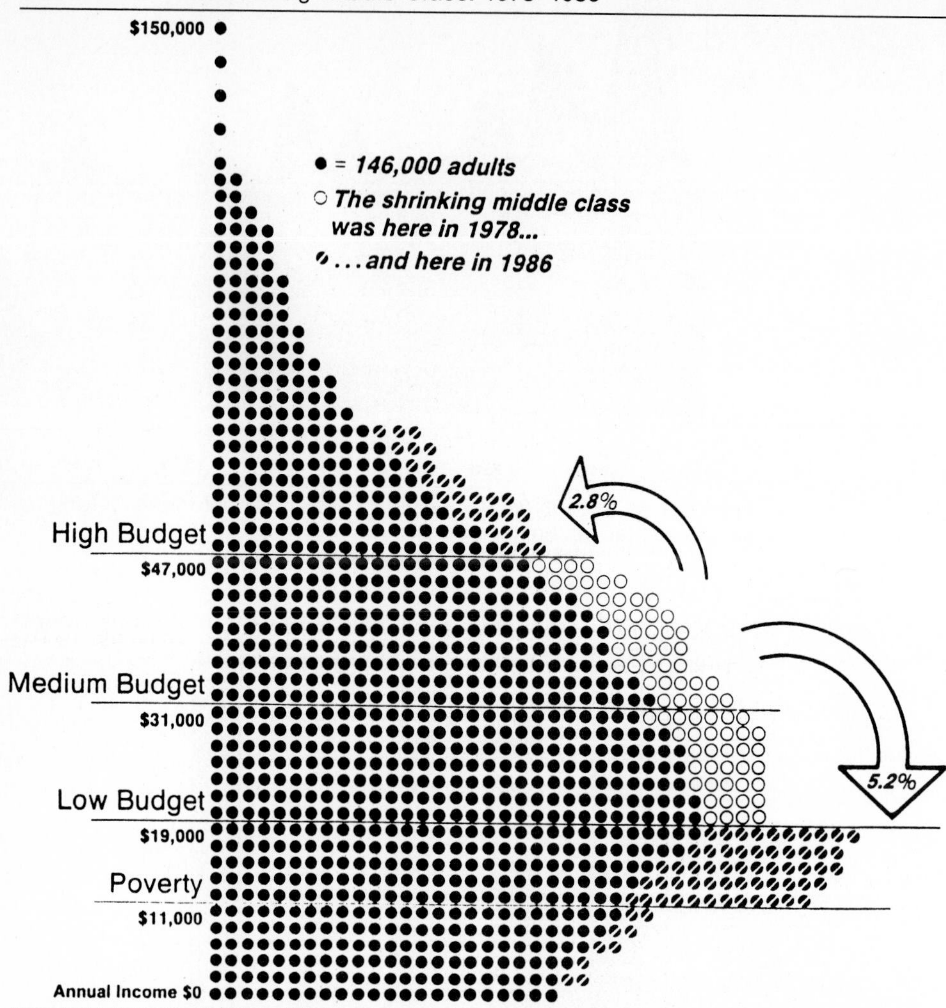


From *The American Profile Poster* by Stephen J. Rose (p. 10). Copyright © 1986 by Social Graphics Co. Reprinted by permission of Pantheon Books, a Division of Random House, Inc.

**Table A-4** Median Weekly Earnings of Full-Time Workers ($1985)

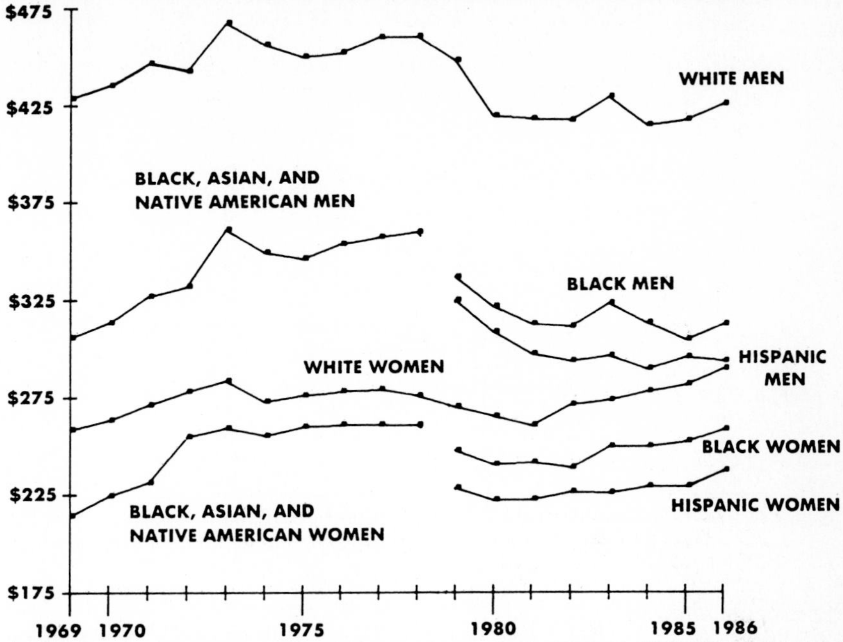

$475
$425
$375
$325
$275
$225
$175

WHITE MEN
BLACK, ASIAN, AND NATIVE AMERICAN MEN
BLACK MEN
WHITE WOMEN
HISPANIC MEN
BLACK WOMEN
HISPANIC WOMEN
BLACK, ASIAN, AND NATIVE AMERICAN WOMEN

1969 1970 1975 1980 1985 1986

From *A Field Guide to the U.S. Economy* by Nancy Folbre (2.6). 

**Table A-5** Years of School Completed by Householder and Average Household Income by Race (1985)

| Years of School Completed by Householder | Average Household Income (Dollars) | | |
|---|---|---|---|
| | White | Black | Hispanic |
| Less than 8 years | $14,470 | $11,612 | $15,247 |
| 8 years | 17,721 | 13,293 | 17,615 |
| 1-3 years high school | 20,379 | 14,750 | 17,786 |
| 4 years high school | 27,343 | 19,429 | 23,709 |
| 1-3 years college | 32,414 | 23,347 | 29,043 |
| 4 years college | 43,405 | 32,670 | 35,842 |
| 5 or more years college | 51,973 | 39,181 | 41,824 |

*Source:* U.S. Bureau of the Census, Current Population Reports, Series P-60, No. 156, *Money Income of Households, Families, and Persons in the United States: 1985,* U.S. Government Printing Office, Washington, D.C., 1987, adapted from pp. 12-16.

**Table A-6** Income Inequality: 1970–1984

| Year | Income Share of Highest Fifth | Income Share of Lowest Fifth | Ratio Highest Fifth: Lowest Fifth |
|---|---|---|---|
| 1984 | 42.9% | 4.7% | 9.13 |
| 1983 | 42.8 | 4.7 | 9.11 |
| 1982 | 42.7 | 4.7 | 9.09 |
| 1981 | 41.9 | 5.0 | 8.38 |
| 1980 | 41.6 | 5.1 | 8.16 |
| 1979 | 41.7 | 5.2 | 8.02 |
| 1978 | 41.5 | 5.2 | 7.98 |
| 1977 | 41.5 | 5.2 | 7.98 |
| 1976 | 41.1 | 5.4 | 7.61 |
| 1975 | 41.1 | 5.4 | 7.61 |
| 1974 | 41.0 | 5.5 | 7.45 |
| 1973 | 41.1 | 5.5 | 7.47 |
| 1972 | 41.4 | 5.4 | 7.67 |
| 1971 | 41.1 | 5.5 | 7.47 |
| 1970 | 40.9 | 5.4 | 7.57 |

*Source:* U.S. Bureau of the Census, Current Population Reports, Series P-60, No. 151 (April 1986), Table 12, p. 37, *Money Income of Householders, Families, and Persons in the United States: 1984.*

**Table A-7** Monthly Earnings in Comparable Occupations in 1982

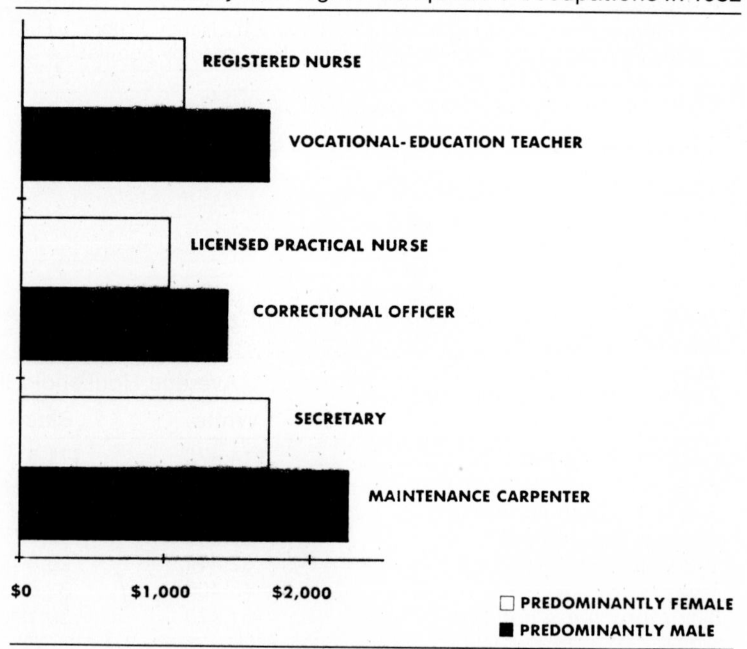


From *A Field Guide to the U.S. Economy* by Nancy Folbre (3.7). Copyright © 1987 by The Center for Popular Economics. Reprinted by permission of Pantheon Books, a Division of Random House, Inc.

**Table A-8** Income Differentials by Gender, Occupation, and Education: 1985 (median incomes for full-time, year-round workers)

| | Men | Women | Women's Income as % Men's Income |
|---|---|---|---|
| Occupation Category | | | |
| Managerial | $30,792 | $17,556 | 57.0% |
| Professional | 29,698 | 17,032 | 57.4 |
| Sales | 20,058 | 5,293 | 26.4 |
| Clerical | 18,127 | 11,310 | 62.4 |
| Craft | 18,956 | 11,185 | 59.0 |
| Operatives | 17,000 | 9,170 | 53.9 |
| Laborers | 7,330 | 6,583 | 89.8 |
| Service workers | 8,038 | 4,224 | 52.6 |
| Educational Attainment | | | |
| 5 + years college | $35,249 | $20,678 | 58.7% |
| 4 years college | 29,698 | 15,256 | 51.4 |
| 1-3 years college | 22,581 | 11,018 | 48.8 |
| 4 years high school | 18,997 | 8,137 | 42.8 |
| 1-3 years high school | 12,870 | 5,689 | 44.1 |
| 8 years elementary | 10,818 | 5,415 | 42.1 |
| Less than 8 years elementary | 7,857 | 4,615 | 58.7 |

*Source:* U.S. Bureau of the Census, Current Population Reports, Series P-60, No. 154 (August 1986), *Money Income and Poverty Status of Families and Persons in the United States: 1985,* pp. 13-14.

**Table A-9** Median Family Income by Race and Spanish Origin (thousands of $1985)

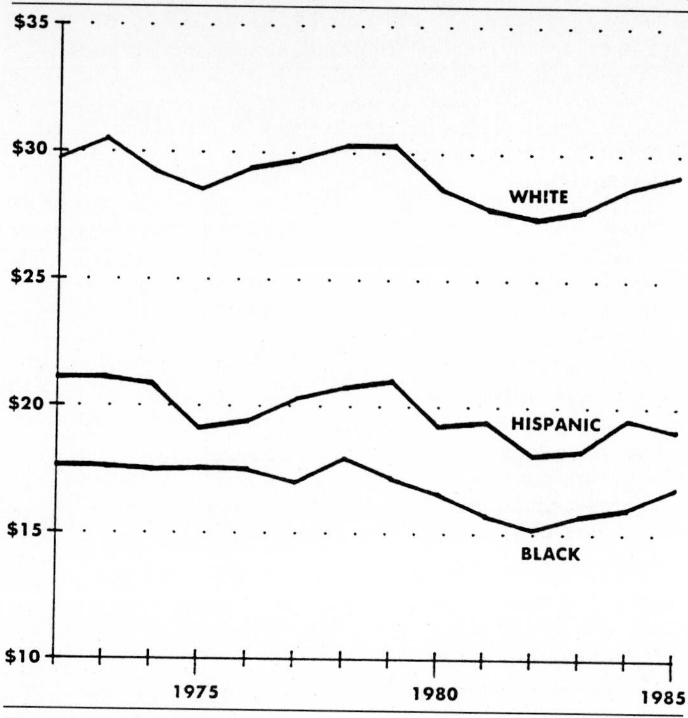


From *A Field Guide to the U.S. Economy* by Nancy Folbre (4.5). Copyright © 1987 by The Center for Popular Economics. Reprinted by permission of Pantheon Books, a Division of Random House, Inc.

**Table A-10** Millions of Persons in Poverty

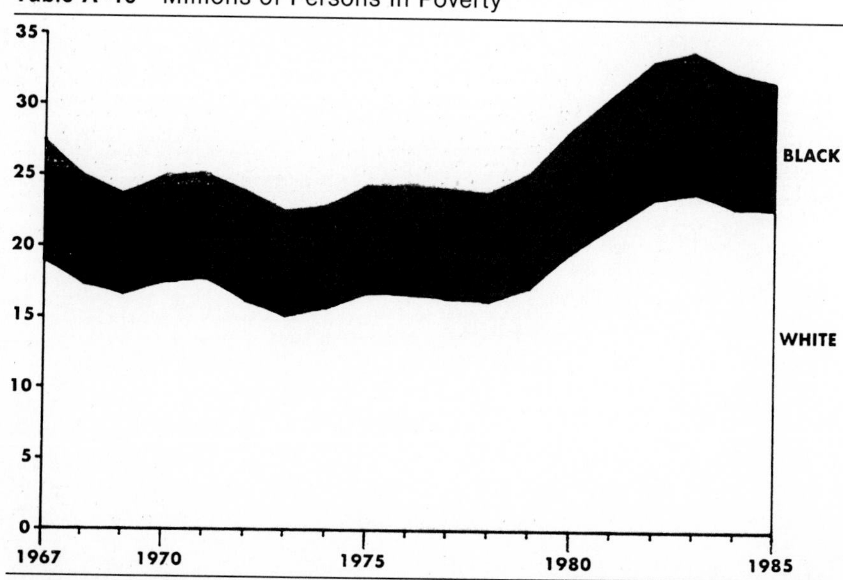


From *A Field Guide to the U.S. Economy* by Nancy Folbre (7.3). Copyright © 1987 by The Center for Popular Economics. Reprinted by permission of Pantheon Books, a Division of Random House, Inc.

**Table A-11** Number of Persons Below the Poverty Level and Poverty Rate, by Race and Hispanic Origin: 1959 to 1985
(Numbers in thousands. Persons as of March of the following year)

| Year | All races | | White | | Black | | Hispanic[1] | |
|---|---|---|---|---|---|---|---|---|
| | Number below the poverty level | Poverty rate | Number below the poverty level | Poverty rate | Number below the poverty level | Poverty rate | Number below the poverty level | Poverty rate |
| 1985 | 33,064 | 14.0 | 22,860 | 11.4 | 8,926 | 31.3 | 5,236 | 29.0 |
| 1984 | 33,700 | 14.4 | 22,955 | 11.5 | 9,490 | 33.8 | 4,806 | 28.4 |
| 1983r | 35,303 | 15.2 | 23,984 | 12.1 | 9,882 | 35.7 | 4,633 | 28.0 |
| 1982 | 34,398 | 15.0 | 23,517 | 12.0 | 9,697 | 35.6 | 4,301 | 29.9 |
| 1981 | 31,822 | 14.0 | 21,553 | 11.1 | 9,173 | 34.2 | 3,713 | 26.5 |
| 1980 | 29,272 | 13.0 | 19,699 | 10.2 | 8,579 | 32.5 | 3,491 | 25.7 |
| 1979 | 26,072 | 11.7 | 17,214 | 9.0 | 8,050 | 31.0 | 2,921 | 21.8 |
| 1978 | 24,497 | 11.4 | 16,259 | 8.7 | 7,625 | 30.6 | 2,607 | 21.6 |
| 1977 | 24,720 | 11.6 | 16,416 | 8.9 | 7,726 | 31.3 | 2,700 | 22.4 |
| 1976 | 24,975 | 11.8 | 16,713 | 9.1 | 7,595 | 31.1 | 2,783 | 24.7 |
| 1975 | 25,877 | 12.3 | 17,770 | 9.7 | 7,545 | 31.3 | 2,991 | 26.9 |
| 1974 | 23,370 | 11.2 | 15,736 | 8.6 | 7,182 | 30.3 | 2,575 | 23.0 |
| 1973 | 22,973 | 11.1 | 15,142 | 8.4 | 7,388 | 31.4 | 2,366 | 21.9 |
| 1972 | 24,460 | 11.9 | 16,203 | 9.0 | 7,710 | 33.3 | (NA) | (NA) |
| 1971 | 25,559 | 12.5 | 17,780 | 9.9 | 7,396 | 32.5 | (NA) | (NA) |
| 1970 | 25,420 | 12.6 | 17,484 | 9.9 | 7,548 | 33.5 | (NA) | (NA) |
| 1969 | 24,147 | 12.1 | 16,659 | 9.5 | 7,095 | 32.2 | (NA) | (NA) |
| 1968 | 25,389 | 12.8 | 17,395 | 10.0 | 7,616 | 34.7 | (NA) | (NA) |
| 1967 | 27,769 | 14.2 | 18,983 | 11.0 | 8,486 | 39.3 | (NA) | (NA) |
| 1966 | 28,510 | 14.7 | 19,290 | 11.3 | 8,867 | 41.8 | (NA) | (NA) |
| 1965 | 33,185 | 17.3 | 22,496 | 13.3 | (NA) | (NA) | (NA) | (NA) |
| 1964 | 36,055 | 19.0 | 24,957 | 14.9 | (NA) | (NA) | (NA) | (NA) |
| 1963 | 36,436 | 19.5 | 25,238 | 15.3 | (NA) | (NA) | (NA) | (NA) |
| 1962 | 38,625 | 21.0 | 26,672 | 16.4 | (NA) | (NA) | (NA) | (NA) |
| 1961 | 39,628 | 21.9 | 27,890 | 17.4 | (NA) | (NA) | (NA) | (NA) |
| 1960 | 39,851 | 22.2 | 28,309 | 17.8 | (NA) | (NA) | (NA) | (NA) |
| 1959 | 39,490 | 22.4 | 28,484 | 18.1 | 9,927 | 55.1 | (NA) | (NA) |

[1]Persons of Hispanic origin may be of any race.
*Source:* U.S. Bureau of the Census, Current Population Reports, Series P-60, No. 158, *Poverty in the United States: 1985,* U.S. Government Printing Office, Washington, D.C. 1987, p. 2.

**Table A-12** Poverty Status of Persons, by Family Relationship, Race, and Hispanic Origin: 1959 to 1986

| Year and characteristic | All persons | | | Persons in families | | | | | | Unrelated individuals | | |
|---|---|---|---|---|---|---|---|---|---|---|---|---|
| | | Below poverty level | | All families | | | Families with female householder, no husband present | | | | Below poverty level | |
| | | | | | Below poverty level | | | Below poverty level | | | | |
| | Total | Number | Percent | Total | Number | Percent | Total | Number | Percent | Total | Number | Percent |
| **WHITE** | | | | | | | | | | | | |
| 1986 | 202 282 | 22 183 | 11.0 | 174 024 | 16 393 | 9.4 | 20 163 | 6 171 | 30.6 | 27 143 | 5 198 | 19.2 |
| 1985 | 200 918 | 22 860 | 11.4 | 172 863 | 17 125 | 9.9 | 20 105 | 5 990 | 29.8 | 27 067 | 5 299 | 19.6 |
| 1984 | 198 941 | 22 955 | 11.5 | 171 839 | 17 299 | 10.1 | 19 727 | 5 866 | 29.7 | 26 094 | 5 181 | 19.9 |
| 1983 | 197 496 | 23 984 | 12.1 | 171 407 | 18 377 | 10.7 | 19 256 | 6 017 | 31.2 | 25 206 | 5 189 | 20.6 |
| 1982 | 195 919 | 23 517 | 12.0 | 170 748 | 18 015 | 10.6 | 18 374 | 5 686 | 30.9 | 24 300 | 5 041 | 20.7 |
| 1981 | 194 504 | 21 553 | 11.1 | 169 868 | 16 127 | 9.5 | 18 795 | 5 600 | 29.8 | 23 913 | 5 061 | 21.2 |
| 1980 | 192 912 | 19 699 | 10.2 | 168 756 | 14 587 | 8.6 | 17 642 | 4 940 | 28.0 | 23 370 | 4 760 | 20.4 |
| 1979 | 191 742 | 17 214 | 9.0 | 168 461 | 12 495 | 7.4 | 17 349 | 4 375 | 25.2 | 22 587 | 4 452 | 19.7 |
| 1978 | 186 450 | 16 259 | 8.7 | 165 193 | 12 050 | 7.3 | 16 877 | 4 371 | 25.9 | 21 257 | 4 209 | 19.8 |
| 1977 | 185 254 | 16 416 | 8.9 | 165 385 | 12 364 | 7.5 | 16 721 | 4 474 | 26.8 | 19 869 | 4 051 | 20.4 |
| 1976 | 184 165 | 16 713 | 9.1 | 165 571 | 12 500 | 7.5 | 15 941 | 4 463 | 28.0 | 18 594 | 4 213 | 22.7 |
| 1975 | 183 164 | 17 770 | 9.7 | 165 661 | 13 799 | 8.3 | 15 577 | 4 577 | 29.4 | 17 503 | 3 972 | 22.7 |
| 1974 | 182 376 | 15 736 | 8.6 | 166 081 | 12 181 | 7.3 | 15 433 | 4 278 | 27.7 | 16 295 | 3 555 | 21.8 |
| 1973 | 181 185 | 15 142 | 8.4 | 165 424 | 11 412 | 6.9 | 14 303 | 4 003 | 28.0 | 15 761 | 3 730 | 23.7 |
| 1972 | 180 125 | 16 203 | 9.0 | 165 630 | 12 268 | 7.4 | 13 739 | 3 770 | 27.4 | 14 495 | 3 935 | 27.1 |
| 1971 | 179 398 | 17 780 | 9.9 | 165 184 | 13 566 | 8.2 | 13 502 | 4 099 | 30.4 | 14 214 | 4 214 | 29.6 |
| 1970 | 177 376 | 17 484 | 9.9 | 163 875 | 13 323 | 8.1 | 13 226 | 3 761 | 28.4 | 13 500 | 4 161 | 30.8 |
| 1969 | 175 349 | 16 659 | 9.5 | 162 779 | 12 623 | 7.8 | 12 285 | 3 577 | 29.1 | 12 570 | 4 036 | 32.1 |
| 1968 | 173 732 | 17 395 | 10.0 | 161 777 | 13 546 | 8.4 | 12 190 | 3 551 | 29.1 | 11 955 | 3 849 | 32.2 |
| 1967 | 172 038 | 18 983 | 11.0 | 160 720 | 14 851 | 9.2 | 12 131 | 3 453 | 28.5 | 11 318 | 4 132 | 36.5 |
| 1966 | 170 247 | 19 290 | 11.3 | 159 561 | 15 430 | 9.7 | 12 261 | 3 646 | 29.7 | 10 686 | 3 860 | 36.1 |
| 1965 | 168 732 | 22 496 | 13.3 | 158 255 | 18 508 | 11.7 | 11 573 | 4 092 | 35.4 | 10 477 | 3 988 | 38.1 |
| 1964 | 167 313 | 24 957 | 14.9 | 156 898 | 20 716 | 13.2 | (NA) | 3 911 | 33.4 | 10 415 | 4 241 | 40.7 |
| 1963 | 165 309 | 25 238 | 15.3 | 155 584 | 21 149 | 13.6 | (NA) | 4 051 | 35.6 | 9 725 | 4 089 | 42.0 |
| 1962 | 162 842 | 26 672 | 16.4 | 153 348 | 22 613 | 14.7 | (NA) | 4 089 | 37.9 | 9 494 | 4 059 | 42.7 |
| 1961 | 160 306 | 27 890 | 17.4 | 150 717 | 23 747 | 15.8 | (NA) | 4 062 | 37.6 | 9 589 | 4 143 | 43.2 |
| 1960 | 158 863 | 28 309 | 17.8 | 149 458 | 24 262 | 16.2 | (NA) | 4 296 | 39.0 | 9 405 | 4 047 | 43.0 |
| 1959 | 156 956 | 28 484 | 18.1 | 147 802 | 24 443 | 16.5 | (NA) | 4 232 | 40.2 | 9 154 | 4 041 | 44.1 |

| Year and characteristic | All persons | | | Persons in families | | | | | | Unrelated individuals | | |
|---|---|---|---|---|---|---|---|---|---|---|---|---|
| | | | | All families | | | Families with female householder, no husband present | | | | | |
| | | Below poverty level | | | Below poverty level | | | Below poverty level | | | Below poverty level | |
| | Total | Number | Percent | Total | Number | Percent | Total | Number | Percent | Total | Number | Percent |
| **BLACK** | | | | | | | | | | | | |
| 1986 | 28 871 | 8 983 | 31.1 | 24 910 | 7 410 | 29.7 | 10 175 | 5 473 | 53.8 | 3 714 | 1 431 | 38.5 |
| 1985 | 28 485 | 8 926 | 31.3 | 24 620 | 7 504 | 30.5 | 10 041 | 5 342 | 53.2 | 3 641 | 1 264 | 34.7 |
| 1984 | 28 087 | 9 490 | 33.8 | 24 387 | 8 104 | 33.2 | 10 384 | 5 666 | 54.6 | 3 501 | 1 255 | 35.8 |
| 1983 | 27 678 | 9 882 | 35.7 | 24 138 | 8 376 | 34.7 | 10 059 | 5 736 | 57.0 | 3 287 | 1 338 | 40.7 |
| 1982 | 27 216 | 9 697 | 35.6 | 23 948 | 8 355 | 34.9 | 9 699 | 5 698 | 58.8 | 3 051 | 1 229 | 40.3 |
| 1981 | 26 834 | 9 173 | 34.2 | 23 423 | 7 780 | 33.2 | 9 214 | 5 222 | 56.7 | 3 277 | 1 296 | 39.6 |
| 1980 | 26 408 | 8 579 | 32.5 | 23 084 | 7 190 | 31.1 | 9 338 | 4 984 | 53.4 | 3 208 | 1 314 | 41.0 |
| 1979 | 25 944 | 8 050 | 31.0 | 22 666 | 6 800 | 30.0 | 9 065 | 4 816 | 53.1 | 3 127 | 1 168 | 37.3 |
| 1978 | 24 956 | 7 625 | 30.6 | 22 027 | 6 493 | 29.5 | 8 689 | 4 712 | 54.2 | 2 929 | 1 132 | 38.6 |
| 1977 | 24 710 | 7 726 | 31.3 | 21 850 | 6 667 | 30.5 | 8 315 | 4 595 | 55.3 | 2 860 | 1 059 | 37.0 |
| 1976 | 24 399 | 7 595 | 31.1 | 21 840 | 6 576 | 30.1 | 7 926 | 4 415 | 55.7 | 2 559 | 1 019 | 39.8 |
| 1975 | 24 089 | 7 545 | 31.3 | 21 687 | 6 533 | 30.1 | 7 679 | 4 168 | 54.3 | 2 402 | 1,011 | 42.1 |
| 1974 | 23 699 | 7 182 | 30.3 | 21 341 | 6 255 | 29.3 | 7 483 | 4 116 | 55.0 | 2 359 | 927 | 39.3 |
| 1973 | 23 512 | 7 388 | 31.4 | 21 328 | 6 560 | 30.8 | 7 188 | 4 064 | 56.5 | 2 183 | 828 | 37.9 |
| 1972 | 23 144 | 7 710 | 33.3 | 21 116 | 6 841 | 32.4 | 7 125 | 4 139 | 58.1 | 2 028 | 870 | 42.9 |
| 1971 | 22 784 | 7 396 | 32.5 | 20 900 | 6 530 | 31.2 | 6 398 | 3 587 | 56.1 | 1 884 | 866 | 46.0 |
| 1970 | 22 515 | 7 548 | 33.5 | 20 724 | 6 683 | 32.2 | 6 225 | 3 656 | 58.7 | 1 791 | 865 | 48.3 |
| 1969 | 22 011 | 7 095 | 32.2 | 20 192 | 6 245 | 30.9 | 5 537 | 3 225 | 58.2 | 1 819 | 850 | 46.7 |
| 1968 | 21 944 | 7 616 | 34.7 | (NA) | 6 839 | 33.7 | (NA) | 3 312 | 58.9 | (NA) | 777 | 46.3 |
| 1967 | 21 590 | 8 486 | 39.3 | (NA) | 7 677 | 38.4 | (NA) | 3 362 | 61.6 | (NA) | 809 | 49.3 |
| 1966 | 21 206 | 8 867 | 41.8 | (NA) | 8 090 | 40.9 | (NA) | 3 160 | 65.3 | (NA) | 777 | 54.4 |
| 1959 | 18 013 | 9 927 | 55.1 | (NA) | 9 112 | 54.9 | (NA) | 2 416 | 70.6 | 1 430 | 815 | 57.0 |
| **HISPANIC**[1] | | | | | | | | | | | | |
| 1986 | 18 758 | 5 117 | 27.3 | 16 880 | 4 469 | 26.5 | 3 631 | 1 921 | 52.9 | 1 685 | 553 | 32.8 |
| 1985 | 18 075 | 5 236 | 29.0 | 16 276 | 4 605 | 28.3 | 3 561 | 1 983 | 55.7 | 1 602 | 532 | 33.2 |
| 1984 | 16 916 | 4 806 | 28.4 | 15 293 | 4 192 | 27.4 | 3 139 | 1 764 | 56.2 | 1 481 | 545 | 36.8 |
| 1983 | 16 544 | 4 633 | 28.0 | 15 075 | 4 113 | 27.3 | 3 032 | 1 670 | 55.1 | 1 364 | 457 | 33.5 |
| 1982 | 14 385 | 4 301 | 29.9 | 13 242 | 3 865 | 29.2 | 2 664 | 1 601 | 60.1 | 1 018 | 358 | 35.1 |
| 1981 | 14 021 | 3 713 | 26.5 | 12 922 | 3 349 | 25.9 | 2 622 | 1 465 | 55.9 | 1 005 | 313 | 31.1 |
| 1980 | 13 600 | 3 491 | 25.7 | 12 547 | 3 143 | 25.1 | 2 421 | 1 319 | 54.5 | 970 | 312 | 32.2 |
| 1979 | 13 371 | 2 921 | 21.8 | 12 291 | 2 599 | 21.1 | 2 058 | 1 053 | 51.2 | 991 | 286 | 28.8 |
| 1978 | 12 079 | 2 607 | 21.6 | 11 193 | 2 343 | 20.9 | 1 817 | 1 024 | 56.4 | 886 | 264 | 29.8 |
| 1977 | 12 046 | 2 700 | 22.4 | 11 249 | 2 463 | 21.9 | 1 901 | 1 077 | 56.7 | 797 | 237 | 29.8 |
| 1976 | 11 269 | 2 783 | 24.7 | 10 552 | 2 516 | 23.8 | 1 766 | 1 000 | 56.6 | 716 | 266 | 37.2 |
| 1975 | 11 117 | 2 991 | 26.9 | 10 472 | 2 755 | 26.3 | 1 842 | 1 053 | 57.2 | 645 | 236 | 36.6 |
| 1974 | 11 201 | 2 575 | 23.0 | 10 584 | 2 374 | 22.4 | 1 723 | 915 | 53.1 | 617 | 201 | 32.6 |
| 1973 | 10 795 | 2 366 | 21.9 | 10 269 | 2 209 | 21.5 | 1 534 | 881 | 57.4 | 526 | 157 | 29.9 |

[1]Hispanic persons may be of any race.

Note: Prior to 1979 persons in unrelated subfamilies were included in persons in families. Beginning in 1979 persons in unrelated subfamilies are included in all persons but are excluded from persons in families.

*Source:* U.S. Bureau of the Census, Current Population Reports, Series P-60, No. 160, *Poverty in the United States: 1986,* U.S. Government Printing Office, Washington, D.C., 1988, pp. 5–6.

**Table A-13** Percentage of Children and Elderly in Poverty

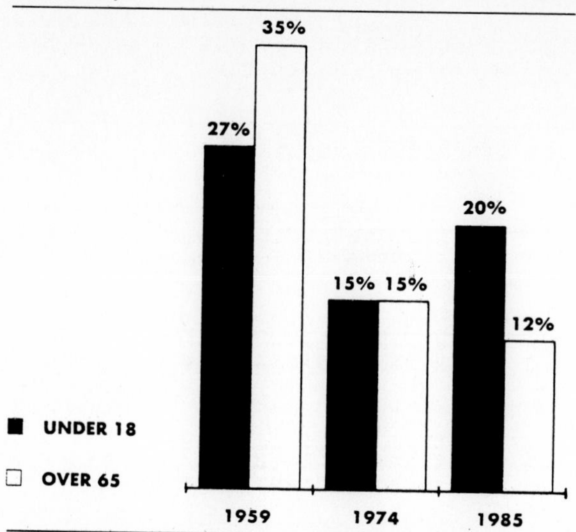




**Table A-14** Age Distribution of Persons, by Poverty Status

| Age | Total | Number Below the Poverty Level | Percent Below the Poverty Level |
|---|---|---|---|
| Total | 236,594 | 33,064 | 14.0 |
| Under 5 years | 18,062 | 4,170 | 23.1 |
| 5 to 9 years | 17,062 | 3,702 | 21.7 |
| 10 to 14 years | 16,643 | 3,239 | 19.5 |
| 15 to 19 years | 18,274 | 3,156 | 17.3 |
| 20 to 24 years | 19,949 | 3,207 | 16.1 |
| 25 to 29 years | 21,619 | 2,642 | 12.2 |
| 30 to 34 years | 20,434 | 2,119 | 10.4 |
| 35 to 39 years | 18,341 | 1,795 | 9.8 |
| 40 to 44 years | 14,166 | 1,343 | 9.5 |
| 45 to 49 years | 11,814 | 985 | 8.3 |
| 50 to 54 years | 10,849 | 926 | 8.5 |
| 55 to 59 years | 11,212 | 1,104 | 9.8 |
| 60 to 64 years | 10,849 | 1,221 | 11.3 |
| 65 to 69 years | 9,415 | 881 | 9.4 |
| 70 to 74 years | 7,466 | 901 | 12.1 |
| 75 to 79 years | 5,283 | 782 | 14.8 |
| 80 to 84 years | 3,122 | 508 | 16.3 |
| 85 years and over | 2,038 | 381 | 18.7 |

*Source:* U.S. Bureau of the Census, Current Population Reports, Series P-60, No. 158, *Poverty in the United States: 1985,* U.S. Government Printing Office, Washington, D.C.: 1987, p. 3.

**Table A-15** The Work Experience of Poor Family Householders in 1984

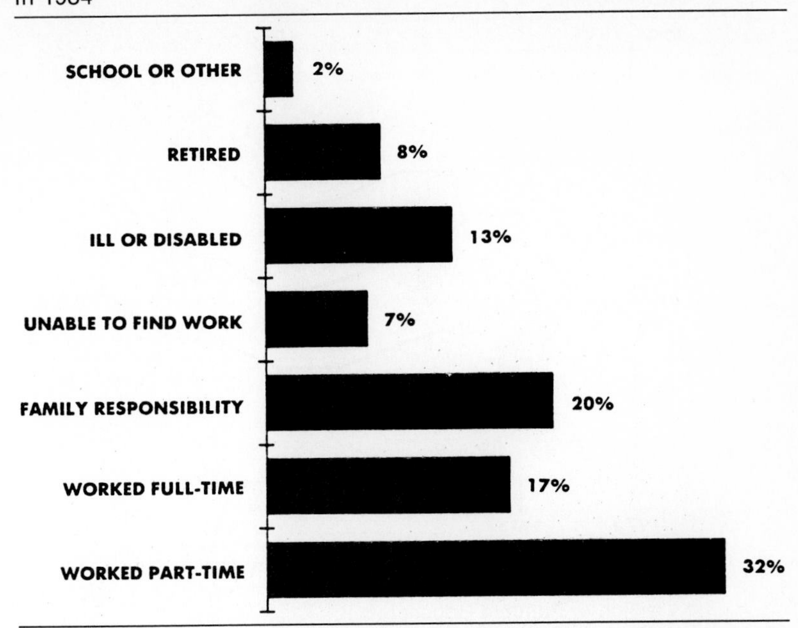




**Table A-16** The Cost of Ending Poverty

The most expensive way to end poverty in the U.S. would be simply to give people enough money every year to lift their incomes over the poverty line. In 1985, as the Census Bureau has calculated, the average poor family would have needed $4,278 in public assistance.

The number of families in poverty that year was 7.46 million. Therefore, an additional income transfer of about $32 billion would have done the job.

How much is $32 billion?

- less than 1% of GNP in 1985
- about 13% of military spending
- about $257 from every employed worker in the U.S.

Poverty could be ended far more cheaply if:

- the unemployment rate were lowered to 4% (because about a third of all poor family householders in 1985 lacked jobs).
- the minimum wage were raised to $5.00 an hour (because 17% of all poor family householders worked full-time in 1985 but didn't earn wages high enough to keep them out of poverty).
- inexpensive high-quality day care were made available (because 20% of all poor family households could not work because of family responsibilities).

**Table A-17** Unemployment Rates by Race and Spanish Origin, Age 16 and Above

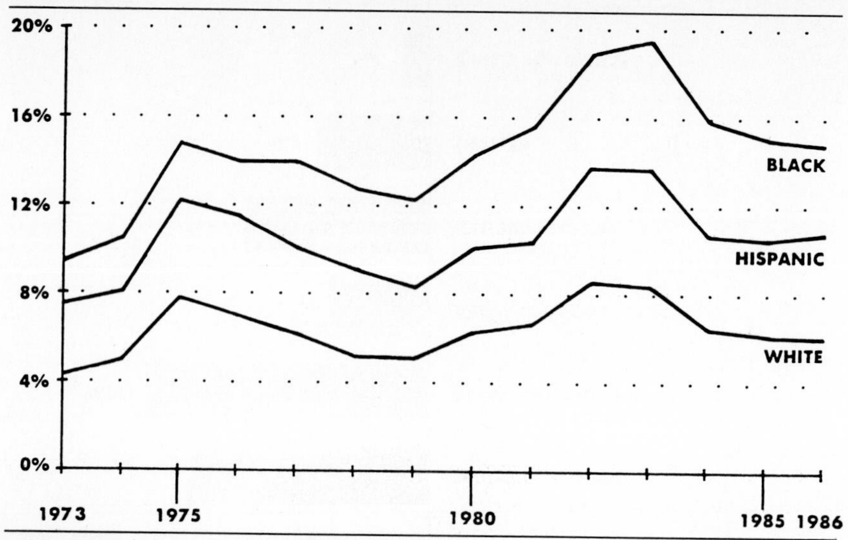


From *A Field Guide to the U.S. Economy* by Nancy Folbre (4.7). Copyright © 1987 by The Center for Popular Economics. Reprinted by permission of Pantheon Books, a Division of Random House, Inc.

**Table A-18** Less Public Assistance for Women and Children

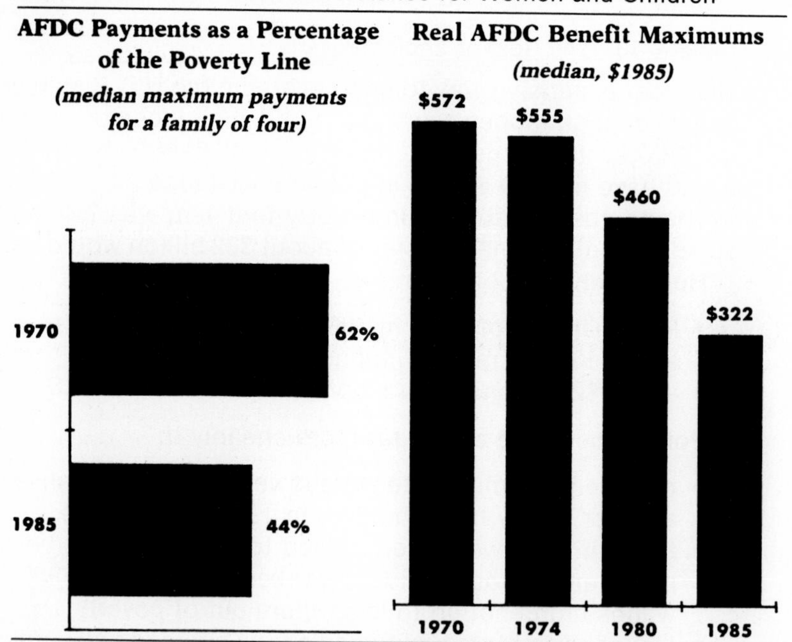


From *A Field Guide to the U.S. Economy* by Nancy Folbre (3.12). Copyright © 1987 by The Center for Popular Economics. Reprinted by permission of Pantheon Books, a Division of Random House, Inc.

**Table A-19** Percentage of Persons 25-Years-Old and Over Who Have Completed High School or College by Race and Sex, 1985

| | White | | Black | | Hispanic | |
|---|---|---|---|---|---|---|
| Educational Attainment | Male | Female | Male | Female | Male | Female |
| Completed 4 years of High School | 75.5 | 76.0 | 58.4 | 60.8 | 48.5 | 47.4 |
| Completed 4 years of College or More | 24.0 | 16.3 | 11.2 | 11.0 | 9.7 | 7.3 |

*Source:* U.S. Bureau of the Census, Current Population Reports, Series P-20, No. 415, *Educational Attainment in the United States: March 1982 to 1985,* U.S. Government Printing Office, Washington, D.C., 1987, adapted from pp. 105–107.

**Table A-20** Households Covered by Health Insurance in 1985

| | Covered by Private Health Insurance | Related to Current or Prior Employment of Self or Family Member | Not Covered by Private or Government Health Insurance |
|---|---|---|---|
| White | 79.6% | 64.9% | 12.4% |
| Black | 55.7% | 46.2% | 19.3% |
| Hispanic | 55.2% | 49.3% | 27.0% |

**Table A-21** Families Maintained by Women by Race and Hispanic Origin (as a percent of all families)

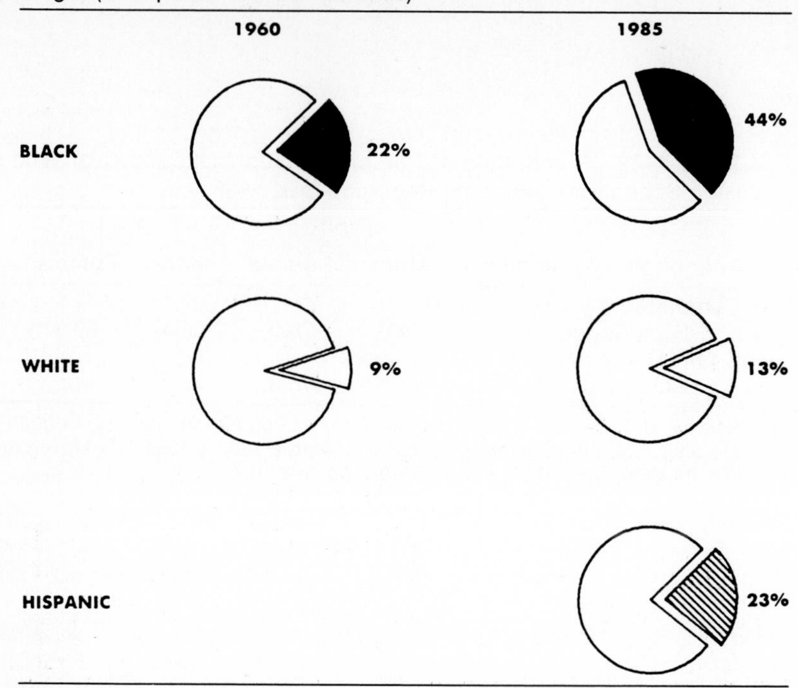


From *A Field Guide to the U.S. Economy* by Nancy Folbre (4.16). 

**Table A-22** Women Who Have Had a Child in the Last Year per 1,000 Women, by Age

| Line no. | Characteristic | Total, 18 to 44 years old | | | 18 to 29 years old | | |
|---|---|---|---|---|---|---|---|
| | | Number of women (thousands) | Women who had a child in the last year | | Number of women (thousands) | Women who had a child in the last year | |
| | | | Total births per 1,000 | First births per 1,000 | | Total births per 1,000 | First births per 1,000 |
| 1 | Total, all women | 51,581 | 70.3 | 26.4 | 24,586 | 99.7 | 44.4 |
| | Race: | | | | | | |
| 2 | White | 43,237 | 68.2 | 26.5 | 20,387 | 96.3 | 44.5 |
| 3 | Black | 6,625 | 78.4 | 23.6 | 3,423 | 112.7 | 41.3 |
| | Hispanic: | | | | | | |
| 4 | Hispanic[1] | 4,061 | 105.6 | 29.1 | 2,177 | 136.7 | 45.3 |
| 5 | Not Hispanic | 47,520 | 67.3 | 26.2 | 22,409 | 96.1 | 44.3 |
| | Marital status: | | | | | | |
| 6 | Currently married | 31,565 | 95.3 | 35.3 | 11,378 | 170.8 | 74.9 |
| 7 | Married, husband present | 29,400 | 97.4 | 36.0 | 10,454 | 175.7 | 76.8 |
| 8 | Married, husband absent[2] | 2,165 | 67.6 | 25.5 | 925 | 114.9 | 53.6 |
| 9 | Widowed or divorced | 5,107 | 27.1 | 3.5 | 1,182 | 58.9 | 12.5 |
| 10 | Single | 14,909 | 32.1 | 15.5 | 12,026 | 36.5 | 18.6 |
| | Educational attainment: | | | | | | |
| 11 | Not a high school graduate | 7,876 | 93.1 | 21.8 | 4,096 | 141.3 | 39.9 |
| 12 | High school: 4 years | 22,241 | 71.0 | 29.1 | 10,762 | 113.9 | 52.9 |
| 13 | College: 1 to 3 years | 11,891 | 58.7 | 24.0 | 6,158 | 68.8 | 36.7 |
| 14 | 4 or more years | 9,573 | 64.3 | 26.9 | 3,570 | 62.4 | 37.0 |
| 15 | 4 years | 6,335 | 60.8 | 27.9 | 2,847 | 62.9 | 39.1 |
| 16 | 5 or more years | 3,238 | 71.3 | 24.8 | 723 | 60.2 | 29.0 |
| | Labor force status: | | | | | | |
| 17 | In labor force | 37,232 | 48.5 | 20.8 | 17,909 | 66.2 | 33.5 |
| 18 | Employed | 34,226 | 46.5 | 19.9 | 15,974 | 62.9 | 32.1 |
| 19 | Unemployed | 3,006 | 74.1 | 32.0 | 1,935 | 92.8 | 44.4 |
| 20 | Not in labor force | 14,349 | 126.9 | 40.8 | 6,678 | 189.7 | 73.6 |
| | Occupation of employed women: | | | | | | |
| 21 | Managerial and professional | 8,300 | 42.9 | 17.3 | 2,869 | 46.8 | 25.5 |
| 22 | Technical, sales, and admin. support | 16,013 | 42.6 | 20.9 | 8,219 | 56.8 | 31.5 |
| 23 | Service occupations | 5,774 | 53.1 | 20.6 | 3,070 | 71.1 | 35.8 |
| 24 | Farming, forestry, and fishing | 417 | 49.0 | 12.8 | 201 | 44.7 | 26.6 |
| 25 | Precision prod., craft, and repair | 798 | 55.7 | 13.5 | 344 | 93.9 | 18.1 |
| 26 | Operators, fabricators, and laborers | 2,924 | 61.9 | 22.6 | 1,270 | 113.3 | 47.1 |
| | Family income: | | | | | | |
| 27 | Under $ 10,000 | 8,523 | 95.3 | 29.8 | 4,918 | 129.1 | 48.2 |
| 28 | $10,000 to $14,999 | 5,713 | 69.7 | 25.9 | 3,252 | 96.4 | 39.2 |
| 29 | $15,000 to $19,999 | 5,506 | 69.3 | 27.6 | 2,871 | 103.2 | 48.3 |
| 30 | $20,000 to $24,999 | 5,512 | 73.3 | 26.2 | 2,650 | 115.8 | 49.5 |
| 31 | $25,000 to $29,999 | 4,650 | 75.4 | 24.9 | 2,087 | 106.4 | 45.5 |
| 32 | $30,000 to $34,999 | 4,691 | 68.3 | 25.7 | 2,072 | 99.3 | 43.3 |
| 33 | $35,000 and over | 15,682 | 55.4 | 24.7 | 6,176 | 66.9 | 39.1 |
| 34 | Income not reported | 1,304 | 68.6 | 30.9 | 560 | 105.5 | 55.3 |
| | Region of residence: | | | | | | |
| 35 | Northeast | 10,656 | 67.4 | 25.6 | 5,010 | 86.7 | 40.9 |
| 36 | Midwest | 12,431 | 66.4 | 24.0 | 5,975 | 98.3 | 40.9 |
| 37 | South | 17,711 | 71.9 | 28.1 | 8,482 | 105.9 | 49.6 |
| 38 | West | 10,783 | 75.0 | 27.2 | 5,120 | 103.7 | 43.1 |

- Zero or rounds to zero.

[1]Persons of Hispanic origin may be of any race.

[2]Includes separated women.

Note: Since the number of women who have had a birth during the 12-month period was tabulated and not the actual numbers of births themselves, some small underestimation of fertility for this period may exist because of the omission of (1) multiple births, (2) two or more live births

*Source:* U.S. Bureau of the Census, Current Population Reports, Series P–20, No. 421, *Fertility of American Women: June 1986,* U.S. Government Printing Office, Washington, D.C., 1987, p. 2.

**Table A-23** Living Arrangements of Children Under 18 years, by Race and Hispanic Origin; 1986, 1980, 1970, and 1960 (Excludes persons under 18 years old who were maintaining households or family groups. Numbers in thousands)

| Living arrangements | 1986 | 1980 | 1970 |
|---|---|---|---|
| All Races | | | |
| Children under 18 years | 62,723 | 63,427 | 69,162 |
| Living with— | | | |
| Two parents | 46,384 | 48,624 | 58,939 |
| One parent | 14,759 | 12,466 | 8,199 |
| Mother only | 13,180 | 11,406 | 7,452 |
| Father only | 1,579 | 1,060 | 748 |
| Other relatives | 1,348 | 1,949 | 1,547 |
| Nonrelatives only | 272 | 388 | 477 |
| White | | | |
| Children under 18 years | 50,931 | 52,242 | 58,790 |
| Living with— | | | |
| Two parents | 40,681 | 43,200 | 52,624 |
| One parent | 9,303 | 7,901 | 5,109 |
| Mother only | 8,021 | 7,059 | 4,581 |
| Father only | 1,282 | 842 | 528 |
| Other relatives | 747 | 887 | 696 |
| Nonrelatives only | 200 | 254 | 362 |
| Black[1] | | | |
| Children under 18 years | 9,532 | 9,375 | 9,422 |
| Living with— | | | |
| Two parents | 3,869 | 3,956 | 5,508 |
| One parent | 5,058 | 4,297 | 2,996 |
| Mother only | 4,827 | 4,117 | 2,783 |
| Father only | 231 | 180 | 213 |
| Other relatives | 542 | 999 | 820 |
| Nonrelatives only | 63 | 123 | 97 |
| Hispanic[2] | | | |
| Children under 18 years | 6,430 | 5,459 | [3]4,006 |
| Living with— | | | |
| Two parents | 4,275 | 4,116 | 3,111 |
| One parent | 1,955 | 1,152 | (NA) |
| Mother only | 1,784 | 1,069 | (NA) |
| Father only | 171 | 83 | (NA) |
| Other relatives | 162 | 183 | (NA) |
| Nonrelatives only | 38 | 8 | (NA) |

[1]Nonwhite for 1960.
[2]Persons of Hispanic origin may be of any race.
[3]Persons under 18 years.
*Source:* U.S. Bureau of the Census, Current Population Reports, Series P-20, No. 418, *Marital Status and Living Arrangements: March 1986,* U.S. Government Printing Office, Washington, D.C., 1986, p. 8.

**Table A-23** (Continued)

| | Percent Distribution | | | |
|---|---|---|---|---|
| 1960 | 1986 | 1980 | 1970 | 1960 |
| 63,727 | 100.0 | 100.0 | 100.0 | 100.0 |
| 55,877 | 73.9 | 76.7 | 85.2 | 87.7 |
| 5,829 | 23.5 | 19.7 | 11.9 | 9.1 |
| 5,105 | 21.0 | 18.0 | 10.8 | 8.0 |
| 724 | 2.5 | 1.7 | 1.1 | 1.1 |
| 1,601 | 2.1 | 3.1 | 2.2 | 2.5 |
| 420 | 0.4 | 0.6 | 0.7 | 0.7 |
| 55,077 | 100.0 | 100.0 | 100.0 | 100.0 |
| 50,082 | 79.9 | 82.7 | 89.5 | 90.9 |
| 3,932 | 18.3 | 15.1 | 8.7 | 7.1 |
| 3,381 | 15.7 | 13.5 | 7.8 | 6.1 |
| 551 | 2.5 | 1.6 | 0.9 | 1.0 |
| 774 | 1.5 | 1.7 | 1.2 | 1.4 |
| 288 | 0.4 | 0.5 | 0.6 | 0.5 |
| 8,650 | 100.0 | 100.0 | 100.0 | 100.0 |
| 5,795 | 40.6 | 42.2 | 58.5 | 67.0 |
| 1,897 | 53.1 | 45.8 | 31.8 | 21.9 |
| 1,723 | 50.6 | 43.9 | 29.5 | 19.9 |
| 173 | 2.4 | 1.9 | 2.3 | 2.0 |
| 827 | 5.7 | 10.7 | 8.7 | 9.6 |
| 132 | 0.7 | 1.3 | 1.0 | 1.5 |
| (NA) | 100.0 | 100.0 | 100.0 | (NA) |
| (NA) | 66.5 | 75.4 | 77.7 | (NA) |
| (NA) | 30.4 | 21.1 | (NA) | (NA) |
| (NA) | 27.7 | 19.6 | (NA) | (NA) |
| (NA) | 2.7 | 1.5 | (NA) | (NA) |
| (NA) | 2.5 | 3.4 | (NA) | (NA) |
| (NA) | 0.6 | 0.1 | (NA) | (NA) |

**Table A-24** Divorced Persons per 1,000 Married Persons With Spouse Present, by Age, Sex, Race, and Hispanic Origin: 1986, 1980, 1970, and 1960

| Year and sex | Race | | | |
|---|---|---|---|---|
| | Total | White | Black | Hispanic[1] |
| Both sexes: | | | | |
| 1986 | 131 | 124 | 248 | 139 |
| 1980 | 100 | 92 | 203 | 98 |
| 1970 | 47 | 44 | 83 | 61 |
| 1960 | 35 | 33 | 62 | (NA) |
| Male: | | | | |
| 1986 | 106 | 102 | 166 | 110 |
| 1980 | 79 | 74 | 149 | 64 |
| 1970 | 35 | 32 | 62 | 40 |
| 1960 | 28 | 27 | 45 | (NA) |
| Female: | | | | |
| 1986 | 157 | 145 | 332 | 166 |
| 1980 | 120 | 110 | 258 | 132 |
| 1970 | 60 | 56 | 104 | 81 |
| 1960 | 42 | 38 | 78 | (NA) |

NA Not Available.

[1]Persons of Hispanic origin may be of any race.

*Source:* U.S. Bureau of the Census, Current Population Reports, Series P-20, No. 418, *Marital Status and Living Arrangements: March 1986,* U.S. Government Printing Office, Washington, D.C., 1986, p. 7.